CCNA Data Center

DCICT 200-155

Official Cert Guide

NAVAID SHAMSEE, CCIE No. 12625
DAVID KLEBANOV, CCIE No. 13791
HESHAM FAYED, CCIE No. 9303
AHMED AFROSE
OZDEN KARAKOK, CCIE No. 6331

Cisco Press
800 East 96th Street
Indianapolis, IN 46240

CCNA Data Center
DCICT 200-155 Official Cert Guide

Navaid Shamsee, CCIE No. 12625

David Klebanov, CCIE No. 13791

Hesham Fayed, CCIE No. 9303

Ahmed Afrose

Ozden Karakok, CCIE No. 6331

Copyright© 2017 Pearson Education, Inc.

Published by:
Cisco Press
800 East 96th Street
Indianapolis, IN 46240 USA

Printed in the United States of America

1   16

Library of Congress Control Number: 2016949728

ISBN-13: 978-1-58720-591-0

ISBN-10: 1-58720-591-2

Warning and Disclaimer

This book is designed to provide information about the 200-155 DCICT exam for CCNA Data Center certification. Every effort has been made to make this book as complete and as accurate as possible, but no warranty or fitness is implied.

The information is provided on an "as is" basis. The authors, Cisco Press, and Cisco Systems, Inc. shall have neither liability nor responsibility to any person or entity with respect to any loss or damages arising from the information contained in this book.

The opinions expressed in this book belong to the authors and are not necessarily those of Cisco Systems, Inc.

Trademark Acknowledgments

All terms mentioned in this book that are known to be trademarks or service marks have been appropriately capitalized. Cisco Press or Cisco Systems, Inc., cannot attest to the accuracy of this information. Use of a term in this book should not be regarded as affecting the validity of any trademark or service mark.

Special Sales

For information about buying this title in bulk quantities, or for special sales opportunities (which may include electronic versions; custom cover designs; and content particular to your business, training goals, marketing focus, or branding interests), please contact our corporate sales department at corpsales@pearsoned.com or (800) 382-3419.

For government sales inquiries, please contact governmentsales@pearsoned.com.

For questions about sales outside the U.S., please contact intlcs@pearson.com.

Feedback Information

At Cisco Press, our goal is to create in-depth technical books of the highest quality and value. Each book is crafted with care and precision, undergoing rigorous development that involves the unique expertise of members from the professional technical community.

Readers' feedback is a natural continuation of this process. If you have any comments regarding how we could improve the quality of this book, or otherwise alter it to better suit your needs, you can contact us through e-mail at feedback@ciscopress.com. Please make sure to include the book title and ISBN in your message.

We greatly appreciate your assistance.

Editor-in-Chief: Mark Taub	**Copy Editor:** Gill Editorial Services
Product Line Manager: Brett Bartow	**Technical Editor:** David Burns
Business Operation Manager, Cisco Press: Ronald Fligge	**Editorial Assistant:** Vanessa Evans
Executive Editor: Mary Beth Ray	**Designer:** Chuti Prasertsith
Managing Editor: Sandra Schroeder	**Composition:** Tricia Bronkella
Development Editor: Ellie Bru	**Indexer:** Ken Johnson
Project Editor: Mandie Frank	**Proofreader:** Debbie Williams

CISCO.

Americas Headquarters
Cisco Systems, Inc.
San Jose, CA

Asia Pacific Headquarters
Cisco Systems (USA) Pte. Ltd.
Singapore

Europe Headquarters
Cisco Systems International BV
Amsterdam, The Netherlands

Cisco has more than 200 offices worldwide. Addresses, phone numbers, and fax numbers are listed on the Cisco Website at **www.cisco.com/go/offices.**

CCDE, CCENT, Cisco Eos, Cisco HealthPresence, the Cisco logo, Cisco Lumin, Cisco Nexus, Cisco StadiumVision, Cisco TelePresence, Cisco WebEx, DCE, and Welcome to the Human Network are trademarks; Changing the Way We Work, Live, Play, and Learn and Cisco Store are service marks; and Access Registrar, Aironet, AsyncOS, Bringing the Meeting To You, Catalyst, CCDA, CCDP, CCIE, CCIP, CCNA, CCNP, CCSP, CCVP, Cisco, the Cisco Certified Internetwork Expert logo, Cisco IOS, Cisco Press, Cisco Systems, Cisco Systems Capital, the Cisco Systems logo, Cisco Unity, Collaboration Without Limitation, EtherFast, EtherSwitch, Event Center, Fast Step, Follow Me Browsing, FormShare, GigaDrive, HomeLink, Internet Quotient, IOS, iPhone, iQuick Study, IronPort, the IronPort logo, LightStream, Linksys, MediaTone, MeetingPlace, MeetingPlace Chime Sound, MGX, Networkers, Networking Academy, Network Registrar, PCNow, PIX, PowerPanels, ProConnect, ScriptShare, SenderBase, SMARTnet, Spectrum Expert, StackWise, The Fastest Way to Increase Your Internet Quotient, TransPath, WebEx, and the WebEx logo are registered trademarks of Cisco Systems, Inc. and/or its affiliates in the United States and certain other countries.

All other trademarks mentioned in this document or website are the property of their respective owners. The use of the word partner does not imply a partnership relationship between Cisco and any other company. (0812R)

About the Authors

Navaid Shamsee, CCIE No.12625, is a senior solutions architect in the Cisco Services organization. He holds a master's degree in telecommunication and a bachelor's degree in electrical engineering. He is also a triple CCIE in routing and switching, service provider, and data center technologies. Navaid has extensive experience in designing, implementing and securing many large-scale enterprise and service provider data centers. In Cisco, Navaid is focused on the security of data center, cloud, and software-defined networking technologies. You can reach Navaid on Twitter: @NavaidShamsee.

David Klebanov, CCIE No.13791 (Routing and Switching), is leading Technical Marketing organization at Viptela, the Software Defined Wide Area Network (SD-WAN) company. David has more than 15 years of diverse industry experience architecting and deploying complex network environments. In his work, David sets strategic direction for industry-leading network platforms, which transform the world of wide area communications for enterprises and service providers alike. David also takes great pride in speaking at industry events, releasing publications, and working on patents. You can reach David on Twitter: @DavidKlebanov.

Hesham Fayed, CCIE No.9303 (Routing and Switching/Data Center), is a consulting systems engineer for data center and virtualization based in California. Hesham has been with Cisco for more than 11 years and has 19 years of experience in the computer industry, working with service providers and large enterprises. His main focus is working with customers in the western region of the United States to address their challenges by doing end-to-end data center architectures.

Ahmed Afrose is a solutions architect at Cisco Cloud and Networking Services (C&NS) Innovation and Delivery team. He is responsible for providing architectural design guidance and leading complex multitech service deliveries. Furthermore, he is involved in demonstrating the Cisco value propositions in data center analytics, application automation, software-defined data centers, and Cisco Unified Computing System (UCS). Ahmed has a bachelor's degree in information systems. He started his career with Sun Microsystem–based technologies and has 17 years of diverse experience in the industry. He's been working for Cisco Systems for 7+ years and was directly responsible for establishing Cisco UCS Advanced Services delivery capabilities while evangelizing the product in the EMEA region. You can reach Ahmed on Twitter: @ahmedafrose.

Ozden Karakok, CCIE No. 6331, is a technical leader from the data center products and technologies team in the Technical Assistant Center (TAC). She has been with Cisco Systems for 17 years and specializes in storage area and data center networks. Prior to joining Cisco, Ozden spent five years working for a number of Cisco's large customers in various telecommunication roles. She is a Cisco Certified Internetwork Expert in routing and switching, SNA/IP, and storage. A frequent speaker at Cisco and data center events, she serves as a member of the patent committee at Cisco Services. Ozden holds a degree in computer engineering from Istanbul Bogazici University. Currently, she is focused on Application Centric Infrastructure (ACI) and software-defined storage (SDS). You can reach Ozden on Twitter: @okarakok.

About the Technical Reviewers

David Burns has in-depth knowledge of routing and switching technologies, network security, data center, and mobility. Dave is currently the Vice President of Engineering & Architecture for QTS DataCenters where he is focused on driving strategy and execution for connectivity, infrastructure, security, and data center and cloud services being delivered to QTS customers and partners. Prior to joining QTS, Dave led various Engineering & Architecture teams for both in the U.S. and internationally-focused on Service Providers and Enterprise IT, covering the spectrum of technologies ranging from security, network, data center, cloud, and connectivity. Dave holds various sales, industry, and Cisco technical certifications, including CISSP, CCNP Security (formerly CCSP), CCDP, and multiple associate-level certifications. Dave is also a published author with Cisco Press and active technical reviewer for multiple titles. Dave has a Masters in Business Administration and a Bachelor of Science in Telecommunications Engineering Technology.

Dedications

Navaid Shamsee: To my parents for their guidance and prayers. To my wife, Hareem, for her love and support, and to my children, Ahsan, Rida, and Maria.

David Klebanov: This book is dedicated to my gorgeous wife, Tanya, and to our two wonderful daughters, Lia and Maya. I wanted you to know how grateful I am to have you in my life, and how your love and support inspire me each and every day. Tanya, your journey to become OTR/L is an inspiration to anyone pursuing personal dreams and a true testament that if you put your mind to it, you can accomplish anything! You are my pride, and I applaud you for your success. Lia, as you become a young adult, keep dreaming big, and remember that life is like a box of chocolates—you never know what you are going to get. Let your talent and perseverance pave the way. Maya, you may still be young, but you have a big heart. Thank you for filling our house with joy and laughter.

This book is also dedicated to all of you who have chosen the path of technology. Together we can make this world a better place.

Hesham Fayed: This book is dedicated to my lovely wife, Eman, and my beautiful children, Ali, Laila, Hamza, Fayrouz, and Farouk. Without your support and encouragement, I would never have been able to finish this book. I can't forget to acknowledge my parents; your guidance, education, and encouragement to strive to be better is what helped in my journey.

Ahmed Afrose: I dedicate this book to my parents, Hilal and Faiziya. Without them, none of this would have been possible. I also dedicate this to those people who are deeply curious and advocate self-advancement.

Ozden Karakok: To my loving husband, Tom, for his endless support, encouragement, and love. Merci beaucoup, Askim.

To Remi and Mira, for being the most incredible miracles of my life and being my number-one source of happiness.

To my wonderful parents, who supported me in every chapter of my life and are an inspiration for life.

To my awesome sisters, Gulden and Cigdem, for their unconditional support and loving me just the way I am.

To the memory of Steve Ritchie, for being the best mentor ever and passionate technology lover.

Acknowledgments

First and foremost, I would like to say thank you to my wife Hareem for her unconditional support throughout my career and writing this book.

To my co-authors, Afrose, David, Hesham, and Ozden: It is my pleasure and honor working with you again on the second edition of this book. Without your support, this book would not have been possible.

I would also like to say thank you to David Burns for reviewing this book and providing us feedback. His input was very valuable and it helped us improve the quality of content.

A big thank-you to the entire Cisco Press team for all their support in getting this book published. Special thanks to Mary Beth and Ellie for keeping us on track and guiding us in the journey of writing this book.

—Navaid Shamsee

My deepest gratitude goes to all the people who have shared my journey over the years and who have inspired me to always strive for more. I would also like to thank my fellow authors for the wonderful team spirit and the entire Cisco Press team for ensuring our success.

—David Klebanov

I'd like to thank my co-authors, Navaid, Afrose, Ozden, and David, for working as a team to complete the second edition of this book. Mary Beth and Ellie, thank you both for your patience and support through my second publication. It has been an honor working with you both, and I have learned a lot during this process.

I want to thank my family for their support and patience while I was working on this book.

—Hesham Fayed

Navaid Shamsee has been a good friend and colleague. I am thankful to him for this awesome opportunity. He has helped me achieve a milestone in my career by offering me the opportunity to be associated with this publication and the world-renowned Cisco Press team.

I'm humbled by this experienced and talented team of co-authors: Navaid, David, Hesham, and Ozden. It was a pleasure working with a team of like-minded professionals.

I am also thankful to all our professional editors, especially Mary Beth Ray and Ellie Bru, for their patience and guidance every step of the way. A big thank-you to all the folks involved in production, publishing, and bringing this book to the shelves.

To our technical reviewer, David Burns, for his keen attention to detail; it helped gauge depth and consistency and improved the overall quality of this certification guide.

—Ahmed Afrose

This book would never have become a reality without the help, support, and advice of a great number of people.

I would like to thank my great co-authors, Navaid, David, Afrose, and Hesham. Thank you for your excellent collaboration, hard work, and priceless time. I truly enjoyed working with each one of you on our second book. I really appreciated Navaid taking the lead and being the glue of this diverse team. It was a great pleasure and honor working with such talented engineers. It would have been impossible to finish this book without your support.

To our technical reviewer, David Burns: Thank you for providing us with your valuable feedback, suggestions, hard work, and quick turnaround. Your excellent input helped us improve the quality and accuracy of the content. It was a great pleasure for all of us to work with you.

To Mary Beth Ray, Ellie Bru, Mandie Frank, and the Cisco Press team: A big thank-you to the entire Cisco Press team for all their support in getting this book published. Special thanks to Mary Beth and Ellie for their endless encouragement and support.

To the extended teams at Cisco: Thank you for being patient while our minds were in the book. Thank you for believing in and supporting us on this journey. Thank you for the innovative organization and development team at Cisco.

To all extended family and friends: Thank you for your patience and endless support.

—Ozden Karakok

Contents at a Glance

On the Companion Website:

Contents

Icons Used in This Book

Layer 2 Switch   Layer 3 Switch   Nexus Switch   Nexus 7000 Switch   Router

Printer   PC   Laptop   Server   IP Phone

WAN Switch   Nexus 9000   Cable Modem   UCS   CSU/DSU

Access Point   Hub   Bridge   Phone   Network Cloud

PIX Firewall   ASA   Ethernet Connection   Virtual Circuit   Ethernet WAN

Wireless

Command Syntax Conventions

The conventions used to present command syntax in this book are the same conventions used in the IOS Command Reference. The Command Reference describes these conventions as follows:

- **Boldface** indicates commands and keywords that are entered literally as shown. In actual configuration examples and output (not general command syntax), boldface indicates commands that are manually input by the user (such as a **show** command).

- *Italic* indicates arguments for which you supply actual values.

- Vertical bars (|) separate alternative, mutually exclusive elements.
- Square brackets ([ ]) indicate an optional element.
- Braces ({ }) indicate a required choice.
- Braces within brackets ([{ }]) indicate a required choice within an optional element.

Introduction

About the Exam

Congratulations! If you are reading far enough to look at this book's Introduction, you've probably already decided to pursue your Cisco CCNA Data Center certification. Cisco dominates the networking marketplace, and after a few short years of entering the server marketplace, Cisco has achieved significant market share and has become one of the primary vendors for server hardware. If you want to succeed as a technical person in the networking industry in general, and in data centers in particular, you need to know Cisco. Getting your CCNA Data Center certification is a great first step in building your skills and becoming a recognized authority in the data center field.

Exams That Help You Achieve CCNA Data Center Certification

Cisco CCNA Data Center is an entry-level Cisco data center certification that is also a prerequisite for other Cisco Data Center certifications. CCNA Data Center itself has no other prerequisites. To achieve the CCNA Data Center certification, you must pass two exams: 200-150 Introduction to Cisco Data Center Networking (DCICN) and 200-155 Introduction to Cisco Data Center Technologies (DCICT), as shown in Figure I-1.

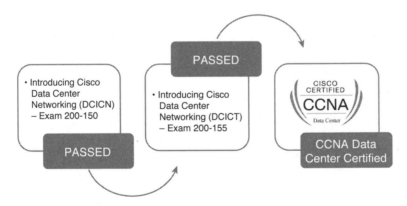

Figure I-1   *Path to Cisco CCNA Data Center Certification*

The DCICN and DCICT exams differ quite a bit in terms of the topics covered. DCICN focuses on networking technology. In fact, it overlaps quite a bit with the topics in the ICND1 100-105 exam, which leads to the Cisco Certified Entry Network Technician (CCENT) certification. DCICN explains the basics of networking, focusing on Ethernet switching and IP routing. The only data center focus on the DCICN exam is that all the configuration and verification examples use Cisco Nexus data center switches.

The DCICT exam instead focuses on technologies specific to the data center. These technologies include Unified Computing, Unified Fabric, network virtualization, Application Centric Infrastructure, cloud computing, automation and orchestration, as well as the other data networking features unique to the Cisco Nexus series of switches.

Types of Questions on the Exams

Cisco certification exams follow the same general format. At the testing center, you sit in a quiet room in front of the PC. Before the exam timer begins, you can complete a few other tasks on the PC; for example, you can take a sample quiz just to get accustomed to the PC and the testing engine. Anyone who has basic skills in getting around a PC should have no problems with the testing environment.

After the exam starts, you are presented with a series of questions, one at a time, on the PC screen. The questions typically fall into one of the following categories:

- Multiple choice, single answer
- Multiple choice, multiple answers
- Testlet
- Drag-and-drop (DND)
- Simulated lab (sim)
- Simlet

The first three items in the list are all multiple-choice questions. The multiple-choice format requires you to point to and click a circle or square beside the correct answer(s).

Cisco traditionally tells you how many answers you need to choose, and the testing software prevents you from choosing too many answers. The testlet asks you several multiple-choice questions, all based on the same larger scenario.

DND questions require you to move some items around in the graphical user interface (GUI). You left-click the mouse to hold the item, move it to another area, and release the mouse button to place the item in its destination (usually into a list). For some questions, to get the question correct, you might need to put a list of items in the proper order or sequence.

The last two types, sim and simlet questions, both use a network simulator to ask questions. Interestingly, the two types enable Cisco to assess two very different skills. First, sim questions generally describe a problem, while your task is to configure one or more routers and switches to fix it. The exam then grades the question based on the configuration you changed or added. Basically, these questions begin with a broken configuration, and you must fix it to answer the question correctly.

Simlet questions also use a network simulator, but instead of answering the question by changing or adding the configuration, they include one or more multiple-choice questions. These questions require you to use the simulator to examine network behavior by interpreting the output of **show** commands you decide to leverage to answer the question. Whereas sim questions require you to troubleshoot problems related to configuration, simlets require you to analyze both working and broken networks, correlating **show** command output with your knowledge of networking theory and configuration commands.

You can watch and even experiment with these command types using the Cisco Exam Tutorial. To find the Cisco Certification Exam Tutorial, go to www.cisco.com and search for "exam tutorial."

What's on the DCICT Exam?

Everyone has always wanted to know what is on the test, for any test, since the early days of school. Cisco openly publishes the topics of each of its certification exams. Cisco wants the candidates to know the variety of topics and get an idea about the kinds of knowledge and skills required for each topic.

Exam topics are very specific, and the verb used in their description is very important. The verb tells us to what degree the topic must be understood and what skills are required. For example, one topic might begin with "Describe...," another with "Configure...," another with "Verify...," and another with "Troubleshoot...." Questions beginning with "Troubleshoot" require the highest skills level, because to troubleshoot, you must understand the topic, be able to configure it (to see what's wrong with the configuration), and be able to verify it (to find the root cause of the problem). Pay attention to the question verbiage.

Cisco's posted exam topics, however, are only guidelines. Cisco's disclaimer language mentions that fact. Cisco makes an effort to keep the exam questions within the confines of the stated exam topics, and we know from talking to those involved that every question is analyzed for whether it fits the stated exam topic.

DCICT 200-155 Exam Topics

The exam topics for both the DCICN and the DCICT exams can be easily found at Cisco.com by searching. Alternatively, you can go to www.cisco.com/go/ccna, which gets you to the page for CCNA Routing and Switching, where you can easily navigate to the nearby CCNA Data Center page.

Over time, Cisco has begun making two stylistic improvements to the posted exam topics. In the past, the topics were simply listed as bullets with indentation to imply subtopics under a major topic. More often today, including for the DCICN and DCICT exam topics, Cisco also numbers the exam topics, making it easier to refer to specific topics. Additionally, Cisco lists the weighting for each of the major topic headings. The weighting tells the percentage of points from your exam, which should come from each major topic area. The DCICT contains five major headings with their respective weighting, shown in Table I-1.

Table I-1 Five Major Topic Areas in the DCICT 200-155 Exam

Number	Exam Topic	Weighting
1.0	Unified Computing	25%
2.0	Network Virtualization	17%
3.0	Cisco Data Center Networking Technologies	26%
4.0	Automation and Orchestration	15%
5.0	Application Centric Infrastructure	17%

Note that while the weighting of each topic area tells you something about the exam, in the authors' opinion, the weighting probably does not change how you study. All five topic areas hold enough weighting so that if you completely ignore an individual topic, you probably will not pass. Furthermore, data center technologies require you to put many concepts together, so you need all the pieces before you can understand the holistic view. The weighting might indicate where you should spend a little more time during the last days before taking the exam, but otherwise, plan to study all the exam topics.

Tables I-2 through I-6 list the details of the exam topics, with one table for each of the major topic areas listed in Table I-1. Note that these tables also list the book chapters that discuss each of the exam topics.

Table I-2 Exam Topics in the First Major DCICT Exam Topic Area

Number	Exam Topic	Chapter
1.0	**Unified Computing**	7, 8, 9, 10, 11
1.1	Describe common server types and connectivity found in a data center	7
1.2	Describe the physical components of the Cisco UCS	7
1.3	Describe the concepts and benefits of Cisco UCS hardware abstraction	9
1.4	Perform basic Cisco UCS configuration	8, 10
1.4.a	Cluster high availability	8, 10
1.4.b	Port roles	8, 10
1.4.c	Hardware discovery	8, 10
1.5	Describe server virtualization concepts and benefits	11
1.5.a	Hypervisors	11
1.5.b	Virtual switches	11
1.5.c	Shared storage	11
1.5.d	Virtual Machine components	11
1.5.e	Virtual Machine Manager	11

Table I-3 Exam Topics in the Second Major DCICT Exam Topic Area

Number	Exam Topic	Chapter
2.0	**Network Virtualization**	2, 4, 5, 6
2.1	Describe the components and operations of Cisco virtual switches	4
2.2	Describe the concepts of overlays	5
2.2.a	OTV	5

Number	Exam Topic	Chapter
2.2.b	NVGRE	5
2.2.c	VXLAN	5
2.3	Describe the benefits and perform simple troubleshooting of VDC STP	6
2.4	Compare and contrast the default and management VRFs	6
2.5	Differentiate between the data, control, and management planes	2

Table I-4 Exam Topics in the Third Major DCICT Exam Topic Area

Number	Exam Topic	Chapter
3.0	**Cisco Data Center Networking Technologies**	1, 2, 3, 6
3.1	Describe, configure, and verify FEX connectivity	6
3.2	Describe, configure, and verify basic vPC features	1
3.3	Describe, configure, and verify FabricPath	1
3.4	Describe, configure, and verify unified switch ports	3
3.5	Describe the features and benefits of Unified Fabric	3
3.6	Describe and explain the use of role-based access control within the data center infrastructure	2

Table I-5 Exam Topics in the Fourth Major DCICT Exam Topic Area

Number	Exam Topic	Chapter
4.0	**Automation and Orchestration**	15, 16, 17
4.1	Explain the purpose and value of using APIs	15
4.2	Describe the basic concepts of cloud computing	15
4.3	Describe the basic functions of a Cisco UCS Director	16
4.3.a	Management	16
4.3.b	Orchestration	17
4.3.c	Multitenancy	16
4.3.d	Chargeback	16
4.3.e	Service offerings	16
4.3.f	Catalogs	16
4.4	Interpret and troubleshoot a Cisco UCS Director workflow	17

Table I-6 Exam Topics in the Fifth Major DCICT Exam Topic Area

Number	Exam Topic	Chapter
5.0	**Application Centric Infrastructure**	12, 13, 14
5.1	Describe the architecture of an ACI environment	12
5.1.a	Basic policy resolution	12
5.1.b	APIC controller	12
5.1.c	Spine leaf	12
5.1.d	APIs	12
5.2	Describe the fabric discovery process	12
5.3	Describe the policy-driven, multitier application deployment model and its benefits	14
5.4	Describe the ACI logical model	13
5.4.a	Tenants	13
5.4.b	Context	13
5.4.c	Bridge domains	13
5.4.d	EPG	13
5.4.e	Contracts	13

NOTE Because it is possible for exam topics to change over time, it might be worth the time to double-check the exam topics as listed on the Cisco website (http://learningnetwork.cisco.com and navigate to the CCNA Data Center page).

About the Book

This book discusses the content and skills needed to pass the 200-155 DCICT certification exam, which is the second and final exam to achieve CCNA Data Center certification. This book's companion title, *CCNA Data Center DCICN 200-150 Official Cert Guide*, discusses the content needed to pass the 200-150 DCICN certification exam.

We strongly recommend that you plan and structure your learning to align with both exam requirements.

Book Features

The most important and somewhat obvious objective of this book is to help you pass the DCICT exam and help you achieve the CCNA Data Center certification. In fact, if the primary objective of this book were different, the book's title would be misleading! At the same time, the methods used in this book to help you pass the exam are also designed to make you much more knowledgeable in the general field of the data center and help you in your daily job responsibilities.

This book uses several tools to help you discover your weak topic areas, to help you improve your knowledge and skills with those topics, and to prove that you have retained your knowledge of those topics. Importantly, this book does not try to help you pass the exams only by memorization, but by truly learning and understanding the topics. CCNA entry-level certification is the foundation for many of the Cisco professional-level certifications, and it would be a disservice to you if this book did not help you truly learn the material. This book helps you pass the CCNA exam by using the following methods:

- Helping you discover which exam topics you have not mastered

- Providing explanations and information to fill in your knowledge gaps

- Supplying exercises that enhance your ability to grasp topics and deduce the answers to subjects related to the exam

- Providing practice exercises on the topics and the testing process via test questions on the companion website

Chapter Features

To help you customize study time using this book, the core chapters have several features that help you make the best use of your time:

- **"Do I Know This Already?" Quizzes:** Each chapter begins with a quiz that helps you determine the amount of time you need to spend studying the chapter.

- **Foundation Topics:** These are the core sections of each chapter. They explain the protocols, concepts, and configuration for the topics in the chapter.

- **Exam Preparation Tasks:** At the end of the "Foundation Topics" section of each chapter, the "Exam Preparation Tasks" section lists a series of study activities that should be completed at the end of the chapter. Each chapter includes the activities that make the most sense for studying the topics in that chapter. The activities include the following:

  - **Review All Key Topics:** The Key Topic icon is shown next to the most important items in the "Foundation Topics" section of the chapter. The "Review All Key Topics" activity lists the key topics from the chapter and their corresponding page numbers. Although the content of the entire chapter could appear on the exam, you should definitely know the information listed in each key topic.

  - **Complete Tables and Lists from Memory:** To help you exercise your memory and memorize certain lists of facts, many of the more important lists and tables from the chapter are included in Appendix B, "Memory Tables." This document lists only partial information, allowing you to complete the table or list.

  - **Define Key Terms:** Although the exam might be unlikely to ask a question such as, "Define this term," the CCNA exams require that you learn and know a lot of networking terminology. This section lists the most important terms from the chapter, asking you to write a short definition and compare your answer to the Glossary at the end of this book.

■ **References:** Some chapters contain a list of reference links for additional information and details on the topics discussed in that particular chapter.

Part Review

The part review tasks help you prepare to apply all the concepts you learned in that part of the book. Each book part contains several related chapters. The part review includes sample test questions that require you to apply the concepts from multiple chapters in that part, uncovering what you truly understood and what you did not quite yet understand.

The part reviews list tasks, along with checklists, so that you can track your progress. The following list explains the most common tasks you will see in the part review:

■ **Repeat All "Do I Know This Already?" Questions:** Although you have already seen the "Do I Know This Already?" questions from the chapters in a part, answering those questions again can be a useful way to review facts. The "Part Review" section suggests that you repeat the "Do I Know This Already?" questions, but use the Pearson IT Certification Practice Test (PCPT) exam software that comes with the book for extra practice in answering multiple-choice questions on a computer.

■ **Answer "Part Review" Questions:** The PCPT exam software includes several exam databases. One exam database holds "Part Review" questions, written specifically for part reviews. These questions purposefully include multiple concepts in each question, sometimes from multiple chapters, to help build the skills needed for the more challenging analysis questions on the exams.

■ **Review Key Topics:** Yes, again! They are indeed the most important topics in each chapter.

■ **Self-Assessment Questionnaire:** The exam is unlikely to ask a question such as, "Define this term," but the CCNA exams require that you learn and know a lot of technology concepts and architectures. This section asks you some open questions that you should try to describe or explain in your own words. This will help you develop a thorough understanding of important exam topics pertaining to that part.

Final Prep Tasks

Chapter 18, "Final Preparation," lists a series of tasks that you can use for your final preparation before taking the exam.

Other Features

In addition to the features in each of the core chapters, this book, as a whole, has additional study resources, including the following:

- **Practice Exam:** The companion website contains the powerful PCPT exam engine. You can answer the questions in study mode or take simulated DCICT exams with the website and activation code included in this book.

- **eBook:** If you are interested in obtaining an e-book version of this title, we have included a special offer on a coupon card inserted in the cardboard sleeve in the back of the book. This offer enables you to purchase the *CCNA Data Center DCICT 200-155 Official Cert Guide, Premium Edition* e-book and practice test at a 70 percent discount off the list price. In addition to three versions of the e-book—PDF (for reading on your computer), EPUB (for reading on your tablet, mobile device, or Nook or other e-reader), and Mobi (the native Kindle version)—you will receive additional practice test questions and enhanced practice test features.

- **Companion website:** The website www.ciscopress.com/title/9781587205910 posts up-to-the-minute material that further clarifies complex exam topics. Check this site regularly for new and updated postings written by the authors that provide further insight into the more troublesome topics on the exam.

- **PearsonITCertification.com:** The website www.pearsonitcertification.com is a great resource for all things IT-certification related. Check out the great CCNA articles, videos, blogs, and other certification preparation tools from the industry's best authors and trainers.

Book Organization, Chapters, and Appendixes

This book contains 17 core chapters—Chapters 1 through 17, with Chapter 18 including some suggestions for how to approach the actual exams. Each core chapter covers a subset of the topics on the 200-155 DCICT exam. The core chapters are organized into sections. The core chapters cover the following topics:

Part I: Data Center Networking Technologies

- **Chapter 1, "Data Center Networking:"** This chapter provides an overview of the data center networking architecture and design practices relevant to the exam. It goes into the detail of multilayer data center network design and technologies, such as port channel, virtual port channel, and Cisco FabricPath. Basic configuration and verification commands for these technologies are also included in this chapter.

- **Chapter 2, "Management and Monitoring of Cisco Nexus Devices:"** This chapter is an overview of operational planes of the Nexus platform—the data plane, control plane, and management plane. It explains the functions performed by each plane and provides an overview of out-of-band and in-band management interfaces. The Nexus platform provides several methods for device configuration and management. These methods are discussed, inclusive of important commands for initial setup, configuration, and verification. Readers will be introduced to Cisco NX-API, which allows using

HTTP/HTTPS as a transport to access and program the Cisco Nexus switches. This chapter also identifies the mechanism available in the Nexus platform to protect the control plane of the switch.

- **Chapter 3, "Unified Fabric Overview:"** This chapter offers an overview of challenges faced by today's data centers. It focuses on how Cisco Unified Fabric architecture addresses those challenges by converging traditionally disparate network and storage environments while providing a platform for scalable, secure, and intelligent services. It also takes a look at some of the technologies allowing extension of the Unified Fabric environment beyond the boundary of a single data center.

Part II: Network Virtualization

- **Chapter 4, "Cisco Nexus 1000V and Virtual Switching:"** This chapter starts by describing the challenges of current virtual switching layers in data centers and then introduces the distributed virtual switches and, in particular, the Cisco vision—Cisco Nexus 1000V. The chapter explains installation options, commands to verify initial configuration of virtual Ethernet modules, virtual supervisor modules, and integration with VMware vCenter Server.

- **Chapter 5, "Data Center Overlay Networks:"** This chapter covers the latest Cisco innovations in the data center extension solutions and in the LAN extension in particular. Readers will learn about OTV, VXLAN, and NVGRE overlay protocols, which provide Layer 2 over Layer 3 connectivity in today's data center networks.

- **Chapter 6, "Virtualizing Cisco Network Devices:"** This chapter covers the virtualization capabilities of the Nexus switches, using virtual device contexts (VDCs) and network interface virtualization (NIV). It details the VDC concept and the VDC deployment scenarios. The different VDC types and commands used to configure and verify the setup are also included in the chapter. Also covered in this chapter is the NIV—what it is, how it works, and how it is configured.

Part III: Cisco Unified Computing

- **Chapter 7, "Cisco UCS Architecture:"** This chapter begins with a quick fly-by on the evolution of server computing, followed by an introduction to the Cisco UCS value proposition, hardware, and software portfolio. Then the chapter explains UCS architecture in terms of component connectivity options and unification of blade and rackmount server connectivity. It also details the Cisco Integrated Management Controller architecture and purpose.

- **Chapter 8, "Cisco UCS Manager:"** This chapter starts by describing how to set up, configure, and verify the Cisco UCS Fabric Interconnect cluster. It then describes the process of hardware and software discovery in Cisco UCS. It also explains how to monitor and verify this process.

- **Chapter 9, "Cisco Unified Computing System Pools, Policies, Templates, and Service Profiles:"** This chapter explains the hardware abstraction layer in more detail and how it relates to stateless computing. Then it explains logical and physical resource pools and the essentials to create templates and aid rapid deployment of service profiles. As a bonus, you also see notes, tips, and most relevant features.

■ **Chapter 10, "Administration, Management, and Monitoring of Cisco UCS:"**
This covers some of the important features used when administering and monitoring
Cisco UCS. It also introduces Cisco UCS XML, goUCS automation toolkit, and the
well-documented UCS XML API using the Python SDK.

■ **Chapter 11, "Server Virtualization Solutions:"** This chapter takes a peek into the
history of server virtualization and discusses fundamental principles behind different
types of server virtualization technologies. It evaluates the benefits and challenges of
server virtualization while offering approaches to mitigate performance and security
concerns.

Part IV: Application Centric Infrastructure

■ **Chapter 12, "ACI Architecture:"** This chapter discusses the ACI in four main areas:
the ACI architecture and how it ties to software-defined networking (SDN), the Cisco
application policy infrastructure controller (APIC) and ACI components, the application programming interface (API), and basic policy resolution in ACI. As a bonus, you
will learn the latest ACI product portfolio, fundamental concepts, and advantages
of ACI.

■ **Chapter 13, "ACI Logical Model and Policy Framework:"** This chapter outlines
the ACI policy model logical constructs. It introduces readers to a basic level of understanding about the model, what this policy model contains, and how to work with
it. The complete object model contains a hierarchy of data center interactions. The
most extensive information resource, which is available at this moment, is the APIC
Management Information Model Reference packaged with the APIC itself.

■ **Chapter 14, "Operating ACI:"** This chapter starts by explaining the three-tier
Application model. It outlines the ACI hypervisor integration from multiple vendors,
service integration, Cisco application virtual switch (AVS), and Openstack integration.
Technologies that deliver telemetry for ACI fabric are also explained.

Part V: Automation and Orchestration

■ **Chapter 15, "Cloud Computing:"** This chapter peeks into the history of cloud
computing and provides an overview of various cloud computing deployment and
services models for public, private, and hybrid environments. It discusses the use
of application programming interfaces (APIs) to power a programmatic approach
to provisioning and operating IT infrastructure elements for an unparalleled
agility.

■ **Chapter 16, "UCS Director:"** This chapter gives readers an overview of UCS
Director features and functions that are relevant to the DCICT exam. It also pro-
vides configuration and troubleshooting guidelines and information about using UCS
Director to simplify data center management.

■ **Chapter 17, "Understanding and Troubleshooting UCSD Workflows:"** This
chapter offers readers a glimpse of UCS Director orchestration. It provides necessary
information about workflow designer to create, validate, execute, and troubleshoot
UCS Director workflows.

Part VI: Final Preparation

- **Chapter 18, "Final Preparation:"** This chapter suggests a plan for exam preparation after you have finished the core parts of the book, in particular explaining the many study options available in the book.

- **Appendix A, "Answers to the 'Do I Know This Already?' Quizzes:"** This includes the answers to all the questions from Chapters 1 through 17.

- **Appendix B, "Memory Tables:"** This holds the key tables and lists from each chapter, with some of the content removed. You can print this appendix and, as a memory exercise, complete the tables and lists. The goal is to help you memorize facts that can be useful on the exams.

- **Appendix C, "Memory Tables Answer Key:"** This contains the answer key for the exercises in Appendix B.

- The **Glossary** contains definitions for all the terms listed in the "Define Key Terms" section at the conclusion of Chapters 1 through 17.

Appendix On the Companion Website

- **Appendix D, "Study Planner:"** This is a spreadsheet with major study milestones enabling you to track your progress through your study.

Reference Information

This short section contains a few topics available for reference elsewhere in the book. You may read these when you first use the book, but you may also skip these topics and refer to them later. In particular, make sure to note the final page of this Introduction, which lists several contact details, including how to get in touch with Cisco Press.

Companion Website

Register this book to get access to the Pearson IT Certification test engine and other study materials plus additional bonus content. Check this site regularly for new and updated postings written by the authors that provide further insight into the more troublesome topics on the exam. Be sure to check the box that you would like to hear from us to receive updates and exclusive discounts on future editions of this product or related products.

To access this companion website, follow these steps:

1. Go to www.pearsonITcertification.com/register and log in or create a new account.

2. Enter the ISBN: 9781587205910.

3. Answer the challenge question as proof of purchase.

4. Click on the "Access Bonus Content" link in the Registered Products section of your account page, to be taken to the page where your downloadable content is available.

Please note that many of our companion content files can be very large, especially image and video files.

If you are unable to locate the files for this title by following the steps above, please visit www.pearsonITcertification.com/contact and select the "Site Problems/Comments" option. Our customer service representatives will assist you.

Pearson IT Certification Practice Test Engine and Questions

The companion website includes the Pearson IT Certification Practice Test engine—software that displays and grades a set of exam-realistic multiple-choice questions. Using the Pearson IT Certification Practice Test engine, you can either study by going through the questions in Study Mode, or take a simulated exam that mimics real exam conditions. You can also serve up questions in a Flash Card Mode, which will display just the question and no answers, challenging you to state the answer in your own words before checking the actual answers to verify your work.

The installation process requires two major steps: installing the software and then activating the exam. The website has a recent copy of the Pearson IT Certification Practice Test engine. The practice exam (the database of exam questions) is not on this site.

NOTE The cardboard sleeve in the back of this book includes a piece of paper. The paper lists the activation code for the practice exam associated with this book. Do not lose the activation code. On the opposite side of the paper from the activation code is a unique, one-time-use coupon code for the purchase of the Premium Edition eBook and Practice Test.

Install the Software

The Pearson IT Certification Practice Test is a Windows-only desktop application. You can run it on a Mac using a Windows virtual machine, but it was built specifically for the PC platform. The minimum system requirements are as follows:

- Windows 10, Windows 8.1, or Windows 7

- Microsoft .NET Framework 4.0 Client

- Pentium-class 1GHz processor (or equivalent)

- 512 MB RAM

- 650 MB disk space plus 50 MB for each downloaded practice exam

- Access to the Internet to register and download exam databases

The software installation process is routine compared with other software installation processes. If you have already installed the Pearson IT Certification Practice Test software from another Pearson product, there is no need for you to reinstall the software. Simply launch the software on your desktop and proceed to activate the practice exam from this book by using the activation code included in the access code card sleeve in the back of the book.

The following steps outline the installation process:

1. Download the exam practice test engine from the companion site.

2. Respond to windows prompts as with any typical software installation process.

The installation process will give you the option to activate your exam with the activation code supplied on the paper in the cardboard sleeve. This process requires that you establish a Pearson website login. You need this login to activate the exam, so please do register when prompted. If you already have a Pearson website login, there is no need to register again. Just use your existing login.

Activate and Download the Practice Exam

Once the exam engine is installed, you should then activate the exam associated with this book (if you did not do so during the installation process) as follows:

1. Start the Pearson IT Certification Practice Test software from the Windows Start menu or from your desktop shortcut icon.

2. To activate and download the exam associated with this book, from the My Products or Tools tab, click the Activate Exam button.

3. At the next screen, enter the activation key from paper inside the cardboard sleeve in the back of the book. Once you've entered the key, click the Activate button.

4. The activation process will download the practice exam. Click **Next**, and then click **Finish**.

When the activation process completes, the My Products tab should list your new exam. If you do not see the exam, make sure that you have selected the **My Products** tab on the menu. At this point, the software and practice exam are ready to use. Simply select the exam and click the **Open Exam** button.

To update a particular exam you have already activated and downloaded, display the **Tools** tab and click the **Update Products** button. Updating your exams will ensure that you have the latest changes and updates to the exam data.

If you want to check for updates to the Pearson Cert Practice Test exam engine software, display the **Tools** tab and click the **Update Application** button. You can then ensure that you are running the latest version of the software engine.

Activating Other Exams

The exam software installation process, and the registration process, only has to happen once. Then, for each new exam, only a few steps are required. For instance, if you buy another Pearson IT Certification Cert Guide, extract the activation code from the cardboard sleeve in the back of that book; you do not even need the exam engine at this point. From there, all you have to do is start the exam engine (if not still up and running) and perform Steps 2 through 4 from the previous list.

Assessing Exam Readiness

Exam candidates never really know whether they are adequately prepared for the exam until they have completed about 30 percent of the questions. At that point, if you are not prepared, it is too late. The best way to determine your readiness is to work through the "Do I Know This Already?" quizzes at the beginning of each chapter and review the foundation and key topics presented in each chapter. It is best to work your way through the entire book unless you can complete each subject without having to do any research or look up any answers.

Premium Edition eBook and Practice Tests

This book also includes an exclusive offer for 70 percent off the Premium Edition eBook and Practice Tests edition of this title. Please see the coupon code included with the cardboard sleeve for information on how to purchase the Premium Edition.

How to View Only "Do I Know This Already?" Questions by Part

Each "Part Review" section asks you to repeat the "Do I Know This Already?" quiz questions from the chapters in that part. Although you could simply scan the book pages to review these questions, it is slightly better to review these questions from inside the PCPT software, just to get a little more practice in how to read questions from the testing software.

To view these "Do I Know This Already?" (book) questions inside the PCPT software, follow these steps:

Step 1.   Start the PCPT software.

Step 2.   From the main (home) menu, select the item for this product, with a name like DCICT 200-155 Official Cert Guide, and click **Open Exam**.

Step 3.   The top of the next window that appears should list some exams; select the box beside DCICT Book Questions, and deselect the other boxes. This selects the "book" questions (that is, the "Do I Know This Already?" questions from the beginning of each chapter).

Step 4.   In this same window, click at the bottom of the screen to deselect all objectives (chapters), and then select the box beside each chapter in the part of the book you are reviewing.

Step 5. Select any other options on the right side of the window.

Step 6. Click **Start** to start reviewing the questions.

How to View Only Part Review Questions by Part

The exam databases you get with this book include a database of questions created solely for study during the part review process. "Do I Know This Already?" questions focus more on facts, with basic application. The part review questions instead focus more on application and look more like real exam questions.

To view these questions, follow the same process as you did with "Do I Know This Already?" book questions, but select the part review database instead of the book database, as follows:

Step 1. Start the PCPT software.

Step 2. From the main (home) menu, select the item for this product, with a name like DCICT 200-155 Official Cert Guide, and click **Open Exam**.

Step 3. The top of the next window should list some exams; select the box beside Part Review Questions, and deselect the other boxes. This selects the questions intended for part-ending review.

Step 4. On this same window, click at the bottom of the screen to deselect all objectives, and then select (check) the box beside the book part you want to review. This tells the PCPT software to give you part review questions from the selected part.

Step 5. Select any other options on the right side of the window.

Step 6. Click **Start** to start reviewing the questions.

For More Information

If you have any comments about the book, submit them via www.ciscopress.com. Just go to the website, select **Contact Us**, and type your message.

Cisco might make changes that affect the CCNA data center certification from time to time. You should always check www.cisco.com/go/certification for the latest details.

The *CCNA Data Center DCICT 200-155 Official Cert Guide* helps you attain the CCNA data center certification. This is the DCICT exam prep book from the only Cisco-authorized publisher. We at Cisco Press believe that this book certainly can help you achieve CCNA data center certification, but the real work is up to you. We trust that your time will be well spent.

Getting Started

It might look like this is yet another certification exam preparation book—indeed, it is. We welcome your decision to become a Cisco Certified Network Associate Data Center professional! You are probably wondering how to get started, and today you are taking a significant step in achieving your goal. A team of five data center professionals came together to carefully pick the content for this book to send you on your CCNA data center certification journey.

Strategizing about your studying is a key element to your success. Spend time thinking about key milestones you want to reach, and plan accordingly to review material for exam topics you are less comfortable with. This "Getting Started" introduction guides you through building a strategy toward success. Take time to review it before starting your CCNA data center certification journey.

A Brief Perspective on the CCNA Data Center Certification Exam

Cisco sets the bar somewhat high for passing its certification exams, including all the exams related to CCNA certifications, such as CCNA data center. These exams pose multidimensional challenges for your ability to analyze, configure, and troubleshoot networking features, as well as understand relevant technology landscape and analyze emerging technology trends. The CCNA data center exam puts your knowledge in network, storage, compute, virtualization, and security to the test.

Many questions in the CCNA data center certification exam apply to connectivity between the data center devices. For example, a question might give you a data center topology diagram and then ask what needs to be considered when designing that topology, what needs to be configured to make that setup work, what is the missing ingredient of the solution, and so on. You will need certain analytical problem-solving skills, skills that require you to prepare by doing more than just reading and memorizing this book's content. This book offers a solid foundation for the knowledge required to pass the CCNA data center certification exam, and, at the same time, it encourages you to continue your journey to become an overall better data center networking professional.

Suggestions for How to Approach Your Study with This Book

Although Cisco certification exams are challenging, many people pass them every day. So, what do you need to do to be ready to pass the exam? Take a two-pronged approach. We encourage you to build your theoretical knowledge by thoroughly reading this book and taking time to remember the most critical facts. At the same time, we encourage you to develop your practical knowledge by having hands-on experience in the topics covered in the CCNA data center certification exam.

Think about studying for the CCNA data center certification exam as preparing for a marathon. It requires a bit of practice every day.

What I Talk About When I Talk About Running is a memoir by Haruki Murakami in which he writes about his interest and participation in long-distance running. Murakami started running in the early 1980s; since then, he has competed in more than 20 marathons and an ultramarathon. On running as a metaphor, he wrote in his book: "For me, running is both exercise and a metaphor. Running day after day, piling up the races, bit-by-bit I raise the bar, and by clearing each level I elevate myself. At least that's why I've put in the effort day after day: to raise my own level. I'm no great runner, by any means. I'm at an ordinary—or perhaps more like mediocre—level. But that's not the point. The point is whether or not I improved over yesterday. In long-distance running the only opponent you have to beat is yourself, the way you used to be."

Similar principles apply here, and the only opponent you have to beat is yourself.

This Book Is Compiled from 17 Short Read-and-Review Sessions

First, look at your study as a series of read-and-review tasks, each on a relatively small set of related topics. These topics are structured to cover main data center infrastructure technologies, such as Network, Compute, Server Virtualization, Unified Fabric, and Application Centricity.

This book has 17 content chapters covering the topics you need to know to pass the exam. Each chapter consists of numerous "Foundation Topics" sections and "Exam Preparation Tasks" at the end. Take time to review this book chapter by chapter and topic by topic. Plan your time accordingly, and make progress every day. Each chapter marks key topics you should pay extra attention to. Review those sections carefully, and make sure you are thoroughly familiar with their content.

This book organizes the content into topics of a more manageable size to give you something more digestible to build your knowledge.

Practice, Practice, Practice—Did I Mention: Practice?

Second, plan to use the practice tasks at the end of each chapter.

Each chapter ends with practice and study tasks under the heading "Exam Preparation Tasks." Doing these tasks, and doing them at the end of the chapter, really helps you get ready. Do not put off doing these tasks until later! The chapter-ending "Exam Preparation Tasks" section helps you with deepening your knowledge and skills of the key topics, remembering terms, and linking the concepts in your brain so that you can remember how it all fits together.

The following list describes the majority of the activities you will find in "Exam Preparation Tasks" sections:

- Review key topics
- Complete memory tables
- Define key terms

Approach each chapter with the same plan. Based on your score in the "Do I Know This Already?" (DIKTA) quiz, you can choose to read the entire core ("Foundation Topics") section of the chapter or just skim the chapter. DIKTA is a self-assessment quiz appearing at the beginning of each content chapter. Remember, regardless of whether you skim or read thoroughly, do the study tasks in the "Exam Preparation Tasks" section at the end of the chapter. Table I-1 shows the suggested study approach for each content chapter.

Table I-1 Suggested Study Approach for the Content Chapter

Take DIKTA Quiz	High Score ➔	Light reading of "Foundation Topics" ➔	Do "Exam Preparation Tasks"
Take DIKTA Quiz	Low Score ➔	Careful reading of "Foundation Topics" ➔	Do "Exam Preparation Tasks"

In Each Part of the Book You Will Hit a New Milestone

Third, view the book as having five major milestones, one for each major topic.

Beyond the more obvious organization into chapters, this book organizes the chapters into five major topic areas called book parts. Completing each part means that you have completed a major area of study. At the end of each part, take extra time to complete "Part Review" tasks and ask yourself where your weak and strong areas are. Acknowledge yourself for completing major milestones. Table I-2 lists the five parts in this book.

Table I-2 Five Major Milestones: Book Parts

Part I, "Data Center Networking Technologies"	Preparation Tasks
Part II, "Network Virtualization"	Preparation Tasks
Part III, "Cisco Unified Computing"	Preparation Tasks
Part IV, "Application Centric Infrastructure"	Preparation Tasks
Part V, "Automation and Orchestration"	Preparation Tasks

Note that the "Part Review" directs you to use the Pearson Certification Practice Test (PCPT) software to access the practice questions. Each "Part Review" instructs you to repeat the DIKTA questions while using the PCPT software. It also instructs you on how to access a specific set of questions reserved for reviewing concepts at the "Part Review." Note that the PCPT software and exam databases included with this book also give you the rights to additional questions. Chapter 18, "Final Preparation," gives some recommendations on how to best use those questions for your final exam preparation.

Consider setting a goal date for finishing each part of the book, and reward yourself for achieving this goal. Plan breaks—some personal time out—to get refreshed and motivated for the next part.

Use the Final Preparation Chapter to Refine Skills

Fourth, do the tasks outlined at the end of the book in Chapter 18.

Chapter 18 helps you plan your exam-taking strategies and no less important gives you invaluable tips for mentally and emotionally preparing yourself for the exam. It may sound unnecessary, but many candidates actually fail certification exams not because of lack of knowledge or experience, but because of improper planning. This chapter helps you with building the right mind-set to avoid some of the pitfalls people experience with the actual exam.

Set Goals and Track Your Progress

Finally, before you start reading the book, take the time to make a plan, set some goals, and be ready to track your progress.

Although making list of tasks may or may not appeal to you, depending on your personality, setting goals can help everyone studying for the exam. To set the goals, you need to know what tasks you plan to do. The list of tasks does not have to be very detailed, such as putting down every single task in the "Exam Preparation Tasks" section, the "Part Review" tasks section, or the "Exam Preparation" chapter. Instead, listing only the major tasks can be sufficient.

You should track at least two tasks for each typical chapter: reading the "Foundation Topics" section and doing the "Exam Preparation Tasks" section at the end of the chapter. Of course, do not forget to list tasks for "Part Reviews" and the "Final Preparation." Table I-3 shows a sample of a task planning table for Part I of this book.

Table I-3   Sample Excerpt from a Planning Table

Element	Task	Goal Date	First Date Completed	Second Date Completed (Optional)
Chapter 1	Read "Foundation Topics"			
Chapter 1	Do "Exam Preparation Tasks"			
Chapter 2	Read "Foundation Topics"			
Chapter 2	Do "Exam Preparation Tasks"			
Chapter 3	Read "Foundation Topics"			
Chapter 3	Do "Exam Preparation Tasks"			
Part I Review	Do "Part Review" Activities			

Use your goal dates as a way to manage your study, and do not get discouraged if you miss a date. Pick reasonable dates you can meet. When setting your goals, think about how fast you read and the length of each chapter's "Foundation Topics" section, as listed in the Table of Contents. If you finish a task sooner than planned, move up the next few goal dates.

If you miss a few dates, do not start skipping the tasks listed at the ends of the chapters. Instead, think about what is impacting your schedule—family commitments, work commitments, and so on—and either adjust your goals or work a little harder on your study.

Other Small Tasks Before Getting Started

You will need to complete a few overhead tasks, such as install software, find some PDFs, and so on. You can complete these tasks now or do them in your spare time when you need a study break during the first few chapters of the book. Do not delay; should you encounter software installation problems, you have sufficient time to resolve them before you need the tool.

Register (for free) at the Cisco Learning Network (CLN, http://learningnetwork.cisco.com) and join the CCNA data center study group. This mailing list allows you to lurk and participate in discussions about CCNA data center topics, for both the DCICN and DCICT exams. Register, join the group, and set up an e-mail filter to redirect the messages to a separate folder. Even if you do not spend time reading all the posts yet, later, when you have time to read, you can browse through the posts to find relevant topics. You can also search the posts from the CLN website. There are many recorded CCNA data center sessions from the technology experts, which you can listen to as much as you want. All the recorded sessions last a maximum of one hour.

Install the PCPT exam software and activate the exams. For more details on how to load the software, refer to the "Introduction," under the heading "Install the Pearson Certification Practice Test Engine and Questions."

Keep calm, and enjoy the ride!

Exam topics covered in Part I:

- 2.5 Differentiate between the data, control, and management planes
- 3.1 Describe, configure, and verify FEX connectivity
- 3.2 Describe, configure, and verify basic vPC features
- 3.3 Describe, configure, and verify FabricPath
- 3.4 Describe, configure, and verify unified switch ports
- 3.5 Describe the features and benefits of Unified Fabric
- 3.6 Describe and explain the use of role-based access control within the data center infrastructure

Part I

Data Center Networking Technologies

This chapter covers the following exam topics:

3.2 Describe, configure, and verify basic vPC features

3.3 Describe, configure, and verify FabricPath

CHAPTER 1

Data Center Networking

Data centers are designed to host critical computing resources in a centralized place. These resources can be utilized from a campus building of an enterprise network, from a branch office over the wide area network (WAN), and from the remote locations over the public Internet. Therefore, the network plays an important role in the availability of data center resources. Data center networking is an important subject addressing many functional areas to ensure that data center services are running around the clock.

This chapter discusses data center networking topics relevant to the certification exam. It is assumed that you are familiar with the Nexus product family and the basics of networking concepts outlined in Introducing Cisco Data Center Networking (DCICN). This chapter goes directly into the key concepts of data center networking and explores the details of topics important for Introducing Cisco Data Center Technologies (DCICT) certification. Basic network configuration and verification commands are also included in this chapter.

"Do I Know This Already?" Quiz

The "Do I Know This Already?" quiz enables you to assess whether you should read this entire chapter thoroughly or jump to the "Exam Preparation Tasks" section. If you are in doubt about your answers to these questions or your own assessment of your knowledge of the topics, read the entire chapter. Table 1-1 lists the major headings in this chapter and their corresponding "Do I Know This Already?" quiz questions. You can find the answers in Appendix A, "Answers to the 'Do I Know This Already?' Quizzes."

Table 1-1 "Do I Know This Already?" Section-to-Question Mapping

Foundation Topics Section	Questions
"Port Channel"	1–6
"Virtual Port Channel"	7–11
"FabricPath"	12–15

CAUTION The goal of self-assessment is to gauge your mastery of the topics in this chapter. If you do not know the answer to a question or are only partially sure of the answer, you should mark that question as wrong for purposes of the self-assessment. Giving yourself credit for an answer you correctly guess skews your self-assessment results and might provide you with a false sense of security.

1. Which of the following are benefits of port channels?

   a. Increased capacity

   b. Load balancing

   c. Quality of service

   d. High availability

2. Which of the following attributes must match to bundle ports into a port channel?

   a. Speed

   b. Duplex

   c. LACP port priority

   d. Flow control

3. Which of the following are valid port channel modes?

   a. Active

   b. Standby

   c. Passive

   d. On

   e. Off

4. LACP is enabled on a port. The port responds to LACP packets that it receives but does not initiate LACP negotiation. Which LACP mode is used?

   a. Progressive

   b. Passive

   c. Active

   d. On

5. LACP is enabled on a port. The port initiates negotiations with a peer switch by sending LACP packets. Which LACP mode is used?

   a. On

   b. Progressive

   c. Passive

   d. Active

6. Cisco Nexus switches support which of the following port channel load-balancing methods?

   a. Source and destination IP address

   b. Source and destination MAC address

   c. Source and destination TCP/UDP port number

   d. None of the above

7. Identify the Cisco switching platform that supports vPC.

    a. Catalyst 6500 switches

    b. Nexus 7000 Series switches

    c. Nexus 5000 Series switches

    d. All Cisco switches

8. Which of the following are benefits of using vPC?

    a. It uses all available uplink bandwidth.

    b. It eliminates Spanning Tree Protocol (STP) blocked ports.

    c. It provides fast convergence if either the link or the device fails.

    d. It is supported on all Cisco switches.

9. In vPC setup, Cisco Fabric Services over Ethernet (CFSoE) uses which of the following links?

    a. vPC peer keepalive link

    b. vPC peer link

    c. vPC ports

    d. vPC peer link and vPC peer keepalive link

10. Cisco Fabric Services over Ethernet (CFSoE) performs which of the following operations?

    a. It performs consistency and compatibility checks.

    b. It performs load balancing of traffic between two vPC switches.

    c. It exchanges Layer 2 forwarding tables between vPC peers.

    d. It monitors the status of vPC member ports.

11. How many vPC domains can be configured on a switch or VDC?

    a. Only one.

    b. Only two.

    c. 255.

    d. There is no limit; you can configure as many as you want.

12. In a FabricPath network, which protocol is used to automatically assign a unique Switch ID to each FabricPath switch?

    a. Dynamic Host Configuration Protocol (DHCP).

    b. Cisco Fabric Services over Ethernet (CFSoE).

    c. Dynamic Resource Allocation Protocol (DRAP).

    d. In FabricPath, the Switch ID must be allocated manually.

13. In a FabricPath network, the root of the first multidestination tree is elected based on which of the following parameters?

   a. Root priority

   b. System ID

   c. Switch ID

   d. MAC address

14. FabricPath routes the frames based on which of the following parameters?

   a. Source Switch ID in outer source address (OSA)

   b. Destination MAC address

   c. Destination Switch ID in outer destination address (ODA)

   d. IP address of packet

15. What is the name of the FabricPath control plane protocol?

   a. IS-IS

   b. OSPF

   c. BGP

   d. EIGRP

Foundation Topics

Port Channel

In this section, you learn about the important concepts of a port channel.

What Is Port Channel?

Data center network topology is built using multiple switches. These switches are connected to each other using physical network links. When you connect two devices using multiple physical links, you can group these links to form a logical bundle. The two devices connected via this logical group of ports see it as a single, big network pipe between the two devices. This logical group is called EtherChannel, or port channel, and physical interfaces participating in this group are called member ports of the group. Therefore, a port channel is an aggregation of multiple physical interfaces that create a logical interface. On the Nexus 5000 Series switch, you can bundle up to 16 links into a port channel. On the Nexus 7000 Series switch, you can bundle 8 active ports on an M-Series module and up to 16 ports on the F-Series module. Figure 1-1 shows how multiple physical interfaces are combined to create a logical port channel between two switches.

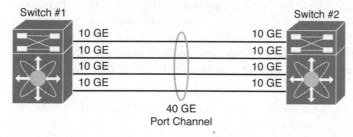

Figure 1-1 *Port Channel*

When a port channel is created, you will see a new interface in the switch configuration. This new interface is a logical representation of all the member ports of the port channel. The port channel interface can be configured with its own speed, bandwidth, delay, IP address, duplex, flow control, maximum transmission unit (MTU), and interface description. You can also shut down the port channel interface, which will result in shutting down all member ports.

Benefits of Using Port Channels

There are several benefits of using port channels, and because of these benefits you will find they're commonly used within data center networks. Some of these benefits are as follows:

- **Increased capacity:** By combing multiple Ethernet links into one logical link, you can increase the capacity of the link. For example, you can combine eight 10-Gbps links to create a logical link with bandwidth of 80 Gbps.

- **High availability:** In a port channel, multiple Ethernet links are bundled together to create a logical link. In case of a physical link failure, the port channel continues to operate even if a single member link is alive. Therefore, it automatically increases availability of the network. As an example, when creating a port channel on a modular network switch, it is recommended that you use member ports from different line cards. This will help you increase network availability in the case of line card failure.

- **Load balancing:** The switch distributes traffic across all operational interfaces in the port channel. This enables you to distribute traffic across multiple physical interfaces, increasing the efficiency of your network. Port channel load balancing configuration is discussed later in this chapter.

- **Simplified network topology:** In some cases, you can use port channels to simplify network topology by aggregating multiple links into one logical link. Typically, if you have multiple links between a pair of switches, to avoid network loops, STP blocks all the links except one. In the case of port channels, multiple links are combined into one logical link; therefore, it simplifies the network topology by avoiding the STP calculation and reducing network complexity by reducing the number of links between switches.

Port Channel Compatibility Requirements

If you want to bundle multiple switch interfaces into a port channel, the interfaces must meet the compatibility requirements. For example, when you add an interface to a port channel, its speed must match with other member interfaces in this port channel. In other words, you cannot put a 1 G interface and a 10 G interface into the same port channel. Other interface attributes are checked by switch software to ensure that the interface is compatible with the channel group. In case of an incompatible attribute, port channel creation will fail. Some of these attributes are speed, duplex, flow control, port mode, VLANs, MTU, and media type.

On the Nexus platform, you can use the **show port-channel compatibility-parameters** command to see the full list of compatibility checks.

If you configure a member port with an incompatible attribute, the software suspends that port in the port channel. You can force ports with incompatible parameters to join the port channel if the following parameters are the same: speed, duplex, and flow control.

Link Aggregation Control Protocol

The Link Aggregation Control Protocol (LACP) provides a standard mechanism to ensure that peer switches exchange information and agree on the necessary details to bundle ports into a port channel. LACP must be enabled on switches at both ends of the link. Network devices use LACP to negotiate an automatic bundling of links by sending LACP packets to the peer. This protocol ensures that both sides of the link have compatible configuration (speed, duplex, flow control, allowed VLAN) to form a bundle.

LACP was initially part of the IEEE 802.3ad standard and later moved to the IEEE 802.1AX standard.

On Nexus 7000 switches, LACP enables you to configure up to 16 interfaces into a port channel. On M-Series modules, a maximum of 8 interfaces can be in an active state, and a maximum of 8 interfaces can be placed in a standby state. Starting from NX-OS Release 5.1, you can bundle up to 16 active links into a port channel on the F-Series module.

NOTE   Nexus switches do not support Cisco proprietary Port Aggregation Protocol (PAgP) to create port channels.

Port Channel Modes

Member ports in a port channel are configured with channel mode. Nexus switches support three port channel modes: On, Active, and Passive. When you configure a static port channel without specifying a channel mode, the channel mode is set to On.

To run LACP, you first enable the LACP feature globally on the device. Then you enable LACP for each channel by setting the channel mode for each interface to Active or Passive. You can configure channel mode Active or Passive for individual links in the LACP channel group when you are adding the links to the channel group.

Table 1-2 shows the port channel modes supported by Nexus switches.

Table 1-2   Port Channel Modes

Port Channel Mode	Description
On	This mode represents a static port channel configuration. In this mode, member ports join the port channel without exchanging information with the peer switch. This mode also means that LACP is not running.
Active	LACP is enabled, and LACP packets are sent on the port. This mode puts the port into an active negotiating state in which the port initiates negotiations with the peer switch by sending LACP packets.
Passive	LACP is enabled, but LACP packets are not initiated. This mode puts the port into a passive negotiating state in which the port responds to LACP packets that it receives but does not initiate LACP negotiation.

If you attempt to change the channel mode to Active or Passive before enabling the LACP feature on the switch, the device returns an error message. After LACP is enabled globally, you can enable LACP on ports by configuring each interface in the channel for the channel mode as either Active or Passive.

When an LACP attempts to negotiate with an interface in the On state, it does not receive LACP packets; therefore, it does not join the LACP channel group, and it becomes an individual link for that interface.

Both the Passive and Active modes enable LACP to negotiate between ports to determine whether they can form a port channel, based on criteria such as the port speed and the trunking state. The Passive mode is useful when you do not know whether the remote system, or partner, supports LACP.

Ports can form an LACP port channel when they are in different LACP modes as long as the modes are compatible, as shown in Figure 1-2.

Port Channel Mode	Compatible Configuration	Description
Active — Active Switch #1 Switch #2	✓	A port in Active mode can form a port channel successfully with a peer switch that is configured with the port in Active mode.
Active — Passive Switch #1 Switch #2	✓	A port in Active mode can form a port channel successfully with a peer switch that is configured with the port in Passive mode.
Passive — Passive Switch #1 Switch #2	✗	A port in Passive mode cannot form a port channel with a peer switch that is also configured with the port in Passive mode because neither port will initiate negotiation.
Active — On Switch #1 Switch #2	✗	A port in the on mode is not running LACP. An Active or Passive mode will not form a port channel with mode on. When using mode on, both sides should be configured with mode on.

Figure 1-2 *Port Channel Mode Compatibility*

Configuring Port Channel

Port channel configuration on the Cisco Nexus switches includes the following steps:

1. Enable the LACP feature. This step is required only if you are using Active mode or Passive mode.

2. Configure the physical interface of the switch with the **channel-group** command and specify the channel number. You can also specify the channel mode On, Active, or Passive within the **channel-group** command. This command automatically creates an interface port channel with the number that you specified in the command.

3. Configure the newly created interface port channel with the appropriate configuration, such as description, trunk configuration, and allowed VLANs.

Figure 1-3 shows configuration of a port channel between two switches.

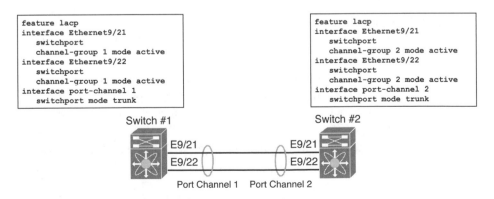

```
feature lacp
interface Ethernet9/21
   switchport
   channel-group 1 mode active
interface Ethernet9/22
   switchport
   channel-group 1 mode active
interface port-channel 1
   switchport mode trunk
```

```
feature lacp
interface Ethernet9/21
   switchport
   channel-group 2 mode active
interface Ethernet9/22
   switchport
   channel-group 2 mode active
interface port-channel 2
   switchport mode trunk
```

Switch #1   Switch #2

E9/21   E9/21
E9/22   E9/22

Port Channel 1   Port Channel 2

Figure 1-3 *Port Channel Configuration Example*

Port Channel Load Balancing

Nexus switches distribute the traffic across all operational ports in a port channel. This load balancing is done using a hashing algorithm that takes addresses in the frame as input and generates a value that selects one of the links in the channel. This provides load balancing across all member ports of a port channel, but it also ensures that frames from a particular address are always forwarded on the same port; therefore, the remote device always receives them in order.

You can configure the device to use one of the following methods to load-balance across the port channel:

- Destination MAC address
- Source MAC address
- Source and destination MAC address
- Destination IP address
- Source IP address
- Source and destination IP address
- Source TCP/UDP port number
- Destination TCP/UDP port number
- Source and destination TCP/UDP port number

Verifying Port Channel Configuration

Several **show** commands are available on the Nexus switch to check port channel configuration. These commands are helpful to verify port channel configuration and troubleshoot the port channel issue. Table 1-3 provides some useful commands.

Table 1-3   Verify Port Channel Configuration

Command	Description
show port-channel summary	Provides a nice summary of all port channels configured on the switch. This command shows the channel number, member ports, status of the channel, and status of the member ports within the channel.
show port-channel traffic interface port-channel 2	Shows traffic distribution on the member ports of port channel 2. Statistics are shown for unicast, multicast, and broadcast traffic in both directions.
show interface port-channel 2	Displays the interface status of port channel 2, its member ports, interface counters, and other interface details.
show port-channel load-balance	Displays the type of load balancing configuration used for the port channel.
show lacp neighbor	Shows the partner's LACP information for each port in the port channel.

Virtual Port Channel

In this section, you learn about important concepts of virtual port channel (vPC).

What Is Virtual Port Channel?

You learned in the previous section that a port channel bundles multiple physical links into a logical link. All the member ports of a port channel belong to the same network switch. A vPC enables the extension of a port channel across two physical switches. These two switches work together to create a virtual domain, so a port channel can be extended across the two devices within this virtual domain. It means that member ports in a virtual port channel can be from two different network switches. In Layer 2 network design, Cisco vPC technology allows dual-homing of a downstream device to two upstream switches. The upstream switches present themselves to the downstream device as one switch from the port channel and STP perspective. Figure 1-4 shows a downstream switch connected to two upstream switches in a vPC configuration.

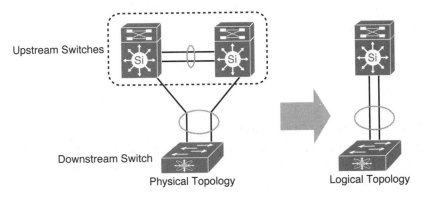

Figure 1-4 *Virtual Port Channel*

In a conventional network design, smaller Layer 2 segments are preferred. However, with the current data center virtualization trend, this preference is changing. A virtualized server running hypervisor software, such as VMware ESX Server, Microsoft Hyper-V, and Citrix XenServer, requires Layer 2 Ethernet connectivity between the physical servers to support seamless workload mobility. There are some other applications, such as high-availability clusters, that require member servers to be on the same Layer 2 Ethernet network to support private interprocess communication and public client-facing communication using a virtual IP of the cluster. These requirements lead to the use of large Layer 2 networks, within and across the data center locations. As a result, data center network architecture is shifting from a highly scalable Layer 3 network model to a highly scalable Layer 2 model. The innovation of new technologies to manage large Layer 2 network environments is the result of this shift in the data center architecture. STP does not provide an efficient way to manage large Layer 2 networks; therefore, it is important to migrate away from STP as a primary loop management technology toward new technologies such as vPC and Cisco FabricPath. FabricPath technology is discussed later in this chapter.

A large Layer 2 network is built using many network switches connected to each other in a redundant topology using multiple network links. Building redundancy is an important design consideration to protect against device or link failure. However, for an Ethernet network, this redundant topology can result in a Layer 2 loop. A Layer 2 loop is a condition in which packets are circulating within the redundant network topology, causing high CPU and link utilization. These loops can cause a meltdown of network resources; therefore, it was necessary to develop protocols and control mechanisms to limit the disastrous effects of a Layer 2 topology loop in the network. STP was the primary solution to this problem because it provides loop detection and loop management capability for Layer 2 Ethernet networks. Over a period of time, and after going through a number of enhancements and extensions, STP became mature and stable. Although STP can support large network environments, it still has a fundamental issue that makes it suboptimal for the network. This issue is related to the STP principle that allows only one active network path from one device to another to break the topology loops in a network. It means that no matter how many connections exist between network devices, only one will be active at any given time.

NOTE   A brief summary of Spanning Tree is provided later in the "FabricPath" section. Detailed discussion on STP is part of Introducing Cisco Data Center Networking (DCICN).

Port channel technology discussed earlier in this chapter was a key enhancement to Layer 2 Ethernet networks. This enhancement enables the use of multiple Ethernet links to forward traffic between the two network devices. It also provides the capability to equally balance traffic by sending packets to all available links using a load-balancing algorithm. In a port channel, Layer 2 loops are managed by bundling multiple physical links into one logical link. It means that if you configure a port channel between two network devices, there is only one logical path between the two switches. This configuration keeps the switches from forwarding broadcast and multicast traffic back to the same link, avoiding loops. Port channel technology has another great benefit. It can recover from a link loss in the bundle within a second, with minimal loss of traffic and no effect on the active network topology.

The limitation of the classic port channel is that it operates between only two devices. In large networks with redundant devices, the alternative path is often connected to a different network switch in a topology that would cause a loop. vPC addresses this limitation by allowing a pair of switches acting as a virtual endpoint, so it looks like a single logical entity to port channel–attached devices. Figure 1-5 shows a comparison of STP topology and vPC topology. It is important to observe that there is no blocking port in the vPC topology, resulting in efficient use of network capacity. Figure 1-5 shows the comparison between STP and vPC topology using the same devices and network links.

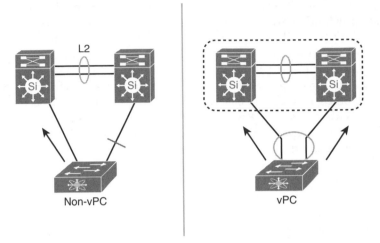

Figure 1-5 *Virtual Port Channel Bi-Section Bandwidth*

The two switches that act as the logical port channel endpoint are still two separate devices. These switches collaborate only for the purpose of creating a vPC. This environment combines the benefits of hardware redundancy with the benefits of port channel.

Benefits of Using vPC

vPC provides the following benefits:

- Enables a single device to use a port channel across two upstream switches
- Eliminates STP blocked ports
- Provides a loop-free topology
- Uses all available uplink bandwidth
- Provides fast convergence in the case of link or device failure
- Provides link-level resiliency
- Helps ensure high availability

Components of vPC

In a vPC configuration, a downstream network device that connects to a pair of upstream Nexus switches sees them as a single Layer 2 switch. These two upstream Nexus switches operate independently with their own control, data, and management planes. However, the data planes of these switches are modified to ensure optimal packet forwarding in vPC configuration. The control planes of these switches also exchange information so it appears as a single logical Layer 2 switch to a downstream device.

> **NOTE**   The operational plane of a switch includes control, data, and management planes. This subject is covered in Chapter 2, "Management and Monitoring of Cisco Nexus Devices."

Before going into the detail of vPC control and data plane operation, it is important to understand the components of vPC and the function of these components. Figure 1-6 shows the components of a vPC.

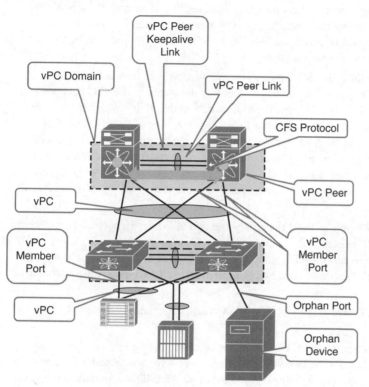

Figure 1-6 *vPC Components*

The vPC architecture consists of the following components:

- **vPC peers:** The two Cisco Nexus switches combined to build a vPC architecture are referred to as vPC peers. This pair of switches acts as a single logical switch, which enables other devices to connect to the two chassis using vPC.

- **PC peer link:** This is a link between two vPC peers to synchronize state. The vPC peer link is the most important connectivity element in the vPC system. Typically, this link is built using two physical interfaces in port channel configuration. This link creates the illusion of a single control plane by forwarding bridge protocol data units (BPDUs) and Link Aggregation Control Protocol (LACP) packets to the primary vPC switch from the secondary vPC switch. The peer link is also used to synchronize MAC address tables between the vPC peers and to synchronize Internet Group Management Protocol (IGMP) entries for IGMP snooping. The peer link provides the necessary transport for data plane traffic, such as multicast traffic, and for the traffic of orphaned ports. If a vPC device is also a Layer 3 switch, the peer link carries Hot Standby Router Protocol (HSRP) and Virtual Router Redundancy Protocol (VRRP) packets.

- **Cisco Fabric Services:** Cisco Fabric Services is a reliable messaging protocol used between the vPC peer switches to synchronize control and data plane information.

It uses the vPC peer link to exchange information between peer switches. When you enable the vPC feature, the device automatically enables Cisco Fabric Services over Ethernet (CFSoE). No CFSoE configuration is required for vPC to function properly. CFSoE carries messages and packets for many features linked with vPC, such as STP and IGMP. To help ensure that the vPC peer link communication for the CFSoE protocol is always available, Spanning Tree has been modified to keep the peer-link ports forwarding.

- **vPC peer keepalive link:** This is a Layer 3 communication path between vPC peer switches. The peer keepalive link is used to monitor the status of the vPC peer when the vPC peer link goes down. It helps the vPC switch to determine whether the peer has failed or whether the vPC peer switch has failed entirely. Peer keepalive is used as a secondary test to make sure that the remote peer switch is operating properly. The vPC peer keepalive link is not used for any data or synchronization traffic; it only sends IP packets to make sure that the originating switch is operating and running vPC. Peer keepalive can also use the management port of the switch and often runs over an out-of-band (OOB) network.

- **vPC:** This is a Layer 2 port channel that spans the two vPC peer switches. The device on the other end of vPC sees the vPC peer switches as a single logical switch. There is no need for this device to support vPC itself. It connects to the vPC peer switches using a regular port channel. This device can be configured to use LACP or a static port channel configuration.

- **vPC member port:** This port is a member of a virtual port channel on the vPC peer switch.

- **vPC domain:** This is a pair of vPC peer switches combined using vPC configuration. A vPC domain is created using two vPC peer devices that are connected using a vPC peer keepalive link and a vPC peer link. A numerical domain ID is assigned to the vPC domain. A peer switch can join only one vPC domain.

- **Orphan device:** The term *orphan device* is used for any device that is connected to only one switch within a vPC domain. It means that the orphan device is not using port channel configuration, and for this device there is no vPC configured on the peer switches.

- **Orphan port:** This is a switch port that is connected to an orphan device. This term is also used for the vPC member ports that are connected to only one vPC switch. This situation can happen in a failure condition in which a device connected to vPC loses all its connection to one of the vPC peer switches.

- **vPC VLANs:** The VLANs that are allowed on vPC are called vPC VLANs. These VLANs must also be allowed on the vPC peer link.

- **Non-vPC VLANs:** These VLANs are not part of any vPC and are not present on a vPC peer link.

vPC Data Plane Operation

vPC technology is designed to always forward traffic locally when possible. In a normal network condition, vPC peer link is not used for the regular vPC traffic and is considered to be an extension of the control plane between the vPC peer switches. The vPC peer link carries the following type of traffic:

■ vPC control traffic, such as Cisco FSoE, BPDUs, and LACP messages

■ Flooding traffic, such as broadcast, multicast, and unknown unicast traffic

■ Traffic from orphan ports

The vPC peer link does not typically forward data packets; it is used specifically for switch management traffic and occasionally for the data packets from failed network ports. This behavior of vPC enables the solution to scale because the bandwidth requirement for the vPC peer link is not directly related to the total bandwidth of all vPC ports.

vPC performs loop avoidance at the data plane by implementing forwarding rules in the hardware. One of the most important forwarding rules for vPC is that a packet that enters the vPC peer switch via the vPC member port, and then goes to other peer switches via peer link, is not allowed to exit the switch on the vPC member port. This packet can exit on any other type of port, such as an L3 port or an orphan port. This rule prevents the packets that are received on a vPC from being flooded back onto the same vPC by the other peer switch. The vPC loop avoidance rule is depicted in Figure 1-7.

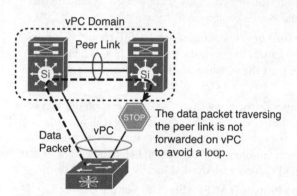

Figure 1-7 *vPC Loop Avoidance*

It is important to understand vPC data plane operation for the orphan ports. The first type of orphan port is the one that is connected to an orphan device and is not part of any vPC configuration. For this type of orphan port, normal switch forwarding rules are applied. The traffic for this type of orphan port can use a vPC peer link as a transit link to reach the devices on the other vPC peer switch.

The second type of orphan port is the one that is a member of a vPC configuration, but the other peer switch has lost all the associated vPC member ports. For this type of orphan port, the vPC loop avoidance rule is disabled. In this special case, the vPC peer switch will be allowed to forward the traffic that is received on the peer link to one of the remaining active vPC member ports.

To implement the specific vPC forwarding behavior, CFSoE is used to synchronize the Layer 2 forwarding tables between the vPC peer switches. Therefore, there is no dependency on the regular MAC address learning between the vPC peer switches. CFSoE-based

MAC address learning is applicable only to the vPC ports. This method of learning is not used for the ports that are not part of vPC configuration.

vPC Control Plane Operation

As discussed earlier, the vPC peer link is used for control plane messaging, such as CFSoE, BPDUs, and LACP messages. The CFSoE is used as the primary control plane protocol for vPC. CFSoE performs the following vPC control plane operations:

- **Exchange the Layer 2 forwarding table between the vPC peers:** If one vPC peer learns a new MAC address, both vPC peer switches know that MAC address, and this MAC is programmed on the Layer 2 Forwarding (L2F) table of both peer devices. This new method of MAC address learning using CFSoE replaces the conventional method of MAC address learning for vPC. It is helpful in reducing data traffic on the vPC peer link by forwarding the traffic to the local vPC member ports.

- **Perform consistency and compatibility checks:** The peer switches exchange information using CFSoE to ensure that vPC configuration is consistent across both switches. It checks the switch configuration for vPC as well as switch-wide parameters that need to be configured consistently on both peer switches. Similar to the conventional port channel, vPC is also subject to the port compatibility checks. CFSoE is used to validate that vPC member ports are compatible and can be combined to form a port channel.

- **Synchronize the IGMP snooping status:** In vPC configuration, IGMP snooping behavior is modified to synchronize the IGMP entries between the peer switches. When IGMP traffic enters a vPC peer switch, it triggers the synchronization of the multicast entry on both vPC peer switches.

- **Monitor the status of the vPC member ports:** For a smooth vPC operation during failure conditions, CFSoE monitors the status of vPC member ports. When all member ports of a vPC go down on one of the peer switches, the other peer switch is notified that its ports are now orphan ports. The switch modifies the forwarding behavior so that all traffic received on the peer link for that vPC is now forwarded locally on the vPC port.

- **Synchronize the Address Resolution Protocol (ARP) table:** This feature enables faster convergence time upon reload of a vPC switch. The ARP table is synchronized between the vPC peer devices using CFSoE. On the Nexus 5000 Series switch, this feature is implemented in Cisco NX-OS Software Release 5.0(2), and for Nexus 7000 it is implemented in Cisco NX-OS Software Version 4.2(6).

- **Determine primary and secondary vPC devices:** When you combine the vPC peer switches in a vPC domain, an election is held to determine the primary and secondary role of the peer switches. This vPC role is nonpreemptive. If the primary vPC peer device fails, the secondary vPC peer device takes the primary role, and it remains primary even if the original device is restored. This role is a control plane function, and it defines which switch will be primarily responsible for the generation and processing of spanning tree BPDUs. It also helps to stabilize the vPC operation during failure conditions. In the case of peer link failure, the peer keepalive mechanism is used to find whether the peer switch is still operational. If both switches are operational and the peer link is down, the secondary switch shuts down all vPC member ports and all switch virtual interfaces (SVIs) that are associated with the vPC VLANs. This mechanism protects from split brain between the vPC peer switches.

■ **Agree on LACP and STP parameters:** In a vPC domain, two peer switches agree on LACP and STP parameters to present themselves as a single logical switch to the device that is connected on a vPC. For LACP, a common LACP system ID is generated from a reserved pool of MAC addresses, which are combined with the vPC domain ID. For STP, the behavior depends on the peer-switch option. When the peer-switch option is used, both primary and secondary switches use the same bridge ID to present themselves as a single switch. In this case, both switches send and process BPDU. If the peer-switch option is not used, only the primary vPC switch sends and processes BPDUs, and it uses its own bridge ID. In this case, the secondary switch only relays BPDUs and does not generate a BPDU.

vPC Limitations

It is important to know the limitations of vPC technology. Some of the key points about vPC limitations are outlined next:

■ **Only two switches per vPC domain:** A vPC domain by definition consists of a pair of switches identified by a shared vPC domain ID. It is not possible to add more than two switches or virtual device contexts (VDCs) to a vPC domain.

■ **Only one vPC domain ID per switch:** Only one vPC domain ID can be configured on a single switch or VDC. It is not possible for a switch or VDC to participate in more than one vPC domain.

■ **Each VDC is a separate switch:** vPC is a per-VDC function on the Cisco Nexus 7000 Series switches. vPCs can be configured in multiple VDCs, but the configuration is entirely independent. A separate vPC peer link and vPC peer keepalive link is required for each of the VDCs. vPC domains cannot be stretched across multiple VDCs on the same switch, and all ports for a given vPC must be in the same VDC.

■ **Peer-link is always 10 Gbps or more:** Only 10 Gigabit Ethernet ports can be used for the vPC peer link. It is recommended that you use at least two 10 Gigabit Ethernet ports in dedicated mode on two different I/O modules.

■ **vPC is a Layer 2 port channel:** A vPC is a Layer 2 port channel. The vPC technology does not support the configuration of Layer 3 port channels. Dynamic routing from the vPC peers to routers connected on a vPC is not supported. It is recommended that routing adjacencies be established on separate routed links.

Configuration Steps of vPC

When you are configuring a vPC, the configuration must be done on both peer switches. Before you start vPC configuration, make sure that peer switches are connected to each other via physical links that can support the requirements of a vPC peer link and that a Layer 3 path is available between the two peer switches. vPC configuration on the Cisco Nexus switches includes the following steps:

1. Enable the vPC feature, which must be enabled on both peer switches. Use the following command to enable the vPC feature:

```
feature vpc
```

2. Create the vPC domain and assign a domain ID to this domain. This domain ID must be unique and should be configured on both vPC switches. Use the following command to create the vPC domain:

```
vpc domain <domain-id>
```

3. Establish peer keepalive connectivity. A peer keepalive link must be configured before you set up the vPC peer link. The peer keepalive link can be in any VRF, including management. Use the following command under the vPC domain to configure the peer keepalive link:

```
peer-keepalive destination <remote peer IP> source <local IP> vrf mgmt
```

4. Create a peer link. The vPC peer link is configured in a port channel configuration. This port channel must be trunked to enable multiple VLANs over the vPC. Use the following commands under the port channel to configure the peer link:

```
Interface port-channel <peer link number>
        switchport mode trunk
        vpc peer-link
```

5. Create the vPC itself. Create a regular port channel and add the **vpc** command under the port channel configuration to create a vPC. This configuration must be the same on both peer switches.

```
Interface port-channel <vPC number>
        vpc <vPC number>
```

Figure 1-8 shows configuration of vPC to connect an access layer switch to a pair of distribution layer switches.

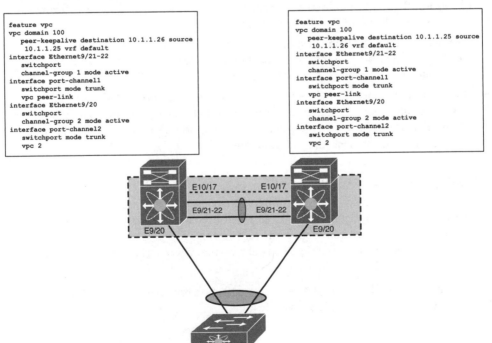

Figure 1-8 *vPC Configuration Example*

Verification of vPC

To verify the status of vPC, you can use all port channel **show** commands discussed earlier. In addition, several **show** commands are available for vPC. These commands are helpful in verifying vPC configuration and troubleshooting the vPC issue. Table 1-4 shows some useful vPC commands.

Table 1-4   Verify Port Channel Configuration

Command	Description
show feature	Provides the status of all the features, including vPC. It shows whether the vPC feature is enabled.
show running-config vpc	Shows the running configuration for all vPCs.
show vpc brief	Displays brief information about all vPCs.
show vpc consistency-parameters	Displays the status of those parameters that must be consistent across all the vPC interfaces.
show vpc statistics	Shows the traffic statistics of vPC.
show vpc peer-keepalive	Displays information about the keepalive messages of vPC.
show vpc role	Shows the peer status, role of the local device, vPC system MAC address and system priority, and MAC address and priority for the local vPC device.

FabricPath

As mentioned earlier in this chapter, server virtualization and seamless workload mobility is a leading trend in the data center. A large-scale, highly scalable, and flexible Layer 2 fabric is needed in most data centers to support distributed and virtualized application workloads. To understand FabricPath, it is important to discuss limitations of STP.

Spanning Tree Protocol

To support high availability within a Layer 2 domain, switches are normally interconnected using redundant links. STP is a Layer 2 control plane protocol that runs on switches to ensure that you do not create topology loops when you have these redundant paths in the network. To create a loop-free topology, STP builds a treelike structure by blocking certain ports in the network. A root bridge is elected, and STP ensures that only one network path to the root bridge exists. All network ports connecting to the root bridge via an alternative network path are blocked. Switches exchange information using BPDUs, and this information is used to elect a root bridge and perform subsequent network configuration by selecting only the shortest path to the root bridge. This tree topology implies that certain links are unused, and traffic does not necessarily take the optimal path. Figure 1-9 shows the STP topology.

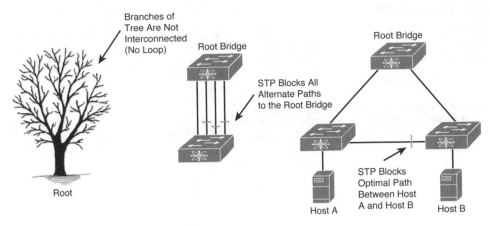

Figure 1-9 *Spanning Tree Topology*

Key limitations of STP are as follows:

- **Lack of multipathing:** In STP, all the switches build only one shortest path to the root switch, and all the redundant links are blocked. Therefore, equal cost multipath cannot be used to efficiently load-balance traffic across multiple network links. This leads to inefficient utilization of network resources.

- **Inefficient path selection:** STP does not always provide a shortest path between two switches. A simple example of inefficient path selection is shown in Figure 1-9, where host A and host B cannot use the direct link between the two switches because STP is blocking it.

- **Slow convergence:** A link failure or any other small change in network topology can cause large changes in the spanning tree that must be propagated to all switches and could take about 30 seconds in older versions of STP. Rapid Spanning Tree Protocol (RSTP) has improved the STP convergence to a few seconds; however, certain failure scenarios are complex and can destabilize the network for longer periods of time.

- **Protocol safety:** A Layer 2 packet header does not have a time to live (TTL), so in a Layer 2 loop condition, packets can continue circulating in the network with no time out. Therefore, there is no safety against STP failure or misconfiguration. Such failures can be extremely dangerous for the switched network because a topology loop can consume all network bandwidth, causing a major network outage.

- **Limited scalability:** Several factors limit scalability of Classic Ethernet. A switch has limited space to store Layer 2 forwarding information. This limit is increasing with improvements in the silicon technology; however, the demand to store more addresses is also growing with computing capacity and the introduction of server virtualization. As you know, the Layer 2 MAC addressing is nonhierarchical, and it is not possible to optimize Layer 2 forwarding tables by summarizing the Layer 2 addresses. Furthermore, packet flooding for broadcast and unknown unicast packets populates all end host MAC addresses in all switches in the network. In addition to the large forwarding table, when there are changes in the spanning tree topology, the switches will clear and rebuild their forwarding table. This results in more flooding to learn new MAC addresses.

What Is FabricPath?

Cisco FabricPath is an innovation to build a simplified and scalable Layer 2 fabric. It combines the benefits of Layer 3 routing with the advantages of Layer 2 switching. Layer 3 routing provides scalability, multipathing, fast convergence, and shortest path selection from any host to any other host in the network. However, Layer 3 creates network segmentation, which makes it less flexible for workload mobility within a virtualized data center. FabricPath brings the stability and performance of Layer 3 routing to the Layer 2 switched network and builds a highly resilient, massively scalable, and flexible Layer 2 fabric.

A FabricPath network is created by connecting a group of switches into an arbitrary topology, combining them in a fabric using a few simple commands. Intermediate System-to-Intermediate System (IS-IS) Protocol is used to provide fabric-wide intelligence and tie the elements together. There is no need to run STP within the FabricPath network. FabricPath can be deployed in any arbitrary topology; however, a typical spine and leaf topology is used in the data center. Figure 1-10 shows the FabricPath topology.

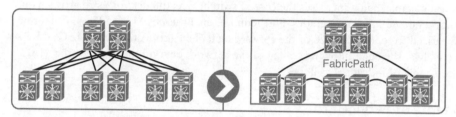

Figure 1-10   *FabricPath Topology*

Benefits of FabricPath

FabricPath converts the entire data center into one big switching fabric. Benefits of Cisco FabricPath technology are as follows:

- **Operational simplicity:** Cisco FabricPath is simple to configure and easy to operate. The switch control plane protocol for FabricPath starts automatically, as soon as the feature is enabled and ports are assigned to the FabricPath network. A single control protocol is used for unicast forwarding, multicast forwarding, and VLAN pruning. This protocol requires less configuration than the STP in the conventional Layer 2 network; therefore, overall complexity of the solution is reduced significantly.

- **Flexibility:** FabricPath provides a single domain Layer 2 fabric to connect all the servers, offering a much more scalable and flexible network fabric. Because all servers within this fabric reside in one common Layer 2 network, they can be moved around within the data center in a nondisruptive manner without constraints on the design. The level of enhanced flexibility translates into lower operational costs.

- **High performance:** High performance in a FabricPath network is achieved using an equal-cost multipath (ECMP) feature. The Ethernet fabric can use all the available paths in the network, and traffic can be load-balanced across these paths. In addition to ECMP, FabricPath supports the shortest path to the destination; therefore, the network latency is reduced and higher performance can be achieved.

- **Reliability based on proven technologies:** Cisco FabricPath uses a reliable and proven control plane mechanism, which is based on the IS-IS routing protocol. This protocol provides fast convergence that has been proven in large service provider networks. The FabricPath data plan also provides robust controls for loop prevention and mitigation. The FabricPath frame includes a time-to-live (TTL) field similar to the one used in IP, and a reverse path forwarding (RPF) check is applied for multidestination frames.

- **High scalability and high availability:** FabricPath delivers highly scalable bandwidth with capabilities such as ECMP and multitopology forwarding, enabling IT architects to start with a small Layer 2 network and build a much bigger data center fabric. In addition, FabricPath provides increased redundancy and high availability with the multiple paths between the end hosts. It means incremental levels of resiliency and bandwidth capacity, which is required as computing and virtualization density continue to grow, driving scale requirements up in the data center.

- **Efficiency:** Conventional Ethernet switches learn the MAC addresses from the frames they receive on the network. Therefore, large networks with many hosts require a large forwarding table, and it increases the cost of switches. As the network size grows, you might require equipment upgrades. Furthermore, the Ethernet MAC address cannot be summarized to reduce the size of the forwarding table. FabricPath learns MAC addresses selectively at the edge, allowing scaling of the network beyond the limits of the MAC address table of individual switches.

Components of FabricPath

To understand FabricPath control and data plane operation, it is important to understand the components of FabricPath. Figure 1-11 shows components of a FabricPath network.

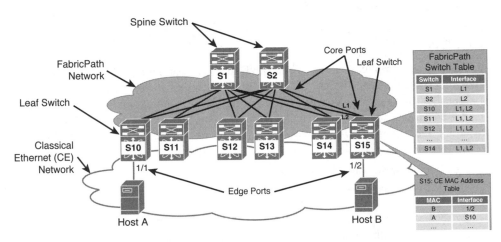

Figure 1-11 *Components of FabricPath*

- **Spine switches:** In a two-tier architecture, spine switches are deployed to provide connectivity between leaf switches. Spine switches act as the backbone of the switching fabric. The role of spine switches is to provide a transit network between the leaf switches.

- **Leaf switches:** Leaf switches provide access layer connectivity for servers and other access layer devices. The hosts on two leaf switches use spine switches to communicate with each other.

- **FabricPath network:** A network that connects the FabricPath switches is called a FabricPath network. In a data center, a typical FabricPath network is built using a spine and leaf topology. In this FabricPath network, packets are forwarded based on a new header, which includes information such as Switch ID and hop count. The FabricPath header is added to the Layer 2 packet when a packet enters the FabricPath network at the ingress switch, and it is stripped when the packet leaves the FabricPath network at the egress switch.

- **Classic Ethernet (CE):** Conventional Ethernet using transparent bridging and running STP is referred to as Classic Ethernet. Nexus switches can be part of both a FabricPath network and a Classic Ethernet network at the same time, with some ports participating in FabricPath and some ports in a Classic Ethernet network.

- **Core port:** Ports that are part of a FabricPath network are called core ports. FabricPath core ports always forward Ethernet frames encapsulated in a FabricPath header. Ethernet frames transmitted on core ports always carry an IEEE 802.1Q VLAN tag and can be considered as a trunk port. Only FabricPath VLANs are allowed on core ports.

- **Edge port:** Edge ports are switch interfaces that are part of Classic Ethernet. These interfaces behave like normal Ethernet ports, and you can connect any Ethernet device to these ports. Because these ports are part of Classic Ethernet, MAC learning is performed as usual, and packets are transmitted using standard IEEE 802.3 Ethernet frames. You can configure an edge port as an access port or as an IEEE 802.1Q trunk.

- **FabricPath VLANs:** The VLANs that are allowed on the FabricPath network are called FabricPath VLANs. When you create a VLAN, by default it operates in Classic Ethernet (CE) mode. To allow a VLAN over the FabricPath network, you must go to the VLAN configuration and change the mode to FabricPath. An edge port can carry both CE as well as FabricPath VLANs. Therefore, devices connected on an edge port in the FabricPath VLAN can send traffic to a remote host over the FabricPath network.

- **FabricPath IS-IS:** FabricPath switches run a Shortest Path First (SPF) routing protocol based on standard IS-IS to build their forwarding table similar to a Layer 3 network. This link state protocol is the core of the FabricPath control plane.

- **Dynamic Resource Allocation Protocol:** DRAP is an extension to FabricPath IS-IS that ensures network-wide unique and consistent Switch IDs and FTAG values.

- **Switch table:** The switch table provides Layer 2 routing information based on Switch ID. It contains Switch IDs and next-hop interfaces to reach the switch.

- **MAC address table:** This table contains MAC address entries and the source from where these MAC addresses are learned. The source could be a local switch interface or a remote switch. If a MAC address table has a local switch interface, the packet is delivered using Classic Ethernet format. In a case in which a MAC address table is pointing to a remote switch, a lookup is done in the switch table to find the next-hop interface. The packet is then encapsulated in the FabricPath header and sent to the next hop within the FabricPath network.

■ **FabricPath topology:** Similar to STP, in which a set of VLANs could belong to one or a different instance, in FabricPath a set of VLANs that have the same forwarding behavior will be mapped to a topology or forwarding instance, and different topologies could be constructed for a different set of VLANs. This could be used for traffic engineering, administrative purposes, or security.

FabricPath Frame Format

When an Ethernet frame enters the FabricPath network, the switch encapsulates the frame with a 16-byte FabricPath header. This header includes a 48-bit outer MAC destination address (ODA), a 48-bit outer MAC source address (OSA), and a 32-bit FabricPath tag. The ODA and SDA contain a 12-bit unique identifier called SwitchID that is used to forward packets within the FabricPath network.

The 48-bit source and destination MAC address contains a 12-bit unique identifier called SwitchID that is used for forwarding in the FabricPath network. The FabricPath tag contains the new Ethertype for the FabricPath header, a forwarding tag called FTAG that uniquely identifies a forwarding graph, and the TTL field that has the same functionality as in the IP header. Figure 1-12 shows the FabricPath frame format.

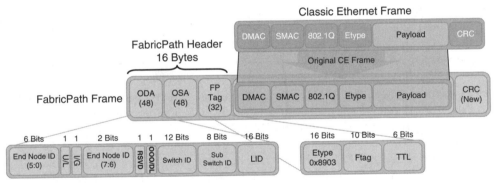

Figure 1-12 *FabricPath Frame Format*

■ **Endnode ID:** This field is currently not in use. The purpose of this field is to provide future capabilities, where a virtual or physical end host located behind a single port can uniquely identify itself to the FabricPath network.

■ **U/L bit:** FabricPath switches set this bit in all unicast OSA and ODA fields, indicating that the MAC address is a locally administered address. This is required because the OSA and ODA fields are not MAC addresses and do not uniquely identify a particular hardware component the way a standard MAC address would.

■ **I/G bit:** The I/G bit serves the same function in FabricPath as in standard Ethernet. Any multidestination addresses have this bit set.

■ **OOO/DL:** This field is currently not in use. The function of the OOO (out of order)/ don't learn (DL) bit varies depending on whether it is used in OSA or ODA. The purpose of this field is to provide future capabilities for per-packet load sharing when multiple equal cost paths are available.

- **Switch ID:** The Switch ID is a 12-bit unique identifier for a switch within the FabricPath network. This Switch ID can be assigned manually within the switch configuration or allocated automatically using DRAP. In the OSA of the FabricPath header, this field is used to identify the switch that originated the packet. In the ODA, this field identifies the destination switch for the FabricPath packet.

- **Sub-SwitchID:** Sub-SwitchID is a unique identifier assigned to an emulated switch within the FabricPath SwitchID. This emulated switch represents a vPC+ port-channel interface associated with a pair of FabricPath switches. In the absence of vPC+, this field is always set to 0. vPC+ is discussed later in this chapter.

- **LID:** Local ID (LID) is also known as port ID. LID is used to identify the specific physical or logical edge port from which the packet is originated or is destined to. The value of this field in the FabricPath header is locally significant to each switch. The forwarding decision at the destination switch can use the LID to send the packet to the correct edge port without additional lookups on the MAC table.

- **Ethertype:** An Ethertype value of 0x8903 is used for FabricPath.

- **FTAG:** FabricPath forwarding tag (FTAG) is a 10-bit traffic identification tag within the FabricPath header. For unicast traffic it identifies the FabricPath topology the frame is traversing. The system selects a unique FTAG for each topology configured within FabricPath. In the case of multicast and broadcast traffic, the FTAG identifies a multidestination forwarding tree within a given topology. The system selects the FTAG value for each multidestination tree.

- **TTL:** This field represents the Time to Live (TTL) of the FabricPath frame. In case of temporary loops during protocol convergence, the TTL prevents Layer 2 frames from circulating endlessly within the network. TTL operates in the same manner within FabricPath as it does in traditional IP forwarding. Each FabricPath switch hop decrements the TTL by 1, and frames with an expired TTL are discarded.

FabricPath Control Plane

Cisco FabricPath uses a single control plane that functions for unicast, broadcast, and multicast packets by leveraging the Layer 2 IS-IS Protocol. There is no need to run STP within the FabricPath network. The Cisco FabricPath Layer 2 IS-IS is a separate process from Layer 3 IS-IS. FabricPath IS-IS provides the following benefits:

- **No IP dependency:** No need for IP reachability to form adjacency between devices.

- **Easily extensible:** Using custom type, length, value (TLV) settings, IS-IS devices can exchange information about virtually anything.

- **Provides Shortest Path First (SPF) routing:** Excellent topology building and reconvergence characteristics.

The FabricPath control plane uses the IS-IS Protocol to perform the following functions:

- **Switch ID allocation:** FabricPath switches establish IS-IS adjacency to the directly connected neighboring switches on the core ports. These switches then start a negotiation process that ensures all FabricPath switches have a unique Switch ID. It also ensures that the type and number of FTAG values in use are consistent. By default, DRAP automatically performs this task. However, a configuration command is also provided for the network administrator to statically assign a Switch ID to a FabricPath switch. While the initial negotiation is in progress, the core interfaces are brought up but not added to the FabricPath topology, and no data plane traffic is passed on these interfaces.

- **Unicast routing:** After IS-IS adjacencies are built and routing information is exchanged, the FabricPath calculates its unicast routing table. This routing table stores the best path to the destination FabricPath switch, which includes the FabricPath Switch ID and its next hop. If multiple equal-cost paths to a particular Switch ID exist, up to 16 next hops are stored in the FabricPath routing table. You can modify the number of next hops installed using the **maximum paths** command in FabricPath-domain configuration mode.

- **Multidestination trees:** To ensure loop-free topology for broadcast, multicast, and unknown unicast traffic, multidestination trees are built within the FabricPath network. FabricPath IS-IS automatically creates multiple multidestination trees connecting to all FabricPath switches and uses them to forward multidestination traffic. As of NX-OS release 6.2(2), two such trees are supported per topology. Figure 1-13 shows a network with two multidestination trees, where switch S1 is the root for tree number 1 and switch S4 is the root for tree number 2.

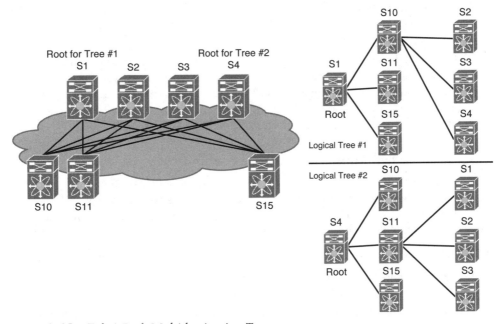

Figure 1-13   *FabricPath Multidestination Trees*

Within the FabricPath domain, first a root switch is elected for tree number 1 in a topology. After a switch becomes the root for the first tree, this root switch selects the root for each additional multidestination tree in the topology and assigns each multidestination tree a unique FTAG value. FabricPath switches use the following three parameters to elect a root for the first tree, and they select a root for any additional trees. A higher value of these parameters is preferred.

- **Root priority:** An 8-bit value. The default root priority is 64.
- **System ID:** A 48-bit value. It is composed of the VDC MAC address.
- **Switch ID:** The unique 12-bit Switch ID.

You can influence root bridge election by using the **root-priority** command. It is recommended to configure a centrally connected switch as the root switch. Therefore, spine switches are the best candidates for the root.

FabricPath Data Plane

The Layer 2 packets forwarded through a FabricPath network are of the following types: known unicast packet, multicast packet, unknown unicast, and broadcast packets.

Known unicast forwarding is done based on the mapping between the unicast MAC address and the Switch ID that is already learned by the network. FabricPath IS-IS computes the SwitchID reachability for each switch in the network. Multiple equal cost paths could exist to a destination Switch ID. In this case, the packets are flow-based load-balanced to distribute traffic over multiple equal cost paths.

Multicast forwarding is done based on multidestination trees computed by IS-IS. For optimized IP multicast forwarding, these trees are further pruned based on IGMP snooping at the edges of the FabricPath network. FabricPath uses IS-IS to propagate multicast receiver locations within the FabricPath network. This allows switches to prune off subtrees that do not have downstream receivers.

Broadcast and unknown unicast forwarding is also done based on a multidestination tree computed by IS-IS for each topology. The FTAG uniquely identifies a topology because different topologies could have different broadcast trees.

When a unicast packet enters the FabricPath network, and as it passes different switches, it goes though different lookups and forwarding logic. This forwarding logic is based on the role that particular switch plays relative to the traffic flow within the FabricPath network. Following are three general roles and the forwarding logic for FabricPath traffic:

- Ingress FabricPath switch
  - Receives the Classic Ethernet (CE) frame from a FabricPath edge port.
  - Performs MAC table lookup to identify the FabricPath Switch ID.
  - Performs Switch ID table lookup to determine FabricPath next-hop interface.
  - Encapsulates frames with the FabricPath header and sends them to the core port for the next-hop FabricPath switch.
- Core FabricPath switch
  - Receives a FabricPath-encapsulated frame on a FabricPath core port.
  - Performs Switch ID table lookup to determine which next-hop interface frame it is destined to.
  - Decrements TTL and sends the frame to the core port for the next-hop FabricPath switch.

- Egress FabricPath switch
    - Receives a FabricPath-encapsulated frame on a FabricPath core port.
    - Performs Switch ID table lookup to determine whether it is the egress FabricPath switch.
    - Uses the LID value in the ODA, or a MAC address table lookup, to determine on which FabricPath edge port the frame should be forwarded.

Conversational Learning

FabricPath switches learn MAC addresses selectively, allowing a significant reduction in the size of the MAC address table. This selective MAC address learning is based on bidirectional conversation of end hosts; therefore, it is called conversational learning. In a FabricPath switch, FabricPath VLANs use conversational MAC address learning, and Classic Ethernet VLANs use traditional MAC address learning. The following are MAC learning rules FabricPath uses:

- Only FabricPath edge switches populate the MAC table and use MAC table lookups to forward frames. FabricPath core switches generally do not learn MAC addresses, and frames are forwarded based on the Switch ID in the ODA.
- For Ethernet frames received from a directly connected access or trunk port, the switch unconditionally learns the source MAC address as a local MAC entry. This MAC learning rule is the same as the Classic Ethernet switch.
- For unicast frames received with FabricPath encapsulation, the switch learns the source MAC address of the frame as a remote MAC entry only if the destination MAC address matches an already learned local MAC entry. In other words, the switch learns remote MAC addresses only if the remote device is having a bidirectional "conversation" with a locally connected device. The unknown unicast frames being flooded in the FabricPath network do not necessarily trigger learning on edge switches.
- Broadcast frames do not trigger learning on edge switches; however, broadcast frames are used to update any existing MAC entries already in the table. For example, if a host moves from one switch to another and sends a gratuitous ARP to update the Layer 2 forwarding tables, FabricPath switches receiving that broadcast will update an existing entry for the source MAC address.
- Multicast frames trigger learning on FabricPath switches (both edge and core) because several key LAN protocols (such as HSRP) rely on source MAC learning from multicast frames to facilitate proper forwarding.

FabricPath Packet Flow Example

In this section, you review an example of packet flow within a FabricPath network. There are two spine switches and three leaf switches in this sample topology. Spine switches are S1 and S2, and leaf switches are S10, S14, and S15. Host A connected to the leaf switch S10 would like to communicate with the Host B connected to the leaf switch S15. FabricPath is configured correctly and the network is fully converged.

Unknown Unicast Packet Flow

In the beginning, the MAC address table of switch S10 and S14 is empty. The MAC address table of switch S15 has only one local entry for Host B pointing to port 1/2. The following steps explain unknown unicast packet flow originated from Host A:

1. Host A sends an unknown unicast packet to switch S10 on port 1/1. This flow is unknown unicast because switch S10 does not know how to reach destination Host B.

2. S10 updates the Classic Ethernet MAC address table with the entry for the source MAC address of Host A and the port 1/1 where the host is connected.

3. A lookup is performed for the destination MAC address of Host B. This lookup is missed because no entry exists for Host B in the switch S10 MAC address table.

4. S10 encapsulates the packet into the FabricPath header and floods it on the FabricPath multidestination tree. This packet has switch S10 Switch ID in its outer source address (OSA).

5. The FabricPath frame is received by switch S14 and switch S15.

6. S14 receives the packet and performs a lookup for Host B in its MAC address table. The MAC address lookup is missed; therefore, the Host A MAC address is not learned on switch S14.

7. S15 receives the packet and performs a lookup for Host B in its MAC address table. The MAC address lookup finds a hit, and the Host A MAC address is added to the MAC table on switch S15. This MAC address is learned on FabricPath and the Switch ID in OSA is S10. The MAC address table on S15 shows Host A pointing to switch S10.

8. The packet is delivered to port 1/2 on switch S15.

Figure 1-14 illustrates these steps for an unknown unicast packet flow.

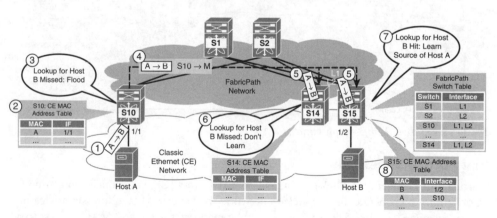

Figure 1-14 *FabricPath Unknown Unicast*

Known Unicast Packet Flow

After the unknown unicast packet flow from switch S10 to S14 and S15, some MAC address tables are populated. Switch S10 has only one entry for Host A connected on port

1/1. Switch S14 has no entry in its MAC address table. Switch S15 has two entries in its MAC address table. The first entry is local for Host B pointing toward port 1/2, and the second entry is remote for Host A pointing toward switch S10. The following steps explain known unicast packet flow originated from Host B:

1. Host B sends a known unicast packet to Host A on switch S15 port 1/2. This flow is known unicast because switch S15 knows how to reach the destination MAC address of Host A.

2. S15 performs the MAC address lookup and finds a hit pointing toward switch S10. Switch S15 performs the Switch ID lookup and selects a FabricPath core port to send the packet.

3. The packet is encapsulated in a FabricPath header, with S15 in the OSA and S10 in the ODA. The packet traverses the FabricPath network to reach the destination switch, which is switch S10.

4. The packet is received by switch S10 and a MAC address of Host B is learned by switch S10. This MAC address is learned on FabricPath and the Switch ID in OSA is S15. The MAC address table on S10 shows Host B pointing to switch S15.

5. Switch S10 performs the MAC address table lookup for Host A, and the packet is delivered on the port 1/1.

Figure 1-15 illustrates these steps for a known unicast packet flow.

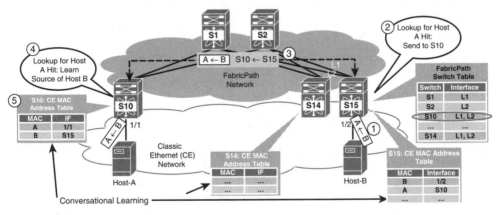

Figure 1-15 *FabricPath Known Unicast*

Virtual Port Channel Plus

A virtual port channel plus (vPC+) enables a Classic Ethernet (CE) vPC domain and Cisco FabricPath to interoperate. In a FabricPath network, the Layer 2 MAC addresses are learned only by the edge switches. The learning consists of mapping the Layer 2 MAC address to a Switch ID, and it is performed in the data plane. In a vPC configuration, a dual-connected host can send a packet into the FabricPath network from two edge switches. When a packet is received at a remote FabricPath switch, with the Switch ID of the first vPC switch in OSA, the MAC address table of this remote FabricPath switch is updated with the Switch ID of the first vPC switch. Because the virtual port channel performs load balancing, the next traffic flow can go via a second vPC switch. When the remote FabricPath switch receives a packet for the same MAC address with the Switch ID of the second vPC switch in its OSA, it sees it as a MAC move. On this remote FabricPath switch, the MAC address table is updated with the Switch ID of the second vPC switch. This behavior is called MAC flapping, and it can destabilize the network.

To address this problem, FabricPath implements an emulated switch. This emulated switch is a logical way of combining two or more FabricPath switches to emulate a single switch to the rest of the FabricPath network. The FabricPath packets originated by the two emulating switches are sourced with the emulated Switch ID. The other FabricPath switches are not aware of this emulation and simply see the emulated switch reachable through both of these emulating switches. The emulated switch implementation in FabricPath where two FabricPath edge switches provide a vPC to a third-party device is called vPC+. It means that the two-emulating switch must be directly connected via peer link, and there should be a peer keepalive path between the two switches.

Figure 1-16 shows an example of a vPC+ configuration.

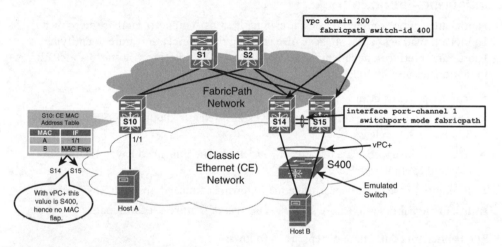

Figure 1-16 *FabricPath with vPC+*

In this example, Host B is connected to switch S14 and S15 in vPC configuration. The packets are load-balanced across the vPC link, and these packets are seen at the remote switch S10, coming from S14 as well as from S15. This results in MAC flapping at switch S10. To solve this problem, configure switch S14 and S15 with a FabricPath-emulated switch using vPC+ configuration.

To configure vPC+, simply configure the vPC peer link as a FabricPath core port, and assign an emulated Switch ID to the vPC. As a result of this configuration, remote switch S10 sees the Host B MAC address entry pointing to the emulated switch.

FabricPath Interaction with Spanning Tree

FabricPath edge ports support direct Classic Ethernet host connections and connections to the traditional Spanning Tree switches. By default, FabricPath switches transmit and process STP BPDUs on FabricPath edge ports. However, BPDUs including TCNs are not transmitted on FabricPath core ports and, as a result, no BPDUs are forwarded or tunneled through the FabricPath network. Therefore, FabricPath isolates STP domains. The entire FabricPath network appears as a single STP bridge to any connected STP domains. To appear as one STP bridge, all FabricPath switches share a common bridge ID, or BID (C84C.75FA.6000). This BID is statically defined and is not user configurable.

Each FabricPath edge switch must be configured as root for all FabricPath VLANs. If you are connecting STP devices to the FabricPath network, make sure you configure all edge switches as STP root. Additionally, if multiple FabricPath edge switches connect to the same STP domain, make sure those edge switches use the same bridge priority value.

To ensure that the FabricPath network acts as STP root, all FabricPath edge ports have the STP root-guard function enabled implicitly. If a superior BPDU is received on a FabricPath edge port, the port is placed in the L2 Gateway Inconsistent state until the condition is cleared.

Configuring FabricPath

FabricPath can be configured using a few simple steps. You perform these steps on all FabricPath switches. These steps involve enabling the FabricPath feature, identifying FabricPath interfaces, and identifying FabricPath VLANs. Before you start FabricPath configuration, ensure the following:

- You have Nexus devices that support FabricPath.
- The system is running at minimum NX-OS 5.1.1 (Nexus 7000)/NX-OS 5.1.3 (Nexus 5500) software release.
- You have the appropriate license for FabricPath. The Enhanced Layer 2 license is required to run FabricPath.
- If required, install the license using the following command: **install license** *<filename>*
- Install the FabricPath feature set by issuing **install feature-set fabricpath**.

The FabricPath configuration steps are as follows:

1. Before you start configuring the FabricPath on a switch, the FabricPath feature set must be enabled. To enable the FabricPath feature set, use the following command in switch global configuration mode:

    feature-set fabricpath

2. **Define FabricPath VLANs**: Identify the VLANs that will be extended across the FabricPath network. By default, all the VLANs are in Classic Ethernet mode. You can change the VLAN mode to FabricPath by going into the VLAN configuration. Use the following command to change the VLAN mode for a range of VLANs:

    vlan <range>

    mode fabricpath

3. **Identify FabricPath interfaces**: Identify the FabricPath core ports. These ports connect to other FabricPath switches to establish IS-IS adjacency. There is no need to configure the IS-IS protocol for FabricPath. Configuring a port in FabricPath mode

automatically enables the IS-IS protocol on the port. The following command is used to configure an interface in FabricPath mode:

interface <name>

switchport mode fabricpath

After performing this configuration on all FabricPath switches in the topology, FabricPath devices will form IS-IS adjacencies. The unicast and multicast routing information is exchanged, and switches will start forwarding traffic. FabricPath Dynamic DRAP automatically assigns a Switch ID to each switch within FabricPath network. You can also configure a static Switch ID using the **fabricpath switch-id** *<ID number>* command.

Figure 1-17 shows an example of FabricPath topology and its configuration.

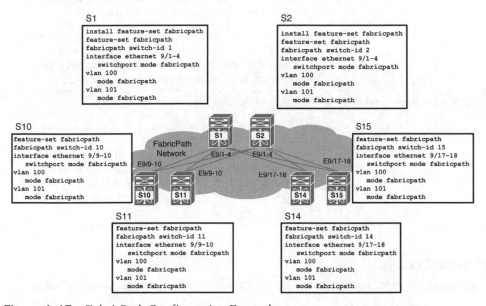

Figure 1-17   *FabricPath Configuration Example*

Verifying FabricPath

The **show mac address table** command can be used to verify that MAC addresses are learned on Cisco FabricPath edge devices. The command shows local addresses with a pointer to the interface on which the address was learned. For remote addresses, it provides a pointer to the remote switch from which this address was learned.

The **show fabricpath route** command can be used to view the Cisco FabricPath routing table that results from the Cisco FabricPath IS-IS SPF calculations. The Cisco FabricPath routing table shows the best paths to all the switches in the fabric. If multiple equal paths are available between two switches, all paths will be installed in the Cisco FabricPath routing table to provide ECMP.

Table 1-5 lists some useful commands to verify FabricPath.

Table 1-5   Verify FabricPath Configuration

Command	Description
show feature-set	Provides the status of FabricPath. It shows whether the FabricPath feature set is enabled.
show running-config fabricpath	Shows the running configuration for FabricPath. It helps quickly verify FabricPath configuration.
show vlan	Shows all the VLANs, including FabricPath, as well as Classic Ethernet VLANs. This command helps you verify whether VLANs are configured with the correct mode.
show fabricpath switch-id	Shows all Switch IDs and their system ID within the FabricPath network. It also shows whether a Switch ID is for a real switch or an emulated switch.
show fabricpath route	Shows the Switch ID, the metric, and the interface from which the switch is reachable. If you know the Switch ID, you can find the path the traffic is taking on the FabricPath network to reach the remote switch.
show fabricpath isis interface brief	Displays FabricPath interface information.
show mac address-table	Displays the MAC address table with all MAC addresses and their reachability. It can help you find whether a MAC is present locally on this switch or connected to a remote switch. If a MAC is connected to a remote switch, you can find the Switch ID that is the owner of the MAC address.

Reference List

Best Practices for Virtual Port Channels (vPC) on Cisco Nexus 7000 Series Switches

http://www.cisco.com/c/dam/en/us/td/docs/switches/datacenter/sw/design/vpc_design/vpc_best_practices_design_guide.pdf

Whitepaper: Nexus 7000 FabricPath

http://www.cisco.com/c/en/us/products/collateral/switches/nexus-7000-series-switches/white_paper_c11-687554.html

Cisco FabricPath Best Practices

http://www.cisco.com/c/dam/en/us/products/collateral/switches/nexus-7000-series-switches/white_paper_c07-728188.pdf

Exam Preparation Tasks

Review All Key Topics

Review the most important topics in the chapter, noted with the key topics icon in the outer margin of the page. Table 1-6 lists a reference for these key topics and the page numbers on which each is found.

Table 1-6   Key Topics for Chapter 1

Key Topic Element	Description	Page
Section	"Benefits of Using Port Channels"	15
Section	"Port Channel Compatibility Requirements"	16
Table 1-2	"Port Channel Modes"	17
List	"Port Channel Load Balancing"	19
Table 1-4	"Verify Port Channel Configuration"	19
List	"Components of vPC"	23
Section	"vPC Data Plane Operation"	24
Section	"vPC Control Plane Operation"	26
Section	"vPC Limitations"	27
Table 1-3	"Verify Port Channel Configuration"	29
Section	"Components of FabricPath"	32
List	"FabricPath Control Plane"	35
List	"FabricPath Data Plane"	37
Section	"Virtual Port Channel Plus (vPC+)"	40
Table 1-5	"Verify FabricPath Configuration"	44

Complete Tables and Lists from Memory

Print a copy of Appendix B, "Memory Tables" or at least the section for this chapter, and complete the tables and lists from memory. Appendix C, "Memory Tables Answer Key" includes completed tables and lists to check your work.

Define Key Terms

Define the following key terms from this chapter, and check your answers in the Glossary:

Virtual LAN (VLAN), Virtual Port Channel (vPC), Maximum Transmit Unit (MTU), Link Aggregation Control Protocol (LACP), Spanning Tree Protocol (STP), Virtual Device Context (VDC), Cisco Fabric Services over Ethernet (CFSoE), Hot Standby Router Protocol (HSRP), Virtual Router Redundancy Protocol (VRRP), Bridge Protocol Data Unit (BPDU), Internet Group Management Protocol (IGMP), Time To Live (TTL), Dynamic Resource Allocation Protocol (DRAP)

This chapter covers the following exam topics:

2.5 Differentiate between the data, control, and management planes

3.6 Describe and explain the use of role-based access control within the data center infra-structure

CHAPTER 2

Management and Monitoring of Cisco Nexus Devices

Management and monitoring of network devices is an important element of data center operations. This includes initial configuration of devices and ongoing maintenance of all the components. An efficient and rich management and monitoring interface enables a network operations team to effectively operate and maintain the data center network. The operational efficiency is an important business priority because it helps in reducing the operational expenditure (OPEX) of the data center. The Cisco Nexus platform provides a rich set of management and monitoring mechanisms.

This chapter offers an overview of the operational planes of the Nexus platform. It explains the functions performed by each plane and the key features of the data plane, control plane, and management plane. It also provides an overview of out-of-band and in-band management interfaces. The Nexus platform has several methods for device configuration and management. These methods are discussed with some important commands for initial setup, configuration, and verification. You will also get introduced to Cisco NX-API, which allows you to use HTTP/HTTPS as a transport to access and program the Cisco Nexus switches. This chapter also identifies the mechanism available in the Nexus platform to protect the control plane of the switch.

"Do I Know This Already?" Quiz

The "Do I Know This Already?" quiz enables you to assess whether you should read this entire chapter thoroughly or jump to the "Exam Preparation Tasks" section. If you are in doubt about your answers to these questions or your own assessment of your knowledge of the topics, read the entire chapter. Table 2-1 lists the major headings in this chapter and their corresponding "Do I Know This Already?" quiz questions. You can find the answers in Appendix A, "Answers to the 'Do I Know This Already?' Quizzes."

Table 2-1 "Do I Know This Already?" Section-to-Question Mapping

Foundation Topics Section	Questions
Control Plane, Data Plane, and Management Plane	1–6
Describe and Explain the Use of "Role Based Access Control" Within the Data Center Infrastructure	7–10

CAUTION The goal of self-assessment is to gauge your mastery of the topics in this chapter. If you do not know the answer to a question or are only partially sure of the answer, you should mark that question as wrong for purposes of the self-assessment. Giving yourself credit for an answer you correctly guess skews your self-assessment results and might provide you with a false sense of security.

1. What is the function of the data plane in a switch?

   a. It stores user data on the switch.

   b. It maintains the routing table.

   c. It forwards user traffic.

   d. It maintains the MAC address table.

2. Which of the following operational planes of a switch is responsible for configuring and monitoring the switch?

   a. Control plane

   b. Data plane

   c. Management plane

   d. User plane

3. Which of the following operational planes is responsible for maintaining routing and switching tables of a multilayer switch?

   a. Control plane

   b. Data plane

   c. Management plane

   d. User plane

4. Select the protocols that belong to the control plane of the switch.

   a. SNMP

   b. NETCONF

   c. STP

   d. LACP

5. Select the protocols that belong to the management plane of the switch.

   a. SNMP

   b. NETCONF

   c. STP

   d. LACP

6. True or False? CMP exists on all Nexus switching families.

   a. True

   b. False

7. Which message format does the NX-API support?

   a. JSON-RPC

   b. JSON

   c. XML

   d. Python

8. User roles contain rules that define the operations allowed on the Nexus 5000 switch. Which of the following options are the default user roles?

   a. network-admin

   b. network-operator

   c. vdc-admin

   d. network-monitor

9. True or False? The vdc-operator has read/write access to a specific operator.

   a. True

   b. False

10. In RBAC, how many rules can be assigned to a single role?

   a. 128

   b. 64

   c. 2

   d. 256

Foundation Topics

Operational Planes of a Nexus Switch

The data center network is built using multiple network nodes or devices. These network nodes are switches and routers, connected to each other and configured in different topologies. In a large network with hundreds of these devices, it is important to build a management framework to monitor and manage these devices. Typically, these network devices talk to each other using different control protocols to find the best network path. The purpose of building such network controls is to provide a reliable data transport for network endpoints. These network endpoints are servers and workstations. When a network endpoint sends a packet (data), it is switched by these network devices based on the best path they learned using the control protocols. This simple explanation of a network node leads to the three operational components of a network node. These components are data plane, control plane, and management plane. Figure 2-1 shows the operational planes of a Nexus switch in a data center.

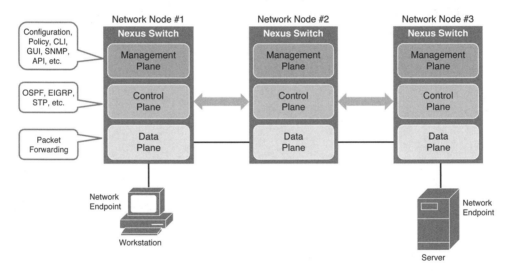

Figure 2-1   *Operational Plane of Nexus*

Data Plane

The data plane is also called a forwarding plane. This component of a network device receives endpoint traffic from a network interface and decides what to do with this traffic. It can process incoming traffic by looking at the destination address in its forwarding table and deciding on an appropriate action. This action could be to forward traffic to an outgoing interface, drop the traffic, or send it to the control plane for further processing.

In a typical Layer 2 switch, the forwarding decisions are based on the destination MAC address of data packets. The advancements in integrated circuit technologies allowed network device vendors to move the Layer 2 forwarding decision from complex instruction set computing (CISC) and reduced instruction set computing (RISC) processors to the application-specific integrated circuits (ASIC) and field-programmable gate arrays (FPGAs). This approach is helpful in reducing the packet-handling time within the network device, thereby improving the data plane latency of network switches to tens of microseconds. The earlier method requires the packet to be stored in the memory before a forwarding decision can be made; however, with ASICs and FPGAs, packets can be switched without storing them in the memory.

Store-and-Forward Switching

In store-and-forward switches, data packets received from an incoming interface must be completely stored in switch memory or ASIC before sending them to an outgoing interface. Following are a few characteristics of store-and-forward switching:

- **Error checking:** Store-and-forward switches receive a frame completely and analyze it using the frame-check-sequence (FCS) calculation to make sure the frame is free from data-link errors. The switch then performs the forwarding process.

- **Buffering:** The process of storing and then forwarding enables the switch to handle various networking conditions. The ingress buffering process offers the flexibility to support any mix of Ethernet speeds. The store-and-forward switch architecture is simple because it is easier to forward a stored packet.

- **Access control list:** Because a store-and-forward switch stores the entire packet, the switch can examine the necessary portions to permit or deny that frame.

Cut-Through Switching

In the cut-through switching mode, switches start forwarding a frame before the frame has been completely received. The forwarding decision is made as soon as the switch sees the portion of the frame with the destination address. Following are a few characteristics of cut-through switching:

- **Low-latency switching:** A cut-through switch can make a forwarding decision as soon as it has looked up the DMAC (Destination MAC) address of the data packet. The switch does not have to wait for the rest of the packet to make its forwarding decision. This technique reduces the network latency.

- **Invalid packets:** A cut-through switch starts forwarding the packet before receiving it completely and making sure it is valid. Therefore, cut-through switching only flags but does not drop invalid packets. In this switching mode, packets with errors are forwarded to other segments of the network.

- **Egress port congestion:** If a cut-through forwarding decision is made but the egress port is busy transmitting a frame coming in from another interface, the switch needs to buffer this packet. In this case, the frame is not forwarded in a cut-through fashion.

Nexus 5500 Data Plane Architecture

Data plane architecture of Nexus switches varies based on the hardware platform; however, the basic principles of data plane operations are the same. The Cisco Nexus 5500 switch data plane architecture is primarily based on two custom-built ASICs developed by Cisco:

- **Unified port controller (UPC):** This provides data plane packet processing on ingress and egress interfaces. Each UPC manages eight ports, and each port has a dedicated data path. Each data path connects to unified crossbar fabric (UCF) via a dedicated fabric interface at 12 Gbps. Therefore, for a 10 Gbps port, it provides a 20 percent over-speed rate, which helps ensure line-rate throughput regardless of the internal packet overhead imposed by ASICs.

■ **Unified crossbar fabric (UCF):** This provides a switching fabric by cross-connecting the UPCs. The UCF is always used to schedule and switch packets between the ports of the UPC. It is a single-stage, high-performance, nonblocking crossbar with an integrated scheduler. The scheduler coordinates the use of the crossbar for a contention-free match between input and output pairs. In Nexus 5500, an enhanced iSLIP algorithm is used for scheduling, which ensures high throughput, low latency, and weighted fairness across all inputs.

Figure 2-2 shows a Nexus 5500 data plane architecture.

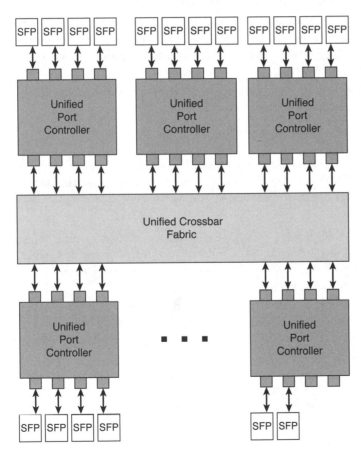

Figure 2-2 *Nexus 5500 Data Plane*

Nexus 5500 utilizes both cut-through and store-and-forward switching. Cut-through switching can be performed only when the ingress data rate is equivalent to or faster than the egress data rate. The switch fabric is designed to forward 10 G packets in cut-through mode. The 1 G to 1 G switching is performed in store-and-forward mode. Table 2-2 shows the interface types and modes of switching.

Table 2-2 Nexus 5500 Switching Modes

Source Interface	Destination Interface	Switching Mode
10 Gigabit Ethernet	10 Gigabit Ethernet	Cut-through
10 Gigabit Ethernet	1 Gigabit Ethernet	Cut-through
1 Gigabit Ethernet	1 Gigabit Ethernet	Store-and-forward
1 Gigabit Ethernet	10 Gigabit Ethernet	Store-and-forward

Control Plane

The control plane maintains the information necessary for the data plane to operate. This information is collected and computed using complex protocols and algorithms. The control plane of a network node can speak to the control plane of its neighbor to share routing and switching information. This information is then processed to create tables that help the data plane to operate. Routing protocols such as Open Shortest Path First (OSPF), Enhanced Interior Gateway Routing Protocol (EIGRP), and Border Gateway Protocol (BGP) are examples of control plane protocols. However, the control plane is not limited to routing protocols. The control plane performs several other functions, including these:

- Cisco Discovery Protocol (CDP)
- Bidirectional Forwarding (BFD)
- Unidirectional Link Detection (UDLD)
- Link Aggregation Control Protocol (LACP)
- Address Resolution Protocol (ARP)
- Spanning Tree Protocol (STP)
- FabricPath

Figure 2-3 shows the Layer 2 and Layer 3 control plane protocols of a Nexus switch.

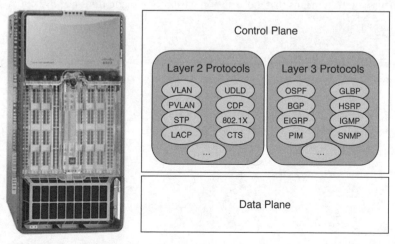

Figure 2-3 *Control Plane Protocols*

Nexus 5500 Control Plane Architecture

The Nexus switches control plane architecture has a similar component for almost all Nexus switches; however, the configuration of these components is different based on the platform and the hardware version. To understand the control plane of Nexus, let's look at the Cisco Nexus 5548P switch. The control plane of this switch runs Cisco NX-OS software on a dual-core 1.7 GHz Intel Xeon Processor C5500/C3500 Series with 8 GB of DRAM. The supervisor complex is connected to the data plane in-band through two internal ports running 1 Gbps Ethernet, and the system is managed in-band, or through the out-of-band 10/100/1000 Mbps management port. Table 2-3 summarizes the control plane specifications of a Nexus 5500 switch.

Table 2-3   Nexus 5500 Control Plane Specifications

Component	Specification
CPU	1.7 GHz Intel Xeon Processor C5500/C3500 Series (dual core)
DRAM	8 GB of DDR3 in two DIMM slots
Program storage	2 GB of eUSB flash memory for base system storage
Boot and BIOS flash memory	8 MB to store upgradable and golden image
Onboard fault log	64 MB of flash memory to store hardware-related fault and reset reasons
NVRAM	6 MB of SRAM to store syslog and licensing information
Management interface	RS-232 console port and 10/100/1000BASE-T mgmt0

Figure 2-4 shows the control plane of a Nexus 5500 switch.

Cisco NX-OS software provides isolation between control and data forwarding planes within the device. This isolation means that a disruption within one plane does not disrupt the other.

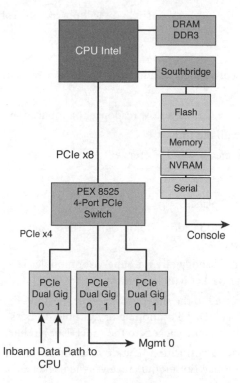

Figure 2-4   *Control Plane of Nexus 5500*

Control Plane Policing

The control plane policing (CoPP) feature prevents unnecessary traffic from overwhelming the control plane resources. The purpose of CoPP is to protect the control plane of the switch from the anomalies within the data plane, such as a broadcast storm, or from a denial of service (DoS) attack. Hence, it ensures network stability, reachability, and packet delivery.

The supervisor module of the Nexus switch performs both the management plane and the control plane function; therefore, it is a critical element for overall network stability and availability. Any disruption or attacks to the supervisor module can bring down the control and management plane of the switch, resulting in serious network outages. For example, a high volume of traffic from the data plane to the supervisor module could overload and slow down the performance of the entire switch. Another example is a DoS attack on the supervisor module. The attacker can generate IP traffic streams to the control plane or management plane at a high rate. In this case, the supervisor module spends a large amount of time handling these malicious packets and preventing the control plane from processing genuine traffic. Some examples of DoS attacks are outlined next:

- Internet Control Message Protocol (ICMP) echo requests
- IP fragments
- TCP SYN flooding

If the control plane of the switch is impacted by excessive traffic, you will observe the following symptoms on the network:

- High CPU utilization
- Route flaps due to loss of the routing protocol neighbor relationship, updates, or keepalives
- Unstable Layer 2 topology
- Reduced service quality, such as poor voice, video, or a slow response for applications
- Slow or unresponsive interactive sessions with the CLI
- Processor resource exhaustion, such as the memory and buffers
- Indiscriminate drops of incoming packets

Different types of packets can reach the control plane:

- **Receive packets:** Packets that have the destination address of a router. These packets include router updates and keepalive messages.
- **Exception packets:** Packets that need special handling by the supervisor module. This includes an ICMP unreachable packet and a packet with IP options set.
- **Redirected packets:** Packets that are redirected to the supervisor module. Features such as Dynamic Host Configuration Protocol (DHCP) snooping or dynamic Address Resolution Protocol (ARP) inspection redirect some packets to the supervisor module.
- **Glean packets:** If a Layer 2 MAC address for a destination IP address is not present in the forwarding information base (FIB), the supervisor module receives the packet and sends an ARP request to the host.

The CoPP feature enables a policy map to be applied to the supervisor bound traffic. This policy map is similar to a normal QoS policy and is applied to all traffic entering the switch from a nonmanagement port. CoPP classifies the packets to different classes and provides a mechanism to individually control the rate at which the supervisor module receives these packets. Packet classification can be done using the following parameters:

- Source and destination IP address
- Source and destination MAC address
- Virtual local area network (VLAN)
- Source and destination port
- Exception cause

After the packets are classified, the rate at which packets arrive at the supervisor module can be controlled by two mechanisms. One is called *policing* and the other is called *rate limiting*. Policing is the monitoring of data rates and burst sizes for a particular class of traffic. A policer determines three colors or conditions for traffic. These conditions or colors are as follows: conform (green), exceed (yellow), and violate (red). You can define only one action for each condition. The actions can transmit the packet, mark down the packet, or drop the packet. You can configure the following parameters for policing:

- **Committed information rate (CIR):** This is the desired bandwidth.
- **Peak information rate (PIR):** The rate above which data traffic is negatively affected.

- **Committed burst (Bc):** The size of a traffic burst that can exceed the CIR within a given unit of time.

- **Extended burst (Be):** The size that a traffic burst can reach before all traffic exceeds the PIR.

Single-rate policers monitor the specified CIR of traffic. Dual-rate policers monitor both CIR and PIR of traffic.

The setup utility allows building an initial configuration file using the system configuration dialog. After the initial setup, the Cisco NX-OS software installs the default CoPP system policy to protect the supervisor module from DoS attacks. Choosing one of the following CoPP policy options from the initial setup can set the level of protection for the control plane of a switch:

- **Strict:** This policy is 1 rate and 2 color and has a Bc value of 250 ms (except for the important class, which has a value of 1000 ms).

- **Moderate:** This policy is 1 rate and 2 color and has a Bc value of 310 ms (except for the important class, which has a value of 1250 ms). These values are 25 percent greater than the strict policy.

- **Lenient:** This policy is 1 rate and 2 color and has a Bc value of 375 ms (except for the important class, which has a value of 1500 ms). These values are 50 percent greater than the strict policy.

- **Dense:** This policy is 1 rate and 2 color. The classes critical, normal, redirect, exception, undesirable, l2-default, and default have a Bc value of 250 ms. The classes important, management, normal-dhcp, normal-dhcp-relay-response, and monitoring have a Bc value of 1000 ms. The class l2-unpoliced has a Bc value of 5 MB.

- **Skip:** No control plane policy is applied. In Cisco NX-OS releases prior to 5.2, this option is named none.

If you do not select a policy, NX-OS software applies strict policy. The Cisco Nexus device hardware performs CoPP on a per-forwarding-engine basis. CoPP does not support distributed policing; therefore, you should choose rates so that the aggregate traffic does not overwhelm the supervisor module.

Control Plane Analyzer

Ethanalyzer is a Cisco NX-OS built-in protocol analyzer, based on the command-line version of Wireshark. You can use Ethanalyzer to troubleshoot your network by capturing and decoding the control-plane traffic. This tool is useful for troubleshooting problems related to the switch itself. The packets captured by Ethanalyzer are only control-plane traffic destined to the supervisor CPU. It does not capture hardware-switched traffic between data ports of the switch. Following are the key benefits of Ethanalyzer:

- It is part of the NX-OS integrated management tool set. It improves troubleshooting and reduces time to resolution.

- It preserves and improves the operational continuity of the network infrastructure.

- Network administrators can learn about the amount and nature of the control-plane traffic within the switch.

Ethanalyzer enables you to perform the following functions:

- Capture packets sent to and received by the switch supervisor CPU
- Set the number of packets to be captured
- Set the length of the packets to be captured
- Display packets with either detailed protocol information or a one-line summary
- Open and save the packet data captured
- Filter packet captures based on many criteria
- Filter packet displays based on many criteria
- Decode the internal header of the control packet

Management Plane

The management plane of the network node deals with the configuration and monitoring of the control plane. The management plane is used in day-to-day administration of the network node. It provides an interface to the network administrators (see Figure 2-5) and NMS tools to perform actions such as the following:

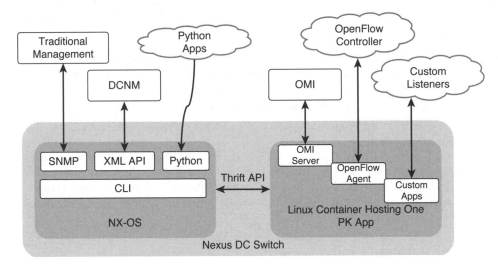

Figure 2-5 *Management Plane of Nexus*

- Configure the network node using the command-line interface (CLI).
- Configure the network node using network management protocols such as Simple Network Management Protocol (SNMP) and Network Configuration Protocol (NETCONF).
- Monitor network statistics by collecting health and utilization data from the network node using network management protocols such as SNMP.
- Manage the network node using an element manager such as Data Center Network Manager (DCNM). DCNM leverages XML application programming interfaces (APIs) of the Nexus platform.

■ Program the network node using One Platform Kit (onePK), JavaScript Object Notation (JSON), Representational State Transfer (REST), API, and guest shell with support for Python.

Nexus Management and Monitoring Features

The Nexus platform provides a wide range of management and monitoring features. Figure 2-6 shows an overview of the management and monitoring tools. Some of these tools are discussed in the following section.

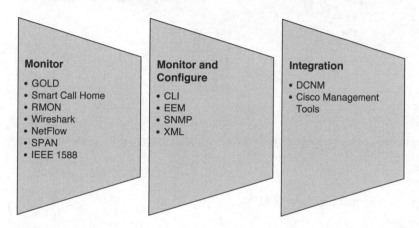

Figure 2-6 *Nexus Management and Monitoring Tools*

Out-of-Band Management

In a data center network, out-of-band (OOB) management means that management traffic is traversing through a dedicated path in the network. The purpose of creating an out-of-band network is to increase the security and availability of management capabilities within the data center.

OOB management enables a network administrator to access the devices in the data center for routine changes, monitoring, and troubleshooting without dependency on the network build for user traffic. The advantage of this approach is that during a network outage, network operators can reach the devices using this OOB management network.

In a data center, dedicated switches, routers, and firewalls are deployed to create an OOB network. This network is dedicated for management traffic only and is completely isolated from the user traffic. This network provides connectivity to management tools, the management port of network devices, and integrated lights-out (ILO) ports of servers. Because this network is built for management of data center devices, it is important to secure it so only administrators can access it. In Figure 2-7, network administrator 1 is using OOB network management, and network administrator 2 is using in-band network management. In-band management is discussed later in this section.

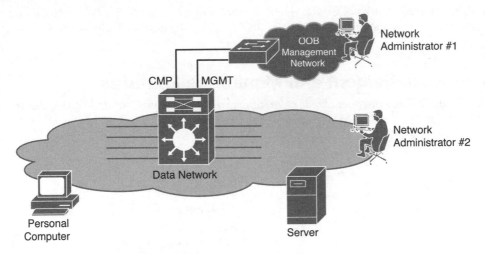

Figure 2-7   *Out-of-Band Management*

Cisco Nexus switches can be connected to the OOB management network using the following methods:

- Console port
- Connectivity management processor (CMP)
- Management port

Console Port

The console port is an asynchronous serial port used for initial switch configuration. It provides an RS-232 connection with an RJ-45 interface. It is recommended to connect all console ports of the devices to a terminal or comm server router such as Cisco 2900 for remotely connecting to the console port of devices. The remote administrator connects to the terminal server router and performs a reverse telnet to connect to the console port of the device. Figure 2-8 shows remote access to the console port via OOB network.

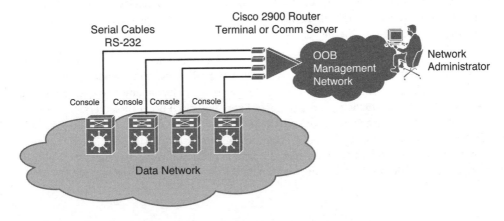

Figure 2-8   *Console Port*

Connectivity Management Processor

For management high availability, the Cisco Nexus 7000 series switches have a connectivity management processor that is known as the CMP. Note that CMP is available only in the Nexus 7000 Supervisor engine 1. The CMP provides OOB management and monitoring capability independent from the primary operating system. The CMP enables lights-out remote monitoring and management of the Cisco Nexus 7000 Series system, its supervisor module, and all other modules without the need for separate terminal servers. Key features of the CMP include the following:

- It provides a dedicated operating environment independent of the switch processor.
- It provides monitoring of supervisor status and initiation of resets.
- It provides complete visibility of the system during the entire boot process.
- It provides the capability to initiate a complete system restart.
- It provides access to critical log information on the supervisor.
- It provides the capability to take complete console control of the supervisor.

You can access the CMP from the active supervisor module. Before you begin, ensure that you are in the default virtual device context (VDC). Figure 2-9 shows how to connect to the CMP from the active supervisor module.

NOTE The CMP is only supported on SUP1 and is not supported on SUP2, SUP2E, Nexus 7700, and the Nexus 9000 series switches.

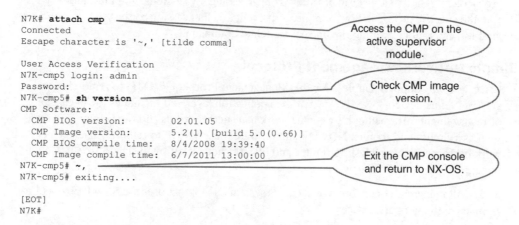

Figure 2-9 *Connectivity Management Processor*

Management Port (mgmt0)

The management port of the Nexus switch is an Ethernet interface to provide OOB management connectivity. It enables you to manage the device using an IPv4 or IPv6 address. The management port is also known as the mgmt0 interface. This port is part of management VRF on the switch and supports speeds of 10/100/1000 Ethernet. The OOB management interface (mgmt0) can be used to manage all VDCs. Each VDC has its own representation for mgmt0 with a unique IP address from a common management subnet for the physical switch that can be used to send syslog, SNMP, and other management information. OOB connectivity via mgmt0 port is shown earlier in Figure 2-7.

In-Band Management

In-band management utilizes the same network as user data to manage network devices. In this method, switches are configured with an in-band IP address on a routed interface, SVI, or loopback interface that is reachable via the same path as user data. The network administrator manages the switch using this in-band IP address. There is no need to build a separate OOB management network. If the network is down, in-band management will not work either.

In-band is done using vty of a Cisco NX-OS device. The administrator uses Secure Shell (SSH) and Telnet to the vty lines to create a virtual terminal session. You can configure an inactive session timeout and a maximum sessions limit for virtual terminals. A vty line is used for all remote network connections supported by the device, regardless of protocol. (SSH, SCP, and Telnet are examples.) To help ensure that you can access a device through a local or remote management session, you must enforce proper controls on vty lines. Cisco NX-OS devices have a limited number of vty lines; the number of configured lines available can be determined by using the **show run vshd** command. By default, up to 16 concurrent vty sessions are allowed. When all vty lines are in use, new management sessions cannot be established.

In Cisco NX-OS, vty lines automatically accept connections using any configured transport protocols. To disable a specific protocol from accessing vty sessions, you must globally disable the specific protocol. For example, to prevent a Telnet session to the vty line, you must disable Telnet globally using the **no feature telnet** command.

Simple Network Management Protocol

Cisco NX-OS supports Simple Network Management Protocol (SNMP) to remotely manage the Nexus devices. SNMP works at the application layer and facilitates the exchange of management information between network management tools and the network devices, such as switches and routers. Network administrators use SNMP to remotely manage network performance, troubleshoot faults, and plan for network growth. There are three components of the SNMP framework:

- **SNMP manager:** A network management system (NMS) that uses the SNMP protocol to manage the network devices.
- **SNMP agent:** A software component that resides on the device that is managed. To enable the SNMP agent, you must define the relationship between manager and agent.
- **Management information base (MIB):** The collection of managed objects on the SNMP agent.

Figure 2-10 shows components of SNMP.

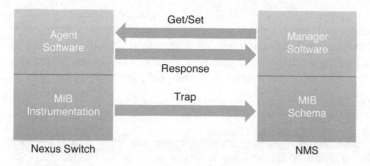

Figure 2-10 *Nexus SNMP*

The Cisco Nexus devices support the agent and MIB. The NMS uses the Cisco MIB variables to perform set operations to configure a device or a get operation to poll devices for specific information. The information collected from polling is analyzed to help troubleshoot network problems, create network performance, verify configuration, and monitor traffic loads.

SNMP Notifications

In case of a network fault or other important event, the SNMP agent can generate notifications without a polling request from the SNMP manager. NX-OS can generate the following two types of SNMP notifications:

■ **Traps:** An unacknowledged message sent from the agent to the SNMP managers listed in the host receiver table. These messages are less reliable because there is no way for an agent to discover whether the SNMP manager has received the message.

■ **Informs:** A message sent from the SNMP agent to the SNMP manager, for which the manager must acknowledge the receipt of the message. These messages are more reliable because of the acknowledgement of the message from the SNMP manager. If the Cisco Nexus device never receives a response for a message, it can send the inform request again.

You can configure Cisco NX-OS to send notifications to multiple host receivers.

SNMPv3

Security was always a concern for SNMP. The community string was sent in clear text and used for authentication between the SNMP manager and agent. SNMPv3 solves this problem by providing security features, such as authentication and encryption, for communication between the SNMP manager and the agent. The security features provided in SNMPv3 are as follows:

■ **Message integrity:** Ensures that a packet has not been tampered with in transit.

■ **Authentication:** Determines the message is from a valid source.

■ **Encryption:** Scrambles the packet content to prevent it from being seen by unauthorized sources.

The Cisco Nexus device supports SNMPv1, SNMPv2c, and SNMPv3. Each SNMP version has different security models and levels. A security model is an authentication strategy that is set up for a user and the role in which the user resides. A security level is the permitted level of security within a security model. A combination of a security model and a security level determines which security mechanism is employed when handling an SNMP packet.

Table 2-4 shows SNMP security models and levels supported by NX-OS.

Table 2-4   NX-OS SNMP Security Models and Levels

Model	Level	Authentication	Encryption	Description
v1	noAuthNoPriv	Community String	No	Uses a community string match for authentication
v2c	noAuthNoPriv	Community String	No	Uses a community string match for authentication
v3	noAuthNoPriv	Username	No	Uses a username match for authentication
v3	authNoPriv	HMAC-MD5 or HMAC-SHA	No	Provides authentication based on HMAC-MD5 or HMAC-SHA algorithm
V3	authPriv	HMAC-MD5 or HMAC-SHA	DES	Provides authentication based on HMAC-MD5 or HMAC-SHA algorithm

Remote Monitoring

Remote monitoring (RMON) is an industry standard remote network monitoring specification, developed by the Internet Engineering Task Force (IETF). RMON allows various network console systems and agents to exchange network-monitoring data. The Cisco NX-OS supports RMON alarms, events, and logs to monitor a Cisco Nexus device. In a Cisco Nexus switch, RMON is disabled by default, and no events or alarms are configured. You can enable RMON and configure your alarms and events by using the CLI or an SNMP-based network management station.

RMON Alarms

An RMON alarm monitors a specific MIB object for a specified interval, triggers an alarm at a specified threshold value, and resets the alarm at another threshold value. You can use alarms with RMON events to generate a log entry or an SNMP notification when the RMON alarm triggers. You can set an alarm on any MIB object that resolves into an SNMP INTEGER type. The specified object must be an existing SNMP MIB object in standard dot notation. (For example, 1.3.6.1.2.1.2.2.1.17 represents ifOutOctets.17.) When you create an alarm, you specify the following parameters:

- **MIB:** The object to monitor.
- **Sampling interval:** The interval to collect a sample value of the MIB object.

- **Sample type:** Absolute sample is the value of the MIB object. Delta sample is the difference between two consecutive sample values.
- **Rising threshold:** Device triggers a rising alarm or resets a falling alarm on this threshold.
- **Falling threshold:** Device triggers a falling alarm or resets a rising alarm on this threshold.
- **Events:** The action taken when an alarm (rising or falling) is triggered.

RMON Events

RMON events are generated by RMON alarms. You can associate an event to an alarm. Different events can be generated for a falling alarm and a rising alarm. RMON supports the following type of events:

- **SNMP notification:** Sends an SNMP notification when a rising alarm or a falling alarm is triggered
- **Log:** Adds an entry in the RMON log table when the associated alarm is triggered
- **Both:** Sends an SNMP notification and adds an entry in the RMON log table when the associated alarm is triggered

Syslog

Syslog is a standard protocol defined in IETF RFC 5424 for logging system messages to a remote server. Nexus switches support logging of system messages. This log can be sent to the terminal sessions, a log file, and syslog servers on remote systems. You can configure the Nexus switch to send syslog messages to a maximum of eight syslog servers. By default, Cisco Nexus switches only log system messages to a log file and output them to the terminal sessions. When the switch first initializes, messages are sent to syslog servers only after the network is initialized. To support the same configuration of syslog servers on all switches in a fabric, you can use Cisco Fabric Services (CFS) to distribute the syslog server configuration.

Table 2-5 describes the severity levels used in system messages. When you configure the severity level, the system outputs messages at that level and lower.

Table 2-5   System Message Severity Levels

Level	Description
0 – emergency	System unusable
1 – alert	Immediate action needed
2 – critical	Critical condition
3 – error	Error condition
4 – warning	Warning condition
5 – notification	Normal but significant condition
6 – information	Informational message only
7 – debugging	Appears during debugging only

Embedded Event Manager

Cisco NX-OS Embedded Event Manager provides real-time network event detection, programmability, and automation within the device. The Embedded Event Manager (EEM) monitors events that occur on the device and takes action to recover or troubleshoot these events, based on the configuration. There are three major components of EEM:

- Event statement
- Action statement
- Policies

Event Statements

An event is any device activity for which some action, such as a workaround or a notification, should be taken. In many cases, these events are related to faults in the device, such as when an interface or a fan malfunctions. EEM defines event filters so only critical events or multiple occurrences of an event within a specified time period trigger an associated action.

Event statements specify the event that triggers a policy to run. In Cisco NX-OS releases prior to 5.2, you can configure only one event statement per policy. However, beginning in Cisco NX-OS Release 5.2, you can configure multiple event triggers.

Action Statements

Action statements describe the action triggered by a policy. These actions could be sending an e-mail or disabling an interface to recover from an event. Each policy can have multiple action statements. If no action is associated with a policy, EEM still observes events but takes no actions. NX-OS EEM supports the following actions in action statements:

- Execute any CLI commands.
- Update a counter.
- Log an exception.
- Force the shutdown of any module.
- Reload the device.
- Shut down specified modules because the power is over budget.
- Generate a syslog message.
- Generate a Call Home event.
- Generate an SNMP notification.
- Use the default action for the system policy.

Policies

NX-OS Embedded Event Manager (EEM) policy consists of an event statement and one or more action statements. The event statement defines the event to look for as well as the filtering characteristics for the event. The action statement defines the action EEM takes when the event occurs.

Figure 2-11 shows a high-level overview of NX-OS EEM.

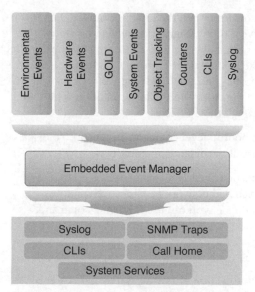

Figure 2-11 *Nexus Embedded Event Manager*

Generic Online Diagnostics

Cisco generic online diagnostics (GOLD) is a suite of diagnostic functions that provide hardware testing and verification. It helps in detecting hardware faults and to make sure that internal data paths are operating as designed. If a fault is detected, the switch takes corrective action to mitigate the fault and to reduce potential network outages. GOLD provides the following tests as part of the feature set:

■ Boot diagnostics

■ Continuous health monitoring

■ On-demand tests

■ Scheduled tests

Figure 2-12 shows an overview of Nexus GOLD.

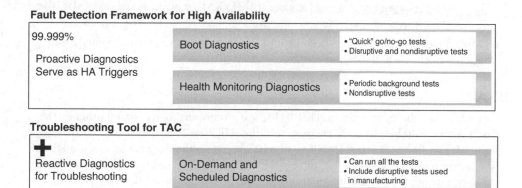

Figure 2-12 *Nexus GOLD*

During the boot diagnostics, GOLD tests are executed when the chassis is powered up or during an online insertion and removal (OIR) event. Boot diagnostics include disruptive tests and nondisruptive tests that run during system boot and system reset. Continuous health checks occur in the background, as per schedule, and on demand from CLI. Runtime diagnostics (also known as health monitoring diagnostics) include nondisruptive tests that run in the background during the normal operation of the switch. If a failure condition is observed during the test, corrective actions are taken through EEM policies.

To enable boot diagnostics, use the **diagnostic bootup level complete** command. To display the diagnostic level that is currently in place, use **show diagnostic boot level**.

You can also start or stop an on-demand diagnostic test. It is recommended to start a disruptive diagnostic test manually during a scheduled network maintenance window. For example, to start an on-demand test on module 6, you can use following command: **diagnostic start module 6 test all**.

Smart Call Home

The Call Home feature provides e-mail-based notification of critical system events. This feature can be used to page a network support engineer, e-mail a network operations center, or use Cisco Smart Call Home services to automatically generate a case with the technical assistance center (TAC). You can use this feature to notify any external entity when an important event occurs on your device. Call Home can deliver alerts to multiple recipients that you configure in destination profiles.

Call Home includes a fixed set of predefined alerts on your switch. These alerts are grouped into alert groups, and CLI commands are assigned to execute when an alert in an alert group occurs. The switch includes the command output in the transmitted Call Home message. Following are advantages of using the Call Home feature:

- Automatic execution and attachment of relevant CLI command output.
- Multiple message format options, such as the following:
    - **Short Text:** Suitable for pagers or printed reports.
    - **Full Text:** Fully formatted message information suitable for human reading.
    - **XML:** Matching readable format that uses the Extensible Markup Language (XML) and the Adaptive Messaging Language (AML) XML schema definition (XSD). The XML format enables communication with the Cisco Systems TAC (Cisco-TAC).
- Multiple concurrent message destinations. You can configure up to 50 e-mail destination addresses for each destination profile.

NX-API

Cisco NX-API allows you to use HTTP/HTTPS as a transport to access and program the Cisco Nexus switches. CLIs are encoded into the HTTP/HTTPS POST body, so rather than using SSH or Telnet to access the CLIs, which only run on the device, you can use NX-API to execute these CLI commands from outside the switch. You can use NX-API to execute **show** commands as well as configuration commands; it supports XML and JSON outputs. Python scripting capability is also available on the devices to provide programmatic access to the switch CLI to perform various tasks.

The NX-API back end uses the Nginx HTTP server. The Nginx process, and all of its children processes, are under Linux cgroup protection, where the CPU and memory usage are capped. If the Nginx memory usage exceeds the cgroup limitations, the Nginx process is restarted and restored.

NX-API is integrated into the authentication system on the device. Users must have appropriate accounts to access the device through NX-API. It is recommended to use HTTPS when communicating with the device so the session and the user credentials will be encrypted.

To enable NX-API, use the following commands:

Example 2-1 *Sample Configuration Showing How to Enable NX-API*

```
nx-osv-1(config)# feature nxapi
nx-osv-1(config)# nxapi sandbox
nx-osv-1(config)# nxapi https port 8001
```

NOTE Port 8001 is just a random port I chose for demonstration purposes only.

The NX-API has a sandbox, which is the web-based user interface that you use to enter the commands, command type, and output type. After enabling the NX-API sandbox as shown in Example 2-1, use HTTP/HTTPS to access it. After posting the request, the output response is displayed.

To access the NX-API sandbox, open a browser (you can use HTTP or HTTPS) and type **http://mgmt_ip**, where **mgmt_ip** is the IP address of the switch you enabled NX-API on. An example of the web page is shown in Figure 2-13.

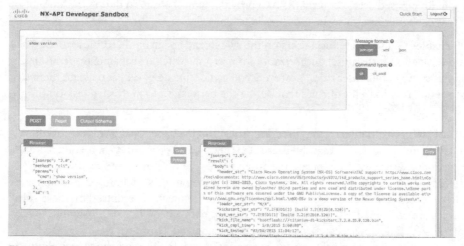

Figure 2-13 *NX-API Sample Request and Sample Response*

As shown in Figure 2-13, in the NX-API sandbox, you type the commands you would like in the left box (I have typed **show version** as an example) and choose the format (JSON-

RPC, XML, or JSON), command type, and output type in the top pane. Click on the POST Request button above the left pane to post the request. Brief descriptions of the request elements are displayed below the left pane. If you like Python, you can click on the Python button shown in Figure 5-13, and you will get the Python-equivalent script.

When choosing the command type before doing a power-on self-test (POST) to the device, you are going to send to the show or configuration commands using the NX-API. The type you choose depends on the actual command you want to send. With a **show** command, you should use the cli_show type. To determine whether a command supports XML/JSON output or not, you can go to the CLI of the switch and run the command with the | xml or | JSON option on the end; you will be able to see whether that command returns XML or JSON output. Example 2-2 shows an example with **show hostname**. If the **show** command is not supported, you will receive a message stating `structured output unsupported` from the API.

Example 2-2   *Sample Configuration Showing cli_show Support for JSON Output*

```
nx-osv-1# show hostname | JSON
{
  "hostname": "nx-osv-1"
}

nx-osv-1#
```

Role-Based Access Control

To manage a Nexus switch, users log in to the switch and perform tasks as per their role in the organization. For example, a network operations center (NOC) engineer might want to check the health of the network, but he is not permitted to make changes to the switch configuration. Role-based access control (RBAC) provides a mechanism to define the amount of access that each user has when the user logs in to the switch.

NX-OS enables you to create local users on the switch and assign a role to these users. The roles are defined to restrict user authorization to perform switch management operations. NX-OS has some default user roles; however, you can define new roles and assign them to the users. Each role has a list of rules that define the permission to perform a task on the switch.

With RBAC, you first define the required user roles and then specify the rules for each switch management operation that the user role is allowed to perform. When you create a user account on the switch, associate the appropriate role with the user account, which then determines what the individual user is allowed to do on the switch. If a user belongs to multiple roles, she can execute a combination of all the commands permitted by these roles. When roles are combined, a permit rule takes priority over a deny rule. For example, a user has Role-A, which denies access to a configuration command. However, this user also has Role-B, which allows access to the configuration command. In this case, the user is allowed access to the configuration commands.

User Roles

User roles contain rules that define the operations allowed on the switch. These roles are assigned to users so they have limited access to switch operations as per their role. Each user can have multiple roles, and each role can contain multiple rules. For example, if Role-A allows access to only configuration operations, and Role-B allows access to only debug operations, users who belong to both Role-A and Role-B can access configuration and debug operations. You can also define roles to limit access to specific virtual storage area networks (VSANs), VLANs, and interfaces of a Nexus switch.

Table 2-6 shows the default roles on a Nexus 5000 switch.

Table 2-6   Default Roles on Nexus 5000

User Role	Description
network-admin	Complete read and write access to the entire switch
network-operator	Complete read access to the switch
san-admin	Complete read and write access to Fibre Channel and FCoE administrative tasks using SNMP or CLI

A Nexus 7000 switch supports features such as VDC, which is a virtual switch within the Nexus chassis. Therefore, a Nexus 7000 supports additional roles to administer and operate the VDCs. Table 2-7 shows the default roles on a Nexus 7000 switch.

Table 2-7   Default Roles on Nexus 7000

User Role	Description
network-admin	Complete read and write access to all the VDCs on the switch
network-operator	Complete read access to all the VDCs on the switch
vdc-admin	Read and write access to a specific VDC
vdc-operator	Only read access to a specific VDC

Rules

A rule is the basic element of a role that defines the switch operations that are permitted or denied by a user role. You can apply rules for the following parameters:

- **Command:** NX-OS command or group of commands defined in a regular expression.

- **Feature:** All the commands associated with a switch feature. You can check the available feature names for this command using the **show role feature** command.

- **Feature group:** Default or user-defined group of features. Enter the **show role feature group** command to display the default feature groups available for this parameter.

The most granular control parameter of the rule is the command. The next level of control parameter is the feature, which represents all commands associated with the feature. The last level of control parameter is the feature group. The feature group combines related features for the ease of management.

User Role Policies

The user role policies are used to limit user access to the switch resources. They allow limiting access to the interfaces, VLANs, and VSANs. Rules defined for a user role override the user role policies. For example, you define a user role policy to access a specific interface, and the user does not have access to the interface unless you configure a command rule to permit the interface command.

RBAC Characteristics and Guidelines

Some characteristics and guidelines for RBAC are outlined next:

- Roles are associated to user accounts in the local database or to the users in a remote Authentication Authorization and Accounting (AAA) database.
- 64 user-defined roles can be configured per VDC.
- 256 rules can be assigned to a single role.
- A user account can belong to 64 roles.
- Role changes do not take effect until the user logs out and logs in again.
- Rules are executed in descending order. (For example, rule 2 is checked before rule 1.)
- If a user account belongs to multiple roles, that user can execute the most privileged union of all the rules in all assigned roles.
- Users see only the CLI commands they are permitted to execute when using context-sensitive help.
- Role features and feature groups should be used to simplify RBAC configuration when applicable.
- Role features and feature groups can be referenced only in the local user account database. They cannot be referenced in an AAA server command authorization policy (for example, AAA/TACACS+).
- RBAC roles can be distributed to multiple Nexus 7000 devices using Cisco Fabric Services (CFS).

Privilege Levels

Privilege levels are introduced in NX-OS to provide IOS-compatible authentication and authorization functionality. This feature is useful in a network environment that uses a common AAA policy for managing Cisco IOS and NX-OS devices. By default, the privilege level feature is disabled on the Nexus switch. To enable privilege-level support on the Nexus switch, use the **feature privilege** configuration command. When this feature is enabled, the predefined privilege levels are created as roles. These predefined privilege levels cannot be deleted. Similar to the RBAC roles, the privilege levels can also be modified to meet different security requirements. On Nexus switches, the privilege level and RBAC roles can be configured simultaneously. A user account can be associated to a privilege level or to RBAC roles.

Table 2-8 shows the IOS privilege levels and their corresponding NX-OS system-defined roles.

Table 2-8   NX-OS Privilege Levels

IOS Privilege Levels	NX-OS System-Defined Role	Description
0	priv-0	All **show** and some Exec and configuration CLI commands
1–13	priv-1 to priv-13	Same as priv-0 by default
14	priv-14	Equivalent to RBAC role vdc-admin
15	priv-15	Equivalent to RBAC role network-admin

Reference List

Cisco Nexus 7000 Series NX-OS Fundamentals Configuration Guide:

http://www.cisco.com/c/en/us/td/docs/switches/datacenter/sw/nx-os/fundamentals/
configuration/guide/b_Cisco_Nexus_7000_Series_NX-OS_Fundamentals_Configuration_
Guide/b_Cisco_Nexus_7000_Series_NX-OS_Fundamentals_Configuration_Guide_
Release_6-x_chapter_010.html

Cisco Nexus 7000 Series NX-OS Programmability Guide:

http://www.cisco.com/c/en/us/td/docs/switches/datacenter/nexus7000/sw/program-
mability/guide/b_Cisco_Nexus_7000_Series_NX-OS_Programmability_Guide/b_Cisco_
Nexus_7000_Series_NX-OS_Programmability_Guide_chapter_0101.html

Exam Preparation Tasks

Review All Key Topics

Review the most important topics in the chapter, noted with the Key Topics icon in the outer margin of the page. Table 2-9 lists a reference of these key topics and the page numbers on which each is found.

Table 2-9   Key Topics for Chapter 2

Key Topic Element	Description	Page
Section	"Data Plane"	50
Section	"Control Plane"	53
Section	"Control Plane Policing"	56
Section	"Management Plane"	58
Section	"Out-of-Band Management"	59
Section	"Simple Network Management Protocol"	62
Section	"Role-Based Access Control"	63
Section	"NX-API"	68
Section	"SNMP Notifications"	70

Complete Tables and Lists from Memory

Print a copy of Appendix B, "Memory Tables" or at least the section for this chapter, and complete the tables and lists from memory. Appendix C, "Memory Tables Answer Key" includes completed tables and lists to check your work.

Define Key Terms

Define the following key terms from this chapter, and check your answers in the Glossary:

Data Center Network Manager (DCNM), Application-Specific Integrated Circuit (ASIC), Frame Check Sequence (FCS), Unified Port Controller (UPC), Unified Crossbar Fabric (UCF), Cisco Discovery Protocol (CDP), Bidirectional Forwarding Detection (BFD), Unidirectional Link Detection (UDLD), Link Aggregation Control Protocol (LACP), Address Resolution Protocol (ARP), Spanning Tree Protocol (STP), Dynamic Host Configuration Protocol (DHCP), Connectivity Management Processor (CMP), Virtual Device Context (VDC), Role-Based Access Control (RBAC), Simple Network Management Protocol (SNMP), Remote Network Monitoring (RMON), Fabric Extender (FEX), Management Information Base (MIB), Generic Online Diagnostics (GOLD), Extensible Markup Language (XML), In Field-Programmable Gate Array (FPGA), Complex Instruction Set Computing (CISC), Reduced Instruction Set Computing (RISC)

This chapter covers the following exam topics:

3.4 Describe, configure, and verify unified switch ports

3.5 Describe the features and benefits of Unified Fabric

CHAPTER 3

Unified Fabric Overview

Unified Fabric is a holistic network architecture that uniquely integrates networking, storage, security, compute elements, and orchestration elements, all designed to seamlessly operate in physical, virtual, and cloud environments. By unifying and consolidating infrastructure components, Cisco Unified Fabric delivers flexibility and consistent architecture across a diverse set of environments.

In this chapter we discuss how Unified Fabric promises to be the architecture that fulfills the requirements for the next generation of Ethernet networks in the data center.

"Do I Know This Already?" Quiz

The "Do I Know This Already?" quiz allows you to assess whether you should read this entire chapter thoroughly or jump to the "Exam Preparation Tasks" section. If you are in doubt about your answers to these questions or your own assessment of your knowledge of the topics, read the entire chapter. Table 3-1 lists the major headings in this chapter and their corresponding "Do I Know This Already?" quiz questions. You can find the answers in Appendix A, "Answers to the 'Do I Know This Already?' Quizzes."

Table 3-1 "Do I Know This Already?" Section-to-Question Mapping

Foundation Topics Section	Questions
"Challenges of Today's Data Center Networks"	1–2
"Cisco Unified Fabric Principles"	3–8
"Inter-Data Center Unified Fabric"	9–10

CAUTION The goal of self-assessment is to gauge your mastery of the topics in this chapter. If you do not know the answer to a question or are only partially sure of the answer, you should mark that question as wrong for purposes of the self-assessment. Giving yourself credit for an answer you correctly guess skews your self-assessment results and might provide you with a false sense of security.

1. Which of the following is one challenge of today's data center networks?

   a. Too Low power consumption is not good for the electric companies.

   b. Multilayer design is not optimal for east-west network traffic flows.

   c. Administrators have a hard time doing unified cabling.

   d. vPC topology causes loss of 50% of bandwidth because of blocked ports.

2. What is one possible way to solve the problem of different application demands in today's data centers?

  a. Rewrite applications to conform to the network on which they are running.

  b. Deploy separate application-specific dedicated environments.

  c. Allow a network to discover application requirements.

  d. Today's networks as they are can accommodate any application demand for network and storage.

3. What does Unified Fabric do?

  a. It leverages the Ethernet network.

  b. It consolidates multiple types of traffic.

  c. It supports virtual, physical, and cloud environments.

  d. It leverages IEEE data center bridging.

4. What are the two types of traffic that are most commonly consolidated with Unified Fabric?

  a. Voice traffic

  b. SAN storage traffic

  c. InfiniBand traffic

  d. Network traffic

5. How does vPC differ from traditional spanning tree topologies?

  a. vPC leverages the IS-IS protocol to construct network topology.

  b. vPC blocks redundant paths toward the STP root bridge.

  c. vPC leverages port channels and has no blocked ports.

  d. Spanning tree is automatically disabled when you enable vPC.

6. What Cisco virtual product is used to secure VM-to-VM communication within the same tenant space?

  a. Virtual Supervisor Module

  b. Virtual Adaptive Security Appliance

  c. Virtual Security Gateway

  d. Virtual Application Security

7. What is vPath?

  a. It is a virtual path selected between two virtual machines in the data center.

  b. It is a feature of Cisco Nexus 7000 series switches to steer the traffic toward physical service nodes.

  c. It is a feature that allows virtual switches to get their basic configuration during boot.

  d. It is a feature of Cisco Nexus 1000v virtual switches to steer the traffic toward virtual service nodes.

8. Which parts of the infrastructure can DCNM products manage?

    a. LAN

    b. SAN

    c. Wireless

    d. vPC

9. What happens when OTV receives a unicast frame and the destination MAC address is not in the MAC address table?

    a. The frame is dropped.

    b. The frame is flooded through the overlay to all remote sites.

    c. The frame is turned into multicast and sent only to some of the remote sites.

    d. The frame is dropped and the ICMP message is sent back to the source.

10. True or false? In LISP, ITR stands for Ingress Transformation Router.

    a. True

    b. False

3

Foundation Topics

Challenges of Today's Data Center Networks

Ethernet is by far the predominant choice for a single, converged fabric that can simultaneously support multiple traffic types. Over the years it has withstood the test of time against other technologies trying to displace it as the popular option for data center network environments. Ethernet enjoys a broad base of engineering and operational expertise resulting from its ubiquitous presence in the data center environments for many years. It is well understood by network engineers and developers worldwide.

IT departments of today's organizations are under increasing pressure to deliver technological solutions that enable strategic business growth and provide a foundation for the continuing trends of the private/public cloud deployments. At the same time, IT departments are under ever-increasing pressure to deliver more for less, where decreasing budgets have to accommodate for innovative technology and process adoption. Operational silos and isolated infrastructure solutions are not optimized for virtualized and cloud environments. This prevents the data centers of today from becoming the engine of enablement for the business growth.

Modern application environments no longer rely on simple client/server transactions, as in years past. Application traffic patterns have shifted from being predominantly north-south to being predominantly east-west, where a single client request for data causes numerous network transactions to take place between the servers in the data center. This shift in network traffic patterns facilitated the transition from traditional multilayer "stove pipe" designs of access, aggregation, and core layers into a flatter data center switching fabric architecture leveraging Spine-Leaf topology. Figure 3-1 depicts traditional north-south and the new east-west data center switching architectures.

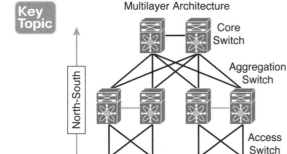

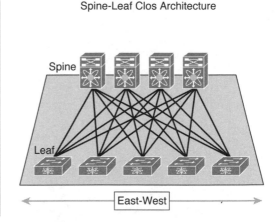

Figure 3-1   *Multilayer and Spine-Leaf Clos Architecture*

Increased volumes of application data led to significant network and storage traffic growth across the infrastructure, which in turn had resulted in greater reliance on the network.

Oftentimes application performance is measured along and coupled with the performance characteristics of the network.

Different types of application traffic carry different characteristics. Client-to-server and server-to-server transactions usually involve short and bursty-in-nature transmissions, whereas most of the server-to-storage traffic consists of long-lasting and steady flows. Networks deployed in high-frequency trading environments have to accommodate ultra-low latency packet forwarding where traditional rules of typical enterprise application deployments do not quite suffice. All these require the network infrastructure to be flexible and intelligent to discover and accommodate the changes in application traffic dynamics.

Bandwidth availability and network latency are significant influencers on the overall application performance, but so is the ability of applications to handle packet drops. Different protocols respond differently to packet drops; some accept packet drops as part of a normal network behavior, whereas others absolutely must have guaranteed no-drop packet delivery. In the converged infrastructure of Unified Fabric, both of the behaviors must be accommodated. The best example is the FCoE protocol, which requires a lossless underlying fabric where packet loss is not tolerated.

Ultimately, growing application demands require additional capabilities from the underlying networking infrastructure. One method to solve this is to deploy multiple, separate, application-specific dedicated environments. It is not uncommon for the data centers of today to deploy an Ethernet network for IP traffic and a Fibre Channel storage-area network (SAN) for block-based storage connectivity. The demands for high performance and cluster computing, as well as services such as Remote Direct Memory Access (RDMA), are at times addressed by leveraging the low latency InfiniBand network, even though this is not a popular technology in the majority of the modern data centers. Some organizations even build separate Ethernet networks for IP-based storage. This highly segmented deployment results in high capital expenditures (CAPEX), high operating expenses (OPEX), and high demands for management. All these combined create an opportunity for consolidation. Figure 3-2 depicts a traditional concept of distinct networks purposely built for specific requirements.

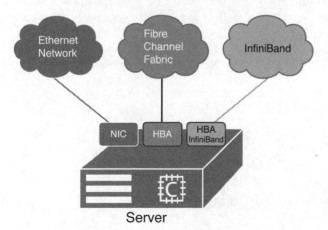

Figure 3-2 *Typical Distinct Data Center Networks*

When these types of separate networks are evaluated against the capabilities of the Ethernet technology, it becomes apparent that Ethernet holds a great promise of consolidation. This is where Cisco Unified Fabric serves as a key building block for ubiquitous infrastructure to deploy applications on top. It provides foundational connectivity service, unifying storage, data networking, and network services onto consistent networking infrastructure across physical, virtual, and cloud environments.

Cisco Unified Fabric Principles

Cisco Unified Fabric is a multidimensional approach where architectures, features, and capabilities are combined with concepts of convergence, scalability, intelligence, high availability, security, and so on. It enables optimized resource utilization, faster application rollout, greater application performance, and overall lower operating costs, while greatly increasing network business value. Cisco Unified Fabric creates a foundational platform for a true multiprotocol environment on a single unified network infrastructure, which breaks organizational silos while reducing technological complexity. The following sections examine in more detail the key properties of the Unified Fabric network.

Convergence of Network and Storage

Convergence properties of the Cisco Unified Fabric architecture are the melding of the SAN with a local-area network (LAN) delivered on top of enhanced Ethernet fabric. Such Ethernet fabric would be simpler to provision and operate, resulting in fewer management points with shorter bring up time.

End-to-end converged Unified Fabric provides the utmost advantages to the organizations. However, at the same time, it allows the flexibility of integrating into existing nonconverged infrastructure, providing investment protection for the current network equipment and technologies. Both the Cisco MDS 9000 family of storage switches and the Cisco Nexus 5000/6000/7000 family of Unified Fabric network switches have features that facilitate network convergence. For instance, Cisco Nexus 5000/6000 and Cisco MDS 9000 family switches provide full, bidirectional bridging between FCoE and traditional Fibre Channel fabric, allowing FCoE servers to connect to older Fibre Channel-only storage arrays. Similarly, servers attached through traditional Fibre Channel HBAs can access newer storage arrays connected through FCoE ports. Figure 3-3 depicts bridging between FCoE and traditional Fibre Channel fabric, where FCoE servers connect to Fibre Channel storage arrays leveraging the principles behind bidirectional bridging on the Cisco Nexus 5000/6000 series switches.

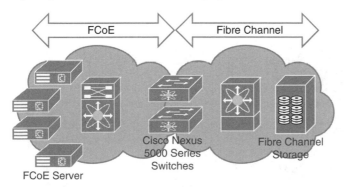

Figure 3-3 *FCoE and Fibre Channel Bidirectional Bridging*

Ultimately, SAN and LAN convergence does not have to happen overnight, and Cisco Unified Fabric architecture is flexible to allow gradual, and many times nondisruptive, migration from disparate isolated environments to unified network infrastructure. Traditionally, server network interface cards (NICs) and host bus adapters (HBAs) are used to provide connectivity into isolated LAN and SAN environments. With convergence of the two, NICs and HBAs make way for a new type of adapter called converged network adapter (CNA). Figure 3-4 depicts elements of CNA.

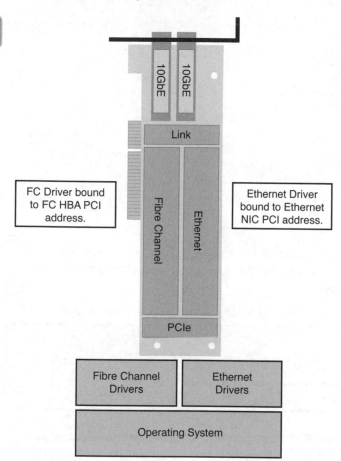

Figure 3-4 *Converged Network Adapter Elements*

Cisco Nexus Unified Fabric switches can leverage unified ports to initially connect systems with traditional Fibre Channel HBAs and later convert to unified FCoE or other Ethernet- and IP-based storage protocols as the time progresses. Figure 3-5 depicts unified port operation.

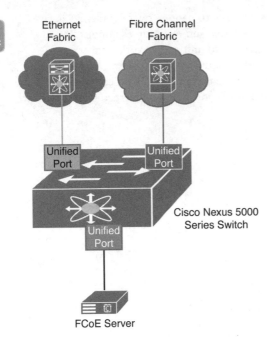

Figure 3-5 *Unified Port Operation*

Example 3-1 shows a configuration example for defining unified ports as port type Fibre Channel on the Cisco Nexus 5500 switches to provide storage connectivity to traditional Fibre Channel initiators or targets.

Example 3-1 *Configuring Unified Port on the Cisco Nexus 5000 Series Switch*

```
nexus5500# configure terminal
nexus5500 (config)# slot 1
nexus5500 (config-slot)# port 32 type fc
nexus5500 (config-slot)# copy running-config startup-config
nexus5500 (config-slot)# reload
```

As we mentioned earlier, Unified Fabric can contribute to significant consolidation. For example, a typical server requires at least five connections: two redundant LAN connections, two redundant SAN connections, and an out-of-band management connection. Separate connections for backup, clustering, and so on, provisioned for each server in the data center, can add up quickly. Figure 3-6 depicts an example of how network adapter consolidation leveraging converged network adapters can greatly reduce the number of server adapters used in the Unified Fabric topology.

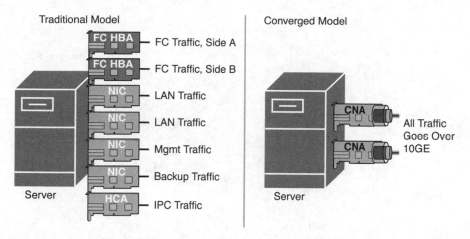

Figure 3-6   *Server Adapter Consolidation Using Converged Network Adapters*

Network adapter virtualization technologies, such as Cisco Adapter-FEX and Cisco VM-FEX, which are also part of Cisco Unified Fabric architecture, contribute to even further consolidation. From the perspective of a large size data center, consolidation of cabling and network adapters translates to fewer ports, fewer switches, fewer network layers, lower power consumption, and improved airflow.

Along with reduction in infrastructure, consolidation carries operational improvements. All switches composing the Unified Fabric environment run the same Cisco NX-OS switch operating system. Such consistency allows IT staff to leverage operational practices of the isolated environments and apply them to the converged environment of the Unified Fabric. At the same time, a converged data center network provides all the functionality of existing disparate network and storage environments. For Ethernet, this includes support for multicast and broadcast traffic, VLANs, link aggregation, equal cost multipathing, and so on. For Fibre Channel, this includes provisioning of all the Fibre Channel services, such as zoning and name servers, and support for virtual storage area networks (VSANs), inter-VSAN routing (IVR), and the like.

One possible concern for delivering converged infrastructure for network and storage traffic is that the Ethernet protocol does not provide guaranteed packet delivery, which is essential for healthy Fibre Channel protocol operation. With FCoE, Fibre Channel frames are encapsulated in outer Ethernet headers for hop-by-hop delivery between initiators and targets where lossless behavior is expected. To enforce Fibre Channel characteristics at each hop along the path between initiators and targets, intermediate Unified Fabric switches operate in either FCoE-NPV or FCoE switching mode. This sometimes is referred to as FCoE Dense Mode. Figure 3-7 depicts the logical concept behind having all FCoE intermediate switches operating in either FCoE-NPV or FCoE switching mode. FCoE switching mode implies running the FCoE Fibre Channel Forwarder function, the FCF, inside the Unified Fabric switch.

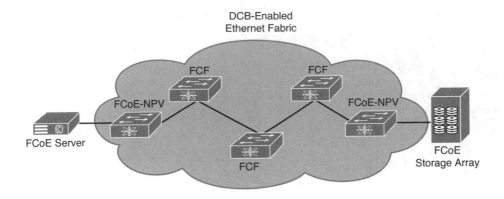

Figure 3-7   *FCoE Dense Mode Operation*

Running FCoE requires additional capabilities added to the Unified Fabric network. IEEE defines a set of standards augmenting standard Ethernet protocol behavior. These are priority flow control (PFC) defined by IEEE 802.1Qbb, enhanced transmission selection (ETS) defined by IEEE 802.1Qaz, quantized congestion notification (QCN) defined by IEEE 802.1Qau, and data center bridging exchange (DCBX) defined by IEEE 802.1AB (LLDP) with TLV extensions. These additional standards make sure that Unified Fabric provides lossless, no-drop, in-order delivery of packets end-to-end, and they are collectively called data center bridging (DCB). DCB is required for successful FCoE operation. Cisco Nexus 5000/6000/7000 series Unified Fabric switches, as well as the MDS 9500/9700 series storage switches with FCoE line cards, support these standards for enhanced Ethernet. For smaller size deployments, Cisco MDS 9250i Multiservice Fabric Switch offers support for the Unified Fabric needs of running Fibre Channel, FCoE, iSCSI, FICON and Fibre Channel over IP. DCB increases overall reliability of the data center networks, which is increasingly necessary not only for the storage traffic, but also for other types of multiprotocol communication across the Unified Fabric.

In environments where storage connectivity has less stringent requirements, Small Computer System Interface over IP (iSCSI) can be considered an alternative to FCoE. iSCSI allows encapsulating original Fibre Channel payload in the TCP/IP packets. Contrary to FCoE, which relies on IEEE DCB standards for efficient operation, iSCSI leverages TCP characteristics to deliver lossless, no-drop, in-order delivery.

Even though DCB is not mandatory for iSCSI operation, some NICs and CNAs connected to Cisco Nexus 5000 series switches can be configured to accept configuration values sent by the switches leveraging Data Center Bridging Exchange protocol, part of DCB. In that case, DCBX would negotiate configuration and settings between the switch and the network adapter by leveraging type-length-value (TLV) and sub-TLV fields. This allows distributing configuration values, for example, class of service (COS) markings, to the connected network adapters in a scalable manner. Potential use of other DCB standards coded in TLV format adds even further flexibility to the iSCSI deployment by allowing underlying Unified Fabric infrastructure separate iSCSI storage traffic from the rest of IP traffic. Example 3-2 shows the relevant command-line interface (CLI) commands to enable a no-drop class for iSCSI traffic on Nexus 5000 series switches for guaranteed traffic delivery.

Example 3-2 *Configuring No-Drop Behavior for iSCSI Traffic*

```
nexus5000# configure terminal
nexus5000(config)# class-map type qos match-all c1
nexus5000(config-cmap-qos)# match protocol iscsi
nexus5000(config-cmap-qos)# match cos 6
nexus5000(config-cmap-qos)# exit

nexus5000(config)# policy-map type qos c1
nexus5000(config-pmap-qos)# class c1
nexus5000(config-pmap-c-qos)# set qos-group 2
nexus5000(config-pmap-c-qos)# exit

nexus5000(config)# class-map type network-qos c1
nexus5000(config-cmap-nq)# match qos-group 2
nexus5000(config-cmap-nq)# exit

nexus5000(config)# policy-map type network-qos p1
nexus5000(config-pmap-nq)# class type network-qos c1
nexus5000(config-pmap-c-nq)# pause no-drop
```

For environments where storage arrays lack iSCSI functionality, organizations can leverage an iSCSI gateway device, such as a Cisco MDS 9250i storage switch, to terminate the iSCSI TCP/IP session, extract the payload, and re-encapsulate it in the FCoE protocol for transmission over the Unified Fabric. Figure 3-8 depicts iSCSI deployment options with and without the gateway service.

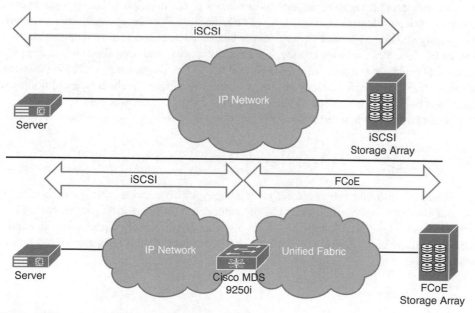

Figure 3-8 *iSCSI Deployment Options*

iSCSI does not support native Fibre Channel services and tools, which are built around traditional Fibre Channel fabrics. iSCSI can also introduce increased CPU cycles resulting from TCP/IP overhead on the server. TCP/IP offload can be leveraged on the network adapter to help with higher CPU utilization, but that increases the cost of network adapters, which are used for this solution.

Although iSCSI continues to be a popular option in many storage applications, particularly with small and medium-sized businesses (SMB), it is not quite replacing the wide adoption of the Fibre Channel protocol, either traditional or FCoE, for critical storage environments.

Scalability and Growth

Scalability is defined as the capability to grow the environment based on changing needs. Unified Fabric is often characterized as having a multidimensional scalability, where individual device performance, as well as the overall fabric and system scalability, is achieved without compromising manageability and cost. Scalability parameters can also stretch beyond the boundary of a single data center, allowing a true geographic span.

Unified Fabric leveraging connectivity speeds of 10G, 40G, and 100G offers substantially higher useable bandwidth for the server and storage connectivity, which contributes to fewer ports, fewer switches, and subsequently fewer network tiers and fewer management points, allowing overall larger scale.

The capability to grow the network in a manner that causes the least amount of disruption to the ongoing operation is a crucial aspect of scalability. Each network deployment has unique characteristics, which cannot be addressed by a rigid architecture. Unified Fabric caters to the needs of ever-expanding scalability by providing flexible architecture, while also following the investment protection philosophy.

Cisco's entire data center switching portfolio adheres to the principles of supporting incremental growth and demands for scalability. For example, Cisco Nexus 7000 series switches offer highly scalable M-series I/O modules for large capacities and feature richness, and F-series I/O modules for lower latency, higher port capacity, and several differentiating features. Through an evolution of the Fabric and the I/O modules, Cisco Nexus 7000 series switches offer expandable pay-as-you-grow scalable switch fabric architecture and nonoversubscribed behavior for high-speed Ethernet fabrics. Figure 3-9 depicts the Cisco Nexus 7000 series switch fabric architecture.

NOTE   Cisco Nexus 7004 and Cisco Nexus 7702 switches have no fabric modules.

Cisco Nexus 5000/6000 series switches offer a highly scalable access layer platform with 10G and 40G Ethernet capabilities and FCoE support for Unified Fabric convergence. The architecture does not include fabric modules but instead uses a unified port controller and unified fabric crossbar. Figure 3-10 depicts the Cisco Nexus 5000/6000 series switch fabric architecture.

Cisco Nexus 7000 Series Switch

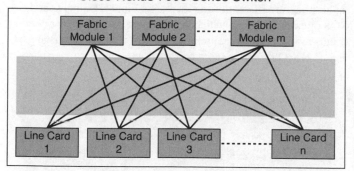

Figure 3-9   *Cisco Nexus 7000 Series Switch Fabric Architecture*

Cisco Nexus 5000/6000 Series Switch

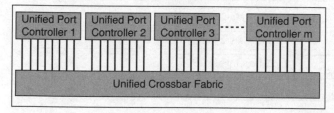

Figure 3-10   *Cisco Nexus 5000/6000 Series Switch Fabric Architecture*

Cisco Nexus 9000 family switches provide fixed and modular switch architecture with high port density and the capability to run Application Centric Infrastructure. Cisco Nexus 9000 series switches are based on a combination of Cisco's own application-specific integrated circuits (ASICs) and Broadcom ASICs. Figure 3-11 depicts Cisco Nexus 9500 series modular switch architecture.

Cisco Nexus 9500 Series Switch

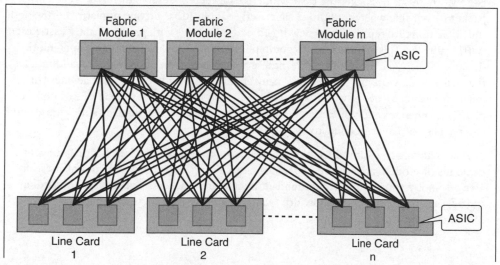

Figure 3-11   *Cisco Nexus 9500 Series Modular Switch Architecture*

On the storage switch side, Cisco MDS switches offer a highly available platform for SANs with expandable and resilient architecture of supporting increased Fibre Channel speeds and services. The Cisco NX-OS operating system, which powers data center network and storage switching platforms, runs modular software architecture based on an underlying Linux kernel. Figure 3-12 depicts NX-OS software architecture components.

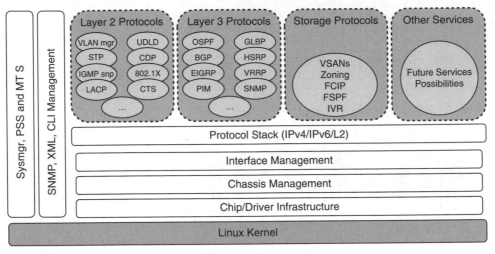

Figure 3-12 *NX-OS Software Architecture Components*

Cisco NX-OS leverages an innovative approach in software development by offering stateful process restart, component patching, persistent storage space (PSS) for process runtime information, in-service software upgrade (ISSU), and so on, coupled with role-based access control (RBAC) and a rich set of remote programmable APIs. Cisco NX-OS software enjoys frequent updates to keep up with the latest feature demands.

In the past, traditional growth implied adding capacity in the form of switch ports or uplink bandwidth; this is no longer the case. Modern data centers observe different trends in packet forwarding where traditional client/server applications driving primarily north-south traffic patterns are replaced by a new breed of applications with predominantly east-west traffic patterns. This shift has significant implications on the data center switching fabric designs, fabric capacities, fabric scale, and service insertion methodologies. In addition to the changing network traffic patterns, many applications reside on virtual machines with inherent characteristics of workload mobility and any workload anywhere design philosophy. This generates additional requirements on the data center switching fabric side around extensibility of Layer 2 connectivity.

Legacy spanning tree–driven topologies lack fast convergence required for the stringent demands of modern applications. Spanning tree Layer 2 loop-free topologies exercise an active/standby approach, where redundant uplinks are blocked from actively forwarding traffic, causing provisioned bandwidth "waste." Figure 3-13 depicts spanning tree Layer 2 operational logic.

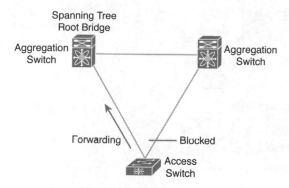

Figure 3-13   *Spanning Tree Layer 2 Operational Logic*

The evolution of spanning tree topologies led to the use of multichassis link-aggregation solutions, where Etherchannels or port channels enable active/active forwarding topologies, allowing faster convergence and full utilization of the provisioned bandwidth. Cisco implements virtual port channel (vPC) technology to help alleviate deficiencies of traditional spanning tree–driven topologies. vPC still runs Spanning Tree Protocol underneath as a safeguard mechanism to break Layer 2 bridging loops should they occur. Figure 3-14 depicts vPC operational logic.

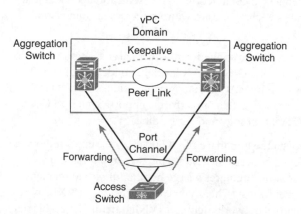

Figure 3-14   *vPC Operational Logic*

Can we do better? Yes. Even with vPC topologies, the scalability of solutions requiring large Layer 2 domains in support of virtual machine mobility can be limited. Cisco FabricPath takes a step further by completely eliminating the dependency on the Spanning Tree Protocol (STP) in constructing loop-free Layer 2 topology. Cisco FabricPath combines the simplicity of Layer 2 with proven scalability of Layer 3 by using the IS-IS routing protocol instead of Spanning Tree Protocol. It leverages Spine-Leaf Clos architecture to construct data center switching fabric with predicable end-to-end latency and vast east-west bisectional bandwidth. It employs the principle of conversational learning to further scale switch hardware forwarding resources. It also allows equal cost multipathing for both unicast and multicast traffic to maximize network resource utilization. Figure 3-15 depicts Cisco FabricPath topology and forwarding.

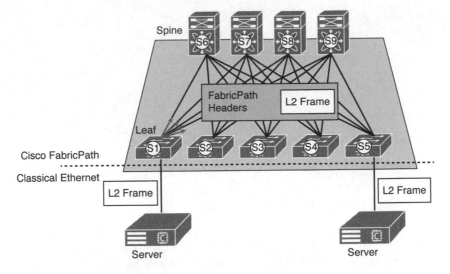

Figure 3-15 *Cisco FabricPath Topology and Forwarding*

By taking data center switching from PODs (points of delivery) to fabric, Cisco FabricPath breaks the boundaries and enables large-scale virtual machine mobility domains. Use of Cisco Nexus 2000 series Fabric Extenders in conjunction with Cisco FabricPath architecture enables building even larger-scale switching fabrics without increasing administrative domain.

Principles of Spine-Leaf topologies can also be applied with other encapsulation technologies, such as virtual extensible LAN, or VXLAN. VXLAN leverages underlying Layer 3 topology to extend Layer 2 services on top (MAC-in-IP), providing similar advantages to Cisco FabricPath while enjoying broader switching platform support. Similar to Cisco FabricPath, Figure 3-16 depicts VXLAN topology and forwarding.

VXLAN also assists in breaking through the boundary of ~4,000 VLANs supported by the IEEE 802.1Q standard widely deployed between switches. This is an important consideration with multitenant Unified Fabric, which requires a large number of virtual segments. Figure 3-17 depicts the VXLAN packet format, where you can see the 24-bit VXLAN ID field, sometimes also known as the virtual network identifier (VNID) field. The 24-bit field potentially enables you to create more than 16 million virtual segments.

VXLAN fabric allows building large-span virtual machine mobility domains with significant scale and bandwidth.

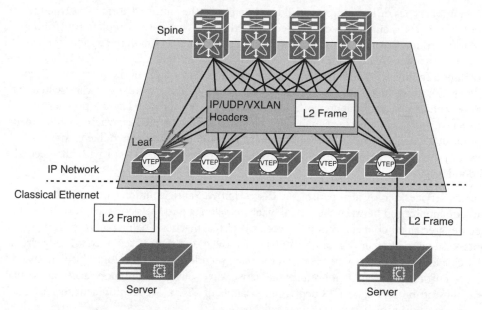

Figure 3-16 *VXLAN Topology and Forwarding*

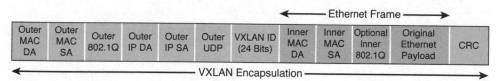

Figure 3-17 *VXLAN Packet Fields*

Security and Intelligence

Network intelligence coupled with security is an essential component of Cisco Unified Fabric. For the Cisco Nexus and Cisco MDS family of switches, the intelligence comes from a common switch operating system, Cisco NX-OS. It provides consistency, a common feature set, and intelligent services delivered to applications residing on physical or virtual network infrastructure alike.

The use of consistent network policies is essential for successful Unified Fabric operation. Policies are applied across the infrastructure and most importantly in the virtualized environment where workloads tend to be rapidly created, removed, and moved around. Consistent use of policies also enables faster application deployment cycles. In the past, deployment of applications required a considerable effort of sequentially configuring various physical infrastructure components. Cisco Unified Fabric policies around security, performance, differentiated service, high availability, and the like can be consistently set across the environment allowing, if necessary, to tune those for special application needs. Policies can be templatized and applied in a consistent repeatable manner, so that creation, removal, or migration of individual workloads has no impact on the overall environment operation. Policies also greatly reduce the risk of human error.

As multiple types of traffic are consolidated on top of the Unified Fabric infrastructure, it raises legitimate security concerns. Cisco Unified Fabric contains a complete portfolio of security products that are virtualization aware. These products run in the hypervisor layer to secure virtual workloads inside a single tenant or across tenants. Cisco Unified Fabric also contains a foundation for traffic switching in the hypervisor layer in the form of a Cisco Nexus 1000v product. Cisco Nexus 1000v is a cross-hypervisor virtual software switch that allows delivering consistent network, security, and Layer 4 through Layer 7 policies for the virtual workloads. It operates in a manner similar to a modular chassis, where switch supervisor modules, called virtual supervisor module (VSM), control the switch line cards called virtual Ethernet module (VEM). VSMs should be deployed in pairs to provide the needed redundancy.

Virtual services deployed as part of the Cisco Unified Fabric solution can secure intratenant communication between the virtual machine belonging to the same tenant, or they can secure intertenant communication between the virtual machines belonging to different tenants. Cisco virtual security gateway (VSG) is deployed on top of Cisco Nexus 1000v virtual switch and it is catering to the case of intratenant security. It provides logical isolation and policy enforcement based on both simple networking constructs and more elaborate virtual machine attributes. Figure 3-18 depicts an example of Cisco VSG deployment to secure a three-tier application within a single tenant space.

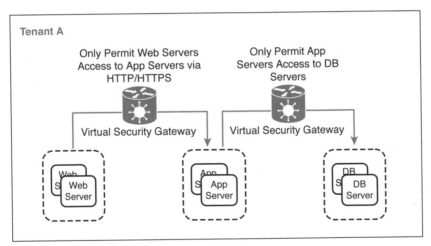

Figure 3-18   *Three-Tier Application Secured by VSG*

The VSG product offers a scalable mode of operation leveraging Cisco vPath technology for traffic steering. With Cisco vPath, the first packet of each flow is redirected to VSG for inspection and policy enforcement. Following inspection, a policy decision is made and programmed into the Cisco Nexus 1000v switch residing in hypervisor kernel space. All the subsequent packets of the flow are switched in a fast-path in the hypervisor kernel, which results in high traffic throughput. Figure 3-19 depicts vPath operation with VSG.

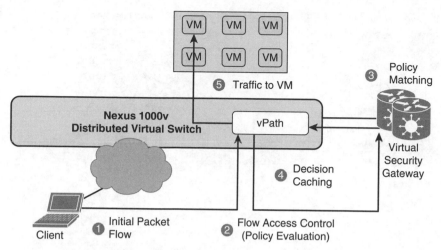

Figure 3-19 *vPath Operation with VSG*

VSG security policies can be deployed in tandem with switching policies enforced by the Cisco Nexus 1000v. This model contributes to consistent policies across the environment. Example 3-3 shows how VSG is inserted into the Cisco Nexus 1000v port-profile for specific tenant use.

Example 3-3 *VSG Port-Profile Configuration*

```
n1000v(config)# vservice node vsg1 type vsg
n1000v(config-vservice-node)# adjacency 10 vlan 90
!
n1000v(config)# port-profile host-profile
n1000v(config-port-prof)# org root/Tenant-A
n1000v (config-port-prof)# vservice node vsg1 profile profile-1
```

Intertenant or tenant edge space can be secured by either a virtual firewall in the form of a virtual Cisco ASA product deployed in the hypervisor layer or by the physical appliances deployed in the upstream physical network. It is also common to use two layers of security with virtual firewalls securing east-west traffic between the virtual machines and physical firewalls securing the north-south traffic in and out of the data center. Physical ASA appliances are many times positioned at the Unified Fabric aggregation layer, and they can also provide security services for the physical nonvirtualized workloads to create consistent policy across virtual and physical infrastructures. In the Spine-Leaf architecture, physical ASAs are connected to the service's leaf nodes. Figure 3-20 depicts typical Cisco ASA topology in a traditional multilayer and Spine-Leaf architecture.

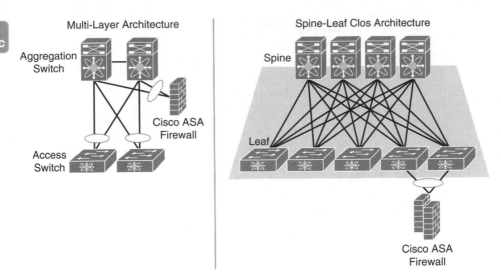

Figure 3-20   *Typical Cisco ASA Deployment Topologies*

Both physical and virtual ASA together provide a comprehensive set of security services for Cisco Unified Fabric.

Management of the network is at the core of the network's intelligence. Cisco Prime Data Center Network Manager (DCNM) manages Cisco Nexus and Cisco MDS families of switches through a single pane of glass. DCNM can set and automatically provision a policy on converged LAN and SAN environments. It dynamically monitors and takes actions when needed on both physical and virtual infrastructures. It provides visibility and control of the unified data center to uphold stringent service-level agreements. DCNM provides a robust set of features by streamlining the provisioning aspects of the Unified Fabric components. These factors contribute to the overall data center infrastructure reliability and uptime, thereby improving business continuity. Figure 3-21 depicts the Cisco Prime DCNM main screen.

Software features provided by Cisco NX-OS can be deployed with Cisco DCNM because it leverages multiple dashboards for the ease of use and representation of the overall network topology. DCNM can also handle provisioning and monitoring aspects of FCoE deployment, including an end-to-end path containing a mix of traditional Fibre Channel and FCoE.

Cisco DCNM has extensive reporting features that allow building custom reports specific to the operating environment. Organizations can also leverage reports available through the preconfigured templates. Cisco DCNM provides automated discovery of the network components, keeping track of all physical and logical network device information. This discovery data can be imported to the change management systems for easier operations.

Figure 3-21 *Cisco Prime DCNM Main Screen*

Inter-Data Center Unified Fabric

Geographically dispersed data centers provide added application resiliency and enhanced application reliability. A network foundation to enable multi-data-center deployment must extend the network properties across the data centers participating in the distributed setup. Such properties are the extension of Layer 2, Layer 3, and storage connectivity between the data centers powered by the end-to-end Unified Fabric approach. Figure 3-22 depicts data center interconnect technology solutions.

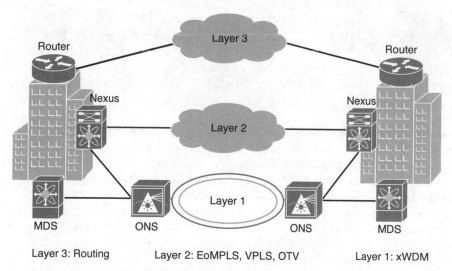

Figure 3-22 *Data Center Interconnect Methods*

Multiple technologies that lay the foundation for the interdata center Unified Fabric extension are in use today. Layer 3 networks allow extending storage connectivity between disparate data center environments by leveraging the Fibre Channel over IP protocol (FCIP), while Layer 2 bridged connectivity is achieved by leveraging overlay transport virtualization (OTV). Layer 1 technologies in the form of DWDM or CWDM allow running any data, storage, or converged protocol on top.

Fibre Channel over IP

Disparate SANs are not uncommon. These could be artifacts of building isolated environments to address local needs, deploying storage environments with different administrative boundaries, or outcomes of acquisitions. As organizations leverage ubiquitous storage services, a need for interconnecting isolated storage networks while maintaining characteristics of performance, availability, and fault tolerance becomes increasingly important.

Disparate storage environments are most often located in topologies segregated from each other by Layer 3 routed networks. These could be long-haul point-to-point links, as well as private or public MPLS networks. Fibre Channel over IP extends the reach of the Fibre Channel protocol across geographic distances by encapsulating Fibre Channel frames in outer TCP/IP headers for transport across interconnecting Layer 3 routed networks. Figure 3-23 depicts the principle of transporting Fibre Channel frames across IP transport.

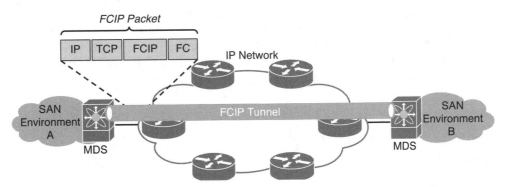

Figure 3-23 *FCIP Operation Principle*

Leveraging the TCP/IP protocol provides FCIP guaranteed traffic delivery required for healthy storage network operation. Should packet drop occur, any packets carrying Fibre Channel payload are retransmitted following standard TCP/IP protocol operation. This lossless storage traffic behavior allows FCIP to extend native Fibre Channel connectivity across greater distances. This, however, cannot come at the expense of storage network performance. Intelligent control over TCP window size is needed to make sure long-haul links are fully utilized while preventing excessive traffic loss and subsequent retransmission. Cisco FCIP-capable platforms allow several features to maximize utilization of the intermediate Layer 3 links, such as leveraging TCP extensions for high performance and scaling up TCP window size. As TCP window size is scaled up, the sustained network throughput increases, but so do the chances of packet drops.

The TCP/IP protocol traditionally achieves its reliability for traffic delivery by leveraging the acknowledgement mechanism for the received data segments. Acknowledgements are used to signal from the receiver back to the sender the receipts of contiguous in-sequence TCP segments. In case of packet loss, segments received after the packet loss occurs are not acknowledged and must be retransmitted. This causes unnecessary traffic load, network capacity "waste," and increased delays, which in turn have a detrimental effect on FCIP storage traffic performance. Cisco implements a selective acknowledgement (SACK) mechanism where the receiver can selectively acknowledge TCP segments received after packet loss occurs. In this case the sender only needs to retransmit the TCP segment lost in transit, rather than all packets beyond the acknowledgement. The SACK mechanism is most effective in environments with long and large transmissions, and it must be enabled and supported on both ends of the FCIP circuit. SACK is not enabled by default on Cisco devices; it must be manually enabled if required by issuing the **sack-enable** CLI command under the FCIP profile configuration.

Large maximum transmission unit size, or MTU, in the transit IP network can also greatly influence the performance characteristics of the storage traffic carried by FCIP. Support for jumbo frames can allow transmission of full-size 2148 bytes Fibre Channel frames without requiring fragmentation and reassembly at the IP level into numerous TCP/IP segments carrying a single Fibre Channel frame. A path MTU Discovery (PMTUD) mechanism can be invoked on both sides of the FCIP connection to make sure the effective maximum supported path MTU is automatically discovered. FCIP PMTUD is not automatically enabled on Cisco devices; it must be manually enabled if required by issuing the **pmtu-enable** CLI command under the FCIP profile configuration.

Deployment of quality of service (QoS) features in the transit Layer 3 routed network is not a requirement for FCIP operation; however, such features are highly advised to make sure that FCIP traffic is subjected to the absolute minimum influence from transient network delays and congestion. Some of the storage traffic types encapsulated inside the FCIP packets can be sensitive to degraded network conditions, and even though FCIP can handle such conditions, overall storage performance will gain benefits from QoS policies operating at the network level.

Along with performance characteristics, FCIP must be designed following high availability and redundancy principles. Utmost attention should be paid to make sure the transit Layer 3 routed network between the sites interconnected by FCIP circuits conforms to the high degree of availability, reliability, and efficiency. Leveraging device, circuit, and path redundancy eliminates the single point of failure, and proper capacity management helps alleviate performance bottlenecks. At the same time, FCIP allows provisioning numerous tunnels interconnecting disparate storage networks. These redundant tunnels are represented as virtual E_port or virtual TE_port types, which are considered by the Fabric Shortest Path First (FSPF) protocol for equal-cost multipathing purposes. These tunnels contribute to connectivity resiliency and allow failover. Just like regular interswitch links, FCIP tunnels can be bound into port channels for simpler FSPF topology and efficient traffic load-balancing operation. Figure 3-24 depicts the principle behind provisioning multiple redundant FCIP tunnels between disparate storage network environments leveraging port-channeled connections.

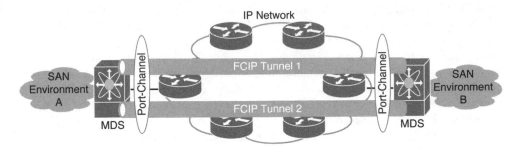

Figure 3-24 *Redundant FCIP Tunnels Leveraging Port Channeled Connections*

The FCIP protocol allows maintaining VSAN traffic segregation by building logically isolated storage environments on top of shared physical storage infrastructure. VSAN segregation is traditionally achieved through data-plane frame tagging. This frame tagging is transparently carried over FCIP tunnels to extend the end-to-end isolation. Each VSAN, either local or extended over the FCIP tunnel, exhibits the same characteristics regarding routing, zoning, fabric services, and fabric management for ubiquitous deployment methodology.

Overlay Transport Virtualization

Certain mechanisms for Layer 2 extension across data centers, or in some cases across PODs of the same data center, introduce challenges that can inhibit their practical use. For example, STP-based extension topologies do not scale well and can cause cascading failures that can propagate beyond the boundaries of a single availability domain. They fall short of making use of multipathing topologies by logically blocking redundant links. A more efficient protocol is needed to leverage all available paths for traffic forwarding, as well as provide intelligent traffic load-balancing across the data center interconnect links.

Other Layer 2 data center interconnect technologies offer a more efficient model than STP–based topologies; however, at the same time, they depend on specific transport network characteristics. The best example is MPLS-based technologies that require label switching between the data center networks for Layer 2 extension. Such a solution can be challenging for organizations not willing to develop operational knowledge around those technologies. Let's now look at a possible alternative.

Cisco OTV technology provides nondisruptive, transport agnostic, multihomed, and multipathed Layer 2 data center interconnect technology that preserves isolation and fault domain properties between the disparate data centers. OTV leverages a MAC-in-IP forwarding paradigm to extend Layer 2 connectivity over any IP transport. Figure 3-25 depicts a basic OTV traffic forwarding principle in which Layer 2 frames are forwarded between the sites attached to OTV overlay.

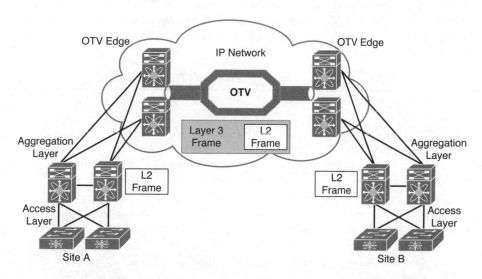

Figure 3-25 *OTV Packet Forwarding Principle*

OTV simulates the behavior of traditional bridged environments while introducing improvements, which greatly reduces the risk often associated with large-scale Layer 2 extensions. OTV leverages the control plane protocol in the form of an IS-IS routing protocol to dissimilate MAC address reachability across the OTV edge devices participating in the overlay. Example 3-4 shows IS-IS neighbor relations established between the OTV edge devices through the overlay.

Example 3-4 *IS-IS Neighbor Relationships Between OTV Edge Devices*

```
OTV_EDGE1_SITEA# show otv isis adjacency


OTV-IS-IS process: default VPN: Overlay1
OTV-IS-IS adjacency database:
System ID        SNPA           Level    State    Hold Time   Interface
NEXUS7K-EDGE2    001b.54c2.43c1  1        UP       00:00:25    Overlay1
OTV_EDGE2_SITE   001b.54c2.43c3  1        UP       00:00:27    Overlay1
OTV_EDGE_SITE3   001b.54c2.43c4  1        UP       00:00:07    Overlay1
```

This approach is different from the traditional bridged environments, which utilize dataplane learning or flood-and-learn behavior. The use of overlay in OTV creates point-to-cloud type connectivity rather than a collection of fully meshed point-to-point links, which are difficult to set up, manage, and scale. After MAC addresses are learned, OTV edge devices leverage the underlying IP transport to carry original Ethernet frames encapsulated in IP protocol between the data centers. The actual hosts on both sides of the connection are unaware of OTV because the transport network is transparently forwarding their traffic. An efficient network core is essential to deliver optimal application performance across the OTV overlay.

Local OTV edge devices hold the mapping between remote host MAC addresses and the IP address of the remote OTV edge device. Example 3-5 shows a MAC address table on an OTV edge device, where you can see locally learned MAC addresses as well as MAC addresses available through the overlay.

Example 3-5 *MAC Address Table Showing Local and OTV Learned Entries*

```
OTV_EDGE1_SITEA# show mac address-table

Legend:
        * - primary entry, G - Gateway MAC, (R) - Routed MAC, O - Overlay MAC
        age - seconds since last seen,+ - primary entry using vPC Peer-Link
   VLAN     MAC Address      Type        age     Secure NTFY   Ports
----------+-----------------+---------+---------+------+-------+------------------
G    -     001b.54c2.43c2   static      -        F      F      sup-eth1(R)
*  110     0000.0c07.ac6e   dynamic     0        F      F      Po1
*  110     0000.6e01.010a   dynamic     0        F      F      Po1
*  110     0000.6e01.016c   dynamic     0        F      F      Po1
*  110     0000.6e01.016d   dynamic     0        F      F      Po1
O  110     0000.6e02.020a   dynamic     0        F      F      Overlay1
O  110     0000.6e02.020b   dynamic     0        F      F      Overlay1
O  110     0000.6e02.026c   dynamic     0        F      F      Overlay1
O  110     0000.6e02.026d   dynamic     0        F      F      Overlay1
```

The control plane protocol, ISIS, includes other Layer 2 semantics, such as VLAN ID, that allow maintaining end-to-end traffic segregation across the data center boundaries. It offers intelligence above and beyond the rudimentary behavior of flood-and-learn techniques and thus is instrumental in implementing OTV value-added features to enhance and safeguard the inter-data-center Layer 2 environment. Such features stretch across loop prevention, multipathing, and multihoming mechanisms and enable First Hop Routing Protocol localization and Address Resolution Protocol (ARP) proxying without creating an additional operational overhead.

As mentioned earlier, OTV can safeguard the Layer 2 environment across the data centers or across IP-separated PODs of the same data center by employing proven Layer 3 techniques. Let's now look a little bit deeper into the main benefits achieved with OTV technology.

■ **Little to no effect on existing network design:** OTV leverages the IP network to transport original MAC encapsulated frames. Any network capable of carrying IP packets can be used for the OTV core. OTV can operate over a unicast-only or multicast-enabled core. In case of OTV operating over a multicast-enabled core, there is a requirement to run multicast routing in the underlying transit network. OTV is also fully transparent to the local Layer 2 domains, where hosts and switches not participating in OTV do not have knowledge of OTV. Local spanning tree topologies are unaffected, too.

■ **Fault isolation and site independence:** Even though local spanning tree topologies are unaware of OTV, OTV does introduce a boundary for the STP, so spanning tree domains in different data centers keep operating independently of each other. This is a huge advantage for OTV. Spanning Tree bridge protocol data units (BPDUs) are not forwarded over the OTV overlay, and ARP traffic is forwarded only in a control manner by offering local ARP response behavior. Because control plane protocol is used to dissimilate MAC address reachability information, OTV does not allow unknown unicast traffic across the overlay unless the administrator specially allows it. These behaviors create site containment similar to one available with Layer 3 routing.

- **Optimal bandwidth utilization and scalability:** OTV can make use of multiple edge devices better utilizing all available ingress and egress points in the data center through the built-in multipathing behavior. Use of multiple ingress and egress points does not require a complex deployment and operational model, as with some of the other Layer 2 data center interconnect technologies. OTV's built-in loop prevention mechanisms avoid loops in the overlay and limit the scope of the loop, should one be formed in the locally attached Layer 2 environments. OTV employs the active-active mode of operation at the edge of the overlay where all ingress and egress points forward traffic simultaneously. Multipathing also applies to the traffic as it crosses the IP transit network, where equal-cost multipath (ECMP) behavior can utilize multiple paths and links between the data centers. Multipathing is an important characteristic of OTV to maximize the utilization of available bandwidth.

- **Fast failover and flexibility:** The OTV control plane protocol, IS-IS, dictates remote MAC address reachability. IS-IS can leverage its own hello/timeout timers, or it can leverage bidirectional forwarding (BFD) for rapid failure detection. Link failure detection in the core is based on routing protocols, which can rapidly reroute around failed sections of the network. OTV also leverages dynamic encapsulation, rather than tunneling, so OTV edge devices do not need to maintain a state of tunnels interconnecting data centers. One of the flexibility attributes of OTV comes from its deployment model at the data center aggregation layer, which provides a convenient topological placement to address the needs of the Layer 2 extension across the data centers. Another flexibility attribute of OTV comes from its incremental deployment characteristics. Because OTV is transport agnostic, it can be seamlessly deployed on top of any existing IP infrastructure, with the exception being multicast-based deployment, where multicast-enabled core is required. OTV can even be deployed over existing Layer 2 data center interconnect solutions, such as vPC, where it can bring the advantages of fault containment and improved scale. If deployed over vPC, in time, OTV can be migrated from vPC to routed links for more streamlined infrastructure.

- **Optimized operations:** The OTV control plane protocol allows the simple addition and removal of OTV sides from the overlay. OTV edge devices express their desire to join the overlay by sending IS-IS hello messages to the multicast control group, which are replicated by the transit network and delivered to all other OTV edge devices that are part of the same overlay (listening to the same multicast group). This behavior automatically establishes IS-IS neighbor relations across the shared medium without the need to define all remote OTV edge devices. Ultimately, the convenience of operations comes from the greatly simplified command-line interface (CLI) needed to enable and configure OTV service on the device. This great simplicity does not come at the expense of deep level troubleshooting that is still available on the platforms supporting OTV functionality.

Layer 2 data center interconnect is not a requirement; however, it can be beneficial in numerous cases. Cross-data center workload mobility, distributed application and server clustering, and simplified disaster recovery are some of the main use cases behind Layer 2 extension.

Locator ID Separation Protocol

Connectivity requirements between data center locations depend on the nature of the applications running in these data centers. Most commonly deployed applications fall into one of the following categories: routable applications, nonroutable applications, clustered applications, distributed applications, and virtualized applications. For routable applications and distributed applications, nothing more than an IP network is required to make sure application components can communicate with each other. Nonroutable applications typically expect to be placed on a share transmissions medium, such as Ethernet, and as such require data center interconnect to exhibit Layer 2 connectivity properties. Clustered applications are a "mixed bag," with some being able to operate over IP-routed network and some requiring Layer 2 adjacency, in which case data center interconnect requirements can be different based on specific clustered application needs. Finally, virtualized applications reside on the virtual hypervisors, such as Xen, KVM, Hyper-V, and ESXi. These applications make use of server virtualization technologies and leverage server virtualization properties, such as virtual machine mobility, fault tolerance, and dynamic resourcing.

As modern data centers become increasingly virtualized, even though at the time of writing the book only about 25% of total servers are estimated to be running a hypervisor virtualization layer, the need to cater to virtualized application needs also increases. The traditional network forwarding paradigm does not distinguish between the identity of an endpoint (virtual machine) and its location in the network topology. As virtual machines move around the network due to administrative actions, various failure conditions, or resource constraints, the network must provide ubiquitous and optimized connectivity services across the entire mobility domain. Endpoint mobility can cause inefficient traffic-forwarding patterns as a traditional network struggles to deliver packets across the shortest path toward an endpoint, which changes its location. Figure 3-26 depicts traffic tromboning cases in which a virtual machine migrates from Site A to Site B; however, ingress traffic is still delivered to Site A because this is where the virtual machine's IP subnet is still advertised out of.

A better mechanism is needed to leverage network intelligence.

LISP, part of the Cisco Unified Fabric holistic architecture, provides a scalable method for network traffic routing, which is based on a true endpoint location in the topology. By decoupling endpoint identifiers (EID) from the routing locators (RLOCs), LISP accommodates virtual machine mobility while maintaining shortest path forwarding through the infrastructure. EIDs, as the name suggests, are the identifiers for the endpoints in the form of either a MAC or an IP address, whereas RLOCs are the identifiers of the edge devices on both sides of a LISP-optimized environment (most likely a loopback interface IP address on the edge router or data center aggregation switch). These edge devices are called tunnel routers. They perform LISP encapsulation sending the traffic from ingress tunnel router (ITR) to egress tunnel router (ETR) on its way toward the destination endpoint. Proxy ingress (PITR) and egress (PETR) tunnel routers are used to integrate a non-LISP environment into the LISP-enabled network. Figure 3-27 shows ITR, ETR, and the proxy tunnel router topology. LISP routers providing both ITR and ETR functionality are called xTRs; similarly, LISP routers providing both PITR and PETR functionality are called PxTRs.

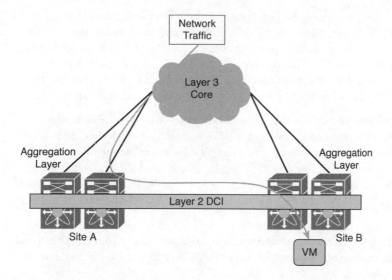

Figure 3-26 *Traffic Tromboning Case*

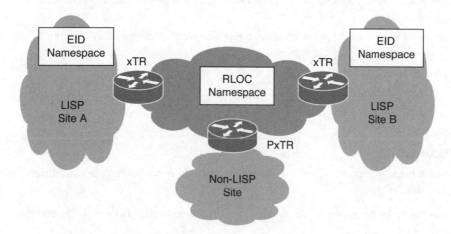

Figure 3-27 *LISP Tunnel Routers*

To derive the true location of an endpoint, a mapping is needed between the EID that represents the endpoint and the RLOC that represents a tunnel router that this endpoint is "behind." This mapping is called an EID-to-RLOC mapping database.

Unlike the approach in conventional databases, LISP mapping entries are distributed rather than centralized. A full mapping database is distributed among all tunnel routers in the LISP environment, with each tunnel router only maintaining entries needed in a particular given time for communication. These entries are derived from the LISP query process and are cached for a certain period of time before being flushed, unless refreshed.

Catering to the virtual machine mobility case, LISP enables a virtual machine to change its network location, while keeping its assigned IP addresses. The endpoint that moves to another subnet or across the same subnet extended between the data centers leveraging technology, such as OTV, is called a roaming device. When endpoints roam, the LISP first-hop router must detect such an event. It compares the source IP address of the received packet to the range of EIDs defined for the interface on which this data packet was received. If matched, first-hop router updates the LISP map server with a new RLOC for the EID. It also updates the tunnel and proxy tunnel routers that have cached this information.

Endpoint mobility events can occur within the same subnet, known as LISP Extended Subnet Mode (ESM), or across subnets, known as LISP Across Subnet Mode (ASM). ESM leverages Layer 2 data center interconnect to extend VLANs and subsequently subnets across multiple data centers. This is where OTV can be leveraged. ASM assumes that there is no VLAN and subnet extension between the data centers. This mode is best suited for cold migration and disaster recovery scenarios where there is no Layer 2 data center interconnect between the sites.

LISP provides an exciting new mechanism for organizations to improve routing system scalability and introduce new capabilities to their networks. Versatility of LISP allows it to be leveraged in a variety of solutions:

■ Simplified and cost-effective multihoming, including ingress traffic engineering

■ IP address portability, including no renumbering when changing providers or adding multihoming

■ IP address (endhost) mobility, including session persistence across mobility events

■ IPv6 transition simplification, including incremental deployment of IPv6 using existing IPv4 infrastructure (or IPv4 over IPv6)

■ Simplified multitenancy and large-scale VPNs

■ Operation and network simplification

Reference List

Unified Fabric: http://www.cisco.com/c/en/us/solutions/data-center-virtualization/unified-fabric/unified_fabric.html

Fibre Channel over IP: http://www.cisco.com/c/en/us/tech/storage-networking/fiber-channel-over-ip-fcip/index.html

iSCSI: http://www.cisco.com/c/en/us/tech/storage-networking/small-computer-systems-interface-over-ip-iscsi/index.html

Overlay Transport Virtualization: http://www.cisco.com/go/otv

Locator ID Separation Protocol: http://www.cisco.com/go/lisp

Exam Preparation Tasks

Review All Key Topics

Review the most important topics in the chapter, noted with the key topics icon in the outer margin of the page. Table 3-2 lists a reference of these key topics and the page numbers on which each is found.

Table 3-2   Key Topics for Chapter 3

Key Topic Element	Description	Page
Figure 3-1	"Multilayer and Spine-Leaf Clos Architecture"	80
Paragraph	"Cisco Unified Fabric Principles"	82
Figure 3-4	"Converged Network Adapter Elements"	83
Figure 3-5	"Unified Port Operation"	84
Paragraph	Considerations for iSCSI deployment (Fibre Channel services and TCP/IP NIC offload)	86
Figure 3-14	"vPC Operational Logic"	91
Figure 3-15	"Cisco FabricPath Topology and Forwarding"	92
Figure 3-16	"VXLAN Topology and Forwarding"	93
Figure 3-18	"Three-Tier Application Secured by VSG"	94
Figure 3-20	"Typical Cisco ASA Deployment Topologies"	96
Paragraph	Overlay Transport Virtualization Operation	100
Paragraph	Virtual Machine Mobility and Locator ID Separation Protocol	104

Complete Tables and Lists from Memory

Print a copy of Appendix B, "Memory Tables" or at least the section for this chapter, and complete the tables and lists from memory. Appendix C, "Memory Tables Answer Key" includes completed tables and lists to check your work.

Define Key Terms

Define the following key terms from this chapter, and check your answers in the Glossary:

Unified Fabric, Local Area Network (LAN), Storage Area Network (SAN), Fibre Channel over Ethernet (FCoE), Fibre Channel (FC), Nexus Switches, Multilayer Director Switch (MDS), Unified Port, Converged Network Adapter (CNA), Internet Small Computer Interface (iSCSI), NX-OS, Spanning Tree Protocol (STP), Virtual Port Channel (vPC), FabricPath, Virtual Extensible Local Area Network (VXLAN), Adaptive Security Appliance (ASA), Virtual Security Gateway (VSG), vPath, Data Center Network Manager (DCNM), Overlay Transport Virtualization (OTV), Locator ID Separation Protocol (LISP)

Part I Review

Keep track of your part review progress with the checklist shown in Table PI-1. Details on each task follow the table.

Table PI-1 Part I Review Checklist

Activity	First Date Completed	Second Date Completed
Repeat all "Do I Know This Already?" questions		
Answer "Part Review" questions		
Review Key Topics		
Self-assessment questionnaire		

Repeat All "Do I Know This Already?" Questions: For this task, answer the "Do I Know This Already?" questions again for the chapters in this part of the book, using the PCPT software. Refer to "How to View Only 'Do I Know This Already?' Questions by Part" in the Introduction to this book for help with how to make the PCPT software show you DIKTA questions for this part only.

Answer "Part Review" Questions: For this task, answer the "Part Review" questions for this part of the book, using the PCPT software. Refer to "How to View Only Part Review Questions by Part" in the Introduction to this book for help with how to make the PCPT software show you "Part Review" questions for this part only.

Review Key Topics: Browse back through the chapters and look for the Key Topic icons. If you do not remember some details, take the time to reread those topics.

Self-Assessment Questionnaire: Each chapter of this book introduces several key learning items. This might seem overwhelming to you initially, but as you read through each new chapter, you will become more familiar and comfortable with them, which will help you remember the concepts and technologies of these key topics as you progress with the book.

For this self-assessment exercise in the book, without looking back at the chapters or your notes, you should try to answer these self-assessment questions to the best of your ability. This exercise lists a set of key self-assessment questions, which are relevant to the particular chapter, shown in the following list. There will be no written answers to these questions in this book; if you are not certain, you should go back and refresh on the key topics.

① **Data Center Networking Architecture**

- Explain different benefits of a port channel
- Discuss the different components of vPC and their functions
- Explain benefits of FabricPath and how it differs from spanning tree protocol
- Describe how FabricPath interoperates with vPC and spanning tree

② **Management and Monitoring of Cisco Nexus Devices**

- Explain operational planes of Nexus devices and their functions
- Describe RBAC and the default user roles on Nexus devices
- Define SNMP notifications and explain the difference between traps and informs
- Define EEM and its main components

③ **Unified Fabric Overview**

- Describe challenges with today's data centers, which resulted in unified fabric innovations
- Describe how unified ports help migrating to FCOE
- List switching platforms supporting unified fabric innovations
- Explain methods for securing virtual machine traffic
- Explain the purpose and function of the LISP protocol

■ Think of each of these open self-assessment questions as being about the chapters you have read. You might or might not find the answer explicitly, but the chapter is structured to give you the knowledge and understanding to be able to discuss and explain these self-assessment questions. For example, number 1 is about data centers, number 2 is about managing and monitoring of Cisco Nexus devices, and so on.

■ Note your answer and try to reference key words in the answer from the relevant chapter. For example, virtual port channel (vPC) would apply to Chapter 1, "Data Center Networking."

Exam topics covered in Part II:

- **2.1** Describe the components and operations of Cisco virtual switches
- **2.2** Describe the concepts of overlays
  - **2.2a** OTV
  - **2.2b** NVGRE
  - **2.2c** VXLAN
- **2.3** Describe the benefits and perform simple troubleshooting of VDC STP
- **2.4** Compare and contrast the default and management VRFs
- **3.1** Describe, configure, and verify FEX connectivity

Part II

Network Virtualization

Chapter 4: Cisco Nexus 1000V and Virtual Switching

Chapter 5: Data Center Overlay Networks

Chapter 6: Virtualizing Cisco Network Devices

This chapter covers the following exam topic:

2.1 Describe the components and operations of Cisco virtual switches

Cisco Nexus 1000V and Virtual Switching

With server virtualization, a physical server can now run multiple workloads as virtual machines. Each virtual machine will be running its own guest operating system and invariably will require access to different networks. The virtual switching layers on hypervisors achieve this by giving you port groups (virtual patch cords), vSwitches (virtual switches in software), and associated uplinks (physical uplinks associated to those vSwitches), for example, on VMware ESX or ESXi hypervisors. Similar constructs are offered in various flavors of hypervisors available today to enable virtual switching, including Hyper-V virtual switch and Open Virtual Switch on KVM.

This chapter begins by describing the limitations of physical access layers. Then, as server virtualization has increased within data centers, the challenges being faced with virtual switching layers and static vSwitches are discussed. After you understand the limitations and challenges, you will start understanding distributed virtual switches and the Cisco virtual network vision. The chapter introduces you to the Cisco Nexus 1000V virtual distributed switch and explains how it solves the challenges in virtual data centers today.

As the chapter progresses, you learn about the Cisco Nexus 1000V virtual switching architecture and understand its integration with VMware ESX or ESXi and VMware vCenter. You also learn the installation methods and commands that enable you to verify the initial configuration and module status of the Cisco Nexus 1000V Series switch and validate connectivity between the virtual Ethernet module (VEM), virtual supervisor module (VSM), and VMware vCenter using VMware ESX command-line interface (CLI), Nexus 1000V CLI, and VMware vCenter vSphere Client.

NOTE The Cisco Nexus 1000V Series switch was developed with close cooperation between Cisco and VMware. This chapter focuses on the Cisco Nexus 1000V integration between VMware ESXi hypervisor and VMware vCenter. At the time of writing this chapter, the Cisco Nexus 1000V distributed virtual switch was also supported on other independent hypervisors, such as Microsoft Hyper-V and Linux/KVM.

Today, there are multiple hypervisor vendors and different implementations of distributed virtual switches. For all intents and purposes in this chapter, explanations and comparisons will be based on the VMware static vSwitch and VMware distributed virtual switch (DVS) technology.

"Do I Know This Already?" Quiz

The "Do I Know This Already?" quiz enables you to assess whether you should read this entire chapter thoroughly or jump to the "Exam Preparation Tasks" section. If you are in doubt about your answers to these questions or your own assessment of your knowledge of the topics, read the entire chapter. Table 4-1 lists the major headings in this chapter and their corresponding "Do I Know This Already?" quiz questions. You can find the answers in Appendix A, "Answers to the 'Do I Know This Already?' Quizzes."

Table 4-1   "Do I Know This Already?" Section-to-Question Mapping

Foundation Topics Section	Questions
"Evolution of Virtual Switching"	1, 2, 3
"Virtual Networking Component"	4
"VMware vDS Overview"	5
"Advantages of VMware vDS and Enhancements"	6
"Cisco Nexus 1000V Series Switch Salient Features and Benefits"	7
"Cisco Nexus 1000V Architecture"	8
"Cisco Nexus 1000V Component Communication"	9
"Cisco Nexus 1000V Port Profiles"	10
"Initial VSM Configuration Verification"	11
"Verifying VEM Agent"	12
"Validating VM Port Groups and Port Profiles"	13

CAUTION   The goal of self-assessment is to gauge your mastery of the topics in this chapter. If you do not know the answer to a question or are only partially sure of the answer, you should mark that question as wrong for purposes of the self-assessment. Giving yourself credit for an answer you correctly guess skews your self-assessment results and might provide you with a false sense of security.

1.   What were key challenges with virtual machines and their hosts' physical access layer prior to Nexus 1000V? (Choose two.)

   a.   VMs could not be moved from one host to another.

   b.   Enforcing policies at the VM vNIC level.

   c.   Virtual machines did not have enough bandwidth and could not scale.

   d.   Making these polices "sticky" and making sure they follow the VM.

2. True or false? You could control a VM's communication belonging to the same VLAN from the virtual access layer, similar to a physical switch port access control prior to Cisco Nexus 1000V Series switch.

   a. True

   b. False

3. What were key challenges with standard VMware static vSwitches? (Choose two.)

   a. A compromised VM could be traced only as far as its host's physical switch port.

   b. VM administrators were suddenly tasked with managing access layer networking, for which they did not have extensive experience around data center networking.

   c. The VMware static vSwitches needed to be upgraded on a regular basis.

   d. The VMware static vSwitch had very limited ports and could connect only a certain number of VMs.

4. What are valid virtual networking components?

   a. Port groups, vNICs, VMNICs, and guest operating systems

   b. IP addresses, NICs, switches, routers, and load balances

   c. vNICs, VMNICs, port groups, physical networks, and virtual networks

   d. VLANs and vSwitches

5. Which statement best describes a VMware vDS?

   a. A VMware vDS is a distributed switch that virtually enables you to manage one switch across multiple VMware ESX/ESXi hosts.

   b. The VMware vDS is the latest version of the VMware vSwitch.

   c. The VMware vDS is an API that enables you to programmatically alter the configuration of VMware vSwitches.

   d. The VMware vDS is a centralized switch management platform that enables you to manage geographically distributed vSwitches from a single location.

6. What are two main advantages of a VMware vDS when compared with VMware vSwitch?

   a. VM LAN, SAN, Admin Pane managed from a single point.

   b. VMware cluster (span across multiple VMware ESX or ESXi hosts)–level network management and configuration capability.

   c. Policies now have the capability to follow the VM as it traverses hosts within a VMware cluster.

   d. Equipment, LAN, SAN, and Admin Panes managed from a single point.

7. True or false? The Cisco Nexus 1000V Series switch is based on a standard Cisco iOS software command-line interface (CLI).

   a. True

   b. False

8. What are the main "components" of a Cisco Nexus 1000V Series switch?

    a. Ncxus 1000, 2000, 3000, 4000, 5000, 6000, 7000, and 9000 Series switches

    b. The Virtual Supervisory Module and Virtual Ethernet Module

    c. The Virtual Chassis and Virtual Line Cards

    d. The Nexus 1010/11000 Series virtual services appliance

9. True or false? The Cisco Nexus 1000V Series switch can be managed and controlled over Layer 2 and Layer 3 networks.

    a. True

    b. False

10. Which statement best describes a Cisco Nexus 1000V port profile?

    a. You can define two types of port profiles in a Cisco Nexus 1000V Series switch (Ethernet, vEthernet). These port profiles are equivalent to VMware port groups and can be assigned to VMs or uplinks on VMware ESX/ESXi hosts.

    b. Port profiles contain a VLAN ID, which can be assigned to a trunk interface.

    c. A port profile is the Cisco terminology to refer to a VM as seen from the Cisco Nexus 1000V Series switch.

    d. Port profiles are defined on VMware vCenter server and can be accessed by all Cisco networking devices within a virtualized data center.

11. Which is the valid CLI command to verify successful VSM connectivity to VMware vCenter?

    a. show running-config

    b. show svs domain

    c. show svs connectivity

    d. show vcenter connectivity

12. True or false? The command to verify whether the VEM agent is running on a VMware ESX or ESXi host is the **vem status** command to be executed on ESX CLI.

    a. True

    b. False

13. Which command do you use to validate and verify a Cisco Nexus 1000V port profile that already exists?

    a. show port-profile name *<name>*

    b. show run port-profile name *<name>*

    c. port-profile list *<name>*

    d. show running-config | port-profile name *<name>*

Foundation Topics

Evolution of Virtual Switching

The effects of virtualization today are felt across the IT spectrum, from the physical layer in a data center, up to the application layer. Particularly, server virtualization has blurred the traditional demarcations between networks, security, servers, application technologies and their respective administration responsibilities. Furthermore, server virtualization has made the enforcement of security policies, rules, and networking fuzzy and hard to pinpoint because a server workload or application can now run from anywhere, any server, and any port. It is dynamic, and that poses a significant challenge in the data center today.

Before Server Virtualization

Traditionally, you were used to a single application running its own operating system on an individual piece of server hardware. That server consisted of network interface cards (NICs) and host bus adapters (HBAs); their ports would connect to redundant network access layer and Fibre Channel switches. Network control security policies, quality of service (QoS), and so on were created at this access layer switch port level, related to that application's usage. These policy enforcements were static and rarely needed modifications.

If that server required maintenance or upgrades and needed to be offline, but the application needed to be available, redundancy was built with a cold or hot standby server or host-based clustering, at a cost. Figure 4-1 shows typical server connectivity in the physical world, before server virtualization.

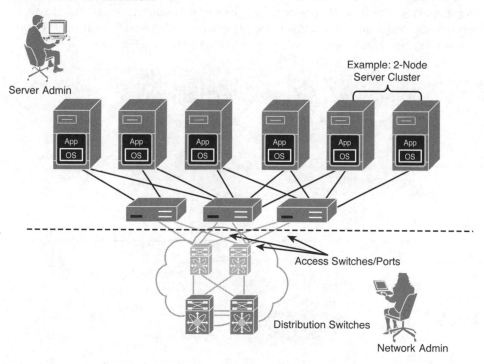

Figure 4-1 *Server Connectivity Before Server Virtualization*

With the advent and adoption of server virtualization technologies, multiple workloads or applications with their own guest operating systems can be hosted on a single server. This increases server utilization, improves efficiency, and keeps server hardware proliferation and costs under control in data centers. All that is achieved without compromising enterprise-class service levels. Features such as VMware vMotion, high availability (HA), and dynamic resource scheduling can move a workload or application running on one host to another in minutes, while in operation. This has essentially driven the need to enforce network policies, security controls, QoS, and the like at the virtual machine (VM) level rather than at the physical host level.

The following are some challenges with VMs and their hosts' physical access layer:

- Enforcing policies at the VM vNIC level

- Making those policies "sticky" and allowing them to follow the VM-in-motion

- Ensuring that a VM that moves to another host is not affected by that host's physical network switch port configuration

- Knowing that most configurations on a physical switch port that the ESX or ESXi host connects to will affect all VMs

- Viewing and controlling the vNIC at VM level from an access switch

- Redirecting traffic to network services, such as load balancers, firewalls, and so on, based on VM vNIC (service chaining)

Given each of these VM workloads or applications, a physical network adapter is not practical and seldom possible. Therefore, VMware developed the vSwitch to help overcome this limitation. Providing each VM one or more virtual network connections (vNIC), they connect to a vSwitch(s), providing access to the physical network (through its uplinks). Figure 4-2 shows typical host server connectivity with server virtualization.

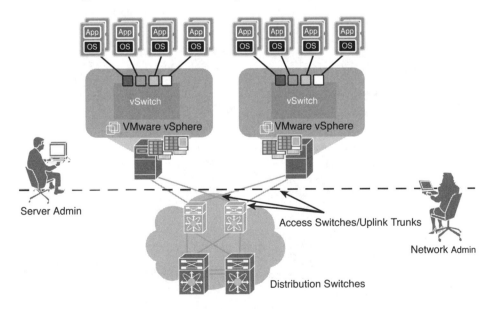

Figure 4-2   *Server Virtualization Effect*

Server Virtualization with Static VMware vSwitch

Server virtualization technologies like VMware ESX and ESXi enable you to run multiple workloads or applications as full virtual machines on physical servers; therefore, a traditional 1:1 relationship between a server and application is seen less in today's data centers. This highlights the requirement to have Layer 2 capabilities closely embedded into the ESX hypervisor to switch packets between VMs and the external world. Therefore, Layer 2 software switches are embedded within the ESX hypervisor to switch packets between VMs and the outside world.

A single host consisting of multiple VMs would utilize the same Ethernet uplinks (VMNICs) to access the network. So how would you differentiate between VM1 and VM2 traffic? This is currently achieved through IEEE 802.1Q VLANs. Therefore, the Ethernet uplinks would be defined as "trunks" for server connectivity into the external network, allowing multiple VLANs to be carried on a single wire, as shown earlier in Figure 4-2.

Interestingly, now server virtualization administrators suddenly owned and managed the virtual network configurations through, for example, VMware vCenter. Figure 4-3 shows a graphical view of standard static virtual switches being utilized on a couple of physical hosts running VMs.

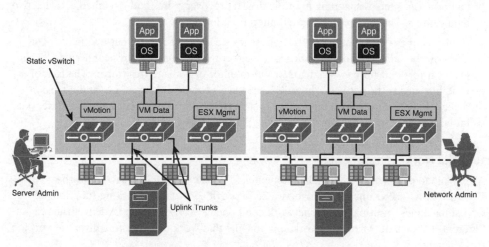

Figure 4-3 *VMware Static vSwitch Configuration at Host Level*

Here are some challenges with standard VMware vSwitch:

- When troubleshooting, the network administration team does not have visibility into the virtual switch layer. The internal vSwitch hides all VMs from the physical network.

- A compromised VM can be traced only as far as its physical switch port to which its host is connected.

- Shutting down a physical network switch port to which an ESX or ESXi host is connected can have severe consequences on production environments, because it would affect all VMs running on that server, and not just the compromised VM.

- In a VMware ESX or ESXi infrastructure, to avail features such as network vMotion and DRS (within a VMware cluster), all vSwitches must have the same port groups available.

Creating a port group on a vSwitch does not automatically propagate to all vSwitches; it needs to be manually created on each concerned ESX or ESXi host.

- As the virtual access layer extends into the ESX or ESXi host (that is, the network closest to the VM), the boundary of server versus network administration responsibilities starts to blur, requiring both functions to up-skill on each other's technology, which can cause some resistance between these functions. Table 4-2 compares the visibilities of physical and virtual network components that contribute to this resistance.

Table 4-2   Network Visibility and Configuration Comparison

Features	Physical Network	Virtual Network
Network visibility	Individual server	Physical server
Port configuration	Individual server	Physical server
Network configuration	Network administrator	VM and network administrator
Security policies	Individual server	Physical server

- As virtualized data centers evolved, more complex virtual network access layer requirements arose, such as spanning multiple disaster recovery sites and stretched active/active data centers. These vSwitches have limited functionalities.

- Many security- and compliance-related issues stem from the fact that traffic between VMs on the same host does not leave the server to run over the physical network. This makes it difficult for networking teams to monitor or manage this traffic. The lack of visibility means the network firewalls, QoS, access control lists (ACLs), and intrusion detection system/intrusion prevention system (IDS/IPS) cannot see this and differentiate individual data transfer activities over the physical network.

Virtual Network Components

As explained earlier, server virtualization extends the network access layer into the VMware ESX or ESXi hypervisor software. To provide virtual networking functions to virtual machines, multiple virtual network components work in union to deliver them. Figure 4-4 shows the virtual network components that work together to deliver networking functionality.

- **Physical NIC:** A VMware ESX or ESXi host requires physical NICs to connect to the external network. These physical NICs will be used as Ethernet uplinks, trunked. Typically, multiple NICs are defined as Ethernet uplinks; they are also known as VMNICs.

- **Port groups:** A subset of ports defined on a vSwitch for connectivity. Virtual machines connect to a virtual Ethernet switch (vSwitch) via port groups; they correspond to patch cords.

- **Virtual Ethernet switch (vSwitch):** Similar to a physical Layer 2 access switch, a vSwitch maintains a table of all connected VMs, similar to a MAC:Port address table and uses it to forward Layer 2 frames. This is a switch and not a hub, whereas it avoids unnecessary deliveries. This vSwitch can be connected to an external network via a physical NIC (VMNICs).

- **vNIC (virtual network interface card):** The virtual equivalent of a physical network interface card or port. It is used by virtual machines to essentially communicate over Layer 2 or Layer 3 protocols.

- **Virtual network:** A network defined in software, where multiple virtual machines share the same system resource.

- **Physical network:** Defined on physical switches that are used to connect VMware ESX or ESXi hosts to physical networks, the same as in regular LANs.

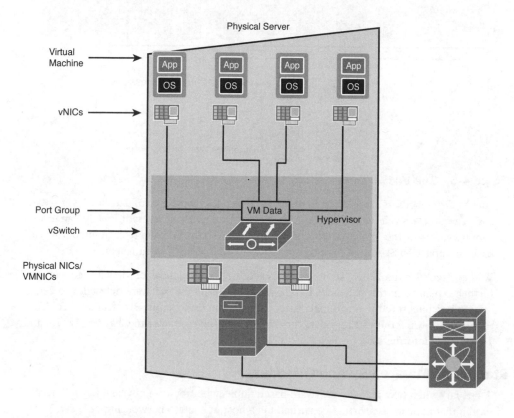

Figure 4-4 *Virtual Network Components*

Virtual Access Layer

In a modern virtualized data center with hundreds and thousands of VMware ESX or ESXi hosts running a large number of virtual machines, you would have multiples of these virtual network components that form a wide virtual access layer. That makes two significant access layers that need to be managed. While the server or virtualization administrator is managing the virtual access layer, your network administrator will manage the physical access layer. Figure 4-5 shows virtual and physical access layers in a data center with multiple VMware ESX or ESXi hosts.

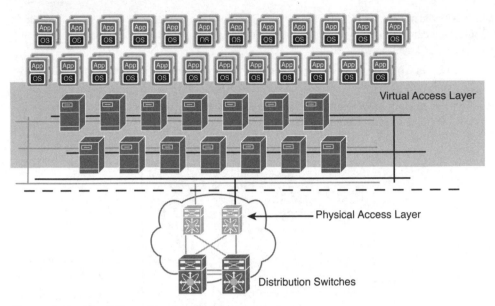

Figure 4-5 *The Virtual and Physical Access Layer*

Due to differences in mode of operation and challenges that the virtual access layer presents, certain tasks that were carried out by network administrators traditionally can move to administrators of the VM environment within a modern data center. Bear in mind, this can have an impact on SLAs and the responsibilities within your IT department.

While Cisco's Nexus 1000V series switches address the challenges of virtual access layers, further explained in this section, Cisco has revolutionized the software defined data center network architecture by introducing Cisco Application Centric Infrastructure (Cisco ACI) that helps to bring out further operational efficiencies. Please refer to Chapters 12, 13, and 14 for some information.

Standard VMware vSwitch Overview

A virtual switch (vSwitch) is a software-based implementation of a physical Layer 2 access switch that appears as a virtual construct. On a host, it enables networking between VMs and the external LAN. It brings together VMNICs and vNICs, facilitating internal and external communications, thus allowing the following:

- VM communications within and between ESX hosts
  - ESX Management (Service Console) communication
  - Port assigned to a VLAN
- VMKernel for vMotion, Fault Tolerance
  - Port assigned to a VLAN
- VMs assigned to port groups
  - Port groups assigned to a VLAN

- Uplinks
  - Used for external network connectivity
  - A VMNIC being associated with a vSwitch only (cannot be shared between vSwitches)

Because it's a software construct, you can create many ports. But note that there are configuration maximums defined by VMware that introduce an upper ceiling limit. Figure 4-6 shows an overview of a VMware ESX or ESXi Virtual Standard Switch (VSS, or vSwitch).

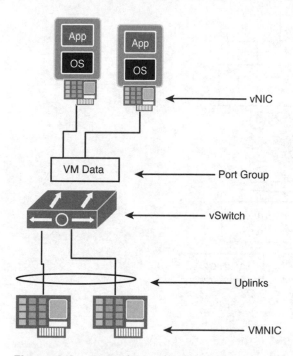

Figure 4-6 *Virtual Standard Switch Overview*

NOTE   You can have multiple vSwitches in a VMware ESX or ESXi host, but the total number of ports per host is 4096. Furthermore, there are limits on the maximum active ports per host: 1016. These are known limits at the time of writing this chapter, defined by VMware. It is recommended that you consult the VMware-defined maximums for the particular VMware version being implemented before designing virtual infrastructure solutions.

Standard VMware vSwitch Operations

A single VMware ESX or ESXi host can consist of multiple vSwitches, such as to separate management and data traffic at the Layer 2 software switch level. As a general rule, there is no means for communication between vSwitches. As mentioned earlier, a vSwitch is a Layer 2 device, which means that only switching of traffic between VMs on the same host or Layer 2 forwarding over the uplinks takes place. These vSwitches cannot perform Layer 3 routing—that is, knowing and communicating with different IP networks. Hence, traffic that does not belong to VMs on the host is forwarded to the uplink port. Figure 4-7 shows some of the operations graphically.

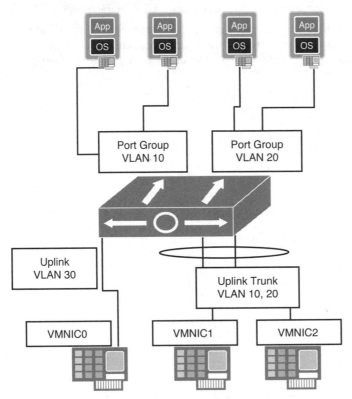

Figure 4-7   *Virtual Standard Switch Operations*

The vSwitch supports the following operations:

- Trunking functionality
- Port channels
- Cisco Discovery Protocol (CDP) for discovering and responding to neighboring network devices
- No participation in Spanning Tree Protocol (STP), Dynamic Trunking Protocol (DTP), or Port Aggregation Protocol (PAgP)
- Virtual guest tagging (reserved VLAN 4095)
    - Tagged traffic passed to guest operating system
- Outbound load balancing only
    - vSwitch port-based
    - Source MAC-based
    - IP Hash-based

Standard VMware vSwitch Configuration

Standard vSwitches on VMware are configured on each VMware ESX or ESXi host via the VMware vCenter Server or by directly connecting to the host using the VMware vSphere client utility. A single ESX or ESXi host can consist of multiple vSwitches, depending on your intended configuration and available physical NICs (VMNICs) available to be designated as uplinks. Figure 4-8 shows two standard vSwitches configured at the host level, via VMware vCenter, and their logical representation, showing the physical and virtual components.

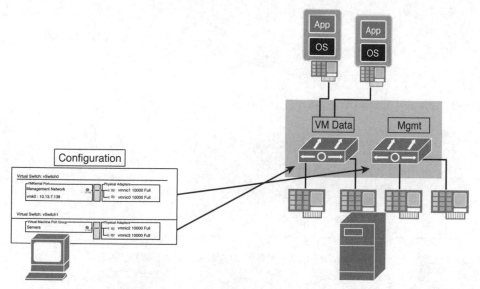

Figure 4-8 *Virtual Standard Switch Configuration*

> **NOTE** A VMware ESX or ESXi host can have a total of 1016 active ports and as many as 32 VMNICs per vSwitch. Refer to the VMware configuration maximums document corresponding to the VMware version for current information.

A VMware standard vSwitch can consist of different port types on a VMware ESX or ESXi host. Figure 4-9 shows the different port types available on VMware ESX/ESXi hosts.

- VM port group types are the most common, used by VMs for their data access.

- VMKernel port types are used for advanced functions, such as vMotion and NIFS/CIFS/ iSCSI storage connectivity and for management communication on ESXi hosts (for example, for console CLI access and vCenter server communication).

These port types usually belong to different logical networks, which allows coexistence of multiple logical networks (VLANs) within the same vSwitch. Or you can segregate networks into different vSwitches. It depends on your intended configuration and circumstances. Figure 4-10 graphically depicts single or multinetworks on vSwitches.

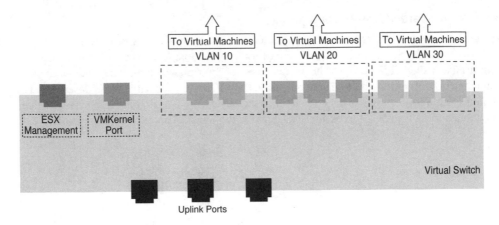

Figure 4-9   *Virtual Standard Switch Port Types*

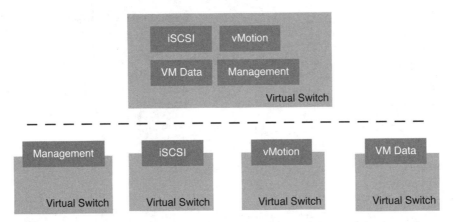

Figure 4-10   *Virtual Standard Switch Single—Multinetwork Examples*

VMware vDS Overview

The VMware Virtual Distributed Switch (vDS) was introduced with VMware vSphere version 4. As opposed to managing static vSwitches on every VMware ESX or ESXi host, the vDS brings the capability to configure and manage a collection of vSwitches in a VMware ESX or ESXi host or multiple hosts within a VMware Cluster. This can be achieved from a central location, via the VMware vCenter Server. Figure 4-11 shows a comparison of a VMware vDS versus standard vSwitches architecture.

> **NOTE**   The VMware vDS feature is licensed and cannot be managed on individual hosts; it requires a VMware vCenter Server.

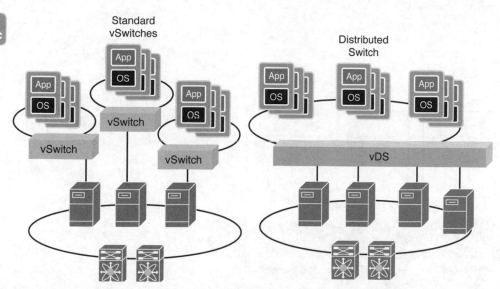

Figure 4-11 *VMware Virtual Distributed Switch (vDS) Overview*

The VMware vDS was an important enhancement to virtual networking or the virtual access layer in data centers. It simplified management while introducing some enhancements, such as private VLAN (PVLAN) support, inbound traffic rate limiting, and tracking VM port state with migrations, to name a few. You will read some explanations of these features in the next sections in this chapter.

The introduction of vDS and enhancement with VMware vSphere version 4 also paved the way to a VMware vNetwork third-party vSwitch API that, as a matter of fact, was used by the Cisco Nexus 1000V Series switch to develop a fully VMware-compatible implementation of a virtual distributed switch. Figure 4-12 shows you an overview of the VMware vDS topology with multiple ESXi hosts.

VMware vDS Configuration

Management of a vDS differs from management of a vSwitch. A vDS is managed from a different management panel. This panel can be opened from any host in that cluster (under network configurations for that host) using the VMware vCenter server, and changes made are reflected on all hosts (within a VMware Cluster) rather than configuring each vSwitch on every host manually, as practiced with standard vSwitches. Figure 4-13 shows the two management panels from a host network configuration window.

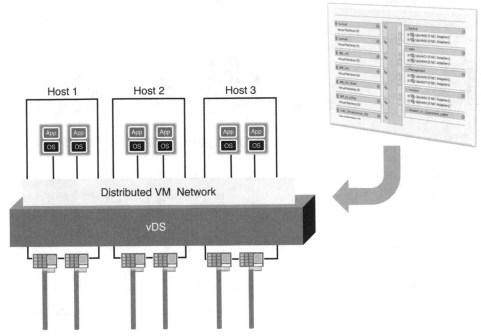

Figure 4-12 *VMware Virtual Distributed Switch (vDS) Topology*

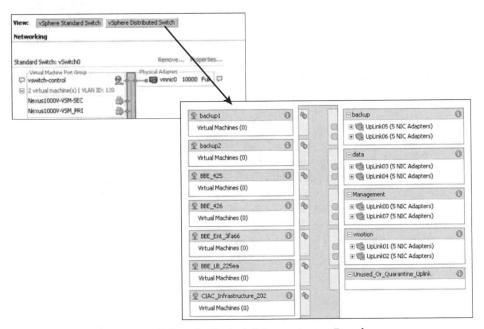

Figure 4-13 *VMware vDS and vSwitch Management Panels*

VMware vDS Enhancements

Apart from the procedural and operational benefits, several feature advancements were introduced with VMware vDS. The following are some of these enhancements, such as PVLANs support, Rx rate limiting, and Port state migration:

- **Port state migration:** When network vMotion is executed on a VM, its network state in terms of counters or port statistics is now tracked or is stateful because the VM moves from host to host on a vDS. So regardless of the location of the VM, its network interface on the vDS is consistent, which helps troubleshooting and network monitoring capabilities immensely.

- **Rx rate limiting:** The vDS builds upon the VM-to-network (Egress) traffic-shaping capabilities by enabling Ingress (from network to VM) as well. Now traffic-shaping policies can be applied on the port group definitions, and these definitions will be applied no matter which host the VM will reside on. Traffic shaping becomes a useful option when you want to prevent oversubscription to and from a VM or other traffic, when faced with limited resources. These policies are defined by average, peak bandwidth, or burst size.

- **PVLAN support:** You must know the concept of VLANs by now, which includes a broadcast domain, a network segment, and implementation over Layer 2 principles. PVLANs enable users to restrict communication between VMs on the same VLAN or network segment. This feature helps reduce the need for a number of subnets, depending upon your network configurations. Within a subnet, PVLANs are implemented on the vDS with allocations made to the following:

  - **Promiscuous PVLAN:** VMs on the promiscuous VLAN can communicate with all VMs.

  - **Community PVLAN:** VMs can communicate among themselves and with VMs on the promiscuous PVLAN.

  - **Isolated PVLAN:** VMs can communicate only with the VMs on promiscuous PVLANs.

> **NOTE**   Adjacent physical network switches must also support PVLANs and should be configured to support the vDS allocations.

VMware vSwitch and vDS

The VMware standard vSwitch and vDS can be used simultaneously on the same VMware ESX or ESXi host and managed by the same VMware vCenter Server, based on your design requirements and circumstances. You can also move the ESX Management and VMKernel ports assigned by default to vSwitch0 to your vDS (dvSwitch0), or you can opt to maintain them on the vSwitch0.

For example, you might want to separate ESX management traffic away from VM data traffic and opt to configure a vSwitch, assign separate uplinks (VMNICs), and connect a VMKernel port group to that vSwitch while you utilize the vDS for all VM data traffic with separate uplinks (VMNICs) assignments. Figure 4-14 shows a graphical view of vDS and vSwitch working in tandem.

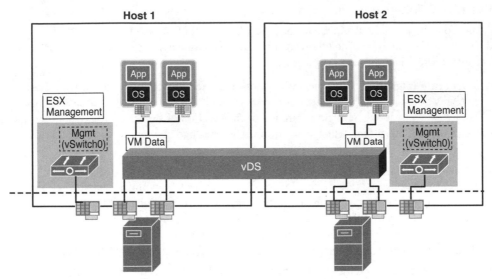

Figure 4-14   *VMware vDS and vSwitch on the Same Host*

The following are some of the advantages and enhancements of VMware vDS:

■ The VMware vDS simplifies and unifies the virtual access layer management function by allowing central management and access.

■ It moves away from the VMware ESX or ESXi host-level management requirement with standard vSwitches, into a VMware Cluster-level network management and configuration capability.

■ With VMware vDS, policies now have the capability to follow the VM as it traverses hosts within a VMware Cluster, enhancing security; it is less prone to errors and has better debugging and troubleshooting capabilities.

■ It forms the foundation for network resource pools and can determine the bandwidth that different network traffic types are given on a VMware virtual distributed switch (vDS).

Cisco Nexus 1000V Virtual Networking Solution

The Cisco virtualized network access layer solution for VM environments uses a technology that Cisco and VMware developed jointly. Primarily, the network access layer is moved further down into the virtual environment to overcome the challenges with the virtual access layers, improving its visibility, management, and enhanced features at the VM level. Figure 4-15 shows the evolution of the VMware vNetwork, virtual access layer.

The Cisco Nexus 1000V solution was introduced with VMware vSphere version 4. It consists of an Ethernet module and a supervisory (management) module. This management module can be deployed on specialized hardware or as a software appliance, depending on your data center design requirements and circumstances. Both these deployment models offer the same improvements and enhancements in terms of VM visibility, policy-based VM connectivity, policy mobility, and a highly available nondisruptive operational model. Figure 4-16 shows you an overview of the Cisco Nexus 1000V distributed virtual software switch architecture.

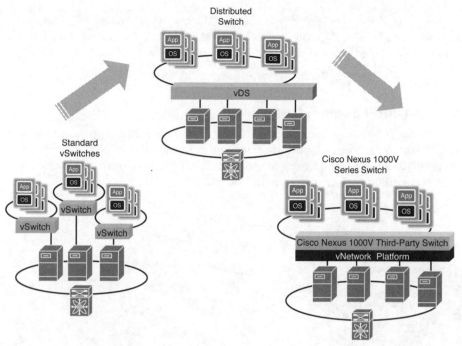

Figure 4-15   *Evolution of VMware vNetwork*

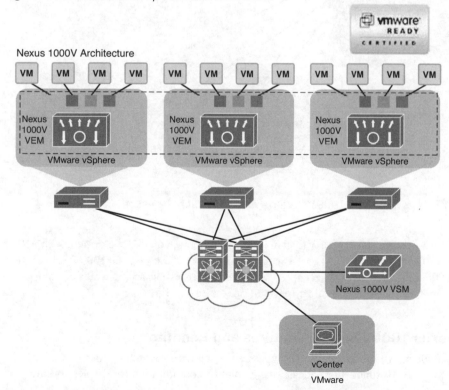

Figure 4-16   *Cisco Nexus 1000V Distributed Virtual Software Switch Architecture*

NOTE The release of VMware vSphere version 4 and the vNetwork vSwitch APIs that were made available by VMware enabled third parties to develop vSwitch implementations. The Cisco Nexus 1000V is the first third-party vDS implementation that is fully supported by VMware.

 ## Cisco Nexus 1000V System Overview

The Cisco Nexus 1000V is a software-based solution that works with any upstream physical switching system to provide standard networking functionality and controls to the virtual machine environment. For your clarity and understanding, Figure 4-17 shows a comparison of a Cisco Nexus 1000V solution to a physical switch.

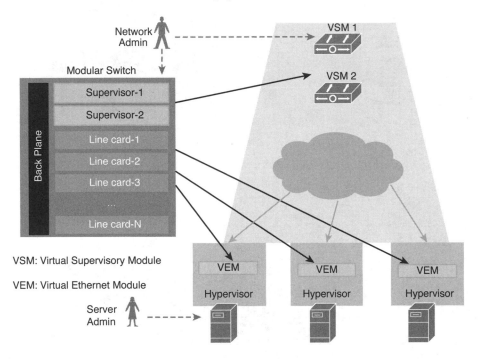

Figure 4-17 *Cisco Nexus 1000V Analogy to a Modular Physical Switch*

NOTE With the introduction of VMware vSphere version 4, you had the option of three virtual networking solutions: VMware vSwitch, vDS, and the Cisco Nexus 1000V Series switch. At the time of writing this chapter, VMware vSphere 6.0 was at general availability. The VMware NSX network virtualization solution was also an option.

Cisco Nexus 1000V Salient Features and Benefits

The Cisco Nexus 1000V Series switch bypasses the standard vSwitch by using a Cisco software switch. This model provides a single point of configuration for the networking environment of multiple ESX or ESXi hosts. Some of the salient features of the Cisco Nexus 1000V Series switch are listed here:

- **Policy-based VM connectivity:** The network administrators, rather than the VM administrators, define these policies, allowing network administrators control of VM-level virtual access layer connectivity. These policies are defined in the form of a port profile containing many characteristics and pushed to VMware vCenter automatically; the VM administrators can then utilize these policies by assigning them to the respective VMs. (Port profiles are discussed later in this chapter.) Figure 4-18 shows you how policy-based VM connectivity is assigned.

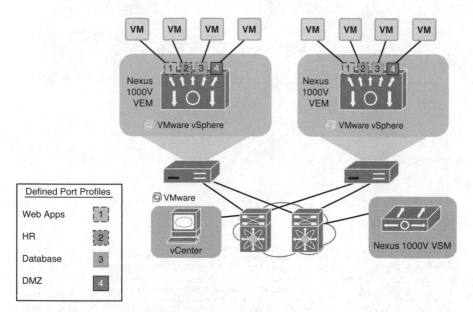

Figure 4-18   *Cisco Nexus 1000V Policy-Based VM Connectivity*

- **Mobility of networking and security properties:** All policies defined in Cisco Nexus 1000V and applied to VMs fully support VMware mobility features, such as VMware vMotion and High Availability (HA). These policies remain attached to the VM, even when the VM moves from host to host. Figure 4-19 shows the mobility of policies along with movement of VMs.

- **Nondisruptive operational model:** The Cisco Nexus 1000V Series switch can be introduced into existing virtual environments nondisruptively by utilizing best practices to migrate from VMware standard virtual networking to the Cisco Nexus 1000V Series switch. Furthermore, this switch unifies the management plane with the rest of the IP network by using the same familiar Cisco NX-OS operating system, commands, and techniques that are available on other Cisco network platforms. Figure 4-20 summarizes the Cisco Nexus 1000V Series switch feature set; for more detailed information, see the links in the "Reference List" section of this chapter.

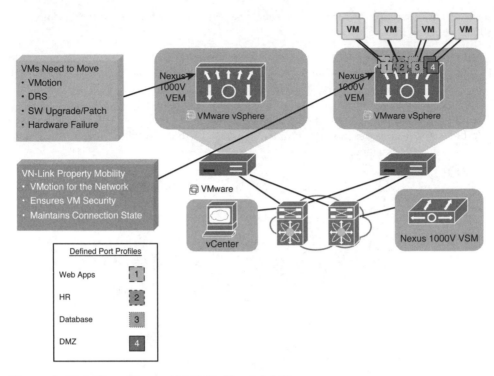

Figure 4-19 *Cisco Nexus 1000V Policy Mobility*

Switching	• L2 switching, 802.1Q tagging, VLAN, rate limiting (TX), VXLAN • IGMP snooping, QoS marking (COS and DSCP), class-based WFQ
Security	• Policy Mobility, Private VLANs w/local PVLAN Enforcement • Access control lists, port security, Cisco TrustSec support • Dynamic ARP inspection, IP Source Guard, DHCP snooping
Network Services	• Virtual Services Datapath (vPath) support for traffic steering and fast-path off-load [leveraged by Virtual Security Gateway (VSG), vWAAS, ASA1000V]
Provisioning	• Port profiles, integration with vC, vCD, SCVMM*, BMC CLM • Optimised NIC teaming with virtual port channel – host mode
Visibility	• VM migration tracking, VC plugin, NetFlow v.9 w/NDE, CDP v.2 • VM-level interface statistics, vTracker • SPAN and ERSPAN (policy-based)
Management	• Virtual Centre VM provisioning, vCenter plugin, Cisco LMS, DCNM • Cisco CLI, Radius, TACACs, Syslog, SNMP (v1, 2, 3) • Hitless upgrade, SW Installer

Figure 4-20 *Cisco Nexus 1000V Series Switch Feature Set Summarized*

Some of the benefits at the server and network levels are summarized here:

- Server Level
  - VM management preserved
  - Reduced operational workload
  - VM-level visibility
  - Compatible with Network vMotion, Storage vMotion, DRS, HA, and FT (Fault Tolerance)
- Network Level
  - Unified management and operations
  - Improved operational security (L2, L3, L4 access lists, port security)*
  - Enhanced network features (VLANs, PVLANs 802.1q, LACP, vPC host mode, QoS)*
  - Policy persistence
  - VM-level visibility
  - SPAN and ERSPAN, NetFlow*

(*Note that some of these additional functionalities are not available on basic vSwitches and vDS; you may require advanced editions.)

Cisco Nexus 1000V Series Virtual Switch Architecture

As mentioned in the overview section, the Cisco Nexus 1000V Series switch has two major components: the VEM, which runs inside the hypervisor, and the VSM, which manages these VEMs.

Cisco Nexus 1000V Virtual Supervisory Module

The VSM is the virtual equivalent of the supervisor module that exists in physical Cisco modular devices running Cisco Nexus Operating System (NX-OS), such as Nexus 7000 Series switches. The VSM is running NX-OS; it manages and controls all other components (VEMs) that are part of the Cisco Nexus 1000V Series switch. All VEMs, equivalent to physical line cards, connect to the VSM and behave as a single virtual modular device. Furthermore, the VSM is responsible for communicating with vCenter and programming, managing the VEMs.

The VSM can be managed via the NX-OS CLI; the CLI has the same syntax and behavior as the CLI on other Cisco Nexus devices. The VSM can reside as a virtual appliance or be hosted on Cisco Nexus 1010/1100 Series virtual services appliances. Figure 4-21 shows the various deployment scenarios for the Cisco Nexus 1000V VSM.

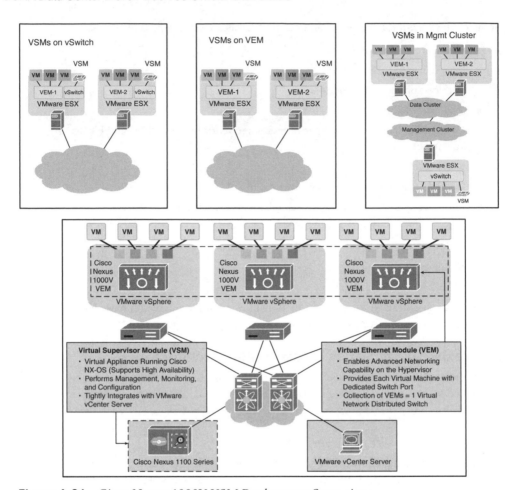

Figure 4-21 *Cisco Nexus 1000V VSM Deployment Scenarios*

Cisco Nexus 1000V Virtual Ethernet Module

The Virtual Ethernet Module (VEM) is the virtual equivalent of a line card that exists in a physical Cisco modular switch. The VEM resides on every VMware ESX or ESXi host; on the hypervisor. The VEM provides all the VMs their connectivity, through physical NICs on the host, and forms that virtual access layer. Multiple VEMs communicating with a VSM or multiple VSMs construct one logical switch.

VEMs on different hosts don't have a direct line of communication with each other; they require an external switch to link them together, such as a physical access layer switch of the VMware ESX or ESXi host. Figure 4-22 graphically represents the Cisco Nexus 1000V VEM.

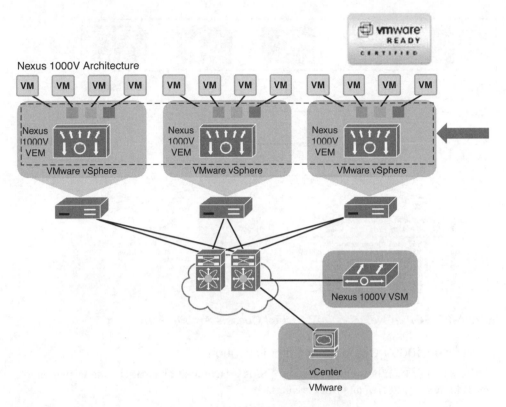

Figure 4-22 *Cisco Nexus 1000V VEM Architecture*

NOTE The VEM-to-VSM communication carries only control traffic. Traditionally, this communication took place over Layer 2 mode. With the later releases of Cisco Nexus 1000V Series switch, Layer 3 mode is valid and is the default option. Every VEM on each VMware ESX or ESXi host requires a VMKernel interface/NIC with an IP address. This VMK interface must be moved to the VEM. The management modes are briefly explained in the subsequent sections.

As described earlier, the Cisco Nexus 1000V can be logically viewed as a virtual modular switch chassis. This virtual chassis contains the Cisco Nexus 1000V Series components, such as redundant VSMs and installed VEMs. Figure 4-23 shows the **show module** command output from the primary VSM, where it displays the VSMs and the VEMs in the same manner as it would display supervisors and line cards on a Cisco Nexus 7000 Series switch.

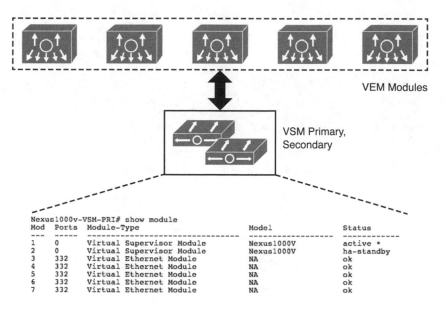

```
Nexus1000v-VSM-PRI# show module
Mod  Ports  Module-Type                  Model         Status
---  -----  ---------------------------  ------------  ------------
1    0      Virtual Supervisor Module    Nexus1000V    active *
2    0      Virtual Supervisor Module    Nexus1000V    ha-standby
3    332    Virtual Ethernet Module      NA            ok
4    332    Virtual Ethernet Module      NA            ok
5    332    Virtual Ethernet Module      NA            ok
6    332    Virtual Ethernet Module      NA            ok
7    332    Virtual Ethernet Module      NA            ok
```

Figure 4-23 *Cisco Nexus 1000V Virtual Chassis Architecture*

Cisco Nexus 1000V Component Communication

The communication between VEMs and VSMs is facilitated by two separate virtual interfaces known as *control* and *packet* interfaces.

- **Control:** The control interface carries "heartbeat" traffic from VEMs to VSM; it's communicated every 2 seconds, with a 6-second timeout to confirm its presence to the VSM. Furthermore, the control interface maintains synchronization between primary and secondary VSMs over this interface.

- **Packet:** The packet interface carries packets such as Cisco Discovery Protocol (CDP) or Internet Group Management Protocol (IGMP) control messages, from VEM to VSM.

> **NOTE** You can use one or separate VLANs for the control and packet interfaces. Usually, two separate VLANs are used for these interfaces; therefore, Layer 2 connectivity between VEMs and VSMs is a prerequisite, unless Layer 3 mode is utilized.

Cisco Nexus 1000V Management Communication

The communication between the VSM and the VMware vCenter server is conducted through this management interface. The VSM uses the VMware virtual infrastructure methodology (VIM) application programming interface (API) over Secure Socket Layer (SSL) to communicate with VMware vCenter server. The connection can be manually set up on the VSM or established during the installation process. After communication between the VSM and VMware vCenter server is established, the Cisco Nexus 1000V is created in the vCenter server.

The management interface is known as the out-of-band management interface. The best practice is to have this interface and the VMware vCenter server ESX management interface on the same VLAN.

> **NOTE**   Cisco Nexus 1000V introduced Layer 3 mode for control, packet, and management traffic since version 1.2. At that time, Layer 3 connection mode was optional; at the time of writing this book, the default when installing the VSM is to establish Layer 3 connectivity instead of Layer 2. With Layer 3 mode, every VEM requires an IP address and all control, packet, and management traffic is carried over this network. Figure 4-24 shows the interaction during VSM installation and the control mode selection.

```
Configure the default domain name? (yes/no) [n]: y

  Default domain name : cisco.com

Enable the telnet service? (yes/no) [n]:

Enable the ssh service? (yes/no) [y]: y

  Type of ssh key you would like to generate (dsa/rsa) [rsa]:

  Number of rsa key bits <768-2048> [1024]:

Enable the http-server? (yes/no) [y]:

Configure the ntp server? (yes/no) [n]: y

  NTP server IPv4 address :

Vem feature level will be set to 4.2(1)SV1(5.1), Do you want to reconfigure? (
yes/no) [n]:

Configure svs domain parameters? (yes/no) [y]:

  Enter SVS Control mode (L2 / L3) : L3_
```

Figure 4-24   *Cisco Nexus 1000V VSM Installation Layer 3 Mode*

Cisco Nexus 1000V Port Profiles

Port profiles are the Cisco Nexus 1000V Series switch equivalent of port groups/dvPortgroups in VMware. When a port profile is created, you will see a corresponding port group being created in VMware vCenter server.

These port profiles are used to configure interfaces on the Cisco Nexus 1000V Series switch. A port profile can be assigned to multiple interfaces (physical or virtual). All changes to a port profile are automatically propagated across all interfaces.

In the VMware vCenter server, port profiles are represented as port groups/dvPortgroups. Both physical and virtual interfaces are assigned in VMware vCenter server to their respective port groups. These port groups perform the following functions:

- Define a port configuration by policy.
- Apply a single policy across all concerned ports.
- Support both virtual and physical Ethernet ports.

When a VMware ESX or ESXi host port (VMNIC) is assigned to the Cisco Nexus 1000V Series switch, an uplink port group/dvPortgroup is assigned to it and its settings are applied to that VMNIC. Similarly, when a NIC is added to a VM (vNIC), an available VM port group/dvPortgroup is assigned, and those network settings associated with that port profile are inherited.

> **NOTE**   When implementing the Cisco Nexus 1000V Series switch, manual configuration of port groups/dvPortgroups via VMware vCenter server is not recommended in general, because it overrides the Cisco Nexus 1000V port profile. Instead, all port profile creation is performed via the VSM.

Types of Port Profiles in Cisco Nexus 1000V

There are two main types of port profile constructs in the Cisco Nexus 1000V Series switch.

- **Type Ethernet:** The Ethernet type port profiles are usually uplink port profiles, normally associated with VMNICs (physical interfaces on ESX or ESXi hosts). All "system VLANs" must be allowed on this uplink.

- **Type vEthernet:** The vEthernet type port profiles are usually assigned to virtual interfaces on VMs (vNICs) and represented as port groups/dvPortgroups in the VMware vCenter server. These port profiles are typically a collection of NX-OS CLI commands, consisting of the port profile name, switch port mode, VLAN number, and so on.

> **NOTE**   System VLANs are Control, Packet, Management VLANs; they are classified as system VLANs in a Cisco Nexus 1000V Series switch implementation.

The Cisco Nexus 1000V Series software switch provides a model in which network administrators define network-related policies that a server administrator can consume as new VMs are provisioned. These port profiles automatically sync with VMware vCenter server and are available as port groups to be assigned by a server administrator.

Cisco Nexus 1000V Administrator View and Roles

This admin model is implemented on Cisco Nexus 1000V Series switches with the port profiles feature. With this port profile feature, server administrators don't need to create and maintain vSwitches or port group configurations on any of their VMware ESX or ESXi hosts.

Port profiles allow separation of the network and server administrator functions. Network administrators now have the ability to define port profiles with the familiar syntax as existing physical Cisco switches and ensure consistent policy enforcement both at physical and virtual machine level.

The server administrator can now focus on server administration tasks; when connectivity is required, the administrator can consume the policies defined through port profiles. Figure 4-25 shows the VMware vCenter view of choosing port groups, which are populated when port profiles are created on a Cisco Nexus 1000V Series switch and assigned to a virtual machine interface (vNIC).

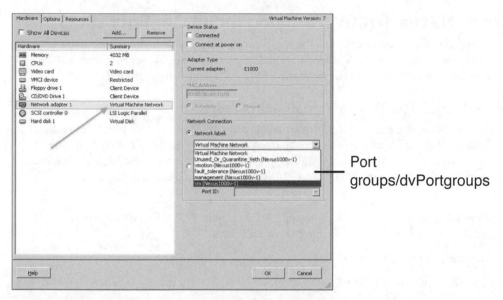

Figure 4-25   *VMware vCenter Port Groups/dvPortgroups*

Table 4-3 compares the typical administrative tasks before and after the Cisco Nexus 1000V Series switch or vDS availability. The network administrators' participation facilitates more focus, control, and manageability around the virtual access layer.

Table 4-3   Administrator Tasks Before and After Cisco Nexus 1000V Series Switch

Tasks	VMware Administrator Before	VMware Administrator After	Network Administrator Before	Network Administrator After
vSwitch config	Per ESX host	Automated	—	Same as physical network
Port group config	Per ESX host	Automated	—	Policy-based
Add ESX host	vCenter-based	vCenter-based	—	—
NIC teaming config	Per vSwitch	Automated	—	Port channel optimized
Virtual machine creation	vCenter-based	vCenter-based	—	—
Security	—	Policy-based	—	ACL, PVLAN, port security, TrustSec
vm visibility	vCenter	VM-specific	—	VM-specific
Management	vCenter	vCenter-based	—	Cisco CLI, XML API, SNMP, DCNM

Cisco Nexus 1000V Verifying Initial Configuration

This section focuses on explaining the initial configuration and validation steps you need to understand when using the VMware ESX and Cisco Nexus 1000V Series switch and the CLI commands to validate connectivity to the VSM, VEM, and VMware vCenter.

Cisco Nexus 1000V VSM Installation Methods

You can use multiple methods to deploy and install your Cisco Nexus 1000V VSM; the preferred installation method is to use an open virtualization appliance (OVA) file. When you download the Cisco Nexus 1000V zipped package from software.cisco.com, it contains a number of folders that include VSM, VEM, XML-APIs, and the like, and a README.txt file.

In the VSM folder, under Install, you will find the required OVA file, which you can use to deploy the VSM directly on to your ESX or ESXi host.

From the .iso file, follow these steps:

Step 1. Create a VSM VM in vCenter.

Step 2. Configure VSM networking.

Step 3. Perform initial VSM setup via the VSM console.

Step 4. Install the VSM plug-in in vCenter.

Step 5. Configure the SVS connection in the VSM console.

Step 6. Add hosts to the virtual distributed switch in vCenter.

From the .ovf file:

Step 1. Use the wizard to deploy an OVF from template (Steps 1 and 2)

Step 2. All other steps are manual as above.

From the .ova file:

Step 1. Use the wizard to deploy an OVF from template (Steps 1–4).

Step 2. All other steps are identical and manual.

NOTE   Open virtualization format (OVF) and open virtualization appliance (OVA) are similar. The main difference is that the OVF folder contains (metadata) structured files—.ovf, .mf, .vmdk/.vhd, and so on—whereas the OVA file is a single zipped file. Figure 4-26 shows the OVA file deployment process.

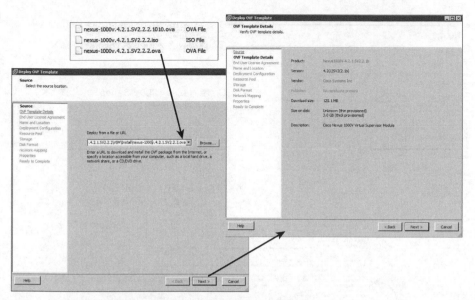

Figure 4-26   *Cisco Nexus 1000V VSM Installation*

Initial VSM Configuration Verification

When installing the Cisco Nexus 1000V Series VSM, as a VM or instantiated in the Cisco Nexus 1010/1100 appliance, the network administrator performs the initial configuration to provide the basic parameters for the Cisco Nexus 1000V Series switch. To verify this initial configuration and subsequent verifications to the configuration, use the **show running-config** command at the Cisco Nexus 1000V CLI. Figure 4-27 shows sample output of this command.

Verifying VMware vCenter Connectivity

During initial configuration, to establish a connection between the Cisco Nexus 1000V Series switch and the VMware vCenter, the network administrator must configure a Software Virtual Switch (SVS) connection. This is required for the Cisco Nexus 1000V Series switch to push configurations and policies such as port profiles to VMware vCenter server.

To verify whether the SVS connection is in place explicitly, use the **show svs connections** command on the Cisco Nexus 1000V Series switch CLI. Figure 4-28 shows sample output of the **show svs connections** command.

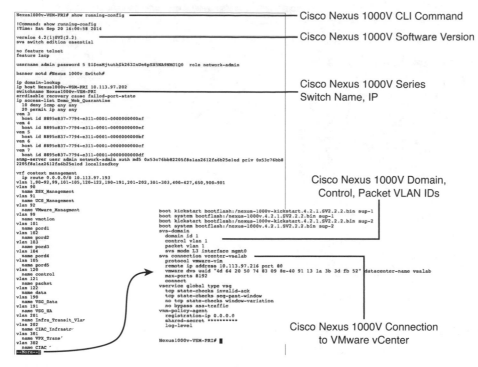

Figure 4-27   *Cisco Nexus 1000V show running-config Command Output*

```
Nexus1000v-VSM-PRI# show svs connections

connection vcenter-vsalab:
    ip address:
    remote port: 80
    protocol: vmware-vim https
    certificate: default
    datacenter name: vsalab
    admin:
    max-ports: 8192
    DVS uuid: 4d 64 20 50 74 83 09 8e-40 91 13 1a 3b 3d fb 52
    config status: Enabled
    operational status: Connected
    sync status: Complete
    version: VMware vCenter Server 5.1.0 build-799731
    vc-uuid: EA62B6C7-0BB4-44B3-A8AF-11E79848C55F
    ssl-cert: self-signed or not authenticated
```

Figure 4-28   *Cisco Nexus 1000V show svs connections Command Output*

You can perform further verifications of the connection between the Cisco Nexus 1000V Series switch and VMware vCenter server by using the **show svs domain** command. It is important to understand that each Cisco Nexus 1000V Series switch uses a domain ID. All ESX or ESXi hosts with a VEM installed are members of a domain and listen to updates from that domain, which demarcates the virtual chassis where they reside. Figure 4-29 shows a sample output of the **show svs domain** command.

> **NOTE**   In the sample output, see the Status field that confirms an operationally successful connection to VMware vCenter server and the use of Cisco-recommended Layer 3 mode for VSM-to-VEM communications, not Layer 2 mode.

```
Nexus1000v-VSM-PRI# show svs domain
SVS domain config:
   Domain id:    1
   Control vlan:  NA
   Packet vlan:   NA
   L2/L3 Control mode: L3
   L3 control interface: mgmt0
   Status: Config push to VC successful.
   Control type multicast: No

Note: Control VLAN and Packet VLAN are not used in L3 mode
Nexus1000v-VSM-PRI#
```

Figure 4-29 *Cisco Nexus 1000V show svs domain Command Output*

Verifying Nexus 1000V Module Status

After an ESX or ESXI host has been added to the distributed switch and the VEM has been installed on it successfully, the VEM appears as a module on the VSM as part of the virtual chassis, similar to modules that are added to a physical module switch chassis.

Figure 4-30 shows a sample output of the **show module** command, demonstrating the primary and standby supervisor modules in slots 1 and 2, respectively, and the VMware ESX or ESXi hosts/modules that have been added to the Cisco Nexus 1000V Series switch instance starting from slot 3.

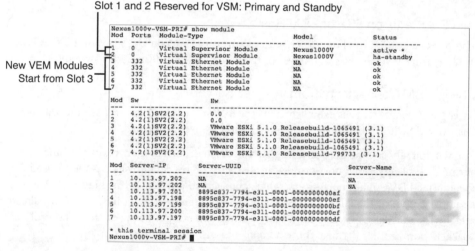

Figure 4-30 *Cisco Nexus 1000V show module Command Output*

> **NOTE**   Slots 1 and 2 are reserved for VSM (primary and standby) supervisory modules; the VEM module slots start from slot 3.

You can further verify module status with the **show module vem map** command, which shows the status of all visible VEMs, as well as their respective hosts (VMware ESX or ESXi), Universally Unique Identifier (UUID), and license status. Figure 4-31 shows a sample output of the **show module vem map** command.

```
Nexus1000v-VSM-PRI# show module vem map
Mod     Status        UUID                                      License Status
-----   ----------    ------------------------------------      --------------
3       powered-up    8895c837-7794-e311-0001-0000000000af      licensed
4       powered-up    8895c837-7794-e311-0001-0000000000ef      licensed
5       powered-up    8895c837-7794-e311-0001-0000000000bf      licensed
6       powered-up    8895c837-7794-e311-0001-0000000000cf      licensed
7       powered-up    8895c837-7794-e311-0001-0000000000df      licensed
Nexus1000v-VSM-PRI# █
```

Figure 4-31 *Cisco Nexus 1000V show module vem map Command Output*

Cisco Nexus 1000V VEM Installation Methods

There are multiple methods to install your Cisco Nexus 1000V VEM. Based on the chosen method, refer to the installation and configuration guides for detailed steps and prerequisites.

■ If you are using the VUM (VMware Update Manager) to install or upgrade, you will have to create a host patch baseline and include the appropriate VMware patch or update bulletin and the corresponding Cisco Nexus 1000V VEM bulletin in the baseline.

■ If you are using the vCLI on the ESX or ESXi host, use the **esxupdate, esxcli** command using the downloaded .vib file.

■ You can also prepare ESXi images with VEMs installed and deploy them along with the ESX installation.

Initial VEM Status on ESX or ESXi Host

This topic will show you how to verify the status of a VEM on the VMware ESX or ESXi host by using VMware vCenter server or the Cisco Nexus 1000V Series switch CLI.

Verifying VSM Connectivity from vCenter Server

After VSM connectivity is established via the SVS connection, you will see the vNetwork Distributed Switch (vDS) in the vCenter networking inventory panel.

You will initially see the port profiles that you created, such as control, packet, and management. Typically, other port profiles are also created by default, such as the Unused_Or_ Quarantined DVUplinks port group, which connects to physical NICs. Figure 4-32 shows a sample output of the initial port profiles. This output also shows physical uplinks already attached to the Cisco Nexus 1000V Series switch and note; it does not show "control" and "packet" port profiles because this environment is using L3 mode.

Verifying VEM Agent Running

If you have SSH enabled on your ESX or ESXi host, you can log in to your host by opening an SSH connection, log in with valid credentials, and at the CLI of the host, you can execute the **vem status** command. This command verifies whether the VEM module is loaded and shows whether the VEM Agent is running on this host. The command also confirms the physical interfaces (VMNICs) that are used as uplinks on this host. Figure 4-33 shows a sample output of the **vem status** command.

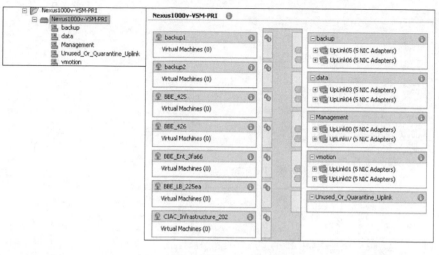

Virtual Side   The Switch   Physical Side

Figure 4-32   *Cisco Nexus 1000V Series Switch from vCenter Server*

Cisco Nexus 1000V Series VEM Module

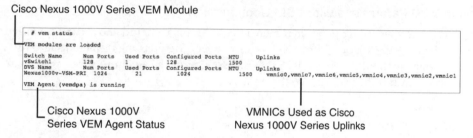

Cisco Nexus 1000V   VMNICs Used as Cisco
Series VEM Agent Status   Nexus 1000V Series Uplinks

Figure 4-33   *VEM Agent Verification on Host*

Verifying VEM Uplink Interface Status

You can also verify the uplink interface status on the VMware ESX or ESXi hosts by using these commands: **vemcmd show port** and **vemcmd show port vlans**.

The **vemcmd show port** command verifies the VEM port that is used on the host (uplink) and the Cisco Nexus 1000V Series switch. It provides details of the port state, link status, and so on. As you can see in Figure 4-34, the port state (F/B*) indicates that it's blocking some VLANs.

The previous command (**vemcmd show port**) showed that certain VLANs were blocked on some uplinks. You can use the **vemcmd show port vlans** command to verify which VLANs are carried across the uplink and whether any VLANs are missing or blocked intentionally. In Figure 4-34, the uplink VMNIC3 on VEM allows only VLAN 99.

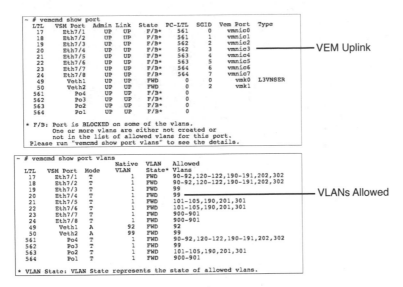

Figure 4-34   *VEM Uplink Interface Status*

Verifying VEM Parameters with VSM Configuration

To ensure that your VEM's parameters match the VSM, the **vemcmd show card** command executed on the VMware ESX or ESXi host can be very useful. Using the command verifies the following components. Figure 4-35 shows the output of the **vemcmd show card** command and identifies the following configurations.

- Card name
- Card domain ID
- Card slot
- Control traffic connectivity mode between VSM and VEM
- VEM control agent MAC ID
- Used VSM MAC address
- Used control and packet VLANs

Validating VM Port Groups and Port Profiles

Now that you have verified the VSM and the VEM configurations and cross-checked the configurations from both perspectives, you will understand how to validate that VMs are using the correct vDS port groups by using VMware vCenter and Cisco Nexus 1000V Series switch CLI.

First, use the **show port-profile name** *<name>* command to verify the details of that port profile configuration and parameters. With this command, you can check which switchport mode this port profile uses, which VLANs are associated with this port profile, and which virtual interfaces are assigned to this port profile. Figure 4-36 shows a sample port profile output using the **show port-profile name** *<name>* command.

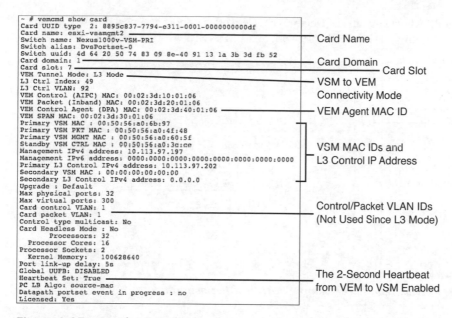

```
~ # vemcmd show card
Card UUID type  2: 8895c837-7794-e311-0001-0000000000df
Card name: esxi-vsamgmt2                               ──────── Card Name
Switch name: Nexus1000v-VSM-PRI
Switch alias: DvsPortset-0
Switch uuid: 4d 64 20 50 74 83 09 8e-40 91 13 1a 3b 3d fb 52
Card domain: 1                                          ──────── Card Domain
Card slot: 7                                            ──────── Card Slot
VEM Tunnel Mode: L3 Mode                                ──────── VSM to VEM
L3 Ctrl Index: 49                                                Connectivity Mode
L3 Ctrl VLAN: 92
VEM Control (AIPC) MAC: 00:02:3d:10:01:06
VEM Packet (Inband) MAC: 00:02:3d:20:01:06
VEM Control Agent (DPA) MAC: 00:02:3d:40:01:06          ──────── VEM Agent MAC ID
VEM SPAN MAC: 00:02:3d:30:01:06
Primary VSM MAC : 00:50:56:a0:6b:97
Primary VSM PKT MAC : 00:50:56:a0:4f:48
Primary VSM MGMT MAC : 00:50:56:a0:60:5f
Standby VSM CTRL MAC : 00:50:56:a0:3c:ce
Management IPv4 address: 10.113.97.197                          VSM MAC IDs and
Management IPv6 address: 0000:0000:0000:0000:0000:0000:0000:0000   L3 Control IP Address
Primary L3 Control IPv4 address: 10.113.97.202
Secondary VSM MAC : 00:00:00:00:00:00
Secondary L3 Control IPv4 address: 0.0.0.0
Upgrade : Default
Max physical ports: 32
Max virtual ports: 300
Card control VLAN: 1                                            Control/Packet VLAN IDs
Card packet VLAN: 1                                     ──────── (Not Used Since L3 Mode)
Control type multicast: No
Card Headless Mode : No
        Processors: 32
   Processor Cores: 16
Processor Sockets: 2
   Kernel Memory:   100628640
Port link-up delay: 5s
Global UUFB: DISABLED
Heartbeat Set: True                                    ──────── The 2-Second Heartbeat
PC LB Algo: source-mac                                          from VEM to VSM Enabled
Datapath portset event in progress : no
Licensed: Yes
```

Figure 4-35 *Verifying VEM Parameters with the **vemcmd show card** Command*

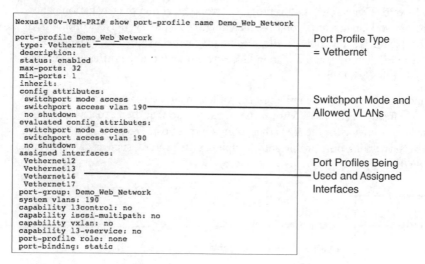

```
Nexus1000v-VSM-PRI# show port-profile name Demo_Web_Network

port-profile Demo_Web_Network
 type: Vethernet                                       ──────── Port Profile Type
 description:                                                   = Vethernet
 status: enabled
 max-ports: 32
 min-ports: 1
 inherit:
 config attributes:
  switchport mode access                                       Switchport Mode and
  switchport access vlan 190                           ──────── Allowed VLANs
  no shutdown
 evaluated config attributes:
  switchport mode access
  switchport access vlan 190
  no shutdown
 assigned interfaces:
  Vethernet12                                                  Port Profiles Being
  Vethernet13                                                  Used and Assigned
  Vethernet16                                          ──────── Interfaces
  Vethernet17
 port-group: Demo_Web_Network
 system vlans: 190
 capability l3control: no
 capability iscsi-multipath: no
 capability vxlan: no
 capability l3-vservice: no
 port-profile role: none
 port-binding: static
```

Figure 4-36 *Cisco UCS Nexus 1000V Sample **show port-profile <name>** Command Output*

After this port profile (Demo_Web_Network) is created on the Cisco Nexus 1000V Series switch and automatically pushed to VMware vCenter server, it will be available for the VMware/server administrator to use and connect a VM to that port profile.

Now let us see that same port profile (Demo_Web_Network) from VMware vCenter server; by right-clicking the VM and choosing Edit Settings, you can add a VM to a port group or port profile. After choosing Edit Settings, you will be presented with the screen shown in Figure 4-37, where you can see Demo_Web_Network as a port group, and now you can assign this port group Demo_Web_Network to a VM's vNIC.

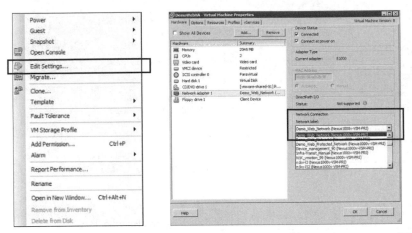

Figure 4-37   *VMware vCenter Sample Port Profile Assignment to VM*

Verifying Port Profile and Groups

From within VMware vCenter, choose Inventory, Networking, and in the navigation pane you will see the networking inventory objects, including the Demo_Web_Networking port profile. This port profile is a VM port profile, meaning it can be assigned to VMs, VMK (they get tied to a vEth number), and not an uplink port profile (note the different symbols); they get tied to an Eth x/x number.

In the same window, you can see the uplink port profiles created on the Cisco Nexus 1000V Series switch and already pushed to VMware vCenter server so that the virtual switch can provide external connectivity for the VMs that reside on that host. Figure 4-38 shows both the Demo_Web_Networking port profile and the uplink port profiles, such as data, backup, vmotion, and the like.

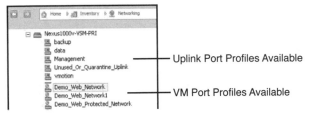

Figure 4-38   *Verifying Port Profiles from VMware vCenter Inventory Networking Pane*

Key New Technologies Integrated with Cisco Nexus 1000V

In addition, here are some brief clarifications and explanations on some concepts and new technologies that have been integrated to work with the Cisco Nexus 1000V Series software switch. In-depth details of these concepts and technologies are beyond the scope of this certification guide.

What Is the Difference Between VN-Link and VN-Tag?

VN-Link (Virtual Network—Link) is not a technology; it is a marketing term that refers to network visibility of nonphysical, nondirect attached devices. This could include virtual machines or virtual interfaces, or it could mean physical interfaces on nonswitching remote devices like Nexus 2000 Series devices. Two approaches offer VN-Link capabilities:

- The Nexus 1000V is VN-Link capable because every virtual machine connected to this software switch receives a virtual Ethernet port that can be configured and controlled just like a physical Ethernet switch port on a standard physical switch.

- The Nexus 5000/2000 Series combination and Cisco UCS Fabric Interconnect/IO module combination both use an additional header in the Ethernet frame called VN-Tag (Virtual Network—Tag), which identifies a remote port (on Nexus 2000 / UCS I/O module) that will be assigned a virtual port on the Cisco Nexus 5000 Series or Cisco UCS 6100/6200/6300 Series Interconnects. This enables the Nexus 2000/UCS I/O module to be managed as a line card on the Cisco Nexus 5000/UCS Fabric 6100/6200/6300 Interconnect. All switching takes place on the Cisco Nexus 5000 or UCS Fabric Interconnects. This same VN-Tag is used to identify a virtual interface on a Cisco Virtual Interface Card (Cisco VIC); the host device (Cisco Nexus 5000 or UCS Fabric Interconnect) can now manage that port as if it were a physical port on the host device.

What Is VXLAN?

Virtual extensible LAN (VXLAN) is an overlay network that is superimposed on top of a traditional network. It is a Layer 2 overlay scheme utilizing Layer 3 networks. Cisco VXLAN is a Layer 2 network isolation technology that uses a 24-bit segment identifier to scale beyond the 4K limitations of VLANs. VXLAN technology creates LAN segments by using an overlay approach with MAC in IP encapsulation.

The Virtual Ethernet Module (VEM) encapsulates the original Layer 2 frame from the VM. Each VEM is assigned an IP address, which is used as the source IP address when encapsulating MAC frames to be sent on the network. This is accomplished by creating virtual network adaptors (VMNIC) on each VEM. You can have multiple VMNICs per VEM and use them for this encapsulated traffic. The encapsulation carries the VXLAN identifier, which is used to scope the MAC address of the payload frame. Figure 4-39 shows a graphical view of a host overlay network with virtual endpoints.

Host Overlays

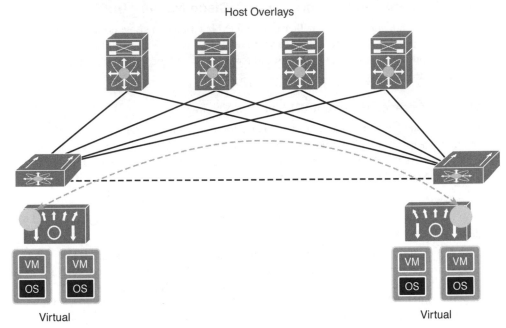

Figure 4-39 *Host Overlay with Virtual Endpoints*

> **NOTE**   Cisco Nexus 1000V Series switches fully support VXLAN technology starting from version 1.5 onward.

What Is vPath Technology?

In virtualized data centers, services such as firewalls, server load balancers, security gateways, and the like are often offered and implemented as virtual services. Given that, the traditional physical connections for these services do not exist, and retrofitting VMs to avail these services causes significant inefficiencies and overheads.

Cisco vPath provides embedded intelligence for virtual services and offers traffic steering capabilities to direct traffic to these virtual services nodes. These topology-agnostic service-chaining capabilities can be built in to the respective Nexus 1000V port profile, for vPath interception. Cisco vPath (Virtual Services Datapath) technology is fully integrated with Cisco Nexus 1000V Series software switches. Figure 4-40 shows an overview of vPath—virtual network services architecture.

What Is Cisco Application Virtual Switch (AVS)?

Cisco AVS is underpinned by Cisco Nexus 1000V Series virtual switch. It is fully integrated with Cisco Application Centric Infrastructure (ACI); thus, the VSM is integrated into the application policy infrastructure controller (APIC), allowing enforcement of application-centric policies automatically, all the way up to the virtual edge of the data center. Please refer to Chapters 12 through 14 for some information.

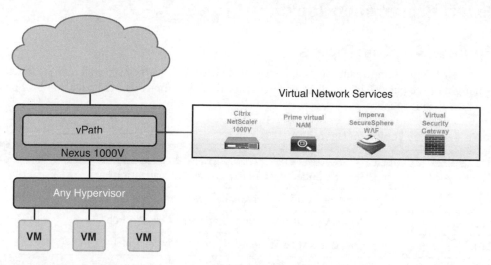

Figure 4-40   *Cisco Virtual Network Services with vPath Technology*

Reference List

VMware Virtual Networking Concepts: http://www.vmware.com/files/pdf/virtual_networking_concepts.pdf

Cisco Nexus 1000V Configuration Guides: http://www.cisco.com/c/en/us/support/switches/nexus-1000v-switch-vmware-vsphere/products-installation-and-configuration-guides-list.html

Cisco Nexus 1000V Installation Guides: http://www.cisco.com/c/en/us/support/switches/nexus-1000v-switch-vmware-vsphere/products-installation-guides-list.html

VMware Configuration Maximums: http://www.vmware.com/pdf/vsphere5/r55/vsphere-55-configuration-maximums.pdf

VMware vSphere 5.1 Documentation: http://pubs.vmware.com/vsphere-51/index.jsp#com.vmware.vsphere.doc/GUID-1B959D6B-41CA-4E23-A7DB-E9165D5A0E80.html

Virtual Networking Features of VMware vDS and Cisco Nexus 1000V: http://www.cisco.com/c/dam/en/us/products/collateral/switches/nexus-1000v-switch-vmware-vsphere/solution_overview_c22-526262.pdf

Cisco Nexus 1100 Series Virtual Services Appliance: http://www.cisco.com/c/en/us/products/collateral/switches/nexus-1100-series-cloud-services-platforms/data_sheet_c78-297641.html

Cisco VXLAN on Nexus 1000V: http://www.cisco.com/c/en/us/products/collateral/switches/nexus-1000v-switch-vmware-vsphere/guide_c07-702975.html

Exam Preparation Tasks

Review All Key Topics

Review the most important topics in the chapter, noted with the key topic icon in the outer margin of the page. Table 4-4 lists a reference for these key topics and the page numbers on which each is found.

Table 4-4   Key Topics for Chapter 4

Key Topic Element	Description	Page
Figure 4-1	"Server Connectivity Before Server Virtualization"	119
List	"Physical Access Layer Challenges"	120
Section	"Server Virtualization with Static VMware vSwitch"	121
List	"Challenges with Standard VMware vSwitch"	121
Section	"Virtual Network Components"	122
Section	"VMware vDS Overview"	128
Figure 4-11	"VMware Virtual Distributed Switch (vDS) Overview"	129
List	"Advantages and Enhancements of VMware vDS"	131
Section	"Cisco Nexus 1000V System Overview"	134
List	"Cisco Nexus 1000V Salient Features and Benefits"	135
Section	"Cisco Nexus 1000V Series Virtual Switch Architecture"	137
List	"Cisco Nexus 1000V Component Communication"	140
Section	"Cisco Nexus 1000V Port Profiles"	141
List	"Types of Port Profiles in Cisco Nexus 1000V"	142
Section	"Initial VSM Configuration Verification"	145
Section	"Verifying Nexus 1000V Module Status"	147
Section	"Verifying VSM Connectivity from vCenter Server"	148
Section	"Verifying VEM Uplink Interface Status"	149
Section	"Validating VM Port Groups and Port Profiles"	150

Complete Tables and Lists from Memory

Print a copy of Appendix B, "Memory Tables" or at least the section for this chapter, and complete the tables and lists from memory. Appendix C, "Memory Tables Answer Key" includes completed tables and lists to check your work.

Define Key Terms

Define the following key terms from this chapter, and check your answers in the Glossary:

Virtual LAN (VLAN), Virtual Extensible LAN (VXLAN), Virtual Services Datapath (vPath), Virtual Network Interface Card (vNIC), VMNIC, Uplink Trunk, VN-Link, VN-Tag, Cisco Virtual Interface Cards (VIC), VMware Update Manager (VUM), vEthernet Ethernet Application Programming Interface (API), Private VLAN (PVLAN), 802.1q, Link Aggregation Control Protocol (LACP), vPC Host Mode, Quality of Service (QoS), Internet Small Computer Interface (iSCSI), VMKernel, Application Centric Infrastructure (ACI), Application Policy Infrastructure Controller (APIC), Application Virtual Switch (AVS)

4

This chapter covers the following exam topics:

2.2 Describe the concepts of overlays

   2.2.a OTV

   2.2.b NVGRE

   2.2.c VXLAN

CHAPTER 5

Data Center Overlay Networks

Applications are the most critical component in the Data Center and businesses are looking for new ways of data center designs, which is more scalable and agile to support the rapid development and deployment of new applications. Server virtualization has been growing exponentially year over year, which allowed data center admins to have more flexibility in provisioning and placement of new compute workloads in the data center. The problem is that network infrastructure didn't develop in the same fast pace with application development. The introduction of data center network overlays and Layer 2 extension technology might help address this gap.

In this chapter, you will learn about the latest Cisco innovations in the Data Center Extension solutions and in the LAN Extension in particular, which is called overlay transport virtualization (OTV). You will learn the fundamentals of OTV and how it can be used as a data center interconnect solution. OTV is the latest innovation. When it comes to Layer 2 extension solutions, you can run OTV over any transport infrastructure; the only requirement is IP connectivity between the sites. OTV uses a concept called MAC address routing. It provides native multihoming and loop prevention end-to-end, and it is simple to configure. With a few command lines, you can extend Layer 2 between multiple sites. I will also cover VXLAN and NVGRE, which is a Layer 2 over Layer 3 overlay used today in the data center. Customers would like to shift from Layer 2-based designs, which rely heavily on STP, and move to Layer 3-based designs. However, they would also like to keep Layer 2 reachability across their data center infrastructure.

"Do I Know This Already?" Quiz

The "Do I Know This Already?" quiz enables you to assess whether you should read this entire chapter thoroughly or jump to the "Exam Preparation Tasks" section. If you are in doubt about your answers to these questions or your own assessment of your knowledge of the topics, read the entire chapter. Table 5-1 lists the major headings in this chapter and their corresponding "Do I Know This Already?" quiz questions. You can find the answers in Appendix A, "Answers to the 'Do I Know This Already?' Quizzes."

Table 5-1 "Do I Know This Already?" Section-to-Question Mapping

Foundation Topics Section	Questions
"Identify Key Differentiators Between DCI and Network Interconnectivity"	1–5
"VXLAN"	6–8
"NVGRE"	9–10

> **CAUTION**   The goal of self-assessment is to gauge your mastery of the topics in this chapter. If you do not know the answer to a question or are only partially sure of the answer, you should mark that question as wrong for purposes of the self-assessment. Giving yourself credit for an answer you correctly guess skews your self-assessment results and might provide you with a false sense of security.

1. Which of the following Cisco products supports OTV?

   a. Nexus 7000 Series

   b. ASR 9000 Series

   c. ASR 1000 Series

   d. Catalyst 6500 Series

2. True or False? For silent hosts, we can set up static MAC-to-IP mappings in OTV.

   a. True

   b. False

3. Which version of IGMP is used on the OTV join interface?

   a. IGMPv1

   b. IGMPv2

   c. IGMPv3

   d. There is no need to enable IGMP on the OTV join interface.

4. How many join interfaces can you create per logical overlay?

   a. 1

   b. 2

   c. 4

   d. 8

5. True or False? You need to do no shutdown for the overlay interface after adding it.

   a. True

   b. False

6. True or False? VXLAN uses MAC in TCP encapsulation.

   a. True

   b. False

7. What is the size of the VXALN VNID?

   a. 8 byte

   b. 16 bit

   c. 24 bit

   d. 32 bit

8. Which BGP address family does EVPN use to advertise MAC/IP information?

   a. L2VPN

   b. L3VPN

   c. VPNv4

   d. IPv4

9. In NVGRE, what is the name of the segment ID?

   a. VSID

   b. VNID

   c. NVID

   d. NVGID

10. What is the size of the VSID in NVGRE?

   a. 16-bit

   b. 4-bytes

   c. 24-bit

   d. 32-bit

5

Foundation Topics

Overlay Transport Virtualization

Overlay transport virtualization (OTV) significantly simplifies extending Layer 2 applications between distributed data centers across any transport. You can deploy data center interconnect (DCI) between different sites as long as you have IP connectivity between them. In the next few sections I will cover OTV and the different concepts around it.

Introduction to Overlay Transport Virtualization

DCI solutions have been available for quite some time; they are mainly used to enable the benefit of geographically separated data centers. Layer 2 extensions might be required at different layers in the data center to enable the resiliency and clustering mechanisms offered by the different applications at the web, application, and database layers. Different types of technologies provide Layer 2 extension solutions:

■ **Ethernet over multiprotocol label switching (EoMPLS):** EoMPLS can be used to provision point-to-point Layer 2 Ethernet connections between two sites with MPLS as the transport.

■ **Virtual private LAN services (VPLS):** Similar to EoMPLS, VPLS uses an MPLS network as the underlying transport network. However, instead of point-to-point Ethernet pseudowires, VPLS delivers a virtual multiaccess Ethernet network.

■ **Dark fiber:** In some cases, dark fiber might be available to build private optical connections between data centers. Dense wavelength-division multiplexing (DWDM) or coarse wavelength-division multiplexing (CWDM) can increase the number of Layer 2 connections that can be run through the fibers. These technologies increase the total bandwidth over the same number of fibers.

Using these technologies to extend the LAN across multiple data centers creates a series of challenges:

■ **Failure isolation:** The extension of Layer 2 domains between multiple data center sites can cause the data centers to share protocols and failures that would normally have been isolated when interconnecting data centers over an IP network. A solution that provides Layer 2 connectivity, yet restricts the reach of the flood domain, is necessary to contain failures and preserve the resiliency achieved by the use of multiple data centers.

■ **Transport infrastructure nature:** The nature of the transport between data centers varies depending on the location of the data centers and the availability and cost of services in the different areas. A cost-effective solution for the interconnection of data centers must be transport agnostic and give the network designer the flexibility to choose any transport between data centers based on business and operational preferences. An IP-capable transport is the most generalized offering, and it provides flexibility and enables long-reach connectivity. A solution capable of using an IP transport is expected to provide the most flexibility.

■ **Multihoming with end-to-end loop prevention:** LAN extension techniques should provide a high degree of resiliency; therefore, multihoming of the Layer 2 sites onto the

VPN is required. Mechanisms must be provided to prevent loops that might be induced when connecting bridged networks that are multihomed.

- **Bandwidth utilization with replication, load balancing, and path diversity:** When extending Layer 2 domains across data centers, the use of available bandwidth between data centers must be optimized to obtain the best connectivity at the lowest cost. Balancing the load across all available paths while providing resilient connectivity between the data center and the transport network requires added intelligence above and beyond that available in traditional Ethernet switching and Layer 2 VPNs. Multicast and broadcast traffic should also be replicated optimally to reduce bandwidth consumption.

- **Complex operations:** Layer 2 VPNs can provide extended Layer 2 connectivity across data centers but will usually involve a mix of complex protocols, distributed provisioning, and an operationally intensive hierarchical scaling model. A simple overlay protocol with built-in capability and point-to-cloud provisioning is crucial to reducing the cost of providing this connectivity.

OTV provides a Layer 2 extension between remote data centers by using a concept called MAC address routing, meaning a control plane protocol is used to exchange MAC address reachability information between network devices providing the LAN extension functionality. This has a huge benefit over traditional data center interconnect solutions, which typically rely on data plane learning and the use of flooding across the transport infrastructure to learn reachability. Bridge protocol data units (BPDUs) are not forwarded on the overlay. This results in failure containment within a data center; failure does not propagate into other data centers and stops at the edge device.

OTV must be deployed only at specific edge devices. Each Ethernet frame is encapsulated into an IP packet and delivered across the transport infrastructure; there is no need to establish virtual circuits between the data center sites. Therefore, addition or removal of an edge device does not affect other edge devices on the overlay.

Finally, OTV does not require additional configuration to offer multihoming; it is built in natively in OTV using the same control plane protocol along with loop prevention mechanisms. The loop prevention mechanisms prevent loops on the overlay and prevent loops from the sites that are multihomed to the overlay. There is no need to extend Spanning-Tree Protocol (STP) across the transport infrastructure. Each site will have its own spanning-tree domain, which is independent from the other site even though all sites have a common Layer 2 domain. This is built-in functionality; no extra configuration is needed to make it work.

Cisco has two main products that currently support OTV: Cisco Nexus 7000 Series switches and Cisco ASR 1000 Series aggregation services routers. Although the features, scale, and convergence times continue to improve, following are the minimum requirements to run OTV on each platform:

- **Cisco Nexus 7000 Series and Cisco Nexus 7700 platform:**
  - Any M-Series (Cisco Nexus 7000 Series) or F3 (Cisco Nexus 7000 Series or 7700 platform) line card for encapsulation
  - Cisco NX-OS Release 5.0(3) or later (Cisco Nexus 7000 Series) or Cisco NX-OS Release 6.2(2) or later (Cisco Nexus 7700 platform)
  - Transport Services license

- **Cisco ASR 1000 Series:**
  - Cisco IOS XE Software Release 3.5 or later
  - Advanced IP Services or Advanced Enterprise Services license

> **NOTE**   This chapter focuses on OTV implementation using the Nexus 7000 Series.

OTV Terminology

Before you learn how the OTV control plane and data plane work, you must know OTV terminology, which is shown in Figure 5-1. This terminology is used throughout the chapter.

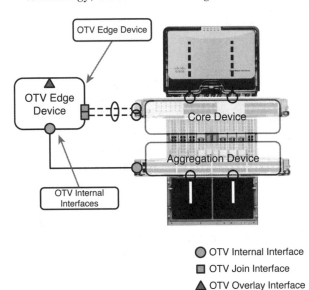

Figure 5-1   *OTV Terminology*

- **OTV edge device:** The edge device performs OTV functions; it receives the Layer 2 traffic for all VLANs that need to be extended to remote sites and dynamically encapsulates the Ethernet frames into IP packets and sends them across through the transport infrastructure. Each site can have one or more edge devices. OTV configuration is done on the edge device and is completely transparent to the rest of the infrastructure. Because the edge device needs to see the Layer 2 traffic, it is recommended to have it at the Layer 3 boundary for the site so it can see all the VLANs. The OTV edge device can be deployed in many places; however, one of the recommended designs is to have a separate virtual device context (VDC) on the Nexus 7000 acting as the OTV edge device. So we create one VDC per each Nexus 7000 to have redundancy.

- **OTV internal interface:** The Layer 2 interface on the edge device that connects to the VLANs to be extended is called the *internal interface*. The internal interface is usually configured as an access or trunk interface and receives Layer 2 traffic. The internal interface does not need specific OTV configuration; typical Layer 2 functions, such as local switching, spanning-tree, and flooding, are performed on the internal interfaces.

- **OTV join interface:** The OTV join interface is a Layer 3 interface. At the time of writing this book, it can be a physical interface or subinterface; it can be a logical interface, such as a Layer 3 port channel, or a Layer 3 port-channel subinterface. You can have only one join interface associated with a given overlay, and you can have one join interface shared across multiple overlays. The join interface "joins" the overlay network and discovers the other overlay remote edge devices. The IP address of the join interface is used to advertise reachability of MAC addresses present in the site.

- **OTV overlay interface:** The OTV overlay interface is a logical multiaccess and multicast-capable interface. The user must define it. All of the OTV configuration is applied to the overlay interface. When the OTV edge device receives a Layer 2 frame that needs to be delivered to a remote data center site, the frame is logically forwarded to the overlay interface, which is encapsulated in an IP unicast or multicast packet and sent to the remote data center.

- **Transport network:** This is the network that connects the OTV sites. It can be owned by the customer or by the service provider or both; the only requirement is to allow IP reachability between the edge devices.

- **Overlay network:** This is a logical network that interconnects OTV edge devices.

- **Site:** An OTV site is the same as a data center, which has VLANs that must be extended to another site—meaning another data center.

- **Site VLAN:** OTV edge devices send hellos on the site VLAN to detect other OTV edge devices in the same site. The edge device uses the site VLAN to elect the authoritative edge device for the VLANs, which need to be extended. It is recommended to use a dedicated VLAN as a site VLAN that is not extended across the overlay.

- **Authoritative edge device:** OTV elects a designated forwarding edge device per site for each VLAN to provide loop-free multihoming. It is part of the OTV control plane and does not need additional configuration. The forwarder is known as the authoritative edge device (AED). The edge devices talk to each other on the internal interfaces to elect the AED. Prior to NX-OS release 5.2(1), OTV used the site VLAN within a site to detect and establish adjacencies with other OTV edge devices. However, the mechanism of electing AEDs that is based only on the communication established on the site VLAN can create situations (resulting from connectivity issues or misconfiguration) in which OTV edge devices belonging to the same site can fail to detect one another, thereby ending up in an Active/Active mode (for the same data VLAN). This could ultimately result in the creation of a loop scenario. To address this concern, starting with the 5.2 (1) NX-OS release, each OTV device maintains dual adjacencies with other OTV edge devices belonging to the same DC site. OTV edge devices continue to use the site VLAN to discover and establish adjacency with other OTV edge devices in a site. This adjacency is called **site adjacency**. In addition to the site adjacency, OTV devices maintain a second adjacency, named **overlay adjacency**, established via the join interfaces across the Layer 3 network domain. To enable this new functionality, it is now mandatory to configure each OTV device with a site-identifier value. All edge devices that are in the same site must be configured with the same site identifier. This site identifier is advertised in IS-IS hello packets sent over both the overlay and on the site VLAN. The combination of the site identifier and the IS-IS system ID is used to identify a neighbor edge device in the same site.

OTV Control Plane

One of the key differentiators of OTV is the use of the control plane protocol, which runs between OTV edge devices. The control protocol function is to advertise MAC address reachability information instead of using data plane learning, which relies on flooding of Layer 2 traffic across the transport infrastructure. To be able to exchange MAC reachability information, OTV edge devices must become adjacent to each other. This can happen in two ways, depending on the nature of the transport infrastructure:

■ **Multicast-enabled transport:** If the transport infrastructure is enabled for multicast, we use a multicast group to exchange control protocol messages between the OTV edge devices.

■ **Unicast-enabled transport:** If the transport infrastructure is not enabled for multicast, starting from NX-OS 5.2(1), you can use one or more OTV edge devices as an adjacency server. All OTV edge devices belonging to a specific overlay register with the available list of the adjacency servers.

Multicast-Enabled Transport Infrastructure

When the transport infrastructure is enabled for multicast, all OTV edge devices should be configured to join a specific any source multicast (ASM) group. The entire edge device will be a source and a receiver on that ASM group. If the service provider owns the transport infrastructure, the enterprise must negotiate the use of this ASM group with the service provider. The following steps explain the sequence, which leads to the discovery of all OTV edge devices belonging to a specific overlay:

1. Each OTV edge device sends an Internet Control Message Protocol (IGMP) report to join the specific ASM group, which is used to carry control protocol exchanges. The edge devices join the group as hosts, leveraging the join interface. This happens without enabling Protocol Independent Multicast (PIM) on this interface; only IGMPv3 is enabled on the interface using the **IP IGMP version 3** command. You need only to specify the ASM group to be used and associate it with a given overlay interface.

2. The OTV control protocol running on each OTV edge device generates hello packets that need to be sent to all other OTV edge devices. This is required to communicate the protocol's existence and to trigger the establishment of control plane adjacencies within the same overlay.

3. The OTV hello messages are sent across the logical overlay to reach all OTV remote edge devices. For this to happen, the original frames must be OTV encapsulated, adding an external IP-header. The source IP address in the external header is set to the IP address of the join interface of the edge device, whereas the destination is the multicast address of the ASM group dedicated to carry the control protocol. The resulting multicast frame is then sent to the join interface toward the Layer 3 network domain.

4. The multicast frames are carried across the transport and optimally replicated to reach all the OTV edge devices that joined that multicast group.

5. The receiving OTV edge devices decapsulate the packets.

6. The hellos are passed to the control protocol process.

The same process occurs in the opposite direction, and the end result is the creation of OTV control protocol adjacencies between all edge devices. The use of the ASM group to transport the hello messages allows the edge devices to discover each other as if they were deployed on a shared LAN segment.

After enabling the OTV overlay interface, the OTV control plane protocol is enabled; it does not require a specific configuration command to do it.

NOTE   To enable OTV functionality, you must use the feature otv command; the device does not display OTV commands until you enable the feature.

The routing protocol used to implement the OTV control plane is IS-IS. It was selected because it is a standard-based protocol, originally designed with the capability of carrying MAC address information in the TLV. For security, it is possible to leverage the IS-IS HMAC-MD5 authentication feature to add an HMAC-MD5 digest to each OTV control protocol message. This prevents unauthorized routing messages from being injected into the network routing domain.

After the OTV devices discover each other, the next step is to exchange MAC address reachability information.

1.   The OTV edge device learns new MAC addresses on its internal interface using traditional data plane learning.

2.   An OTV update message is created containing information for the MAC address learned through the internal interface. The message is OTV encapsulated and sent into the OTV transport infrastructure. The source IP address in the external header is set to the IP address of the join interface of the OTV edge device. The IP destination address of the packet in the outer header is the multicast group used for OTV control protocol exchanges.

3.   The OTV update is replicated in the transport infrastructure and delivered to all the remote OTV edge devices on the same overlay. The OTV edge devices receiving the update decapsulate the message and deliver it to the OTV control process.

4.   The MAC address reachability information is imported to the MAC address tables of the edge devices. The only difference with the traditional MAC address table entry is that for the MAC address in the remote data center, instead of pointing to a physical interface, it will point to the joint interface of the remote OTV edge device.

Unicast-Enabled Transport Infrastructure

OTV can be deployed with a unicast-only transport infrastructure; the unicast deployment of OTV is used when a multicast-enabled transport infrastructure is not an option. The OTV control plane over unicast transport infrastructure works in the same way the multicast transport works. The only difference is that each OTV edge device must create a copy of the control plane packet and send it to each remote OTV edge device.

To be able to send control protocol messages to all the OTV edge devices, each OTV edge device needs to know the list of the other devices that are part of the same overlay. This is achieved by having one or more OTV edge devices as an adjacency server. Each OTV edge device must join a specific overlay register with the adjacency server. When the adjacency server receives hello messages from the remote OTV edge devices, it builds the list of all the OTV edge devices that are part of the same overlay. The list is called a unicast-replication list. This list is periodically sent to all the listed OTV edge devices.

Data Plane for Unicast Traffic

After all OTV edge devices are part of an overlay establish adjacency and MAC address reachability information is exchanged, traffic can start flowing across the overlay. There are two types of Layer 2 communication: intrasite (traffic within the same site) and intersite (traffic between two different sites on the same overlay). The following process details the communication:

■ **Intrasite unicast communication:** Intrasite means that both servers that need to talk to each other reside in the same data center. As shown in Figure 5-2, MAC 1 needs to talk to MAC 2. They both belong to Site A, and they are in the same VLAN. When a Layer 2 frame is received at the aggregation device, which is the OTV edge device in this case, a normal Layer 2 lookup determines how to reach MAC 2; the information in the MAC table points to Eth1, and the frame is delivered to the destination.

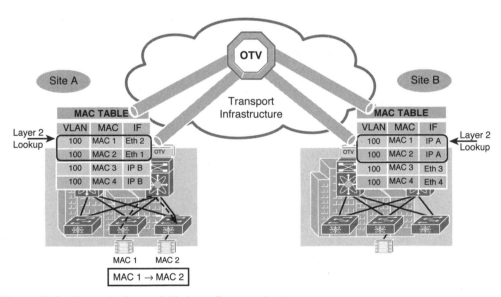

Figure 5-2 *Intrasite Layer 2 Unicast Communication*

■ **Intersite unicast communication:** Intersite means that the servers that need to talk to each other reside in different data centers but belong to the same overlay. As shown in Figure 5-3, MAC 1 needs to talk to MAC 3. MAC 1 belongs to Site A and MAC 3 belongs to Site B. The following procedure details the process for MAC 1 to establish communication with MAC 3:

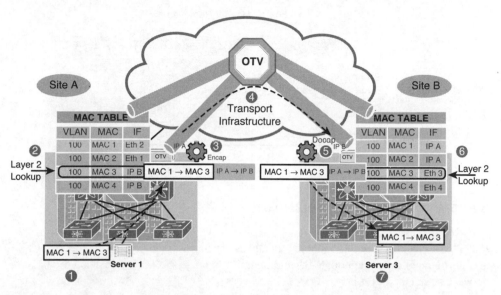

Figure 5-3   *Intersite Layer 2 Unicast Communication*

1. The Layer 2 frame is received at the aggregation device, which is the OTV edge device at Site A in this case; a normal Layer 2 lookup happens. MAC 3 in the MAC table in Site A points to the IP address of the remote OTV edge device in Site B.

2. The OTV edge device in Site A encapsulates the Layer 2 frame; the source IP of the outer header is the IP address of the joint interface of the OTV edge device in Site A. The destination IP address in the outer header is the IP address of the joint interface of the remote OTV edge device in Site B; after that, a normal IP unicast packet is sent across the transport infrastructure.

3. When the remote OTV edge device receives the IP packet, it decapsulates it and exposes the original Layer 2 packet.

4. The OTV edge device at Site B performs another Layer 2 lookup on the original Ethernet frame. This time, MAC 3 points to a local physical interface, and the frame is delivered to the MAC 3 destination.

Figure 5-4 shows the OTV data plane encapsulation on the original Ethernet frame. The OTV encapsulation increases the overall MTU size by 42 bytes. The OTV edge device removes the CRC and the 802.1Q fields from the original Layer 2 frame and adds an OTV shim (containing the VLAN and the overlay information) and an external IP-header.

All OTV control and data plane packets originate from an OTV edge device with the don't fragment (DF) bit set. In a Layer 2 domain, the assumption is that all intermediate LAN segments support at least the configured interface MTU size of the host. This means that mechanisms like path MTU discovery (PMTUD) are not an option in this case.

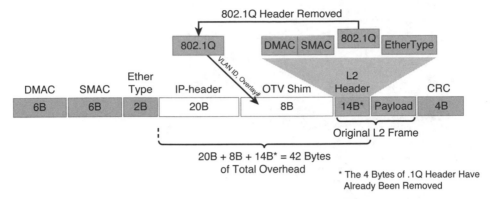

Figure 5-4   *OTV Data Plane Encapsulation*

NOTE   Nexus 7000 does not support fragmentation and reassembly capabilities. That means you need to accommodate the additional 42 bytes in the MTU size along the path between source and destination OTV edge devices.

There are two ways to overcome the issue of the increased MTU size:

- Configure a larger MTU on all interfaces where traffic will be encapsulated, including the join interface and any links between the data centers that are in the OTV transport.

- Lower the MTU on all servers so that the total packet size does not exceed the MTU of the interfaces where traffic is encapsulated.

Data Plane for Multicast Traffic

You might be faced with situations in which there is a need to establish multicast communication between remote sites. This can happen when the multicast sources are deployed in one site and the multicast receivers are in another remote site. In the "OTV Control Plane" section, we distinguished between two scenarios in which the transport infrastructure is multicast enabled or not.

The multicast traffic needs to flow across the OTV overlay; in this case, we use a set of source-specific multicast (SSM) groups in the transport to carry the Layer 2 multicast streams. These groups are different from the ASM groups used for the OTV control plane.

Step 1 starts when a multicast source is activated in a given data center site. The mapping happens between the site multicast groups and the SSM group range in the transport infrastructure, which is explained in the following steps and shown in Figure 5-5.

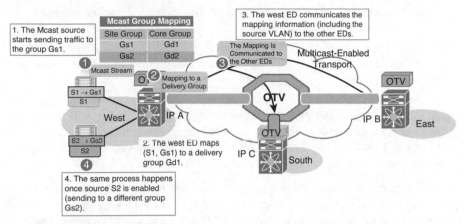

Figure 5-5 *Mapping of the Site Multicast Group to the SSM Range*

1. A multicast source is activated on the west side and starts streaming traffic to the multicast group Gs.

2. The local OTV edge device receives the first multicast frame and creates a mapping between the group Gs and a specific SSM group Gd available in the transport infrastructure. The range of SSM groups to be used to carry Layer 2 multicast data streams is specified during the configuration of the overlay interface.

3. The OTV control protocol is used to communicate the Gs-to-Gd mapping to all remote OTV edge devices. The mapping information specifies the VLAN (VLAN A) to which the multicast source belongs and the IP address of the OTV edge device that created the mapping.

In the figure, Step 2 starts when a receiver in the remote site deployed in the same VLAN as the multicast source decides to join the multicast group Gs, which is explained in the following steps and shown in Figure 5-6.

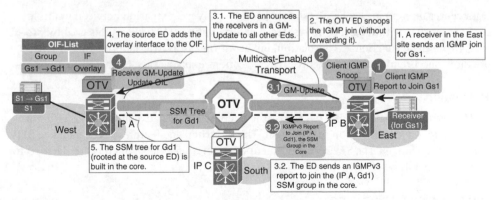

Figure 5-6 *Receiver Joining Multicast Group Gs*

1. The client sends an IGMP report inside the east site to join the Gs group.

2. The OTV edge device snoops the IGMP message and realizes there is an active receiver in the site interested in group Gs, belonging to VLAN A.

3. The OTV device sends an OTV control protocol message to all the remote edge devices to communicate this information.

4. The remote edge device in the west side receives the GM-Update and updates its outgoing interface list (OIL) with the information that group Gs needs to be delivered across the OTV overlay.

5. The edge device in the east side finds the mapping information previously received from the OTV edge device in the west side identified by the IP address IP A. The east edge device, in turn, sends an IGMPv3 report to the transport to join the (IP A, Gd) SSM group. This allows building an SSM tree (group Gd) across the transport infrastructure that can be used to deliver the multicast stream Gs.

When the OTV transport infrastructure is not multicast enabled, Layer 2 multicast traffic can be sent across the overlay using head-end replication by the OTV edge device deployed in the DC where the multicast source is enabled. IGMP snooping is used to ensure that Layer 2 multicast traffic is sent to the remote DC only when an active receiver exists. This helps to reduce the amount of head-end replication.

When we have a multicast-enabled transport, we leverage the same ASM multicast groups in the transport already used for OTV control protocol. Broadcast traffic will be handled the same way as the OTV hello messages. For a unicast only transport infrastructure, head-end replication performed on the OTV device in the site originating the broadcast would ensure traffic delivery to all the remote OTV edge devices that are part of the unicast-only list.

NOTE Cisco NX-OS 6.2(2) introduces a new optional feature called *dedicated broadcast group*. This feature enables the administrator to configure a dedicated broadcast group to be used by OTV in the multicast core network. By separating the two multicast addresses, you can now enforce different QoS treatments for data traffic and control traffic.

Failure Isolation

Data center interconnect solutions should provide a Layer 2 extension between multiple data center sites without giving up resilience and stability. OTV achieves this goal by providing four main functions: STP isolation, unknown Unicast traffic suppression, ARP suppression, and broadcast policy control. These sections explains each of these functions.

STP Isolation

OTV does not forward STP BPDUs across the overlay. This is native in OTV; you do not need to add any configuration to achieve it. This control plane feature makes each site STP domain independent. The STP root placement configuration and parameters are decided for each site separately.

Unknown Unicast Handling

OTV control protocol advertises MAC address reachability information between OTV edge devices. If the MAC address is in a remote data center, the OTV control protocol will map the MAC address to the destination IP address of the join interface of the remote data center.

When the OTV edge device receives a frame destined to a MAC address that is not in the MAC address table, the Layer 2 traffic is flooded out the internal interfaces. This is the normal behavior of a classical Ethernet interface; however, that does not happen via the overlay. It is assumed that no silent hosts are available, and eventually the OTV edge device will learn the MAC address of the host and advertise it to the other OTV edge devices on the overlay. As a workaround, you can statically add the MAC address of the silent host in the OTV edge device MAC address table.

Starting with NX-OS 6.2(2), selective unknown unicast flooding based on the MAC address is supported. This feature is important, for example, in the case of Microsoft network load balancing services (NLBS), which require the flooding of Layer 2 traffic to function. The command **otv flood mac** *mac-address* **vlan** *vlan-id* must be added; otherwise, all unknown unicast frames will not be forwarded across the logical overlay.

ARP Optimization

ARP optimization is one of the native features in OTV that helps to reduce the amount of traffic sent across the transport infrastructure. When a device in one of the data centers, such as Site A, sends out an ARP request, which is a broadcast message, this request is sent across the OTV overlay to Site B. The ARP request eventually reaches the destination machine, which in turn creates an ARP reply message and sends it back to the originating host. When a subsequent ARP request originates to the same IP address in Site A, it will not be forwarded across the OTV overlay but will be locally answered by the OTV edge device.

The OTV edge device in Site A can snoop the ARP reply and cache the contained mapping information. This reduces the amount of traffic sent across the transport infrastructure.

> **NOTE**   For the ARP caching, consider the interaction between ARP and CAM table aging timers because incorrect settings can lead to traffic black holing. The ARP aging timer on the OTV edge devices should always be set lower than the CAM table aging timer.

If the default gateway of the host is placed on a device different from Nexus 7000, you should put the ARP aging timer of the device to a value lower than its MAC aging timer. By default on the Nexus 7000, the OTV ARP aging timer is 480 seconds, and the MAC aging timer is 1800 seconds.

OTV Multihoming

Multihoming is a native function in OTV in which two or more OTV edge devices provide a LAN extension for a given site. Having more than one OTV edge device at a given site, because OTV does not send spanning-tree BPDUs across the overlay, can lead to an end-to-end loop.

To be able to support multihoming, and to avoid creating an end-to-end loop, an AED concept is introduced. The AED role is elected on a per-VLAN basis at a given site. OTV uses a VLAN called *Site VLAN* within a site to detect adjacency with other OTV edge devices. In addition to the site adjacency, OTV maintains a second adjacency named *overlay adjacency*, which happens via the OTV join interface across the Layer 3 network domain. To enable this functionality, the OTV device must be configured with a site-identifier value. All OTV edge devices in the same site are configured with the same site-identifier value. The site identifier is advertised through IS-IS hello packets. The combination of the system ID and the site identifier identifies a neighbor edge device belonging to the same site.

First Hop Redundancy Protocol Isolation

Another capability introduced by OTV is to filter the First Hop Redundancy Protocol (FHRP—HSRP, VRRP, and so on) messages across the overlay. This is necessary to localize the gateway at a given site and optimize the outbound traffic from that site. Because we have the same VLANs in multiple sites, if we do not filter the hello messages between the sites, it will lead to the election of a single default gateway for a given VLAN that will lead to a suboptimal path for the outbound traffic.

It is important that you enable the filtering of FHRP messages across the overlay; it allows the use of the same FHRP configuration in different sites. In this case, the same default gateway is available, and it is characterized by the same virtual IP and virtual MAC addresses in each data center. In this case, the outbound traffic will be able to follow the optimal and shortest path, always using the local default gateway.

OTV Configuration Example with Multicast Transport

This configuration example addresses OTV deployment at the aggregation layer with a multicast transport infrastructure. Examples 5-1 through 5-5 use a dedicated VDC to do the OTV function. It is assumed the VDC is already created, so you will not see steps to create the Nexus 7000 VDC. You will be using VLANs 10 and 5 to be extended to VLAN 15 as the site VLAN. Figure 5-7 shows the topology used.

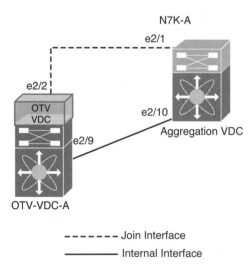

Figure 5-7 *OTV Topology for Multicast Transport*

Example 5-1 *Sample Configuration for How to Enable OTV VDC VLANs*

```
OTV-VDC-A(config)# vlan 5-10, 15
```

Example 5-2 *Sample Configuration of the Join Interface*

```
OTV-VDC-A(config)# interface ethernet 2/2
OTV-VDC-A(config-if)# description [ OTV Join-Interface ]
OTV-VDC-A(config-if)# ip address 172.26.255.98/30
OTV-VDC-A(config-if)# ip igmp version 3
OTV-VDC-A(config-if)# no shutdown
```

Example 5-3 *Sample Configuration of the Point-to-Point Interface on the Aggregation Layer Facing the Join Interface*

```
AGG-VDC-A(config)# interface ethernet 2/1
AGG-VDC-A(config-if)# description [ Connected to OTV Join-Interface ]
AGG-VDC-A(config-if)# ip address 172.26.255.99/30
AGG-VDC-A(config-if)# ip pim sparse-mode
AGG-VDC-A(config-if)# ip igmp version 3
AGG-VDC-A(config-if)# no shutdown
```

Example 5-4 *Sample PIM Configuration on the Aggregation VDC*

```
AGG-VDC-A# show running pim
feature pim
interface ethernet 2/1
  ip pim sparse-mode
interface ethernet 1/10
  ip pim sparse-mode
interface ethernet 1/20
  ip pim sparse-mode
ip pim rp-address 172.26.255.101
ip pim ssm range 232.0.0.0/8
```

Example 5-5 *Sample Configuration of the Internal Interfaces*

```
interface ethernet 2/10
description [ OTV Internal Interface ]
switchport
switchport mode trunk
switchport trunk allowed vlan 5-10, 15
no shutdown
```

Before creating and configuring the overlay interface, you must do certain configurations. The following shows a sample configuration for the overlay interface for a multicast-enabled transport infrastructure:

Step 1. Enable the OTV feature; otherwise, you will not see OTV commands:

```
OTV-VDC-A(config)# feature otv
```

Step 2. Configure the OTV site identifier. (It should be the same for all the OTV edge devices belonging to the same site.)

```
OTV-VDC-A(config)# otv site-identifier 0x1
```

Step 3. Configure the OTV site VLAN:

```
OTV-VDC-A(config)# otv site-vlan 15
```

Step 4. Create and configure the overlay interface:

```
OTV-VDC-A(config)# interface overlay 1
OTV-VDC-A(config-if)# otv join-interface ethernet 2/2
```

Step 5. Configure the OTV control group:

```
OTV-VDC-A(config-if)# otv control-group 239.1.1.1
```

Step 6. Configure the OTV data group:

```
OTV-VDC-A(config-if)# otv data-group 232.1.1.0/26
```

Step 7. Configure the VLAN range to be extended across the overlay:

```
OTV-VDC-A(config-if)# otv extend-vlan 5-10
```

Step 8. Create a static default route to point out to the join interface. This is required to allow communication from the OTV VDC to the Layer 3 network domain:

```
OTV-VDC-A(config)# ip route 0.0.0.0/0 172.26.255.99
```

Step 9. You must bring up the overlay interface; it is shut down by default:

```
OTV-VDC-A(config-if)# no shutdown
```

To confirm that the OTV edge device joined the overlay, run the **Show otv overlay 1** command as shown in Example 5-6.

Example 5-6 *Verify That the OTV Edge Device Joined the Overlay*

```
OTV-VDC-A# show otv overlay 1
OTV Overlay Information
Overlay interface Overlay1
 VPN name                 : Overlay1
 VPN state                : UP
 Extended vlans           : 5-10 (Total:6)
 Control group            : 239.1.1.1
 Data group range(s)      : 232.1.1.0/26
 Join interface(s)        : Eth2/2 (172.26.255.98)
 Site vlan                : 15 (up)
OTV-VDC-A# show otv adjacency
Overlay Adjacency database
```

```
Overlay-Interface Overlay1 :
Hostname          System-ID      Dest Addr          Up Time    Adj-State
OTV-VDC-C         0022.5579.7c42 172.26.255.90      1w0d       UP
OTV-VDC-D         0022.5579.36c2 172.26.255.94      1w0d       UP
```

After confirming that the OTV edge device joined the overlay, check to make sure that the OTV edge device started learning MAC addresses by running **Show otv route** as shown in Example 5-7.

Example 5-7   *Check the MAC Addresses Learned Through the Overlay*

```
OTV-VDC-A# show otv route
OTV Unicast MAC Routing Table For Overlay1
VLAN MAC-Address     Metric Uptime   Owner     Next-hop(s)
---- -------------- ------ -------- --------- -----------
10   0000.0c07.ac64 1      00:00:55 site      ethernet 2/10
10   001b.54c2.3dc1 1      00:00:55 Overlay   OTV-VDC-C
```

OTV Configuration Example with Unicast Transport

Examples 5-8 through 5-13 show sample configurations for an OTV deployment in a unicast-only transport. The first step is to define the role of the adjacency server, one of the OTV edge devices. The second step is to do the required configuration on the OTV edge device not acting as an adjacency server, meaning acting as a client. The client devices are configured with the address of the adjacent server. When a new site is added, only the OTV edge devices for the new site need to be configured with adjacency server addresses. It is always recommended to configure a pair with a secondary adjacency server in another site for redundancy. Figure 5-8 shows the topology that will be used in Examples 5-8 through 5-13.

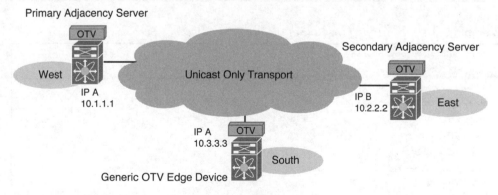

Figure 5-8   *OTV Topology for Unicast Transport*

Example 5-8 *Primary Adjacency Server Configuration*

```
feature otv
otv site-identifier 0x1
otv site-vlan 15
interface Overlay1
   otv join-interface e2/2
   otv adjacency-server unicast-only
   otv extend-vlan 5-10
```

Example 5-9 *Secondary Adjacency Server Configuration*

```
feature otv
otv site-identifier 0x2
otv site-vlan 15
interface Overlay1
   otv join-interface e1/2
   otv adjacency-server unicast-only
   otv use-adjacency-server 10.1.1.1 unicast-only
   otv extend-vlan 5-10
```

Example 5-10 *Client OTV Edge Device Configuration*

```
feature otv
otv site-identifier 0x3
otv site-vlan 15
interface Overlay1
   otv join-interface e1/1
   otv use-adjacency-server 10.1.1.1 10.2.2.2 unicast-only
   otv extend-vlan 5-10
```

Example 5-11 *Identifying the Role of the Primary Adjacency Server*

```
Primary_AS# show otv overlay 1
OTV Overlay Information
Site Identifier 0000.0000.0001
Overlay interface Overlay1
 VPN name              : Overlay1
 VPN state             : UP
 Extended vlans        : 5-10 (Total:6)
 Join interface(s)     : E2/2 (10.1.1.1)
 Site vlan             : 15 (up)
 AED-Capable           : Yes
 Capability            : Unicast-Only
 Is Adjacency Server   : Yes
 Adjacency Server(s)   : [None] / [None]
```

Example 5-12 *Identifying the Role of the Secondary Adjacency Server*

```
Secondary_AS# show otv overlay 1
OTV Overlay Information
Site Identifier 0000.0000.0002
Overlay interface Overlay1
 VPN name                  : Overlay1
 VPN state                 : UP
 Extended vlans            : 5-10 (Total:6)
 Join interface(s)         : E1/2 (10.2.2.2)
 Site vlan                 : 15 (up)
 AED-Capable               : Yes
 Capability                : Unicast-Only
 Is Adjacency Server       : Yes
 Adjacency Server(s)       : 10.1.1.1 / [None]
```

Example 5-13 *Identifying the Role of the Client OTV Edge Device*

```
Generic_OTV# show otv overlay 1
OTV Overlay Information
Site Identifier 0000.0000.0003
Overlay interface Overlay1
 VPN name                  : Overlay1
 VPN state                 : UP
 Extended vlans            : 5-10 (Total:6)
 Join interface(s)         : E1/1 (10.3.3.3)
 Site vlan                 : 15 (up)
 AED-Capable               : Yes
 Capability                : Unicast-Only
 Is Adjacency Server       : No
 Adjacency Server(s)       : 10.1.1.1 / 10.2.2.2
```

Virtual Extensible LAN

In today's data centers, there is an increased demand on server virtualization. A virtualized server today runs more than one virtual machine (VM). In most cases, each VM will have more than one network adapter, which eventually will be placed in its own VLAN. Having VM sprawl in a data center will increase the demand on VLANs. Using the standard 802.1Q, you can have up to 4094 VLANs, but that will not be enough.

In many cases in big data centers and in public clouds, customers ask for multitenancy, which is a way to isolate traffic between a VLAN or a group of VLANs. For administration purposes or for security reasons, sometimes there is a need to use the same VLAN IDs or overlapping IP addressing. Virtual extensible LAN (VXLAN) can solve this issue, which we will discuss later in this chapter.

Current data centers use STP. To avoid loops in Layer 2 environments, STP needs to block redundant links. Despite there being many ways to configure STP to benefit from redundant links, it is still inefficient and requires a special way to configure it. Because VXLAN can extend Layer 2 over Layer 3, we can have all the links be forwarding traffic and use equal-cost multipath (ECMP) to load-balance traffic on those links.

VXLAN is a MAC in IP/UDP encapsulation that allows the overlay of the Layer 2 network over an IP network. We call each overlay a segment. We identify each segment by a 24-bit segment ID, as shown in Figure 5-9. We call the segment ID a VXLAN network identifier (VNI). This VNI allows us to create 16M VXLAN segments.

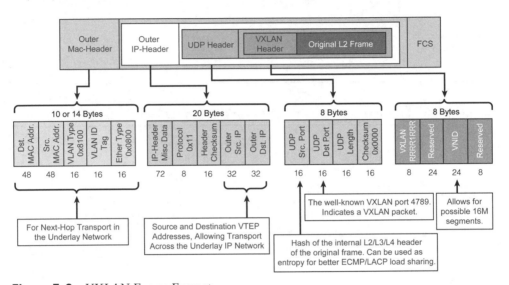

Figure 5-9 *VXLAN Frame Format*

VXLAN Terminology

VTEP

VTEP stands for VXLAN tunnel end point. VXLAN tunnels originate at the VTEP and terminate at the VTEP, as shown in Figure 5-10. This is where the encapsulation and de-encapsulation of VXLAN traffic happen. The VTEP function has two interfaces: one Layer 2 interface in the local LAN to communicate with the local endpoints, and one Layer 3 interface to communicate with other VTEPs in the IP transport network.

In a virtual environment, when VTEPs are located in the hypervisors and a tunnel starts and ends at the hypervisor level, it is known as host-based overlay. VTEPs can also be located on physical switches; this is known as network-based overlay. Today, data centers usually have both virtual endpoints and physical endpoints where the VTEPs run in the hypervisors and on local physical switches. In this case, the overlay is called hybrid overlay.

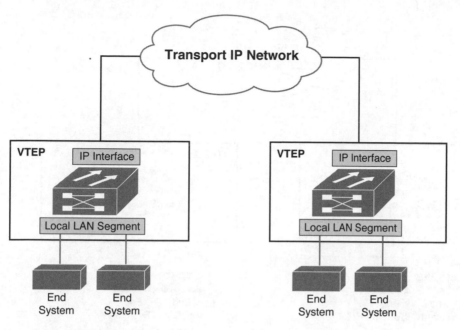

Figure 5-10   *VXLAN Gateway Function*

VNID

VNID stands for VXLAN network identifier. As previously shown in Figure 5-9, VXLAN has an 8-byte VXLAN header that consists of a 24-bit VNID. The VNID is used to uniquely identify a Layer 2 segment and maintain Layer 2 isolation between segments.

VXLAN Gateway Types

A VXLAN gateway is a function of the VTEP device to connect different VXLAN segments or connect between VXLAN segments and VLANs. There are two types that I will discuss next.

VXLAN Bridging

VXLAN bridging is a way to extend VLAN to VXLAN or a VXLAN to VXLAN. The idea in bridging here is that it is always going within the same IP subnet. Figure 5-11 shows this scenario.

VXLAN Routing

VXLAN routing is a way to extend VLAN to VXLAN or one VXLAN segment to another VXLAN segment. The idea in routing is that you need to do additional lookup in the inner IP-header. Figure 5-12 shows this scenario.

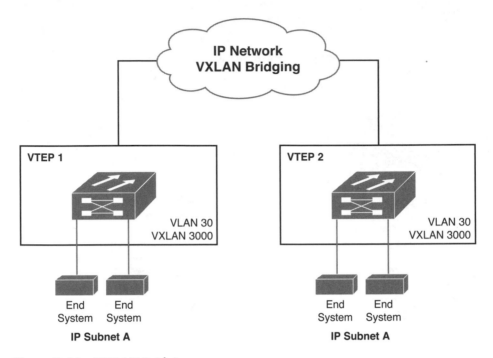

Figure 5-11   *VXLAN Bridging*

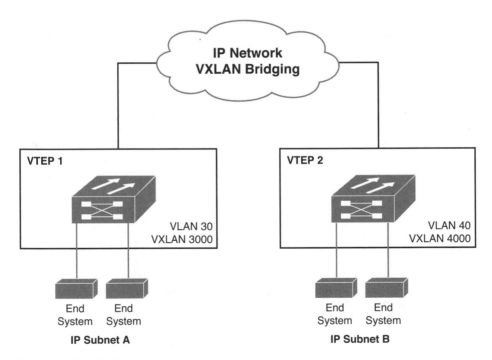

Figure 5-12   *VXLAN Routing*

VXLAN Packet Forwarding

As shown in Figure 5-13, Host-A wants to talk to Host-B. Both belong to VXLAN segment 10. In this case, we are doing VXLAN bridging. It is assumed that both VTEPs already have the MAC-to-VTEP mapping. (I will explain the methods of address learning later in this chapter.)

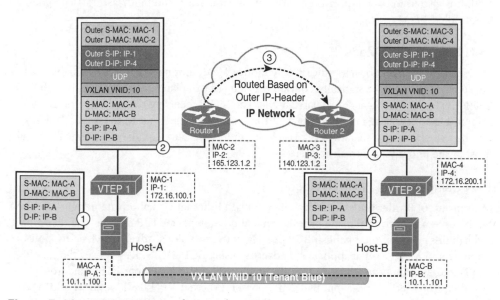

Figure 5-13 *VXLAN Forwarding Packet Walk*

- Host-A creates an Ethernet frame with MAC-A as the source MAC and MAC-B for Host-B as the destination MAC and sends it to VTEP-1.

- VTEP-1 checks its mapping table and finds that MAC-B is learned through VXLAN VTEP-2.

- VTEP-1 does VXLAN encapsulation and adds the outer IP-header, UDP header, and outer MAC-header to send to the next hop router, which is Router-1.

- Packets are routed to Router-2 in the IP network based on the outer IP-header.

- Router-2 does a lookup on the IP address of VTEP-2 and adds the outer MAC-header to send the packet to VTEP-2.

- VTEP-2 receives the packet it removes from the outer MAC-header: the outer IP-header and the VXLAN header. Then it forwards the packet to Host-B, based on the Dest MAC in the inner MAC-header.

VXLAN VTEP Discovery and Address Learning

There are multiple ways to build the VXLAN mapping database, which is VTEP IP address-to-MAC address mapping. It is essential to be able to forward traffic. The VXLAN standard, which is defined in RFC 7384, discusses two types: data plane learning and control plane learning. In addition to these two methods, you can have a database to hold this information. The database concept is used in ACI.

VXLAN Data Plane Learning

VXLAN data plane learning utilizes flood-and learn mechanisms to build its VTEP-to-MAC address information. It requires multicast to be running in the underlying network to reduce flooding scope. Each VNI is mapped to a multicast group, so only the hosts participating in a specific VXLAN segment will receive the traffic. The multicast group is mapped to the VNI. It is also used to transport broadcast, unknown unicast, and multicast traffic (sometimes called *BUM traffic*).

VXLAN Unicast-Only Mode

This scenario is also known as unicast-only mode. We do not need a multicast-enabled transport. VTEPs can be statically configured, or a control plane can announce to each VTEP the list of VTEPs and associated VNIs. The VTEP receiving the BUM traffic is responsible for creating multiple copies of the traffic and sending it to the remote VTEPs, which are mapped to a specific VNI. Using this mode, we can relax the requirement of multicast in the underlying infrastructure.

VXLAN Using Control Plane Protocol

Multiprotocol Border Gateway Protocol (MP-BGP) Ethernet virtual private network (EVPN) can be used as the control plane protocol. It can provide peer VTEP discovery and end-host reachability information, establish BGP peering between VTEPs, advertise MAC-to-VNI mapping and MAC-to-IP mapping, and advertise using BGP EVPN. EVPN uses the L2VPN EVPN address family to advertise this information. EVPN is based on IETF standards, including **draft-ietf-l2vpn-evpn**, BGP MPLS-based Ethernet VPN (EVPN), **draft-sd-l2vpn-evpn-overlay**, a network virtualization overlay solution using EVPN, and **draft-sajassi-l2vpn-evpn-inter-subnet-forwarding-03**, IP Inter-Subnet Forwarding in EVPN.

Network Virtualization Using Generic Routing Encapsulation

Network Virtualization Using Generic Routing Encapsulation (NVGRE) is like VXLAN; it allows you to create Layer 2 overlay networks on top of Layer 3 underlying networks. You basically tunnel Ethernet frames in an IP packet and send them over an IP network. As shown in Figure 5-14, NVGRE has a 24-bit virtual subnet identifier (VSID). Similar to VXLAN, it can provide up to 16 million segments. Unlike VXLAN, which uses the VXLAN header, NVGRE uses generic routing encapsulation (GRE). GRE was developed by Cisco long ago and made available in many hardware platforms. For forwarding broadcast, multicast, and unknown unicast (BUM) traffic, the NVGRE encapsulation uses IP multicast, where each VSID is mapped to a multicast group. Multiple VSIDs can share the same multicast groups. To distribute the location and VSID information, NVGRE draft RFC 7637 (**draft-sridharan-virtualization-nvgre-01**) suggests the usage of data plane learning or control plane learning.

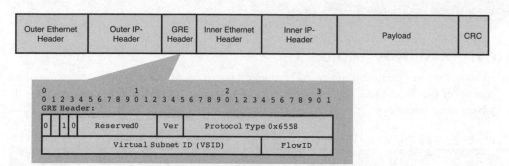

Figure 5-14 *NVGRE Frame Format*

A main difference between VXLAN and NVGRE is that the NVGRE header includes an optional flow ID field. In multipathing deployments, network routers and switches that can parse this header can use this field with the VSID to add flow-based entropy, although this feature requires additional hardware capabilities.

Reference List

Data Center Overlay Technologies: http://www.cisco.com/c/en/us/products/collateral/switches/nexus-9000-series-switches/white-paper-c11-730116.html

Overlay Transport Virtualization (OTV): http://www.cisco.com/c/en/us/solutions/data-center-virtualization/overlay-transport-virtualization-otv/index.html

Cisco Overlay Transport Virtualization Technology Introduction and Deployment Considerations: http://www.cisco.com/c/en/us/td/docs/solutions/Enterprise/Data_Center/DCI/whitepaper/DCI3_OTV_Intro/DCI_1.html

VXLAN Overview: Cisco Nexus 9000 Series Switches: http://www.cisco.com/c/en/us/products/collateral/switches/nexus-9000-series-switches/white-paper-c11-729383.html

VXLAN Network with MP-BGP EVPN Control Plane Design Guide: http://www.cisco.com/c/en/us/products/collateral/switches/ncxus-9000-series-switches/guide-c07-734107.html

Cisco Nexus 1000V Switch for Microsoft Hyper-V: http://www.cisco.com/c/en/us/products/collateral/switches/nexus-1000v-switch-microsoft-hyper-v/qa_c67-727680.html

Exam Preparation Tasks

Review All Key Topics

Review the most important topics in the chapter, noted with the key topics icon in the outer margin of the page. Table 5-2 lists a reference of these key topics and the page numbers on which each is found.

Table 5-2   Key Topics for Chapter 5

Key Topic Element	Description	Page
Section	"OTV Terminology"	164
Section	"OTV Control Plane"	166
Section	"Unknown Unicast Handling"	172
Section	"OTV Multihoming"	173
Section	"VXLAN Terminology"	180
Section	"VXLAN Gateway Types"	181
Section	"VXLAN VTEP Discovery and Address Learning"	183
Section	"Network Virtualization Using Generic Routing Encapsulation"	184

Define Key Terms

Define the following key terms from this chapter, and check your answers in the Glossary:

Overlay Transport Virtualization (OTV), Data Center Interconnect (DCI), Ethernet over Multiprotocol Label Switching (EoMPLS), Multiprotocol Label Switching (MPLS), Virtual Private LAN Services (VPLS), Coarse Wavelength-Division Multiplexing (CWDM), Spanning-tree Protocol (STP), Authoritative Edge Device (AED), Virtual LAN (VLAN), Bridge Protocol Data Unit (BPDU), Media Access Control (MAC), Address Resolution Protocol (ARP), Virtual Router Redundancy Protocol (VRRP), First Hop Redundancy Protocol (FHRP), Hot Standby Router Protocol (HSRP), Internet Group Management Protocol (IGMP), Protocol Independent Multicast (PIM), Virtual Extensible LAN (VXLAN), VXLAN Tunnel End Point, VXLAN Network Identifier (VNID), Network Virtualization Using Generic Routing Encapsulation (NVGRE), Virtual Subnet Identifier (VSID)

This chapter covers the following exam topics:

2.3 Describe the benefits and perform simple troubleshooting of VDC STP

2.4 Compare and contrast the default and management VRFs

3.1 Describe, configure, and verify FEX connectivity

CHAPTER 6

Virtualizing Cisco Network Devices

There are two types of device virtualization when it comes to Nexus devices. The first is how to partition one physical switch and make it appear as multiple switches, each with its own administrative domain and security policy. That approach has its own benefits and business requirements.

The other option is how to make multiple switches appear as if they are one big modular switch. That approach has its own benefits and business requirements, too. This chapter covers the virtualization capabilities of the Nexus switches using virtual device context (VDC) and network interface virtualization (NIV).

This chapter covers the virtualization capabilities of the Nexus switches using virtual device context (VDC). VDC is a feature on the Nexus 7000 switches, enabling true device virtualization; each VDC will have its own management domain, allowing the management plane to be virtualized.

VDCs are treated as separate STP bridges. All STP rules apply, and all verification commands apply when dealing with VDCs in Layer 2 environments. To further virtualize each VDC, I will cover VRFs (Virtual Routing and Forwarding). Multiple VRFs can be configured in a single VDC. Each VRF has its own forwarding table and routing process.

This chapter also covers network interface virtualization (NIV). Cisco Nexus 2000 utilizes the NIV technology. Cisco Nexus 2000 cannot operate in a standalone mode; it needs a parent switch to connect to. Part of NIV is the Adapter-FEX and VM-FEX, which also uses the NIV technology. Adapter-FEX can be extended to the hypervisor while VM-FEX is extended to the virtual machine running on the hypervisor itself.

"Do I Know This Already?" Quiz

The "Do I Know This Already?" quiz enables you to assess whether you should read this entire chapter thoroughly or jump to the "Exam Preparation Tasks" section. If you are in doubt about your answers to these questions or your own assessment of your knowledge of the topics, read the entire chapter. Table 6-1 lists the major headings in this chapter and their corresponding "Do I Know This Already?" quiz questions. You can find the answers in Appendix A, "Answers to the 'Do I Know This Already?' Quizzes."

Table 6-1 "Do I Know This Already?" Section-to-Question Mapping

Foundation Topics Section	Questions
"Describing VDCs on the Cisco Nexus 7000 Series Switch"	1–4, 8, 9
"Describing Network Interface Virtualization"	5–7, 10

CAUTION   The goal of self-assessment is to gauge your mastery of the topics in this chapter. If you do not know the answer to a question or are only partially sure of the answer, you should mark that question as wrong for purposes of the self-assessment. Giving yourself credit for an answer you correctly guess skews your self-assessment results and might provide you with a false sense of security.

1. How many VDCs are supported on Nexus 7000 SUP 1 and SUP 2E? (Don't count admin VDC.)

    a. SUP 1 supports four VDCs, and SUP 2E supports four.

    b. SUP 1 supports four VDCs, and SUP 2E supports six.

    c. SUP 1 supports two VDCs, and SUP 2E supports eight.

    d. SUP 1 supports four VDCs, and SUP 2E support eight.

2. Choose the different types of VDCs that can be created on the Nexus 7000. (Choose 3.)

    a. Default VDC

    b. Admin VDC

    c. Storage VDC

    d. OTV VDC

3. True or False? We can assign physical interfaces to an admin VDC.

    a. True

    b. False

4. Which command is used to access a nondefault VDC from the default VDC?

    a. connectTo

    b. switchto vdc{vdc name}

    c. VDC {id}

    d. switchto {vdc name}

5. True or False? The Nexus 2000 Switch Series can be used as a standalone access switch.

    a. True

    b. False

6. The VN-Tag is being standardized under which IEEE standard?

    a. 802.1qpg

    b. 802.1Qbh

    c. 802.1BR

    d. 802.Qbr

7. In the VN-Tag fields, what does the acronym VIF stand for?

    a. VN-Tag initial frame

    b. Virtual interface

    c. Virtualized interface

    d. vntag interface

8. What is the default STP mode in NX OS ?

    a. MST

    b. Rapid-PVST+

    c. VDC

    d. PVST

9. Which of the commands can display the STP root for all VLANs for a given switch?

    a. Show spanning-tree root

    b. Show spanning-tree vlan all

    c. Show spanning-tree bridge root

    d. Show stp root

10. Which of the following adapters can be used to enable adapter-fex?

    a. Cisco 1240 Card

    b. Cisco 1385 Card

    c. Intel I350

    d. Broadcom 5709

6

Foundation Topics

Describing VDCs on the Cisco Nexus 7000 Series Switch

The VDC is used to virtualize the Nexus 7000 switch, meaning presenting the Nexus 7000 switch as multiple logical switches. Within a VDC, you can have a unique set of VLANs and virtual routing and forwarding (VRF) instances allowing the virtualization of the control plane. Each VDC will have its own administrative domain allowing the management plane as well to be virtualized. You can assign a line card to a VDC or a set of ports to the VDC.

> **NOTE** VDC is supported only on Nexus 7000 and Nexus 7700.

Without creating a VDC on the Nexus 7000, the control plane runs a single VDC; within this VDC are multiple processes and Layer 2 and Layer 3 services running, as shown in Figure 6-1. This VDC is always active and cannot be deleted.

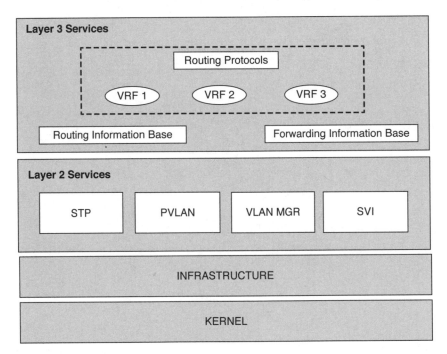

Figure 6-1 *Single VDC Operation Mode Structure*

Virtualization using VLANS and VRFs within this VDC can still be used. When enabling multiple VDCs, these processes are replicated for each VDC. Within each VDC, you can have duplicate VLAN names and VRF names, meaning you can have VRF production in VDC1 and VRF production in VDC2.

When enabling role-based access control (RBAC) for each VDC, each VDC administrator will interface with the process for his or her own VDC. Figure 6-2 shows what the structure looks like when creating multiple VDCs. You can have fault isolation, separate administration per VDC, separate data traffic, and hardware partitioning.

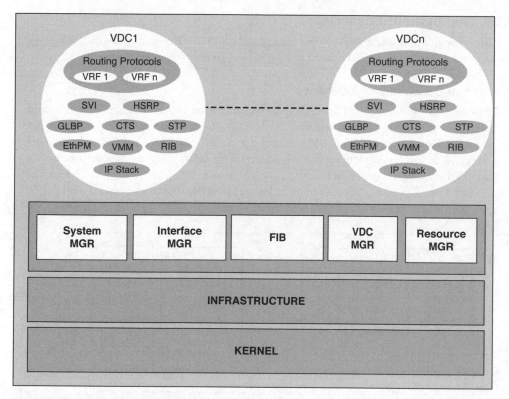

Figure 6-2 *Multiple VDC Operation Mode Structure*

The following are typical use cases for the Cisco Nexus 7000 VDC, which can be used in the design of the data center:

- Creation of separate production, development, and test environments
- Creation of intranet, extranet, and demilitarized zone (DMZ)
- Creation of separate organizations on the same physical switch
- Creation of separate application environments
- Creation of separate departments for the same organization due to different administration domains

VDC separation is industry certified; it has NSS labs certification for payment card industry (PCI)–compliant environments, Federal Information Processing Standards (FIPS 140-2) certification, and Common Criteria Evaluation and Validation Scheme (CCEVS) 10349 certification with EAL4 conformance.

VDC Deployment Scenarios

There are multiple deployment scenarios using the VDCs. They enable the reduction of the physical footprint in the data center, which in turn saves space, power, and cooling.

Horizontal Consolidation Scenarios

VDCs can consolidate multiple physical devices that share the same function role. In horizontal consolidation, you can consolidate core functions and aggregation functions. For example, using a pair of Nexus 7000 switches, you can build two redundant data center cores, which can be useful in facilitating migration scenarios. This can happen by creating two VDCs, as shown in Figure 6-3. VDC1 will accommodate Core A and VDC2 will accommodate Core B. You can allocate ports or line cards to the VDCs, and after the migration you can reallocate the old core ports to the new core.

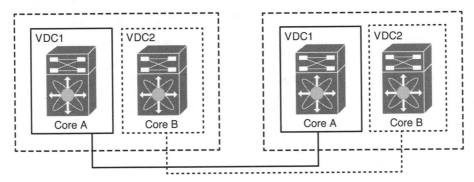

Figure 6-3   *Horizontal Consolidations for Core Layer*

Aggregation layers can also be consolidated, so rather than building a separate aggregation layer for test and development, you can create multiple VDCs called Aggregation 1 and Aggregation 2. Aggregation 1 and Aggregation 2 are completely isolated with a separate role-based access and separate configuration file. Figure 6-4 shows multiple aggregation layers created on the same physical devices.

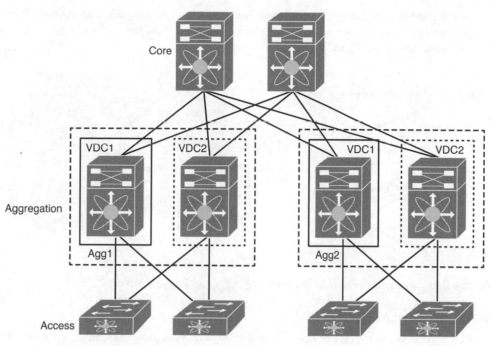

Figure 6-4   *Horizontal Consolidation for Aggregation Layers*

Vertical Consolidation Scenarios

When using VDCs in vertical consolidation, you can consolidate core functions and aggregation functions. For example, using a pair of Nexus 7000 switches, you can build a redundant core and aggregation layer. Although the port count is the same, it can be useful because it reduces the number of physical switches. This can happen by creating two VDCs, as shown in Figure 6-5. VDC1 accommodates Core A and Aggregation Λ; VDC2 accommodates Core B and Aggregation B. You can allocate ports or line cards to the VDCs.

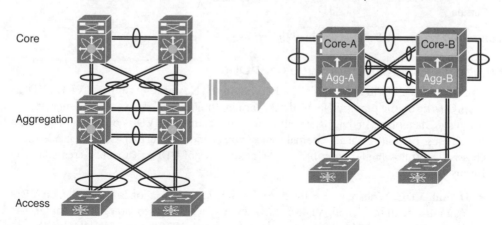

Figure 6-5   *Vertical Consolidation for Core and Aggregation Layers*

Another scenario is consolidation of core aggregation and access while you maintain the same hierarchy. Figure 6-6 shows that scenario; as you can see, we used a pair of Nexus 7000 switches to build a three-tier architecture.

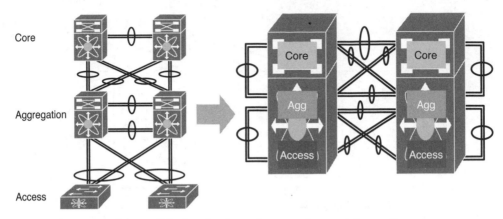

Figure 6-6 *Vertical Consolidation for Core, Aggregation, and Access Layers*

VDCs for Service Insertion

VDCs can be used for service insertion and policy enforcement. By creating two separate VDCs for two logical areas inside and outside, as shown in Figure 6-7, for traffic to cross VDC-A to go to VDC-B it must pass through the firewall. This design can make service insertion more deterministic and secure. Each VDC has its own administrative domain, and traffic must go out VDC-A to reach VDC-B. The only way is through the firewall.

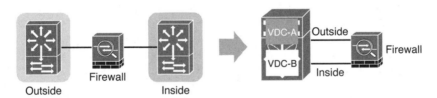

Figure 6-7 *Using VDCs for Firewall Insertion*

Understanding Different Types of VDCs

As explained earlier in the chapter, the NX-OS on the Nexus 7000 supports VDCs. VDCs simply partition the physical Nexus device into multiple logical devices with a separate control plane, data plane, and management plane. Connecting two VDCs on the same physical switch must be done through external cables; you cannot connect VDCs from inside the chassis. The following list describes the different types of VDCs that can be created on the Nexus 7000:

- **Default VDC:** When you first log in to the Nexus 7000, you log in to the default VDC. You must be in the default VDC or the Admin VDC (discussed later in the chapter) to do certain tasks, which can be done only in these two VDC types. The default VDC is a full-function VDC; the admin always uses it to manage the physical device and other

VDCs created. The default VDC has certain characteristics and tasks that can only be done in the default VDC, which can be summarized in the following:

- VDC creation/deletion/suspend
- Resource allocation—interfaces, memory
- NX-OS upgrade across all VDCs
- EPLD upgrade—as directed by technical assistance center (TAC) or to enable new features
- Ethanalyzer captures—control plane traffic
- Feature-set installation for Nexus 2000, FabricPath, and FCoE
- Control plane policing (CoPP)
- Port channel load balancing
- Hardware intrusion detection system (IDS) checks control
- ACL capture feature enabled

- **Nondefault VDC:** The nondefault VDC is a fully functional VDC that can be created from the default VDC or the admin VDC. Changes in the nondefault VDC affect only that VDC. An independent process is started for each protocol per VDC created. There is a separate configuration file per VDC, and each VDC has its own RBAC, Simple Network Management Protocol (SNMP), and so on.

- **Admin VDC:** The admin VDC is used for administration functions, things like CoPP (Control Plane Policing), ISSU (In Service Software Upgrades), EPLD (Electronic Programmable Logical Device), VDC creation, suspension and deletion. You can enable starting from NX-OS 6.1 for SUP2/2E modules, and starting from the NX-OS 6.2(2) for SUP1 module, you can create the admin VDC in different ways:

  - During a fresh switch boot, you will be prompted to select an admin VDC.
  - Enter the **system admin-vdc** command after boot. In that case, the default VDC becomes the admin VDC, and all nonglobal configuration in the default VDC is lost.
  - Enter the **system admin-vdc migrate** *new vdc name* command. All nonglobal configuration on the default VDC will be migrated to the new VDC.
  - The admin VDC has certain characteristics that are unique.
  - Features and feature sets cannot be enabled in an admin VDC.
  - You cannot assign an interface to the admin VDC; only mgmt0 can be assigned to the admin VDC.
  - When you enable the admin VDC, it replaces the default VDC. You must be careful or you will lose the nonglobal configuration.
  - After the admin VDC is created, it cannot be deleted or changed back to the default VDC. To change back to the default VDC, you must erase the configuration and do a fresh boot script.

NOTE The admin VDC does not count toward the total number of VDCs. Creating the admin VDC does not require the advanced package license or VDC license.

■ **Storage VDC:** The storage VDC is a nondefault VDC that helps maintain the operation model when the customer has a local-area network (LAN) admin and a storage-area network (SAN) admin. The storage VDC relies on the Fibre Channel over Ethernet (FCoE) license and does not need a VDC license. The storage VDC counts toward the total number of VDCs. We can create only one storage VDC on the physical device. After the creation of the storage VDC, we assign interfaces to it. There are two types of interfaces—dedicated FCoE interfaces or shared interfaces—that can carry both Ethernet and FCoE traffic. Figure 6-8 shows the two types of ports.

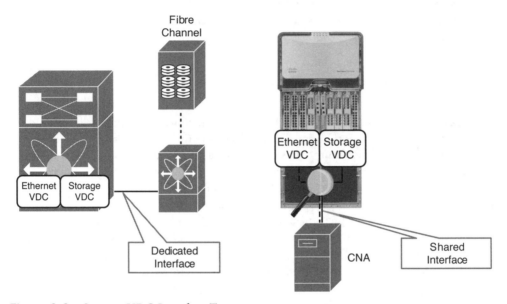

Figure 6-8 *Storage VDC Interface Types*

NOTE   Sup2/2e is required to run FCoE.

With Supervisor 1, you can have up to four VDCs and one admin VDC, which requires 8 GB of RAM because you must upgrade to NX-OS 6.2. Supervisor engine 2 can have up to four VDCs and one admin VDC. With Supervisor engine 2E, you can have up to eight VDCs and one admin VDC. Beyond four VDCs on Supervisor 2E, we require a license to increment the VDCs with an additional four.

Interface Allocation

The only thing you can assign to a VDC is the physical ports. At the beginning and before creating a VDC, all interfaces belong to the default VDC. After you create a VDC, you start assigning interfaces to it. A physical interface can belong to only one VDC at a given time. When you create a shared interface, the physical interface belongs to one Ethernet VDC and one storage VDC at the same time. When you allocate the physical interface to a VDC, all configurations that existed on it are erased. The physical interface is configured within the VDC. Logical interfaces, such as tunnel interfaces and switch virtual interfaces, are created within the VDC, and within a VDC, physical and logical interfaces can be assigned to VLANs or VRFs.

> **NOTE**   All members of a port group are automatically allocated to the VDC when you allocate an interface. For example, in the N7K-M132XP-12 and N7K-M132XP-12L (4 interfaces × 8 port groups = 32 interfaces), you are required to allocate ports to a VDC in groups of four ports, and you can configure eight port groups. Interfaces belonging to the same port group must belong to the same VDC. See the example for this module in Figure 6-9.

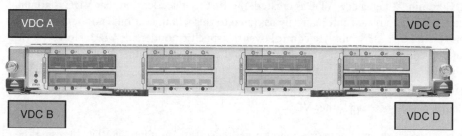

Figure 6-9   *VDC Interface Allocation Example*

VDC CPU Shares and Hardware Resources

CPU Shares Enables per-VDC CPU access and **prioritization,** it provides more control and protection per VDC for users. CPU shares are controlled by VDC priority and user **configurable;** it only comes into effect when CPU utilization increases, **meaning during times of contention. The** more VDCs **are configured,** the lower overall percentage per VDC. This feature, which is available **on SUP2/SUP2E, only helps** ensure that higher **priority VDCs** have access to the CPU and lower-priority. VDCs don't affect higher-priority VDCs.

> **NOTE**   With CPU shares, you do not dedicate a CPU to a VDC; rather priorities VDC access to CPUs.

Access to the physical device resources can be controlled when the user creates a VDC. This can be accomplished using a VDC resource template. By default, the NX-OS reserves the minimum for the resource when a VDC is created. If the user changed the default and allocated resources to the VDC beyond the minimum, it will be based on the maximum limit and the resources available on the device. An example of resources that can be part of a VDC resource template are IPv4 multicast route memory, IPv6 multicast route memory, IPv4 unicast route memory, port channels, VLANs, SPAN (Switch Port Analyzer) sessions, and VRFs (virtual routing and forwarding instances).

VDC Administration

The operations allowed for a user in VDC depend on the role assigned to that user. Users can have multiple roles assigned to them, and the NX-OS provides four default user roles:

- **Network-admin:** The first user account that is created on a Cisco Nexus 7000 Series switch in the default VDC is admin. The network-admin role is automatically assigned to this user. The network-admin role gives a user complete read and write access to the device, and it is available only in the default VDC. This role includes the ability to create, delete, or change nondefault VDCs.

- **Network-operator:** The second default role that exists on Cisco Nexus 7000 Series switches is the network-operator role. This role grants the user read-only rights in the default VDC. The network-operator role includes the right to issue the **switchto** command, which can be used to access a nondefault VDC from the default VDC. By default, no users are assigned to this role. The role must be assigned specifically to a user by a user who has network-admin rights.

- **VDC-admin:** When a new VDC is created, the first user account on that VDC is admin. The VDC-admin role is automatically assigned to this admin user on a nondefault VDC. This role gives a user complete control over the specific nondefault VDC. However, this user does not have rights in any other VDC and cannot access other VDCs through the **switchto** command.

- **VDC-operator:** The VDC-operator role has read-only rights for a specific VDC. This role has no rights to any other VDC.

When a network-admin or network-operator user accesses a nondefault VDC by using the **switchto** command, that user is mapped to a role of the same level in the nondefault VDC. That means a user with the network-admin role is given the VDC-admin role in the nondefault VDC. A user with the network-operator role is given the VDC-operator role in the nondefault VDC.

> **NOTE**   You can create custom roles for a user, but you cannot change the default user roles for a VDC. User roles are not shared between VDCs; each VDC maintains its user role database.

VDC Requirements

An advanced license is required to create VDCs. The license is associated with the serial number of a Cisco Nexus 7000 switch chassis. The storage VDC is enabled using the storage license associated with a specific line card. You can try the feature for the 120-day grace period. When the grace period expires, any nondefault VDCs will be removed from the switch configuration.

> **NOTE**   The grace period operates across all features in a license package; the license package can contain several features. When you enable a feature, the countdown for the 120 days does not stop if a single feature of the license package is already enabled. To stop the grace period, all the features of the license package must be stopped, so if you enable a feature to try it, but another feature was enabled, for example, 100 days before, you are left with 20 days to install the license.

As stated before, VDCs are created or deleted from the default VDC only. You need network admin privileges to do that. Physical interfaces also are assigned to nondefault VDCs from the default VDC.

Verifying VDCs on the Cisco Nexus 7000 Series Switch

The next few lines show certain commands to display useful information about the VDC. As shown in Example 6-1, the **show feature-set** command is used to verify and show which feature has been enabled or disabled in a VDC.

Example 6-1   *Displaying the Status of a Feature Set on a Switch*

```
N7K-VDC-A# show feature-set
Feature Set Name          ID          State
-------------------       --------    --------
fabricpath                2           enabled
fex                       3           disabled
N7K-VDC-A#
```

The **show feature-set** command in Example 6-1 shows that the FabricPath feature is enabled and the FEX feature is disabled.

The **show vdc** command in Example 6-2 displays different outputs depending on where you are executing it from. If you are executing the command from the default VDC, this command displays information about all VDCs on the physical device.

Example 6-2   *Displaying Information About All VDCs (Running the Command from the Default VDC)*

```
N7K-Core# show vdc
vdc_id    vdc_name      state       mac
------    --------      -----       ----------
1         prod          active      00:18:ba:d8:3f:fd
2         dev           active      00:18:ba:d8:3f:fe
3         MyVDC         active      00:18:ba:d8:3f:ff
```

If you are executing the **show vdc** command as shown in Example 6-3 within the nondefault VDC, which in our case is the N7K-Core-Prod, the output displays information about the current VDC.

Example 6-3   *Displaying Information About the Current VDC (Running the Command from the Nondefault VDC)*

```
N7K-Core-Prod# show vdc
vdc_id    vdc_name      state       mac
------    --------      -----       ----------
1         prod          active      00:18:ba:d8:3f:fd
```

To display the detailed information about all VDCs, execute **show vdc detail** from the default VDC, as shown in Example 6-4.

Example 6-4 *Displaying Detailed Information About All VDCs*

```
N7K-Core# show vdc detail
vdc id: 1
vdc name: N7K-Core
vdc state: active
vdc mac address: 00:22:55:79:a4:c1
vdc ha policy: RELOAD
vdc dual-sup ha policy: SWITCHOVER
vdc boot Order: 1
vdc create time: Thu May 14 08:14:39 2012
vdc restart count: 0
vdc id: 2
vdc name: prod
vdc state: active
vdc mac address: 00:22:55:79:a4:c2
vdc ha policy: RESTART
vdc dual-sup ha policy: SWITCHOVER
vdc boot Order: 1
vdc create time: Thu May 14 08:15:22 2012
vdc restart count: 0
vdc id: 3
vdc name: dev
vdc state: active
vdc mac address: 00:22:55:79:a4:c3
vdc ha policy: RESTART
vdc dual-sup ha policy: SWITCHOVER
vdc boot Order: 1
vdc create time: Thu May 14 08:15:29 2012
vdc restart count: 0
```

You can display the detailed information about the current VDC by executing **show vdc {vdc name} detail** from the nondefault VDC, as shown in Example 6-5.

Example 6-5 *Displaying Detailed Information About the Current VDC When You Are in the Nondefault VDC*

```
N7K-Core-prod# show vdc prod detail
vdc id: 2
vdc name: prod
vdc state: active
vdc mac address: 00:22:55:79:a4:c2
vdc ha policy: RESTART
vdc dual-sup ha policy: SWITCHOVER
vdc boot Order: 1
vdc create time: Thu May 14 08:15:22 2012
vdc restart count: 0
```

To verify the interface allocation per VDC, execute **show vdc membership** from the default VDC, as shown in Example 6-6.

Example 6-6 *Displaying Interface Allocation per VDC*

```
N7K-Core# show vdc membership
vdc_id: 1 vdc_name: N7K-Core interfaces:
            Ethernet2/1              Ethernet2/2              Ethernet2/3
            Ethernet2/4              Ethernet2/5              Ethernet2/6
            Ethernet2/7              Ethernet2/8              Ethernet2/9
            Ethernet2/10             Ethernet2/11             Ethernet2/12
            Ethernet2/13             Ethernet2/14             Ethernet2/15
            Ethernet2/16             Ethernet2/17             Ethernet2/18
            Ethernet2/19             Ethernet2/20             Ethernet2/21
            Ethernet2/22             Ethernet2/23             Ethernet2/24
            Ethernet2/25             Ethernet2/26             Ethernet2/27
            Ethernet2/28             Ethernet2/29             Ethernet2/30
            Ethernet2/31             Ethernet2/32             Ethernet2/33
            Ethernet2/34             Ethernet2/35             Ethernet2/36
            Ethernet2/37             Ethernet2/38             Ethernet2/39
            Ethernet2/40             Ethernet2/41             Ethernet2/42
            Ethernet2/43             Ethernet2/44             Ethernet2/45
            Ethernet2/48
vdc_id: 2 vdc_name: prod interfaces:
        Ethernet2/47
vdc_id: 3 vdc_name: dev interfaces:
        Ethernet2/46
```

If you execute **show VDC membership** from the VDC you are currently in, it will show the interface membership only for that VDC.

You can save all the running configurations to the startup configuration for all VDCs using one command. Use the **copy running-config startup-config vdc-all** command as shown in Example 6-7, which is executed from the default VDC.

Example 6-7 *Saving All Configurations for All VDCs*

```
N7K-Core# copy running-config startup-config vdc-all
[########################################] 100%
```

To display the running configurations for all VDCs, use the **show running-config vdc-all** command, executed from the default VDC. You cannot see the configuration for other VDCs except from the default VDC.

You can navigate from the default VDC to the nondefault VDC using the **switchto** command, as shown in Example 6-8.

Example 6-8   *Navigating Between VDCs on the Nexus 7000 Switch*

```
N7K-Core# switchto vdc Prod
TAC support: http://www.cisco.com/tac
Copyright (c) 2002-2008, Cisco Systems, Inc. All rights reserved.
The copyrights to certain works contained in this software are
owned by other third parties and used and distributed under
license. Certain components of this software are licensed under
the GNU General Public License (GPL) version 2.0 or the GNU
Lesser General Public License (LGPL) Version 2.1. A copy of each
such license is available at
http://www.opensource.org/licenses/gpl-2.0.php and
http://www.opensource.org/licenses/lgpl-2.1.php
N7K-Core-Prod#
```

To switch back to the default VDC, use the **switchback** command. You cannot execute the **switchto** command from the nondefault VDC; you must do **switchback** to the default VDC before going to another VDC. Use these commands for the initial setup; after that, when you create the user accounts and configure the IP connectivity, you use Secure Shell (SSH) and Telnet to connect to the desired VDC.

Describing Layer 3 Virtualization Within VDCs

In addition to using VDCs to virtualize Nexus 7000 and Nexus 7700, you can further virtualize each VDC to support VRFs. Multiple VRFs can be configured in a single VDC. VRF names are local to the VDC, which means you can have two VRFs with the same name as long as they are in two separate VDCs.

VRFs associate to one or more Layer 3 interfaces. Each VRF has its own forwarding table and routing process. An interface associated with one VRF cannot be assigned to another VRF.

VRFs allow you to have overlapping IP addresses in case of multitenant environments. Because each VRF has its own address space, each will have separate unicast and multicast routing tables for IPv4 and IPv6 that make routing decisions independent within each VRF by default. Each router has a default VRF and a management VRF. The characteristics of each one are described next.

- Management VRF
    - This is used for management purposes only.
    - Only the mgmt 0 interface can be a member of the management VRF.
    - The mgmt 0 interface is shared among multiple VDCs.
    - The mgmt 0 interface cannot be assigned to another VRF.
    - It has no routing protocols (static only).
- Default VRF
    - By default, all Layer 3 interfaces exist in the default VRF until they are assigned to another VRF.
    - The default VRF uses the default routing context for all **show** and **exec** commands.

- All IPv4 and IPv6 routing protocols run in a default VRF context unless other VRF context is specified.

- The default VRF is similar to the IOS global routing table.

NOTE if you decided to move the interface from an existing VRF to another existing VRF, all Layer 3 configuration on the interface is removed.

Examples 6-9 through 6-12 will show you how to create and verify that the VRF is created successfully.

Example 6-9 *Sample Configuration of Creating VRF*

```
CCNAv2-SW1(config)# vrf context VRF1
CCNAv2-SW1(config-vrf)#
```

Example 6-10 *Sample Configuration to Display VRF Information*

```
CCNAv2-SW1# show vrf
VRF-Name                     VRF-ID State   Reason
VRF1                              3 Up       --
default                           1 Up       --
management                        2 Up       --
CCNAv2-SW1#
```

Example 6-11 *Sample Configuration to Add an Interface to a VRF*

```
CCNAv2-SW1(config)# inter eth 2/1
CCNAv2-SW1(config-if)# vrf member VRF1
CCNAv2-SW1(config-if)#
```

Example 6-12 *Sample Configuration to Display the Routes of Management VRF*

```
CCNAv2-SW2%VRF1# show ip route vrf management
IP Route Table for VRF "management"
'*' denotes best ucast next-hop
'**' denotes best mcast next-hop
'[x/y]' denotes [preference/metric]
'%<string>' in via output denotes VRF <string>

40.40.40.0/24, ubest/mbest: 1/0, attached
    *via 40.40.40.1, mgmt0, [0/0], 00:13:48, direct
40.40.40.1/32, ubest/mbest: 1/0, attached
    *via 40.40.40.1, mgmt0, [0/0], 00:13:48, local
CCNAv2-SW2%VRF1#
CCNAv2-SW2%VRF1#
```

6

```
CCNAv2-SW2%VRF1# show ip route
IP Route Table for VRF "VRF1"
'*' denotes best ucast next-hop
'**' denotes best mcast next-hop
'[x/y]' denotes [preference/metric]
'%<string>' in via output denotes VRF <string>

20.20.20.1/32, ubest/mbest: 1/0
    *via 192.168.1.100, Eth2/1, [110/41], 00:19:18, ospf-1, intra
30.30.30.0/24, ubest/mbest: 1/0, attached
    *via 30.30.30.1, Lo0, [0/0], 00:20:01, direct
30.30.30.1/32, ubest/mbest: 1/0, attached
    *via 30.30.30.1, Lo0, [0/0], 00:20:01, local
192.168.1.0/24, ubest/mbest: 1/0, attached
    *via 192.168.1.101, Eth2/1, [0/0], 00:19:30, direct
192.168.1.101/32, ubest/mbest: 1/0, attached
    *via 192.168.1.101, Eth2/1, [0/0], 00:19:30, local
```

As you can see from Example 6-12, the **show ip route** command shows that the VRF1 routing table and mgmt0 are not there because mgmt0 is in the management VRF.

As you saw in Example 6-12, when we wanted to display the routing table of VRF management, we had to put the **vrf management** at the end of the **show ip route** command. You must do the same for commands such as **ping** and **traceroute** to verify connectivity. A better way is to use the **routing-context** command, as shown in Example 6-13.

Example 6-13   *Sample Configuration to Show the Usage of VRF routing-context Command*

```
CCNAv2-SW2%VRF1# routing-context vrf vrf1
CCNAv2-SW2%VRF1#
CCNAv2-SW2%VRF1# ping 20.20.20.1
PING 20.20.20.1 (20.20.20.1): 56 data bytes
64 bytes from 20.20.20.1: icmp_seq=0 ttl=254 time=3.377 ms
64 bytes from 20.20.20.1: icmp_seq=1 ttl=254 time=1.847 ms
64 bytes from 20.20.20.1: icmp_seq=2 ttl=254 time=1.709 ms
64 bytes from 20.20.20.1: icmp_seq=3 ttl=254 time=1.745 ms
64 bytes from 20.20.20.1: icmp_seq=4 ttl=254 time=1.782 ms

--- 20.20.20.1 ping statistics ---
5 packets transmitted, 5 packets received, 0.00% packet loss
round-trip min/avg/max = 1.709/2.091/3.377 ms
CCNAv2-SW1#
```

Describe the Benefits and Perform Simple Troubleshooting of VDC STP

The job of Spanning Tree Protocol (STP) is to provide redundant loop-free Layer 2 topologies. To achieve this, Layer 2 switches send and receive bridge protocol data units (BPDUs) to build a loop-free Layer 2 path.

To ensure a loop-free path, some links will be in a forwarding state, whereas others will be in a blocking state. Using something like Rapid Per-VLAN Spanning Tree (Rapid PVSTP+), the links that will be blocking for some VLANs will be active for others.

- **Rapid-PVST+:** Rapid PVST+, which is the IEEE 802.1w, is the default spanning tree mode for the NX-OS software. For the default VLAN and each newly configured VLAN, a single instance of RSTP runs is enabled by default. Each instance of Rapid PVST+ has a single root bridge. All other devices in that instance determine what is the lowest cost to the root device. Because per-VLAN we have an instance of Rapid PVST+ running, any changes affect only this VLAN. Rapid PVST+ is backward compatible with legacy IEEE 802.1d for integration and migration purposes.

- **Multiple Spanning Tree (MST):** The NX-OS also supports MST, which can be used in case of a large Layer 2 domain, where using PVST+ is complex to manage from a configuration perspective. MST maps multiple VLANs into a spanning tree instance. An MST instance with the same name, revision number, and VLAN-to-instance mapping form a region. The MST region appears as a single bridge to adjacent MST regions, other Rapid PVST+ regions, and 802.1D spanning tree protocols.

NOTE   In a given VDC, you can run either Rapid PVST+ or MST. You cannot run both in one VDC.

- **Bridge ID:** As shown in Figure 6-10, the bridge ID is a 64-bit ID that consists of a bridge priority (4 bits); an extended system ID (12 bits), which is IEEE 802.1t; and an STP MAC (6 bytes).

Cisco switches let you configure the BID, but only the priority part. The switch fills in its universal (burned-in) MAC address as the system ID. It also plugs in the VLAN ID of a VLAN in the 12-bit System ID Extension field. The only part configurable by the network engineer is the 4-bit Priority field.

You will be able to configure the bridge priority using **spanning-tree vlan** *vlan-id* **priority** *value*, where the value will be a multiple of 4096. The lowest value will be 4096; the lowest value is better. You can also set the switch to the lowest priority by using **spanning-tree vlan** *vlan-id* **root {Primary | Secondary}**.

For the same VLAN, if the bridge priority is the same, which usually happens if we leave it as the default (32768), the network device with the lowest MAC address in the VLAN will become the root bridge.

Bridge ID Priority

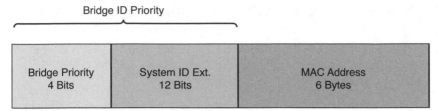

Figure 6-10   *STP Bridge ID*

So now you know the criteria for a switch to become an STP root for a given VLAN. For the switches to elect that STP root bridge, they exchange BPDUs. The BPDUs, which are transmitted through the STP instance, will have the Bridge-ID of the transmitting bridge, the STP path cost to the root, and other information. Based on this information, the STP root bridge is elected for a given STP instance, and the shortest path cost to the root is calculated for each given bridge based on the path cost to the root. Example 6-14 shows how to change the STP cost on an interface.

Example 6-14   *Sample Configuration to Show How to Change STP Cost for an Interface*

```
CCNAv2-SW1(config)# interface eth2/3
CCNAv2-SW1(config-if)# spanning-tree vlan 100 cost 4
CCNAv2-SW1(config-if)#
```

As you can see in Figure 6-11, CCNAv2-SW1 is the root bridge. All the ports of the CCNAv2-SW1 are placed in forwarding mode, and they are called designated ports (DPs). Based on the shortest path cost to the root CCNAv2-SW2 and CCNAv2-SW3, the ports that lead to the STP root (with the lowest path cost to the root bridge) are placed in the forwarding state; these ports are known as root ports (RPs). For the LAN segment between CCNAv2-SW2 and CCNAv2-SW3, both ports cannot be in the forwarding state because it would lead to a network loop. Therefore, from the BPDUs sent on that segment, the switches compare cost. Based on the cost, one switch will be DP and will be forwarding and the other will be blocking.

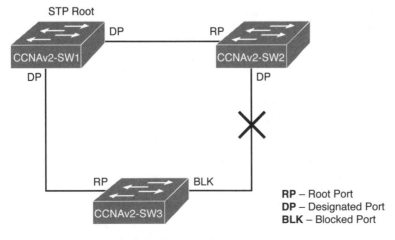

Figure 6-11   *Example for LAN Topology*

Verifying STP Operation

As stated previously, each VDC is considered a separate STP bridge. To go from one VDC to another VDC, you need a physical cable.

Example 6-15 shows how to verify the root bridge for VLAN 100 and set the local switch. Running the command **show spanning-tree vlan 100** shows that CCNAv2-sw1 is the STP root for VLAN 100. It also shows that all the port roles are DPs.

Example 6-15 *Verify the STP Status of Switch CCNAv2-sw1*

```
CCNAv2-SW1# show spanning-tree vlan 100


VLAN0100
  Spanning tree enabled protocol rstp
  Root ID    Priority    4196
             Address     fa16.3e5a.4e6c
             This bridge is the root
             Hello Time   2  sec  Max Age 20 sec  Forward Delay 15 sec


  Bridge ID  Priority    4196    (priority 4096 sys-id-ext 100)
             Address     fa16.3e5a.4e6c
             Hello Time   2  sec  Max Age 20 sec  Forward Delay 15 sec


Interface        Role Sts Cost      Prio.Nbr Type
---------------- ---- --- --------- -------- --------------------------------
Eth2/1           Desg FWD 4         128.257  P2p
Eth2/2           Desg FWD 4         128.258  P2p
Eth2/3           Desg FWD 4         128.259  P2p
```

Example 6-16 shows the output of the same command but on CCNAv2-sw3. However, as you can see, **interface Ethernet 2/2** is in BLK, meaning it is blocked for VLAN 100.

Example 6-16 *Verify the STP Status of Switch CCNAv2-sw3*

```
CCNAv2-SW3# show spanning-tree vlan 100


VLAN0100
  Spanning tree enabled protocol rstp
  Root ID    Priority    4196
             Address     fa16.3e5a.4e6c
             Cost        4
             Port        257 (Ethernet2/1)
             Hello Time   2  sec  Max Age 20 sec  Forward Delay 15 sec


  Bridge ID  Priority    32868   (priority 32768 sys-id-ext 100)
             Address     fa16.3ee9.ddaa
             Hello Time   2  sec  Max Age 20 sec  Forward Delay 15 sec
```

```
Interface         Role Sts Cost       Prio.Nbr Type
----------------  ---- --- ---------  -------- --------------------------------
Eth2/1            Root FWD 4          128.257  P2p
Eth2/2            Altn BLK 4          128.258  P2p
```

Another useful command you can run to display the STP root for all VLANs for a given bridge is **show spanning-tree root**, as shown in Example 6-17.

Example 6-17 *Show How to Verify STP Root Bridge for All VLANs for a Specific Switch*

```
CCNAv2-SW3# show spanning-tree root

                                Root  Hello Max Fwd
Vlan                 Root ID    Cost  Time  Age Dly  Root Port
----------------  --------------------  -------  ----- --- ---  ----------------
VLAN0001          32769 fa16.3e39.8439      4     2   20  15       Ethernet2/2
VLAN0100           4196 fa16.3e5a.4e6c      4     2   20  15       Ethernet2/1
VLAN0200           4296 fa16.3e39.8439      4     2   20  15       Ethernet2/2
VLAN0300           4396 fa16.3ee9.ddaa      0     2   20  15  This bridge is root

VLAN0400          33168 fa16.3e39.8439      4     2   20  15       Ethernet2/2
```

Describing Network Interface Virtualization

You can deliver an extensible and scalable fabric solution using the Cisco FEX technology. The FEX technology can be extended all the way to the server hypervisor. This technology enables operational simplicity by having a single point of management and policy enforcement on the access parent switch.

Cisco Nexus 2000 FEX Terminology

The following terminology and acronyms are used with the Nexus 2000 fabric extenders:

- **Network Interface (NIF):** Port on FEX, connecting to parent switch.

- **Host Interface (HIF):** Front panel port on FEX, connecting to server.

- **Virtual Interface (VIF):** Logical construct consisting of a front panel port, VLAN, and several other parameters.

- **Logical interface (LIF):** Presentation of a front panel port in parent switch.

- **Fabric links (Fabric Port Channel or FPC):** Links that connect FEX NIF and FEX fabric ports on parent switch.

- **Parent switch:** Switch (N7K/N5K) where FEX is connected.

- **FEX A/A or dual-attached FEX:** Scenario in which the fabric links of FEX are connected, actively forwarding traffic to two parent switches.

- **Fabric Extender (FEX):** NEXUS 2000 is the instantiation of FEX.

- **Fabric Port:** N7K side of the link connected to FEX.
- **Fabric Port Channel:** Port channel between N7K and FEX.
- **FEX uplink:** Network-facing port on the FEX side of the link connected to N7K. The FEX uplink is also a NIF.
- **FEX port:** Server-facing port on FEX, also referred to as a server port or host port in this presentation. The FEX port is also a HIF.

Figure 6-12 shows the ports with reference to the physical hardware.

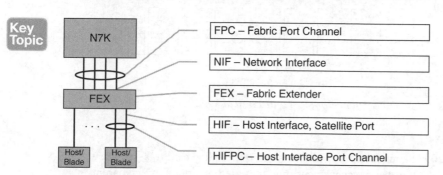

Figure 6-12 *Nexus 2000 Interface Types and Acronyms*

Nexus 2000 Series Fabric Extender Connectivity

The Cisco Nexus 2000 Series cannot run as a standalone switch; it needs a parent switch. This switch can be a Nexus 9000, Nexus 7000, Nexus 7700, Nexus 6000, Nexus 5600, or Nexus 5000 Series. This type of design combines the benefit of the top-of-rack (ToR) design with the benefit of the end-of-row (EoR) design.

Based on the type and the density of the access ports required, dual redundant Nexus 2000 fabric extenders are placed at the top of the rack. The uplink ports from the Nexus 2000 will be connected to the parent switch, as stated previously, and be installed at the EoR. From a cabling point of view, this design is a ToR design. The cabling between the servers and the Nexus 2000 Series fabric extenders is contained within the rack. Only a small number of cables will run between the racks, which will be 10/40 Gbps.

From the logical network deployment point of view, this design is an EoR design. The FEX acts as a remote line card. The server appears as if it is connected directly to the parent switch. From an operation perspective, this design has the advantage of the EoR design; all configuration and maintenance tasks are done from the parent switch, and no operation tasks are required to be performed from the FEXs. Figure 6-13 shows the physical and the logical architecture of the FEX implementation.

NOTE You can connect a switch to the FEX host interfaces, but it is not recommended. To make this work, you need to turn off BPDUs from the access switch and turn on "bpdufilter" on the Nexus 2000, which might create a loop in the network. The Nexus 2000 host ports (HIFs) do not expect to receive BPDUs on the host ports; they expect only end hosts, such as servers.

Figure 6-13 shows the physical and logical view for the Nexus 2000 fabric extender deployment.

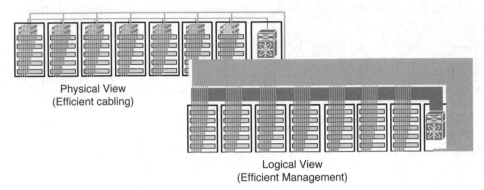

Physical View
(Efficient cabling)

Logical View
(Efficient Management)

Figure 6-13 *Nexus 2000 Deployment Physical and Logical View*

VN-Tag Overview

The Cisco Nexus 2000 Series fabric extender acts as a remote line card to a parent switch, as already stated. All control and management functions are performed by the parent switch, as is forwarding. The physical ports on the Nexus 2000 fabric extender appear as logical ports on the parent switch, and the hosts connected to the Nexus 2000 fabric extender appear as if they are directly connected to the parent switch.

A frame exchanged between the Nexus 2000 fabric extender and the parent switch will have an information tag inserted in it called VN-Tag, which enables advanced functions and policies to be applied to it. The host connected to the Nexus 2000 fabric extender is unaware of any tags.

At the time of writing this book, there is no local switching happening on the Nexus 2000 fabric extender, so all traffic must be sent to the parent switch.

VN-Tag is a NIV technology. At the beginning, VN-Tag was being standardized under the IEEE 802.1Qbh working group. However, 802.1Qbh was withdrawn and is no longer an approved IEEE project. The effort was moved to the IEEE 802.1BR in July 2011. Figure 6-14 shows the VN-Tag fields in an Ethernet frame.

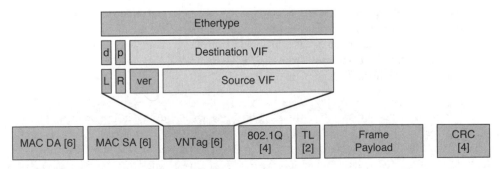

Figure 6-14 *VN-Tag Fields in an Ethernet Frame*

- **d:** Direction bit (0 is host-to-network forwarding; 1 is network-to-host)
- **p:** Pointer bit (set if this is a multicast frame requiring egress replication)
- **L:** Looped filter (set if sending back to source Cisco Nexus 2000 Series)
- **VIF:** Virtual interface

Cisco Nexus 2000 FEX Packet Flow

The packet processing on the Nexus 2000 happens in two parts: when the host sends a packet to the network, and when the network sends a packet to the host. Figure 6-15 shows the two scenarios.

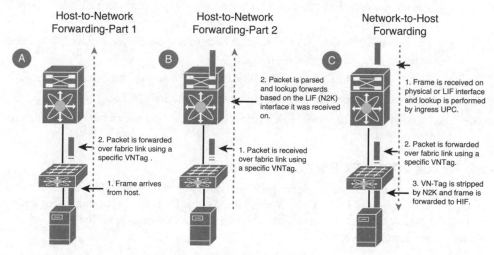

Figure 6-15   *Cisco Nexus 2000 Packet Flow*

When the host sends a packet to the network (diagrams A and B), these events occur:

1. The frame arrives from the host.

2. The Cisco Nexus 2000 Series switch adds a VN-Tag, and the packet is forwarded over a fabric link using a specific VN-Tag. The Cisco Nexus 2000 Series switch adds a unique VN-Tag for each Cisco Nexus 2000 Series host interface. These are the VN-Tag field values:

   - The direction bit is set to 0, indicating host-to network forwarding.
   - The source virtual interface is set based on the ingress host interface.
   - The p (pointer), l (looped), and destination virtual interface are undefined (0).

3. The packet is received over the fabric link using a specific VN-Tag. The Cisco Nexus switch extracts the VN-Tag, which identifies the logical interface that corresponds to the physical host interface on the Cisco Nexus 2000 Series. The Cisco Nexus switch applies an ingress policy that is based on the physical Cisco Nexus Series switch port and logical interface:

   - Access control and forwarding are based on frame fields and virtual (logical) interface policy.
   - Physical link-level properties are based on the Cisco Nexus Series switch port.

4. The Cisco Nexus switch strips the VN-Tag and sends the packet to the network.

When the network sends a packet to the host (diagram C), these events occur:

1. The frame is received on the physical or logical interface. The Cisco Nexus switch performs standard lookup and policy processing when the egress port is determined to be a logical interface (Cisco Nexus 2000 Series) port. The Cisco Nexus switch inserts a VN-Tag with these characteristics:

    ■ The direction is set to 1 (network to host).

    ■ The destination virtual interface is set to be the Cisco Nexus 2000 Series port VN-Tag.

    ■ The source virtual interface is set if the packet was sourced from a Cisco Nexus 2000 Series port.

    ■ The l (looped) bit filter is set if sending back to a source Cisco Nexus 2000 Series switch.

    ■ The p bit is set if this frame is a multicast frame requiring egress replication.

2. The packet is forwarded over a fabric link using a specific VN-Tag.

3. The Cisco Nexus 2000 Series switch strips the VN-Tag, and the frame is forwarded to the host interface.

Cisco Nexus 2000 FEX Port Connectivity

You can connect the Nexus 2000 Series fabric extender to one of the following Ethernet modules that are installed in the Cisco Nexus 7000 Series. There is a best practice for connecting the Nexus 2000 fabric extender to the Nexus 7000, depending on the type and model of card installed in it.

■ 12-port 40-Gigabit Ethernet F3-Series QSFP I/O module (N7K-F312FQ-25) for Cisco Nexus 7000 Series switches

■ 24-port Cisco Nexus 7700 F3 Series 40-Gigabit Ethernet QSFP I/O module (N77-F324FQ-25)

■ 48-port Cisco Nexus 7700 F3 Series 1/10-Gigabit Ethernet SFP+ I/O module (N77-F348XP-23)

■ 32-port 10-Gigabit Ethernet SFP+ I/O module (N7K-M132XP-12)

■ 32-port 10-Gigabit Ethernet SFP+ I/O module (N7K-M132XP-12L)

■ 24-port 10-Gigabit Ethernet I/O M2 Series module XL (N7K-M224XP-23L)

■ 48-port 1/10-Gigabit Ethernet SFP+ I/O F2 Series module (N7K-F248XP-25)

■ Enhanced 48-port 1/10-Gigabit Ethernet SFP+ I/O module (F2e Series) (N7K-F248XP-25E)

■ 48-port 1/10-Gigabit Ethernet SFP+ I/O module (F2e Series) (N77-F248XP-23E)

Figure 6-16 shows the connectivity between the Cisco Nexus 2000 fabric extender and the N7K-M132XP-12 line card.

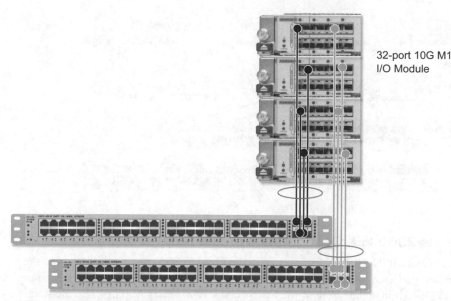

32-port 10G M1
I/O Module

Figure 6-16 *Cisco Nexus 2000 Connectivity to N7K-M132XP-12*

There are two ways to connect the Nexus 2000 to the parent switch: either use static pinning, which makes the FEX use individual links connected to the parent switch, or use a port channel when connecting the fabric interfaces on the FEX to the parent switch. This is explained in more detail in the next paragraphs.

In static pinning, when the FEX is powered up and connected to the parent switch, its host interfaces are distributed equally among the available fabric interfaces. As a result, the bandwidth that is dedicated to each end host toward the parent switch is never changed by the switch but instead is always specified by you.

The drawback here is that if the fabric link goes down, all the associated host interfaces go down and will remain down as long as the fabric port is down. You must use the **pinning max-links** command to create several pinned fabric interface connections so that the parent switch can determine a distribution of host interfaces. The host interfaces are divided by the number of the max-links and distributed accordingly. The default value is max-links 1.

To provide load balancing between the host interfaces and the parent switch, you can configure the FEX to use a port channel fabric interface connection. This connection bundles 10-Gigabit Ethernet fabric interfaces into a single logical channel. A fabric interface that fails in the port channel does not trigger a change to the host interfaces. Traffic is automatically redistributed across the remaining links in the port channel fabric interface. If all links in the fabric port channel go down, all host interfaces on the FEX are set to the down state.

When you have VDCs created on the Nexus 7000, you must follow certain rules. All FEX fabric links belong to the same VDC; all FEX host ports belong to the same VDC; FEX IDs are unique across VDCs. (The same FEX ID cannot be used across different VDCs.) Figure 6-17 shows the FEX connectivity to the Nexus 7000 when you have multiple VDCs.

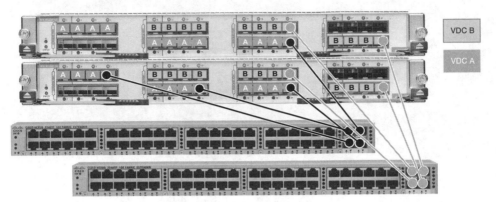

Figure 6-17   *Cisco Nexus 2000 and VDCs*

Cisco Nexus 2000 FEX Configuration on the Nexus 7000 Series

The Cisco Nexus 2000 Series configuration on the Cisco 7000 Series is different from the configuration on Cisco Nexus 5000, 6000, and 5600 Series switches. The difference comes from the VDC-based architecture of the Cisco Nexus 7000 Series switches. Use the steps shown in Example 6-18 through 6-21 to provision the Cisco Nexus 2000 when connected to the Cisco 7000 Series parent switch using one of the supported line cards.

Example 6-18   *Installing the Fabric Extender Feature Set in Default VDC*

```
N7K-Agg(config)#
N7K-Agg(config)# install feature-set fex
```

Example 6-19   *Enabling the Fabric Extender Feature Set*

```
N7K-Agg(config)#
N7K-Agg(config)# feature-set fex
```

By default, when you install the fabric extender feature set, it is allowed in all VDCs. You can disallow the installed fabric extender feature set in a specific VDC on the device.

Example 6-20   *Entering the Chassis Mode for the Fabric Extender*

```
N7K-Agg(config)# fex 101
N7K-Agg(config-fex)# description Rack8-N2k
N7K-Agg(config-fex)# type N2232P
```

Example 6-21   *Defining the Number of Uplinks*

```
N7K-Agg(config-fex)# pinning max-links 1
```

You can use this command if the fabric extender is connected to its parent switch using one or more statically pinned fabric interfaces. There can be only one port channel connection.

Sometimes you want to disallow the ability to provision FEXs in a specific VDC; Example 6-22 shows how to do that

Example 6-22   *Disallowing the Fabric Extender Feature Set in a VDC*

```
N7K-Agg# configure terminal
N7K-Agg (config)# vdc 1
N7K-Agg (config-vdc)# no allow feature-set fex
N7K-Agg (config-vdc)# end
N7K-Agg #
```

NOTE   The **N7k-agg#** VDC1 is the VDC_ID, so it might be different depending on which VDC you want to connect to.

The next step is to associate the fabric extender to a port channel interface on the parent device. Example 6-23 creates a port channel with four member ports.

Example 6-23   *Associate the Fabric Extender to a Port Channel Interface*

```
N7K-Agg# configure terminal
N7K-Agg (config)# interface ethernet 1/28
N7K-Agg (config-if)# channel-group 4
N7K-Agg (config-if)# no shutdown
N7K-Agg (config-if)# exit
N7K-Agg (config)# interface ethernet 1/29
N7K-Agg (config-if)# channel-group 4
N7K-Agg (config-if)# no shutdown
N7K-Agg (config-if)# exit
N7K-Agg (config)# interface ethernet 1/30
N7K-Agg (config-if)# channel-group 4
N7K-Agg (config-if)# no shutdown
N7K-Agg (config-if)# exit
N7K-Agg (config)# interface ethernet 1/31
N7K-Agg (config-if)# channel-group 4
N7K-Agg (config-if)# no shutdown
N7K-Agg (config-if)# exit
N7K-Agg (config)# interface port-channel 4
N7K-Agg (config-if)# switchport
N7K-Agg (config-if)# switchport mode fex-fabric
N7K-Agg (config-if)# fex associate 101
```

After the FEX is associated successfully, use the commands shown in Examples 6-24 through 6-27 to verify that everything is configured properly.

Example 6-24 *Verifying FEX Association*

```
N7K-Agg# show fex
FEX        FEX             FEX       FEX
Number     Description     State     Model             Serial
-----------------------------------------------------------------------
101        FEX0101         Online    N2K-C2248TP-1GE   JAF1418AARL
```

Example 6-25 *Display Detailed Information About a Specific FEX*

```
N7K-Agg# show fex 101 detail
FEX: 101 Description: FEX0101       state: Online
   FEX version: 5.1(1) [Switch version: 5.1(1)]
   FEX Interim version: 5.1(0.159.6)
   Switch Interim version: 5.1(1)
   Extender Model: N2K-C2248TP-1GE,    Extender Serial: JAF1418AARL
   Part No: 73-12748-05
   Card Id: 99, Mac Addr: 54:75:d0:a9:49:42, Num Macs: 64
   Module Sw Gen: 21    [Switch Sw Gen: 21]
 pinning-mode: static        Max-links: 1
   Fabric port for control traffic: Po101
   Fabric interface state:
      Po101 - Interface Up. State: Active
      Eth2/1 - Interface Up. State: Active
      Eth2/2 - Interface Up. State: Active
      Eth4/1 - Interface Up. State: Active
      Eth4/2 - Interface Up. State: Active
   Fex Port              State    Fabric Port    Primary Fabric
            Eth101/1/1     Up        Po101           Po101
            Eth101/1/2     Up        Po101           Po101
            Eth101/1/3    Down       Po101           Po101
            Eth101/1/4    Down       Po101           Po101
```

Example 6-26 *Display Which FEX Interfaces Are Pinned to Which Fabric Interfaces*

```
N7K-Agg# show interface port-channel 101 fex-intf
Fabric          FEX
Interface       Interfaces
--------------------------------------------------
Po101           Eth101/1/2    Eth101/1/1
```

Example 6-27 *Display the Host Interfaces That Are Pinned to a Port Channel Fabric Interface*

```
N7K-Agg# show interface port-channel 4 fex-intf
Fabric                 FEX
Interface              Interfaces
--------------------------------------------------
Po4                    Eth101/1/48   Eth101/1/47   Eth101/1/46   Eth101/1/45
                       Eth101/1/44   Eth101/1/43   Eth101/1/42   Eth101/1/41
                       Eth101/1/40   Eth101/1/39   Eth101/1/38   Eth101/1/37
                       Eth101/1/36   Eth101/1/35   Eth101/1/34   Eth101/1/33
                       Eth101/1/32   Eth101/1/31   Eth101/1/30   Eth101/1/29
                       Eth101/1/28   Eth101/1/27   Eth101/1/26   Eth101/1/25
                       Eth101/1/24   Eth101/1/23   Eth101/1/22   Eth101/1/21
                       Eth101/1/20   Eth101/1/19   Eth101/1/18   Eth101/1/17
                       Eth101/1/16   Eth101/1/15   Eth101/1/14   Eth101/1/13
                       Eth101/1/12   Eth101/1/11   Eth101/1/10   Eth101/1/9
                       Eth101/1/8    Eth101/1/7    Eth101/1/6    Eth101/1/5
                       Eth101/1/4    Eth101/1/3    Eth101/1/2    Eth101/1/1
```

Cisco Adapter FEX Technology

Cisco Adapter FEX is a technology to virtualize 10GE/40G adapters for a bare metal server. The physical adapter can be logically partitioned to multiple vNICS and vHBAs and will be visible to the main operating system installed on the server as separate interface cards as if there are multiple physical adapters installed in the server itself. The advantage of this approach is that it allows you to reduce power and cooling needs and reduce the number of network ports.

> **NOTE** Another technology that complements Adapter-FEX but for virtualized servers is Cisco Virtual Machine Fabric Extender (VM-FEX), which is a Cisco technology that extends Cisco fabric extender technology to the virtual machines.

As shown in Figure 6-18, the server is a bare metal server with a Cisco virtual interface card (VIC) and two 10G ports, The server is connected to the Nexus 5500 using the two 10G physical ports. As an option, you can deploy this solution using the Nexus 2000 connected to the Nexus 5000 as a parent switch.

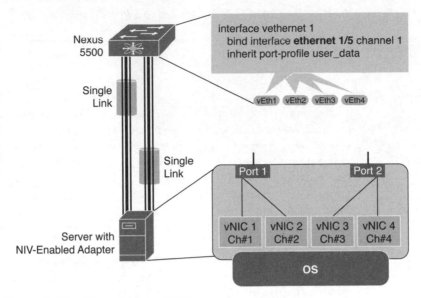

Figure 6-18   *Cisco Adapter FEX*

The Cisco Adapter FEX requires an adapter that supports VN-Tag technology like the Cisco UCS VIC-1225/1385 for the Cisco UCS C-Series rack-mount server, the Cisco UCS VIC-1240/1380 for the Cisco UCS B-Series server, or third-party adapters that support the VN-Tag technology. We require a switch that also supports adapter FEX, such as the Nexus 5500/6000. In addition to the hardware, we need the software component, which is the Cisco NX-OS that combines the advantages of the FEX link architecture with server I/O virtualization to create multiple virtual interfaces over a single Ethernet interface.

Figure 6-19 shows examples of Cisco Nexus 5500 platform switch adapter FEX topologies with server network adapters.

Topologies 4 and 5 support active/standby teaming of uplinks. The active/standby topologies that are shown have one uplink as active and the other uplink as standby. With some server network adapters, you can select the active and standby uplinks per each vNIC. In this case, each uplink is an active uplink for a specific vNIC and becomes a standby for the remaining uplinks. Selecting the active and standby uplinks per vNIC is recommended.

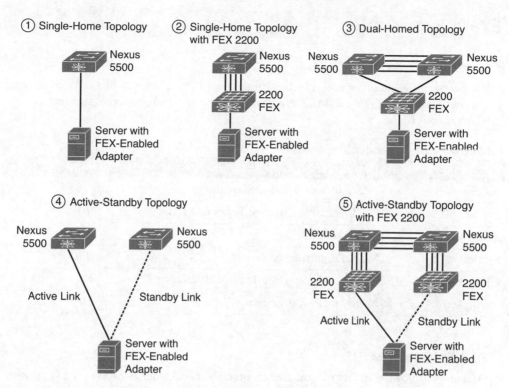

Figure 6-19 *Cisco Adapter FEX Supported Topologies*

Reference List

Cisco Nexus 7000 Series NX-OS Virtual Device Context Configuration Guide: http://
www.cisco.com/c/en/us/td/docs/switches/datacenter/sw/nx-os/virtual_device_context/
configuration/guide/b-7k-Cisco-Nexus-7000-Series-NX-OS-Virtual-Device-Context-Config-
uration-Guide.html

**Data Center Routed Access Design with Cisco Nexus 5500 Platform and 2000 Series
Fabric Extenders:** http://www.cisco.com/c/en/us/products/collateral/switches/nexus-
5000-series-switches/guide_c07-673997.html

Using Adapter FEX: http://www.cisco.com/en/US/docs/switches/datacenter/nexus5000/
sw/mkt_ops_guides/513_n1_1/n5k_ops_adapter_fex.html

Exam Preparation Tasks

Review All Key Topics

Review the most important topics in the chapter, noted with the key topics icon in the outer margin of the page. Table 6-2 lists a reference for these key topics and the page numbers on which each is found.

Table 6-2   Key Topics for Chapter 6

Key Topic Element	Description	Page
Section	"Vertical Consolidation Scenarios"	195
Section	"Understanding Different Types of VDCs"	197
Section	"VDC Administration"	199
Section	"VDC Requirements"	200
Figure 6-12	"Nexus 2000 Interface Types and Acronyms"	211
Example 6-24	"Verifying FEX Association"	218

Define Key Terms

Define the following key terms from this chapter, and check your answers in the Glossary:

Virtual Device Context (VDC), Supervisor Engine (SUP), Demilitarized Zone (DMZ), Erasable Programmable Logic Device (EPLD), Fabric Extender (FEX), Role-Based Access Control (RBAC), Network Interface (NIF), Host Interface (HIF), Virtual Interface (VIF), Logical Interface (LIF), End-of-Row (EoR), Top-of-Rack (ToR), VN-Tag, Root Port (RP), Designated Port (DP)

Part II Review

Keep track of your part review progress with the checklist shown in Table PII-1. Details on each task follow the table.

Table PII-1   Part II Review Checklist

Activity	First Date Completed	Second Date Completed
Repeat all "Do I Know This Already?" questions		
Answer "Part Review" questions		
Review Key Topics		
Self-assessment questionnaire		

Repeat All "Do I Know This Already?" Questions: For this task, answer the "Do I Know This Already?" questions again for the chapters in this part of the book, using the PCPT software. Refer to "How to View Only 'Do I Know This Already?' Questions by Part" in the Introduction to this book for help with how to make the PCPT software show you "Do I Know This Already?" questions for this part only.

Answer "Part Review" Questions: For this task, answer the "Part Review" questions for this part of the book, using the PCPT software. Refer to "How to View Only Part Review Questions by Part" in the Introduction to this book for help with how to make the PCPT software show you "Part Review" questions for this part only.

Review Key Topics: Browse back through the chapters and look for the Key Topic icons. If you do not remember some details, take the time to reread those topics.

Self-Assessment Questionnaire: Each chapter of this book introduces several key learning items. This might seem overwhelming to you initially, but as you read through each new chapter, you will become more familiar and comfortable with them, which will help you remember the concepts and technologies of these key topics as you progress with the book.

For this self-assessment exercise in the book, without looking back at the chapters or your notes, you should try to answer these self-assessment questions to the best of your ability. This exercise lists a set of key self-assessment questions, which are relevant to the particular chapter, shown in the following list. There will be no written answers to these questions in this book; if you are not certain, you should go back and refresh on the key topics.

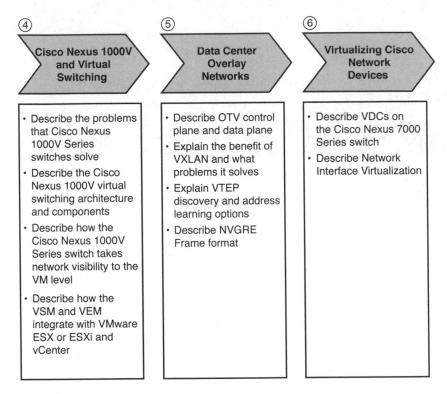

④ **Cisco Nexus 1000V and Virtual Switching**

- Describe the problems that Cisco Nexus 1000V Series switches solve
- Describe the Cisco Nexus 1000V virtual switching architecture and components
- Describe how the Cisco Nexus 1000V Series switch takes network visibility to the VM level
- Describe how the VSM and VEM integrate with VMware ESX or ESXi and vCenter

⑤ **Data Center Overlay Networks**

- Describe OTV control plane and data plane
- Explain the benefit of VXLAN and what problems it solves
- Explain VTEP discovery and address learning options
- Describe NVGRE Frame format

⑥ **Virtualizing Cisco Network Devices**

- Describe VDCs on the Cisco Nexus 7000 Series switch
- Describe Network Interface Virtualization

■ Think of each of these open self-assessment questions as being about the chapters you have read. You might or might not find the answer explicitly, but the chapter is structured to give you the knowledge and understanding to be able to discuss and explain these self-assessment questions. For example, number 4 is about Cisco Nexus 1000V and virtual switching, number 5 is about data center overlay networks, and so on.

■ Note your answer and try to reference key words in the answer from the relevant chapter. For example, VXLAN would apply to Chapter 5, "Data Center Overlay Networks."

Exam topics covered in Part III:

- 1.1 Describe common server types and connectivity found in a data center
- 1.2 Describe the physical components of the Cisco UCS
- 1.3 Describe the concepts and benefits of UCS hardware abstraction
- 1.4 Perform basic Cisco UCS configuration
    - 1.4.a Cluster high availability
    - 1.4.b Port roles
    - 1.4.c Hardware discovery
- 1.5 Describe server virtualization concepts and benefits
    - 1.5.a Hypervisors
    - 1.5.b Virtual switches
    - 1.5.c Shared storage
    - 1.5.d Virtual Machine components
    - 1.5.e Virtual Machine Manager

Part III

Cisco Unified Computing

This chapter covers the following exam topics:

1.1 Describe common server types and connectivity found in a data center

1.2 Describe the physical components of the UCS

CHAPTER 7

Cisco UCS Architecture

The Cisco Unified Computing System (UCS) journey started many years ago, culminating in its first customer shipment (FCS) around 2009. Since then, the x86 server market has been transformed and reshaped by Cisco UCS. Having started with a clean slate, Cisco clearly changed the industry with a true shift in computing paradigm around x86 server systems. This shift was initially focused on x86 blade server legacy computing architectures, and then Cisco transferred those benefits to Cisco x86 rackmount servers and paved the way for Cisco's hyperconverged infrastructure with Cisco UCS.

The Cisco UCS infrastructure hardware is now in its third generation. This chapter focuses on the second generation of infrastructure and computer server hardware. Where necessary, you will learn the key differences in third-generation hardware as we progress through this chapter.

The Cisco UCS servers have undergone faster, more frequent upgrades because Cisco UCS servers are released in lock step with Intel's tick-tock processor development model and market requirements. Figure 7-1 shows an overview of the Cisco UCS product family.

This chapter is structured into two sections. The first section aims to explain the Cisco UCS value proposition, Cisco UCS hardware, and software portfolio. The objective is to provide you with an up-to-date product overview and explain how it fits within the Cisco UCS family of products and solutions.

The second section focuses on Cisco UCS architecture, describing the various options for connectivity, north and south to the Cisco UCS fabric interconnects, I/O module connectivity, and key server components. The core Cisco UCS architecture remains firm and solid, while Cisco has unified blade, rackmount, and modular server management into it. This is explained later in this chapter.

This chapter is written to clearly outline the product portfolio, fundamentals, concepts, valid architectures, and advantages. This chapter is not an official product or configuration guide, however; refer to the appropriate official documents to evaluate products, design, and configure solutions with Cisco UCS products.

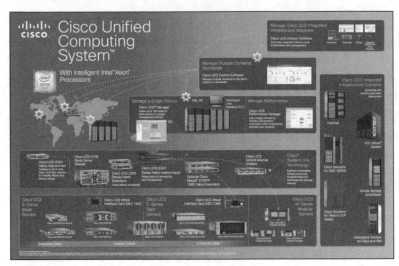

Figure 7-1 *Cisco UCS Product Family Overview*

"Do I Know This Already?" Quiz

The "Do I Know This Already?" quiz enables you to assess whether you should read this entire chapter thoroughly or jump to the "Exam Preparation Tasks" section. If you are in doubt about your answers to these questions or your own assessment of your knowledge of the topics, read the entire chapter. Table 7-1 lists some of the major headings in this chapter and their corresponding "Do I Know This Already?" quiz questions. You can find the answers in Appendix A, "Answers to the 'Do I Know This Already?' Quizzes."

Table 7-1   "Do I Know This Already?" Section-to-Question Mapping

Foundation Topics Section	Questions
"Evolution of Server Computing in a Nutshell"	2, 3, 4
"Cisco Unified Computing System Architecture"	1, 8
"Describing the Cisco UCS Product Family"	5, 6
"Cisco UCS Connectivity Architecture"	7, 10
"Cisco Integrated Management Controller (CIMC) Architecture"	9

CAUTION   The goal of self-assessment is to gauge your mastery of the topics in this chapter. If you do not know the answer to a question or are only partially sure of the answer, you should mark that question as wrong for purposes of the self-assessment. Giving yourself credit for an answer you correctly guess skews your self-assessment results and might provide you with a false sense of security.

1. Which of the following is true?

   a. Cisco UCS is the newest unified communications system architecture by Cisco.

   b. Cisco UCS is a blade server.

   c. Cisco UCS is a unified computing system composed of hardware and software.

   d. Cisco UCS is a rackmount server.

2. Which of the following are not physical form factors of computing in a data center? (Choose two.)

   a. Blade and rackmount servers

   b. High performance or grid computing

   c. Mainframes and symmetric multiprocessing computing systems in rack cabinets

   d. Cloud computing

3. True or False? Cisco UCS M-Series modular servers use System Link Technology to share common, disaggregated resources; this is composed via Cisco UCS Service Profiles.

   a. True

   b. False

4. True or false? Cisco UCS computing blades and rackmount servers are part of the x86 microprocessor architecture.

   a. True

   b. False

5. What is the difference between Cisco UCS B, C-Series naming conventions, and the trailing reference to M#?

   a. Cisco UCS B-Series, C-Series, and so on is the release of computing hardware based on alphabetical order, and the trailing M# refers to the processor family.

   b. The Cisco B-Series refers to AC-powered blades, the Cisco C-Series refers to DC-powered blades, and the trailing M# refers to the processor family.

   c. Cisco UCS B-Series and C-Series refer to blade and rackmount form factors, respectively. The trailing M# is a reference to the processor family.

   d. Cisco UCS B-Series refers to high-density servers, and Cisco C-Series refers to low-density servers.

6. Which of the following is the configuration for optimal performance when populating DRAM in a Cisco UCS B-Series B200 M3 blade server with 2x E5-2600v2 processors?

   a. 1DPC

   b. 2DPC

   c. 3DPC

   d. 4DPC

7. Which of the following is the configuration maximum of a Cisco UCS C460 M2 C-Series rackmount server?

  a. 2 CPU sockets, 512 GB RAM, 10 SAS disk drives

  b. 4 CPU sockets, 1 TB RAM, 10 SAS disk drives

  c. 2 CPU sockets, 1 TB RAM, 12 SAS disk drives

  d. 4 CPU sockets, 2 TB RAM, 12 SAS disk drives or SATA SSDs

8. Which of the following are valid fabric link configurations (discrete) on a Cisco UCS 2104XP, 2208XP, or IOM 2304 I/O module? (Choose all that apply.)

  a. 1 link

  b. 2 links

  c. 3 links

  d. 4 links

9. Where is the Cisco Integrated Management Controller (CIMC) chip located within Cisco UCS?

  a. It is located in every Cisco UCS B- and C-Series server motherboard.

  b. On the Cisco UCS 61xx and 62xx Fabric Interconnects.

  c. It is located in every Cisco UCS IOM 2104XP and 2208XP module.

  d. It is located in the Cisco UCS 5108 chassis that contains all blade servers.

10. When connecting a Cisco UCS chassis-to-fabric interconnect cluster, can you connect a single IOM module to both fabric interconnects?

  a. Yes, it can be connected.

  b. No, it cannot be connected.

Foundation Topics

Evolution of Server Computing in a Nutshell

Not so long ago, mainstream servers were designed as large rack-cabinet mounted systems. Some server computing systems were large enough to consume an entire rack or even multiple racks. In fact, such systems still exist today. These systems required a large footprint to house enough power and capacity to service a large number of users.

In an enterprise data center, you would see a mixture of these server-computing footprints, mainly because of the silo approach to computing dictated by minimum computing requirements, to host a particular vendor's application. An enterprise utilizes applications from multiple vendors. Therefore, there is a mixture of reduced instruction set computing (RISC) and complex instruction set computing (CISC) based system footprints in an enterprise data center.

RISC-based systems (RISC architecture includes DEC-ALPHA, PA-RISC, SPARC, PowerPC, MIPS, and so on) were mainly running UNIX operating systems, whereas the CISC-based systems (CISC architecture includes AMD K5, x86-64, Opteron, Intel 8086, 8088, 80286, 80386, 80486, Pentium, Xeon, and so on) were running MS-DOS, Novell, Windows, and now Linux operating systems.

RISC has existed for many years and has not been able to kick CISC architecture out of the market. In fact, the price-performance ratio of CISC-based microprocessors has improved tremendously, and with robust operating systems to support it and many more application vendors porting their critical applications onto CISC architecture today, the x86 architecture is growing. A point to note: the x86 standard, as used by Intel and AMD, for example, is based on this CISC architecture.

As the x86 architecture started to grow, the next change in server computing came with commoditized rackmount servers, which were smaller, cost-effective computing nodes. It did not have the mighty processing power of the symmetric multiprocessing systems (SMPs), so it had a smaller footprint and was used purposefully to host a single service or application per physical server. That gave way to proliferation of commoditized servers, also known as physical server sprawl in an enterprise data center, leading to a multitude of issues with having to provide cabling, space, power, cooling, networking, storage-area network (SAN) connectivity, and management (to name a few) for each server.

The next wave in computing was to combine the compute resources of commoditized rackmount servers into a blade form factor and house it within a smaller enclosure. The proliferation was somewhat curtailed by maximizing on physical space, shared power, shared networking, and storage access; the industry started focusing on blade server architecture and realizing the benefits.

Today, it is all about doing more with less; variable-ratio composable and hyperconverged servers. How has Cisco UCS improved legacy x86 server architectures? Servers are composable, compact, and more densely populated and utilize more shared resources, less cabling, and converged network fabrics. The key driver has been server virtualization technologies applied to these server systems within an enterprise/cloud data center, which allows a single

7

server to host many virtual servers of varying workloads or a single application to be distributed across multiple servers that can be composed using atomic components.

What Is a Socket?

In the server-computing world, you will hear reference to terminologies such as socket, CPU, core, and hyperthreading. A socket is a reference to a physical microprocessor receptacle, which is visible and present on your server motherboard. It is also referred to as the physical CPU. Figure 7-2 shows a CPU socket in a Cisco UCS B-Series blade server.

Cisco UCS B-Series Blade Server (Front View)

Cisco UCS B-Series Blade Server (Half-Width, Top View)

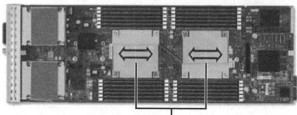

CPU Sockets (with Heat Sinks)

Figure 7-2 *A CPU Socket*

What Is a Core?

A socket or physical CPU can consist of a single core or multiple cores. Each core is a physical processing unit embedded within that socket. An operating system will always see the number of CPUs as equal to the number of cores. Figure 7-3 shows the overlay of a core on a physical socket.

Cisco UCS B-Series Blade Server (Front View)

Physical CPU Cores

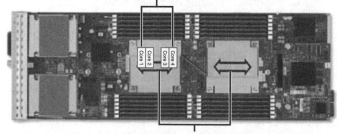

CPU Sockets (with Heat Sinks)

Figure 7-3 *A Core*

What Is Hyperthreading?

If an operating system sees more cores than existing physical cores, that is the effect of hyperthreading. CPUs have the capability to signal each core to emulate two or more processors. These emulated processors are called threads. Each of these emulated processors can execute multiple queues of instructions by means of a time-sharing resource (clever multitasking techniques) and increase the efficiency and throughput of a CPU. Figure 7-4 shows a graphical representation of hyperthreading.

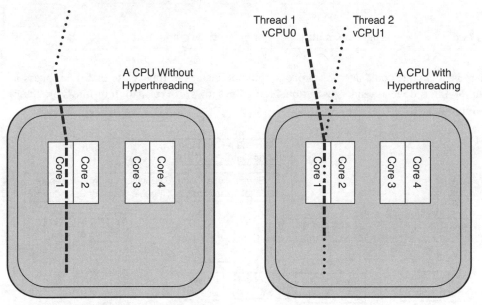

Figure 7-4   *Hyperthreading*

Understanding Server Processor Numbering

In the server class microprocessor family, you are most likely familiar with Intel stickers, nameplates advertising Pentium and Xeon-based servers. These are marketing terms. The corresponding actual microprocessor architecture of these chips has different code names.

At the time of writing this chapter, the latest server-class microprocessor architecture was code-named Haswell, Broadwell, which are the successors to the Ivy Bridge microprocessor architecture by Intel. Since the Nehalem microprocessor architecture, Intel started to introduce a two-letter code EP or EX to differentiate between 2-socket and 4-socket capable microprocessor architectural variants, respectively. Older Intel CPUs had numerical processor numbers; the first digit in these numbers signified scalability. Table 7-2 shows numerical processor numbers and their relationship.

Table 7-2   Numerical Processor Numbers (Intel's Nehalem Family)

Processor	Scalability
3xxx	1-Socket / 1-Way
5xxx	2-Socket / 2-Way
7xxx	4-Socket / 4-Way

At the time of writing this chapter, the latest generation of Intel's microprocessors started using a different naming convention: E3/E5/E7 classes signifying enterprise class. Table 7-3 contains the latest generation of processor naming and their positioning.

Table 7-3   Latest Generation of Processor Naming

Processor	Positioning
E3-xxxx	Microprocessor for workstations
E5-xxxx	Midclass servers
E7-xxxx	High-end, multiprocessor enterprise computing

Here is how you should interpret processor numbering at this time. Note that the processor numbering is done at vendor discretion. Figure 7-5 shows an explanation of Intel's processor numbering.

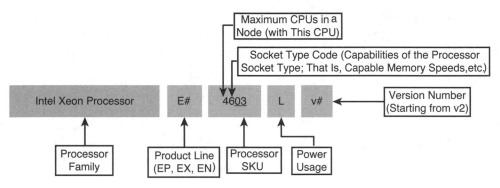

Figure 7-5   *Intel's Processor Numbering*

Value of Cisco UCS in the Data Center

As you know, x86-architecture–based servers have been in existence for a while. The industry has been upgrading these computer server nodes over time with newer, faster resources and components, but it has not necessarily improved or optimized the legacy computing approach or architecture.

Cisco has taken a clean-slate approach to improving that legacy computing approach or architecture and brought about a paradigm shift in computing architecture with clear, tangible benefits in an enterprise data center.

Cisco reinvented the legacy architectures, where each computer server chassis or enclosure was equipped with its own LAN, SAN switches, or pass-through capabilities and various other active peripherals to an architecture based on open standards that enable sharing and pooling of computer resources, wire-once capabilities, and unified management, with a single pane of glass. Some of the key Cisco UCS improvements are explained in detail in the following sections.

One Unified System

Simply said, a computer server is a set of resources needed to process or execute a set of defined tasks/jobs and produce a result. A UCS is a collection of such computer servers that are no longer tied to its chassis boundary. This system is wired once to networks (for data, management access) and to central storage to boot or store file/block-level data. LAN and SAN connectivity is set up on a system-by-system basis and does not require the administrator to redo it when a new computer server is added to the infrastructure. And this unified system is managed through a single pane of glass rather than multiple points of management with layers of software.

The entire Cisco UCS is seen as one domain. The Cisco UCS is not tied to an individual blade chassis or to a server; instead, it is tied to the first level aggregation point of a collection of these blade chassis and computer servers—that is, fabric interconnects running the UCS Manager software. This allows better scalability and flexibility, faster modifications, and reduced management endpoints today. Figure 7-6 shows a logical view of a Cisco UCS domain.

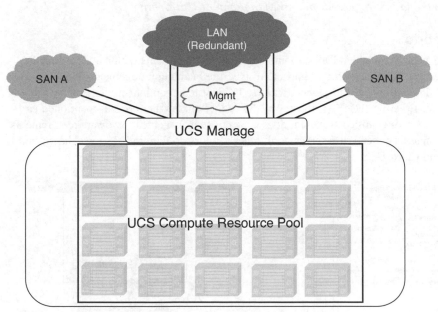

Figure 7-6   *Cisco UCS—One Unified System*

The Cisco UCS is the only system to provide "management uniformity" across multiple form factors, bringing all the advantages of the UCS to all form factors. Through stateless computing capabilities (discussed later in this section and subsequent chapters), the UCS system allows various workloads/applications to run on the best suited hardware configuration that it requires. This makes better use of hardware resources independent of the compute form factor. Figure 7-7 shows the management uniformity across form factors.

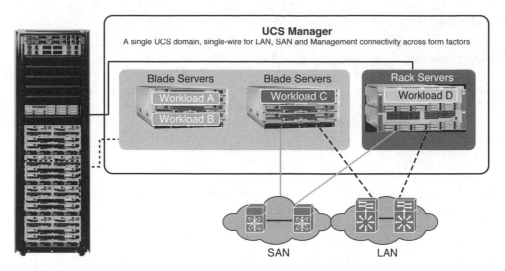

Figure 7-7   *Form Factor Freedom and Management Uniformity*

Unified Fabric

Cisco UCS utilizes a Unified Fabric to interconnect all components within a UCS domain. The Unified Fabric has a profound impact on structured cabling requirements within a server rack(s). Its single point of management within a UCS system, combined with running Fibre Channel over Ethernet (FCoE), is the key to this reduction. Furthermore, as mentioned earlier, Cisco UCS is one unified system; it does not impose management hardware requirements chassis-by-chassis or server-by-server, as all other vendors do. Figure 7-8 shows the unified fabric within Cisco UCS.

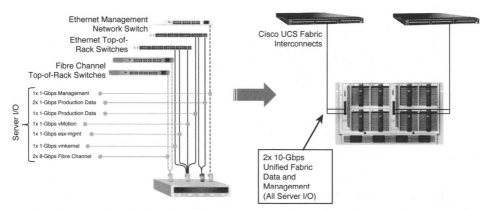

Figure 7-8   *Unified Fabric*

Unified Management and Operations

The Cisco UCS Manager software manages a UCS domain. This software is designed with current organizational IT functional responsibilities in mind; it is designed to be nondisruptive but integral. The UCS Manager software enables multiple teams (such as storage, network, compute, and security) to control their area of responsibility within the UCS domain.

The UCS Manager controls all aspects of a server other than the operating system of a server or LUN provisioning. Details of faults, computer service profiles, LAN, SAN access management and communication, logging, UCS backup, and so on are all managed by a piece of unified management software—Cisco UCS Manager. There is no need to purchase additional external solution to achieve this level of consolidated, highly available, and open interface (XML API)–based management. Figure 7-9 shows the Cisco UCS Management layer and open standards.

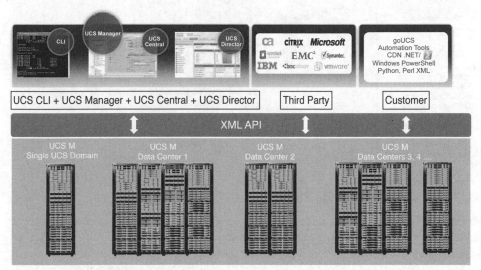

Figure 7-9 *Unified Management and Operations*

Cisco UCS Stateless Computing

The Cisco UCS system operates on a stateless x86-based computing infrastructure model. It offers programmable computer hardware. Until the computer hardware is programmed with predefined identities, the computer hardware (blade/modular/rackmount server) is nothing but bare metal.

This programmability is extended to all firmware, BIOS settings, adapters, LAN, SAN edge, and quality of service (QoS) parameters, to name a few. The list of programmable attributes is the most extensive list of settings offered in the market today. All these settings are defined in an object called a service profile, which is a definition of a server. When a service profile is attached to a bare metal server, it assumes the connectivity, configuration, and identities defined in that service profile, and it boots. Figure 7-10 shows some of the key Cisco UCS service profile's attributes.

This level of hardware abstraction allows great flexibility. A simple, yet straightforward analogy: do you remember the concept of hot-spares in storage arrays? When disks functioning in a RAID configuration encounter a faulty disk, an unused hot-spare disk located anywhere in that array can assume the function of that failed disk and allow the RAID to be reconstructed. That was made possible because that unused disk did not have state and could assume the identity of the failed disk. With Cisco UCS service profiles, you can achieve the same on a blade or rackmount server.

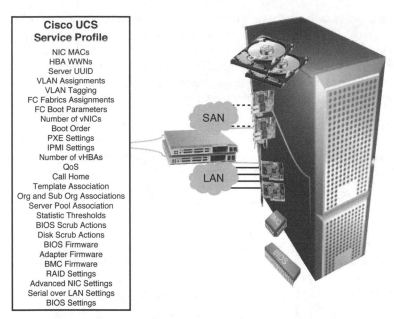

Cisco UCS Service Profile

NIC MACs
HBA WWNs
Server UUID
VLAN Assignments
VLAN Tagging
FC Fabrics Assignments
FC Boot Parameters
Number of vNICs
Boot Order
PXE Settings
IPMI Settings
Number of vHBAs
QoS
Call Home
Template Association
Org and Sub Org Associations
Server Pool Association
Statistic Thresholds
BIOS Scrub Actions
Disk Scrub Actions
BIOS Firmware
Adapter Firmware
BMC Firmware
RAID Settings
Advanced NIC Settings
Serial over LAN Settings
BIOS Settings

Figure 7-10 *Cisco UCS Service Profile*

Numerous benefits arise given different circumstances with stateless computing. Various applications may require different levels of firmware support on a blade. You can package these updates into service profiles and perform a coordinated update or ensure that the level of firmware always follows the service profile that is designated for that particular application.

Intelligent Automation, Cloud-Ready Infrastructure

The Cisco UCS system is fundamentally designed with multitenancy in mind and ready to enable automation. The Cisco UCS system allows multilevel tiers of organizational structures. This provides the flexibility to define organizational business units; for example, marketing and finance can correspond to Tenant 1 and Tenant 2 within the system. The UCS system can be logically carved out (with all the benefits it offers) to a given organization or tenant. The ability to define resources per organization allows for shared resources/pools within the UCS system and the architecture moving away from traditional silo deployments.

Cisco UCS can be configured to automatically qualify, classify, and optionally insert server computer resources into pools for use. The classification can be based on various attributes (memory, CPU types, adapter types) with minimum and maximum ranges. When an organization or tenant wants to assign its server templates to a computer resource, it needs only to select the appropriate pool. This capability helps with automation of server assignments to an organization or tenant.

As mentioned earlier, with stateless computing, all resources utilized for computing—such as network interface cards (NICs), host bus adapters (HBAs), firmware, BOIS, SAN and LAN settings, and so on—can be templatized for rapid automated deployment. The Cisco UCS system has many integrated features to help in automating common functions, allowing the management of larger server footprints without much administrator overhead. By making use of the XML application programming interface (API; discussed later in another chapter), you have all the tools needed to implement a custom user or admin portal for self-service provisioning and the ability to tie into governance, chargeback, trouble ticketing, business process, and other manager of manager (MoM) solutions.

Describing the Cisco UCS Product Family

The Cisco UCS product family consists of both hardware and software. Over the years, the Cisco UCS hardware product portfolio has been evolving and growing with key innovations and acquisitions; as a result, the Cisco UCS hardware product portfolio has grown. The Cisco UCS hardware product family includes blade, rackmount, modular servers, and the associated components to house the blade/rackmount, modular servers and their connectivity. This chapter will primarily focus on mainstream Cisco UCS B-Series and C-Series server connectivity, while highlighting M-Series servers where appropriate for your understanding. Figure 7-11 shows the building blocks of Cisco UCS.

> **NOTE**   At the time of writing this chapter, End-of-Sale of Cisco M-Series modular server hardware was announced.

UCS Manager
• Embedded–Manages Entire UCS Domain

Fabric Interconnect
• 10GE Unified Fabric Switch

Chassis IO Module
• Remote Line Card

Blade Server Chassis
• Flexible Bay Configurations

Blade and Rack Servers
• x86 Industry Standard
• Patented Extended Memory

I/O Adapters
• Choice of Multiple Adapters

Figure 7-11   *Building Blocks of Cisco UCS*

Cisco UCS Computer Hardware Naming

The Cisco UCS computing hardware (blades or rackmount servers) is numbered; examples are B200 M3, C220 M1, M142, and so on. This numbering is primarily to indicate four key aspects of that computer hardware. Depending on the intents and purposes of utilizing the computer node within an enterprise, you should understand the following. Figure 7-12 explains the Cisco UCS computer hardware naming convention.

1. This is a Blade Server (B-Series), a Rackmount Server (C-Series), or Modular Servers (M-Series).

2. This blade/rackmount/modular server can scale in CPU (for example, a maximum of 1-Socket, 2-Sockets, or 4-Sockets).

3. This blade/rackmount server can scale in terms of memory and internal storage capacity.

4. This blade has the capability to house a generation of microprocessor (for example, M4 [Ivy Bridge]).

NOTE Cisco M-Series modular servers have a similar naming convention; it consists of compute cartridges (Cisco UCS M142, M1414, or M2814s) and requires a modular chassis (Cisco M4308) to house these compute cartridges.

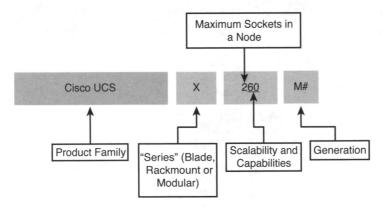

Figure 7-12 *Cisco UCS Computer Hardware Naming*

Cisco UCS Fabric Interconnects

The Cisco UCS Fabric Interconnects provide northbound access to LAN, SAN, and out-of-band management segments. The Cisco UCS Fabric Interconnects are Top-of-Rack devices that provide unified access to the Cisco UCS domain. Figure 7-13 shows a logical view of a Cisco UCS domain with multiple server form factors and north/south connectivity.

As mentioned earlier, the Cisco UCS infrastructure hardware (at the time of writing this chapter) is in its third generation. Table 7-4 summarizes all three generations of UCS Fabric Interconnect hardware.

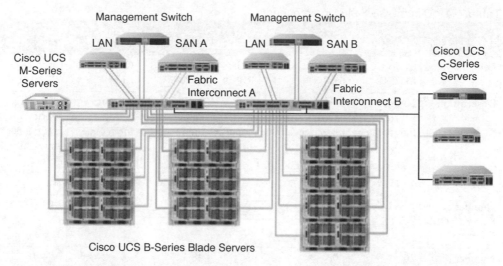

Figure 7-13 *Cisco UCS Domain*

NOTE The Cisco UCS 61xx series Fabric Interconnects and Cisco UCS 2104 I/O modules have reached end-of-life, End-of-Sale status but continue to be supported until a certain time period, at the time of writing this chapter. Refer to the Cisco website for more information. Figure 7-14 shows all three generations of Cisco UCS Fabric Interconnects and expansion modules, and Table 7-4 tabulates their key attributes.

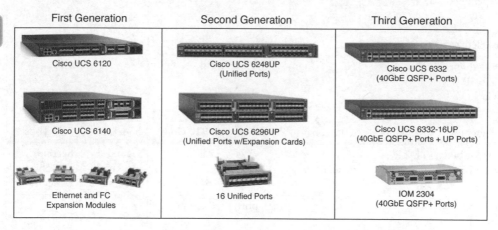

Figure 7-14 *Cisco UCS Fabric Interconnects and Expansion Modules*

Table 7-4   Cisco UCS Fabric Interconnects

	First Generation		Second Generation		*Third Generation	
Item	Cisco UCS 6120XP	Cisco UCS 6140XP	Cisco UCS 6248UP	Cisco UCS 6296UP	Cisco UCS 6332	Cisco UCS 6332-16UP
Description	20-Port Fabric Interconnect	40-Port Fabric Interconnect	48-Port Fabric Interconnect	96-Port Fabric Interconnect	32-Port Fabric Interconnect	40-Port Fabric Interconnect with Unified Ports
Form Factor	1 RU	2 RU	1 RU	2 RU	1RU	1RU
Number of Fixed 40 GB Interfaces					32	24
Number of Fixed 10 GB Interfaces	20	40	32	48	96 + 2 (Using breakout cables + QSA module)	72 + 16 (Using breakout cables)
Number of 1 GB/10 GB Interfaces (Depending on SFP Module Installed)	Ports 1–8	Ports 1–16	—	—	—	Ports 1–16
Unified Ports (1 GB/10 GB, 8 Gb/s FC, FCoE)	No	No	All	All	—	1-16
Throughput	520 Gbps	1.04 Tbps	960 Gbps	1920 Gbps	2.56 Tbps	2.43 Tbps
Compatibility with all IOMs	First generation only	First generation only	All	All	Second and Third Generation	Second and Third Generation
Expansion Slots	1	2	1 (16 port)	3 (16 port)	—	—
Fan Modules	2	5	2	5	4	4
Power Supplies	2 (AC only)	2 (AC only)	2 (AC/DC available)	2 (AC/DC available)	2	2

NOTE   The first-generation UCS Fabric Interconnects had the XP suffix to indicate 10 GbE and FCoE capability, whereas the second- and third-generation Fabric Interconnects have a UP suffix to indicate Unified Port capability.

What Is a Unified Port?

A unified port is a physical interface/port on the Cisco UCS Fabric Interconnect, where its characteristics (protocol, associated speeds) can be changed dynamically. These physical ports' characteristics can be changed to behave as an Ethernet or Native FC port and 1G/10G or 8/4/2/1 Gbps FC speeds. This applies to the expansion module, too. It increases design flexibility and allows LAN and storage convergence based on business needs. You can configure this via the Configure Unified Ports slider action and by right-clicking the desired port within the Cisco UCS Manager. You must ensure the appropriate optics are used—SFP/SFP+ transceivers—to achieve functionality.

What Are QSA Modules and Breakout Cables?

The Cisco QSFP to SFP or SFP+ Adapter (QSA) Module offers 10 Gigabit Ethernet and 1 Gigabit Ethernet connectivity for QSFP 40G-only platforms. The breakout cables plug into a 40GBase port and provide 4x10GBase-CU SFP+ connections. The QSA module is a 40-Gigabit Ethernet transceiver module.

Cisco UCS Fabric Interconnect—Expansion Modules

The Cisco UCS Fabric Interconnect expansion modules exist to accommodate customer business requirements, design flexibility, and scalability. Figure 7-14 refers to these expansion modules, and Table 7-5 summarizes those expansion module options available for both Cisco UCS 6100 and 6200 Fabric Interconnects only.

Table 7-5   Cisco UCS Fabric Interconnect—Expansion Modules

Description	Cisco UCS 6120XP	Cisco UCS 6140XP	Cisco UCS 6248UP	Cisco UCS 6296UP
16-Port Unified Expansion Module	No	No	Yes	Yes
8-Port 1, 2, 4 Gbps Fibre Channel (FC)	Yes	Yes	—	—
6-Port 1, 2, 4, or 8 Gbps Fibre Channel (FC)	Yes	Yes	—	—
6-Port 10 GE	Yes	Yes	—	—
4-Port 10 GE/4-Port Fibre Channel	Yes	Yes	—	—

NOTE   The Cisco UCS 6300 Fabric Interconnects were released at the time of writing this chapter. They consist of physical/fixed ports only.

Cisco UCS 5108 Blade Server Chassis

The Cisco UCS 5108 blade server chassis is second to no other vendor in the market. As mentioned earlier, Cisco had a clean slate to innovate and remove all inherent weaknesses of the legacy blade and chassis architecture. A Cisco UCS 5108 blade server chassis backplane is 63% open. It contains only two I/O bays and nothing else apart from power supplies and fans. Figure 7-15 shows a Cisco UCS 5108 chassis backplane.

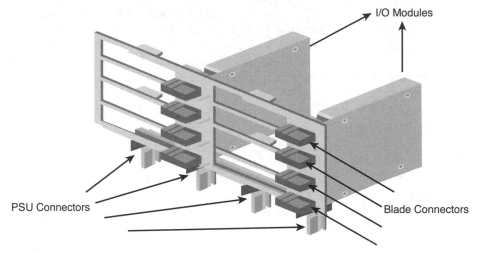

Figure 7-15   *Cisco UCS 5108 Blade Chassis Backplane*

The Cisco UCS 5108 blade server chassis is only 6 rack units (RU) in height with standard front-to-back cooling. A single chassis can contain eight half-width or four full-width Cisco UCS B-Series blade servers or a combination. Cisco UCS blade servers and power supplies are accessed from the front of the chassis, whereas the power inputs, fan, and I/O modules are accessed from the back of the chassis. All components are hot-swappable or field-replaceable units (FRU). The Cisco UCS 5108 blade server chassis supports multiple genera-tions of blade servers, I/O modules, power supplies, and fans. Figure 7-16 shows the front and rear view of a Cisco UCS 5108 blade server chassis.

Cisco UCS 5108 Blade Server Chassis—Power Supply and Redundancy Modes

The Cisco UCS 5108 blade server chassis consists of four power supplies, each at 110/220V, 2500W (autosensing), single-phase, AC power supplies or −48 to −60V, 2500W DC power supplies.

> **NOTE**   Do not mix the AC and DC power supplies within a Cisco 5108 blade server chas-sis, and ensure the right powered version of 5108 blade server chassis is utilized.

Two redundancy modes are available for these power supplies. In N+1 mode, the Cisco UCS 5108 blade server chassis tolerates a single power supply failure, without service interrup-tion. However, in the N+N (Grid) mode, if you have 4x power supplies and have set N+N redundancy, all 4x power supplies will be active, taking one-fourth of the load each. In the event of a single power supply failure, the load will be redistributed across the remaining 3x power supplies.

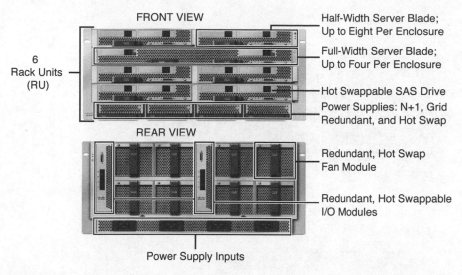

Figure 7-16 *Cisco UCS 5108 Blade Server Chassis Front and Rear View*

In either case, the output powers of these power supplies are in a matrix, pooled together, and all chassis components can draw power from this matrix. There are standard, high-density power cappings and policies that can be applied to the Cisco UCS 5108 blade server chassis power subsystems, which is discussed under the "Cisco UCS Chassis and Blade Power Capping" section in Chapter 9, "Cisco Unified Computing System Pools, Policies, Templates, and Service Profiles."

NOTE   For N+1 redundancy (standard-density), the chassis should have at least 3x power supplies active, and for redundant (high-density), the chassis should have 4x active power supplies. High-density mode is not supported in grid-redundant configuration.

Cisco UCS M4308 Chassis

The Cisco M4308 chassis is a 2RU chassis designed to house Cisco modular (M-Series) servers. It consists of a chassis management controller and eight cartridge slots. The chassis also consists of 2.5-inch, small form factor solid-state drive (SSD) bays and an internal RAID controller. 2x AC power modules (1+1 redundant) supply power to the chassis; 6x hot swappable fans provide the cooling. The chassis consists of 2x40GbE ports for data, management, and console ports. The Cisco UCS M4308 chassis also includes Cisco's System Link Technology, which allows creating 1024 PCIe devices on application-specific integrated circuits (ASIC) to be utilized by cartridge servers. Figure 7-17 shows the front and rear view of a modular server chassis.

FRONT VIEW

REAR VIEW

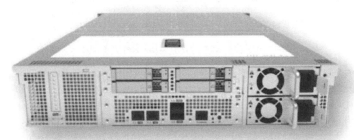

Figure 7-17   *Cisco UCS M4308 Modular Server Chassis Front and Rear View*

Cisco UCS I/O Modules (FEX)

The Fabric Extender (also referred to as the I/O Module, IOM, or FEX) logically extends the fabric interconnects to the blade server. Think of it as a remote line card that is embedded into the blade server chassis, allowing blade connectivity to the external world. I/O module settings are pushed via the UCS Manager and not managed directly. The primary functions of this module are to facilitate blade server I/O connectivity (internal and external), multiplex all I/O traffic up to the fabric interconnects, and monitor and manage the Cisco UCS infrastructure.

Apart from multiplexing blade server I/O, it also contains some key components: the Chassis Management Controller (CMC) and Chassis Management Switch (CMS) are vital components utilized to manage and monitor the chassis hardware and blade-server hardware components, also providing keyboard, video, mouse (KVM) access. Detailed architecture and connectivity options are discussed later in this chapter. Figure 7-18 shows pictures of first-, second-, and third-generation Cisco UCS I/O Modules, and Table 7-6 tabulates their key product capabilities.

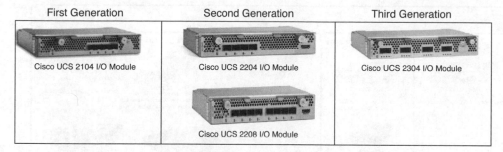

Figure 7-18 *Cisco UCS I/O Modules*

Table 7-6 Cisco UCS I/O Module Details

Description	Cisco UCS 2104 IOM	Cisco UCS 2204 IOM	Cisco UCS 2208 IOM	Cisco UCS 2304 IOM
Fabric Interconnect facing ports (Fabric Ports)	4	4	8	4
Fabric Interconnect facing bandwidth	40	40	80	160
Port channeling fabric ports	No	Yes	Yes	Yes
Host/blade facing ports/per IOM	8	32	32	4
Host/blade facing bandwidth/per IOM	80G	160G	320G	320G
Compatibility with different generation fabric interconnects	No	Yes	Yes	No
Max bandwidth per blade (per I/O module)	5G	40G	80G	40G

Cisco UCS B-Series Blade Servers

Cisco UCS B-Series blade servers are available in half- and full-width form factors. All blades are based on current (Nehalem) microprocessor architecture and share many features, such as being stateless and hot swappable, and each Cisco UCS blade server contains a Cisco Integrated Management Controller (CIMC). The CIMC architecture and the Cisco UCS blade server connectivity options are discussed later in this chapter. Table 7-7 summarizes the current Cisco UCS B-Series blade servers and their specifications to give you an overview of the product offering. Figure 7-19 shows a summary of Cisco UCS B-Series blade server products.

NOTE   The Cisco UCS B-Series blade servers B200 M1, B250 M1, B230 M1, and B440 M1 have all reached end-of-sale status but continue to be supported until a certain time period, at the time of writing this chapter. Please refer to the Cisco website for more information.

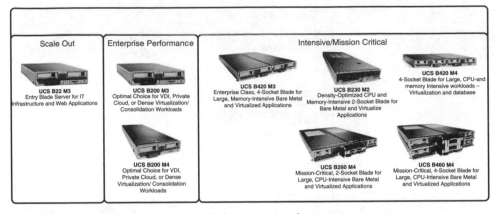

Figure 7-19 *Cisco UCS B-Series Blade Server Products*

Table 7-7 Cisco UCS B-Series Blade Server Products

Description	B22 M3	B200 M3	B230 M2	B260 M4	B420 M3	B420 M4	B460 M4	B200 M4
Width	Half	Half	Half	Half	Half	Half	Half	Half
Processor Sockets	Up to 2	Up to 2	Up to 2	Up to 2	2 or 4	2 or 4	2 or 4	Up to 2
Processors Supported	E5-2400	E5-2600 (Sandy Bridge), E5-2600 v2 (Ivy Bridge)	E7-2800, E7-8800	E5-2800 v2 E7-4800 v2 E7-8800 v2	E5-4600 v2	E5-4600 v3	E7-4800 v2, E7-8800 v2	E2600 v3
Memory Capacity	Up to 384 GB (12 slots)	Up to 768 GB (24 slots)	Up to 512 GB (32 slots)	Up to 3 TB (48 slots)	Up to 1.5 TB (48 slots)	Up to 3 TB (48 slots)	Up to 6 TB (96 slots)	Up to 768 GB (24 slots)
Extended Memory Technology	No	No	Yes	Yes	No	No	Yes	No
Memory DIMM Sizes	4, 8, 16, 32 GB DIMMS	4, 8, 16, 32 GB DIMMS	4, 8, 16 GB DIMMS	8, 16, 32 GB DIMMS	4, 8, 16, 32 GB DIMMS	8, 16, 32, 64 GB DIMMS	8, 16, 32 GB DIMMS	8, 16, 32 GB DIMMS (DDR4)
Internal Disk Drives	Max 2 (SATA, SAS)	Max 2 (SATA, SAS)	Max 2 (SATA)	Max 2 (SAS, SATA)	Max 4 (SAS, SATA)	Max 4 (SAS, SATA)	Max 4 (SAS, SATA)	Max 2 (SAS, SATA,)

Description	B22 M3	B200 M3	B230 M2	B260 M4	B420 M3	B420 M4	B460 M4	B200 M4
Maximum Internal Storage (Raw)	2 TB	2 TB	800 GB	2.4 TB	4 TB	6.4 TB	4.8 TB	3.2 TB
Integrated RAID Controller	0,1	0,1	0,1	0,1	0,1,10, 5	0,1,10, 5, 6,50,60	0,1	0,1
I/O Throughput	Up to 80 Gbps	Up to 80 Gbps	Up to 80 Gbps	Up to 160 Gbps	Up to 160 Gbps	Up to 160 Gbps	Up to 160 Gbps	Up to 80 Gbps

NOTE   The configurable options for Cisco virtual interface cards, port extenders, and adapter combinations differ based on the Cisco B-Series blade server model and CPU configuration. To achieve configuration maximums, it is a best practice to view the spec sheet of the corresponding Cisco UCS blade server(s) (available online) to understand the configuration maximums and validity of configurations.

Cisco UCS B-Series Best Practices for Populating DRAM

The Intel Nehalem microprocessor architecture fundamentally changed the server platform architecture by introducing a QuickPath Interconnect (QPI—high-speed point-to-point connections between processor, I/O, and other subsystems) and by integrating a memory controller within a CPU. This allowed delegating control of DRAM to each processor.

As a result, each processor or socket on the system board has "memory channels" directly connecting the processor and array of memory DIMMs available for that channel. These memory channels form a logical DIMM. It is important to note that if you mix different DIMM speeds on a single channel, the memory channel operates at the lowest common denominator. For example, if there is a mix of 1066 MHz and 1333 MHz memory modules on the same channel, the channel will operate at 1066 MHz.

It is equally important to note that memory interleaving is a technique to further improve the access of DRAM through spreading memory addresses evenly across memory banks for better contiguous memory read and write performance. To benefit from this, you must populate channels evenly across the system board.

The best practices and guidelines to operate DRAM at top speeds and performance greatly depend on the configuration of CPU, core, socket frequency, and so on of the blade and model. Following is an indicative summary of the best practices per the blade model. It is assumed that these blade servers consist of ideal CPU configurations and socket speeds. Table 7-8 tabulates the best practices when populating DRAM on Cisco UCS B-Series blade servers.

Table 7-8   Cisco UCS Blade Server Populating DRAM

Description	Best Practice
B22 M3	1DPC or 2DPC
B200 M3, M4	2DPC
B230 M2	2DPC
B260 M4	2DPC
B420 M3, M4	2DPC
B460 M4	2DPC

DPC = DIMM per channel

NOTE   Please refer to the spec sheet of each blade server to understand the configuration maximums and best practices for populating DRAM. The table is an indicative summary of populating DRAM per server type at the time of writing this chapter.

Cisco Adapters (Mezzanine Cards) for UCS B-Series Blade Servers

Cisco offers three types of adapters. The suitable adapter must be chosen based on the bandwidth requirements, the ultimate workload intended to run on that blade server, and you must pay attention to the configuration rules and maximums as defined in the respective spec sheets. Figure 7-20 shows adapters for Cisco UCS B-Series blade servers.

Figure 7-20   *Cisco UCS B-Series Adapters*

Cisco Converged Network Adapters (CNA)

CNAs are available from OEM partners, such as Emulex and Qlogic. When a CNA is installed on a server, the running operating system will see regular PCIe Ethernet and HBA adapters. The physical ports will then transmit FC traffic over Ethernet (encapsulated) and regular Ethernet traffic on the same wire (converged). Table 7-9 lists the adapters available from OEM partners.

NOTE Cisco UCS has transitioned from CNAs to VICs. However, customers might still be running the older CNAs due to host OS supportability or nonupgraded UCS environments. The M73KR is the closest equivalent to the older M72KR CNA.

Table 7-9 Cisco UCS Nonvirtualized Adapter Portfolio

Description	CNA M73KR-Q Qlogic Adapter	CNA M73KR-E Emulex Adapter
Total Physical Interfaces	2	2
Interface Type	Fixed (2 Eth, 2 FC)	Fixed (2 Eth, 2 FC)
Interface Failover Support	Software driver required	Software driver required
Compatibility	Supports first and second generation UCS hardware only.	Supports first and second generation UCS hardware only.

Cisco Virtual Interface Cards

Virtual interface cards (VICs) are Cisco engineered, developed interface cards. The initial VIC developed by Cisco was the M81KR (Palo interface card), with its capability to create multiple virtual NIC and HBA devices. The physical ports will run FC traffic over Ethernet and regular Ethernet traffic on the same wire (FCoE). Table 7-10 lists the key attributes of Cisco VIC adapters.

Table 7-10 Cisco UCS Virtual Interface Cards

Description	Cisco UCS Virtual Interface Card 1240	Cisco UCS Virtual Interface Card 1280	Cisco UCS Virtual Interface Card 1340	Cisco UCS Virtual Interface Card 1380	Cisco UCS M81KR Virtual Interface Card (Palo)
Port Interface Speeds	10 GbE	10 GbE	10–40 GbE	10–40 GbE	10 GbE
Total Virtual Interfaces	256	256	256 and above	256 and above	128
Interface Type	Dynamic	Dynamic	Dynamic	Dynamic	Dynamic
Ethernet Interfaces	0–256	0–256	0–256+	0–256+	0–128
FC Interfaces	0–256	0–256	0–256+	0–256+	0–128
Virtual Machine Fabric Extender	VM-FEX or Cisco Adapter FEX	VM-FEX or Cisco Adapter FEX	VM-FEX		VM-FEX or Cisco Adapter FEX

Description	Cisco UCS Virtual Interface Card 1240	Cisco UCS Virtual Interface Card 1280	Cisco UCS Virtual Interface Card 1340	Cisco UCS Virtual Interface Card 1380	Cisco UCS M81KR Virtual Interface Card (Palo)
Compatibility	Requires second generation UCS hardware	Requires second generation UCS hardware	Second and third generation UCS hardware Exclusive for B200 M3, M4	Second and third generation UCS hardware Exclusive for B200 M3, M4	Supports first and second generation UCS hardware
Interface Fabric Failover Support	Hardware, no driver needed	Hardware, no driver needed	Hardware, no driver needed	Hardware, no driver needed	Hardware, no driver needed
RoCE, NVGRE, VXLAN Offload, Netflow Support	No	No	Yes	Yes	No

Cisco UCS VIC 1340/1380

Cisco UCS VICs are now in their third generation. They come with 2x 40 GbE ports and support new features such as NVGRE, VXLAN offload, Netflow, and more. At the time of writing this chapter, they were exclusive to Cisco B-Series M3, M4 blade servers.

NOTE The Cisco UCS M81KR card can no longer be ordered. However, customers might still be running these adapters due to host OS supportability or nonupgraded UCS hardware/software environments.

NOTE Cisco UCS VICs have a unique feature, known as Fabric Failover, for vNICs on Cisco adapters. When enabled, if a vNIC fails to communicate from an application or operating systems view point, all traffic will be redirected to the alternative path automatically by Cisco UCS Manager, without a bonding or teaming driver (done in hardware). It is important to determine the responsibility of bonding or teaming, such as in ESX environments. It is a Cisco best practice recommendation to allow VMware ESX to control the network adapter failover management.

Cisco UCS Port Expander

Starting with the M3 blade server release, the system boards included a second slot apart from the standard mezz slot, which means the B200 M3 has two PCIe slots instead of just one. This second slot is called an mLOM slot. This mLOM slot allows a second VIC card, and it accommodates the Cisco VIC 1240 only. The standard mezz slot could accommodate a VIC 1280, port expander, third-party cards, or a Generation3 card in the future. Figure 7-21 shows the M3 blade layout with VIC and Port Expander.

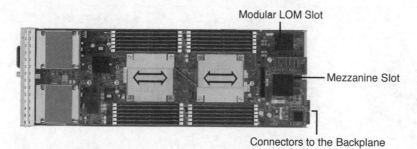

Figure 7-21   *Cisco UCS B-Series VIC 1240 + Port Expander*

With Cisco UCS M3 blade servers and second-generation Cisco UCS infrastructure hardware, you have the option to maximize bandwidth to each Cisco UCS blade server. The port expander card is a passive device; it does not have PCIe presence, and it enables you to energize the additional 10 GBASE-KR internal links from each blade server to I/O module within the Cisco UCS 5108 chassis, allowing 4x lanes per I/O module, each operating at 10 GbE per blade server. This allows a total of 40 GbE 10 GBase-KR internal links to a blade server from a single I/O module.

What Is Cisco Adapter FEX?

Cisco VICs enable you to dynamically create virtual NIC and HBA devices. The Cisco UCS server (blade or rack server) operating system sees them as physical devices, and they can be used as virtual machine host server uplinks. When those virtualized adapters appear on the upstream switch (Nexus 7K, 5K), as if they were physical ports on that switch, that is the fabric extension (control pane) from adapter to upstream switch, based on a prestandard implementation of IEEE 802.1Qbh Bridge Port Extension; this is referred to as Adapter-FEX.

What Is Cisco Virtual Machine-Fabric Extender?

This Adapter-FEX technology can be extended to the virtual machine. The dynamically created virtual NIC device is seen as a physical device. When such a PCIe device on the adapter is assigned directly to the virtual machine (VM), for example, through VMDirectPath or PCIe pass-through mode, it enables that interface to be controlled via the northbound Nexus (7K, 5K) as if they were physical ports on that switch. That fabric extension (control plane) from VM-adapter to upstream switch, based on a prestandard implementation of IEEE 802.1Qbh Bridge Port Extension, is referred to as virtual machine-fabric extender (VM-FEX).

Cisco UCS Storage Accelerator Adapters

These storage accelerator adapters are based on Fusion-IO/LSI technology. Cisco UCS storage accelerator adapters are designed specifically for the Cisco UCS B-Series and C-Series servers and integrate seamlessly to allow improvement in performance and relief of I/O bottlenecks. They are available in various form factors; for Cisco UCS blade servers, they are available as a mezzanine card. Figure 7-22 shows the available Cisco UCS storage adapters, and Table 7-11 contains the descriptions.

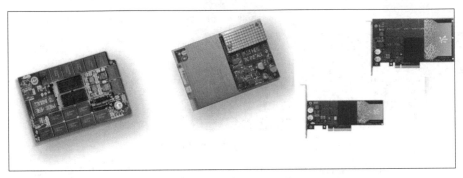

Figure 7-22   *Cisco UCS Storage Accelerator Adapters*

Table 7-11   Cisco UCS Storage Accelerator Adapters

Manufacturer	Description
Fusion-IO	Cisco UCS 365 GB MLC Fusion-io ioDrive2
Fusion-IO	Cisco UCS 785 GB MLC Fusion-io ioDrive2
LSI	LSI 400 GB SLC WarpDrive
Fusion-IO	SX300 ioMemory3 Adapter
Fusion-IO	PX600 ioMemory3 Adapter

NOTE   The suitable adapter must be chosen based on the ultimate workload intended to run on that blade server. You must pay attention to the configuration rules and maximums as defined in the respective spec sheets.

Cisco UCS C-Series Rackmount Servers

The Cisco UCS C-Series rackmount servers bring all the Cisco UCS benefits into the rackmount server form factor that can operate standalone or be integrated with the Cisco UCS Manager. The Cisco UCS connectivity options are discussed later in this chapter. Figure 7-23 shows the Cisco UCS C-Series rackmount server products, and Table 7-12 tabulates their key attributes.

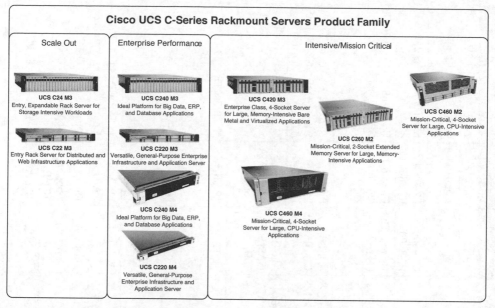

Figure 7-23   *Cisco UCS C-Series Rackmount Server Products*

NOTE   The Cisco UCS C-Series Rackmount Servers C200 M2, C210 M2, and C250 M2 have all reached end-of-sale notifications. At the time of writing this chapter, Cisco UCS C-Series C22 M3, C24 M3, C260 M2, C420 M3, and C460 M2 servers were nearing end-of-life. Please check the End-of-life and End-of-Sale notifications published by Cisco.

7

Table 7-12   Cisco UCS C-Series Rackmount Server Product Details

Description	C22 M3	C24 M3	C220 M3	C240 M3	C260 M2	C420 M3	C460 M2	C460 M4	C220 M4	C240 M4
Form Factor	1 RU	2 RU	1 RU	2 RU	2 RU	2 RU	4 RU	4 RU	1 RU	2 RU
Processor Sockets	Up to 2	Up to 2	Up to 2	Up to 2	Up to 2	2 or 4	2 or 4	2 or 4	Up to 2	Up to 2
Processors Supported	E5-2400 Or E5-2400 v2	E5-2400 Or E5-2400 v2	E5-2600 Or E5-2600 v2	E5-2400 Or E5-2400 v2	E7-2800	E7-4600	E7-4800 E7-8800	E7-4800 v2 E7-8800 v2	E5-2600 v3	E5 2600 v3
Memory Capacity	Up to 384 GB (12 slots)	Up to 384 GB (12 slots)	Up to 512 GB (16 slots)	Up to 3 TB (24 slots)	Up to 1 TB (64 slots)	Up to 1.5 TB (48 slots)	Up to 2 TB (64 slots)	Up to 6 TB (96 slots)	Up to 768 GB (24 slots)	Up to 76 GB (24 slots)
Extended Memory Tech	No	No	No	No	Yes	No	Yes	Yes	No	No
Memory DIMM Sizes	4, 8, 16, 32 GB DIMMS	4, 8, 16, 32 GB DIMMS	4, 8, 16, 32 GB DIMMS	4, 8, 16, 32 GB DIMMS	8, 16, 32 GB DIMMS	4, 8, 16, 32 GB DIMMS	4, 8, 16, 32 GB DIMMS	8, 16, 32 GB DIMMS	8, 16, 32 GB DIMMS (DDR4)	8, 16, 32 GB DIMMS (DDR4)
Internal Disk Drives	*Max 8/4 (SSD, SATA, SAS)	*Max 16-24/12 (SSD, SATA, SAS)	*Max 8/4 (SSD, SATA, SAS)	*Max 16-24/12 (SSD, SATA, SAS)	Max 16 (SAS, SATA, SSD)	Max 16 (SAS, SATA, SSD)	Max 12 (SAS, SATA, SSD)	Max 12 (SAS, SATA, SSD)	*Max 8 (SAS, SATA, SSD)	*Max 24 (SAS, SATA, SSD)
Maximum Internal Storage (Raw)	*8 TB/16 TB	*16-24 TB/48 TB	*8 TB/16 TB	*19-28 TB/14 TB	16 TB	16 TB	12 TB	19 TB	*7 TB/3.8 TB	*23 TB/7.6 TB
Integrated or Mezz RAID Controller Option	Yes	No	Yes	Yes	No	No	No	No	Yes	Yes
PCIe RAID Controller	Yes	Yes	Yes	Yes	Yes	Yes	Yes	LSI Mega-RAID	PCIe RAID Controller	PCIe RAID Controller
Embedded Ethernet Controller	Dual 1 Gbps	Dual 1 Gbps	Dual 1 Gbps	Quad 1 Gbps	Dual 1 Gbps and 10 GE	Quad 1 Gbps	Dual 1 Gbps and 10 GE	Dual 1 Gbps and 10 GE	Dual 1 Gbps	Quad 1 Gbps
PCIe Slots	2x PCIe Gen 3 slots	5x PCIe Gen3 slots	2x PCIe Gen 3 slots	5x PCIe Gen3 slots	7x PCIe Gen3 slots	7x PCIe Gen3 slots	10x PCIe Gen3 slots	10x PCIe Gen3 slots	2x PCIe Gen3 slots	6x PCIe Gen3 slots

* These Cisco UCS C-Series servers have short and long form factor drive options (either 2.- inch or 3.5- inch hard disk drives) based on the number of drives, RAID controllers, and capacities.

** The Cisco UCS C-Series M4 server details are preliminary; they were being released at the time of writing this chapter.

NOTE   The configurable options for Cisco VICs, network adapters, and storage accelerator combinations differ based on the Cisco C-Series rackmount server model and CPU configuration. To achieve configuration maximums, view the spec sheet of the corresponding Cisco UCS C-Series rackmount servers (available online) to understand the configuration maximums and valid configurations.

Cisco UCS C-Series Dense Storage Rack Server

These are modular, dense storage rack servers with dual server nodes, with storage capacity optimized for large datasets used in environments such as big data, cloud, object storage, and content delivery. The enterprise-class UCS C-Series dense rack servers extend the capabilities of Cisco's Unified Computing System portfolio in a 4U form factor that delivers the best combination of performance, flexibility, and efficiency gains. At the time of writing this chapter, Cisco UCS C-Series dense rack servers C3160 and C3260 were currently available. Figure 7-24 shows the front and rear views of these two dense storage rack server models.

Cisco UCS C-Series Rackmount Servers Product Family

UCS C3160 Dense Rack Server   UCS C3260 Dense Rack Server

Figure 7-24   *Cisco UCS C-Series Dense Rack Server Products*

Cisco UCS C-Series Best Practices for Populating DRAM

Because both UCS C-Series and B-Series computer servers are based on the same underlying microprocessor architecture, the premise described earlier regarding populating memory on these systems is the same. Nevertheless, the best practice for C-Series rackmount servers still depends on the server model, the number of CPUs configured, and the type of memory DIMM/speed utilized. Table 7-13 shows the best practice for populating DRAM for best performance and assumes the server consists of the ideal CPU configurations.

NOTE   Please refer to the spec sheet of each blade server to understand the configuration maximums and best practices for populating DRAM. The table is an indicative summary of memory modules inserted per channel at the time of writing this chapter. Also, you will have to go into the BIOS or via service profiles and set up the performance mode.

Table 7-13   Cisco UCS C-Series Rackmount Server Populating DRAM

Description	C22 M3	C24 M3	C220 M3	C240 M3	C260 M2	C420 M3	C460 M2	C460 M4	C220 M4	C240 M4
Best Practice	1 DPC	1 DPC	1 DPC/2 DPC	1 DPC/2 DPC	2 DPC	3 DPC	2 DPC	2 DPC	2DPC	2DPC

*DPC = DIMM per channel

Cisco Adapters for UCS C-Series Rackmount Servers

Cisco offers different types of adapters for UCS C-Series rack servers. Each of these adapters performs different functions. Based on the intended workload, bandwidth, connectivity design, and redundancy requirements, you must configure and order the server accordingly. Before you configure a server, pay attention to the configuration rules and maximums as defined in their respective spec sheets.

Cisco UCS C-Series RAID Adapter Options

Do you know what a disk RAID configuration is? What are the common RAID configurations today? Here is a brief explanation of each of these common RAID configurations and their salient points.

A redundant array of independent disks is referred to as RAID. RAID configurations exist today to provide disk-level redundancy and a means to protect data stored in disks by duplicating or distributing the data across a collection of disks. Figures 7-25 and 7-26 are graphical representations of basic and advanced RAID configurations. Table 7-14 lists details and key attributes of these RAID configurations.

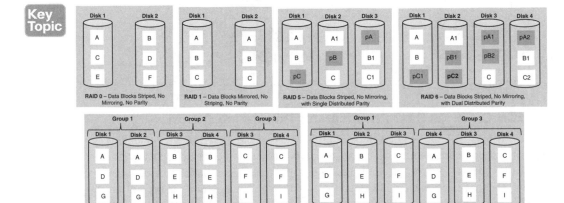

Figure 7-25   *Basic RAID Configurations*

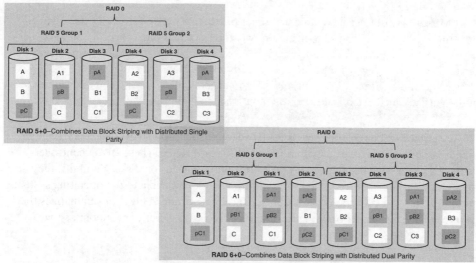

Figure 7-26 *Advanced RAID Configurations RAID 5+0 and 6+0*

Table 7-14 Common RAID Configurations

RAID Level	RAID 0 (Stripe)	RAID 1 (Mirror)	RAID 5, Distributed Parity	RAID 6, Dual Distributed Parity	RAID 1+0	RAID 0+1	RAID 5+0	RAID 6+0
Minimum Disks	2.	2.	3.	3.	4.	4.	6.	8.
Redundancy	No.	Yes.	Yes.	Yes.	Yes.	Yes.	Yes.	Yes.
Parity	No.	No.	Yes.	Yes.	No.	No.	Yes.	Yes.
Performance (Read/ Write)	Excellent.	Good.	Good writes. Excellent for read-intensive operations.	Good writes. Excellent for read-intensive operations.	Excellent.	Excellent.	Excellent.	Excellent.
Popular Use	Noncriti-cal data.	Critical data.	Critical data.	Critical data.	Critical data. Better fault tolerance. Best option, but needs more disks.	Critical data. Slightly less fault tolerant.	Critical data. Most cost effective.	Critical data.

> **NOTE**   Mirroring disks ensure redundant copies of data are maintained but with a significant overhead because they need to maintain two copies of that data. Data redundancy can also be achieved via parity, which is a technique used to provide redundancy with minimum overhead. Parity uses the XOR operation to data bytes to create the parity byte. If an XOR b = Parity, then an XOR parity = b; this mechanism enables you to create any one data byte using the parity, which can be repeated to reconstruct an entire disk.

There are combinations and options of RAID adapters for Cisco UCS C-Series rackmount servers that are built in to the system board or PCIe card based. These RAID controllers take on the processing responsibilities of RAID configurations on disks. Naturally, they also enable you to group these disks and form logical volumes available to the operating system. Figure 7-27 shows a collection of available RAID adapters, and Table 7-15 summarizes the attributes of RAID adapter options available for Cisco UCS C-Series rackmount servers.

Figure 7-27   *Cisco UCS C-Series RAID Adapters*

Table 7-15   Cisco UCS C-Series Server RAID Adapter Details

Description	C22 M3	C24 M3	C220 M3	C240 M3	C260 M2	C420 M3	C460 M2	C460 M4	C220 M4	C240 M4
Built-In Option and Support	Yes	—	Yes	Yes	No	No	No	No	Yes	Yes
RAID Levels	RAID 0, 1, 5, 10		RAID 0, 1, 5, 10	RAID 0, 1, 5, 10					RAID 0, 1, 5, 10	RAID 0, 1, 5, 10
Mezz Card	No	No	Yes	Yes	No	No	No	No	Yes	Yes
RAID Option and Supported RAID Levels			RAID 0, 1, 5, 10	RAID 0, 1, 5, 10					RAID 0, 1, 5, 10, 6, 50, 60	RAID 0, 1, 5, 10, 6, 50, 60
PCIe Adapter Options and Supported RAID Levels	Yes	Yes	Yes	Yes	Yes	Yes	Yes	Yes	Yes	Yes
	RAID 0, 1, 5, 6, 1+0, 5+0, 6+0	RAID 0, 1, 5, 6, 1+0, 5+0, 6+0	RAID 0, 1, 1+0, 5, 6, 5+0, 6+0	RAID 0, 1, 1+0, 5, 6, 5+0, 6+0	RAID 0, 1, 5, 6, 1+0	UCS-RAID-9286CV-8E RAID 0, 1, 1+0, 5, 6	RAID 0, 1, 1+0, 5, 6, 5+0, 6+0	RAID 0, 1, 5, 10, 6, 50, 60, & JBOD (Just a Bunch Of Disks)	RAID 0, 1, 5, 10, 6, 50, 60, & JBOD (Just a Bunch Of Disks)	RAID 0, 1, 5, 10, 6, 50, 60, & JBOD (Just a Bunch Of Disks)

NOTE The supported list of both built-in and PCI-based RAID controllers will vary according to the Cisco UCS C-Series short- and long-form factor models. Based on the RAID controller chosen, the supported RAID configurations and maximum RAID groups (virtual drives) will also differ accordingly. At the time of writing this chapter, these were the available options. Refer to the spec sheet of each server for current information before choosing the best RAID controller for your configuration and intended workloads.

Cisco UCS C-Series Virtual Interface Cards and OEM CNA Adapters

Cisco UCS adapters have transitioned from converged network adapters (CNAs) to VICs. Figure 7-28 shows the available Cisco VIC and OEM adapters available, and Table 7-16 lists their key attributes.

NOTE One of the initial Cisco VIC cards developed by Cisco was the M81KR (Palo interface card), capable of creating multiple NIC and HBA devices. The physical ports will run FC traffic over Ethernet and regular Ethernet traffic on the same wire (FCoE). At the time of writing this chapter, this card was discontinued.

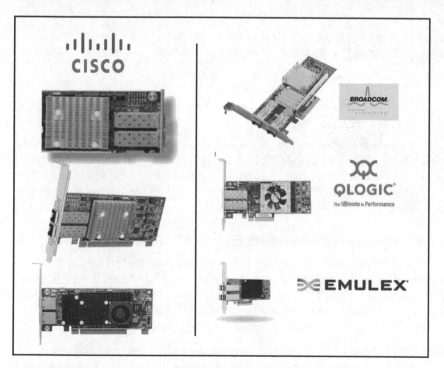

Figure 7-28 *Cisco UCS C-Series VIC and OEM CNA Adapters*

Table 7-16 Cisco UCS C-Series Virtual Interface Cards

Description	Cisco UCS Virtual Interface Card 1225	Cisco UCS Virtual Interface Card 1225T	Cisco UCS Virtual Interface Card 1285	Cisco UCS Virtual Interface Card 1227 (Exclusive M4)	Cisco UCS Virtual Interface Card 1227T	Cisco UCS Virtual Interface Card 1385
Total Virtual Interfaces	256	256	256	256	256	256 & above
Interface Type	Dynamic	Dynamic	Dynamic	Dynamic	Dynamic	Dynamic
Interface Speeds	2x10Gb	2x10Gb (10GBASE-T only)	2x40Gb (QSFP)	2x10Gb (SFP+)	2x10Gb (10GBase-T only)	2x40Gb (QSFP+ Ports)
Ethernet Interfaces	0–256	0–256	0–256	0–256	0–256	0–256
FC Interfaces	0–256	0–256	0–256	0–256	0–256	0–256
Virtual Machine Fabric Extender Support	Yes	Yes	Yes	Yes	Yes	Yes
Interface Fabric Failover Support	Yes (In Hardware)	Yes (In Hardware)	Yes (In Hardware)	Yes (In Hardware)	Yes (In Hardware)	Yes (In Hardware)
SR-IOV Capable	Yes	Yes	Yes	Yes	Yes	No

Cisco UCS VIC 1387 mLOM

The VIC 1387 is based on third-generation Cisco ASIC technology and is ideally suited for next-generation networks requiring up to 40 Gb bandwidth. It supports network overlay technologies such as VXLAN and carries forward support for advanced Cisco features such as VMFEX, Netflow, and usNIC. The VIC 1387 is supported with the C220 M4, C240 M4, and C3160 servers.

What Is SR-IOV (Single Root-IO Virtualization)?

Created by the PCI Special Interest Group (PCI-SIG), this standard enables a PCIe device to emulate itself as multiple physical PCIe devices to the operating system. It uses physical function (PF) analogs to a physical NIC port, and the emulated port is the virtual function (VF). Each of these VFs can be spawned as an emulated-NIC and assigned to a VM directly (vNICs), if you want to serve as virtual machine host uplinks, for example (VMNICs).

The Cisco UCS VIC achieves the same; it does not employ SR-IOV but uses alternate, standards-based PCIe methods of presenting virtual hardware to the operating system or hypervisor (on ASICs). Nevertheless, the Cisco VICs are capable of SR-IOV but do not utilize SR-IOV to emulate devices. Cisco VIC cards on UCS C-Series can be configured for Classical Ethernet (CE); then it operates with fixed ports (NIC, HBAs) or network interface virtualization (NIV) mode where, at the time of writing this chapter, you can create dynamic interfaces.

Apart from Cisco UCS VICs, OEM CNA adapters are supported on Cisco UCS C-Series. There are Emulex, Qlogic, and Broadcom CNA PCIe cards that are supported on Cisco UCS C-Series rackmount servers. At the time of writing this chapter, these were the available OEM Adapter options. Table 7-17 lists the supported OEM adapters and their key attributes.

Table 7-17   Cisco UCS C-Series OEM CNA Adapters

Description	Emulex OCe11102-FX	Emulex OneConnect OCe10102-F	Emulex OCe 14102-UX	Qlogic QLE8362	Broadcom 57810	Broadcom 57712	Qlogic QLE8242-CU
Total Physical Interfaces	2	2	2	2 (can be partitioned)	2 (can be partitioned)	2 (can be partitioned)	2 (intended for use with copper cables)
Interface Type	Fixed	Fixed	Dynamic (SR-IOV)	Dynamic (SR-IOV)	Dynamic (SR-IOV)	Dynamic (SR-IOV)	Fixed
Ethernet Interfaces	2	2	Fixed/ Dynamic	Fixed/ Dynamic	Fixed/ Dynamic	Fixed/ Dynamic	2
FC Interfaces	2	2	Fixed/ Dynamic	Fixed/ Dynamic	Fixed/ Dynamic	Fixed/ Dynamic	2
Virtual Machine Fabric Extender	No	No	No	No	No	Yes	No
Interface Failover Support on OS	Driver required	Driver required	Driver required	Driver required	Driver required	Driver required	Driver required

NOTE   The supported lists of Cisco VICs or OEM adapters depend on the server model and configuration of that server. Refer to the spec sheet of each server for current information before choosing the appropriate VIC or OEM adapter for your configuration and intended workloads.

Cisco UCS C-Series Network Interface Card

There are NICs available for Cisco UCS C-Series rackmount servers through supported OEMs. Some of them are CNAs, with FCoE requirements. Figure 7-29 shows the available NICs for Cisco UCS C-Series rackmount servers, and Table 7-18 summarizes their key attributes.

NOTE At the time of writing this chapter, these were the available NIC options. Refer to the latest spec sheet of each server for current information before choosing the appropriate NIC for your configuration and intended workloads.

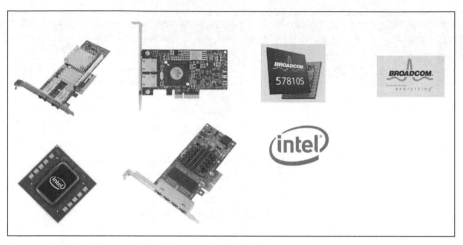

Figure 7-29 *Cisco UCS C-Series OEM NICs*

Table 7-18 Cisco UCS C-Series OEM NIC Adapter Details

Description	Broadcom 5709 Dual Port	Broadcom 5709 Quad Port	Broadcom 57712	Broadcom 57810 (LOM)	Intel 10GbE X520	Intel Quad Port i350	Intel X540 (10GBASE-T— LOM)
Total Physical Interfaces	2	4	2	2	2	4	2
Speed	10/100/1 Gb	10/100/1 Gb	10 GbE	10 GbE	10 GbE	10/100/1 Gb	100/1/10 GbE
iSCSI HBA Support, Boot	HBA function for iSCSI	HBA function for iSCSI	Both	Both	Both	Both	Yes
FCoE Support/ FCoE Boot from SAN	No	No	Yes	Yes	Yes	No	Yes
SR-IOV Support	No	No	Yes	Yes	Yes	Yes	Yes

Cisco UCS C-Series Host Bus Adapter

These are HBA cards available for Cisco UCS C-Series rackmount servers. They are from OEM vendors and are fully tested and supported by Cisco UCS C-Series rackmount servers. Figure 7-30 shows the available HBA adapter for Cisco UCS C-Series rackmount servers.

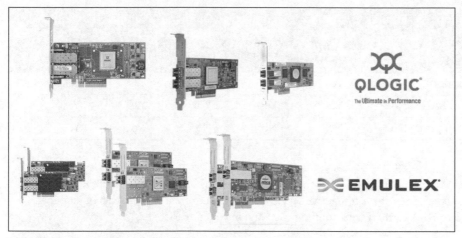

Figure 7-30 *Cisco UCS C-Series HBAs*

What Is N_Port ID Virtualization (NPIV)?

There are different types of port classifications in the Fibre Channel T11 standards, such as N_Port, F_Port, E_Port, and so on. N_Port refers to the host/server side port (HBA port), and that port consists of a unique ID (24-bit), assigned by the FC switch during the FLOGI (Fabric Log-In process).

This N_Port ID is not the same as the world wide port name (WWPN) / worldwide node name (WWNN). In fact, each N_Port ID will have a corresponding WWPN associated with it.

Essentially, the NPIV capability enables an N_Port to carry multiple N_Port IDs and associated WWPNs. The F_Port on the FC switch should also have this NPIV capability and be enabled to understand the multiple N_Port IDs and WWPNs coming from the host/HBA port. Why do we need it? Because of the effect of server virtualization and I/O consolidation, these FC links are now trunks and must be capable of understanding the fact that multiple servers (VMs) will now log in and communicate via the same Fibre Channel uplink.

The best analogy would be to perceive that port as a network trunk_port, which allows transporting multiple VLAN_IDs on a single-wire. Do not confuse NPV and NPIV. Whereas NPIV is host side facing, NPV is switch side used in conjunction with NP_Ports. For more details and explanation, refer to the SAN topics under the DCICN certification guide. Table 7-19 lists the supported HBAs for Cisco UCS C-Series rackmount servers.

Key Topic

Table 7-19 Cisco UCS C-Series OEM HBA Adapters

Description	Emulex LPe 11002	Emulex LPe 12002	Emulex LPe 16002-M6	Qlogic QLE2462	Qlogic QLE2562	Qlogic QLE2672-CSC
Total Physical Interfaces	2	2	2	2	2	2
Speed	1/2/4 Gb	2/4/8 Gb	4/8/16 Gb	1/2/4 Gb	2/4/8 Gb	4/8/16 Gb

Description	Emulex LPe 11002	Emulex LPe 12002	Emulex LPe 16002-M6	Qlogic QLE2462	Qlogic QLE2562	Qlogic QLE2672-CSC
NPIV Support	Yes	Yes	Yes	Yes	Yes	Yes
Boot from SAN	No	Yes	Yes	Yes	Yes	Yes
SR-IOV Support	No	No	No	No	No	Yes

NOTE At the time of writing this chapter, these were the available HBA options. Refer to the latest spec sheet of the respective server for current information before choosing the appropriate HBA card for your configuration and intended workloads.

Cisco UCS Storage Accelerator Adapters

These storage accelerator adapters are based on Fusion-IO/LSI technology. Cisco UCS storage accelerator adapters are designed specifically for the Cisco UCS B-Series M4 blade servers and integrate seamlessly to allow improvement in performance and relief of I/O bottlenecks. They are available in various form factors; for Cisco UCS blade servers they are available as a mezzanine card. Figure 7-31 shows the available storage accelerator adapters for B- and C-Series rackmount servers, and Table 7-20 contains brief descriptions.

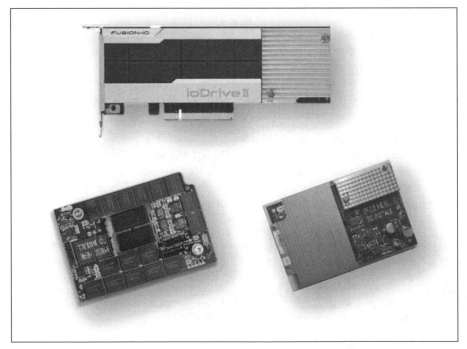

Figure 7-31 *Cisco UCS C-Series Storage Accelerator Adapters*

Table 7-20 Cisco UCS Storage Accelerator Adapters

Manufacturer	Description
Fusion-io	Cisco UCS 365 GB MLC Fusion-io ioDrive2
Fusion-io	Cisco UCS 785 GB MLC Fusion-io ioDrive2
Fusion-io	Cisco UCS 1205 GB MLC Fusion-io ioDrive2
Fusion-io	Cisco UCS 3.0 TB MLC Fusion-io ioDrive2
Fusion-io	ioMemory3 PX / SX Series for B/C-Series Servers
LSI	LSI 400 GB SLC WarpDrive

NOTE   Refer to the latest spec sheet of the respective server for current information before choosing the appropriate accelerator card for your configuration and intended workloads.

Cisco UCS E-Series Servers

Cisco UCS E-Series servers are power-optimized, x86, Intel Xeon 64-bit blade servers designed to be deployed in Cisco Integrated Services Routers Generation 2 (ISR G2). These price-to-performance-optimized, single-socket blade servers balance simplicity, performance, reliability, and power efficiency. They are well suited for applications and infrastructure services typically deployed in small offices and branch offices.

Cisco UCS E-Series servers are available in two form factors. The first is a single-width blade server powered by a high-performance yet power-efficient Intel Xeon E3 processor with four cores, up to 16 gigabytes of RAM, and two terabytes of local storage. The second is a double-width blade server powered by a high-performance Intel Xeon E5-2400 processor with up to six cores and support for up to 48 gigabytes of RAM and three terabytes of local storage.

These blades utilize the same CIMC chip and have a similar management interface and capabilities as standalone C-Series rackmount servers. Figure 7-32 shows the available E-Series components.

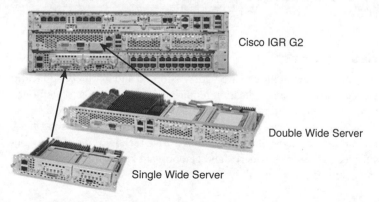

Cisco IGR G2

Double Wide Server

Single Wide Server

Figure 7-32   *Cisco UCS E-Series Servers*

Cisco UCS Mini

As the name implies, this is a compact solution optimized for branch offices and remote sites. A Cisco UCS Mini solution will include Cisco UCS 5108 blade server chassis, Cisco UCS 6324 Fabric Interconnects, and Cisco UCS Manager. All servers, networking, and management are integrated into a single chassis. The Cisco UCS 6324 Fabric interconnects will fit into the I/O module bays. Supported Cisco UCS C-Series rack servers can be added to a Cisco UCS Mini solution to further enhance storage, I/O capabilities, and so on. Figure 7-33 shows a representation of a Cisco UCS Mini domain.

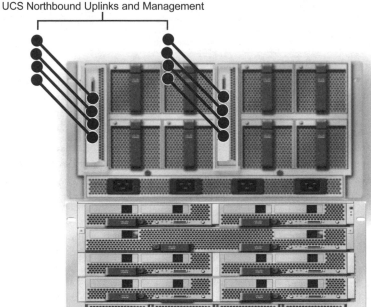

Figure 7-33 *Cisco UCS Mini Overview*

> **NOTE** At the time of writing this chapter, the Cisco UCS Mini solution required a unique version of the Cisco UCS Manager software to manage it.

Cisco UCS M-Series Servers

As server virtualization and cloud computing have widely adopted and matured, application architectures have evolved, too; from an application requiring a server to more scaled-out application architecture. This is also referred to as cloud scale architectures, where a service is distributed across multiple servers. Figure 7-34 graphically depicts the Cisco UCS M-Series architecture. Various demands in e-services, innovative technology platforms, and web services such as Docker, Node.js, AngularJS, and Hadoop are key contributors to this shift in application architectures.

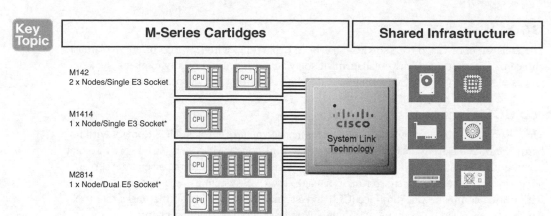

Figure 7-34 *Cisco UCS M-Series Architecture*

The goal of Cisco UCS M-Series servers is to meet this requirement of cloud scale application architectures. They do this by disaggregating the server components; Cisco UCS M-Series provides a platform that offers flexible and rapid deployment of compute, storage, and networking resources. The System Link Technology in Cisco M-Series servers is based on Cisco VIC, which uses standard PCIe to present an endpoint device to compute resources. In Cisco M-Series servers, this same technology has been extended to provide access to PCIe resources local to the M-Series chassis. Figure 7-35 shows currently available M-Series server offerings and the 2RU chassis to house them.

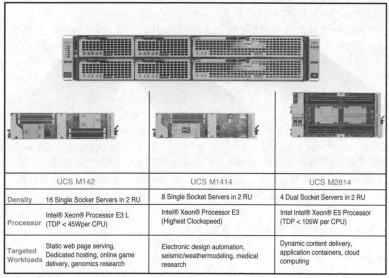

	UCS M142	UCS M1414	UCS M2814
Density	16 Single Socker Servers in 2 RU	8 Single Socket Servers in 2 RU	4 Dual Socket Servers in 2 RU
Processor	Intel® Xeon® Processor E3 L (TDP < 45Wper CPU)	Intel® Xeon® Processor E3 (Highest Clockspeed)	Intel Intel® Xeon® E5 Processor (TDP < 105W per CPU)
Targeted Workloads	Static web page serving, Dedicated hosting, online game delivery, genomics research	Electronic design automation, seismic/weathermodeling, medical research	Dynamic content delivery, application containers, cloud computing

Figure 7-35 *Cisco UCS M-Series Servers*

7

Cisco UCS Software

The ecosystem of Cisco UCS software has been expanding; with it, Cisco offers the largest choice of Cisco or third-party management software. This section briefly explains the key pieces of Cisco UCS software available at the time of writing this chapter.

Cisco UCS Manager

The Cisco UCS Manager provides end-to-end management of a Cisco UCS domain with no hardware boundaries; it creates a unified management domain. It is web-based software that is embedded into the Cisco UCS fabric interconnects. Without requiring a separate server/host with an operating system to run, it manages the UCS system using an intuitive GUI, with both a command-line interface (CLI) and a standards-based API so that tasks that took days and weeks can be executed in minutes. You learn more in the next chapter.

> **NOTE** A Cisco UCS domain can consist of one or two Cisco UCS Fabric Interconnects (HA Cluster), under one instance of Cisco UCS Manager, which is considered a Cisco UCS domain. Within this UCS domain, you could have multiple Cisco UCS 5100 chassis, IOMs, blade, or rackmount servers.

Cisco UCS Central

The Cisco UCS Central software is a multi-UCS domain management software. It is a MoM that extends all the capabilities of the Cisco UCS Manager across multiple UCS domains, even across geographical boundaries. The Cisco UCS Central software enables you to standardize and enforce configuration settings, pools, policies, and identities centrally while enabling consistent deployment across multiple UCS domains. It can be used in a multimaster model, which enables settings to be managed by UCS Central or by the individual UCS Manager. The Cisco UCS Central software runs as a VM, ideally situated in your out-of-band management network segment.

Cisco UCS StorMagic SvSAN

Cisco and StorMagic have designed an enterprise-class software defined storage solution that addresses the needs of remote office, branch office (ROBO) environments and is simple to deploy and manage. The solution is built on best-in-class Cisco UCS servers, an industry-leading hypervisor, and software-defined storage components from StorMagic. This combination creates a single addressable storage pool across multiple nodes. At the time of writing this chapter, the software-defined storage (SDS) solution was supported on Cisco UCS C220 M4, UCS C240 M4, and UCS Mini with B200 M4 blades.

Cisco UCS Director

The Cisco UCS Director software manages both physical and virtual infrastructure and virtualization resources from a single web-based service portal. It is capable of automating and orchestrating the end-to-end IT process of devices, hypervisors, and virtual/physical resources across the data center infrastructure stack—that is, compute, storage, and networks. All infrastructure consumers, such as IT administrators and end users, can use the web-based service portal. Similar to other UCS software, Cisco UCS Director contains northbound APIs to integrate into higher platforms and has an SDK allowing for ecosystem partner integration.

Cisco IMC Supervisor

The Cisco IMC Supervisor software is a tool that will enable centralized management of Standalone C-Series and E-Series servers (B and M-Series servers cannot be managed) located across multiple sites, spread across multiple geographic locations. Figure 7-36 shows the IMC Supervisor GUI and lists some of its main features.

Figure 7-36 *Cisco IMC Supervisor Main Features*

The Cisco IMC Supervisor is downloadable from Cisco Software as a virtual appliance with a web-based interface. Here is a summary of its features:

- Hardware Health Status (Monitoring)
- Platform Hardware Inventory
- Platform Management with vKVM Launcher
- Firmware Inventory + Management
- Diagnostic Tools Management (Non-Interactive Diagnostics)
- Scheduler (System Discovery & Firmware Updates)
- Call Home (E-mail Alerting)
- Cisco Smart Call Home
- Platform Grouping & Tagging
- Group Discovery
- Server Utilization Stats Collection
- REST/XML API
- Policy Import & Deletion
- Policy Deployment
- Profile Deployment (Policy Group)
- Server Group Deployment

NOTE Cisco IMC Supervisory version 2.0 had been released when this chapter was written. Please refer to its release notes for latest updates, minimum required firmware on target servers, and supported hardware (currently C-Series M3 & M4, E-Series M1 & M2).

The following menu options are available in the Cisco IMC Supervisor, where you can obtain full inventories, faults, manage each system, firmware, groups, policies, and administer the software user accounts, IMC patch updates, licenses, and so on.

System Menu

This menu is used to manage rack groups, where you can monitor all discovered C-Series and E-Series servers. Furthermore, you can create, edit, and delete rack groups and CIMC accounts. You can also manage firmware images, upgrade profiles, and actually upgrade the server devices. Figure 7-37 shows the IMC Supervisor systems menu tab.

Figure 7-37   *Cisco IMC Supervisor Systems Menu*

Policies Menu

This menus consists of a collection of policies and profiles that can be defined and utilized across multiple managed C-Series or E-Series servers. Credential policies allow you to create usernames, passwords, protocols, and ports that can be used to access C/E-Series servers. Hardware policies are used to configure various CIMC attributes, for example BIOS, RAID policy, and allowing repeatability of configurations across servers. You can create, edit, delete, and clone policies as necessary.

Multiple policies combined together will form a hardware profile. This profile then can be assigned to multiple rackmount severs. You can create, edit, and delete these profiles as necessary. Figure 7-38 shows the IMC supervisor policies menu.

Figure 7-38   *Cisco IMC Supervisory Policies Menu*

Administration Menu

This menu allows you to manage IMC supervisor licenses, system information, user access, and integration. Using this tab, you can view license keys and utilization, upgrades, and update licenses. This menu also allows you to view system information, for example IP addresses in use, uptime, and configure email alerts, too. User accounts that can access the IMC supervisor can also be defined under this menu. Figure 7-39 shows the IMC supervisor administration menu.

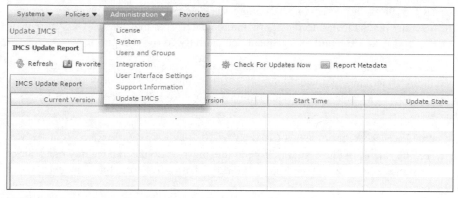

Figure 7-39 *Cisco IMC Supervisor Administration Menu*

Cisco UCS Platform Emulator

The UCS Platform Emulator is a version of the Cisco UCS Manager that runs on a hypervisor as a virtual machine. As the name states, it is an emulator; therefore, it does not require actual UCS hardware. It is ideal for training IT administrators, for demonstrations, and for customer hardware setup emulation. One of its key capabilities is that it consists of the UCS XML API that you can interact with without the requirement of actual hardware. The latest version of this software allows testing firmware upgrades, too, and it is available in the Cisco Developer Network.

Cisco goUCS Automation Tool

This toolkit was developed as a proof of concept to show the capabilities of interacting with the UCS XML API. It showcases the inherent power of this XML API to the UCS system administrator by automating tasks across multiple UCS domains. It is available in the Cisco Developer Network.

Cisco UCS Connectivity Architecture

Cisco UCS unified fabric enables a "wire-once" deployment model, where the Cisco UCS 5108 blade server chassis is connected to Fabric Interconnects, and these Fabric Interconnects are extended to LAN and SAN access just once. This eliminates the task of wiring/patching each server adapter to the network or SAN when you add or remove server infrastructure in your data center.

Cisco UCS 5108 Chassis to Fabric Interconnect Physical Connectivity

> **NOTE** This section is primarily based on Cisco UCS second-generation hardware—62xx Fabric Interconnects and 22xx I/O modules and their capabilities. The fundamentals of physical connectivity discussed here are valid with third-generation Cisco UCS Fabric Interconnects and I/O modules; the main difference would be the introduction of QSA (Cisco QSFP to SFP/SFP+ Adapter) modules and breakout cables with 40GbE support.

The Cisco UCS 5108 blade server chassis contains the Cisco UCS B-Series blade servers. These chassis must be connected to the Fabric Interconnects that manage the UCS system and provide data (LAN, SAN) and management connectivity to the computing system.

Consider a non-UCS standalone server; if you need to connect that server redundantly to the LAN and SAN mediums, you would require a Path A and a Path B, right? Would you connect both paths to a single switch? That would not be wise because you will not have redundancy.

Similarly, consider each I/O module in a Cisco UCS 5108 blade server chassis as your Path A and Path B. The rule is, the links of any I/O module must be connected to only one Fabric Interconnect. Figure 7-40 shows some valid and invalid chassis to Fabric Interconnect connectivity schemes.

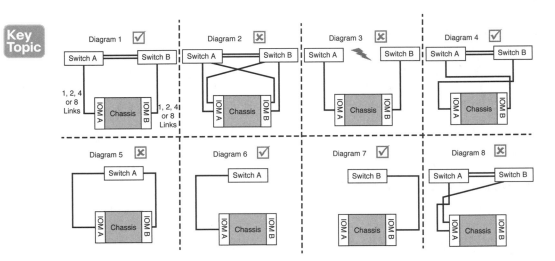

Figure 7-40   *Cisco UCS 5108 Blade Server Chassis Physical Connectivity*

Cisco UCS C-Series Rackmount Server Physical Connectivity

Cisco UCS is the only vendor offering one integrated computing and management system across both blade and rack form factors, with stateless computing features extended to both form factors. This enables a user to move server workloads from blade to rack servers seamlessly. Cisco UCS C-Series rackmount server connectivity has evolved; at the time of writing this chapter, the latest release of Cisco UCS Manager firmware supported Direct-Connect (to Fabric Interconnect) management for Cisco UCS-C-Series rack servers.

Three connectivity methods for C-Series rack servers are available today. You can have combinations of these connectivity methods within a single UCS domain as long as you adhere to the configuration rules and prerequisites. Figure 7-41 shows a picture of both dual- and single-wire connectivity of UCS C-Series rackmount servers.

■ **Dual-Wire Management:** Introduced with UCS Manager version 2.0(2). This connectivity method requires the use of a Cisco Nexus 2232PP FEX, which provides converged I/O at 10 GbE (through supported VIC, CNAs). Separate network interfaces (1Gb Ethernet

LOM ports) are used for management. The FEX will then uplink to the Cisco UCS Fabric Interconnects, through 10 GbE connections to server ports on the Cisco UCS Fabric Interconnects.

> **NOTE**   Prerequisites: a pair of UCS Fabric Interconnects (HA Cluster), a pair of Cisco 2232PP FEXs, and either Cisco UCS P81E VIC or the Cisco VIC 1225 is supported. If you're using the latter, please ensure it is installed in the stipulated PCIe slot for dual-wire integration (varies based on server model) and note the management traffic utilizes the LoM ports, while converged data traffic flows via the chosen VIC card. Please refer to the C-Series integration guide for the latest details.

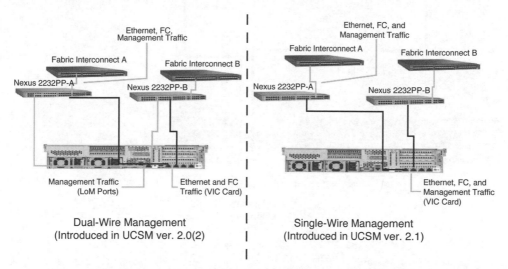

Figure 7-41   *Cisco UCS C-Series Dual and Single-Wire Management*

- **Single-wire Management Connect:** Introduced with UCS Manager version 2.1. This connectivity method requires the use of redundant Cisco Nexus 2232PP FEX, which provides converged I/O and management traffic (through the Cisco VIC 1225). This method requires the Cisco 1225 VIC. The FEX will then uplink to the Cisco UCS Fabric Interconnects over 10 GbE connections to server ports on the Cisco UCS Fabric Interconnect.

> **NOTE**   Prerequisites include a pair of UCS Fabric Interconnects (HA Cluster), a pair of Cisco 2232PP FEXs, and a Cisco VIC 1225 (Cisco P81E not supported). Please ensure it is installed in the stipulated PCIe slot for single-wire integration (varies based on server model). Uplinks on the FEX can be either static pinned for deterministic traffic flow or port channeled for better redundancy and scaling. Please refer to the C-Series integration guide for the latest details.

- **Direct Connects to Fabric Interconnects:** Introduced with UCS Manager version 2.2. This connectivity method does not require additional hardware. Converged I/O and management traffic is connected directly to the Cisco UCS Fabric Interconnects (through VIC

1225). Redundant VIC cards can be used. Figure 7-42 shows the direct connectivity of UCS C-Series rackmount servers.

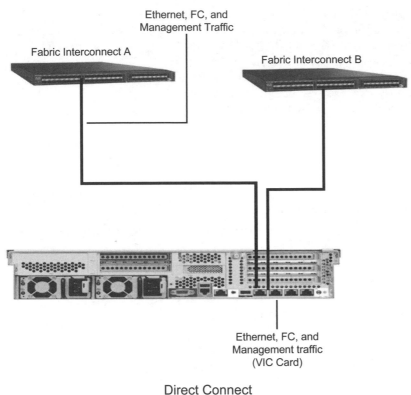

Figure 7-42 *Cisco UCS C-Series Direct Connect to Cisco UCS Fabric Interconnects*

Cisco UCS 6200 Fabric Interconnect to LAN, SAN Connectivity

The Cisco UCS 6200 series Fabric Interconnects are top-of-rack devices. They are not exactly Cisco Nexus 5000 Series switches, although there are similarities. However, they do differ around the software stack they run on.

NOTE The Cisco UCS 6300 Fabric Interconnects were released at the time of writing this chapter. There are two models, Cisco UCS FI 6332 (Ethernet/FCoE only) and UCS FI 6332-UP (Ethernet/FCoE and FC) with 40GbE ports/options. The fundamentals of LAN, SAN connectivity discussed here are valid with third-generation Cisco UCS Fabric Interconnects and I/O modules.

Different types of port modes and types are configurable on the Fabric Interconnects. Top-level port mode selection is either Ethernet or Fibre Channel; these port modes are further classified into port types, and they will be made available for configuration. Table

7-21 lists the different port types configurable on the Cisco UCS 6200/6300 series Fabric Interconnects. In the next chapter we discuss some of these port types and where these port types and states are configured.

Table 7-21   Cisco UCS Fabric Interconnect Port Types

Port Types	Description
Server Ports	Used to connect to the I/O modules (FEX) on the UCS chassis.
Uplink Ports	Used to connect via Ethernet/FC/FCoE ports to LAN/SAN/FCoE devices.
Appliance Ports	Used to directly connect with NFS/iSCSI storage devices.
FCoE/FC Storage Port	Used only in switch mode to connect directly to storage devices.
Breakout Ports	Breakout ports are used to connect 40GE interfaces to 10GE capable equipment.

CAUTION   When configuring port modes (Ethernet/Fibre Channel) or breakout ports on the fixed or expansion modules and when transitioning to or from switch and end-host modes, the Cisco UCS Fabric Interconnect must be restarted or expansion modules power cycled. Hence, it would be advised to predetermine the requirement and ensure that port types are configured initially after required firmware upgrades are completed. Also note that the main port modes can be configured only as a continuous set of ports; you cannot configure them as staggered.

Cisco UCS Fabric Interconnect Switching Modes

Cisco UCS Fabric Interconnects can be operated in two main switching modes: End-Host or Switch mode, for either Ethernet or Fibre Channel traffic. These modes are independent of each other and determine how the Fabric Interconnect behaves and handles traffic, as a device in between the server and network and storage device/network.

Ethernet Switching Mode

- **End-Host Mode:** In this mode, the Fabric Interconnects do not forward frames based on MAC addresses and do not run Spanning Tree Protocol (STP). Forwarding is based on server-to-uplink/port channel pinning. Therefore, UCS Fabric Interconnects do not learn MAC addresses from external switches and uplinks; they learn MAC addresses from server ports only.

  To an external switch, the UCS Fabric Interconnect looks like a host with many NICs. A number of operating rules are in place to prevent packet looping, such as Deja-Vu check, reverse path forwarding, no uplink-to-uplink packet forwarding, and special attention to handling broadcast and multicast traffic. This is the default and recommended mode of operation for UCS Fabric Interconnects.

Following is a brief explanation of some of the key operating rules in end-host mode:

■ All source blade server traffic goes out via its pinned uplink port only, regardless of the MAC it is trying to reach.

■ Server-to-server traffic on the same VLAN connected to the same Fabric Interconnect is locally switched.

■ Reverse Path Forwarding: A packet destined for a blade server is accepted only on its pinned border interface for that blade. The upstream switch MAC table should point to the link where the destination MAC exists.

■ Deja-Vu check: Packets arriving with source UCS blade server MACs are dropped by comparing the source MAC and local MAC address table on Cisco UCS Fabric Interconnects.

■ All incoming broadcast/multicast traffic will be received via one uplink per Fabric Interconnect (not per VLAN). This is possible because all VLANs are active on all uplinks.

NOTE   Cisco UCS allows connecting to Layer 2 disjoint network environments in end-host mode. This enables you to connect multiple redundant uplinks to different Layer 2 networks—such as DMZ, Prod-Applications, and Prod-Database segmented networks within your organization—and utilize static and dynamic pinning of Cisco UCS blade server vNICs to communicate via specific uplinks only.

■ **Switch Mode:** This is the traditional Ethernet switch mode. The UCS Fabric Interconnects act as a switch; they start running STP and broadcast, and multicast packets are handled in the traditional manner. Switch mode is not the default and recommended mode of operation and should be used only if the UCS Fabric Interconnects are directly connected to a router or the upstream is L3 aggregation.

Fibre Channel Switching Mode

■ **End-Host Mode:** In this mode, the Fabric Interconnect acts as an end host to the connected storage network. All server FC vHBA ports are seen as endpoints (N_Ports). This mode is the default mode of operation.

■ **Switch Mode:** This mode allows the Fabric Interconnect to connect directly to a storage device, with no SAN and limited FC switching features.

Based on your requirements, Cisco UCS Fabric Interconnects must be configured appropriately. Here is an example of a UCS Fabric Interconnect connected to a LAN (via Ethernet uplink ports in a port channel), SAN (via FC uplink ports), out-of-band management (via Management Ports), and interconnects-clustered (via cluster ports). This type of connectivity is the most commonly used. Figure 7-43 shows physical connectivity of Cisco UCS 6248 Fabric Interconnects to LAN and SAN.

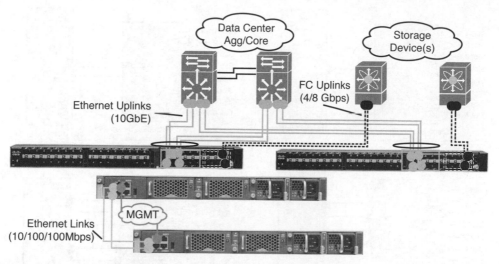

Figure 7-43   *Cisco UCS Fabric Interconnect LAN, SAN Connectivity*

Cisco UCS I/O Module and Fabric Interconnect Connectivity

The number of links and connectivity mode from the I/O module to Fabric Interconnects, also known as fabric ports, determines the total available bandwidth per blade and the over-subscription ratio at the fabric link level. The second-generation Cisco UCS 2200 series Fabric Extenders support 1/2/4/8 physical links, each at 10 GbE. Figure 7-44 shows the blade server oversubscription at the I/O module level.

> **NOTE**   The Cisco UCS 2304 I/O modules were released and consist of 4x40GbE, FCoE capable QSFP+ ports that connect the blade chassis to Cisco UCS 6300 series Fabric Interconnects (configured redundantly will provide 320 Gbps per chassis). In addition, they support 8x 40GbE server ports connected through the mid-plane to each half-width blade slot.

With the Cisco UCS I/OM modules in discrete mode, the number of fabric links determines bandwidth oversubscription. See Table 7-22 for a summary of oversubscription rates.

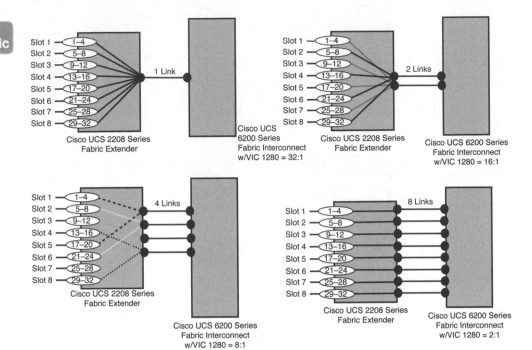

Figure 7-44 *Blade Server Oversubscription Summarized*

Table 7-22 Cisco UCS 2100XP and 2200UP Series IOM Discrete-Mode Connectivity Ratios

Device	Blade Pinning	Based on Cisco UCS 2104XP	*Based on Cisco UCS 2204XP	*Based on Cisco UCS 2208XP with VIC 1280	*Based on Cisco UCS 2208XP with VIC 1240	Cisco UCS 2304
I/O Module Mode	Discrete	Discrete	Discrete	Discrete	Discrete	Discrete
I/O Module Links	Blade slot to FEX link pinning	Over-subscription	Over-subscription	Over-subscription	Over-subscription	Over-subscription
1	Blade slot (1–8)	8:1	16:1	32:1	16:1	8:1
2	Blade slot (1, 3, 5, 7), (2, 4, 6, 8)	4:1	8:1	16:1	8:1	4:1

Device	Blade Pinning	Based on Cisco UCS 2104XP	*Based on Cisco UCS 2204XP	*Based on Cisco UCS 2208XP with VIC 1280	*Based on Cisco UCS 2208XP with VIC 1240	Cisco UCS 2304
4	Blade slot (1, 5), (2, 6), (3, 7), (4, 8)	2:1	1:1	8:1	4:1	2:1
8	Blade slot (1–8)	—	—	1:1	2:1	-

* When the Cisco UCS 2204XP FEX module is used, the oversubscription ratio changes due to 16x 10 GbE connections that exist from FEX to blade slots—that is, two per blade slot internally. With the Cisco UCS 2208XP FEX model, there are 32x 10 GbE connections, which is four per blade slot internally.

These fabric links can be operated in two modes today: either in Discrete (as you see mentioned in the preceding table) or Fabric Port Channel mode. If the I/O module in the blade chassis supports it and is configured in Fabric Port Channel mode, the server traffic shares the entire Fabric Port Channel. In Discrete mode, the server slots are pinned to a fabric link. Figure 7-45 shows the differences between Discrete and Fabric Port Channel mode.

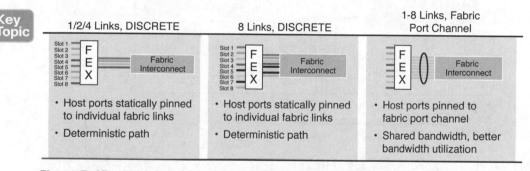

Figure 7-45 *UCS I/O Module Connectivity Summarized*

TIP   As a best practice, when connecting a Cisco UCS I/O module to Fabric Interconnects, always maintain symmetrical cabling connections between both Cisco UCS Fabric Interconnects in a cluster. Also, Cisco UCS Fabric Interconnect ports (groups of 8 ports) are managed by a single ASIC; it is recommended to connect a set of fabric port channels (from I/O module) to a contiguous set of ports managed by an ASIC. Please refer to Cisco configurations guides for detailed information.

Cisco UCS I/O Module Architecture

The Cisco UCS I/O module is analogous to a line card on a switch, but in this case, it is completely "unmanaged." This module facilitates blade connectivity to Cisco UCS Fabric

Interconnects. Cisco I/O module settings are pushed transparently via the UCS Manager. (It is not a point of management.)

> **TIP** In a Cisco UCS blade server chassis, to start configurations, you can install one IOM as a minimum. However, it gives you only partial bandwidth, no redundancy. If you do so, be sure to install it on the "left" side of the chassis (Slot A).

The I/O module is sometimes referred to as an FEX similar to a Nexus 2000 series device. However, the Cisco UCS I/O module consists of some additional components that are not found in the Nexus 2000 series Fabric Extenders and are key to the innovation with Cisco UCS. See the following list, which also explains the purpose and functionality of these components. Figure 7-46 shows the internal architecture of a Cisco UCS I/O module.

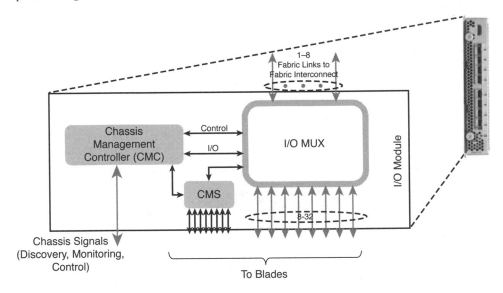

Figure 7-46 *UCS I/O Module Architecture*

- **CMC:** Within the Cisco UCS, it is not an independent point of management. You do not interact or log in to the CMC directly. The Cisco UCS Fabric Interconnects deploy and receive settings and real-time data based on your interaction with the Cisco UCS Manager software. The CMC is used to monitor chassis sensors such as fan speeds, temperature, and so on, and is used in Cisco UCS component discovery. The CMC (in the I/O module), the CIMC (on the blade), and the UCS Manager (Fabric Interconnects) work together to manage the entire Cisco UCS domain.

- **CMS:** This is an unmanaged, ASIC-based Ethernet switch that enables communication internally between the CIMC (on the blade), the CMC (on the I/O module), and UCS Fabric Interconnects. It is the main conduit to carry control traffic and aides the discovery, monitoring, and control processes within the UCS domain.

- **I/O Multiplexer (MUX):** This device multiplexes the I/O traffic from Fabric Interconnects to hosts and blade servers, based on the number of ports connected or the fabric port channel and internal 10GBASE-KR links energized based on the VIC cards used, as shown in Figure 7-42.

Fabric and Adapter Port Channel Architecture

We discussed Fabric Port Channels in the preceding section; essentially, that is the capability to create port channels between the Cisco UCS 6200 series Fabric Interconnects and the Cisco 2200 series I/O modules. Here we briefly explain adapter port channels, which is not a visible link but embedded internal 10G (10GBASE-KR) connections between the adapter on a blade server and the Cisco 2200 series I/O module. Figure 7-47 shows the architecture of port channels between blade, I/O module, and Fabric Interconnects.

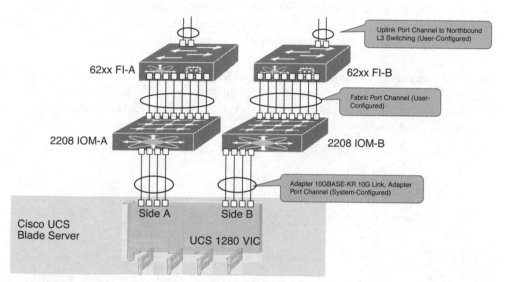

Figure 7-47 *Cisco UCS Fabric and Adapter Port Channel*

As mentioned earlier, these are embedded connections on the Cisco UCS 5108 server chassis. However, you can view these connections via the UCS Manager—Internal Fabric Manager. For more explanation of UCS Manager, refer to the next chapter.

Cisco Integrated Management Controller Architecture

The CIMC is an important piece of hardware that makes the UCS system architecture efficient and a step away from the legacy architecture. The legacy approach was to stitch together agents, pieces of hardware and software, and an out-of-band approach to each computer server or enclosure.

As a key component, the Cisco CIMC is present in both Cisco UCS B-Series blade servers and Cisco C-Series rackmount server systems, allowing Cisco UCS to unify the management of these servers. The CIMC provides three important functions, explained next, and Figure 7-48 shows the CIMC architecture and integration within Cisco UCS.

- **KVM (keyboard, video, and mouse) access to the server:** A KVM console is essentially your video/screen output of the blade, but instead of a physical cable it is transmitted over IP—video-over-IP. The IP referred to here is the management IP assigned to that server or associated service profile.

> **NOTE** When you connect the UCS Manager, you will also see an option to launch a KVM Manager, which is the same KVM capability available as a standalone application accessed over a web browser, but it authenticates via the UCS Manager. The KVM console also provides a utility to access media, virtual CD-ROM, .iso files, client PC-based files, and so on.

- **Serial over LAN (SoL) functionality:** This is the capability to communicate with a COM port over IP (SSH). It is primarily command-line access only. You will have to create an SoL policy that contains a baud rate. At this point, you would be able to login via SSH into the CIMC management IP address assigned to that blade or profile. (It is recommended that you create an intelligent platform management interface (IPMI) policy, and you might have to redirect the console in the BIOS.)

- **IPMI capability:** This is used to monitor and report blade temperature and power readings. CIMC does not take action unless directed by the UCS Manager. The CIMC can also receive IPMI commands over the network via the assigned CIMC management IP address. Therefore, it is recommended that you create an IPMI access profile to control access.

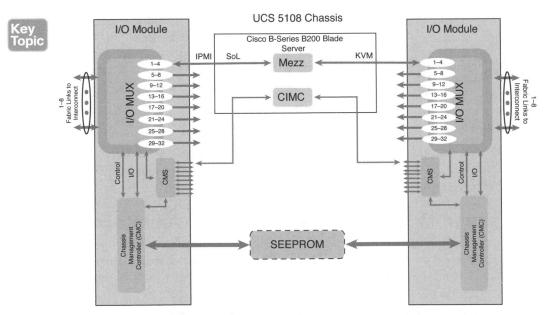

Figure 7-48 *Cisco Integrated CIMC Architecture*

> **NOTE** The CIMC was formerly known as the Baseboard Management Controller (BMC). Cisco has reengineered the management controller to be tightly integrated and work in tandem with the Cisco UCS Manager. It is based on the IPMI specification and standard.

Reference List

Cisco UCS Product Data and Spec Sheets: http://www.cisco.com/c/en/us/products/servers-unified-computing/ucs-c-series-rack-servers/datasheet-listing.html

Cisco UCS Configuration Guides: http://www.cisco.com/c/en/us/support/servers-unified-computing/ucs-manager/products-installation-and-configuration-guides-list.html

Cisco Storage Networking White Paper: http://www.cisco.com/c/en/us/products/collateral/storage-networking/mds-9000-nx-os-software-release-4-1/white_paper_c11-459263.html

IPMI Standards: http://www.intel.com/content/www/us/en/servers/ipmi/ipmi-specifications.html

Cisco Adapter FEX Technology: http://www.cisco.com/c/en/us/products/collateral/switches/nexus-5000-series-switches/data_sheet_c78-657397.html

Relevant Cisco Live Sessions: http://www.ciscolive.com

Cisco Development Network: https://developer.cisco.com/web/unifiedcomputing/ucsemulatordownload

Exam Preparation Tasks

Review All Key Topics

Review the most important topics in the chapter, noted with the key topic icon in the outer margin of the page. Table 7-23 lists a reference of these key topics and the page numbers on which each is found.

Table 7-23   Key Topics for Chapter 7

Key Topic Element	Description	Page
Section	"Cisco UCS Fabric Interconnects"	244
Figure 7-14	"Cisco UCS Fabric Interconnects and Expansion Modules"	245
Table 7-4	"Cisco UCS Fabric Interconnects"	246
Table 7-5	"Cisco UCS Fabric Interconnect—Expansion Modules"	247
Section	"Cisco UCS 5108 Blade Server Chassis"	248
Figure 7-16	"Cisco UCS 5108 Blade Server Chassis Front and Rear View"	249
Section	"Cisco UCS I/O Modules (FEX)"	250
Table 7-6	"Cisco UCS I/O Module Details"	251
Section	"Cisco UCS B-Series Blade Servers"	251
Table 7-7	"Cisco UCS B-Series Blade Server Products"	252
Table 7-8	"Cisco UCS Blade Server Populating DRAM"	254
Section	"Cisco Adapters (Mezzanine Cards) for UCS B-Series Blade Servers"	254
Table 7-9	"Cisco UCS Nonvirtualized Adapter Portfolio"	255
Table 7-10	"Cisco UCS Virtual Interface Cards"	255
Section	"Cisco UCS Port Expander"	257
Section	"Cisco UCS C-Series Rackmount Servers"	258
Table 7-12	"Cisco UCS C-Series Rackmount Server Product Details"	260
Table 7-13	"Cisco UCS C-Series Rackmount Server Populating DRAM"	262
Section	"Cisco Adapters for UCS C-Series Rackmount Servers"	262
Figure 7-25	"Basic RAID Configurations"	262
Figure 7-26	"Advanced RAID Configurations RAID 5+0 and 6+0"	263
Table 7-14	"Common RAID Configurations"	263
Figure 7-27	"Cisco UCS C-Series RAID Adapters"	264
Table 7-15	"Cisco UCS C-Series Server RAID Adapter Details"	264

7

Complete Tables and Lists from Memory

Print a copy of Appendix B, "Memory Tables," or at least the section for this chapter, and complete the tables and lists from memory. Appendix C, "Memory Tables Answer Key," includes completed tables and lists to check your work.

Define Key Terms

Define the following key terms from this chapter, and check your answers in the Glossary:

Basic Input/Output System (BIOS), Network Interface Card (NIC), Host Bus Adapter (HBA), Dynamic Random Access Memory (DRAM), Fabric Extender (FEX), Ethernet, Fibre Channel, Port Channel, Fabric Port Channel, Adapter Port Channel, Storage-Area Network (SAN), Logical-Area Network (LAN), Virtual Storage-Area Network (VSAN), Redundant Array of Independent Disks (RAID), N_Port ID Virtualization (NPIV), N_Port Serial over LAN (SoL), Intelligent Platform Management Interface (IPMI), Cisco Integrated Management Controller (CIMC), Extensible Markup Language (XML), Application Programming Interface (API), Quality of Service (QoS), Chassis Management Controller (CMC), Keyboard, Video, and Mouse (KVM), Input/Output Operations per Second (IOPS), MUX (Multiplexer), SSH (Secure Shell)

This chapter covers the following exam topics:

1.4 Perform basic UCS configuration

1.4a Cluster high availability

1.4b Port roles

1.4c Hardware discovery

CHAPTER 8

Cisco UCS Manager

The Cisco Unified Computing System (UCS) Manager does not require a separate server/host; it is embedded in the Cisco UCS Fabric Interconnects. It is fully redundant and provides a single pane of glass to manage an entire Unified Computing System. The Cisco UCS Manager has a management model that maps to an organization's IT administration functions, such as network/server/storage-area network (SAN) administrators, enabling asynchronous operations between those teams, and allowing full reusability of their work when installing or setting up a server. Thus, Cisco UCS Manager enables individual teams to define, operate, and secure their respective technology elements while achieving consistent server deployments efficiently. Figure 8-1 shows the Cisco UCS Manager Interface with discovered hardware and unconfigured Fabric Interconnects.

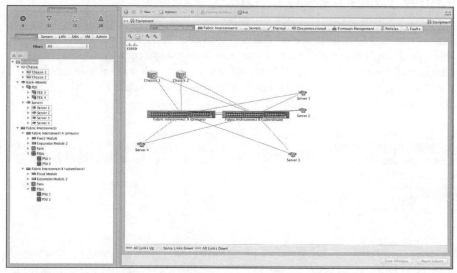

Figure 8-1 *The Cisco UCS Manager*

NOTE It is not mandatory to deploy highly available Cisco UCS Fabric Interconnects, but it is a best practice to deploy a solution that has no single points of failure.

This chapter begins by describing how to set up a Cisco Unified Computing System (UCS) Fabric Interconnect cluster, starting with cabling requirements, console connectivity, and the essential parameters that you need to supply for the Cisco UCS Fabric Interconnects to initialize, establish a cluster relationship, and start running the Cisco UCS Manager.

Before attempting any configurations, you must understand the Cisco UCS Manager layout, functions, and essential configuration element locations and their purpose. This will help you understand the operational model, enable you to swiftly navigate to the required configuration item, and determine its necessity.

NOTE It is recommended to follow a UCS low-level design that captures your configuration requirements in detail before starting any configuration on the Cisco UCS Manager. The holistic view and prerequisites, such as physical cabling, port assignments, and LAN/SAN settings, must be understood and ironed out before beginning any configuration work on the Cisco UCS Manager.

You learn and understand the processes that Cisco UCS Manager follows to discover all Cisco UCS hardware and software components. You also learn and understand the Cisco UCS Manager discovery process and how to monitor and verify whether the process is completed.

After the Cisco UCS Manager has discovered hardware and software components within the UCS domain, you can start configuring the settings, templates, pools, and policies required to match your configuration requirements. Cisco UCS Manager pools, policies, templates, and service profiles are detailed in the next chapter.

"Do I Know This Already?" Quiz

The "Do I Know This Already?" quiz enables you to assess whether you should read this entire chapter thoroughly or jump to the "Exam Preparation Tasks" section. If you are in doubt about your answers to these questions or your own assessment of your knowledge of the topics, read the entire chapter. Table 8-1 lists the major headings in this chapter and their corresponding "Do I Know This Already?" quiz questions. You can find the answers in Appendix A, "Answers to the 'Do I Know This Already?' Quizzes."

Table 8-1 "Do I Know This Already?" Section-to-Question Mapping

Foundation Topics Section	Questions
"Cisco UCS Cluster High Availability"	3–5
"Cisco UCS Hardware Discovery"	9

CAUTION The goal of self-assessment is to gauge your mastery of the topics in this chapter. If you do not know the answer to a question or are only partially sure of the answer, you should mark that question as wrong for purposes of the self-assessment. Giving yourself credit for an answer you correctly guess skews your self-assessment results and might provide you with a false sense of security.

1. What is a Cisco UCS Manager?

   a. It refers to the same product: Cisco Unified Computing System.

   b. Cisco UCS is the newest Unified Communications System Manager software by Cisco.

   c. Cisco UCS Manager is an embedded device manager: a single pane of glass to manage and monitor a Cisco Unified Computing System.

   d. Cisco UCS Manager runs on every blade server and helps manage that system.

2. True or false? You can perform the initial setup of a Cisco UCS Fabric Interconnect via its management virtual/floating IP address.

    a. True

    b. False

3. What are the L1 and L2 ports on Cisco UCS Fabric Interconnects meant for? Mark all statements that are true. (Choose two.)

    a. These ports are used to interconnect Cisco UCS Fabric Interconnects.

    b. These ports are used as a synchronization channel between Cisco UCS Fabric Interconnects in a cluster pair (private network).

    c. The L1 and L2 ports on a UCS Fabric Interconnect are redundant console ports.

    d. These two ports are used to carry data traffic from server ports to uplink Ethernet and FC ports.

    e. These two ports are not in use in the current version of Cisco UCS Fabric Interconnects.

4. How do you connect to the console port of a Cisco UCS Fabric Interconnect?

    a. You can connect to the console port via the management port.

    b. Connect via the RJ-45 console port physical on the Cisco UCS Fabric Interconnect using a Cisco DB-9 to RJ-45 console cable.

    c. Connect via a DB-9 serial console cable by attaching it to the serial port on the Cisco UCS Fabric Interconnect.

    d. Connect via the USB port by connecting to the USB port on the Cisco UCS Fabric Interconnect.

5. Which commands do you use to verify the primary/subordinate roles and the state of a Cisco UCS Fabric Interconnect cluster pair? (Choose two.)

    a. **show system config all**

    b. **show cluster state**

    c. **show cluster extended-state**

    d. **show cluster virtual state**

    e. All of the above

6. What are the three main "panes" in the UCS Manager GUI?

    a. LAN, SAN, Admin pane

    b. Equipment, LAN, SAN pane

    c. Navigation trail, Navigation pane, Content pane

    d. LAN, SAN and VM pane

7. True or false? Is it recommended to use the Cisco UCS Manager GUI to configure the entire system.

    a. True

    b. False

8

8. What are the main tabs in the UCS Manager GUI?

   a. LAN, SAN, Admin tabs

   b. Equipment, Server, LAN, SAN, VM, and Admin tabs

   c. Navigation trail, Navigation pane, Content tabs

   d. Equipment, LAN, SAN, and Admin tabs

9. True or false? When you add new hardware to a Cisco UCS domain, you must manually initiate a discovery.

   a. True

   b. False

10. Which sentence best describes the Finite State Machine (FSM) in the Cisco UCS Manager?

   a. It's a virtual machine that maintains the state of the Cisco UCS hardware and software.

   b. The Cisco UCS manager uses FSM to manage endpoints by monitoring their state transitions.

   c. It's another name for the main configuration database of the Cisco UCS Manager.

   d. It helps monitor the Cisco UCS server and chassis discovery process only.

Foundation Topics

Cabling a Cisco UCS Fabric Interconnect HA Cluster

This chapter starts by explaining the Cisco UCS Fabric Interconnect high availability (HA) concept and architecture, after which you will understand the essential cabling requirements and appropriate port, purpose, and various options with cabling Cisco UCS Fabric Interconnects.

Cisco UCS Fabric Interconnect HA Architecture

Essentially, each Cisco UCS Fabric Interconnect runs an instance of the Cisco UCS Manager (UCSM). In an HA cluster setup, these Cisco UCSM instances (maximum of two in a domain) communicate privately over the L1-L2 links. These dual links are utilized as cluster interconnects to carry heartbeat, command, and configuration database synchronization only.

The UCSM management plane instance runs in an active/standby architecture while the data plane remains fully active/active. The active UCSM instance is known as *primary*, whereas the standby instance is known as *subordinate*. It is important to note that the main configuration database is maintained by the primary instance and replicated onto the subordinate.

When a Fabric Interconnect is down for some time, its configuration database can be out of date. How does Cisco UCSM know which database is the latest and most current? Ingeniously, the Cisco UCS Manager utilizes a Fabric Interconnect-owned area within the SEEPROM/Flash, located on the Cisco UCS 5108 blade server chassis to write and maintain a simple counter, representing the database version. The same is also utilized as a mediator, to guard against a "split-brain" syndrome, where Cisco UCS Fabric Interconnects contend to become primary due to L1-L2 failures.

Each Cisco UCS Fabric Interconnect has a static, physical IP address assigned to its management port, which is used to access the Cisco UCS Manager (out-of-band). There is also a virtual/floating IP address configured during setup, which is always associated with the active/primary UCSM instance. If the active/primary UCSM instance fails, it is associated with the standby/subordinate instance, and vice versa. Figure 8-2 shows a picture of the HA architecture and graphically depicts the static, floating IP addresses.

8

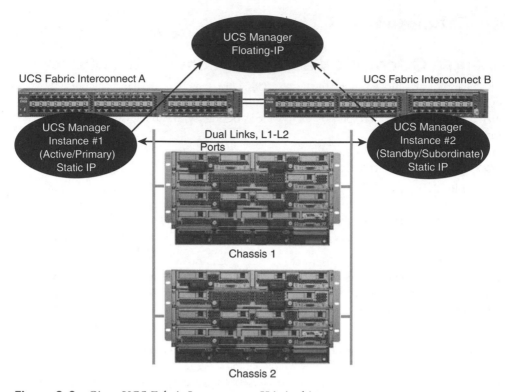

Figure 8-2 *Cisco UCS Fabric Interconnect HA Architecture*

> **NOTE**   An out-of-box initial setup of the Cisco UCS Fabric Interconnects can be performed only via the console connection, and it is important to maintain symmetric UCSM versions between Cisco UCS Fabric Interconnects in a domain. Please refer to the release notes and relevant firmware upgrade guides of the UCSM version to determine the supported/interoperable firmware versions.

Cisco UCS Fabric Interconnect Cluster Connectivity

The management and console ports in a Cisco UCS 6200/6300 series Fabric Interconnect are located in front of the device. Figure 8-3 shows the front and rear view of a Cisco UCS 6248 Fabric Interconnect.

> **NOTE**   Cisco UCS 6100 series Fabric Interconnects have all the management ports on the rear side of the Fabric Interconnect, whereas the Cisco UCS 6200/6300 series Fabric Interconnects have them on the front side, accessible next to the fan modules. Also, next to the console port, Cisco UCS 6200/6300 Fabric Interconnects have a USB port (usb1:) for storing firmware, configuration files, and so on.

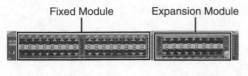

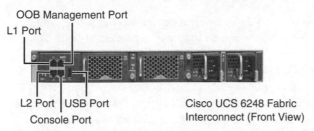

Figure 8-3 *Cisco UCS Fabric Interconnects Cabling Connectivity*

In both 6100/6200 series Fabric Interconnects, the L1 and L2 ports (private network) are located next to the management and console ports in the front, whereas in the third-generation 6300 series Fabric Interconnects, these ports are located separately on the rear side. These ports are not in the data path of the server application traffic; they operate at 10/100/1000 Mbps speeds and connect back-to-back using a straight-through standard Category 6 Ethernet copper cable. Figure 8-4 shows the physical connectivity in preparation for a Cisco UCS Fabric Interconnect HA cluster setup.

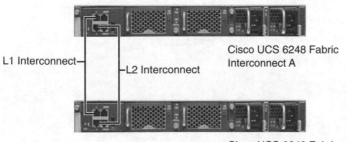

Figure 8-4 *Cisco UCS Fabric Interconnect L1 and L2 Connections*

TIP Figure 8-4 is valid for both UCS 6100 and 6200 series Fabric Interconnects. In the 6300 series Fabric Interconnects, they are located on the rear side. They are all ToR (top-of-rack) devices, and it is recommended to mount Cisco UCS Fabric Interconnects next to each other, thus allowing short 5–10-inch cables to connect these ports back to back. It can be cabled via patch panels when mounted on separate racks, depending on your scale and rack layout options.

Initial Setup Script for Primary Fabric Interconnect

TIP Ensure that you have a Cisco DB-9 to RJ-45 console cable. If your client workstation does not consist of a serial COM port, you need a DB-9 to USB converter with the appropriate USB driver software installed, tested, and ready. Make sure you have collected the information that you require to input during the initial setup dialog.

The serial console connection is a standard VT100 terminal emulation connection. You can use your preferred terminal emulation software and configure it to connect at 9600 baud, 8-bits data, 1 stop-bit, and no parity (9600-8-1-N). With the emulation software running on your client workstation, start with the designated Cisco UCS Fabric Interconnect "A" to begin the cluster configuration. Connect your DB-9/USB interface to your client workstation and the RJ-45 connector into the console port of the Fabric Interconnect A. Figure 8-5 shows the information needed for initial setup of the primary Fabric Interconnects.

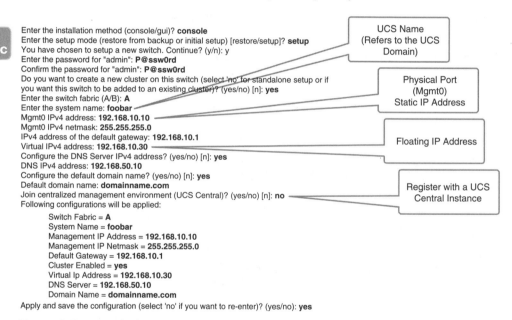

Figure 8-5 *Initial Cluster Setup for Primary Fabric Interconnect Dialog*

Cisco UCS Fabric Interconnects can be accessed via their individual static IPs through the command-line interface (CLI). (You can directly log in via Secure Shell (SSH) to that IP address.) However, the UCS Manager GUI instance is always bound to the primary node; hence, it can be accessed only via its floating IP or the primary node's static IP.

NOTE It is an implicit dependency to have both static management interfaces and virtual IP addresses from the same IP subnet. With Cisco UCS Manager software version 2.2 and later, IPv6 capability for management connectivity and external services, such as NTP, SSH, and HTTP/HTTPS, is also available.

> **NOTE** At a minimum, the third-generation Cisco UCS 6300 series Fabric Interconnects will require Cisco UCS Manager version 3.1(1x) or later. At the time of writing this chapter, Cisco UCS Manager 3.1(1e) had just been released.

Initial Setup Script for Subordinate Secondary Fabric Interconnect

After the primary UCS Fabric Interconnect is configured, remove the RJ-45 connection from the Cisco UCS Fabric Interconnect A and plug it into the same port on Fabric Interconnect B. Reestablish the console connection, and you will be prompted with this dialog. Make sure you have cabled the L1-L2 connections correctly (as per Figure 8-3) and collected the information that you need to input during the subordinate peer setup dialog. Figure 8-6 shows the information needed for the initial setup of the subordinate Fabric Interconnects.

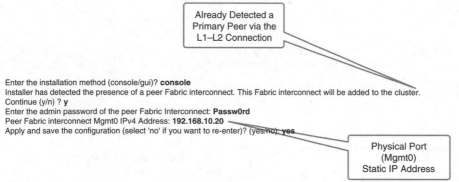

Figure 8-6 *Initial Cluster Setup for Subordinate Fabric Interconnect Dialog*

> **NOTE** As you can see, the dialog is short; because the L1-L2 connectivity is already in place and this is a cluster setup, the subordinate detects a primary peer, its details, and upon completion will perform a full synchronization of configuration databases, UCS Manager, firmware version, and so on. Hence, it requires only minimal details. More information and best practices when upgrading firmware are discussed in Chapter 10, "Administration, Management, and Monitoring of Cisco UCS."

Verify Cisco UCS Fabric Interconnect Cluster Setup

Immediately after both Cisco UCS Fabric Interconnect configurations are complete, how do you verify the cluster state? It is recommended to log in to the UCS Fabric Interconnect via SSH and verify the cluster status through CLI. Two main commands can be used to verify the cluster state: **show cluster state** and **show cluster extended-state**. Figures 8-7 and 8-8 show the output of these commands.

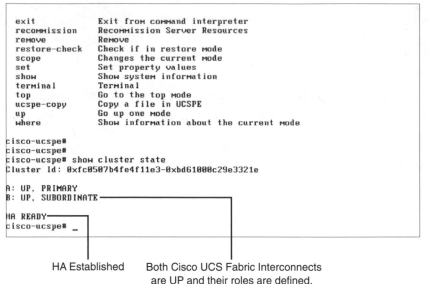

```
exit              Exit from command interpreter
recommission      Recommission Server Resources
remove            Remove
restore-check     Check if in restore mode
scope             Changes the current mode
set               Set property values
show              Show system information
terminal          Terminal
top               Go to the top mode
ucspe-copy        Copy a file in UCSPE
up                Go up one mode
where             Show information about the current mode

cisco-ucspe#
cisco-ucspe#
cisco-ucspe# show cluster state
Cluster Id: 0xfc0507b4fe4f11e3-0xbd61000c29e3321e

A: UP, PRIMARY
B: UP, SUBORDINATE

HA READY
cisco-ucspe# _
```

HA Established   Both Cisco UCS Fabric Interconnects
                      are UP and their roles are defined.

Figure 8-7 *Command/Output to Verify Cluster State*

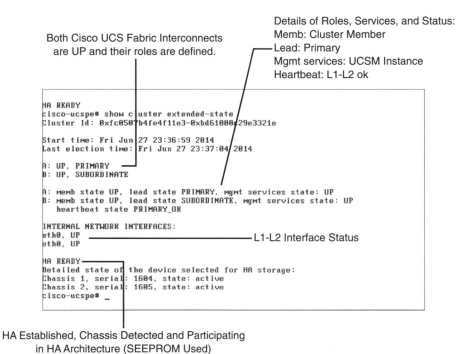

Both Cisco UCS Fabric Interconnects
are UP and their roles are defined.

Details of Roles, Services, and Status:
Memb: Cluster Member
Lead: Primary
Mgmt services: UCSM Instance
Heartbeat: L1-L2 ok

```
HA READY
cisco-ucspe# show cluster extended-state
Cluster Id: 0xfc0507b4fe4f11e3-0xbd61000c29e3321e

Start time: Fri Jun 27 23:36:59 2014
Last election time: Fri Jun 27 23:37:04 2014

A: UP, PRIMARY
B: UP, SUBORDINATE

A: memb state UP, lead state PRIMARY, mgmt services state: UP
B: memb state UP, lead state SUBORDINATE, mgmt services state: UP
   heartbeat state PRIMARY_OK

INTERNAL NETWORK INTERFACES:
eth0, UP
eth0, UP

HA READY
Detailed state of the device selected for HA storage:
Chassis 1, serial: 1604, state: active
Chassis 2, serial: 1605, state: active
cisco-ucspe# _
```

L1-L2 Interface Status

HA Established, Chassis Detected and Participating
in HA Architecture (SEEPROM Used)

Figure 8-8 *Command/Output to Verify Cluster Extended State*

As you can see, the **show cluster extended-state** command gives you more details about the cluster state and typically is used when troubleshooting cluster issues. The output in

Figure 8-8 shows that the UCS Fabric Interconnect A is operating in lead Primary state, management services are Up, L1-L2 interfaces are Up, and HA status is Ready.

When logged in via the Cisco UCS Manager GUI, all configurations are performed on the Primary/Active node; when updates occur on the primary, they are first replicated to the subordinate, acknowledged by its DME (Data Management Engine), and only then the primary node's DME will commit it locally.

NOTE In an HA architecture, both Cisco UCS Fabric Interconnects are active in the data plane and will communicate server-application traffic; that is, data planes are always Active/Active.

Changing Cluster Addressing via Command-Line Interface

After the initial configuration, you can directly log in to the Cisco UCS Fabric Interconnects to change cluster or management IP addressing via the CLI.

Command Modes

The Cisco UCS Manager is designed to use a managed object model. Each physical element, such as blade, chassis, I/O module, and adapter, and every logical element, such as service profile, policy, VLAN, resource pools, and so on, is represented as a managed object within the UCS Manager. Multiple CLI command modes are available in Cisco UCS. Each command mode enables you to administer different types of privileged tasks. Table 8-2 briefly describes the command modes available on the Cisco UCS Fabric Interconnects.

Table 8-2   Cisco UCS Fabric Interconnect Command Modes

Command Modes	Brief Description
EXEC	Default mode; manage/configure UCS Manager physical and logical objects, firmware management via CLI, and so on.
#connect local-mgmt	Enters local management mode, which allows operations of UCS Fabric Interconnect management-related tasks, such as set mgmt0 IP address, install a license, test network reachability of management ports, erase configuration, and the like.
#connect nxos	NX-OS CLI and all the networking properties of the UCS Fabric Interconnects. The command syntax is NX-OS; an example is **show mac-address-table**.

NOTE In default mode, you can use the **scope** command to move down level by level and navigate to the particular object you want to manage. If you want to move back up one level, use the **up** or **exit** command. If you want to go to the top level directly, use the **top** command. The **scope** command does not create a new object; for this you must use the **create** or **enter** command. When you use these commands, remember to use the **commit-buffer** command to apply the command.

Changing Cluster IP Addresses via Command-Line Interface

A standalone Cisco UCS Fabric Interconnect can be converted to a cluster configuration using CLI commands by first enabling it for cluster operation with a floating/virtual IP address and then adding the second UCS Fabric Interconnect into the cluster. Figure 8-9 shows the command usage.

```
cisco-ucspe# scope system
cisco-ucspe /system # set virtual-ip
  a.b.c.d  System IP Address
  ipv6     System IPv6 Address

cisco-ucspe /system # set virtual-ip a.b.c.d_
```

Figure 8-9 *Changing the Virtual IP*

Changing Static IP Addresses via Command-Line Interface

After the initial configuration, it is also possible to change the static IP address assigned to the management port of the Cisco UCS Fabric Interconnects via the command line. Figure 8-10 shows the command usage.

```
cisco-ucspe# scope system
cisco-ucspe /system # set virtual-ip
  a.b.c.d  System IP Address
  ipv6     System IPv6 Address

cisco-ucspe /system # UP
cisco-ucspe# scope fabric-interconnect a
cisco-ucspe /fabric-interconnect # set out-of-band
  gw       Gw
  ip       Ip
  netmask  Netmask

cisco-ucspe /fabric-interconnect # up
cisco-ucspe# scope fabric-interconnect b
cisco-ucspe /fabric-interconnect # set out-of-band
  gw       Gw
  ip       Ip
  netmask  Netmask

cisco-ucspe /fabric-interconnect # set out-of-band _
```

Figure 8-10 *Changing the Static IP of UCS Fabric Interconnects*

Following are some other useful commands you can use to switch the Primary and Subordinate roles in a Cisco UCS Fabric Interconnect HA cluster setup. Can you think of a reason why you might want the ability to do this?

The purpose of the **cluster lead** command is to allow an administrator to switch over the Primary and Subordinate roles in a Cisco UCS HA cluster. It can be run only when HA is at the READY state. This command is typically run on the Primary/Active Cisco UCS Fabric Interconnect, requesting the Subordinate to be elected as the new primary. Figure 8-11 shows the **cluster lead** command usage.

The **cluster force** command is typically not used, but it comes in handy in an emergency when a switchover is stuck (unable to decide who the primary should be) and you want the Cisco UCS Fabric Interconnect you have logged into to become the lead. Figure 8-12 shows the **cluster force** command usage.

```
Cisco Nexus Operating System (NX-OS) Software
TAC support: http://www.cisco.com/tac
Copyright (c) 2009, Cisco Systems, Inc. All rights reserved.
The copyrights to certain works contained in this software are
owned by other third parties and used and distributed under
license. Certain components of this software are licensed under
the GNU General Public License (GPL) version 2.0 or the GNU
Lesser General Public License (LGPL) Version 2.1. A copy of each
such license is available at
http://www.opensource.org/licenses/gpl-2.0.php and
http://www.opensource.org/licenses/lgpl-2.1.php

cisco-ucspe(local-mgmt)#

cisco-ucspe(local-mgmt)#
cisco-ucspe(local-mgmt)# cluster
  force  Force local fabric interconnect to become primary
  lead   Make subordinate fabric interconnect primary

cisco-ucspe(local-mgmt)# cluster lead
  <CR>
  a      Fabric A
  b      Fabric B

cisco-ucspe(local-mgmt)# cluster lead _
```

Figure 8-11 *cluster lead Command*

```
cisco-ucspe# connect local-mgmt
Cisco Nexus Operating System (NX-OS) Software
TAC support: http://www.cisco.com/tac
Copyright (c) 2009, Cisco Systems, Inc. All rights reserved.
The copyrights to certain works contained in this software are
owned by other third parties and used and distributed under
license. Certain components of this software are licensed under
the GNU General Public License (GPL) version 2.0 or the GNU
Lesser General Public License (LGPL) Version 2.1. A copy of each
such license is available at
http://www.opensource.org/licenses/gpl-2.0.php and
http://www.opensource.org/licenses/lgpl-2.1.php

cisco-ucspe(local-mgmt)# cluster lead
  <CR>
  a      Fabric A
  b      Fabric B

cisco-ucspe(local-mgmt)# cluster force
  primary  Primary

cisco-ucspe(local-mgmt)# cluster force ▊
```

Figure 8-12 *cluster force Command*

Cisco UCS Manager Operations

The Cisco UCS Manager is a single pane of glass to discover, monitor, and manage a Cisco UCS domain.

Cisco UCS Manager Functions

Now that you have established a Cisco UCS Fabric Interconnect cluster and checked the cluster status, you can point your shiny new web browser to the virtual/floating IP address assigned during the initial setup process to access your new Cisco UCS Manager. But before that, read these two sections that describe the functions and layout of the UCS Manager to give you a better understanding of what you can configure and where to find those configuration elements within the Cisco UCS Manager.

Following is a graphical representation of Cisco UCS Manager's brief history. This is not in reference to any future roadmap or trend; this is based on the released versions over the year(s). The spaces between the stilts do not indicate a timeline. Cisco UCS Manager version 3.1 is the current major version at the time of writing this chapter. Figure 8-13 shows the Cisco UCS Manager releases.

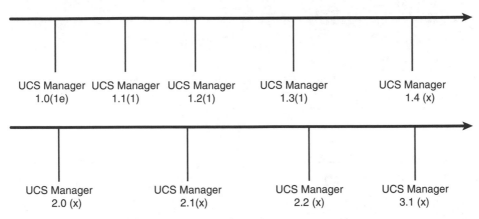

Figure 8-13 *Cisco UCS Manager Brief History*

The Cisco UCS Manager is unique; it provides one point of management for the entire Cisco UCS domain and is embedded in the Cisco UCS Fabric Interconnects. It utilizes a managed object hierarchical model and enables you to manage both physical and logical elements within a Cisco UCS domain as described in the previous section. Under the hood, the Cisco UCS Manager consists of three main modules: an External Interface Layer, a Data Management Engine (DME) and Endpoint Gateways, which enable you to manage endpoints. Figure 8-14 graphically depicts the Cisco UCS Manager module structure and its purpose.

The native language of Cisco UCS Manager is XML. All configurations in the database within UCS Manager are stored in XML format. The GUI and CLI for Cisco UCS Manager utilize the same XML application programming interfaces (APIs), which are also available to you or any third party to interface with the Cisco UCS Manager.

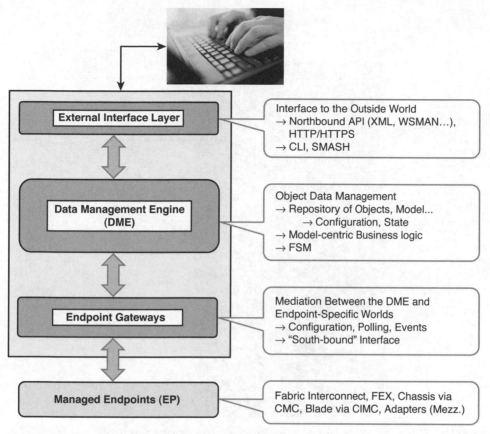

Figure 8-14 *Cisco UCS Manager Layered Architecture*

When a UCS administrator submits a configuration request pertaining to a logical/physical element, the DME calls the appropriate Endpoint Gateway to set that configuration. The state of this element is then communicated to the UCS Manager and reflected in the GUI/CLI. The Cisco UCS Manager database stores all running states of all configurations in nonvolatile flash memory.

The Cisco UCS Manager offers a variety of options for management and monitoring protocols, straight out of the box. Figure 8-15 shows the variety of industry standard protocols for management, monitoring, and logging available on the Cisco UCS Manager. The color/shading represents the protocol/options focusing on the blade hardware versus Cisco UCS domain wide.

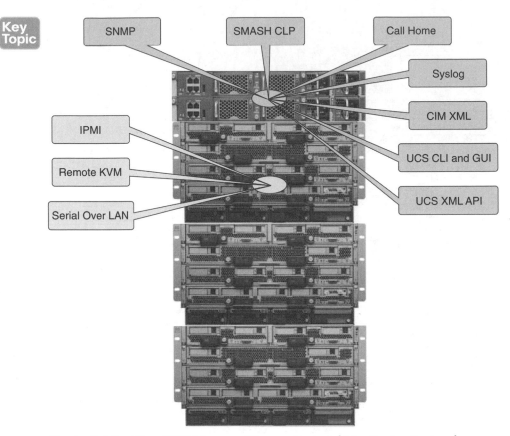

Figure 8-15 *Cisco UCS Manager Management and Monitoring Protocols*

The Cisco Developer Network (DevNet) is a key location to visit and access the Software Development Kits (SDKs) and user guides readily available for various software languages, such as Python SDK, that can be used to create wrappers to access the Cisco UCS XML APIs. Here are some sample use cases in which you would utilize these SDKs to integrate with Cisco UCSM; more details are discussed in Chapter 10.

- Integrating with other operations managers, such as Zenoss and Microsoft SCOM
- Scripting your own UCS provisioning utilities
- Integrating with custom automation tools

Cisco UCS Manager GUI Layout

When you point your web browser to the Cisco UCS Manager IP address (floating/virtual IP address), you are first presented with a landing page. Figure 8-16 shows you the Cisco UCS Manager landing page, where you immediately see the Cisco UCSM version and two main buttons: Launch UCS Manager and Launch KVM Manager.

Click here to launch the UCS Manager.

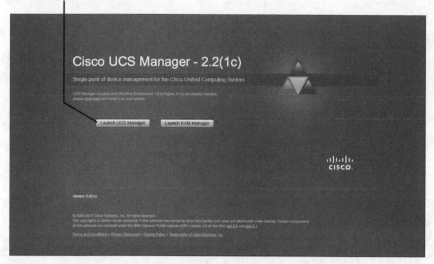

Figure 8-16   *Cisco UCS Manager Main Landing Page*

NOTE   The Cisco UCS Manager versioning follows the standard X.Y (Z) notation, where X=Major, Y=Minor, and Z=fixes version/release; for example, UCSM Version 2.2(2c).

The Launch KVM Manager button initiates the KVM application (separately) that enables you to access the KVMs of individual blade servers. The KVM application can also be accessed from within the Cisco UCS Manager.

Because you want to log in to the Cisco UCS Manager, click that button and you are presented with the banner momentarily before the login screen appears. Figure 8-17 shows the banner and login screen.

After you log in to the UCS Manager, you see that the GUI consists of multiple panes. It consists of three main areas, which are explained in detail, and at the bottom right of the content pane are the functions associated with committing, saving, and discarding changes. Figure 8-18 shows the UCS Manager GUI layout.

■ A navigation pane that shows your current location/selection (expandable tree structure) and an overall fault summary.

■ A content pane that shows you more granular details of the component you have selected and a top toolbar, with a Back button, a new object creation drop-down list, and a question and information button. The second toolbar contains a navigation trail that allows you to rapidly return to the previous locations along the trail; the rightmost component is the current location.

■ Six tabs: Equipment, Servers, LAN, SAN, VM, and Admin, which are detail views of physical and logical managed objects. This is explained in the following section.

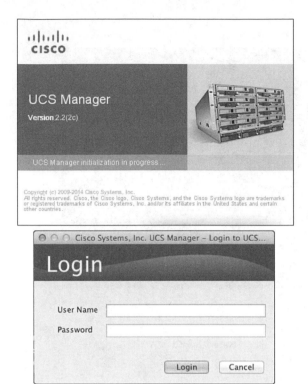

Figure 8-17 *Cisco UCS Manager Banner and Login Screen*

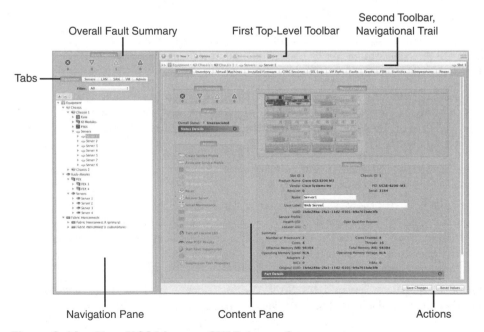

Figure 8-18 *Cisco UCS Manager GUI Primary Components*

> **NOTE** All the operations performed via the GUI can also be executed via the CLI or via XML API programming. However, the GUI is intuitive, and it is the recommended point of Cisco UCS configuration management.

Cisco UCS Manager: Navigation Pane—Tabs

The navigation pane consists of tabs that can be aligned with different IT functional responsibilities within a typical organization. Also note that the Servers tab onward consists of suborganizations, which allow multitenancy through logical containment of pools, policies, service profiles, and more. This section briefly describes what configuration elements can be found and configured under each tab.

Equipment Tab

This tab shows and enables you to interact with all your discovered physical hardware and its configurations. The physical equipment is divided into major categories: Fabric Interconnect, Chassis, Rack Mount, and so on. It also enables you to define global policies that affect the overall UCS domain; most perform firmware management operations. When you select a component, its details will be displayed in the content pane. Figure 8-19 shows the Equipment tab.

Figure 8-19 *Cisco UCS Manager—Equipment Tab*

Servers Tab

It is important to understand that the Servers tab contains a set of logical parameters configured and applied to a physical server. This is where server administrators create service profiles, templates, policies, schedules, and server and identity pools. Figure 8-20 shows the Servers tab.

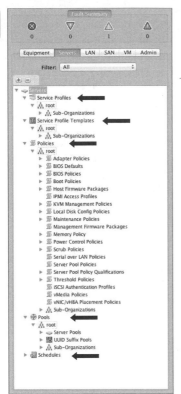

Figure 8-20   *Cisco UCS Manager—Servers Tab*

> **NOTE**   Cisco UCS server pools (server pool policy) enable you to qualify physical servers as they are discovered and automatically classify them into predefined resource pools. You can qualify these server pools based on CPU type, memory, HDD, adapter type, server location, server model, and so on. It is recommended to group servers with similar characteristics into one pool. These server pools can be associated with service profiles/templates, which will associate a new service profile to a server from the pool automatically. (They also can be used with autoconfiguration policies.)

LAN Tab

The Cisco UCS administrators can create, modify, and delete configuration elements related to Ethernet networks via this tab. Some of the main elements that can be configured are the following: create port channels, quality of service (QoS), VLANs, policies, vNIC templates, pools, monitoring, and internal LAN. Figure 8-21 shows the LAN tab.

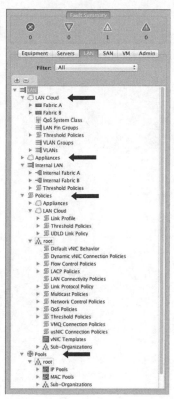

Figure 8-21 *Cisco UCS Manager—LAN Tab*

SAN Tab

The UCS administrator can create, modify, and delete configuration elements related to SANs (FC, iSCSI) or direct attached Fibre Channel/Fibre Channel over Ethernet (FC/FCoE) or network-attached storage (NAS) appliances via this tab. The major categories that are accessible in this tab are vSANs, policies, pools, SAN port channels, uplinks, vHBA templates, and monitoring. Figure 8-22 shows the SAN tab.

VM Tab

The UCS administrator can create, modify, and delete configuration elements related to VMware vSphere and Microsoft Hyper-V VM networks via this tab. You can configure integration with virtual machine managers and discover their configured clusters, hosts, and VMs. You can create port profiles and assign them to dynamic vNICs, which contain VM-FEX technology. Items in this tab are logical configurations that are applied to physical network adapters. Figure 8-23 shows the VM tab.

Figure 8-22   *Cisco UCS Manager—SAN Tab*

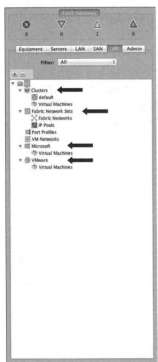

Figure 8-23   *Cisco UCS Manager—VM Tab*

Admin Tab

The UCS administrators can perform administrative tasks on this UCS domain via this tab. You can create, modify, and delete configuration elements that are related to Cisco UCS administrative tasks. There are many elements in this tab; therefore, applying filters to limit the scope of the display is a helpful feature. Some of the main categories in this tab are the following: user management, communications management, faults-events and audit logs, and time zone management. Figure 8-24 shows the Admin tab.

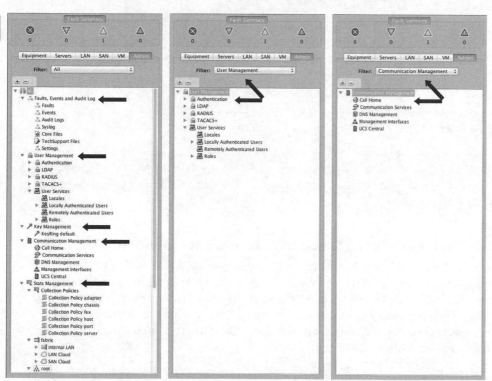

Figure 8-24   *Cisco UCS Manager—Admin Tab*

> **TIP**   All Cisco UCS Manager tabs have filters (just below the tab selection) that will help you filter the relevant configuration elements.

Storage Tab

In Cisco UCS Manager version 2.2(5a) onward, a Storage tab (see Figure 8-25) has been introduced, allowing flexibility in defining logical LUNs and other storage parameters as storage profiles. A storage profile encapsulates the storage requirements for one or more service profiles.

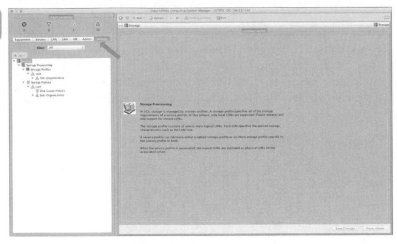

Figure 8-25   *Cisco UCS Manager—Storage Tab*

> **TIP**   LUNs configured in a storage profile can be used as boot LUNs or data LUNs and can be dedicated to a specific server. At the time of writing this chapter, this function had only local LUN support.

Basic Port Roles in the Cisco UCS Fabric Interconnects

Cisco UCS Fabric Interconnect Unified Ports have two main port modes: Ethernet and Fibre Channel (FC). All Ethernet ports in a Fabric Interconnect are in an unconfigured state by default. This applies to all Cisco UCS Fabric Interconnects and their fixed or expansion modules. When changing port modes, fixed/expansion modules need a reboot. Figure 8-26 shows the unconfigured state of a port in Cisco UCS Manager and the available personalities that it can be configured as.

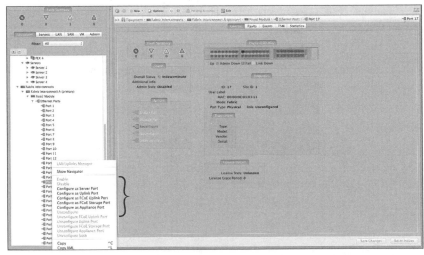

Figure 8-26   *Cisco UCS Manager Ethernet Port Personalities*

The Cisco UCS 6200/6332-16UP series Fabric Interconnects consist of unified ports. A unified port can assume different port modes, such as Ethernet and Fibre Channel. The Cisco UCS hardware device discovery takes place via (Ethernet) server ports. Therefore, this role (server port) indicates that this port is connected to a Cisco UCS I/O module fabric port on a Cisco UCS 5108 blade server chassis. Figure 8-27 shows a configured server port.

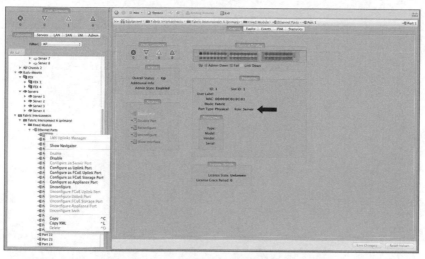

Figure 8-27   *Cisco UCS Manager—Configured Server Port*

> **NOTE**   Cisco UCS 6332 Fabric Interconnects consist of Ethernet and FCoE ports only.

Cisco UCS Manager Hardware Discovery

The UCS Manager is continuously in discovery mode; through its presence sensors and voltage detectors, Cisco UCS Manager realizes the presence of new hardware. Cisco UCS chassis discovery takes place as soon as a chassis is connected to a Cisco UCS Fabric Interconnect or Cisco UCS Manager recognizes a new server port link is active (shown in Figure 8-27). When this happens, a connection is made to the Chassis Management Controller (CMC). The CMC sends all inventory data including serial numbers and part IDs back to the UCS Manager. The DME then stores the data in the configuration database. Figure 8-28 shows the chassis discovery process.

> **NOTE**   Reacknowledging the chassis starts the chassis discovery process manually. However, note that doing so will cause an interruption in communication to and from the chassis because the Cisco I/O modules located within the UCS chassis will reset and be rediscovered while their fabric port/links will be reestablished in the process.

If a server presence is detected, the server inventory is also sent to the Cisco UCS Manager. The details of the inventory include serial numbers, part IDs, CPU information, memory details, installed DIMMs, adapter cards, hard drives, BIOS and CIMC details, and so on. The DME stores them in the configuration database. Figure 8-29 shows the server discovery process.

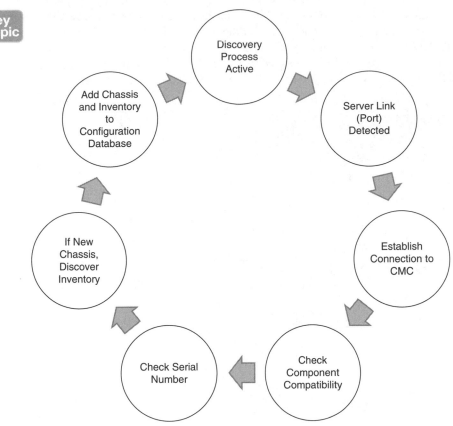

Figure 8-28   *Cisco UCS Manager—Chassis Discovery Process*

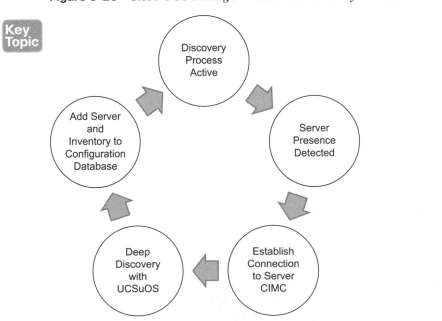

Figure 8-29   *Cisco UCS Manager—Server Discovery Process*

NOTE   Cisco UCS utility operating system (UCSuOS) is a small utility that resides on the Cisco UCS Fabric Interconnect flash memory. It is PXE booted on a blade server when a blade server is initially detected. This utility boots on a blade (with no OS or service profile) and provides inventory discovery services. It is also used to preboot and provide firmware management and service profiles association/disassociation services.

Verifying Device Discovery in Cisco UCS Manager

The Cisco UCS Manager uses the Finite State Machine (FSM) to monitor the progress of configuration and discovery-related states. Every action that requires a set/retrieve action within the UCS Manager is perceived as a set of state transitions; there are "worker" processes performing these highly complex state transitions, and their progress and validity can be monitored and audited via the FSM. Here are some examples of components that are subject to FSM validation/monitoring:

- Physical components
    - Chassis
    - I/O module
    - Blade/rackmount servers and their elements within
- Logical components
    - Pools
    - Policies
- Workflows
    - Chassis discovery
    - Server discovery
    - Service profiles association/disassociation
    - Firmware downloads, upgrades
    - Backup and import jobs

Figure 8-30 shows the option to acknowledge a server blade chassis from within the Cisco UCS Manager. After the Cisco UCS 5108 blade server chassis is acknowledged, you can visit the FSM tab in the content pane of either I/O module and observe the process shown earlier in Figure 8-28 as a series of logical transitions. Figure 8-31 shows the progress bar and current FSM name (this name indicates the current FSM stages as it progresses until the end) and completion of the state transitions.

You can also manually reset a Cisco I/O module. The progress indicator provides a graphical representation of the FSM progress. Often you will see long pauses at particular stages; these pauses are process specific and nothing to be alarmed about. If the FSM stops responding, there is a specific timeout, and that will take effect classifying the operation as failed.

8

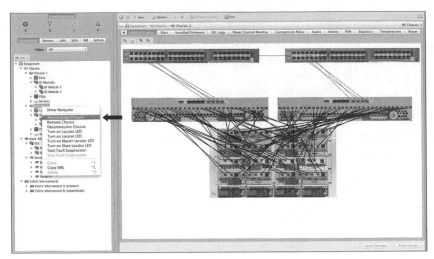

Figure 8-30   *Cisco UCS Manager Chassis—Acknowledgement*

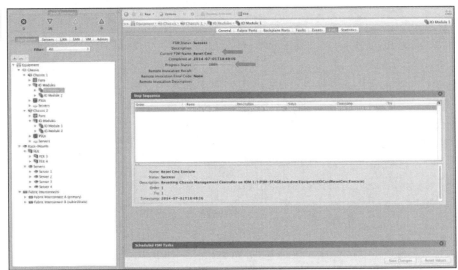

Figure 8-31   *Cisco UCS Manager—Chassis Discovery I/O Module FSM Tab*

Figure 8-32 shows the successful completion of the I/O module reset execute operation. Notice the current FSM name and error code (if any), which shows that the operation executed successfully. Figure 8-33 illustrates the corresponding Events tab, which clearly shows you the state transitions that transpired when executing the I/O module reset and their descriptions.

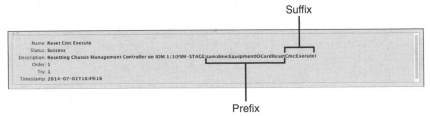

Figure 8-32   *Cisco UCS Manager—I/O Module Reset & FSM Notation*

Figure 8-33 also shows the FSM description and its format for this corresponding operation, which is clearly readable. Although the FSM description looks cryptic at the end, it has a clear notation. Each FSM stage name has a **prefix** that identifies the FSM and a **suffix** that identifies a stage within the FSM. The prefix notation is FsmObjectWorkflow, and the suffix notation is OperationWhere-is-it-executed.

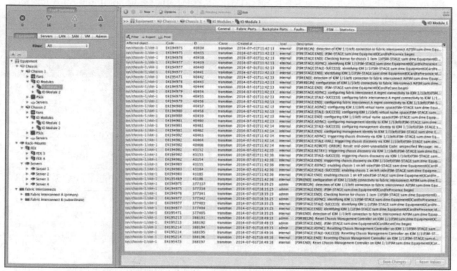

Figure 8-33 *Cisco UCS Manager—Chassis Discovery I/O Module Events Tab*

Reference List

Cisco Console Cable Guide: http://www.cisco.com/c/en/us/support/docs/routers/7000-series-routers/12223-14.html

Cisco UCS FSM: http://www.cisco.com/c/en/us/td/docs/unified_computing/ucs/ts/guide_old_FM/TS_FSM.html

Cisco UCS CLI Configuration Guide: http://www.cisco.com/c/en/us/td/docs/unified_computing/ucs/sw/cli/config/guide/2-2/b_UCSM_CLI_Configuration_Guide_2_2.html

Cisco DevNet: https://developer.cisco.com/site/devnet/home/index.gsp#comboFilters[devnettech]=.datacenter&comboFilters[datacentertech]=.ucssystemsmanagement)

Cisco UCS Manager Release Notes: http://www.cisco.com/c/en/us/support/servers-unified-computing/ucs-manager/products-release-notes-list.html

Cisco UCS Firmware Management: http://www.cisco.com/c/en/us/td/docs/unified_computing/ucs/sw/firmware-mgmt/cli/2-2/b_CLI_Firmware_Management_22/b_CLI_Firmware_Management_22_chapter_011.html

Cisco UCS Manager Install and Upgrade Guides: http://www.cisco.com/c/en/us/support/servers-unified-computing/ucs-manager/products-installation-guides-list.html

Cisco UCS Firmware Management Best Practices: http://www.cisco.com/c/en/us/support/docs/servers-unified-computing/ucs-manager/110511-ucs-fw-mgmt-00.html

Exam Preparation Tasks

Review All Key Topics

Review the most important topics in the chapter, noted with the key topic icon in the outer margin of the page. Table 8-3 lists a reference for these key topics and the page numbers on which each is found.

Table 8-3   Key Topics for Chapter 8

Key Topic Element	Description	Page
Section	"Cisco UCS Fabric Interconnect HA Cluster"	299
Paragraph	"Cisco UCS Fabric Interconnect HA Architecture"	299
Figure 8-4	"Cisco UCS Fabric Interconnect L1-L2 Port Connectivity"	301
Figure 8-5	"Initial Cluster Setup for Primary Fabric Interconnect Dialog"	302
Figure 8-6	"Initial Cluster Setup for Subordinate Fabric Interconnect Dialog"	303
Figure 8-7	"Command/Output to Verify Cluster State"	304
Figure 8-9	"Changing the Virtual IP"	306
Paragraph	"Cisco UCS Manager Functions"	307
Figure 8-15	"Cisco UCS Manager Management and Monitoring Protocols"	310
Section	"Cisco UCS Manager GUI Layout"	310
Figure 8-19	"Cisco UCS Manager—Equipment Tab"	313
Figure 8-20	"Cisco UCS Manager—Servers Tab"	314
Figure 8-21	"Cisco UCS Manager—LAN Tab"	315
Figure 8-22	"Cisco UCS Manager—SAN Tab"	316
Figure 8-23	"Cisco UCS Manager—VM Tab"	316
Figure 8-24	"Cisco UCS Manager—Admin Tab"	317
Figure 8-25	"Cisco UCS Manager—Storage Tab"	318
Section	"Basic Port Roles in the Cisco UCS Fabric Interconnects"	318
Figure 8-26	"Cisco UCS Manager Ethernet Port Personalities"	318
Section	"Cisco UCS Manager Hardware Discovery"	319
Figure 8-28	"Cisco UCS Manager—Chassis Discovery Process"	320
Figure 8-29	"Cisco UCS Manager—Server Discovery Process"	320
Section	"Verifying Device Discovery in Cisco UCS Manager"	321
Figure 8-31	"Cisco UCS Manager—Chassis Discovery I/O Module FSM Tab"	322
Figure 8-33	"Cisco UCS Manager—Chassis Discovery I/O Module Events Tab"	323

Define Key Terms

Define the following key terms from this chapter, and check your answers in the Glossary:

Graphical User Interface (GUI), Command-Line Interface (CLI), Local-Area Network (LAN), Storage-Area Network (SAN), Virtual Machine (VM), Finite State Machine (FSM), Pane, Boot, Hard Disk Drive (HDD), Serial Electrically Erasable Programmable Read Only Memory (SEEPROM), Data Management Engine (DME), Pre-Boot Execution Environment (PXE)

8

This chapter covers the following exam topic:

1.3 Describe the concepts and benefits of UCS hardware abstraction

CHAPTER 9

Cisco Unified Computing System Pools, Policies, Templates, and Service Profiles

The Cisco Unified Computing System (UCS) Manager is fully redundant and provides a single pane of glass to manage an entire Cisco UCS. The Cisco UCS Manager is the UI to configure various settings, templates, pools, policies, and service profiles required to commission a Cisco UCS solution.

This chapter starts by explaining the hardware abstraction layer in more detail that translates into a service profile object. This enables the Cisco UCS to offer such features as stateless computing and consistent server deployments by utilizing resource pools, policies, and templates. These resource pools can be further classified as logical and physical resource pools. You will learn the usage, benefits, and Cisco best practices of the UCS.

You will understand the organizational tree structure, locales within the Cisco UCS Manager, and the essential policies and pools you can create that affect the Cisco UCS domain, such as MAC, World Wide Name (WWN) identity pools, power capping policies, and so on, utilized within various templates. Multiple templates can be created that assist rapid and consistent provisioning with unique identities; details are discussed within this chapter.

Furthermore, you also learn the Cisco best practices and considerations in terms of naming conventions and defining identities when creating logical identity pools and templates. Where applicable, you will see notes and tips about the useful, most relevant features that currently exist at the time of writing this chapter; these features are explained briefly.

NOTE It is recommended to follow a UCS low-level design that captures your configuration requirements in detail before starting any configuration on the Cisco UCS Manager. The holistic view and prerequisites, such as physical cabling, port assignments, LAN/SAN settings, and so on, must be understood and ironed out before beginning any configuration work on the Cisco UCS Manager.

"Do I Know This Already?" Quiz

The "Do I Know This Already?" quiz enables you to assess whether you should read this entire chapter thoroughly or jump to the "Exam Preparation Tasks" section. If you are in doubt about your answers to these questions or your own assessment of your knowledge of the topics, read the entire chapter. Table 9-1 lists some of the major headings in this chapter and their corresponding "Do I Know This Already?" quiz questions. You can find the answers in Appendix A, "Answers to the 'Do I Know This Already?' Quizzes."

Table 9-1   "Do I Know This Already?" Section-to-Question Mapping

Foundation Topics Section	Questions
"Cisco UCS Service Profiles"	1, 2, 3, 7
"Cisco UCS Templates"	6
"Cisco UCS Logical Resource Pools"	4, 5
"Cisco UCS Physical Resource Pools"	10
"Policies Consumed by Cisco UCS Service Profiles/Service Profile Templates"	8
"Cisco UCS Chassis and Blade Power Capping"	9

CAUTION   The goal of self-assessment is to gauge your mastery of the topics in this chapter. If you do not know the answer to a question or are only partially sure of the answer, you should mark that question as wrong for purposes of the self-assessment. Giving yourself credit for an answer you correctly guess skews your self-assessment results and might provide you with a false sense of security.

1. What is a Cisco UCS service profile?

   a. A software object that contains all the hardware identifiers and firmware details available on a typical server; it can be associated with a Cisco UCS blade or rackmount server to instantiate a server.

   b. All the servers and their hardware configurations are known as Cisco UCS service profiles.

   c. The Cisco UCS Manager is also known as a Cisco UCS service profile.

   d. A service profile is the physical hardware profile of a Cisco UCS blade server.

2. True or false? You can power on and start deploying an operating system on a Cisco UCS blade or rackmount server and later assign a service profile.

   a. True

   b. False

3. A virtual machine is also a form of hardware abstraction. What are the key differences between a virtual machine and a service profile? Choose all statements that you think are valid.

   a. A virtual machine's hardware abstraction layer resides on top of a hypervisor, which provides hardware abstraction capabilities. The Cisco UCS service profile is yet another hypervisor.

   b. A virtual machine's hardware abstraction layer resides on top of a hypervisor, which provides that hardware abstraction capability. A Cisco UCS service profile hardware abstraction layer resides before the hypervisor.

   c. A Cisco UCS blade or rackmount server requires a service profile associated and ready to install a hypervisor and subsequently create virtual machines.

   d. To install an operating system on a virtual machine, you must first associate a Cisco UCS service profile to that virtual machine.

4. What is the difference between a logical and a physical resource pool?

    a. It is a group of identities; they are both identical and differ only in the way they are utilized.

    b. Logical resource pools are user-defined identities used in service profiles, whereas physical resource pools are computer nodes consumed by associating service profiles to them.

    c. Logical resource pools are user-defined identities that are utilized by physical resource pools.

    d. Physical resource pools refer to all the hardware components within a UCS domain; logical resource pools are all the software components within the Cisco UCS domain.

5. What is a WWN address, and what is the length of this address?

    a. It is the worldwide number that is unique and assigned to a blade, and it is an 8-bit address.

    b. It is the worldwide node number; it contains a prefix and a suffix and is used to identify a computer node/server. It is a 16-bit address.

    c. It is the worldwide node number, and it contains a prefix and a suffix. It is assigned to a manufacturer by IEEE and used to identify a computer node/server in Fibre Channel Protocol. It is a 32-bit address.

    d. It is the worldwide number and contains multiple fields. It also contains an OUI that is assigned to a manufacturer by IEEE and, together with a sequence number, it identifies a computer node/port in Fibre Channel Protocol. It can be a 64-bit or 128-bit address, depending on the component it addresses.

6. Why do you create a Cisco UCS service profile template? Mark all valid statements.

    a. It is used for automated, rapid provisioning of Cisco UCS service profiles.

    b. It is mandatory to create a Cisco UCS service profile template to create service profiles.

    c. It gives you the capability to create Cisco UCS service profiles with different attributes to suit the target application and allow rapid provisioning at the same time.

    d. You can utilize the template to pre-create the required service profiles and utilize the derived identities to already preconfigure the external SAN, LAN environment in preparation of new servers and applications.

7. True or false? You can "move" a service profile from one location to another and rename it within a Cisco UCS domain.

    a. True

    b. False

9

8. What is a Cisco UCS adapter policy, and what is its primary benefit? Mark the statement that describes it the best.

   a. This policy enables you to place an adapter in a particular PCIe order via interrupt queues.

   b. This policy enables you to set low-level attributes of an adapter, such as queues, interrupt handing, and the like. The default values are based on OS and software vendor recommendations.

   c. This policy enables you to create the required number of dynamic adapters and allows it to be consumed by service profile templates.

   d. This policy enables you to set the adapter firmware level on vNICs only.

9. What are the different types of UCS Power Management policies available?

   a. Minimum, Average, and Maximum UCS power management policies.

   b. Low, Medium, and High UCS power management policies for each Cisco UCS blade or rackmount server.

   c. Manual blade level, policy-driven chassis groups, and power control policies (priority based option).

   d. There are only two types of power-capping policies: single blade and chassis-based.

10. True or false? A blade server can belong to multiple server pools.

   a. True

   b. False

Foundation Topics

Cisco UCS Service Profiles

Cisco UCS service profiles are fundamental to the Cisco UCS solution. They are instrumental in providing the hardware abstraction discussed in this chapter. You must clearly understand the concept of a service profile, which becomes a key building block in this software-defined computing infrastructure.

Cisco UCS Hardware Abstraction and Stateless Computing

It is important that you understand the service profile software object and the concept in Cisco UCS technology. As you know, in every server there are installed hardware components and settings, such as a BIOS, network interface cards (NICs), host bus adapters (HBAs), VLAN assignments, disks, RAID configurations, and so on. Each has an identity/parameter associated with it, such as a MAC address, a WWN number, a VLAN ID, BIOS settings, and the like. These identities are fixed; they are burned in to the physical hardware component itself. Figure 9-1 shows you a list of some identities and parameters that are fixed—burned in on a bare metal server.

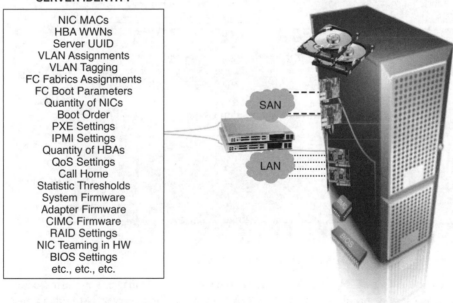

SERVER IDENTITY

NIC MACs
HBA WWNs
Server UUID
VLAN Assignments
VLAN Tagging
FC Fabrics Assignments
FC Boot Parameters
Quantity of NICs
Boot Order
PXE Settings
IPMI Settings
Quantity of HBAs
QoS Settings
Call Home
Statistic Thresholds
System Firmware
Adapter Firmware
CIMC Firmware
RAID Settings
NIC Teaming in HW
BIOS Settings
etc., etc., etc.

SAN

LAN

Figure 9-1   *Cisco UCS Service Profile Software Object*

NOTE   A bare metal server is a physical server with hardware, such as CPU, NICs, HBAs, DRAM, and hard disks, that are installed in it, ready for power-up and direct operating system installation onto those hard drives.

Traditionally, when you install an operating system directly on to a bare metal server, the operating system utilizes these fixed identities to interface with internal and external entities. An example is the MAC address built in to the NIC card that is used for all network communications. The Cisco UCS service profile object contains the entire server personality (BIOS settings, MACs, WWNs, RAID configuration, connectivity information, and the like, discussed later) and boot requirements.

This service profile can then be associated with a single blade, rackmount, or cartridge server at a time to give it that personality. The concept of a Cisco UCS service profile was invented to support the notion of mobility—or transferring of identities transparently from one blade or rackmount server to another (stateless computing), as well as resource pooling concepts discussed later in this chapter. Figure 9-2 shows the hardware abstraction layer between the physical hardware and the operating system or hypervisor.

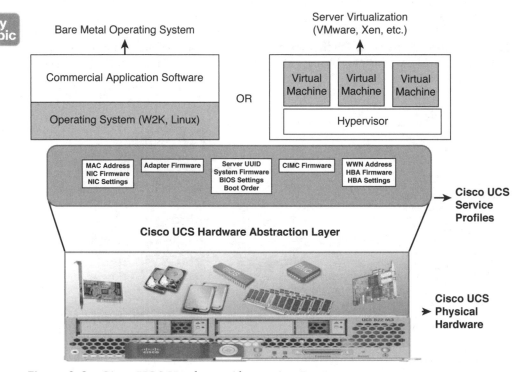

Figure 9-2 *Cisco UCS Hardware Abstraction Layer*

As long as you manage Cisco UCS hardware via the Cisco UCS Manager, you must create and manage a service profile for the blade, rackmount, or cartridge servers. Although you can power on a blade or rackmount server without a service profile, it would have no identities, network, or storage-area network (SAN) connectivity; instead, it would remain at default BIOS after the power-on self-test (POST) stage.

The capability to achieve true "stateless computing" is a phenomenal advantage in server computing. With Cisco UCS service profiles, resource pooling, and SAN-boot technologies, in the event of hardware failure the entire service profile can be reassociated with another

Cisco UCS blade or rackmount server with the same identities and settings. Today, with high vm:host server consolidation ratios, the capability to recover the host server with the same OS/identities within minutes translates to huge benefits and savings. Traditionally, you would have to reinstall the operating system, reconfigure it, reinstall all software on a new bare metal server, and then establish external connectivity to LAN, SAN—all of which are time-consuming tasks.

Server mobility (stateless computing) gives you the opportunity to right-size your environment and better utilize your hardware. You might want to run your application on lower hardware configurations and reassociate the Cisco UCS service profile to a blade with higher hardware configurations for peak-time utilization only and move it back in a timely manner. There is no need to build expensive additional capacity on every piece of hardware to counter any or all eventualities during that application's life cycle.

NOTE   When a Cisco UCS service profile is moved from server to server, the SAN node and LAN port identities will move with it. The Cisco UCS service profile running on a new blade will be indistinguishable from an external entity compared to the same service profile previously running on the original server. You can access the same external storage, without reconfiguration on the external Fibre Channel fabric (zones, for example) or remapping of storage LUNs or L2/L3 communications. It is important to understand that SAN-boot is a prerequisite to achieving the advantages of true stateless computing.

Contents of a Cisco UCS Service Profile

As discussed, Cisco UCS service profiles take the lowest level of identities and settings in the hardware—those settings that were previously known to be fixed and burned in to the hardware and allow them to be configurable, controlled via software.

More than 120 parameters can be controlled within a single Cisco UCS service profile. You can even define the versions of firmware you need to run on an adapter and what the identities of those adapters are going to be—such as the worldwide names, MAC addresses, BIOS versions, and BIOS settings. It also extends to LAN and SAN connectivity settings, such as the VLAN that the NIC needs to be a part of, the VSAN membership on the HBA, quality of service (QoS) settings for the vNICs, and so on. Figure 9-3 shows a partial list of the identities, settings that can be maintained within a single Cisco UCS service profile software object.

As you can see, many characteristics and settings are captured in a Cisco UCS service profile and applied to the server hardware at the time you associate a service profile to a Cisco UCS server. The construct of a Cisco UCS service profile enables the LAN/Network, SAN/Storage, and server administration teams to populate settings and identity details around their areas of autonomy through the Cisco UCS Manager.

Then eventually, you as the UCS administrator can draw upon these pre-created values, such as named VLANs and definitions of how the service profile must access the upper layers of the network, settings at the adapter level, MAC addresses, QoS settings, virtual storage area network (VSAN) memberships, WWNs, boot order, and so on, and create a service profile.

9

A UCS Service Profile:

120 + server settings in a single object...

BIOS: Quiet Boot
BIOS: Post Error Pause
BIOS: Resume A/C on Power Loss
BIOS: Front Panel Lockout
BIOS: Turbo Boost
BIOS: ACPI10 Support
BIOS: Enhanced Intel Speedstep
BIOS: Hyper Threading
BIOS: Core Multi Processing
BIOS: Virtualization Technology (VT)
BIOS: Execute Disabled Bit
BIOS: Direct Cache Access
BIOS: Processor C State
BIOS: Processor C1E
BIOS: Processor C3 Report
BIOS: Processor C6 Report
BIOS: CPU Performance
BIOS: Max Variable MTRR Setting
BIOS: VT for Directed IO
BIOS: Interrupt Remap
BIOS: Coherency Support
BIOS: ATS Support
BIOS: Passthrough DMA Support
BIOS: Memory RAS Config
BIOS: NUMA
BIOS: Low Voltage DDR Mode
BIOS: Serial Port A state
BIOS: USB Make Device Non Bootable
BIOS: USB System Idle Power Optimizing Setting
BIOS: USB Front Panel Access Lock
BIOS: PCI Max Memory Below 4G

BIOS: PCI Memory Mapped IO Above 4Gb Config
BIOS: Boot Option Retry
BIOS: UCSM Boot Order Rule Control
BIOS: Intel Entry SAS RAID
BIOS: Intel Entry SAS RAID Module
BIOS: Assert Nmi on Serr
BIOS: Assert Nmi on Perr
BIOS: OS Boot Watchdog Timer
BIOS: Console Redirection
BIOS: Console Flow Control
BIOS: Console BAUD rate
BIOS: Console Terminal Type
BIOS: Console Legacy OS Redirect
Server Boot Order (HDD, CD-ROM, SAN, USB, Floppy, RXE)
Server BIOS Firmware
Ethernet Adapter Firmware
Fiber Channel Adapter Firmware
HBA Option ROM Firmware
Storage Controller Firmware
Remote Management Controller (e.g. HP iLO) Firmware
Server UUID
Virtual Server Serial Number
Define Number of vNICs on Server
Define Number of Dynamic vNICs (for VMware Pass-through)
Settable vNIC/FlexNIC Speed (reflected in OS)
PXE Boot Setting
Fabric Failover (NIC Teaming) Settings
VLAN Assignment per NIC

VLAN Tagging Settings per NIC
NIC Transmit Rate Limiting
NIC MAC Address Assignment
NIC Maximum Transmission Unit (MTU)
Number of NIC Transmit Queues
NIC Transmit Queue Ring Size
NIC Receive Queues
NIC Receive Queue Ring Size
NIC Completion Queues
NIC Interrupts
NIC Transmit Checksum Offload
NIC Receive Checksum Offload
NIC TCP Segmentation Offload
NIC TCP Large Receive Offload
NIC Receive Side Scaling (RSS)
NIC Failback Timeout
NIC Interrupt Mode
NIC Interrupt Coalescing
NIC Interrupt Timer
NIC QoS Host Control Option
Enable/Disable Cisco Discovery Protocol for VMware vSwitch
MAC Security per NIC
QoS settings per NIC
NIC action on Switch uplink failure
Distribution Enet Switch Uplink Assignment Per NIC (Pin Group)
Server Pool Assignment
Maintenance Policy
IPMI Usernames & Passwords
IPMI User Roles
Server Management IP Address
Serial over LAN Configuration
Power Control Policy Capping and Priority
PCIe Bus Device Scan Order for NICs/HBAs
PCIe Virtual Device Slot Placement for NIC/HBA
BIOS Scrub Actions

Figure 9-3   *Cisco UCS Service Profile Parameters*

Through the UCS Manager, you can select a service profile and associate it to an individual Cisco UCS blade, rackmount server, or server pool. By doing so, Cisco UCS Manager will essentially take that set of configurations (service profile object) and apply it to the selected physical server or, if associated to a server pool, it will pick the next available unassociated server and associate the service profile. In doing so, it will utilize the UCS utility operating system (UCSuOS) to program/set service profile parameters onto hardware. At the end of this process, you essentially will have a bare metal server with your identities ready for operation system installation. Figure 9-4 shows you the actions available when you select an existing service profile object in the Cisco UCS Manager.

NOTE   It is easy to copy or clone a service profile or template (provided you utilize identity pools; you will have unique identities once copied or cloned). However, at the time of writing this chapter, it is not possible to "move" a service profile software object from one organization or location to another within the Cisco UCS Manager.

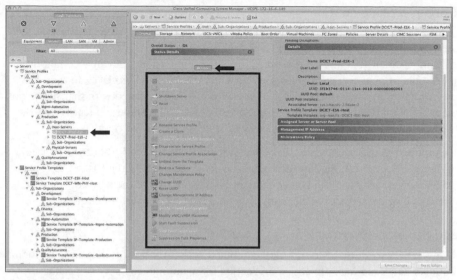

Figure 9-4 *Cisco UCS Service Profile Actions*

Other Benefits of Cisco UCS Service Profiles

Apart from some of the leading benefits explained in the preceding section, such as stateless computing, some other benefits exist that you should understand and can utilize as part of your Cisco UCS design, adoption, and operational processes.

Ease of Incremental Deployments

As you start deploying servers incrementally, you can realize significant benefits because the process of deploying servers by creating service profiles is now an automated process. You spend little time upfront to create the service profile templates; after you do that, deploying or redeploying those servers and their workloads is much more efficient than it has been in the past. To reap this benefit, you must adhere to Cisco best practices and utilize identity pools and service profile templates.

Plan and Preconfigure Cisco UCS Solutions

This advantage stems from the hardware abstraction capabilities, resource pooling, and UCS architecture itself; the wire-once UCS concept with LAN, SAN connectivity and pooling of computer resources provides a significant operational benefit. The UCS Manager UI—with its concept of various administration teams interacting with one portal, nondisruptive nature, and reusability of work—enables a Cisco UCS solution to be preconfigured and progressively deployed.

You will have the network team creating network policies on defining the NICs, MAC pools, VLANs, and QoS characteristics (if any), and they insert those into readable policy names. Then you can simply reuse those policy names inside your service profiles or templates. Similarly, on the SAN side, the SAN admin creates server-SAN related policies that can be reused when deploying a server. This combination enables you to plan ahead and preconfigure server deployments that will result in efficient deployment times and scalability.

Ease of Server Replacement

You can extend the concept of hot sparing made popular in enterprise storage solutions to a pool of computer resources with Cisco UCS. You can designate a Cisco UCS server as a hot spare and ensure it contains a minimum hardware configuration that can accommodate the requirements of your average applications currently hosted on Cisco UCS. In the event of a server or hardware component failure, the service profile associated with that server can be reassociated with the designated hot spare server, which will assume all identities of the failed hardware. Within minutes, you will have the same server up and running.

In the meantime, the failed hardware can be hot swapped and replaced. When the replacement hardware arrives, it can be plugged back in again, discovered by the Cisco UCS Manager, and when ready for use, you could either designate that as the new hot spare or reassociate the original service profile, with planned downtime for that application.

Right-Sized Server Deployments

With the use of Cisco UCS service profiles, combined with SAN-boot techniques, you don't have to budget and build each project or application for maximum capacity or peak usage and preprovision more hardware from day one. The benefit is reduced hardware rollout in the overall data center. Start with bare-minimum hardware configurations and perhaps a few nodes with higher capacities that can be shared among applications at peak usage/times. With Cisco UCS service profiles, you can disassociate and reassociate service profiles on different hardware configurations to accommodate peak usage during certain operational hours or days of the month and revert back to initial allocations otherwise.

> **NOTE**   Server virtualization is a widely adopted concept, but organizations are still going to have a number of physical x86 servers that run in their data center. The Cisco UCS and service profiles are essentially valuable in both cases.

Cisco UCS Templates

The Cisco UCS Manager utilizes templates to promote reusability, automation, and domain-specific grouping of parameters. This helps specialist administration teams, such as LAN, SAN within an organization to create the required pools and policies to be consumed in service profile templates. Cisco UCS can also consist of physical resource pools, which are mainly server pools either grouped based on certain qualification criteria or treated as a holding area for available computer nodes. Figure 9-5 identifies the various Cisco UCS template types and resource pools available for consumption.

> **NOTE**   There are two main types of templates: initial and updating templates in the Cisco UCS Manager. The main difference between them is that an updating template will reflect any changes made to it, to all its child service profiles, whereas the initial template will not propagate changes to its child service profiles. With initial templates, changes can be propagated to its child service profile by unbinding the child from the parent, making the necessary changes, and rebinding it.

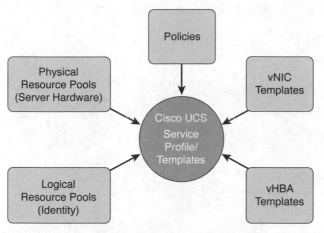

Figure 9-5 *Cisco UCS Template Types, Resource Pools, and Policies*

NOTE Because certain updates to child service profiles require a reboot of a server, it is recommended to implement a maintenance policy and include it in service profile templates to defer immediate reboot to a user-defined maintenance window. You can also define a schedule to release that maintenance task.

These deferrals are not available for certain tasks, such as initial association, final disassociation, decommissioning, reacknowledging, and resetting a server. Furthermore, depending on your use cases and scale, it is recommended to use nested updating templates, such as updating vNIC and VSAN templates, within an initial service profile template.

Organizational Awareness with Service Profile Templates

Cisco UCS offers the capability to compartmentalize the UCS configuration into an organizational tree structure, which can be helpful in multitenant environments. This can be a hard enforcement (using org structure, locales, and role-based access control [RBAC], for instance) or a soft enforcement (at task level). It is important to decide early on whether an organizational tree structure will be utilized. Cisco UCS service profile templates are organization-structure aware; when you create a child service profile from a template, it will be created within the same organization to which the template belonged. If you require it to be created further down the suborganization's structure, you can initiate the service profile creating process from within that particular suborganization or from its respective template. Figure 9-6 shows the organization-aware service profile creation using the respective template.

NOTE Consider maintaining a maximum of two levels under an organizational structure and try not to scale deeper. When planning for multitenancy, you can create multiple organizations, such as Development, Production, and Quality Assurance, instead of creating multiple levels under one high-level organization, such as Production/project1/test/QA. Also note that logical and physical resource pools created at higher levels of the organization structure can be utilized by suborganizations, but organizations at the same level cannot share resource pools.

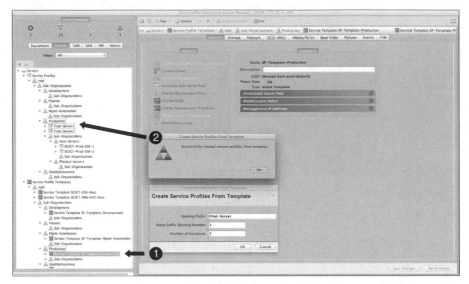

Figure 9-6   *Cisco UCS Organization-Aware Template Creation*

Cisco UCS Service Profile Templates

Cisco UCS service profile templates are used to rapidly create multiple service profiles with similar characteristics. For example, if you require a physical server and virtual host server to have different characteristics, you would create two separate Cisco UCS service profile templates and use them to generate multiple child service profiles. Figure 9-7 shows multiple Cisco UCS service profile templates created and ready to spawn child service profiles.

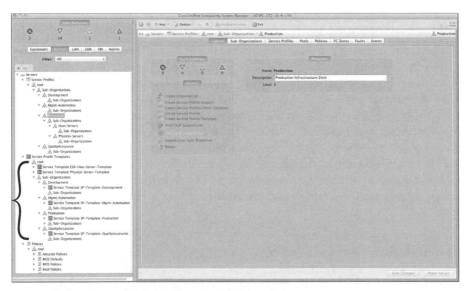

Figure 9-7   *Cisco UCS Service Profile Templates*

> **NOTE** When creating service profiles or templates, plan to use a naming convention that is descriptive enough to indicate where they are placed, the function, and the owner. Subsequently, when creating child service profiles, use purposeful naming and clear numbering, such as Prod-ESX-01 and Prod-WEB-01.

Cisco UCS vNIC Templates

The Cisco UCS vNIC template defines how a vNIC on a server connects to the LAN. It is also referred to as a LAN connectivity policy, which is another layer of abstracting vNIC templates. The vNIC template consumes the MAC pools and relevant policies. Figure 9-8 shows sample vNIC templates in the Cisco UCS Manager.

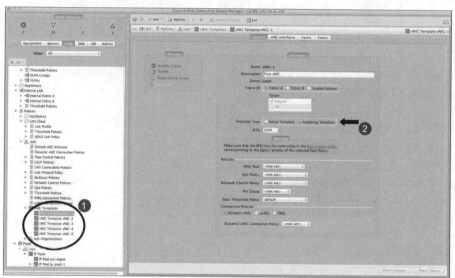

Figure 9-8 *Cisco UCS vNIC Template*

Cisco UCS vHBA Templates

The Cisco UCS vHBA template defines how a vHBA on a server connects to the SAN. This is also referred to as a SAN connectivity policy, which is another layer of abstracting vHBA templates. The vHBA template consumes the WWN pools (1x WWNN per compute node, 1x WWPN per vHBA) and relevant policies. Figure 9-9 shows sample vHBA templates in the Cisco UCS Manager.

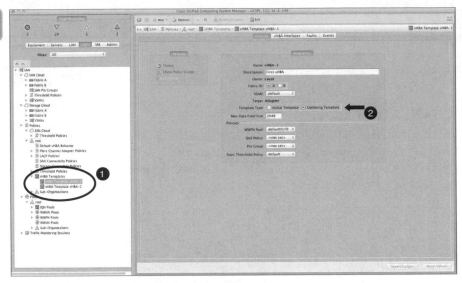

Figure 9-9 *Cisco UCS vHBA Template*

Cisco UCS Logical Resource Pools

The Cisco UCS can consist of multiple identity pools for all types of server identity requirements. A service profile or template consumes the relevant identities from a pool, appropriately. These identity pools are logical resource pools. Figure 9-10 shows the various Cisco UCS identity pools that can be created for consumption by Cisco UCS service profiles.

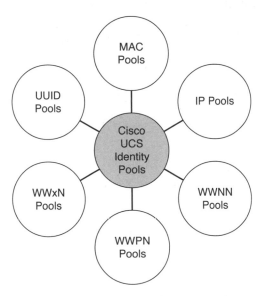

Figure 9-10 *Cisco UCS Identity Pool Types*

NOTE   These are identities that belong to a service profile until you delete that service profile or specify a different identity. Picking an identity from a pool can be specified to be sequential and deterministic to preplan and preconfigure certain external entities. For example, SAN zoning configurations can take place much earlier in the deployment process when the required WWNs are known in advance. It is the service profile that is the consumer of the pool, not the physical blade. These identities (virtualized) retrieved from their respective pools can still move from blade to blade along with their respective service profile.

Using pools can be a management advantage in all scenarios requiring virtualized identities. With pools, you will be actively prevented from virtualized identity conflicts within the same UCS system. Pools have a particular advantage in a server farm model; clones and templates offer ways of easily creating multiple similar service profiles to be used simultaneously for consumption. Table 9-2 shows the challenges and advantages with Cisco UCS identity pool usage.

Table 9-2   Cisco UCS Identity Pools and Their Advantages

The Challenge	With Identity Pools	Without Identity Pools
Managing virtual identities	Consumed and associated, if resources are available, or waits	Must manually assign, reassign, and manage identities
Templates	Allows greater speed and flexibility in server creation and in conjunction with updating templates; many service profiles can be updated	Must manually assign, reassign, and manage identities
Cloning	Allows greater speed and flexibility in server creation	Must manually assign, reassign, and manage identities

UUID Identity Pools

The universally unique identifier (UUID) is standardized by the Open Software Foundation; it is a 128-bit address spread over five fields. There is a prefix and a suffix element to the UUID; typically, the prefix is fixed (utilize the default pool, root level) and unique to that UCS domain, whereas the suffix is optionally modified to indicate a domain ID and the host ID, sequentially assigned. You could also modify the prefix to match the Cisco organization unique identifier (OUI; 24-bit) as used in the WWN pools and pad the suffix as necessary.

NOTE   These two schemes are for reference only; you should determine the best approach at the time of a Cisco UCS low-level design based on the requirements.

The UUID is typically leveraged by software vendors to fingerprint a machine and is often used to bind or associate a software license. If the underlying computer node fails, the service profile carries the UUID to the replacement computer node. Figure 9-11 shows the UUID prefix and suffix format with a sample pool.

9

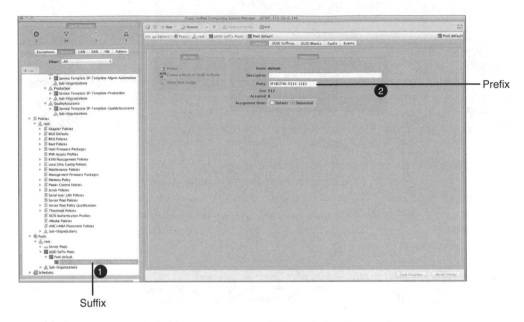

Prefix

Suffix

Figure 9-11 *Cisco UCS UUID Format and Sample Pool*

MAC Address Identity Pools

The MAC addresses are unique identifiers assigned to NICs; each port on a NIC would have a unique MAC address. The MAC address is a 48-bit address, represented in hexadecimal format. IEEE allocates an OUI per manufacturer (the initial 24 bits); the Cisco OUI is 00:25:B5:xx:xx:xx. As a Cisco best practice, create custom pools (do not use the default pool) and create two pools of MAC addresses representing Path A and B as a minimum. It is recommended to create MAC pools that at least identify the UCS domain and fabric and optionally identify operating system and organization. Figure 9-12 shows sample MAC address pools.

> **NOTE**   Keep the pool sizes the same, which allows consistent allocation between A and B pools, and choose sequential allocation for a deterministic approach. Sequential allocation is set on a per-pool basis. If used, ensure all pools are sequential and contain fewer than 256 entries per pool, if you want to maintain low-order byte ordering depending on the number of bytes used for the host ID. This will help consistency and self-documentation.

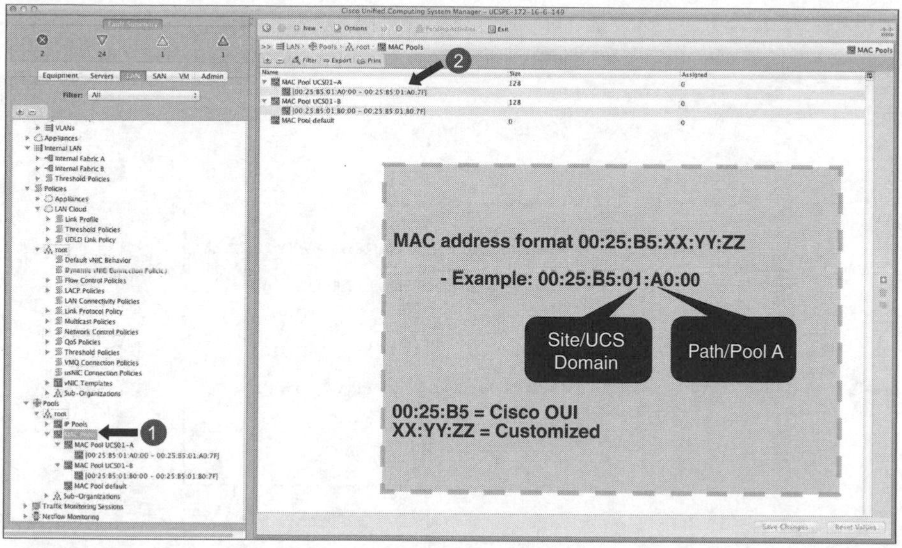

Figure 9-12   *Cisco UCS MAC Address Identity Pool*

WWN Address Identity Pools

Key Topic

A Fibre Channel node and port must have a globally unique World Wide Number; in Cisco UCS they are created as identity pools. A Fibre Channel node (a whole server, storage array) must have a World Wide Node Name (WWNN), and a Fibre Channel port must have a World Wide Port Name (WWPN). Both WWNNs and WWPNs are 64-bit addresses. These WWN identities are not the same as FCIDs; they are intended for a different purpose, such as routing in SAN. However, there is a correlation between WWPNs and FCIDs.

WWNN Pools

The WWNN pool is created as one large pool for the Cisco UCS domain. You can use the default pool in the Cisco UCS Manager SAN tab. However, it is recommended that you create a custom WWNN pool for that UCS domain, which makes your Cisco UCS solution unique and self-documenting. Figure 9-13 shows a sample WWNN pool.

> **NOTE**   Zoning and masking do not use the WWNN. You must ensure WWNN and WWPN pools do not overlap, and for clarity they must contain fewer than 256 entries per pool if you want to maintain low-order byte ordering depending on the number of bytes used for the host ID. You can always create multiple pools, if need be, following the same guideline.

9

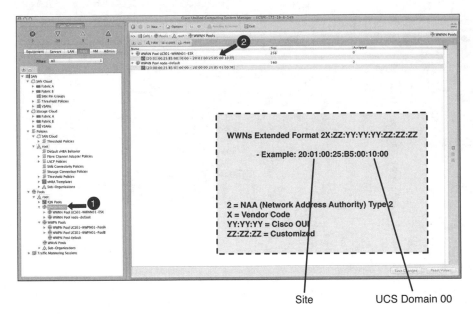

Figure 9-13   *Cisco UCS WWNN Address Identity Pool*

WWPN Pools

You will create two WWPN pools. Typically, a computer node consists of at least two vHBA ports, each requiring a WWPN and assigned to Path A and B, respectively. Create a custom pool for each path in the Cisco UCS Manager SAN tab. Figure 9-14 shows a sample WWPN pool.

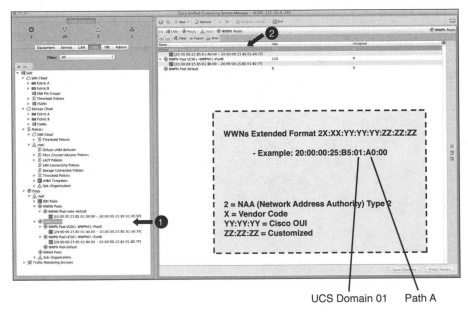

Figure 9-14   *Cisco UCS WWPN Identity Pool*

NOTE You must ensure WWNN and WWPN pools do not overlap and for clarity, ensure pools contain fewer than 256 entries if you want to maintain low-order byte ordering depending on the number of bytes used for the host ID. You can always create multiple pools, following the same guidelines, if required.

NOTE It is recommended not to use WWxN pools in production setup because it would skew the deployment of IDs, and you would have no control over path identification, pool separation, and customizations as servers are deployed.

Cisco UCS Physical Resource Pools

Cisco UCS physical blade and rackmount server hardware can be grouped to form a physical resource pool that can be associated with a service profile or template.

Server Pools

These server pools can be populated manually or automatically. Typically, such server pools are grouped based on either common hardware configurations or SLA boundaries. It is important to understand that a server can be part of multiple pools; a Cisco UCS service profile that associates itself to the blade owns that blade, regardless of which pool that server resides in.

A Cisco UCS service profile or template can be associated with a server pool rather than manually assigning it to a blade or rackmount server. When associated with a server pool, a service profile will automatically select an unused blade or rackmount server; a server resource that is in the process of being disassociated is also considered unavailable.

Cisco UCS Server Qualification and Pool Policies

The server qualification policy enables you to create patterns of qualification criteria. These patterns can be based on CPU, memory, adapter, Part ID, and disk criteria. Under each main criterion, you can further qualify at a granular level; for example, if you want to qualify based on CPU category, you have the option to choose CPU type, cores, speed/MHz, and so on. Figure 9-15 shows the CPU criteria and the granular options for qualifications.

These patterns can then be referred to from a server pool policy, which enables you to select the respective qualification pattern and the action in terms of which server pool the positively qualified servers should reside in. The content pane shows details of the physical server identity; if allocated to a service profile, it will show you a hyperlink to that service profile. Figure 9-16 shows a group of qualified servers (criteria based on physical memory) in their respective server pools.

9

Qualification Pattern, Grouped Under One Name

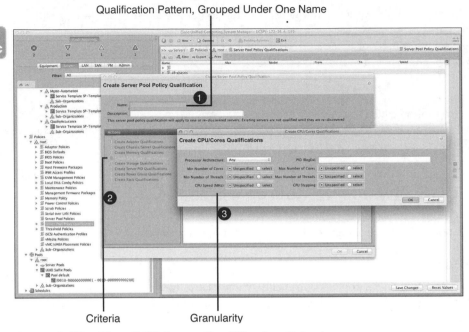

Criteria   Granularity

Figure 9-15 *Cisco UCS Server Qualification Criteria*

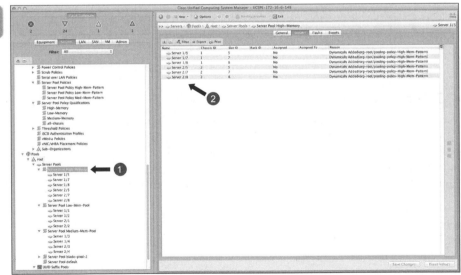

Figure 9-16 *Cisco UCS Qualified Server Pools*

Server Auto-Configuration Policies

The server pool and qualification process is taken to another level with the server auto-configuration policy; when a server is discovered and qualified, a service profile can be automatically created using a specified template, placed in the appropriate organization structure, and associated with a qualified server from the pool. The entire process is automated. Figure 9-17 shows the server auto-configuration policy creation window.

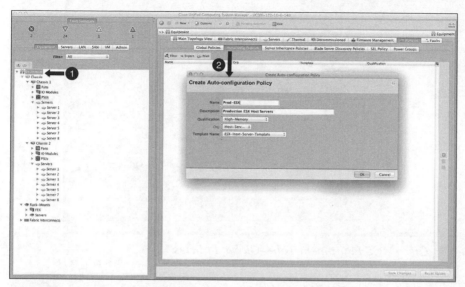

Figure 9-17   *Cisco UCS Server Auto-Configuration Policy*

Creation of Policies for Cisco UCS Service Profiles and Service Profile Templates

Cisco UCS policies exist mainly around the equipment, server, and LAN and SAN tabs within the Cisco UCS Manager. Policies can be created at the root organization level and its children can see them, but policies created at the suborganization level will be not visible to all and are effective at that level only. Therefore, it is a Cisco best practice to create common policies at the root organization level, which can be leveraged by all organizations and managed centrally. Unless the policy is unique to a suborganization only, it can be located within an organization, such as a boot policy that applies to a suborganization's storage system only.

Frequently Used Policies Explained

Many Cisco UCS polices can be defined in a Cisco UCS solution that you can use to tune and tweak your Cisco UCS domain to suit your operational or infrastructure requirements. Although some policies apply to Cisco UCS domain-wide, most policies map to service profiles and service profile templates and eventually are applied to their associated Cisco UCS server.

Equipment Tab—Global Policies

This is a set of policies that are effective Cisco UCS domain-wide and are used to define various aspects, such as chassis/FEX discovery policy (discrete versus port channel), chassis power redundancy mode, rack server discovery policy, auto configuration, SEL policy, blade server discovery policy, and so on. These policies can be found in the Equipment tab in the content pane of the Cisco UCS Manager. Figure 9-18 shows the policies under the Equipment tab.

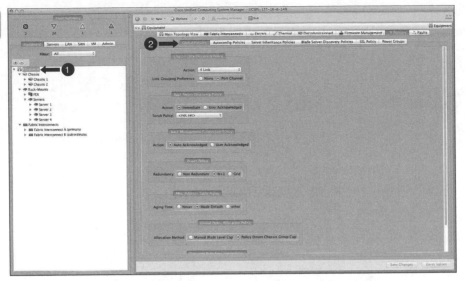

Figure 9-18 *Cisco UCS Equipment Tab—Global Policies*

NOTE   With the chassis/FEX discovery policy, the number of links specified is a minimum required during initial discovery only. If it is not per minimum, the discovery process will still continue with warnings. Additional links can be added later and would require reacknowledging the chassis for all available links to be used. In the link grouping preference, you can choose either option, but if the Cisco UCS I/O module hardware in a certain chassis does not support port channels, it will fall back to discrete mode.

BIOS Policy

The BIOS policy is used to optimize your BIOS parameters and is available for assignment to a Cisco UCS service profile or service profile template. These BIOS policies traverse with the assigned service profile. This policy is listed under the Servers tab, and details are shown in its content pane. Figure 9-19 shows BIOS policies available for assignment to Cisco UCS service profiles and templates.

Boot Policy

A boot policy is a boot order, such as floppy, CD-ROM, hard disk, and target/path information for a boot from SAN requirement. You can have multiple boot policies associated with, for example, odd/even service profiles to balance the boot storm in a large Cisco UCS environment onto different target storage ports. This policy is listed under the Servers tab, and details are shown in its content pane. Figure 9-20 shows the sample boot policies available for assignment to a Cisco UCS service profile and template.

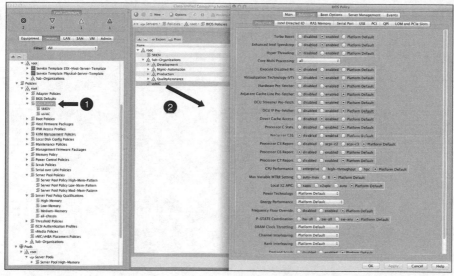

Figure 9-19   *Cisco UCS BIOS Policy*

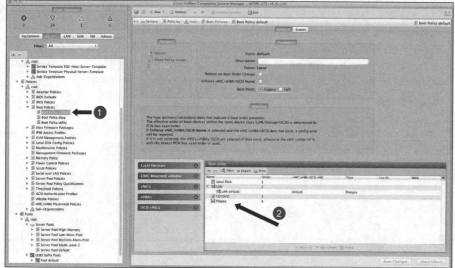

Figure 9-20   *Cisco UCS Boot Policy*

Local Disk Configuration Policy

The local disk configuration policy enables you to define the required RAID configuration on a server's local disks and protect and unprotect it if that service profile is disassociated from that particular blade or rackmount server. This policy is listed under the Servers tab, and details are shown in its content pane. Figure 9-21 shows a sample local disk configuration policy.

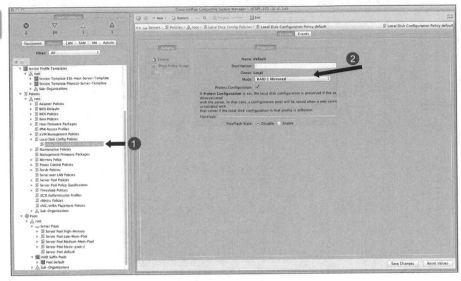

Figure 9-21 *Cisco UCS Local Disk Configuration Policy*

Maintenance Policy

As discussed earlier, certain changes to a service profile or template may require that associated server to reboot. To prevent immediate reboots and defer it to either user acknowledgement or a scheduled maintenance window is where this policy comes in handy. This policy is listed under the Servers tab, and details are shown in its content pane. Figure 9-22 shows a sample maintenance policy.

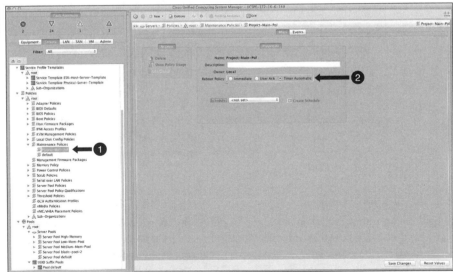

Figure 9-22 *Cisco UCS Maintenance Policy*

Scrub Policy

The scrub policy is utilized to remove any configuration on disk, BIOS, or flash. The scrub policy can be invoked during the server discovery process or when a service profile is disassociated from that particular Cisco UCS blade or rackmount server. This policy is listed under the Servers tab, and details are shown in its content pane. Figure 9-23 shows a sample scrub policy.

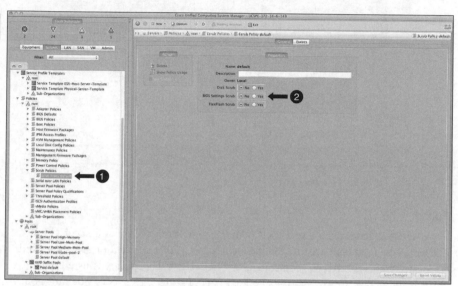

Figure 9-23 *Cisco UCS Scrub Policy*

Host Firmware Packages

This policy enables you to choose suitable firmware versions for various blade server components, such as adapter, BIOS, CIMC, and so on, and reference them from a Cisco UCS service profile or template. This policy is listed under the Servers tab, and details are shown in its content pane. Figure 9-24 shows a default host firmware package policy available for assignment to a Cisco UCS service profile or template.

NOTE   Cisco VIC 12xx adapters must be upgraded using this host firmware package.

9

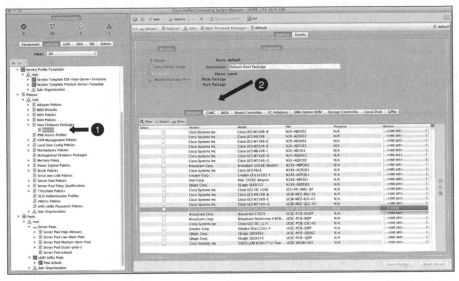

Figure 9-24   *Cisco UCS Host Firmware Package*

Adapter Policy

This policy is created and attached to a vNIC template and referenced in a Cisco UCS service profile or template. It contains the independent settings that are vendor recommended, such as VMware low-level settings for a standard vNIC/vHBA. This policy is listed under the Servers tab and details are shown in its content pane. Figure 9-25 shows a default policy available for assignment to a Cisco UCS service profile or template.

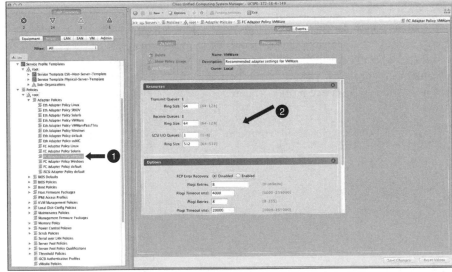

Figure 9-25   *Cisco UCS Adapter Policy*

Cisco UCS Chassis and Blade Power Capping

Power capping is one of the main differentiators of the Cisco Unified Computing System. This feature provides increasing benefits as each individual Cisco UCS instance scales. Power capping is the capability to limit the power consumption of a system, be it a blade server or a rack server, to some threshold that is less than or equal to the system's maximum rated power. In Cisco UCS, when policy-driven power capping is selected in the global cap policy, Cisco UCS, at chassis level, can start dividing the amount of power required within that chassis group; or at blade level, the amount of power available is divided among the blades based on priority levels.

What Is Power Capping?

The Cisco UCS chassis with four power supplies has a maximum power limit of approximately 5000 watts. Cisco UCS blade servers can draw varying power depending on the configuration and utilization of that blade server; typically, the allowance for a half-width blade server is approximately 550 watts. With newer, faster Cisco UCS blades, such as B200 M4 and B440 M2, the blade power requirement is between 600 and 800 watts, depending on configuration and server utilization levels.

Hence, Cisco UCS provides the option to manage the overall power consumption through power capping to share the power draw between blade servers utilizing power management policies and priorities.

Cisco UCS Power Capping Strategies

Cisco UCS can manage power across groups of blade and rack servers within a Cisco UCS domain. This capability is integrated into the Cisco UCS architecture. Figure 9-26 shows the global power allocation policy in the Cisco UCS Manager, which enables a policy-driven or manual blade-level capping.

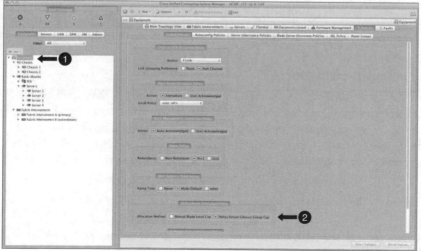

Figure 9-26   *Cisco UCS Global Power Allocation Policy*

Static Power Capping (Explicit Blade Power Cap)

Explicit power capping for blades is calculated at 550 or 600W per blade approximately. When a power cap is applied to a blade, the CPU steps down to a lower power or performance level, and Cisco UCS Manager ensures the blade does not exceed its power budget allowance based on the defined priority.

Dynamic Power Capping (Implicit Chassis Power Cap)

This enables the Cisco UCS system to distribute the total pool of power across multiple chassis. The system will adhere to the maximum limits; power will be dynamically allocated to the blade that requires it. This is the default behavior. If the global power allocation policy is set to manual blade level, this policy capping will not be effective. Figure 9-27 shows the power control policy in the Cisco UCS Manager.

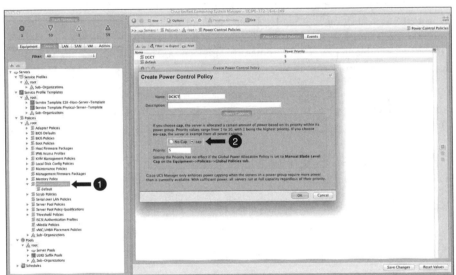

Figure 9-27   *Cisco UCS Power Control Policy*

Power Cap Groups (Explicit Group)

This is one or more chassis sharing a common power allocation, which is then applied dynamically to servers within that chassis group. You can create power control policies and assign them to the Cisco UCS service profile that contains priorities in terms of blade level power allocation. These priorities are set from 1–10 (highest to lowest, respectively). Figure 9-28 shows a sample power cap group creation and associated parameters in the Cisco UCS Manager.

- Absolute values for the power cap group can be set by the facilities or operations manager.

- IT administrators can set the relative priority through the power control policy of each service profile.

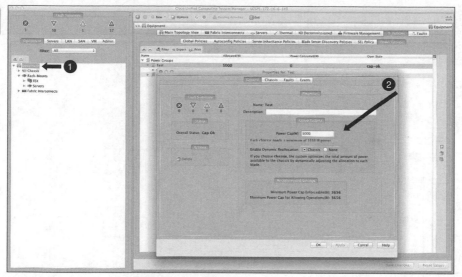

Figure 9-28   *Cisco UCS Power Groups*

The advantages of Cisco UCS power management are that Cisco UCS Manager ensures there is available power for booting, power caps are applied globally or at the chassis level, and power can be managed within minimum and maximum range. These capabilities provide better management of facility power, better utilization, and help to even out any spikes.

Utilizing Cisco UCS Service Profile Templates

In Cisco UCS, when service profile templates are utilized, you can quickly create several service profiles with the same parameters, such as vNICs and vHBAs drawn from pools and relevant policies. Furthermore, you can update and manage service profiles via updating templates, where planned changes can be distributed easily.

Creating Cisco UCS Service Profile Templates

The process of creating a Cisco UCS service profile template is nearly identical to creating a service profile. A Cisco UCS service profile template cannot be directly associated with a Cisco UCS blade or rackmount server; it is solely used to generate child service profiles that can be associated with Cisco UCS server hardware.

Cisco UCS service profile templates utilize all the identity pools, physical, logical resource pools, policies, and vNIC/vHBA templates (discussed in the previous sections of this chapter) and generate child service profiles. They cannot be associated with an individual server, but they can be associated with a server pool or server assignments can be opted to be manual. Figure 9-29 shows the Cisco UCS service profile template creation window, invoked by right-clicking the organization or selecting the option to create a service profile template from the content pane.

9

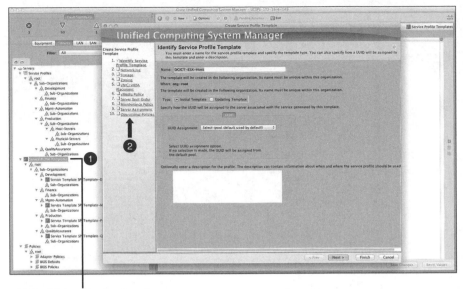

Right-Click at the Org Level
and Create Your SP Template

Figure 9-29 *Cisco UCS Creating a Service Profile Template*

> **NOTE** See the Cisco UCS service profile template creation steps on the left pane of the creation window.

Modifying a Cisco UCS Service Profile Template

Cisco UCS service profile templates can be modified after they have been created and utilized to generate child service profiles. Figure 9-30 shows the actions possible on a service profile template, under the storage category. As you can see, all categories are listed in the contents page.

> **NOTE** Bear in mind, depending on whether the service profile template is initializing or updating, certain changes made to a service profile template might or might not propagate to its child service profiles, and if propagated, certain changes will cause the child-service profile to require a reboot. Hence, ensure that you have a maintenance policy assigned to a service profile to manually acknowledge a change.

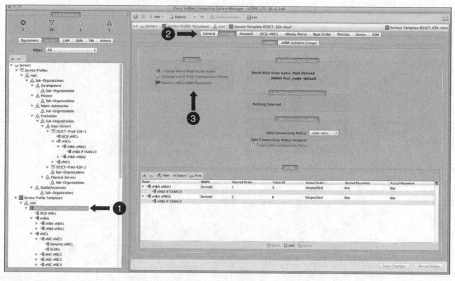

Figure 9-30 *Cisco UCS Modifying a Service Profile Template*

Utilizing Cisco UCS Service Profile Templates for Different Workloads

The use of Cisco UCS service profile templates enables you to consistently apply resource pools and policies to different workloads or application requirements in your data center. A good example is the vNIC requirements for physical servers versus virtual machine host servers, where they would require consistency in terms of resource pool assignments but would differ in terms of policies and number of vNICs required. Table 9-3 shows an example of different applications and workloads that can be addressed via multiple Cisco UCS service profile templates.

Table 9-3 Cisco UCS Service Profile Templates for Multiple Workloads

Physical Server	Virtual Machine Host Server	Web Server
B200 M3 with E5-2600 series	B260 M34 with E5-2800 series	B230 M2 with E5-2800 series
256 GB RAM	1 TB RAM	256 GB RAM
Local hard disk drive for swap only	No local drives	Local hard disk drive for swap only
Boot from SAN	Boot from SAN	Boot from SAN

Creating Service Profiles from Templates

After you create the required service profile templates, the Cisco UCS administrator can automate the provisioning of hundreds of service profiles into a simple operation. In the navigation pane, select the service profile template in the organization you would like it to be created, and in the content pane, choose Create Service Profile from Template. Figure 9-31 shows the selection of a service profile template under the root organization.

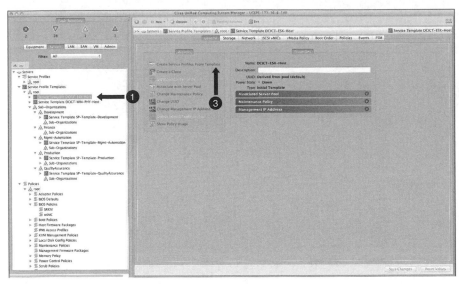

Figure 9-31 *Creating Cisco UCS Service Profiles from Template*

The dialog box that appears prompts you for naming the prefix, the suffix, and the total number of service profiles to spawn from this particular service profile template. Immediately after you click OK, the new service profiles will appear under the relevant organization in the service profile section (navigation pane). If the server assignment in the template points to a server pool, the service profile immediately starts association with an unused blade or rackmount server from that pool. Figure 9-32 shows the dialog box that appears when creating service profiles from a service profile template.

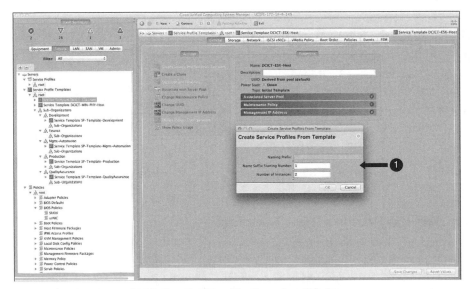

Figure 9-32 *Cisco UCS Service Profile Creation Dialog*

Reference List

Cisco UCS Manager Release Notes: http://www.cisco.com/c/en/us/support/servers-unified-computing/ucs-manager/products-release-notes-list.html

Cisco UCS Firmware Management Best Practices: http://www.cisco.com/c/en/us/support/docs/servers-unified-computing/ucs-manager/110511-ucs-fw-mgmt-00.html

Cisco UCS Firmware Management: http://www.cisco.com/c/en/us/td/docs/unified_computing/ucs/sw/firmware-mgmt/cli/2-2/b_CLI_Firmware_Management_22/b_CLI_Firmware_Management_22_chapter_011.html

Cisco UCS Manager Install and Upgrade Guides: http://www.cisco.com/c/en/us/support/servers-unified-computing/ucs-manager/products-installation-guides-list.html

Cisco UCS Manager Configuration Guides: http://www.cisco.com/c/en/us/support/servers-unified-computing/ucs-manager/products-installation-and-configuration-guides-list.html

EMC Community Notes on WWN: https://community.emc.com/servlet/JiveServlet/previewBody/5136-102-1-18154/WWN_Notes_v1.3.pdf

How to Interpret World Wide Names: http://howto.techworld.com/storage/156/how-to-interpret-worldwide-names/

IEEE OUI Registry: http://standards.ieee.org/develop/regauth/oui/oui.txt

9

Exam Preparation Tasks

Review All Key Topics

Review the most important topics in the chapter, noted with the key topic icon in the outer margin of the page. Table 9-4 lists a reference of these key topics and the page numbers on which each is found.

Table 9-4   Key Topics for Chapter 9

Key Topic Element	Description	Page
Section	"Cisco UCS Hardware Abstraction and Stateless Computing"	331
Figure 9-2	"Cisco UCS Hardware Abstraction Layer"	332
Section	"Cisco UCS Templates"	336
Section	"Cisco UCS Service Profile Templates"	338
Figure 9-8	"Cisco UCS vNIC Template"	339
Figure 9-9	"Cisco UCS vHBA Template"	340
Section	"Cisco UCS Logical Resource Pools"	340
Section	"UUID Identity Pools"	341
Section	"MAC Address Identity Pool"	342
Section	"WWN Address Identity Pools"	343
Figure 9-15	"Cisco UCS Server Qualification Criteria"	346
Figure 9-16	"Cisco UCS Qualified Server Pools"	346
Section	"Creation of Policies for Cisco UCS Service Profiles and Service Profile Templates"	347
Figure 9-18	"Cisco UCS Equipment Tab—Global Policies"	348
Figure 9-19	"Cisco UCS BIOS Policy"	349
Figure 9-20	"Cisco UCS Boot Policy"	349
Figure 9-21	"Cisco UCS Local Disk Configuration Policy"	350
Figure 9-22	"Cisco UCS Maintenance Policy"	350
Figure 9-23	"Cisco UCS Scrub Policy"	351
Figure 9-24	"Cisco UCS Host Firmware Package"	352
Figure 9-25	"Cisco UCS Adapter Policy"	352
Figure 9-26	"Cisco UCS Global Power Allocation Policy"	353
Figure 9-27	"Cisco UCS Power Control Policy"	354
Figure 9-28	"Cisco UCS Power Groups"	355

Key Topic Element	Description	Page
Section	"Creating Cisco UCS Service Profile Templates"	355
Section	"Modifying a Cisco UCS Service Profile Template"	356
Section	"Utilizing Cisco UCS Service Profile Templates for Different Workloads"	357
Section	"Creating Service Profiles from Templates"	357

Complete Tables and Lists from Memory

Print a copy of Appendix B, "Memory Tables" or at least the section for this chapter, and complete the tables and lists from memory. Appendix C, "Memory Tables Answer Key" includes completed tables and lists to check your work.

Define Key Terms

Define the following key terms from this chapter, and check your answers in the Glossary:

Media Access Control (MAC), World Wide Port Name (WWPN), World Wide Node Name (WWNN), Local-Area Network (LAN), Storage-Area Network (SAN), Basic Input Output System (BIOS), Virtual LAN (VLAN), Redundant Array of Inexpensive Disks (RAID), Virtual Machine (VM), Host Bus Adapter (HBA), Dynamic Random Access Memory (DRAM), Hypervisor, Universally Unique Identifier (UUID), Intel VT, Maximum Transmission Unit (MTU), UCS Manager (UCSM)

9

This chapter covers the following exam topics:

Cisco UCS Administration

Cisco UCS Management

Cisco UCS Monitoring

CHAPTER 10

Administration, Management, and Monitoring of Cisco UCS

This chapter offers an overview of the administration, management, and monitoring functions of Cisco Unified Computing System (UCS) and best practices. The Cisco UCS Manager is fully redundant and provides a single pane of glass to manage an entire Cisco Unified Computing System. The Cisco UCS Manager is the user interface (UI) that is utilized to configure the control plane of the system and that constitutes the management plane of the Cisco UCS solution.

This chapter starts by explaining the salient points of UCS administration in the section "Cisco UCS Administration." It discusses user management, role-based access control (RBAC), firmware management, and Cisco UCS backup operations to give you an overview of typical administrative tasks and Cisco best practices.

The "Cisco UCS Management" section is divided into two sections. First you learn the differences between in-band and out-of-band management, direct KVM accessibility, and Cisco UCS remote connectivity. The second section introduces you to UCS XML, goUCS automation toolkit, and XML API-based operations with Cisco UCS Manager using the Python software development kit (SDK) with some basic examples.

In the "Cisco UCS Monitoring" section, you learn Simple Network Management Protocol (SNMP usage, smart call home features, UCS fault monitoring, suppression, collection, and threshold policies). You will also understand their functionality and usage.

This chapter should give you an overview of administration, management, and monitoring of Cisco UCS infrastructure; it is not meant to be a comprehensive configuration guide. For this, refer to the Cisco UCS Manager configuration guides in the "Reference List" section.

"Do I Know This Already?" Quiz

The "Do I Know This Already?" quiz enables you to assess whether you should read this entire chapter thoroughly or jump to the "Exam Preparation Tasks" section. If you are in doubt about your answers to these questions or your own assessment of your knowledge of the topics, read the entire chapter. Table 10-1 lists the major headings in this chapter and their corresponding "Do I Know This Already?" quiz questions. You can find the answers in Appendix A, "Answers to the 'Do I Know This Already?' Quizzes."

Table 10-1   "Do I Know This Already?" Section-to-Question Mapping

Foundation Topics Section	Questions
"Cisco UCS Administration"	3, 4, 5, 6
"Cisco UCS Management"	1, 2, 9, 10
"Cisco UCS Monitoring"	7, 8, 11

CAUTION   The goal of self-assessment is to gauge your mastery of the topics in this chapter. If you do not know the answer to a question or are only partially sure of the answer, you should mark that question as wrong for purposes of the self-assessment. Giving yourself credit for an answer you correctly guess skews your self-assessment results and might provide you with a false sense of security.

1. What is the difference between Cisco UCS Manager in-band and out-of-band management access?

   a. If the management access traffic traverses the data path, it is known as in-band management; if management access traffic is separate from the data traffic path, it is known as out-of-band.

   b. If you can log in to a server directly, it is called in-band management; if you have to access the server via a jump server, it is known as out-of-band management.

   c. If the server KVM can be accessed directly via a spider cable, it is called out-of-band management; if the server KVM needs to be accessed over the LAN, it is called in-band management.

   d. If a blade chassis consists of a management module, it is referred to as in-band management; if it does not, it is referred to as out-of-band management access.

2. True or false? Cisco UCS Manager can be accessed via its out-of-band management interface only.

   a. True

   b. False

3. What is the main purpose of a host firmware package? Mark the statement that you think is most accurate.

   a. A host firmware package is a piece of utility software that must be installed on every Cisco UCS server that provides hardware-level performance statistics to the host operating system.

   b. This host firmware package is the firmware level of a Cisco UCS system.

   c. The host firmware package consists of all the firmware versions required for a Cisco UCS blade server, consisting of all blade server-based hardware, such as BIOS, adapters, CIMC, local disks, and storage controllers. This can be referenced in a Cisco UCS service profile or template.

   d. The host firmware package is the Cisco UCS Manager version installed on the Cisco UCS Fabric Interconnects.

4. What are the different types of firmware bundles available for Cisco UCS, and does it support cross-version firmware levels? Choose the most accurate explanation.

   a. There is one Cisco UCS firmware bundle; it is not possible to mix UCS Manager firmware levels because it is not a Cisco-supported procedure.

   b. There are three main types of Cisco UCS firmware bundles: Cisco UCS infrastructure, B-Series, and C-Series. The mixing of firmware levels between infrastructure and blade/rack server is supported, but only specific version levels can be mixed.

   c. There are three main types of Cisco UCS firmware bundles: Cisco UCS infrastructure, B-Series, and C-Series. You can mix firmware only between B-Series and C-Series server firmware bundles.

   d. There are three main types of Cisco UCS firmware bundles: Cisco UCS infrastructure, B-Series, and C-Series. The mixing of firmware levels between infrastructure and blade/rack server is supported without limitations or restrictions.

5. What are the different types of backups available with Cisco UCS Manager?

   a. There are four types of backup methods available on the Cisco UCS Manager: logical, system, all configurations, and full state backups.

   b. There are two backup types available: full state and all configurations only.

   c. There are two backup types available: physical configuration and logical configuration.

   d. You can perform only full state backups with Cisco UCS Manager, which does a complete backup of the entire Cisco UCS Manager configuration and state.

6. Which Cisco UCS backup types can be used to restore a new Cisco UCS Fabric Interconnect in a disaster recovery situation?

   a. All backup types can be used to restore a new Cisco UCS Fabric Interconnect.

   b. Only a full state backup can be used to restore the state of a Cisco UCS Fabric Interconnect, and it is a .bin file.

   c. The all configurations backup type should be used to restore a new Cisco UCS Fabric Interconnect.

   d. The system configuration backup type should be used to restore a new Cisco UCS Fabric Interconnect.

7. True or false? You can suppress faults with Cisco UCS Manager.

   a. True

   b. False

10

8. What are collection and threshold policies in Cisco UCS Manager? Choose the statement that defines it best.

   a. These policies define Cisco UCS statistics collection intervals and notification thresholds of these statistics of adapter, chassis, server, and ports.

   b. They define the interval of fault collections; their thresholds clear these faults automatically.

   c. These policies provide overall usage statistics in terms of user login/logouts; you can define the threshold for multiple simultaneous logins.

   d. The collection policies collect all input/output transmission statistics of all FCoE connections (Ethernet, Fibre Channel interfaces) and allow them to be displayed/graphed. The threshold policy defines upper and lower limit (red/yellow/green) lines in graphs.

9. What is the most unique feature of the goUCS Automation Toolkit? Mark the statement that best describes it.

   a. It is a proof-of-concept tool that can be used to showcase XML interaction.

   b. It is a prerequisite to run the Firefox HttpRequester plug-in that enables XML communication with Cisco UCS Manager.

   c. It enables you to filter Cisco UCS GUI operations based on its Java log file and retrieve, anonymize, and reuse XML methods and create your own XML-wrappers.

   d. It is an automation and orchestration tool that runs as a virtual machine and allows automation of all operations and tasks executed via the Cisco UCS Manager.

10. What are the four main XML methods that are available to interact with Cisco UCS Manager?

   a. XML APIs, REST APIs, XML Wrappers, and XML CMDs

   b. PUSH, PULL, SET, and QUERY

   c. PUT, GET, SET, and QUERY

   d. Authentication, Query, Configuration Change, and Event Subscription

11. True or false? Cisco UCS SNMP can be used to set and configure elements.

   a. True

   b. False

Foundation Topics

Cisco UCS Administration

The Cisco UCS Manager will be utilized by server administrators to perform various server management tasks and administer the Cisco UCS solution overall. In this section you learn some essential administrative tasks and capabilities; for detailed administrative capabilities, you should refer to the Cisco UCS configuration guides for a comprehensive list of administration guidelines.

Organization and Locales

The Cisco UCS Manager is inherently multitenant oriented. It is capable of subdividing logical and physical resource pools into multiple logical entities within a single UCS domain. In the Cisco UCS Manager, under the root organization structure, you can create multiple suborganization structures. You can create various physical and logical identity resource pools for each of these organizations, making them self-sufficient and fenced. The Cisco UCS Manager is intelligent to understand the hierarchy, and if a resource or policy is not found, it can search the upper-level hierarchical order. Figure 10-1 shows a sample organizational structure in Cisco UCS Manager.

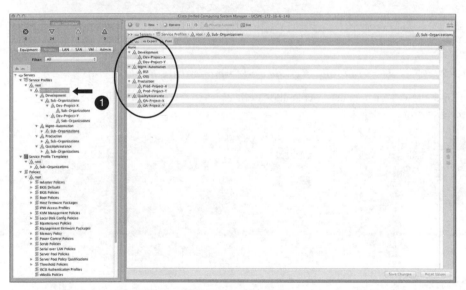

Figure 10-1 *Cisco UCS Manager Organization Structure*

NOTE   Although this capability exists, it is recommended that you create an appropriate level for clarity, representation, and ease of management. When you create an organizational structure, it is also seen in the Server, LAN, and SAN tabs in parallel.

These organizations can be further allocated to "locales." These locales allow one or more "organizations" to belong together, and they allow a user (with adequate assigned privileges) to manage an organization(s) within that locale, which is popularly known as delegated administration. A user can manage more than one locale. A single UCS domain can consist of up to 48 locales. Figure 10-2 shows the creation of the development-QA locale and assigning of organization members to that locale.

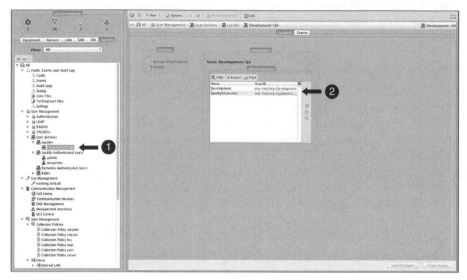

Figure 10-2 *Cisco UCS Manager Locale and Organization Membership*

Figure 10-3 shows a custom user being allocated access to the respective locale, with defined roles and privileges.

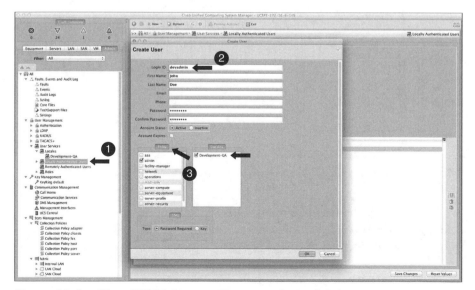

Figure 10-3 *Cisco UCS Manager User, Locale, and Role Assignment*

Role-Based Access Control

RBAC enables you to restrict or authorize the type of access to a user. Type of access implies the role to which the user is assigned. A role consists of a privilege or multiple privileges. A total of 11 roles are available with Cisco UCS Manager. For example, Figure 10-4 shows the facilities manager role and the assigned privilege in the content pane. For details of what a Power Mgmt privilege can execute or view, refer to the Cisco UCS configuration guide.

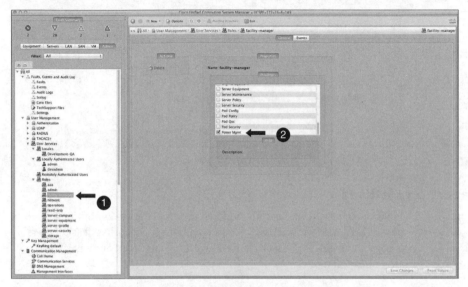

Figure 10-4 *Cisco UCS Manager Roles and Privileges*

> **NOTE**   Administrators can create custom roles by selecting specific privileges. Privileges available on the Cisco UCS Manager cannot be modified.

In the Cisco UCS Manager, RBAC can also be integrated with Lightweight Directory Access Protocol/Active Directory (LDAP/AD) authentication. It allows integration of Active Directory group roles with Cisco UCS roles by way of LDAP group maps. Figure 10-5 shows the LDAP group mapping in Cisco UCS Manager, where certain roles along with their privileges are mapped to an LDAP group DN. More details of Active Directory authentication are discussed in the next section.

10

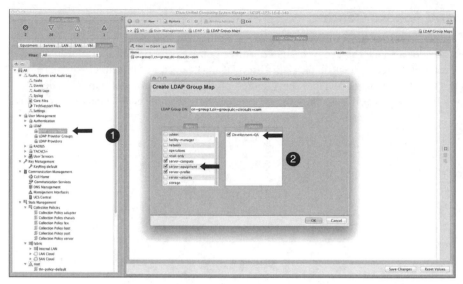

Figure 10-5   *Cisco UCS Manager LDAP Group Maps*

Authentication Methods

The Cisco UCS Manager allows various central and local user authentication options, such as LDAP (MS AD, Open LDAP), RADIUS, TACACS+, and default/native authentication (local). In this section you learn about the Microsoft Active Directory integrated authentication setup, a popular authentication mode.

> **NOTE**   Cisco UCS Manager also supports two-factor authentication methods. At the time of writing this chapter, they are supported under RADIUS and TACACS+ methods only. Please see validated and supported vendors prior to designing or implementing two-factor authentication.

LDAP Providers

The Cisco UCS Manager supports up to 16 servers per authentication method. Figure 10-6 shows the screen and location of where to define a provider server.

LDAP Provider Groups

Provider servers can be defined into provider groups. You can define a total of 16 provider groups if you require. The providers can be listed in the order of preference within a provider group so that it queries for authentication in that order. Figure 10-7 shows a sample list of provider servers in a hypothetical provider group.

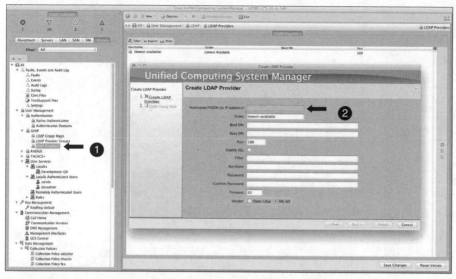

Figure 10-6 *Cisco UCS Manager LDAP Provider Server*

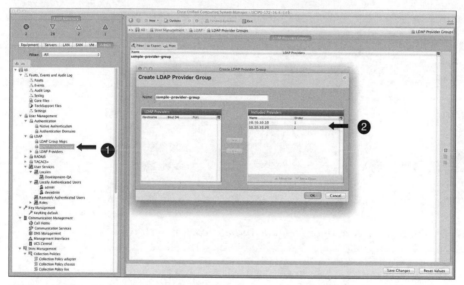

Figure 10-7 *Cisco UCS Manager LDAP Provider Groups*

Domain, Realm, and Default Authentication Settings

After defining the providers, groups, and LDAP mappings accordingly, to instruct the Cisco UCS Manager to interrogate the directory server to authenticate a user, you must define a domain and a realm and select the providers. Figure 10-8 shows the parameters required to achieve LDAP-based authentication. Figure 10-9 shows the default authentication and console authentication settings.

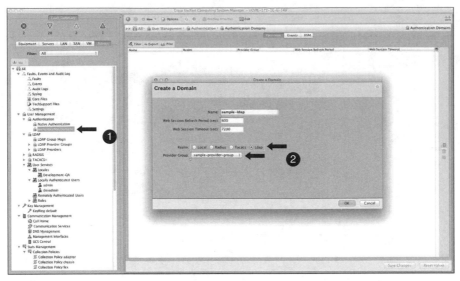

Figure 10-8 *Cisco UCS Manager Authentication Domains*

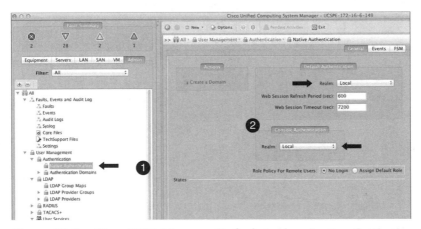

Figure 10-9 *Cisco UCS Manager Default Authentication Settings*

NOTE Console authentication is used when a user logs in via the management console port of the Cisco UCS Fabric Interconnects. Default authentication occurs when the user logs in via SSH/Telnet/GUI/XML without specifying a domain. It is a good practice to keep local authentication as an option in case you cannot reach your LDAP providers.

Communication Management

In the Cisco UCS Manager Admin tab, you will find the communication management settings. They consist of communication service settings for SSH, Telnet, HTTP, HTTPS, SNMP, web session limits, Call Home settings, Domain Name System (DNS) management, and management interfaces. Figure 10-10 shows you the communications management in Cisco UCS Manager.

TIP   As a preconfiguration step (post initial setup), it is important to visit this configuration and ensure that all communication settings are configured appropriately.

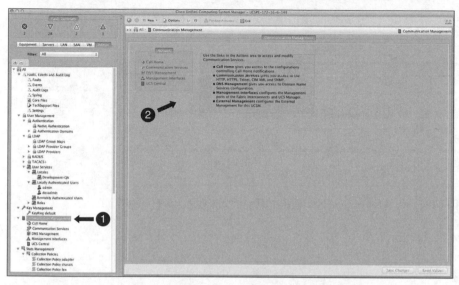

Figure 10-10   *Cisco UCS Manager Communication Settings*

NOTE   Cisco UCS Central is a multi-UCS domain management solution. It enables you to manage multiple UCS domains in terms of cross-domain policy control, global identity/resource pools, global service profiles, and a dashboard feature that allows centralized hardware inventory and faults/logs/backup management. This chapter does not discuss details of the Cisco UCS Central product and its capabilities.

UCS Firmware, Backup, and License Management

With Cisco UCS, the relevant firmware is carved out into bundles. These bundles (.bin files) contain the relevant firmware bundle that would effectively touch and upgrade the intended target endpoints. The main reason for these bundles is to ease distribution and management. Figure 10-11 shows the endpoints on the left and the different firmware bundles that apply to them on the right.

Firmware Terminology

It is important that you review and understand all release notes for the appropriate version of firmware upgrading or downgrading. You can find the release notes and upgrade guides at the Cisco website. The Cisco UCS Manager refers to three versions of firmware that are currently visible to Cisco UCS Manager: running, startup, and backup versions.

The running version is the firmware version that is actively being used by the endpoint. The startup version is the firmware that will be used after the next reboot of that endpoint, and the backup version is the previous firmware version that used to run on that endpoint.

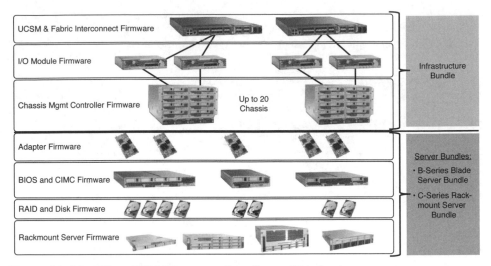

Figure 10-11   *Cisco UCS Firmware Bundles and Endpoints*

Firmware Definitions

In the Cisco UCS Manager, under the Equipment tab, when you choose the Installed Firmware button in the content pane, you will see these options:

■ Download the Firmware refers to copying the firmware onto the Cisco UCS Fabric Interconnect/bootflash partition from an external source/location. This process is nondisruptive.

■ Update Firmware copies the firmware to the backup partition on the endpoint (I/O Module); this process is nondisruptive.

■ Activate Firmware is disruptive. It places the firmware from the backup partition into the active partition and activates the startup version on the endpoint. Figure 10-12 shows the firmware definitions listed in the Cisco UCS Manager.

NOTE   Activating firmware should be executed according to the upgrade guides and most often requires following a particular sequence of activation of endpoints. Refer to the release notes and upgrade guides available on the Cisco website.

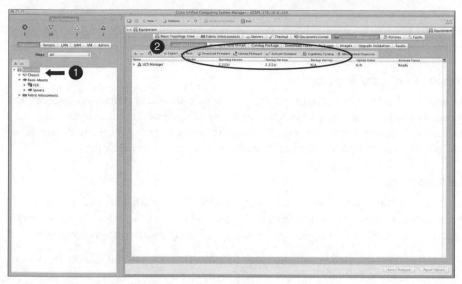

Figure 10-12 *Cisco UCS Manager Firmware Definitions*

Firmware Update Guidelines

As a general practice, you should adhere to or understand the following guidelines and their implications when planning to update Cisco UCS firmware:

- Ensure the Cisco UCS Manager HA state is healthy before starting any upgrades.
- Back up all configurations using the Cisco UCS Manager backup mechanism.
- Do not perform any chassis or server maintenance during upgrades.
- Disable call home features.
- Redundant Cisco UCS Fabric Interconnects can be updated without disrupting data traffic.
- Administratively shut down uplinks and check whether the data path is still available prior to upgrade.
- Do not activate all endpoints simultaneously.
- Update adapters through host firmware packages.

CAUTION   Refer to the firmware release notes and upgrade guides available on the Cisco website before upgrading, and plan accordingly.

Host Firmware Packages

Host firmware packages enable you to defer the upgrade and activation of firmware on certain endpoints through host firmware packages (until the time of associating a service profile to a blade or rack server), such as server BIOS, RAID controller, host HBA, and network adapters. However, you cannot defer the direct deployment of firmware images for components that do not use host firmware packages, such as Cisco UCS Manager, fabric

10

interconnects, and I/O modules. Host firmware packages were introduced in Chapter 9, "Cisco Unified Computing System Pools, Policies, Templates, and Service Profiles;" refer to it for a brief explanation.

Cross-Version Firmware Support

Starting with the Cisco UCS Manager version 2.1 release, cross-version firmware support was introduced. This states that Cisco UCS Manager enables the server bundle version to be one version prior to the infrastructure bundle. Refer to the firmware release notes and upgrade guides available on the Cisco website before planning any cross-firmware operations.

Firmware Auto Install

This feature is available starting with Cisco UCS Manager version 2.1(1) onward, the minimum base version required to use this feature. Figure 10-13 shows the firmware auto-install setup page in the Cisco UCS Manager. The auto-install feature gives you two options:

- **Install infrastructure firmware:** Upgrades all infrastructure endpoints, including Cisco UCS Manager, to the selected software bundle version.

- **Install server firmware:** Utilizes the host firmware packages feature to upgrade all Cisco UCS server components to the selected software bundle version.

CAUTION   Refer to the firmware release notes and upgrade guides available on the Cisco website and ensure that you have a thorough understanding of the process prior to using this feature.

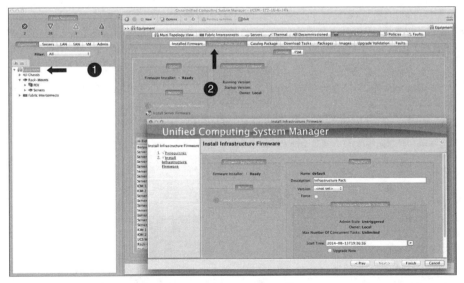

Figure 10-13   *Cisco UCS Firmware Auto Install*

TIP In the Cisco UCS Manager, a Firmware Conformance Checker enables you to check whether a downloaded firmware version is at support level for that hardware. Figure 10-14 shows a screenshot of this feature accessed in the Cisco UCS Manager.

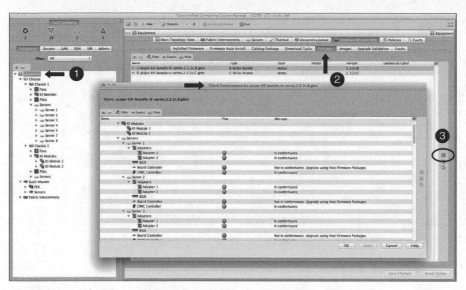

Figure 10-14   *Cisco UCS Manager Check for Conformance*

UCS Backups

The Cisco UCS Manager consists of four backup operation types:

- **Full State:** A full state backup is a binary file (.bin). This is the only type of backup that can be used to restore a new, bare metal Cisco UCS Fabric Interconnect. However, this type of backup cannot be used in a backup import operation.

- **All Configurations:** This is an XML file. It cannot be used to restore a new, bare metal Cisco UCS Fabric Interconnect. It contains all system and logical configurations of the Cisco UCS domain. It is ideal to import the entire current configuration into a new Cisco UCS system and allow it to preserve or maintain consumed logical identities and associated pools.

- **System Configuration:** This is an XML file. It contains all system configurations (usernames, roles, locales, and so on) and cannot be used to restore a new, bare metal Cisco UCS Fabric Interconnect. It is ideal to import the current configuration into a new Cisco UCS system.

- **Logical Configuration:** This is an XML file. It contains all logical configurations (service profiles, VLANs, VSAN, and so on) and cannot be used to restore a new, bare metal Cisco UCS Fabric Interconnect. It is ideal to import the entire current configuration into a new Cisco UCS system and allow it to preserve or maintain consumed logical identities and associated pools.

10

Figure 10-15 shows the window to create a backup operation in Cisco UCS Manager.

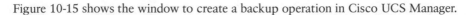

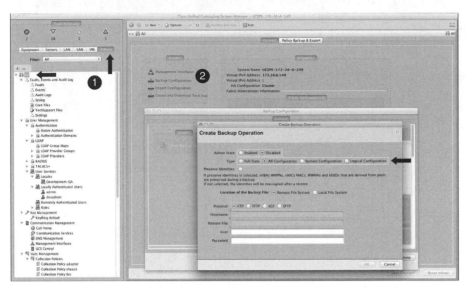

Figure 10-15   *Cisco UCS Manager Backup Operation Creation*

Backup Automation

Starting with release 2.1(1) of Cisco UCS Manager, backup automation capability has been introduced. The backup automation policy allows you to create regular, automated backups—daily, weekly, and bi-weekly—of full state and all configuration backup types. Figure 10-16 shows the backup automation configuration capability through policies in the Cisco UCS Manager.

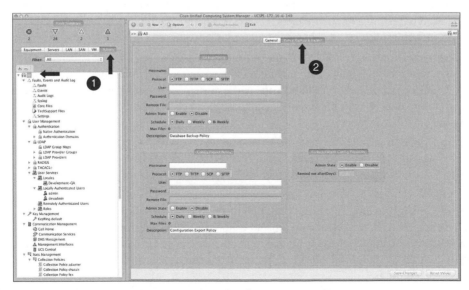

Figure 10-16   *Cisco UCS Manager Backup Automation*

License Management

The Cisco UCS Fabric Interconnect ports must be licensed. When a license expires, the functionality of that port will remain (as per general understanding, at the time of writing this chapter), but you will be notified about a license violation.

On Cisco UCS 6200 Series Fabric Interconnects, each of the fixed ports or expansion module ports can be used as 1G/10G Ethernet, FCoE, or FC ports. To use a port, you must have the correct SFP (Small Form factor Pluggable) modules and configure the port appropriately.

- Second-Generation Cisco UCS Fabric Interconnects
  - The 6248UP has 12 ports prelicensed.
  - The 6296UP has 18 ports prelicensed.
- Expansion Module
  - The 10-port unified expansion module has 16 physical ports. Of these, 8 ports are prelicensed.
- Third-Generation Cisco UCS Fabric Interconnects
  - The 6332 Fabric Interconnect has 8 ports prelicensed.
  - The 6332-16UP has 4x QSFP+ and 8x Unified Ports prelicensed.

NOTE   The First Generation Cisco Fabric Interconnect model UCS 6120XP has 8 ports with preinstalled licenses, and the UCS 6140XP has 16 preinstalled licenses.

NOTE   The Third-Generation Cisco Fabric Interconnect models 6332 and 6332-16UP were released at the time of writing this chapter.

If you start using an unlicensed port, a 120-day grace period is initiated for that port—this was the case at the time of writing this chapter. Additional licenses can be purchased and managed via Cisco license support and administered via the Cisco UCS Manager. Figure 10-17 shows the license management content pane under the Admin tab, which enables you to view, download, install, and determine license grace periods in use.

NOTE   These licenses are not portable across Cisco UCS Fabric Interconnect hardware generations; that is, between 6100, 6200, and 6300 Series.

10

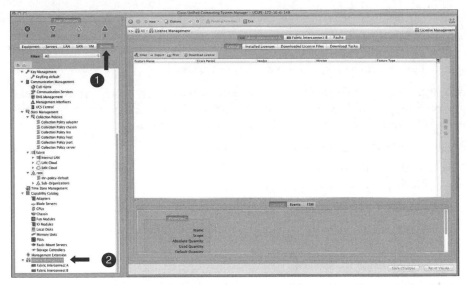

Figure 10-17 *Cisco UCS Manager License Management*

Cisco UCS Management

In this section you learn the operational planes of Cisco UCS, in-band and out-of-band management, remote accessibility, direct KVM access capability, and an introduction to advanced UCS management through its XML API. Under the advanced management topic, you will be briefly introduced to the goUCS automation toolkit, basic usage, and XML API usage via the Python SDK. As an example, you will learn how to query the Cisco UCS via XML to understand its inventory or set a value.

Operational Planes

The Cisco UCS Fabric Interconnects act as a single point of management providing independent data plane (based on application-specific integrated circuits [ASIC]), control plane (Ethernet and FC switching), and management plane (Cisco UCS Manager) functions. The management plane is redundant and clustered, active/passive to ensure availability of the management plane in case of component failure. Figure 10-18 shows the Cisco UCS Fabric Interconnect architecture and its operational planes.

> **NOTE** The control plane of the Cisco UCS Fabric Interconnect is configured only through the Cisco UCS Manager.

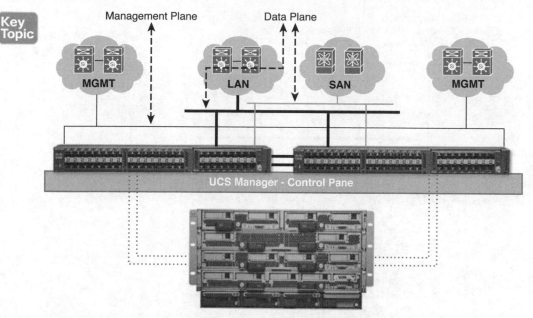

Figure 10-18 *Cisco UCS Fabric Interconnect Operational Planes*

In-Band Versus Out-of-Band Management

The Cisco UCS Manager provides both options: in-band and out-of-band management. However, note that the in-band option is for server CIMC/KVM access only. Typically, the CIMC management IP addresses are used to access the server KVM via the out-of-band (OOB) management network. This KVM can now be accessed via an in-band network, too, where the traffic path is via the fabric interconnect Ethernet uplink ports and not via the out-of-band management network.

> **NOTE** The in-band and out-of-band management IP address pool will be from separate L3 subnets. The out-of-band IP subnet should be from the same subnet as the physical and virtual-IP L3 subnet range. At the time of writing this chapter, this in-band access was supported on M3 and M4 Cisco UCS blades only.

Although the KVM can be accessed either in-band, out-of-band, or direct-KVM, the Cisco UCS Manager will be accessed via the out-of-band IP address (virtual-IP) assigned to the Cisco UCS Manager instance. This cannot be accessed via in-band access. Figure 10-19 shows a diagram of Cisco in-band and out-of-band management access.

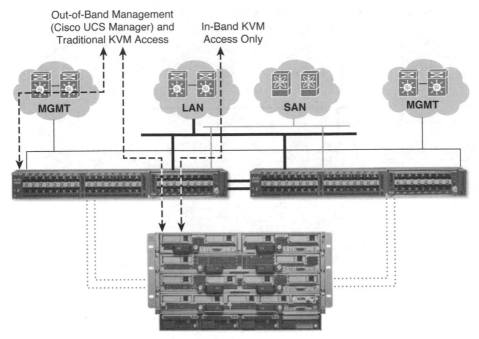

Figure 10-19 *Cisco UCS In-Band Versus Out-of-Band Management*

Remote Accessibility

The Cisco UCS Manager can be accessed remotely via different protocols/ports and programmatically. Some of these options are disabled by default and can be administered from the communications settings section, under the Admin tab in the Cisco UCS Manager. Following is a list of remote accessibility options:

- HTTP (Port 80)
- HTTPS (Port 443)
- SSH (Port 22)
- Telnet (Port 23), disabled by default
- SNMP (Port 161), disabled by default
- CIM-XML (Port 5988), disabled by default

Direct KVM Access

UCS administrators can now access the server KVMs without going through the Cisco UCS Manager. You can point your browser (http/https) to the blade server management IP address (https://<cimc-blade_mgmt_ip>) and access the blade KVM directly. Figure 10-20 shows the direct KVM access screen.

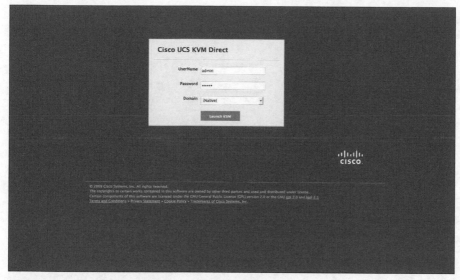

Figure 10-20   *Cisco UCS Direct KVM Access*

NOTE   Direct KVM can now be accessed via the OOB management network or in-band via the data path. You can configure OOB and in-band management IP ranges in Cisco UCS so that you can access the CIMC/KVM via multiple sessions and routes.

Advanced UCS Management

In this section you are briefly introduced to the programmatic nature of the Cisco UCS Manager. We discuss two methods of accessing the Cisco UCS Manager via its XML APIs, programmatically. As examples in this section, you will see the XML code that creates a VLAN in the LAN tab, LAN cloud under object VLANs, and obtaining an inventory via the goUCS automation toolkit. Then you will see how a backup operation is invoked programmatically via the Python SDK method.

Cisco UCS Manager XML API

The Cisco UCS Manager XML API communicates over http/https with a standard request/ response cycle. The XML schema for Cisco UCS Manager is published and readily available to the general public. (See the reference list for the Cisco DevNet link.) The XML API is used to manage multiple UCS domains, monitor event streams, integrate with manager of managers (MoMs), and enable rapid deployment, to name a few use cases.

NOTE   The Cisco UCS Manager GUI natively uses XML to communicate with Cisco UCS endpoints and gateways. It even enables UCS administrators to copy XML that is used to reference an object within the Cisco UCSM GUI. Figure 10-21 shows a right-click operation on an object and the ability to copy the object's XML code, which then can be used to address that object programmatically.

10

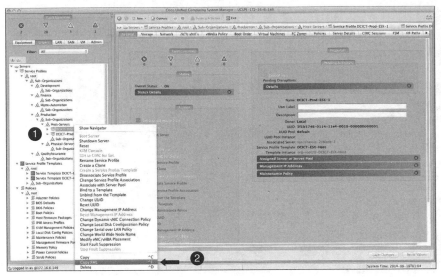

Figure 10-21 *Cisco UCS Manager Copy Object XML*

goUCS Automation Toolkit

The goUCS automation toolkit was primarily developed for Cisco UCS administrators who are not quite familiar with XML API programming. The goUCS automation toolkit gives a UCS system admin the capability to automate anything a Cisco UCS Manager GUI can do by allowing an administrator to extract the XML code that was used by the Cisco UCS Manager GUI, anonymize it, add variables, and reuse the code to perform a task repeatedly.

There are ready-made XML wrappers included in the toolkit that can be utilized to modify or query Cisco UCS Manager objects. Figure 10-22 shows a list of these ready-made CMD and XML wrappers available in the toolkit.

After downloading, installing, and setting up the environment/shell variables for the goUCS automation toolkit, you can access the goUCS toolkit command-line interface (CLI) by using the **#goucs** command from the shell/command prompt. The sample output shown in Figure 10-23 is the output of the **#goucs default listblades** command (query function). This output can be displayed as a table in .csv format, or you can redirect this output into files that can be manipulated or used to update a CMDB.

> **NOTE** Ensure that you specify the path to where Java Runtime Environment (JRE) stores its logs on your local machine. You can edit the goucs variables (clienv.cfg) file to point to that directory, where you should see log files with the name "centrale" and a number with extension .log when logs are successfully created.

Although the available CMD and XML wrappers are quite useful, the unique feature of the goUCS tool is that it enables you to trace the actions performed on the Cisco UCS Manager GUI using the **#goucs filterlog logtail** command. This method enables you to filter the last XML document/action sent from the Cisco UCS Manager GUI to UCS endpoints via its Java log file and enables you to anonymize it and then reuse the action/XML code in the future. This way, a UCS admin can convert GUI operations to scriptable, reusable code.

```
The following XML wrapper commands are available (Total:37):

all
automate
automatetest
autotrans
autotranstest
begin
cache
class
clonesp
connect
connectkvm
createvlan
dn
end
exportdn
filterlog
filterlogc
importdn
listautomate
listautotrans
listcurrentsessions
listexported
listimportable
listtransactions
login
logout
paramimportable
raw
rmautomate
rmautotrans
rmexported
rmimportable
rmtransaction
run
setkey
transaction
version

The following CMD wrapper commands are available (Total:13):

createvlan
listblades
listchassis
listfaults
listlocatorleds
listpowerblades
listpowerchassis
listpowerchassispsu
listpowerfis
listsps
reassociatesp
showfault
waitfor

XML wrapper syntax:
goucs [<session>] <wmlwrapper> ExecType PrintType [<arg1> ... <arg10>]
Example: goucs my_ucs1 class realtime indent /class:computeBlade

CMD wrapper syntax:
goucs [<session>] <cmdwrapper> [<arg1> ... <arg10>]
Example: goucs listblades

XML wrapper with answer file syntax:
goucs [<session>] args:<answerfile>
Example: goucs args:Sample

XML wrapper with options only answer file syntax:
goucs [<session>] <xmlwrapper> ExecType PrintType /args:<answerfile>
Example: goucs class realtime table:* /args:Sample

For help on a specific command use:
goucs <command> -?
```

Figure 10-22 *goUCS Automation Toolkit CMD/XML Wrappers*

dn	assignedToDn	model	numOfCpus	availableMemory	name
sys/chassis-1/blade-2		UCSB-B200-M3	2	98304	
sys/chassis-1/blade-1		UCSB-B200-M3	2	98304	
sys/chassis-1/blade-8		UCSB-B200-M3	2	393216	
sys/chassis-1/blade-7		UCSB-B200-M3	2	393216	
sys/chassis-1/blade-5		UCSB-B420-M3	4	786432	
sys/chassis-1/blade-4		UCSB-B200-M3	2	196608	
sys/chassis-1/blade-3		UCSB-B200-M3	2	196608	
sys/chassis-2/blade-2	org-root/org-Production/org-Host-Servers/ls-DCICT-Prod-ESX-1	UCSB-B200-M3	2	98304	
sys/chassis-2/blade-1		UCSB-B200-M3	2	98304	
sys/chassis-2/blade-7		UCSB-B200-M3	2	393216	
sys/chassis-2/blade-5		UCSB-B420-M3	4	786432	
sys/chassis-2/blade-4		UCSB-B200-M3	2	196608	
sys/chassis-2/blade-3	org-root/org-Production/org-Host-Servers/ls-DCICT-Prod-ESX-2	UCSB-B200-M3	2	196608	
sys/chassis-2/blade-8		UCSB-B200-M3	2	393216	

Figure 10-23 *Command #goucs listblades Output*

As an example, see the **#goucs filterlog logtail** output when creating and deleting a VLAN called "management" with VLAN ID "500". Figure 10-24 shows the output of these actions in XML via Java logs. This output can be anonymized using the **#goucs filterlog trueco ignore management:NAME @id:500:ID** command and converted into a custom XML wrapper.

```
sh-3.2# goucs filterlog logtail
[------------- Sending Request to Server ------------
<configConfMos
inHierarchical="false">
     <inConfigs>
<pair key="fabric/lan/net-management">
     <fabricVlan
     compressionType="included"
     defaultNet="no"
     dn="fabric/lan/net-management"
     id="500"
     mcastPolicyName=""
     name="management"
     policyOwner="local"
     pubNwName=""
     sharing="none"
     status="created">
     </fabricVlan>
</pair>
     </inConfigs>
</configConfMos>
-------------------------------------------------]

[------------- Sending Request to Server ------------
<configConfMos
inHierarchical="false">
     <inConfigs>
<pair key="fabric/lan/net-management">
     <fabricVlan
     dn="fabric/lan/net-management"
     status="deleted">
     </fabricVlan>
</pair>
     </inConfigs>
</configConfMos>
-------------------------------------------------]
```

Figure 10-24 *#goucs filterlog logtail Command Output*

For more information, visit the Cisco DevNet site and download the required tools, kits, and documentation.

Using the Python SDK

You can download the Python SDK at Cisco DevNet and utilize its libraries to interface with Cisco UCS Manager. The Cisco UCS XML API utilizes four main types of methods: authentication, querying, configuration change, and event subscription. The Cisco UCS Python SDK contains the required libraries and methods. As an example, using these Python SDK–based libraries and methods, you will see below a backup operation executed in the Cisco UCS Manager programmatically.

NOTE It is essential that you have an average understanding of Python-based scripting. You must develop these Python scripts, utilizing the methods supplied in the software development kit, including the logic, validation, and string/text manipulations as required. Before you begin any scripting work, ensure that the Python utilities and SDKs are installed correctly. You should also follow the Cisco UCS Python SDK User Guide (included with the Python SDK from DevNet).

TIP You can utilize the Cisco UCS Platform Emulator (UCSPE) for testing, development, and validation purposes. Interacting with its XML API simulates the same behavior as a live system.

Figure 10-25 shows the Python CLI, importing the Cisco UCS SDK libraries, creating a variable for the handle, and executing a login operation via the API. All subsequent XML API calls should be preceded by the "handle.(operation)" syntax. An example is **handle.Login** (IP address, username, password) until you wish to logout via the **handle.logout()** call, which signifies login and logout operations.

```
Python 2.7.2 (default, Oct 11 2012, 20:14:37)
[GCC 4.2.1 Compatible Apple Clang 4.0 (tags/Apple/clang-418.0.60)] on darwin
Type "help", "copyright", "credits" or "license" for more information.
>>> from UcsSdk import *
>>> handle = UcsHandle()
>>> handle.Login("172.16.6.149",username="cliuser",password="cliuser")
True
>>>
```

Figure 10-25 *Cisco UCS Python SDK—Login to Cisco UCS Manager*

Following is an example of executing the sample script provided in the Python SDK to back up a Cisco UCS Manager domain/instance programmatically. Figure 10-26 shows the command-line syntax, the required parameter switches, and the results. Please note that the "handle" as explained in the earlier section is embedded within this sample Python script.

```
sh-3.2# python backupUcsManager.py --ip=172.16.6.149 --username=cliuser --password=cliuser --type=config-logical --pathPattern=/ucspebackup.xml

Managed Object             :      MgmtBackup
------------------
Status                     :None
PostAction                 :remove
MaxFiles                   :0
Name                       :
Descr                      :
Proto                      :http
Hostname                   :aafrose-m-403b20140907182926
AdminState                 :disabled
OwnerPolicy                :
Rn                         :backup-aafrose-m-403b20140907182926
PreservePooledValues       :no
Dn                         :sys/backup-aafrose-m-403b20140907182926
PolicyLevel                :0
Type                       :config-logical
PolicyOwner                :local
Pwd                        :
Job                        :immediate
User                       :
RemoteFile                 :/ucspebackup.xml
Ucs                        :UCSPE-172-16-6-149

Downloading: ucspebackup.xml Bytes: 114484
sh-3.2#
```

Figure 10-26 *Cisco UCS Python SDK—Calling Sample Backup*

NOTE The Cisco Developer Network (https://developer.cisco.com/site/devnet/home/index.gsp) is the prime source of resources, tools, and documentation.

Multi-UCS Management

The Cisco UCS Central solution is a VM-appliance-based application available for both VMware and Hyper-v hypervisors. This solution extends the Cisco UCS Manager paradigm to a multi-UCS domain management tool. It provides centralized inventory management, usage and availability summaries, fault summaries, centralized firmware management, and the ability to manage global service profiles and identities. This topic is beyond the scope of this certification guide; for further details, refer to the Cisco website, release notes, and configuration guides.

Cisco UCS Monitoring

The recommendation for monitoring a UCS Manager environment is to monitor all faults of either severity, critical or major. FSM-related faults are transient in nature because they

10

are triggered when an FSM transition is occurring in UCS Manager. This section discusses monitoring UCS via SNMP, UCS fault suppression capabilities, system logs, and collection threshold policies that are essential to understanding Cisco UCS monitoring.

Cisco UCS System Logs

Two main types of logs exist in the Cisco UCS Manager. One is holistic, around the UCS system faults, failures, and alarm thresholds (Syslog). Another specific set of logs covers system hardware events around servers and chassis components in terms of their internal hardware components (SEL logs).

Fault, Event, and Audit Logs (Syslogs)

There are three kinds of syslog entries: Fault, Event, and Audit. This can be viewed from the Cisco UCS Manager. It labels each fault with a severity term, as shown in Figure 10-27; the fault events are categorized as per the legend shown.

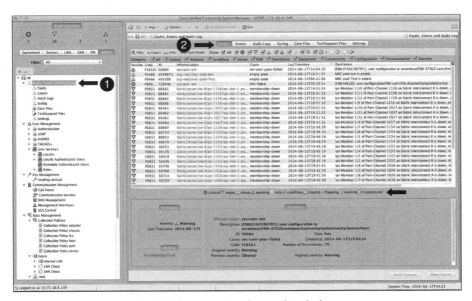

Figure 10-27   *Cisco UCS Manager Faults and Labels*

In the Faults tab, you can see the severity level, the description, the affected object, and so on. They are all self-descriptive and easy to understand. Apart from other faults listed in Figure 10-27, you might notice [FSM] faults listed; these are event messages generated when an FSM transitions from one state to another. The finite state machine (FSM) monitors configuration changes. Every action that requires a set/retrieve action within the UCS Manager is perceived as a set of state transitions. These transitions (based on severity) are monitored and listed here.

In general, all FSM transitions can be monitored in the Events tab, as shown in Figure 10-28. Note the Cause column in Figure 10-28, which shows the cause of this event.

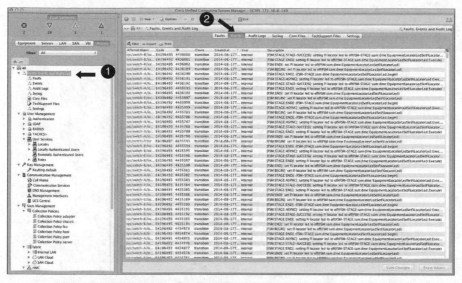

Figure 10-28   *Cisco UCS Manager Events Tab*

In the Audit Logs tab, you can see the events that took place, where, and who was responsible for that event. These logs track actions that users initiated. Figure 10-29 shows the Audit Logs tab in the Cisco UCS Manager.

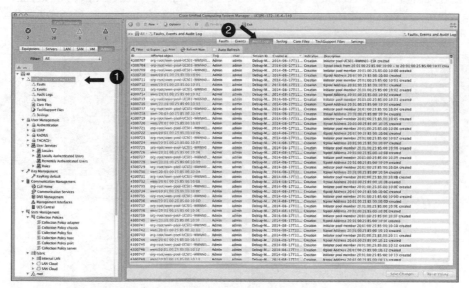

Figure 10-29   *Cisco UCS Manager Audit Logs Tab*

The global fault policy is used to control the settings around faults, events, and audit logs. For example, you can set the retention interval of cleared faults, flapping and soaking intervals, and so on. Figure 10-30 shows the global fault policy settings page in Cisco UCS Manager.

10

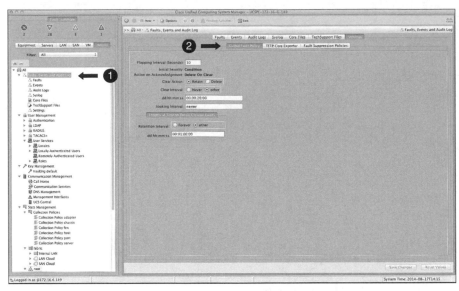

Figure 10-30   *Cisco UCS Manager Global Fault Policy Settings*

It is a best practice to periodically download the fault, event, and audit logs. It is also recommended to use an external syslog server to periodically download these logs. You could use a maximum of three different syslog servers and send specific types of logs to different syslog servers, if need be. Figure 10-31 shows the syslog settings screen in the Cisco UCS Manager.

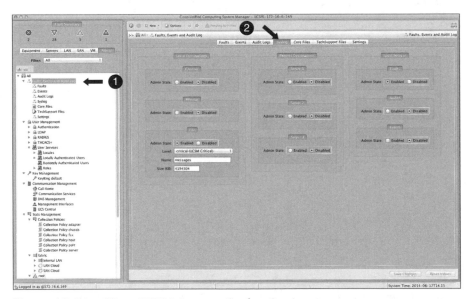

Figure 10-31   *Cisco UCS Manager Syslog Settings*

System Event Logs

The system event log (SEL) resides on the CIMC in NVRAM. The SEL records most server-related events, such as over and under voltage, temperature events, fan events, and events from BIOS to the CIMC buffer. SEL is an effective health-monitoring tool and is usually used for troubleshooting purposes.

The types of events supported by SEL include BIOS events, memory unit events (ECC errors, address parity, and so on), processor events (memory mirroring, parsing, and the like), and motherboard events (PCIe, QPI uncorrectable errors, Legacy PCI errors). It is a best practice to periodically download and clear the SEL logs because they are stored in the CIMC NVRAM, through an SEL log policy.

The SEL file is approximately 40 KB in size, and no further events can be recorded when it is full. Therefore, it is recommended to periodically back up the SEL log file onto an external server and clear the SEL. Figure 10-32 shows the SEL policy settings on Cisco UCS Manager.

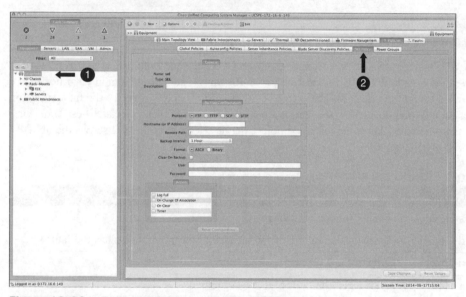

Figure 10-32   *Cisco UCS Manager SEL Policy*

UCS SNMP

Cisco UCS supports read-only access to SNMP MIBs. All traps/notifications from Cisco UCS can be sent to multiple SNMP hosts. Figure 10-33 shows the SNMP host and user configuration settings in the Cisco UCS Manager.

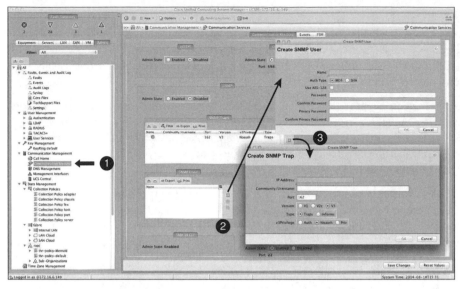

Figure 10-33 *Cisco UCS Manager SNMP Settings*

Cisco UCS supports SNMP v1, v2, and v3. Cisco UCS will send only two types of traps to an SNMP host: a fault active notification (when the fault is active) and a fault clear notification (when the fault is cleared). These traps contain information to identify the fault type and cause. An external host with the appropriate MIBs loaded can then correlate these traps via OIDs to specifically know the managed object that is affected. Table 10-2 shows the SNMP fault trap attributes.

Table 10-2 Cisco UCS SNMP Fault Trap Attributes

Field	Description
Fault Instance	Unique integer identifying the fault
Affected Object	Distinguished name of the managed object (MO) that has the fault
Affected Object	OID of the MO that has the fault
Creation Time	Time when the fault object was created
Last Modification	Time when any of the attributes below were modified
Code	A code providing specific information about the nature of the fault
Type	The type of the fault (broad)
Cause	Fault probable causes
Severity	Fault severity
Occurrence	Number of times fault has occurred since it was created
Description	Human-readable string providing more information about the fault

Fault Suppression

SNMP traps and call home notifications can be suppressed based on UCS administrative events, such as maintenance windows. It can be stopped for a fixed time, manually stopped, or scheduled. Also, fault suppression can be activated for a specific device, such as chassis, I/O module, server blade, service profile, or an organization. Figure 10-34 shows a manually configurable fault suppression screen for a chassis within the Cisco UCS Manager.

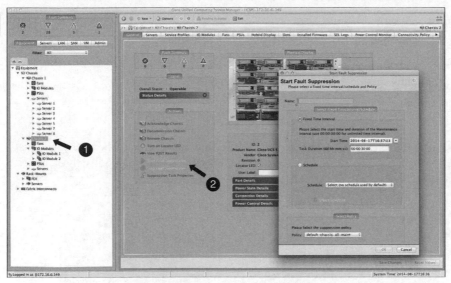

Figure 10-34   *Cisco UCS Start Fault Suppression*

Figure 10-35 shows a list of available fault suppression policies that will be utilized and their respective fault types that will be suppressed. These policies can be expanded to understand the components and the type of fault that would be suppressed if chosen.

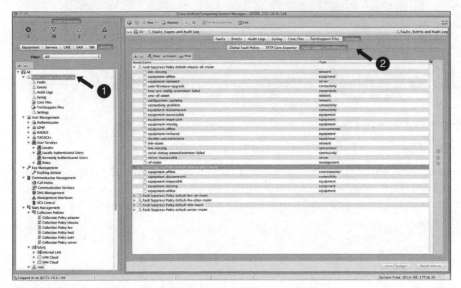

Figure 10-35   *Cisco UCS Fault Suppression Policies*

10

Collection and Threshold Policies

A collection policy in Cisco UCS Manager defines the frequency of statistic collection (collection interval) and reporting (reporting interval). Ideally, you want a larger reporting interval than a collection interval, thereby allowing multiple data points to be reported and enabling the Cisco UCS Manager to report minimum, maximum, and average values.

In the Cisco UCS Manager, statistics can be collected for five functional areas:

- **Adapter:** Converged adapter
- **Chassis:** Blade chassis
- **Host:** Future use
- **Port:** All uplink (Ethernet and FC) and server ports
- **Server:** Physical server

> **NOTE**   Cisco UCS Manager consists of default collection policies predefined per functional area. You cannot create additional collection policies. However, you can modify them, as shown in Figure 10-36, and edit the collection and reporting intervals.

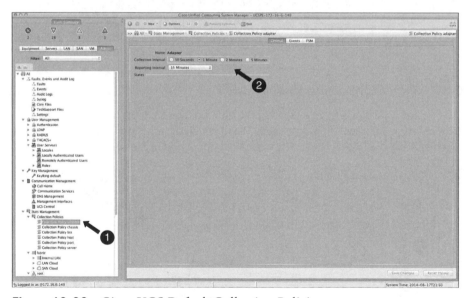

Figure 10-36   *Cisco UCS Default Collection Policies*

The output of these statistics can be viewed from the Cisco UCS Manager Equipment tab and by selecting the relevant hardware. Figure 10-37 shows the Cisco UCS Chassis and the associated statistics based on the collection/reporting interval defined earlier.

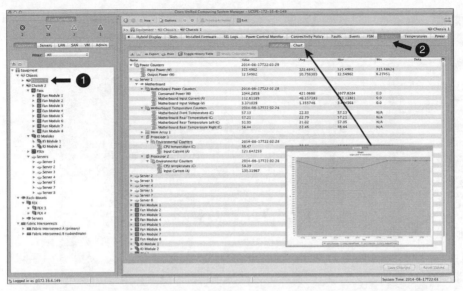

Figure 10-37 *Cisco UCS Statistic Reporting*

Based on these statistics, you can also create threshold policies. These threshold policies can generate an event based on whether a predefined statistic threshold has been crossed. The threshold policy does not control the hardware; it raises an event/alarm only.

Threshold policies can be created in any of these tabs: Servers, LAN, SAN, and Admin. Cisco UCS Manager has threshold classes already defined for the following areas:

- Servers and server components
- Uplink Ethernet ports
- Ethernet server ports, chassis, and Fabric interconnects
- Fibre Channel ports

You cannot delete these classes. However, you can create your custom threshold policies by choosing a class and defining values to monitor. As an example, you will see a custom-defined threshold policy to monitor server "runtime memory available," as shown in Figure 10-38. When the runtime memory available value is greater than 25 GB, UCS Manager will send an info notification; if the value is lower than 25 GB, UCS Manager will send a warning notification.

After defining the threshold policy, attach it to either a Cisco UCS service profile or a service profile template, under the Stats Policy section, as shown in Figure 10-39.

10

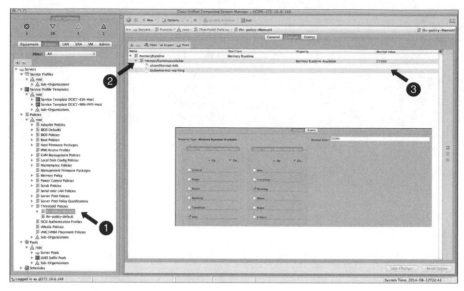

Figure 10-38 *Cisco UCS Threshold Policy Definitions*

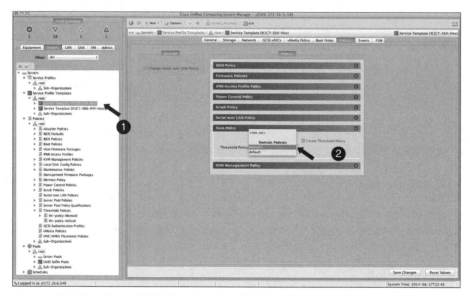

Figure 10-39 *Cisco UCS Service Profile Template Stats Policy*

Call Home and Smart Call Home

Basically, the Cisco Call Home feature provides e-mail–based notification of system events. It is important that you understand the difference between Cisco UCS Call Home (CH) and Smart Call Home (SCH) features.

The primary differences are that Cisco TAC cannot maintain an inventory; faults/alerts are not sent to Cisco TAC, no auto-case creation occurs, and there is no access to the Cisco

Smart Call Home portal with CH. SCH actually leverages the CH feature and enables proactive diagnostics and sends real-time e-mail alerts.

NOTE Configuring SCH will send automatic alerts/notifications to Cisco TAC via Simple Mail Transfer Protocol (SMTP). SCH also requires a valid Cisco ID associated with an active support contract for your company. This active support contract must cover the devices (Cisco UCS). Also, it is recommended that you use a secure transport gateway to send e-mails to the SCH system to ensure secure communications.

First, you must enable Cisco UCS CH via the Cisco UCS Manager, Admin tab. By default, the call home feature is disabled. You must enable call home, throttling (controlling of duplicate messages within a timeframe), and input details in the following sections: Contact information, Contract IDs (if you plan to use SCH), e-mail addresses, and SMTP server details. Figure 10-40 shows the call home configuration screen.

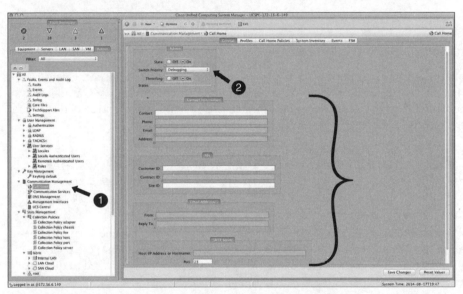

Figure 10-40 *Cisco UCS Call Home Configuration*

TIP Log in to the Cisco UCS Fabric Interconnect *connect local-mgmt*. Use the **ping** command and test reachability to the SMTP gateway configured when enabling Cisco Call Home.

After enabling call home, you must configure Cisco CH profiles. These profiles define the alert level and the recipients of the e-mail. By default, there are three profiles: CiscoTAC-1, full_txt, and short_txt. You can add multiple profiles, with different alert levels (all faults greater than or equal to this fault level trigger call home) and e-mail addresses associated with it, such as different mailboxes for operations teams depending on the type of alert. Figure 10-41 shows the call home profile configuration.

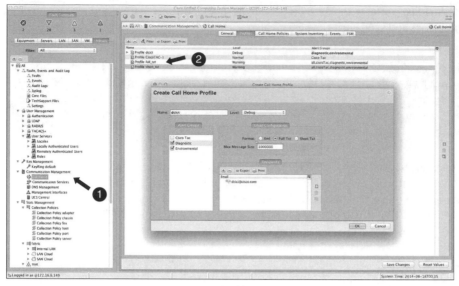

Figure 10-41   *Cisco UCS Call Home Profiles*

The full_txt and short_txt profiles are not for SCH. If you use secure transport gateway software, this e-mail address should have a specific inbox that all e-mails are sent to locally, and the transport gateway software should pick e-mails from this inbox and send them on in a secure fashion to SCH.

NOTE   If you want to enable SCH, you must configure the already available CiscoTAC-1 call home profile with the relevant e-mail address. This profile sends XML-based messages; do not configure additional recipients here.

The next step is to enable Cisco UCS CH policies. These policies determine whether a specific cause should raise an alert. By enabling different types of "causes" in these policies, you ensure that a cause generates the alert; it is this alert that is communicated to the e-mail recipients. Figure 10-42 shows the Create Call Home Policy screen.

NOTE   If you want to enable SCH and you have configured the necessary information as outlined earlier in this section—Cisco IDs, CiscoTAC-1 profile, and so on—you must trigger a call home inventory message to start the registration process.

A call home inventory message can be triggered via the system inventory tab in the content pane. With SCH, this starts the registration process; when Cisco support receives the inventory, an e-mail is sent back to the e-mail address you configured earlier in the contact information area. Figure 10-43 shows system inventory generation.

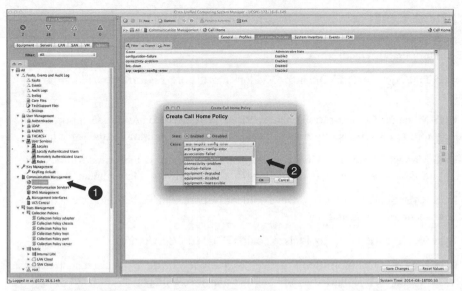

Figure 10-42   *Cisco UCS Call Home Policies*

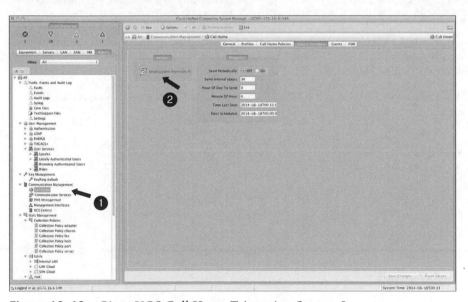

Figure 10-43   *Cisco UCS Call Home Triggering System Inventory*

Reference List

Cisco UCS Hardware-Software Interoperability Matrix: http://www.cisco.com/web/tech-doc/ucs/interoperability/matrix/matrix.html

Firefox HTTP Requester Add-On: https://addons.mozilla.org/En-us/firefox/addon/httpre-quester/

Cisco UCS Manager Configuration Guides: http://www.cisco.com/c/en/us/support/servers-unified-computing/ucs-manager/products-installation-and-configuration-guides-list.html

Cisco UCS Manager Firmware Management: http://www.cisco.com/c/en/us/td/docs/uni-fied_computing/ucs/sw/firmware-mgmt/gui/2-1/b_GUI_Firmware_Management_21.html

Cisco UCS XML Schema and Cisco Development Network: https://developer.cisco.com/site/ucs-dev-center/documentation/

Cisco UCS SNMP MIB: http://tools.cisco.com/ITDIT/MIBS/servlet/index

Cisco UCS Manager Configuration Practices Whitepaper: http://www.cisco.com/c/en/us/products/collateral/servers-unified-computing/ucs-manager/whitepaper_c11-697337.html

Cisco UCS Monitoring Using Syslog: http://www.cisco.com/c/en/us/td/docs/unified_com-puting/ucs/sw/ucsm_syslog/b_Monitoring_Cisco_UCSM_Using_Syslog.pdf

Cisco UCS Smart Call Home: http://www.cisco.com/c/en/us/td/docs/unified_computing/ucs/sw/gui/config/guide/2-0/b_UCSM_GUI_Configuration_Guide_2_0/b_UCSM_GUI_Configuration_Guide_2_0_chapter_0101100.html

Cisco UCS Manager XML Schema: https://developer.cisco.com/site/ucs-dev-center/docu-mentation/

Exam Preparation Tasks

Review All Key Topics

Review the most important topics in the chapter, noted with the key topic icon in the outer margin of the page. Table 10-3 lists a reference for these key topics and the page numbers on which each is found.

Table 10-3   Key Topics for Chapter 10

Key Topic Element	Description	Page
Section	"Organization and Locales"	367
Section	"Role-Based Access Control"	369
Section	"Authentication Methods"	370
Section	"Communication Management"	372
Section	"UCS Firmware, Backup, and License Management"	373
Section	"Operational Planes"	380
Figure 10-18	"Cisco UCS Fabric Interconnect Operational Planes"	381
Section	"In-Band Versus Out-of-Band Management"	381
Section	"Fault, Event, and Audit Logs (Syslogs)"	388
Section	"System Event Logs"	391
Section	"UCS SNMP"	391
Table 10-2	"Cisco UCS SNMP Fault Trap Attributes"	392
Section	"Fault Suppression"	393
Figure 10-34	"Cisco UCS Start Fault Suppression"	393
Section	"Collection and Threshold Policies"	394
Section	"Call Home and Smart Call Home"	396

10

Define Key Terms

Define the following key terms from this chapter, and check your answers in the Glossary:

Cisco Technical Assistance Center (TAC), Local-Area Network (LAN), Storage-Area Network (SAN), Cisco Integrated Management Controller (CIMC), Nonvolatile RAM (NVRAM), Keyboard Video and Mouse (KVM), Finite State Machine (FSM), Simple Network Management Protocol (SNMP), System Event Log (SEL), Application Programming Interface (API), Software Development Kit (SDK), Microsoft (MS), Active Directory (AD), Remote Authentication Dial-In User Service (RADIUS), Lightweight Directory Access Protocol (LDAP), Terminal Access Controller Access Control System (TACACS), Role-Based Access Control (RBAC)

This chapter covers the following exam topics:

1.5 Describe server virtualization concepts and benefits

1.5.a Hypervisors

1.5.b Virtual switches

1.5.c Shared storage

1.5.d Virtual Machine components

1.5.e Virtual Machine Manager

CHAPTER 11

Server Virtualization Solutions

Server virtualization is a technology that allows abstracting physical x86 server hardware components, such as CPU, memory, disk, and network interface cards (NICs). Once abstracted, those physical resources can be shared across multiple isolated instances of the server operating systems running inside the virtual machines created on top of the abstraction layer, otherwise known as the virtual hypervisor.

The virtual hyperlvisor schedules access to the actual underlying physical server resources. Virtual machines do not realize they run on top of virtualized hardware, thus neither server operating system nor the applications need to be modified to run in a server virtualized environment. In this chapter we briefly review the history of server virtualization and discuss its main operational characteristics, benefits, and challenges.

"Do I Know This Already?" Quiz

The "Do I Know This Already?" quiz enables you to assess whether you should read this entire chapter thoroughly or jump to the "Exam Preparation Tasks" section. If you are in doubt about your answers to these questions or your own assessment of your knowledge of the topics, read the entire chapter. Table 11-1 lists the major headings in this chapter and their corresponding "Do I Know This Already?" quiz questions. You can find the answers in Appendix A, "Answers to the 'Do I Know This Already?' Quizzes."

Table 11-1 "Do I Know This Already?" Section-to-Question Mapping

Foundation Topics Section	Questions
Describe Server Virtualization Concepts and Benefits	8-9
Hypervisors	1-2, 7
Virtual Switches	3, 10
Virtual Machine Components	4-6

CAUTION The goal of self-assessment is to gauge your mastery of the topics in this chapter. If you do not know the answer to a question or are only partially sure of the answer, you should mark that question as wrong for purposes of the self-assessment. Giving yourself credit for an answer you correctly guess skews your self-assessment results and might provide you with a false sense of security.

1. What is a hypervisor?

    a. A software layer installed on top of a bare metal server to provide access to the physical server resources in a shared manner.

    b. A software layer installed on top of a bare metal server and operating at Ring 1 privilege access.

    c. It is also called Virtual Machine Monitor.

    d. It is also called Virtual Machine Manager.

2. What is a Type-2 hypervisor?

    a. It is a hypervisor that does not run directly on top of the physical server hardware; instead, it runs as an application on top of the server operating system.

    b. It is a hypervisor that runs directly on top of the physical server hardware.

    c. It is a deployment model where two Type-1 hypervisors are deployed in the same data center.

    d. It is a default mode of VMware ESXi hypervisor operation.

3. What type of technology is most often used between the virtual switch in the hypervisor and a physical switch the host is connected to?

    a. 802.1X

    b. 802.3X

    c. 802.1Q

    d. 802.1AE

4. Can you install any guest operating system inside the virtual machine?

    a. Yes

    b. No

    c. Only ones supported by the virtualization vendor

    d. Only ones that support paravirtualization

5. The paravirtualization method requires the server operating system installed in the virtual machine to be modified.

    a. Yes

    b. No

    c. Only if it is Type-1 hypervisor

    d. Only if it is Type-2 hypervisor

6. Operating system virtualization allows installing different types of operating systems on top of the shared kernel.

    a. True

    b. False

7. Which events can trigger a virtual machine mobility event?

   a. Physical server failure

   b. Insufficient hardware resources

   c. Manually initiated by administrator

   d. All of the above

8. Which conditions must be met for successful live virtual machine mobility to occur?

   a. Layer 2 connectivity must exist between source and destination host.

   b. Live virtual machine mobility is never supported in the server virtualization products.

   c. The source and destination physical server must be connected to the same physical switch.

   d. Live virtual machine mobility requires changing TCP/IP settings, such as the IP address, during the mobility event

9. Traditional data center POD architecture helps deploy server virtualization.

   a. Yes, because it allows flat Layer 2 architecture

   b. No, because it breaks Layer 2 domain continuity between source and destination hosts

   c. Yes, because it provides plenty of bisectional traffic

   d. No, because local aggregation layer switches do not have routing information for subnets in the other PODs

10. The physical network can provide security for network traffic between two virtual machines.

   a. Only if the two virtual machines are on the same physical server.

   b. Only if the two virtual machines are on different physical servers.

   c. The physical network can never provide security for traffic between two virtual machines.

   d. Only if you install a virtual firewall.

11

Foundation Topics

Brief History of Server Virtualization

Server virtualization is a popular technology leveraged in a variety of environments. From its inception, server virtualization has dramatically increased in popularity, and it is an enabling force behind innovative cloud computing models. To understand where we are going, we must understand where we have been. Let's briefly look at the history of server virtualization.

Server virtualization is not a new concept. Generally, its roots can be traced back to the 1960s when IBM released a first server virtualization technology on its mainframe products. At that time, computers performed serialized or batch processing with a single operator being able to use the machine at any given time. Such operation resulted in resource under-utilization and raised concerns about the economical model around highly priced mainframe systems. Something needed to be done about it.

At the end of the 1960s and into the early 1970s, IBM released Control Program/ Cambridge Monitor System (CP/CMS), which implemented the first virtual machine architecture. The CP/CMS virtual machine concept constituted a significant step forward in an operating system design. It allowed interactive time-sharing use of resources, where instead of dividing server hardware resources between system users, which was the traditional approach, each user was provided with a simulated standalone computer system. By creating isolated computer environments, CP/CMS improved overall system reliability and security and allowed running any software in the time-sharing environment, and not software specifically written for this purpose.

In the subsequent decades, industry moved away from centralized computing design and adopted a more distributed approach of server/client operation where expensive mainframes gave way to a plethora of relatively inexpensive x86 commodity servers. The x86 server architecture did not initially provide sufficient hardware support to successfully implement server virtualization, and this approach was largely abandoned in the 1980s and 1990s.

Over time, complex software operations and application fault containment drove system administrators to dedicate servers for a single application use. Convenient x86 price points encouraged organizations to increase their server footprint, resulting in significant server sprawl, while according to the market research, individual server utilization stood at only approximately 5%–15%. This approach increased physical infrastructure demands, management costs, and overall operational expenditures.

Things changed in 1998 when a company called VMware figured out a way to effectively virtualize the x86 platform. As mentioned earlier, x86 platforms did not initially provide support for server virtualization, and server operating systems were designed to run in a fashion in which they had direct access to the underlying physical server resources. Running server virtualization on x86 platforms required placing a virtualization layer between the guest operating systems running in the virtual machines and the underlying physical server resources. The virtualization layer leveraged a technique known as binary translation, where the software interpreter layer, known as the Virtual Machine Monitor, intercepted privileged instructions, converting them into instructions that could be virtualized.

In 2006, both Intel and AMD introduced enhancements to their processors to allow addressing the issue of privileged instructions. Intel's technology was called VT-x, and AMD's technology was called AMD-V. Subsequent chipsets addressed low performance of the virtualized system memory. Introduction of hardware acceleration pushed server virtualization over the edge, turning it into a predominant technology leveraged in many organizational computing environments.

Today, several vendors implement server virtualization in their products. The most common solutions for commercial server virtualization offerings come from VMware in the form of ESXi hypervisor and from Microsoft in the form of Hyper-V hypervisor. Xen and KVM are examples of open source hypervisors.

Server Virtualization Components

Server virtualization comprises several components working in synergy to deliver a holistic solution. In this section we look at the main components for building a server virtualization environment.

Hypervisor

Hypervisor, also known as the Virtual Machine Monitor, is a piece of software running on the bare metal x86 server. It allows virtualizing underlying physical server resources and presenting them as components to be consumed by the virtual machines running on top. The hypervisor can virtualize all major server hardware components, such as CPU, disk, memory, and network. Figure 11-1 depicts the general principle behind server virtualization.

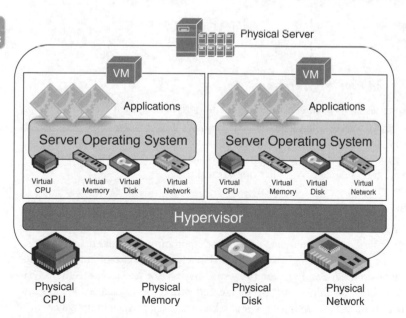

Figure 11-1 *Server Virtualization Principles*

Hypervisors are usually described as being either Type 1 or Type 2. Type-1 hypervisors, also known as the bare metal, run directly on top of the physical server hardware, and they represent the original idea behind server virtualization developed by IBM in the 1960s and 1970s. Virtual machines run on top, and guest operating systems installed on those virtual machines leverage virtual hardware exposed by the hypervisor. More popular examples of Type-1 hypervisors include Microsoft Hyper-V, VMware ESXi, XenServer, and KVM.

Type-2 hypervisors, also known as hosted, do not run directly on top of the physical server hardware. Instead, they run as an application on top of the server operating system. Type-2 hypervisors coordinate a call to the physical server resources through the host operating system installed on the server. The actual virtual machines run one level higher. Examples of Type-2 hypervisors include VMware Workstation, VMware Fusion, Oracle VM VirtualBox, and others.

Figure 11-2 depicts the Type-1 and Type-2 hypervisor approach.

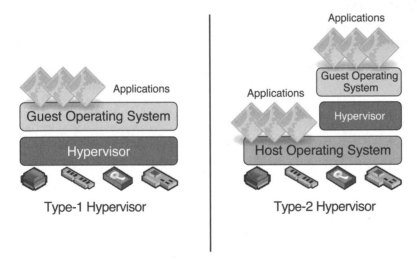

Figure 11-2   *Type-1 and Type-2 Hypervisors*

Because Type-1 hypervisors have direct access to the underlying physical server resources, they often offer better performance characteristics for the running workloads. At the same time, Type-2 hypervisors may offer easier implementation and maintenance because they rely on the underlying host operating system to provide hardware driver compatibility, configuration flexibility, and reliance on familiar operational tools.

Virtual Machines

Virtual machines are a software construct operating on top of the virtual hypervisor. Guest operating systems run inside the virtual machines; most commonly, a virtual machine runs a single instance of the guest operating system. Virtual machines emulate operation of the physical computing environment and rely on the virtual hypervisor for access to the physical server resources. Virtual machines can also be created within the virtualization environment running on top of the server operating system, known as the host operating system.

It is important to note that not all guest operating systems are supported on all virtual hypervisor products, but if they are, they can be installed on top of virtual machines the same as they would be installed on top of physical server hardware. For example, a guest operating system can have several NICs defined in its settings, when in reality those network interfaces are presented and scheduled by the virtual hypervisor for access into the actual physical server network interfaces.

Using virtual machines instead of bare metal nonvirtualized servers can provide significant advantages. Guest operating system isolation allows running multiple instances of a server operating system on the same physical server hardware without having them interfere with each other. This allows dedicating servers for specific application use while not contributing to server sprawl. Server virtualization can also be viewed as a form of hardware abstraction. When abstracted from the underlying physical server hardware, virtual machines can be easily moved around, copied, paused, and so on. Abstraction can also greatly facilitate simplified backup and disaster recovery procedures.

Virtual Switching

In the pre-server virtualization days, all traffic forwarding functions across the data center networks were carried out by the physical switching infrastructure. Servers were attached through either IEEE 802.1Q VLAN trunks or single-VLAN switch ports sending their network traffic toward the data center access layer switches, which in turn forwarded it to its destination. With the advent of server virtualization, servers were turned into software constructs running on top of the shim hypervisor layer running in turn on top of the bare metal physical server hardware. This introduced a challenge of handling virtual machine network traffic.

A solution came in the form of virtual switches deployed at the server virtualization layer. Virtual switches took care of forwarding the network traffic between the virtual machines residing on the same or different physical hosts. They also leveraged physical network interfaces to send traffic between the virtual machines and nonvirtualized servers. Figure 11-3 depicts the principle behind virtual switching traffic forwarding.

Virtual switching is important in the case of virtual machine mobility. As virtual machines move around the virtualization layer, they many times traverse physical network boundaries; in other words, virtual machines migrate between physical hosts connected to different physical switches. In this case, virtual switches make sure to maintain configuration consistency for the virtual machine attachment points in terms of network and security settings.

11

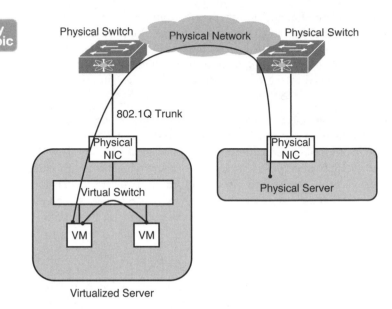

Figure 11-3 *Virtual Switching Traffic Forwarding*

Shared Storage

In the server virtualized environment, the entire state of the virtual machine is decoupled from the underlying server physical resources. That state needs to be stored, so it can be started, stopped, copied, moved, or deleted, just like the traditional servers that can be brought up, taken down, cloned, reracked, or decommissioned, respectively. Server virtualization makes use of a hosting file system; in essence, what used to be a server with CPU, memory, disks, and network cards is now encapsulated in a single file residing either on the local physical hardware or on remote shared storage.

In many situations, using remote shared storage has distinct advantages over local storage on each physical server. With remote shared storage, all the physical hosts are able to access the same disk space, which effectively allows virtual machines to be run on any of them. Figure 11-4 depicts the principle of remote shared storage leveraged for server virtualization.

Shared storage access also allows administrators to move a virtual machine from one host to another, in some cases with zero disruption to the service offered by that virtual machine. It is referred to as live migration. Such moves can also be prompted by availability or underlying physical resources, such as a virtual machine moving from one physical server to another due to insufficient physical memory.

Remote shared storage can be accessed from the hosts in a variety of ways over Ethernet (such as Fibre Channel over Ethernet [FCoE]), IP (such as iSCSI), or Fibre Channel networks. Shared storage itself can consist of traditional storage arrays (network-attached storage [NAS] or storage-area network [SAN]) or increasingly popular hyper-converged systems based on x86 distributed storage.

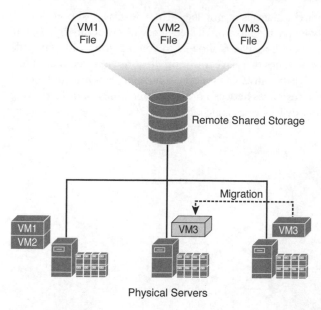

Figure 11-4 *Remote Shared Storage for Server Virtualization*

Management Tools

Server virtualization probably would have not taken off in such a dramatic fashion if not for the management tools it offered. Consolidation of computing resources in a form of virtual machines increased server infrastructure utilization and allowed building a larger computing power footprint. Unfortunately, an increase in the amount of virtual servers also resulted in increased administration overhead. Because IT organizations remained under the ever-increasing pressure of doing more for less, the need for better management tools became absolutely necessary.

The virtualization management tool is also referred to as Virtual Machine Manager. Virtual Machine Manager products exist for all the major types of server virtualization solutions. They help create, edit, clone, start, stop, and move virtual machines (VMs). They help view performance characteristics and utilization of the individual VMs and a virtualization system as a whole. Through a set of application programming interfaces (APIs), virtual machine management tools also provide a programmatic way of interacting with the server virtualization environment.

Two more popular examples of the Virtual Machine Manager product are VMware's vCenter and Microsoft's System Center. Virtual machine management tools also exist for Linux-based open hypervisors, such as KVM and Xen.

Types of Server Virtualization

Server virtualization is not a one-size-fits-all approach. Over the years there have been several approaches to implementing server virtualization technology. In this chapter we will look at three main approaches powering server virtualization, but before we step into it, it is important to understand the relevant portion of x86 architecture revolving around its levels of privileges.

11

x86 architecture defines four hierarchical levels of privilege. These levels are also known as rings. Rings are layered in the way where the most privileged access is given through Ring 0, where the operating system running on the server is allowed to communicate with physical resources, such as CPU and memory. Rings that have lower privilege are allowed to communicate to the rings having higher privilege only in a predefined manner. This provides a level of control to prevent misuse of the resources between programs operating on different ring levels. Figure 11-5 depicts the x86 privilege rings concept.

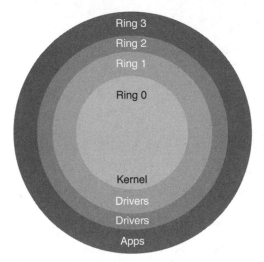

Figure 11-5 *Privilege Rings of the x86 Architecture*

Full Virtualization

Operating systems written for x86 architecture were designed to work on top of bare metal servers having direct access to the underlying server hardware components. By residing in Ring 0 of the x86 privilege access architecture, these operating systems assume that they are the sole owners of the server hardware resources allowing them to execute privileged instructions. Applications running on those operating systems typically leverage Ring 3.

To achieve x86 virtualization with a full virtualization model, a shim layer of software is put below the server operating system to manage shared access to the underlying physical resources. This software is called the hypervisor or Virtual Machine Monitor. Hypervisor software interacts directly with the physical server components, such as CPU, memory, disk, and network, and serves as a platform for deploying virtual machine constructs on top. This requires the hypervisor to operate in Ring 0 privileged access level, while the actual server operating system, also referred to as the guest operating system, operates in Ring 1. User applications still operate in Ring 3. Figure 11-6 depicts the ring privileged access layer in virtualized x86 architecture.

Full virtualization achieves complete separation between the virtual machines, so each virtual machine is not aware of the other virtual machine's existence. At the same time, each guest operating system believes it has exclusive access to the server resources. In reality, hypervisor software takes care of allocating and scheduling this access. Not all instructions can be virtualized, and it is the function of the hypervisor to replace such instructions with new sequences that have the intended effect on the virtual hardware. Binary translation and direct execution make this possible.

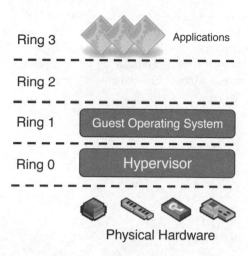

Figure 11-6 *Full Virtualization Privileged Access*

Because virtual machines are fully isolated, each virtual machine can run a completely different type of the server operating system; for example, Windows and Linux operating systems can coexist on the same virtualized server independently.

Paravirtualization

Paravirtualization is another form of server virtualization technology in which the guest operating system running inside the virtual machine communicates with the hypervisor to improve its performance characteristics.

Contrary to the full virtualization technique in which the guest operating system is unaware it is running on top of the virtualized hardware, with paravirtualization the guest operating system is allowed additional communication channels with the underlying hypervisor to make better use of the physical server hardware. Paravirtualization offers guest operating system software interfaces, which are close to the real physical server hardware, but not identical. Performance characteristics gains are achieved by having the guest operating system communicate directly with the hypervisor without going through the emulation process of a full virtualization technique.

To support paravirtualization, most of the guest operating systems need to be modified. This is different from the full virtualization, where the entire operating system is encapsulated in the virtual machine construct. This can be good and bad. The obvious bad side is that most operating systems cannot run as is on top of the paravirtualization solution, which limits deployment choices for the operating systems that cannot be modified to support paravirtualization. The good side is that paravirtualized guest operating systems have direct control over underlying resources, which allows them to achieve better performance. Because paravirtualized guest operating systems are aware of the demands placed on the

11

physical server, the result is that fewer system resources, traditionally required for the emulation process, are consumed by the hypervisor software itself.

For the privileged access, paravirtualization leverages a method somewhat similar to full virtualization. In this case, the paravirtualized guest operating system runs in Ring 0, communicating with the virtualization layer below by issuing what is known as hypercalls to replace nonvirtualizable instructions. Hypercalls are also used for other critical kernel operations. Figure 11-7 depicts the privileged access structure in a paravirtualized environment.

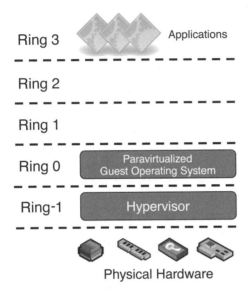

Figure 11-7 *Paravirtualization Privileged Access*

Operating System Virtualization

Operating system virtualization offers a different approach to server virtualization. It describes the model where separate environments run on top of a single shared operating system kernel without the use of hypervisor software. In other words, the host operating system running on the server performs functions that otherwise would have been performed by the hypervisor software. Separate environments run in a form of multiple isolated user space instances, sometimes also referred to as containers. Figure 11-8 depicts the operating system virtualization concept.

Examples of operating systems supporting the operating system virtualization model include FreeBSD Jail, Solaris containers, and OpenVZ. In addition to isolation, shared kernel provides an underlying physical resource management function to make sure a single user space instance does not starve other instances.

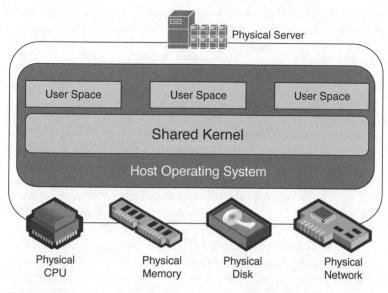

Figure 11-8 *Operating System Virtualization Concept*

The most significant advantage of the operating system virtualization model is that leveraging a single host operating system has far fewer resource demands than using full or paravirtualization techniques. This ultimately allows deploying a higher density of virtual machine instances per server and drives an even higher rate of server consolidation. The downside is that because all virtual machines rely on the same shared host operating system kernel, the operating system virtualization technique does not allow running different flavors of the guest operating system. In other words, you cannot run Linux and Microsoft Windows on the same server leveraging operating system virtualization model. It might, however, be possible to run different versions of the same Linux operating system on a single system.

Because operating system virtualization supports only homogeneous operating system environments, it might not fit all server virtualization scenarios. However, its low resource overhead makes it a compelling option where full encapsulation is not required.

Server Virtualization Benefits and Challenges

From the onset of x86 server virtualization, and definitely in the latest era when server virtualization became a popular technology across vast market segments, organizations have been reaping significant benefits from it. Server virtualization, however, is not without its own challenges. In this section we look at the main benefits and challenges of the server virtualization.

Server Virtualization Benefits

Cloud computing changed the economics of deploying private infrastructure inside organizations. It allowed organizations to achieve greater deployment agility in accordance with changing business needs. It also promoted deployment flexibility by offering new services in a fraction of the time. For service providers, cloud computing meant the capability to capture market segments by offering and reselling cloud services to organizations interested in consuming this capacity only on an as-needed basis, rather than owning it. The linkage of private and public cloud concepts created a notion of hybrid cloud, where public cloud resources can be leveraged to augment private cloud capacity with the capability to burst into the public cloud during the times of high resource demand. With its capability to abstract underlying server physical resources while maintaining strict control over their utilization, server virtualization plays a key role in enabling cloud computing.

Decoupling the server operating system from the underlying physical server hardware has significant implications for reliability of virtual machines. This manifests itself in the ability to have virtual machines move across the physical hosts in real time without incurring application downtime. Administrators wanting to perform maintenance tasks on the physical host can migrate virtual machines off of it before commencing work. Virtual machine migration can also occur as a result of unexpected failures or resource shortage. Live virtual machine migration is supported on all major hypervisor platforms. The ability to migrate virtual machines between main and backup sites can assist in disaster recovery situations. Such migration can occur in real time if the distance between the data centers is not significant; otherwise, the virtual machine can be migrated offline.

Instantiation of virtual machines happens in no time when compared to the similar task performed on the bare metal servers. Virtual machines can also be provisioned to allow an elastic capacity that can grow and shrink based on the computing resource requirements in the environment. Virtual machines can be copied or cloned for even faster provisioning. Agility is the key in today's data center environments.

The basic premise of server virtualization is to maximize server resource utilization by creating several instances of the server operating system running on the same physical server hardware, which results in consolidation of computing resources. Having fewer, and many times significantly fewer, physical servers results in reduced facility expenses, such as space, power, and cooling, as well as fewer administrative touch points.

Servers are usually the most vulnerable components of the solution, and keeping them compliant with organizational security policy is a daunting task. The ability to clone virtual machines allows creating what is many times known as a "golden image." This image includes all server-side security protections in accordance with organizational security policy. Any new virtual machine brought online can be cloned from the "golden image," automatically inheriting its operating system security properties. If the virtual machine becomes compromised, it can be quickly decommissioned, and a new instance of it can be created. Note that the new instance might not have all application components existing in the old one, so restoring from backup might still be required.

Server Virtualization Challenges

Server virtualization makes use of virtual switching components to establish connectivity between the virtual machines on the same physical server, between virtual machines on different physical servers, and between virtual machines and bare metal nonvirtualization servers. Network connectivity in and out of the virtualized server relies on the switching design implemented in the data center network. At the time of writing this book, the most predominant design for data center networks is still a multilayer design, where servers are connected to access layer switches operating at OSI Layer 2. With this design, access layer switches are provisioned with trunked Ethernet links toward the virtualized servers. VLANs added to the trunk represent IP subnets existing on that virtualized server. Virtual switches in the hypervisor need to be configured to trunk the same VLANs back to the data center network. Figure 11-9 depicts networking concepts between data center access layer switches and virtualized servers.

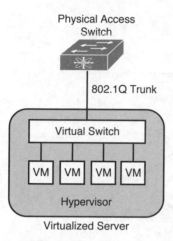

Figure 11-9 *Networking Between Data Center Access Layer Switch and Virtualized Server*

Server virtualization administrators most often have exclusive access to the Virtual Machine Manager tools. When new IP subnets or VLANs are provisioned for the server virtualization environment in the physical data center network, server virtualization administrators are required to make necessary changes on the trunks provisioned between the virtual and physical switches. Coordination between network administrators and server virtualization administrators is required. This pain-point is the focus of the most recent data center architectures, such as Cisco's Application Centric Infrastructure (ACI), where provisioning of virtual switching in the hypervisor and physical switching in the data center switching fabric are coordinated through the use of software-defined networking (SDN) principles.

Although VLANs provide a basic means for connectivity, other concepts, such as quality of service (QoS), should also be coordinated. Should the guest operating system running inside the virtual machine decide to mark its packets with priority bits, those bits will be honored and acted upon in the physical data center network.

During live virtual machine migration events, the guest operating system running inside the virtual machine is expected to keep servicing user requests, so it must retain its TCP/IP properties throughout the migration event. Such properties also refer to virtual machine IP address. This means that source and destination physical hosts, which virtual machine migrates from and to respectively, have to accommodate the same VLAN and IP subnet. This requirement can be quite challenging in environments employing the data center design principle of POD, where VLANs and IP subnets are contained within a specific building block defined by a pair of data center aggregation layer switches. Typically in POD design, VLANs and IP subnets are not extended across the aggregation layer switch boundary, which limits the scope of the

11

virtual machine mobility domain and may hinder the ability to deliver on cross-organizational server virtualization policy. Popularity of POD designs stems from their capability to limit the stretch of Spanning Tree Protocol (STP) domains, which was and still is a strong recommendation for data center networks making use of STP. Figure 11-10 depicts the constricting nature of POD design on the virtual machine mobility domain.

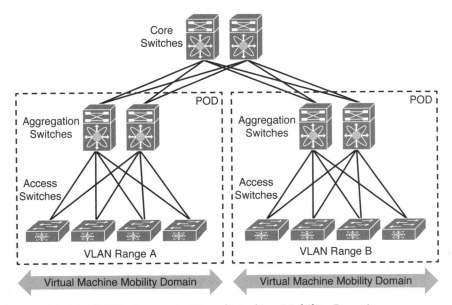

Figure 11-10   *PODs Constrain Virtual Machine Mobility Domain*

One solution is to leverage the data center switching fabric approach, which does not rely on STP for constructing forwarding topology. At the time of writing this book, Cisco offers three solutions for such a fabric: ACI, VXLAN, and FabricPath. These solutions use overlay tunneling technology and Spine-Leaf architecture, which can safely extend Layer 2 connectivity allowing a larger virtual machine mobility domain. Overlay tunnels can be provisioned between the hypervisors, between the hypervisors and physical switches, or between the physical switches only. Figure 11-11 depicts overlay tunnel deployment options. At the time of writing this book, Cisco FabricPath technology can be deployed only on physical switches.

Consolidation of servers through the use of server virtualization technology has implications on data center network capacities. The more virtual machines are deployed on a physical server, the more network traffic can be potentially generated out of that physical server onto a data center network. As virtual machines migrate between the physical servers, they can contribute to network bandwidth "hot spots," where network capacity provisioned in that particular part of the data center network may not be sufficient to accommodate traffic generated by those virtual machines. The somewhat unpredictable nature of virtual machine migration makes the task of planning for sufficient network capacity across the board a daunting one. Figure 11-12 depicts a possible scenario where virtual machine mobility can contribute to network bandwidth hot spots.

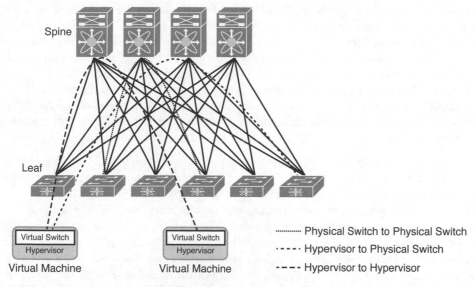

.... Physical Switch to Physical Switch

---- Hypervisor to Physical Switch

---- Hypervisor to Hypervisor

Figure 11-11   *Overlay Tunnel Deployment Options*

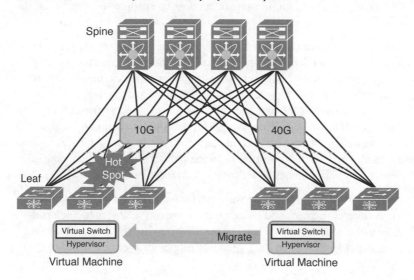

Figure 11-12   *Virtual Machine Migration and Network Bandwidth Hot Spots*

Tighter integration between virtual machine management tools and tools responsible for network infrastructure provisioning is required to make sure the two do not operate in silos.

Security is top of mind for nearly all data center networks. In the pre-server virtualization world, each port on the physical switch was connected to a single server. Communication between the servers and communication between clients and servers could be subjected to security policy. Server virtualization introduces a new paradigm of virtual switching, where virtual machines are connected to virtual switches both residing on the virtualized physical server. These virtual machines can belong to the same or a different Layer 2 segment, the VLAN.

11

Network traffic between virtual machines belonging to the same Layer 2 segment on the same physical server is switched locally within the virtual switch and is never forwarded through the physical network. Network traffic between virtual machines belonging to different Layer 2 segments on the same physical server, between virtual machines residing on different physical servers, or between virtual machines and physical nonvirtualized servers, is forwarded through the physical network. The second case is similar to the pre-server virtualization operation; however, the first case introduces a new set of challenges securing virtual machine traffic. A solution is needed to make sure that all possible traffic forwarding patterns can be secured.

One approach is in-hypervisor security, where traffic between two virtual machines belonging to the same Layer 2 segment and being on the same physical server is secured by tools operating in synergy with virtual switching. Cisco offers its Virtual Security Gateway product, which leverages Cisco vPath technology to steer virtual machine traffic toward the security inspection point for security policy validation. When the security policy is validated, the resulting decision is cached within the hypervisor, so subsequent network traffic can be switched in fast-path. The Cisco VSG product relies on a Cisco Nexus 1000v virtual switch installed in the hypervisor. Cisco also offers virtual Adaptive Security Appliance, the ASA, which runs in the hypervisor to secure network traffic at the tenant boundary. Both VSG and virtual ASA products provide in-hypervisor services to enforce security at the virtual machine level.

A different approach relies on mechanisms of "extracting" or punting network traffic from the hypervisor into the physical network for inspection. This approach can increase the latency incurred by the network traffic between two virtual machines residing on the same physical server, where rather than being switched locally by the virtual switch, traffic is now forwarded to a physical upstream switch and back into the physical server for delivery to a destination virtual machine. This traffic "hairpinning" through the upstream physical switch can sound inefficient; however, it contributes to ubiquitous security policy across physical and virtual infrastructure, which in turn contributes to the overall security policy consistency. Figure 11-13 depicts both approaches to securing virtual machine traffic.

Similar considerations apply to QoS for the network traffic between the virtual machines belonging to the same Layer 2 segment and being on the same physical server. Such traffic is switched locally within the virtualized server and never reaches the physical network boundary. The virtual switch deployed in the hypervisor is responsible for enforcing QoS characteristics in that case.

If virtual machines belong to different Layer 2 segments, or if they reside on different physical servers, the physical network can take part in enforcing QoS characteristics. In this case, the virtual machine or the virtual switch can set desired network traffic priority markings in the form of IP precedence or differentiated services code point (DSCP) on the outbound packets, which can be acted upon by the physical network to make sure that QoS characteristics are enforced for this type of traffic.

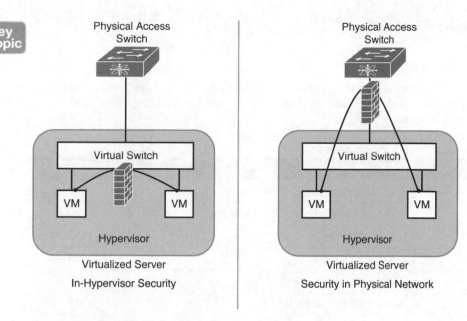

Figure 11-13 *Methods of Securing Virtual Machine Traffic*

Reference List

Security and Virtualization in the Data Center: http://www.cisco.com/c/en/us/td/docs/solutions/Enterprise/Data_Center/DC_3_0/dc_sec_design.html

Securing Virtual Applications and Servers: http://www.cisco.com/c/en/us/solutions/collateral/data-center-virtualization/unified-network-services-uns/white_paper_c11-652663.pdf

Four Steps to Virtualization: How to Start a Server Project: http://www.cisco.com/cisco/web/solutions/small_business/resource_center/articles/do_business_better/four_steps_to_vitualization/index.html

The ROI of Virtualization: Get Big Results from Your Servers: http://www.cisco.com/cisco/web/solutions/small_business/resource_center/articles/do_business_better/the_roi_of_virtualization/index.html

11

Exam Preparation Tasks

Review All Key Topics

Review the most important topics in the chapter, noted with the key topic icon in the outer margin of the page. Table 11-2 lists a reference of these key topics and the page numbers on which each is found.

Table 11-2   Key Topics for Chapter 11

Key Topic Element	Description	Page
Figure 11-1	"Server Virtualization Principles"	407
Figure 11-3	"Virtual Switching Traffic Forwarding"	410
Paragraph	Full Virtualization	412
Paragraph	Paravirtualization	413
Paragraph	Operating System Virtualization	414
Paragraph	Server Virtualization Benefits	415
Paragraph	Server Virtualization Challenges	416
Figure 11-10	"PODs Constrain Virtual Machine Mobility Domain"	418
Figure 11-11	"Overlay Tunnel Deployment Options"	419
Figure 11-13	"Methods of Securing Virtual Machine Traffic"	421

Define Key Terms

Define the following key terms from this chapter, and check your answers in the Glossary:

Hypervisor, Virtual Machine Monitor, Full Virtualization, Paravirtualization, Operating System Virtualization, Guest Operating System

Part III Review

Keep track of your part review progress with the checklist shown in Table PIII-1. Details on each task follow the table.

Table PIII-1 Part III Review Checklist

Activity	First Date Completed	Second Date Completed
Repeat all "Do I Know This Already?" Questions		
Answer "Part Review" Questions		
Review Key Topics		
Self-Assessment Questionnaire		

Repeat All "Do I Know This Already?" Questions: For this task, answer the "Do I Know This Already?" questions again for the chapters in this part of the book, using the PCPT software. Refer to "How to View Only 'Do I Know This Already?' Questions by Part" in the Introduction to this book for help with how to make the PCPT software show you DIKTA questions for this part only.

Answer "Part Review" Questions: For this task, answer the "Part Review" questions for this part of the book, using the PCPT software. Refer to "How to View Only Part Review Questions by Part" in the Introduction for help with how to make the PCPT software show you "Part Review" questions for this part only.

Review Key Topics: Browse back through the chapters and look for the Key Topic icons. If you do not remember some details, take the time to reread those topics.

Self-Assessment Questionnaire: Each chapter of this book introduces a number of key learning items. This might seem overwhelming to you initially, but as you read through each new chapter, you will become more familiar and comfortable with them, which will help you remember the concepts and technologies of these key topics as you progress with the book.

For this self-assessment exercise in the book, without looking back at the chapters or your notes, you should try to answer these self-assessment questions to the best of your ability. This exercise lists a set of key self-assessment questions, which are relevant to the particular chapter, shown in the following list. There will be no written answers to these questions in this book; if you are not certain, please go back and refresh on the key topics.

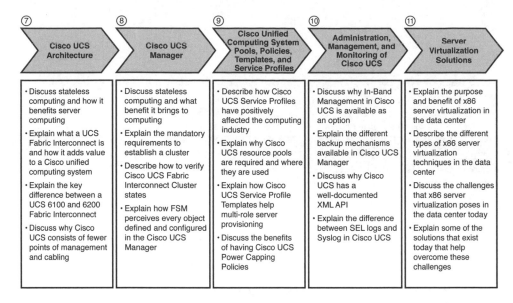

- Think of each of these open self-assessment questions as being about the chapters you have read. You may or may not find the answer explicitly, but the chapter is structured to give you the knowledge and understanding to be able to discuss and explain these self-assessment questions. For example, number 7 is about UCS product and architecture, number 8 is about operating Cisco UCS Manager, number 11 is about server virtualization solutions, and so on.

- Note your answer and try to reference key words in the answer from the relevant chapter. For example, Cisco UCS service profile would apply to Chapter 9, "Cisco Unified Computing System Pools, Policies, Templates, and Service Profiles."

Exam topics covered in Part IV:

- 5.1 Describe the architecture of an ACI environment
  - 5.1a Basic policy resolution
  - 5.1b APIC Controller
  - 5.1c Spine leaf
  - 5.1d APIs
- 5.2 Describe the fabric discovery process
- 5.3 Describe the policy-driven, multitier application deployment model and its benefits
- 5.4 Describe the ACI logical model
  - 5.4a Tenants
  - 5.4b Context
  - 5.4c Bridge domains
  - 5.4d EPG
  - 5.4e Contracts

Part IV

Application Centric Infrastructure

This chapter covers the following exam topics:

5.0 Application Centric Infrastructure

5.1 Describe the Architecture of an ACI Environment

5.1a Basic Policy Resolution

5.1b APIC Controller

5.1c Spine Leaf

5.1d APIs

5.2 Describe the Fabric Discovery Process

CHAPTER 12

ACI Architecture

The Cisco Application Centric Infrastructure journey started a couple of years ago, culminating in its first customer shipment (FCS) on July 31, 2014. A team of veteran leaders and engineers from the Cisco Insieme Business Unit (*Insieme* is an Italian word that means *together* in English) decided to continue to disrupt markets to drive industry transformation. Their latest disruption is focused on leapfrogging software-defined networks (SDN) with a holistic approach to the future of networking: application centric infrastructure, or ACI for short. Cisco Insieme Business Unit engineers had a simple goal: to design an infrastructure for customers that meets the needs of applications today and in the future. These applications require a dynamic, agile, fast, secure, scalable, reliable infrastructure that is automated as a native, baseline requirement.

The Cisco approach to SDN is very different from other models. In this chapter we will demystify SDN. ACI goes beyond SDN to help customers deliver business outcomes and network device programmability. By looking at the problem holistically, Cisco has taken into account the variety of needs from a wide range of customers. ACI was designed to provide an infrastructure with the intent for co-existence of both physical and virtual networking worlds.

By focusing on the delivery of the application, Cisco built a network based on its business requirements, including security and user experience services (Layer 4 through Layer 7). Simplicity is a core part of ACI. The simplicity comes through the use of a common policy framework that empowers teams across the IT environment with the ability to more rapidly and cost-effectively deploy applications. ACI automates across network, security, and application teams driving consistency of policies, and at the core—as there should be—scale, security, and support for multitenancy. This means a single network can run workloads for multiple purposes: existing and emerging cloud applications, and development lifecycles spanning enterprise, service provider, and cloud provider customers.

Today's data center has workloads that are 70 percent virtualized, not 100 percent, and servers are only about one-third virtualized. With new high-growth applications being bare metal in nature—such as Big Data and the emerging Linux containers disrupting virtual machines—in 5 to 7 years, it will be less virtual in the traditional sense.

The networks of the future will be an elaboration of the mixed workloads of today. Virtual machines will be used for specific workloads, bare metal for others, and Linux containers like Docker for another set.

ACI took an approach that normalizes each of these, allowing them to be used where required and without the need for separate network tools. With the inherent flexibility of deploying ACI, customers can gracefully transition to the required 10G, 40G, and 100G speeds without the need for rip-and-replace of existing networks and cabling plants.

ACI supports service insertion and chaining for *any* service device. Therefore, customers can leverage their existing model of deploying and operating their Layer 4 through Layer 7 device while automating network connectivity. ACI is delivering consistent policy-driven automation across multiple data centers to enable application mobility and disaster recovery. ACI provides flexibility to perform any operation through NX-OS style command-line interface (CLI) leveraging application policy infrastructure controller (APIC) as a single point of management—providing a single switch view for the entire ACI Fabric.

This chapter discusses the ACI in four main areas: the ACI architecture and how it ties to SDN, the Cisco APIC and ACI components, the application programming interface (API), and basic policy resolution in ACI.

This chapter is written to clearly outline the product portfolio, fundamental concepts, valid architectures, and advantages of ACI. This chapter is not an official product or configuration guide, however; refer to the appropriate official documents to evaluate products, design, and configure solutions with Cisco ACI. This chapter goes directly into the key concepts of ACI and discusses topics relevant to "The 200-155 DCICT Introducing Cisco Data Center Technologies" certification.

"Do I Know This Already?" Quiz

The "Do I Know This Already?" quiz enables you to assess whether you should read this entire chapter thoroughly or jump to the "Exam Preparation Tasks" section. If you are in doubt about your answers to these questions or your own assessment of your knowledge of the topics, read the entire chapter. Table 12-1 lists the major headings in this chapter and their corresponding "Do I Know This Already?" quiz questions. You can find the answers in Appendix A, "Answers to the 'Do I Know This Already?' Quizzes."

Table 12-1   "Do I Know This Already?" Section-to-Question Mapping

Foundation Topics Section	Questions
"What's an Application Programming Interface (API)?"	1
"Network Management Options"	2
"Cisco Software-Defined Networking (SDN)"	3, 4, 5, 6
"The Policy-Based Model"	9
"Spine-Leaf Data Center Design"	7
"ACI Fabric Hardware—Cisco Nexus 9000 Family"	8, 13
"Application Policy Infrastructure Controller (APIC)"	10
"VXLAN Forwarding"	11
"Mapping Database"	12
"ACI Fabric Provisioning and Startup Discovery"	14

1. Which of the following options are true for primary components of application programming interface (API)? (Choose two.)

   a. The data can be represented in JSON.

   b. A uniform resource identifier is a string of characters used to identify a resource.

   c. The API call is described as a noun.

   d. ERASE is an example of the commonly used API operations.

   e. Projects describe the mechanism of the API implementations.

2. Which of the following options are the key requirements for management protocols as expressed in RFC 3535? (Choose two.)

   a. The payload must be human readable.

   b. The payload must be text based.

   c. Transactions must be dependent and short lived.

   d. The payload must be in HTML format.

3. Which of the following options are true for software-defined networking? (Choose three.)

   a. SDN is decoupling of the control plane and the data plane.

   b. In the SDN architecture, network intelligence is centralized in a controller.

   c. SDN is coupling of the control plane and the digital plane.

   d. The programmable control APIs are exposed in the SDN environment.

   e. SDN is most effectively used in cloud computing.

4. What are the core components of OpenFlow? (Choose three.)

   a. Controller

   b. OpenFlow Agent

   c. South APIs

   d. Northbound APIs

   e. OpenControl Protocol

5. Which of the following options are the common use cases for software-defined networking beyond general cloud and data center? (Choose three.)

   a. DevOps

   b. Big Data

   c. IT automation

   d. Change management

   e. Business recovery

12

6. What are the advantages of a group-based policy? (Choose three.)

   a. An easier, application-focused way of expressing policy

   b. Improved automation

   c. Extensible policy model, Layers 4 through 7 services

   d. Everything-as-a-Service

   e. Advanced security

7. Which of the following options are the main benefits of Cisco application centric infrastructure? (Choose three.)

   a. Simplified automation with an application-based policy model

   b. Open software flexibility for development and operations (DevOps)

   c. Scalable performance and secure multitenancy

   d. Open storage resources

   e. Practices of imperative management model

8. Which of the following options are the components of Cisco ACI? (Choose three.)

   a. Cisco application policy infrastructure controller (APIC)

   b. Cisco Nexus 9000 Series switches

   c. Cisco Nexus 1000 Series switches

   d. Cisco application virtual switch (AVS)

   e. Cisco FabricPath protocol

9. Which of the following approaches is used in the Cisco application centric infrastructure?

   a. Imperative management model

   b. Declarative management model

10. Which of the following tools are used to access APIC? (Choose three.)

   a. GUI

   b. Cisco UCS Director

   c. Cisco VTS

   d. POSTMAN

   e. CLI on Cisco Nexus 7000

11. Which of the following statements are correct for VXLAN? (Choose three.)

   a. VXLAN provides greater scalability in the number of Layer 2 segments that are supported.

   b. VXLAN can scale up to 4000 individual segments.

   c. VXLAN uses MAC-in-UDP.

   d. VXLAN uses a 24-byte header.

   e. Cisco ACI uses VXLAN in ACI Fabric.

12. Which of the following options explain how ACI Fabric learns the location of the endpoint in the fabric? (Choose three.)

    a. The administrator can statically program the identity-to-location mapping.

    b. DHCP packets can be used.

    c. Learning can occur through ARP.

    d. Learning can occur through VMware host discovery.

    e. The unknown unicast flooding can be eliminated for the learning.

13. Which of the following Cisco Nexus switches can be used as the spine? (Choose three.)

    a. Nexus 9516

    b. Nexus 9508

    c. Nexus 9336PQ

    d. Nexus 9736PQ

    e. Nexus 9372PX

14. Which of the following protocols are used in ACI Fabric discovery? (Choose two.)

    a. LLDP

    b. DHCP

    c. THRILL

    d. EBGP

    e. REST

12

Foundation Topics

What's an Application Programming Interface (API)?

An application programming interface (API) is a specification of how some software components should interact with each other and a set of routines, protocols, and tools for building software.

Most applications expose some sort of API that governs how an application can be accessed by other applications. APIs represent a means through which elements or applications can be programmatically controlled and describe how external applications can gain access to capabilities and functions within another application. APIs have four primary components:

- **Methods:** Describe the mechanism of the API implementation including how resources communicate, provide encapsulation, and more.

- **Actions:** This is the intent of the API call, often referred to as a verb. It describes the operations available, such as GET, PUT, POST, and DELETE.

- **Objects:** This is the resource the user is trying to access. It is often referred to as a noun, and it is typically a uniform resource identifier (URI). A URI is a string of characters that identify a resource.

- **Formats:** This is how the data is represented, such as JSON or XML.

The following characteristics of an API enable users to build a more efficient, manageable, and reliable network via automation:

- **Modularity:** Applications can be built leveraging clearly defined and reusable modules.

- **Abstraction:** APIs abstract the details of the underlying implementation from the higher level logic that invokes it.

- **Stability:** APIs provide a stable and consistent interface.

Network Management Options

The networking industry has developed various approaches to network management. The industry's network management technologies and protocols that are currently used the most include REST, Network Configuration Protocol (NETCONF), and Simple Network Management Protocol (SNMP). Table 12-2 outlines the differences.

Table 12-2   Comparison of REST, NETCONF, and SNMP

	REST	NETCONF	SNMP
Transport	HTTP/HTTPS	SSH	UDP
Payload formatting	XML, JSON	XML	BER
Schema		YANG	MIBs
Identification of resources	URLs	Paths	OIDs

The following are the key requirements for management protocols as expressed in RFC 3535:

- The payload must be human readable.
- The payload must be text based for ease of revision control.
- Transactions must follow the ACID rules; they must be atomic, consistent, independent, and durable.

Over the past several years, vendors realized that just offering a standard CLI was not going to cut it anymore and that using a CLI severely held back operations. The major pain point was that scripting with legacy, or CLI-based network devices, was not object oriented and did not return structured data. This meant data was returned from the device to a script in a raw text format—that is, the output of a *show version*—and then the individual writing the script needed to parse that text manually to extract attributes such as *uptime* and *operating system version*. Although this approach was all administrators had, vendors are gradually migrating to API-driven network devices.

The Cisco APIC supports a comprehensive RESTful API over HTTP(S) with XML and JSON encoding bindings. The API provides both class-level and tree-oriented data access.

Representational state transfer (REST) is a style of software architecture for distributed systems such as the World Wide Web. REST has emerged over the past few years as a predominant web services design model. It has increasingly displaced other design models such as SOAP and Web Services Description Language (WSDL) due to its simpler style.

The uniform interface that any REST interface must provide is considered fundamental to the design of any REST service; thus, the interface has these guiding principles:

- **Identification of resources:** Individual resources are identified in requests, such as using URIs in web-based REST systems. The resources themselves are conceptually separate from the representations that are returned to the client.
- **Manipulation of resources through these representations:** When a client holds a representation of a resource, including any metadata attached, it has enough information to modify or delete the resource on the server, provided it has permission to do so.
- **Self-descriptive messages:** Each message includes enough information to describe how to process the message. Responses also explicitly indicate their cache ability.
- An important concept in REST is the existence of resources (sources of specific information), each of which is referenced with a global identifier, such as a URI in HTTP. To manipulate these resources, components of the network (user agents and origin servers) communicate through a standardized interface such as HTTP and exchange representations of these resources (the actual documents conveying the information).

Any number of connectors (clients, servers, caches, tunnels, and more) can mediate the request, but each does so without seeing past its own request (referred to as layering, another constraint of REST and a common principle in many other parts of information and networking architecture). Thus, an application can interact with a resource by knowing two things: the identifier of the resource and the action required. The application does not need to know whether there are caches, proxies, gateways, firewalls, tunnels, or anything else between it and the server actually holding the information. The application does, however, need to understand the format of the information (representation) returned, which is typi-cally an HTML, XML, or JSON document of some kind, although it may be an image, plain text, or any other content.

Cisco Software-Defined Networking (SDN)

The Open Network Foundation (ONF) defines SDN as a decoupling of the control plane and the data plane. Traditional network devices have an integrated control plane and data plane. In classic SDN architecture, network intelligence is logically centralized in a controller, and there is a physical separation between the control plane and the data plane. As the central control point, the controller can simplify and automate the orchestration of the network, enabling organizations to improve the intelligence, agility, scalability, and cost effectiveness of their overall infrastructure. It does this by using the programmable control APIs that are exposed in an SDN environment; these APIs enable the controller to communicate to the switches/routers below (via southbound APIs) and applications/services above (via north-bound APIs). Figure 12-1 demonstrates an SDN stack. When conceptualized by networking researchers at Stanford back in 2008, it was meant to manipulate the data plane to optimize traffic flows and make adjustments, so the network could quickly adapt to changing requirements.

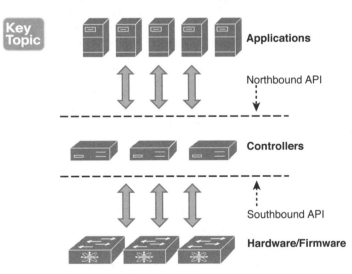

Figure 12-1 *SDN Stack*

The controllers expose open northbound APIs, which applications use. These applications use the controller to gather network intelligence, run algorithms to perform analytics, and then use the controller to orchestrate the new rules, if any, throughout the network.

The controller platform itself contains a collection of dynamically pluggable modules to per-form needed network tasks. There are base network services for such tasks as understanding what devices are contained within the network and the capabilities of each, statistics gather-ing, and so on. In addition, platform-oriented services and other extensions can be inserted into the controller platform for enhanced SDN functions.

The southbound interface is capable of supporting multiple protocols (as separate plug-ins), such as OpenFlow 1.0, OpenFlow 1.3, and BGP-LS. Version 1.0 of the OpenFlow specification was released in December 2009; it continues to be enhanced under the management of the ONF, which is a user-led organization focused on advancing the development of open standards and the adoption of SDN technologies. Figure 12-2 demonstrates four core components of OpenFlow.

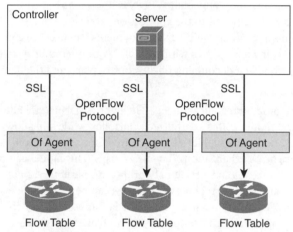

Four Parts of OpenFlow

- **Controller** – resides on a server and provides control plane function for the network.
- **OpenFlow Agent** – resides on a network device and fulfills requests from the Controller.
- **Northbound APIs** – enable applications to interface with the Controller.
- **OpenFlow Protocol** – the Layer 2 protocol that the Controller and Agents use to communicate.

Figure 12-2 *OpenFlow Components*

OpenFlow is the protocol that specifies the interactions between the control plane running in the controller and the infrastructure. The intent of this architecture is agility, automation, and a decrease in the overall costs of the network. This complete separation of the entire control plane from the data plane in a classic SDN model—removing it from the network to a centralized controller—is a radical departure from the design and operation of most networks today. OpenFlow provides an open protocol to program the flow-table in different switches and routers. If a switch (or router) supports OpenFlow, it does not mean that every packet sent through the device has to be processed through the protocol. Standard "built-

12

in" algorithms can be used for the majority of traffic, and specific destination addresses (or other packet characteristics) can be used to determine the subset that should be handled via OpenFlow. OpenFlow itself does not provide a network abstraction; that takes software that implements the protocol. Based on the spec, a controller programs the flow table of an OpenFlow switch to forward traffic in a way that you specify based on certain criteria of the frame or packet.

The classic SDN approach to network architecture introduces potential challenges in availability, performance, scale, and security. When all control plane functionality is moved to a central controller, the controller must be highly available. The performance should meet the rapid requests and extreme load conditions on the network. The controller must be able to scale to very large networks, with thousands of nodes. It must be highly secure, with only approved applications able to modify or change the underlying network. Although the classic SDN model takes advantage of network programmability, SDN is not a requirement for programmability. Network devices can be exposed to the application layer through APIs. This hybrid approach to network programmability and SDN deployments can take advantage of hardware intelligence as well as existing feature sets within the network operating system. This can be accomplished without a complete decoupling of the control plane and the data plane.

Figure 12-3 shows different network programmability models. The hybrid SDN model allows many of the benefits of a classic SDN model with a centralized controller, while still allowing users to benefit from the existing network capabilities many have come to rely upon. The third model in this figure is Network Virtualization Virtual Overlays. This model can be defined as a logical network created on top of an existing networking infrastructure. In an environment where network overlays are used, virtual network planes can be created independently from the original network. The policy intent model is the last approach for network programmability in SDN. The policy authority resides in the controller and enables the policies by talking to the policy agent, which sits in the actual network devices.

Network Programmability Models

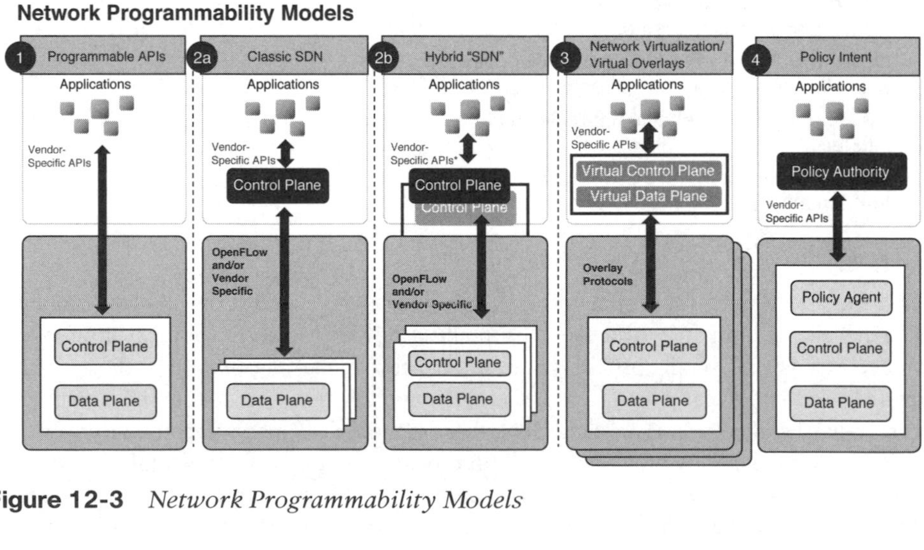

Figure 12-3 *Network Programmability Models*

SDN is rapidly changing the way that organizations view and operate networks. It primarily seeks to address the lack of agility found in existing networks. Various implementations of SDN have emerged within the industry, each seeking to address specific environments and use cases.

The Cisco position on SDN is that one size does not fit all. At the operational level, for example, manufacturing, medical, public sector, and cloud environments all have very different IT requirements. At the technology level, data center, WAN, and campus networks also have very different requirements. These differences in requirements create the need for a portfolio of solutions to address SDN and achieve the agility, portability, security, and cost savings that it promises. Figure 12-4 demonstrates requirements in different networks.

Different Networks, Different Needs

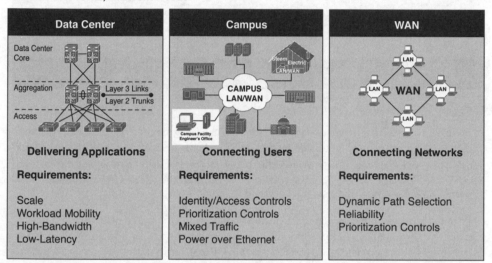

Figure 12-4 *Different Requirements with Different Needs in Data Center, Campus, and WAN Environments*

Although different, campus and WAN environments have many similarities, and in most cases their requirements can be addressed by the same SDN solutions. For these networks, Cisco supports the Cisco application policy infrastructure controller enterprise module (APIC EM) or commercially available versions of OpenDaylight (ODL).

In the data center, the landscape is much more varied. Different business requirements, sizes, and scales create disparate demands on data center networks. The needs of massively scalable data centers, service providers, and the mass market are unique. Even a single organization may have multiple data centers, each with dissimilar requirements. For example, a cloud provider may have one data center for its cloud offering and another for its internal IT resources.

The Cisco lead solution for SDN in the data center is Cisco ACI. Cisco ACI is the industry's most comprehensive SDN solution, with ready-to-use automation from the physical hardware through virtual services. This solution is targeted at the mass market as well as at specific service and cloud provider environments. Figure 12-5 demonstrates Cisco Data Center SDN solutions.

12

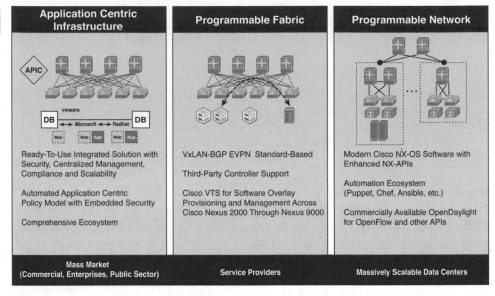

Figure 12-5 *Cisco Data Center SDN Solutions*

For service provider customers with expertise in managing separate underlay and overlay fabrics, Cisco offers programmable fabrics. These fabrics are based on industry standards such as Border Gateway Protocol and Ethernet VPN (BGP-EVPN) and virtual extensible LAN (VXLAN) and support central provisioning through the Cisco virtual topology system (VTS) controller or third-party controllers.

For massively scalable data centers, typically cloud providers, Cisco offers the industry's leading programmable network options. In these environments, the software delivering infrastructure as a service (IaaS), platform as a service (PaaS), or software as a service (SaaS) to the end customer is already designed to do most of the work. These environments need network switching with a robust set of programmability and automation tools to give customers flexible options for integrating their custom software offerings. Table 12-3 summarizes Cisco SDN solutions.

Table 12-3 Cisco Solutions

Category	Use Case	Cisco Solution
Data Center	Integrated Overlay and Underlay Policy-Based Automation	Cisco ACI
Data Center	Overlay Automation	Virtual Topology System
Data Center, Campus and WAN	OpenFlow Traffic Engineering Other Open-Source Modules	OpenDaylight Version Supported by Cisco
Campus, Branch, and WAN	WAN and LAN Automation	APIC EM

Overall, the Cisco SDN stance is customer choice. Cisco strives to provide the right options for the unique challenges of different customer environments and business models. Figure 12-6 demonstrates different Cisco SDN solutions.

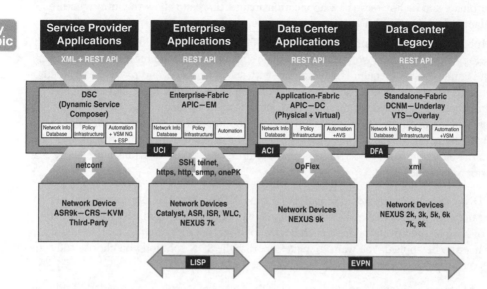

Figure 12-6 *Cisco SDN Solutions*

As networks grow, they become much more complex to manage and maintain. In the traditional model, this complexity means that ever-more IT resources are needed to handle processes such as provisioning, configuration, and remediation. These have typically been manual processes, so growing your network from 10 to 100 nodes meant that someone had to manually touch and configure 10 times as many devices.

SDN changes that equation in a fundamental way: It automates processes like provisioning, configuration, and remediation via software. Rather than requiring an IT worker to physically configure each piece of hardware, SDN enables you to roll out network changes by sending out software updates. Some common use cases for SDN beyond general cloud, data center, and IT automation include these:

- **DevOps:** DevOps, the synergistic integration of *development* and *operations,* is a rapidly emerging method of developing applications for IT organizations, with the goal of accelerating IT innovation and service delivery (coincidently, some of the same objectives as SDN). Including an SDN technology-based approach can facilitate DevOps through the automation of application updates and deployments and the automation of IT infrastructure components as the DevOps applications and platforms are deployed. DevOps gives developers more control over the IT environment, which not only implies an underlying SDN capability, but also is facilitated by an application centric approach to policies because DevOps is software application oriented.

- **Big Data and Everything-as-a-Service:** Data is routinely collected and traded in the new economy. Big Data brings with it a new class of data and server-intensive applications that present an enormous opportunity to make organizations more efficient and more competitive. But systems must be in place to efficiently and effectively harness, manage, and access it.

12

■ Clouds are taking many forms—private, public, and hybrid. Business processes are changing; service industries are exploring as-a-service, online, and virtual models to accelerate business and their engagement with customers, partners, and suppliers. SDN can help automate and deploy these new application architectures and allow the infrastructure to adapt quickly to the changing application requirements.

■ **Mobility apps and the Internet of things (IoT):** Consumer technology is reshaping technology expectations at work. A demographic shift to mobile, and more social customers and employees will require IT to integrate with social networks and provide expanded options for flexible workspaces and collaboration technologies. Also, more and more *things* are being linked (via an Internet of things, or IoT) with a view to further expansion into linking people, process, data, and devices (the Internet of everything, or IoE). The changing nature of these application types and the demands for flexibility that they place on the entire network infrastructure can be addressed by SDN solutions more easily than prior approaches.

All SDN implementations are not equal. For example, the Cisco ACI fabric encompasses smart network devices that make automating network processes much easier because you do not have to specifically address each device to properly propagate those processes where they need to be applied. You want to make sure that the SDN solution you choose fully supports the automation features you need.

Cisco has taken a different approach to policy than many SDN solution providers. Traditional SDN policies specified how the network should behave in networking terms. A better approach is to build a policy language that specifies what the business applications need from the network. Policies are defined for groups or classes of applications, and the network adjusts to the application requirements.

How the network is implemented is not directly relevant to the overall business policies of the organization. But how applications work and perform is closely related to high-level business policies and objectives. This immediately aligns IT and business policies and makes IT more responsive to business requirements.

Cisco calls this new approach *group-based policy*—an application centric policy model that separates information about application connectivity requirements from information about the underlying details of the network infrastructure. Group-based policy (GBP) makes managing the network much easier and is one of the benefits of the Cisco SDN solution. Figure 12-7 illustrates GBP.

A GBP offers a number of advantages:

■ **An easier, application-focused way of expressing policy:** By creating policies that mirror application semantics, this framework provides a simpler, self-documenting mechanism for capturing policy requirements.

■ **Improved automation:** Grouping policies allows higher level automation tools to easily manipulate groups of network endpoints and applications simultaneously.

■ **Consistency:** By grouping endpoints and applying policy to application groups, the framework offers a consistent and concise way to handle policy changes, as well as consistency across both physical and virtual workloads, and physical and virtual application services and security devices.

■ **Extensible policy model:** Because the policy model is open and can be extended to other vendors and other device types, it can easily incorporate switches, routers, security, Layer 4 through 7 services, and so on.

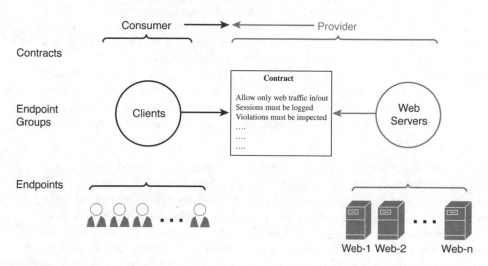

Representation of Group-Based Policy (GBP)

Figure 12-7 *Group-Based Policy*

The Policy-Based Model

The Cisco ACI addresses the need of the data center operator for automated provisioning, programmatic management, and comprehensive orchestration. Rather than decoupling the control plane from the data plane, ACI applies a policy model designed to capture application requirements and automate deployment across the network, regardless of whether the applications are virtualized or running on bare metal. This type of approach is called a *declarative management model*, and it involves the agents that publish their intentions via commitments to each other. The intentions are abstract; thus, for example, an application policy would state its requirements, and the underlying infrastructure (for example, the data center switches) would interpret how best to satisfy those requirements based on their inherent capabilities.

There are two main approaches to the SDN control plane: imperative and declarative:

■ **Imperative** describes a centralized SDN controller that acts as the brains for the SDN environment; the controller receives requests from applications via a northbound API and dictates downstream to the forwarding plane how the switches/routers need to be configured to answer the needs of the application. There is the potential for the centralized controller to become a bottleneck and a single point of failure in the network, which different implementations attempt to address. OpenFlow supports an imperative control plane, with no control/intelligence embedded in the data path. OpenFlow centralizes the network control plane on a controller and can push commands down to OpenFlow-enabled network devices.

- **Declarative** describes a model in which the SDN controller declares what the application needs and sends that message to the network fabric for the switches and routers to determine how to meet the application requirements. A declarative control plane allows for more distributed intelligence; it sets a central policy, but it gives power to network nodes to make more decisions about how to execute said policies. It is based on a concept called *promise theory*. *OpFlex* is an extensible policy protocol designed to exchange abstract policy between a network controller and a set of smart devices capable of rendering policy. OpFlex supports a declarative control plane, focusing on centralizing the policy and then pushing out some of the intelligence to the data path. For a second, let us look at how things operate at an airport. You could think of the air traffic control system as a good example of a declarative control system. Air traffic controllers tell pilots to take off or land in particular places, but they do not describe how to actually reach them. The job of actually flying the plane and adjusting the air speed, flaps, and landing gear falls on the intelligent, capable, and independent pilot. Cisco ACI and APIC support this declarative approach.

Let us talk about promise theory. In promise theory, promises are the statements of a request of a desired behavior to be performed by an agent. Promises, which are not transient or transferable, are made between agents. The agent is asked to fulfil a promise, which is a broadcast declaration of intent that contains a body, a quality/quantity, trust, and other characteristics of the desired state. We are often concerned about how we really know the configurations of all our IT infrastructure at any given time. Imagine how all the autonomous independent elements in an IT environment could be talking with one another in a loosely coupled configuration. Through promises, they form expectations of each other's behavior for cooperation and building a complete end-to-end working system.

Promise theory offers a declarative control model based on scalable control of intelligent objects, proposed in 2004 by Mark Burgess, founder of CFEngine. Mark started out as a physicist and received a PhD in theoretical physics in 1990. His interest shifted to computers, networks, and system administration. He started working on his promise theory research when he was professor of network and system administration at Oslo University College from 1994 to 2011. Mark was the coauthor of the paper titled "A Promise Theory Perspective on Data Networks" (May 2014). Cisco was one of the companies that worked with Mark on this paper.

In a system managed through the declarative control model, underlying objects handle their own configuration state changes and are responsible only for passing exceptions or faults back to the control system. This approach reduces the burden and complexity of the control system and allows greater scale. This system increases scalability by allowing the methods of underlying objects to request state changes from one another and from lower-level objects.

Declarative control systems such as Cisco ACI offer a number of advantages over imperative systems. They inherently separate out application, operation, and infrastructure requirements and allow each to be specified independently. This separation can accelerate application deployment by allowing the system, rather than the administrator, to coalesce these requirements. This policy model helps application developers, who no longer need to understand the details of the underlying systems; the solution also creates an accurate, auditable record of each developer's requests that can be a huge benefit to a cloud administrator. Systems built on declarative control can achieve high performance at scale with strong resiliency by moving complexity to edge devices, which do most of the processing. Finally, declarative systems, which allow policies to be specified in abstract terms, have strong interoperability characteristics. Multiple vendors can consume and honor the same policy without the need to have identical hardware configurations or software versions. Different vendors can continue to innovate on their platforms and expose new features as long as they honor the semantics of the abstract policy.

Within this theoretical model, ACI builds an object model for the deployment of applications, with the applications as the central focus. Traditionally, applications have been restricted by the capabilities of the network and by requirements to prevent misuse of the constructs to implement policy. Concepts such as addressing, VLAN, and security have been tied together, limiting the scale and the mobility of the application. As applications are being redesigned for mobility and web scale, this traditional approach hinders rapid and consistent deployment.

OpFlex

OpFlex is an extensible policy protocol designed to exchange abstract policy between a network controller and a set of smart devices capable of rendering policy. OpFlex relies on a separate information model understood by agents in both the controller and the devices. This information model, which exists outside the OpFlex protocol itself, must be based on abstract policy, giving each device the freedom and the flexibility to render policy within the semantic constraints of the abstraction. For this reason, OpFlex can support any device, including hypervisor switches, physical switches, and Layer 4 through 7 network services. OpFlex includes a native mechanism for identity resolution used to define declarative policies between two network endpoints.

Cisco, along with partners including Intel, Microsoft, Red Hat, Citrix, F5, Canonical, and Embrane, developed OpFlex. Cisco and its partners are working through the Internet Engineering Task Force (IETF) and open source community to standardize OpFlex and provide a reference implementation.

Spine-Leaf Data Center Design

Traditional data centers are built on a three-tier architecture with core, aggregation, and access layers (Figure 12-8), or a two-tier collapsed core with the aggregation and core layers combined into one layer.

Smaller data centers may even take advantage of a single pair of switches. This architecture accommodates a north-south traffic pattern where client data comes in from the WAN or Internet to be processed by a server in the data center and is then pushed back out of the data center. This is common for applications like web services, where most communication is between an external client and an internal server. The north-south traffic pattern permits hardware oversubscription because most traffic is funneled in and out through the lower-bandwidth WAN or Internet bottleneck.

12

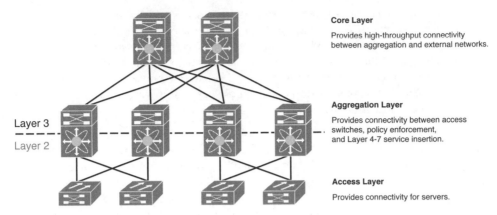

Core Layer

Provides high-throughput connectivity between aggregation and external networks.

Aggregation Layer

Provides connectivity between access switches, policy enforcement, and Layer 4-7 service insertion.

Access Layer

Provides connectivity for servers.

Figure 12-8 *Traditional Three-Tier Design*

Customers with a two- or three-tier design who want to route to the access layer yet still maintain Layer 2 reachability between servers can take the next step in the data center evolution by implementing a virtual overlay fabric. In a Cisco Nexus 9000 fabric design, dynamic routing is configured between switches down to the access layer so that all links are active. This eliminates the need for Spanning Tree on the fabric and can enable equal-cost multipath (ECMP) using the dynamic routing protocol.

A VXLAN is used to provide Layer 2 adjacencies over the Layer 3 fabric for servers and other devices that require Layer 2 reachability in the Cisco Nexus 9000 design. Combining VXLAN and a dynamic routing protocol offers the benefits of an intelligent Layer 3 routing protocol, yet can also provide Layer 2 reachability across all access switches for applications like virtual-machine workload mobility and clustering. The details of VXLAN are discussed in Chapter 5, "Data Center Overlay Networks."

The limitations of Spanning Tree in three-tier designs and the needs of modern applications are driving a shift in network design toward a spine-leaf or access-aggregation architecture. Two- and three-tier designs are still a valid and prevalent architecture; spine-leaf simply provides another easily integrated option.

Spine-leaf topologies are based on the Clos network architecture. The term originates from Charles Clos at Bell Laboratories. He published a paper in 1953 describing a mathematical theory of a multipathing, nonblocking, multiple-stage network topology to switch telephone calls through.

Today, Clos's original thoughts on design are applied to the modern spine-leaf topology. It is also known as "fat-tree" topology. Spine-leaf is typically deployed as two layers: spines (like an aggregation layer) and leaves (like an access layer). Spine-leaf topologies provide high-bandwidth, low-latency, nonblocking server-to-server connectivity.

Leaf switches give devices access to the fabric (the network of spine and leaf switches) and are typically deployed at the top of the rack. All devices connect to the leaf switches. Devices may include servers, Layer 4 through 7 services (firewalls and load balancers), and WAN or Internet routers. Leaf switches do not connect to other leaf switches. However, every leaf should connect to every spine in a full mesh. Some ports on the leaf will be used for end devices (typically at 1 Gb or 10 Gb), and some ports will be used for the spine connections (at 40 Gb).

Spine switches are used to connect to all leaf switches and are typically deployed at the end or in the middle of the row. Spine switches do not connect to other spine switches. Spines serve as backbone interconnects for leaf switches. Spines only connect to leaves.

All devices connected to the fabric are an equal number of hops away from one another. This delivers predictable latency and high bandwidth between servers. Figure 12-9 depicts a sample spine-leaf design.

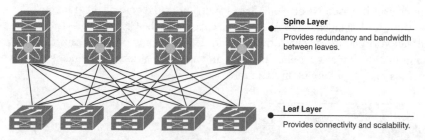

Figure 12-9 *Spine-Leaf Topology*

ACI Physical Topology and Software

Cisco ACI uses a holistic systems-based approach, with tight integration between physical and virtual elements, an open ecosystem model, and innovation-spanning ASICs, hardware, and software. It uses a common policy-based operating model across a network that supports Cisco ACI along with security elements (and computing and storage in the future).

Following are the main benefits of Cisco ACI:

- Simplified automation with an application-based policy model
- Common platform for managing physical, virtual, and cloud-based environments
- Centralized visibility with real-time application health monitoring
- Operation simplicity, with common policy, management, and operation models across application, network, and security resources (and computing and storage resources in the future)
- Open software flexibility for development and operations (DevOps) teams and ecosystem partner integration
- Scalable performance and secure multitenancy

Cisco ACI consists of the following:

- Cisco APIC
- Cisco Nexus 9000 Series switches (Cisco ACI spine and leaf switches)
- Cisco ACI ecosystem (we will discuss the ecosystem in Chapter 14, "Operating ACI")

The ACI architecture relies on the spine-leaf model, or Clos network described in the previous section. This design is well suited to the east-west traffic patterns of modern data centers, moving traffic between application tiers or components. All leaf nodes connect to all spine nodes, but a full mesh is not required. The leaf switches have two types of ports: fabric ports for connecting to spine switches and access ports for connecting servers, service appliances, routers, Fabric Extender (FEX), and so forth. Spine nodes do not connect to each other; neither do leaf nodes. Servers can be connected to two leaf switches, in a PortChannel or virtual PortChannel (vPC). Any leaf switch can also be a border leaf switch (node) for outside connectivity from each tenant. All devices can be connected through the mgmt0 port to an out-of-band management network. You can connect the out-of-band management network to the mgmt0 port of the switches and the REST API of the APIC.

Cisco ACI fabrics use the Cisco Nexus 9000 Series switches as the core of the transport system. Above this physical layer, Cisco ACI uses a controller—the Cisco APIC—to manage the data center network and its policy centrally. Cisco APIC not only provides central management and automation, but also a policy model that maps application requirements. Figure 12-10 illustrates a simple topology of an ACI fabric.

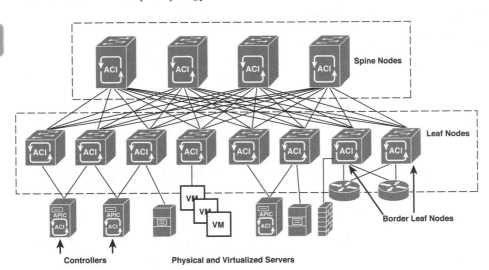

Figure 12-10 *ACI Physical Topology*

The Cisco Nexus 9000 Series can run in two modes. The first mode is called NX-OS or standalone, and it functions as a classical Nexus switch. The second mode is called ACI or fabric, and it provides an ACI. The Cisco ACI mode fabric software is an optimized version of the Cisco NX-OS Software operating system that offers a foundation for building a programmable network infrastructure. NX-OS has been rewritten as a fully object-based switch operating system for Cisco ACI. The object model enables fluid programmability and full access to the underlying components of the infrastructure using REST APIs.

NOTE   Cisco NX-OS Release 11.X works only on Cisco Nexus 9000 Series switches in ACI Mode. Between releases, patches are published on a regular basis. For every patch, there is an accompanying release note. Please refer to the Release Notes at www.cisco.com/go/aci.

The Cisco Nexus 9000 switches run on Cisco ACI software on a 64-bit Linux kernel (Release 3.4.10) with a single binary image that supports both Cisco ACI modular spine switches (Cisco Nexus 9500 platform) and fixed-port switches (Cisco Nexus 9300 platform). The software image is based on Cisco ACI Release 11.0. The single image incorporates both the Linux kernel and Cisco ACI software so that the switch can be booted through a standard Linux kickstart process.

The Cisco APIC is a physically distributed but logically centralized controller that offers Dynamic Host Configuration Protocol (DHCP), bootstrap configuration, and image management to the fabric for automated startup and upgrades. The Cisco Nexus ACI fabric software is bundled as an ISO image, which can be installed on the Cisco APIC appliance server through the serial console. The Cisco Nexus ACI Software ISO contains the Cisco APIC image, the firmware image for the leaf node and the spine node, default fabric infrastructure policies, and the protocols required for operation.

Each firmware image has corresponding image metadata that identifies supported types and switch models. The Cisco APIC maintains a catalog of the firmware images and switch types and models allowed to use that firmware image. The Cisco APIC performs image management and has an image repository for both Cisco APIC and switch images.

The Cisco NX-OS Software image runs in ACI mode and contains a major release identifier, a minor release identifier, and a maintenance release identifier. It can also contain a rebuild identifier, which might be referred to as a support patch. Cisco NX-OS Software for Nexus 9000 Series switches running in ACI mode use the numbering scheme that is shown in Figure 12-11. The Cisco NX-OS software that you use for ACI mode deployments is not the same image that you load on Cisco Nexus 9000 Series switches used in standalone mode. It is possible to convert a Cisco Nexus 9000 standalone switch to ACI mode with an ACI NX-OS software upgrade.

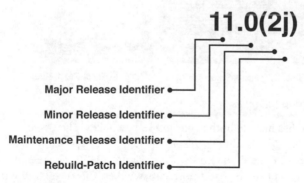

11.0(2j)

Major Release Identifier ●

Minor Release Identifier ●

Maintenance Release Identifier ●

Rebuild-Patch Identifier ●

Figure 12-11 *Cisco Nexus 9000 Series ACI-Mode Switches NX-OS Software Numbering*

12

Each APIC runs software that matches the equivalent of Cisco Nexus 9000 Series ACI-Mode NX-OS software. Figure 12-12 illustrates the software scheme for APIC.

The ACI software licenses are required only for leaf switches and Cisco Nexus 2000 Series Fabric Extenders that are connected to leaf Nexus 9300 Series switches.

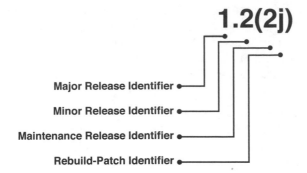

Figure 12-12 *Cisco Application Policy Infrastructure Controller Software Numbering*

ACI Fabric Hardware—Cisco Nexus 9000 Family

The Nexus 9000 Series switches include both modular and fixed-port switches. The modular Cisco Nexus 9504, 9508, and 9516 switches (Figure 12-13) are Cisco ACI spine devices enabled by nonblocking 100 and 40 Gigabit Ethernet line cards, supervisors, system controllers, and power supplies. This chapter covers the different product types available at the time this chapter was written.

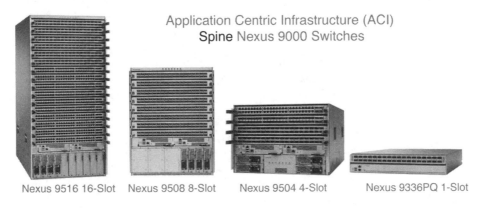

Figure 12-13 *ACI Spine Nexus 9000 Switches*

The Cisco Nexus 9300 Series switches include both spine and leaf switches. The Cisco Nexus 9336PQ ACI Spine Switch is a 2-rack-unit (2RU) spine switch for Cisco ACI that supports 2.88 Tbps of bandwidth across 36 fixed 40 QSFP+ ports (Figure 12-14). The rest of the Cisco Nexus 9300 platform is composed of fixed-port leaf switches. Cisco Nexus 9300 platform leaf switches are Layer 2 and 3 nonblocking 10 and 40 Gigabit Ethernet switches with up to 2.56 terabits per second (Tbps) of internal bandwidth. The Cisco Nexus 9336PQ form factor is well suited for smaller deployments because it provides 36 ports of 40-Gigabit Ethernet.

The Cisco Nexus 9500 platform enables scalable Cisco ACI deployments. Customers can choose from 4-, 8-, or 16-slot chassis options to build a Cisco ACI spine to fit their deployment scale. Table 12-4 shows the comparison between different models of Nexus 9500 modular ACI switches.

Table 12-4   Cisco Nexus 9500 Modular ACI Switch Comparison

	Nexus 9504 4-Slot	Nexus 9508 8-Slot	Nexus 9518 16-Slot
Height	7 RU	13 RU	20 RU
Max 1/10/40 Ports	192/576/144	384/1152/288	768/2304/576
Supervisor Slots	Up to 2	Up to 2	Up to 2
Fabric Modules	Up to 6	Up to 6	Up to 6
I/O Module Slots	Up to 4	Up to 8	Up to 16
Power Supplies	4 × 3KW AC PSUs	6 × 3KW PSUs	10 × 3KW PSUs
Fan Trays	Up to 3	Up to 3	Up to 3
System Controllers	Up to 2	Up to 2	Up to 2

The Cisco Nexus 9500 platform supports a nonblocking 40 Gigabit Ethernet line card for the spine. (Table 12-5 summarizes the platform line card for Cisco ACI.)

Table 12-5   Cisco Nexus 9500 Platform Line Card for Cisco ACI

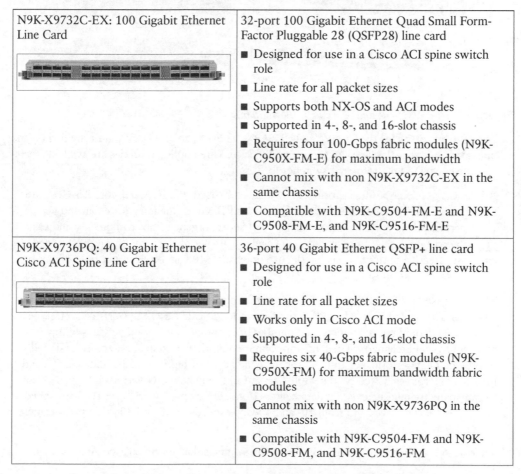

N9K-X9732C-EX: 100 Gigabit Ethernet Line Card	32-port 100 Gigabit Ethernet Quad Small Form-Factor Pluggable 28 (QSFP28) line card <ul><li>Designed for use in a Cisco ACI spine switch role</li><li>Line rate for all packet sizes</li><li>Supports both NX-OS and ACI modes</li><li>Supported in 4-, 8-, and 16-slot chassis</li><li>Requires four 100-Gbps fabric modules (N9K-C950X-FM-E) for maximum bandwidth</li><li>Cannot mix with non N9K-X9732C-EX in the same chassis</li><li>Compatible with N9K-C9504-FM-E and N9K-C9508-FM-E, and N9K-C9516-FM-E</li></ul>
N9K-X9736PQ: 40 Gigabit Ethernet Cisco ACI Spine Line Card	36-port 40 Gigabit Ethernet QSFP+ line card <ul><li>Designed for use in a Cisco ACI spine switch role</li><li>Line rate for all packet sizes</li><li>Works only in Cisco ACI mode</li><li>Supported in 4-, 8-, and 16-slot chassis</li><li>Requires six 40-Gbps fabric modules (N9K-C950X-FM) for maximum bandwidth fabric modules</li><li>Cannot mix with non N9K-X9736PQ in the same chassis</li><li>Compatible with N9K-C9504-FM and N9K-C9508-FM, and N9K-C9516-FM</li></ul>

12

The Cisco Nexus 9300 platform leaf switches for Cisco ACI are fixed-port switches designed for top-of-rack (ToR) and middle-of-row (MoR) deployment in data centers that support enterprise applications, service provider hosting, and cloud computing environments. Figure 12-14 illustrates ACI ToR leaf Nexus 9300 switches at the time of writing this book.

Application Centric Infrastructure (ACI)
Top-of-rack Leaf Nexus 9300 Switches

Nexus 9396TX

Nexus 93128TX

Nexus 9396PX

Nexus 93180YC-EX

Nexus 9332PQ

Nexus 93120TX

Nexus 9372TX & Nexus 9372TX-E

Nexus 9372PX & Nexus 9372PX-E

Figure 12-14   *ACI ToR Leaf Nexus 9300 Switches*

The 40-Gbps ports for the Cisco Nexus 9396PX, 9396TX, and 93128TX are provided on an uplink module that the user can service and replace. Three uplink modules are available for Cisco Nexus 9300 platform leaf switches for Cisco ACI.

All the Cisco Nexus 9300 platform leaf switches for Cisco ACI use dual-core 2.5-GHz x86 CPUs with a 64-GB solid-state disk (SSD) drive and 16 GB of memory for enhanced network performance. With the Cisco Nexus 9000 Series, organizations can quickly and easily upgrade existing data centers to carry 40 Gigabit Ethernet to the spine through advanced and cost-effective optics that enable the use of existing 10 Gigabit Ethernet fiber (a pair of multimode fiber strands).

The Cisco Nexus 9300-EX platform is the next generation of fixed Cisco Nexus 9000 Series switches. The new platform, based on the Cisco Cloud Scale ASIC, supports cost-effective cloud-scale deployments, an increased number of endpoints, and cloud services with wire-rate security and telemetry. The platform is built on modern system architecture designed to provide high performance to meet the evolving needs of highly scalable data centers and growing enterprises. Cisco Nexus 9300-EX platform switches offer various interface options to transparently migrate existing data centers from 100-Mbps, 1-Gbps, and 10-Gbps speeds to 25 Gbps at the server, and from 10- and 40-Gbps speeds to 50 and 100 Gbps at the aggregation layer.

Table 12-6 lists the Cisco Nexus 9300 platform switches that support Cisco ACI.

Table 12-6   Cisco Nexus 9300 Platform Line Card for Cisco ACI

Model	Description
Cisco Nexus 9332PQ Switch Nexus 9332PQ	32 × 40-Gbps Quad Enhanced Small Form-Factor Pluggable (QSFP+) ports. The switch offers 25 MB of additional packet buffer space shared with all ports for more resilient operations.
Cisco Nexus 9372PX-E Switch Nexus 9372PX & Nexus 9372PX-E	48 × 1/10-Gbps SFP+ and 6 × 40-Gbps QSFP+ ports. The Cisco Nexus 9372PX-E Switch is a minor hardware revision of the Cisco Nexus 9372PX. Enhancements include hardware capability for IP-based endpoint group (EPG) classification in Cisco ACI mode.
Cisco Nexus 9372TX-E Switch Nexus 9372TX & Nexus 9372TX-E	48 × 1/10GBASE-T and 6 × 40-Gbps QSFP+ ports. The Cisco Nexus 9372TX-E Switch is a minor hardware revision of the Cisco Nexus 9372TX. Enhancements include hardware capability for IP-based EPG classification in Cisco ACI mode.
Cisco Nexus 9372PX Switch Nexus 9372PX & Nexus 9372PX-E	48 × 1/10-Gbps SFP+ and 6 × 40-Gbps QSFP+ ports.
Cisco Nexus 9372TX Switch Nexus 9372TX & Nexus 9372TX-E	48 × 1/10GBASE-T and 6 × 40-Gbps QSFP+ ports.
Cisco Nexus 9396PX Switch Nexus 9396PX	48 × 1/10-Gbps SFP+ and up to 12 × 40-Gbps QSFP+ ports.
Cisco Nexus 9396TX Switch Nexus 9396TX	48 × 1/10-Gbps SFP+ and up to 12 × 40-Gbps QSFP+ ports.
Cisco Nexus 93128TX Switch Nexus 93128TX	96 × 1/10GBASE-T and up to 8 × 40-Gbps QSFP+ ports.
Cisco Nexus 93180YC-EX Switch Nexus 93180YC-EX	48 × 10/25-Gbps and 6 × 40/100-Gbps QSFP28 ports.

12

The Cisco Nexus 9396PX, 9396TX, and 93128TX require an uplink module to be installed for normal switch operation that the user can service and replace. Two uplink module options are available.

The Cisco Nexus M6PQ and M6PQ-E uplink module provides up to six QSFP+ ports for 40 Gigabit Ethernet connectivity to spine-layer switches. The uplink module provides six active ports when installed in the Cisco Nexus 93128TX, 9396TX, and 9396PX. Cisco Nexus M6PQ-E is a minor hardware revision of Cisco Nexus M6PQ. Enhancements include hardware capability for IP-based EPG classification in Cisco ACI mode.

The Cisco Nexus M12PQ uplink module provides up to 12 QSFP+ ports for 40 Gigabit Ethernet connectivity to spine-layer switches. The uplink module provides 8 active ports when installed in the Cisco Nexus 93128TX, and 12 active ports when installed in the Cisco Nexus 9396PX and 9396TX.

Application Policy Infrastructure Controller (APIC)

The infrastructure controller is the main architectural component of the Cisco ACI solution. It is the unified point of automation and management for the Cisco ACI fabric, policy enforcement, and health monitoring. The APIC appliance is a centralized, clustered controller that optimizes performance and unifies operation of physical and virtual environments. The controller manages and operates a scalable multitenant Cisco ACI fabric. The Cisco APIC is a distributed system implemented as a cluster of controllers. The Cisco APIC provides a single point of control, a central API, a central repository of global data, and a repository of policy data for the Cisco ACI. The Cisco ACI is conceptualized as a distributed overlay system with external endpoint connections controlled and grouped through policies.

The Cisco APIC communicates in the infrastructure VLAN (in-band) with the Cisco ACI spine and leaf nodes to distribute policies to the points of attachment (Cisco leaf) and provide a number of key administrative functions to the Cisco ACI. The Cisco APIC is not directly involved in data plane forwarding, so a complete failure or disconnection of all Cisco APIC elements in a cluster will not result in a loss of existing data center functionality.

In general, policies are distributed to nodes as needed upon endpoint attachment or by an administrative static binding. You can, however, specify "resolutional immediacy," which regulates when policies are delivered into Cisco nodes. "Prefetch," or early resolution, is one of the modes. The most scalable mode is the "just-in-time mode," in which policies are delivered to nodes just in time upon detection of the attachment. Attachment detection is based on analysis of various triggers available to the Cisco APIC.

A central Cisco APIC concept is to express application networking needs as an extension of application-level metadata through a set of policies and requirements that are automatically applied to the network infrastructure. The Cisco APIC policy model allows specification of network policy in an application- and workload-centric way. It describes sets of endpoints with identical network and semantic behaviors as endpoint groups. Policies are specified per interaction among such endpoint groups.

Following are the main features of the controller:

■ Application centric network policies

■ Data-model-based declarative provisioning

- Application and topology monitoring and troubleshooting

- Third-party integration (Layer 4 through Layer 7 [L4–L7] services and VMware vCenter and vShield)

- Image management (spine and leaf)

- Cisco ACI inventory and configuration

- Implementation on a distributed framework across a cluster of appliances

- Health scores for critical managed objects (tenants, application profiles, switches, and so on)

- Fault, event, and performance management

- Cisco application virtual switch (AVS), which can be used as a virtual leaf switch

The controller framework enables broad ecosystem and industry interoperability with Cisco ACI. It enables interoperability between a Cisco ACI environment and management, orchestration, virtualization, and L4-L7 services from a broad range of vendors. Figure 12-15 illustrates the Cisco APIC policy model.

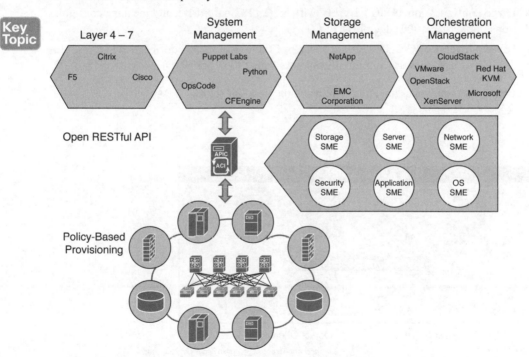

Figure 12-15 *Centralized Automation and Fabric Management of Cisco APIC*

The infrastructure controller provides centralized access to the Cisco ACI through an object-oriented REST API framework with XML and JavaScript Object Notation (JSON) binding. It also supports a modernized, user-extensible CLI and GUI. APIs have full read and write access to Cisco ACI, providing tenant- and application-aware programmability, automation, and system access.

The ACI fabric object-oriented operating system (OS) runs on each Cisco Nexus 9000 Series node. It enables programming of objects for each configurable element of the system.

The APIC appliance is deployed as a cluster. A minimum of three infrastructure controllers are configured in a cluster to provide control of the scale-out Cisco ACI fabric. The ultimate size of the controller cluster is directly proportionate to the size of the Cisco ACI deployment and is based on the transaction-rate requirements. Any controller in the cluster can service any user for any operation, and a controller can be transparently added to or removed from the cluster. The minimum size of the cluster is 3 APIC nodes, and the maximum is 31. The APIC clusters run with N+2 redundancy.

The controller is a physical server appliance like a Cisco UCS C220 M3 or M4 Rack Server with two 10 Gigabit Ethernet interfaces that are designed to be connected to the leaf switches and with 1 Gigabit Ethernet interfaces for out-of-band management. The APIC appliance is available in four form factors:

- **Medium configuration:** [APIC-M2] APIC with medium-size CPU, hard drive, and memory configurations (up to 1000 edge ports)

- **Medium cluster:** [APIC-CLUSTER-M2] Cluster of three APIC devices with medium-size CPU, hard drive, and memory configurations (up to 1000 edge ports)

- **Large configuration:** [APIC-L2] APIC with large CPU, hard drive, and memory configurations (more than 1000 edge ports)

- **Large cluster:** [APIC-CLUSTER-L2] Cluster of three Cisco APIC devices with large CPU, hard drive, and memory configurations (more than 1000 edge ports)

Figure 12-16 summarizes the unified information model of the Cisco ACI.

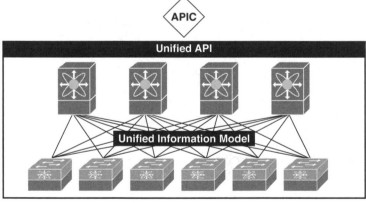

Figure 12-16 *Unified Information Model of the Cisco ACI*

The ACI fabric OS renders policies from the APIC into a concrete model that runs in the physical infrastructure. The concrete model is analogous to compiled software; it is the form of the model that the switch operating system can execute. Figure 12-17 shows the relationship of the logical model to the concrete model and the switch OS.

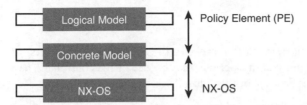

Figure 12-17   *Logical Model Rendered into a Concrete Model*

A Data Management Engine (DME) in the Cisco ACI Fabric OS provides the framework that serves read and write requests from a shared lockless datastore. The datastore is object oriented, with each object stored as chunks of data.

A chunk is owned by one Cisco ACI Fabric OS process, and only the owner of this process can write to the data chunk. However, any Cisco ACI Fabric OS process can read any of the data simultaneously through the CLI, the Simple Network Management Protocol (SNMP), or an API call. A local policy element (PE) enables the Cisco APIC to implement the policy model directly in the Cisco ACI Fabric OS.

All the switch nodes contain a complete copy of the concrete model. When an administrator creates a policy in the APIC that represents a configuration, the APIC updates the logical model. The APIC then performs the intermediate step of creating a fully elaborated policy that it pushes into all the switch nodes where the concrete model is updated.

NOTE   The Cisco Nexus 9000 Series switches can only execute the concrete model. Each switch has a copy of the concrete model. If the APIC goes offline, the fabric keeps functioning, but modifications to the fabric policies are not possible.

The APIC is responsible for fabric activation, switch firmware management, network policy configuration, and instantiation. Although the APIC acts as the centralized policy and network management engine for the fabric, it is completely removed from the data path, including the forwarding topology. Therefore, the fabric can still forward traffic even when communication with the APIC is lost.

The Cisco APIC contains the database for the policies that govern the fabric. The controller automatically archives the following data:

- Policies (are also replicated)
- Statistics
- Endpoint database (which is also replicated)

Because of this design, the Cisco APIC database is based on these principles:

- High-performance computing (HPC)-type clustering with all active nodes
- High availability (three controllers are recommended, although the fabric can be managed with just one)

12

- Low latency
- Incremental scalability
- Consistency
- Partition tolerance

The fabric continues to forward traffic even in the absence of the controller. New servers or VMs can be added and VMs can move in the fabric in the absence of the controller. The only thing that cannot be done in the absence of the controller is to change the policy.

The Cisco APIC controller should be dual-attached to two leaf devices. No configuration is required to build the NIC teaming interface; the 10-Gigabit Ethernet ports of the Cisco APIC appliance are preconfigured for NIC teaming.

The fabric needs at least one Cisco APIC server to provide switch bootup, policy management, and fault and statistics correlation. Three controllers are recommended for redundancy, although you can still provision and configure policies for the fabric with a single controller. Three controllers provide optimal redundancy and support both Cisco APIC software upgrades and failure scenarios. More than three controllers can be used for geographical redundancy and in cases in which you need additional transactional scale (high transaction rate for the API for policy creation or monitoring of the network).

The members of the Cisco APIC cluster do not need to form a full cluster prior to switch node bootstrapping. The controller cluster is designed to operate in split-brain mode, which occurs on bootup and during a partitioning network failure (large-scale failure).

Connectivity between Cisco APIC cluster members takes place through the management port and infrastructure virtual routing and forwarding (VRF), so an out-of-band management network is not needed for the cluster to form. But the cluster does not have to form before each node can initiate the fabric and switch.

When you define the Cisco APIC cluster, you are asked how many members you want to be present at steady state. This number tells the cluster how many other nodes to expect so that each node can track bootup scenarios (only the first node has been attached), partitioned fabrics, and other cases in which only a subset of the total target number of Cisco APIC nodes is active.

To support greater scale and resilience, a concept known as data sharding is supported both for data stored in the APIC and for data stored in the endpoint mapping database located at the spine layer. The basic idea behind sharding is that the data repository is split into several database units, known as shards. Data is placed in a shard, and that shard is replicated three times, with each replica assigned to an APIC appliance

When all nodes are active, the distributed management information tree (DMIT) for the Cisco APIC cluster has the database shards (containers for the managed objects representing the system and policy) replicated across the servers and assigns one of the shard copies as the primary, with transactions performed against that copy. If three servers are defined in a cluster, when all three are active, each supports transactions against one-third of the DMIT. If only two servers are active, each has half of the shards marked as primary, and the system load is shared across the two active Cisco APIC nodes. Figure 12-18 illustrates the APIC cluster.

APIC—Distributed Multi-Active Database

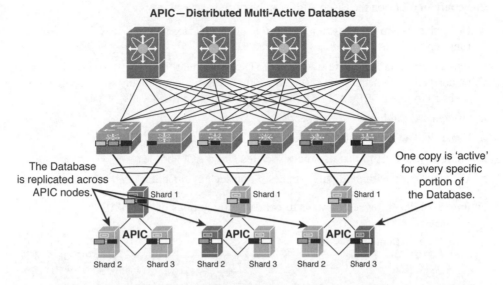

The Database is replicated across APIC nodes.

One copy is 'active' for every specific portion of the Database.

• Processes are active on all nodes (not active/standby).
• The Database is distributed as active + 2 backup instances (shards) for every attribute.

Figure 12-18 *Cisco Application Infrastructure Controller Distributed Multiactive Database*

Cisco ACI is changing network management from a traditional feature-by-feature, link-by-link approach to a declarative model, in which the controller relies on each node to render the declared desired end state. The user configures policies on the Cisco APIC, and it propagates the policy configuration through the OpFlex protocol to all the leaf devices in the fabric, as shown in Figure 12-19. If the server and the software switching on the server support OpFlex, the policy can also be applied within the server. Each networking element (physical or virtual) then renders the policies according to the local capabilities.

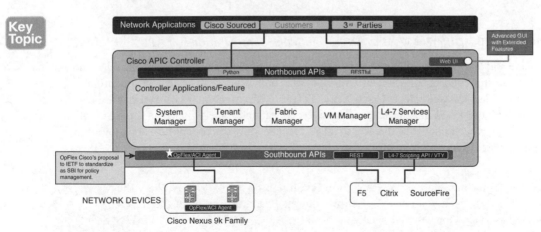

Figure 12-19 *Cisco Application Infrastructure Controller*

12

The configurations on the Cisco APIC can be done in several ways.

- Using the easy-to-use GUI running on the same appliance that provides the controller function
- Using representational state transfer (REST) calls with intuitive XML- or JSON-formatted payloads that are sent to the Cisco APIC; these can be sent in many ways, using tools such as Google POSTMAN or Python scripts that send REST calls
- Using a custom-built GUI that sends REST calls
- Using the CLI to navigate the object model from the Cisco APIC
- Using Python scripts that use the associated Cisco ACI libraries
- Via integration with third-party orchestration such as OpenStack

Figure 12-20 illustrates several ways to define configurations on Cisco APIC.

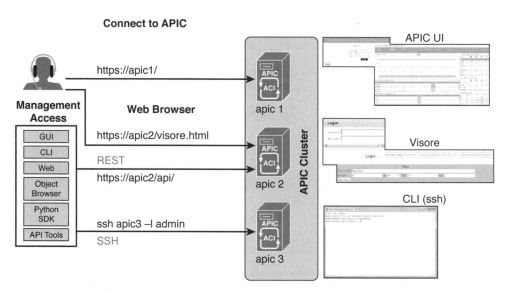

Figure 12-20 *Different Ways to Access and Make Configurations on APIC*

Spine and leaf devices will be receiving the policy configurations from the controller, and you can still connect to each device through the console or the management (mgmt0) port and use the well-known Cisco Nexus Software CLI to monitor how policies are rendered. Figure 12-21 illustrates how to connect to leaf and spine switches in the ACI fabric. However, when connecting directly to a leaf or spine, only read operations are allowed to prevent state synchronization issues with the APIC controller.

> **NOTE** You can use Visore, the APIC Object Store Browser, to directly query the Managed Objects (MO) when you point your browser to the IP address of one of the APICs or a physical switch. One would typically point to the APIC, which is generally HTTPS (default) but could also be HTTP if configured.
> ```
> https://<APIC or Switch IP ADDRESS>/visore.html
> ```

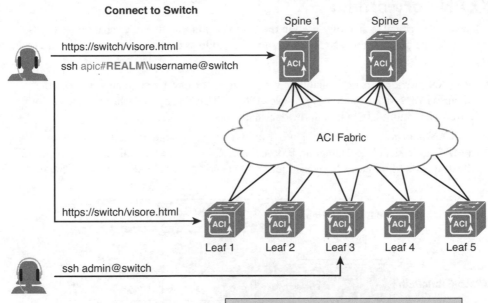

Connect to Switch

https://switch/visore.html

ssh apic#**REALM**\\username@switch

Spine 1   Spine 2

ACI Fabric

https://switch/visore.html

Leaf 1   Leaf 2   Leaf 3   Leaf 4   Leaf 5

ssh admin@switch

We could connect directly to switches as well.
- ssh or Console
- Visore
- REST

Figure 12-21 *Different Ways to Access Leaf and Spine ACI Switches*

Different teams in organizations will have different preferred tools to access the APIC.

- **GUI:** Mostly for the infrastructure administration and for monitoring and troubleshooting purposes. It is also used to generate templates.

- **CLI on Cisco APIC:** Mainly to create shell scripts and for troubleshooting.

- **POSTMAN and other REST tools:** Mostly to test and define configurations to be automated. The scripts are based on XML, JSON, or REST calls with simple scripts for the operator. A scripting language can be used, such as Python, or it can be directly done via POSTMAN.

- **Python scripts:** Mainly to create comprehensive provisioning. The software development kit (SDK) provided with Cisco ACI performs this.

- **PHP and web pages with embedded REST calls:** Mostly to create simple user interfaces for operators or IT customers.

- **Advanced orchestration tools like OpenStack or Cisco Intelligent Automation for Cloud (IAC) or Cisco UCS Director:** Mainly for end-to-end provisioning of compute and network resources.

12

VXLAN Forwarding

VXLAN is a critical technology used in the Cisco ACI fabric. In earlier chapters, we discussed details of VXLAN. VXLAN is designed to address the shortcomings associated with regular VLANs:

- VXLAN provides greater scalability in the number of Layer 2 segments supported. Whereas VLANs are limited to just over 4000, VXLAN can scale (through the use of a 24-bit ID) to up to 16 million individual segments.

- VXLAN allows an extension of Layer 2 across Layer 3 boundaries through the use of a MAC address in User Datagram Protocol (MAC-in-UDP) encapsulation. Figure 12-22 illustrates the differences between the VXLAN and Cisco FabricPath frame formats.

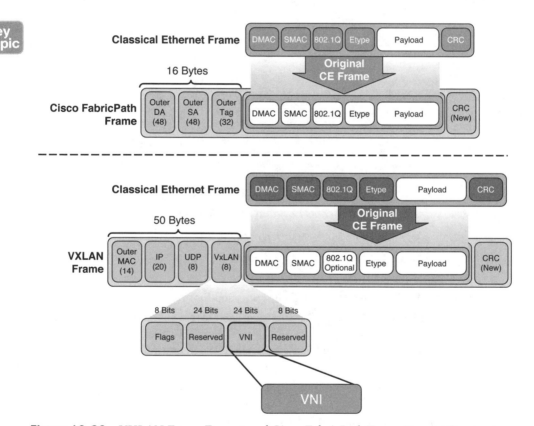

Figure 12-22 *VXLAN Frame Format and Cisco FabricPath Frame Format Comparison*

VXLAN uses an 8-byte header consisting of a 24-bit virtual network identifier (VNID) and a number of reserved bits, as shown in Figure 12-23.

The VTEP is the device that terminates a VXLAN tunnel. A VTEP is a virtual or physical device that maps end devices to VXLAN segments and performs encapsulation and deencapsulation. A VTEP has two interfaces: one on the local LAN segment, used to connect directly to end devices, and the other on the IP transport network, used to encapsulate Layer 2 frames into UDP packets and send them over the transport network.

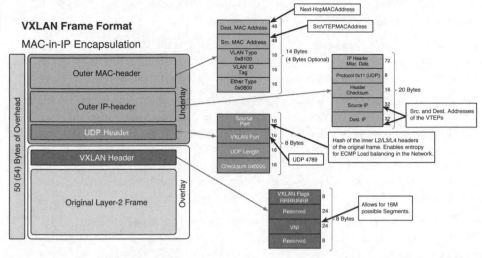

Figure 12-23 *VXLAN Frame Format*

In a Cisco ACI environment, VXLAN is used to encapsulate traffic inside the fabric. In other words, each leaf switch acts as a hardware VTEP, as shown in Figure 12-24.

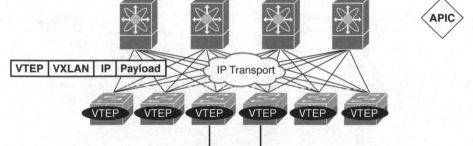

Figure 12-24 *VTEPs in a Cisco ACI Fabric*

In addition to its scalability, VXLAN allows the separation of location from identity. In a traditional IP-based environment, the IP address is used to provide information about an endpoint's identity, as well as information about where that endpoint resides in the network. An overlay technology such as VXLAN separates these functions and creates two name spaces: one for the identity, and another to signify where that endpoint resides.

12

In the case of the Cisco ACI, the endpoint's IP address is the identifier, and a VTEP address designates the location of an endpoint in the network.

In the Cisco ACI fabric, some extensions have been added to the VXLAN header to allow the segmentation of End Point Groups (EPGs) and the management of filtering rules, as well as to support the enhanced load-balancing techniques used in the fabric.

Forwarding within the fabric is between VTEPs. The mapping of the internal tenant MAC or IP address to a location is performed by the VTEP using a distributed mapping database. After a lookup is done, the VTEP sends the original data packet encapsulated in VXLAN with the destination address (DA) of the VTEP on the destination leaf. The packet is then de-encapsulated on the destination leaf and sent down to the receiving host. With this model, we can have a full mesh, loop-free topology without the need to use the Spanning-Tree Protocol to prevent loops.

The enhanced VXLAN header used in the Cisco ACI fabric is shown in Figure 12-25.

IETF VXLAN Group-based Policy

ACI VXLAN (VXLAN) header provides a tagging mechanism to identify properties associated with frames forwarded through an ACI capable fabric. It is an extension of the Layer 2 LISP protocol (draft-smith-lisp-layer2-01) with the addition of a policy group, load and path metric, counter and ingress port, and encapsulation information. The VXLAN header is not associated with a specific L2 segment or L3 domain but provides a multifunction tagging mechanism used in ACI Application Defined Networking enabled fabric.

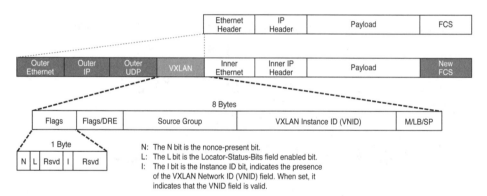

Figure 12-25 *VXLAN Header*

Notice that the Cisco ACI uses the reserved fields of the regular VXLAN header for other purposes. The Source Group field is used to represent the End Point Groups (hosts) to which the endpoint that is the source of the packet belongs. This information allows the filtering policy to be consistently applied regardless of the location of an endpoint.

Traffic within the fabric is encapsulated as VXLAN. External VLAN/VXLAN/NVGRE tags are mapped at ingress to an internal VXLAN tag. Figure 12-26 shows encapsulation normalization.

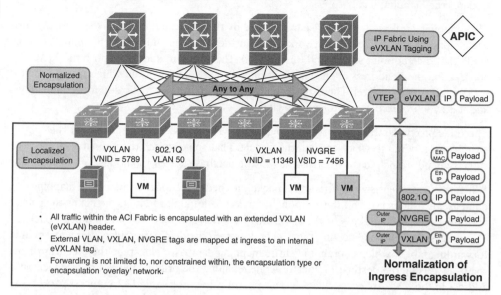

Figure 12-26 *Encapsulation Normalization*

Forwarding is not limited to or constrained by the encapsulation type or encapsulation overlay network. External identifiers are localized to the leaf or leaf port, which allows reuse or translation if required.

Mapping Database

For the Cisco ACI to forward traffic through the fabric, the fabric must know the identity and the location of the endpoint. The fabric can learn the location of the endpoint in the following ways:

■ The administrator can statically program the identity-to-location mapping.

■ Upon creation of a new virtual machine, the virtual machine manager (VMM) can update the APIC with the identity and location information. The location—that is, the port to which the virtual machine is connected—is known through a combination of what the virtual machine manager tells the APIC (the ESXi host on which the virtual machine is located) and the information that the APIC retrieves from the leaf (the Link Layer Discovery Protocol [LLDP] or Cisco Discovery Protocol neighbor, to identify the interface to which the ESXi host is connected).

■ DHCP packets can be used to learn identity-to-location mapping.

■ Learning can occur through Address Resolution Protocol (ARP), Gratuitous ARP (GARP), and Reverse ARP (RARP) traffic. The CPU on the leaf switch, upon receiving a copy of the ARP, GARP, or RARP packet, updates its local mapping cache with a static entry for this host and informs the centralized mapping database of the update for the host address through Council of Oracles Protocol (COOP).

■ Learning can be based on the arrival of the first packet.

12

Upon learning the endpoint information, the leaf switch to which the endpoint is connected updates the mapping database.

The mapping database is a database maintained by the fabric and contains the mapping for each endpoint attached to the network (the identifier) and the address of the tunnel endpoint (TEP) that the endpoint sits behind (the locator). The endpoint address is both the MAC address and the IP address of the endpoint plus the logical network in which the endpoint resides (the VRF instance). The mapping database in the spine is replicated for redundancy, and it is synchronized across all spine switches.

The spine proxy database is updated using COOP. The leaf switch selects one of the spine switches at random to which to send the update. That spine switch then updates all the other spine switches to help ensure consistency of the database across the nodes.

When an ingress leaf switch forwards a packet, it checks the local cache of the mapping database. If it does not find the endpoint address it is looking for, it encapsulates the packet with the destination address of the spine proxy anycast and forwards it as a unicast packet. The spine switch, upon receiving the packet, looks up the destination identifier address in its forwarding tables, which contain the entire mapping database. The spine then reencapsulates the packet using the destination locator while retaining the original ingress source locator address in the VXLAN encapsulation. This packet is then forwarded as a unicast packet to the intended destination. This process eliminates unknown unicast flooding and ARP flooding.

ACI Fabric Provisioning and Startup Discovery

Cisco ACI automation and self-provisioning offers operation advantages over the traditional switching infrastructure:

- A clustered logically centralized but physically distributed APIC provides policy, boot-strap, and image management for the entire fabric.
- The APIC startup topology auto discovery, automated configuration, and infrastructure addressing uses these industry-standard protocols: Intermediate System-to-Intermediate System (IS-IS), LLDP, and DHCP.
- The APIC provides a simple and automated policy-based provisioning and upgrade pro-cess, and automated image management.
- APIC provides scalable configuration management. Because ACI data centers can be large, configuring switches or interfaces individually does not scale well, even using scripts. APIC pod, controller, switch, module, and interface selectors (all, range, specific instances) enable symmetric configurations across the fabric. To apply a symmetric con-figuration, an administrator defines switch profiles that associate interface configurations in a single policy group. The configuration is then rapidly deployed to all interfaces in that profile without the need to configure them individually.

The clustered APIC controller provides DHCP, bootstrap configuration, and image manage-ment to the fabric for automated startup and upgrades.

The Cisco Nexus ACI fabric software is bundled as an ISO image, which can be installed on the Cisco APIC server through the KVM interface on the Cisco Integrated Management

Controller (CIMC). The Cisco Nexus ACI Software ISO contains the Cisco APIC image, the firmware image for the leaf node, the firmware image for the spine node, the default fabric infrastructure policies, and the protocols required for operation.

The ACI fabric bootstrap sequence begins when the fabric is booted with factory-installed images on all the switches. The Cisco Nexus 9000 Series switches that run the ACI firmware and APICs use a reserved overlay for the boot process. This infrastructure space is hard-coded on the switches. The APIC can connect to a leaf through the default overlay, or it can use a locally significant identifier.

The ACI fabric uses an infrastructure space, which is securely isolated in the fabric and is where all the topology discovery, fabric management, and infrastructure addressing are performed. ACI fabric management communication within the fabric takes place in the infrastructure space through internal private IP addresses. This addressing scheme allows the APIC to communicate with fabric nodes and other Cisco APIC controllers in the cluster. The APIC discovers the IP address and node information of other Cisco APIC controllers in the cluster using the LLDP–based discovery process. Figure 12-27 shows the ACI Fabric Initialization steps.

Fabric Initialization and Maintenance

⑥ Fabric will self-assemble starting from multiple APIC sources.

③ Spine switch discovers attached Leaf via LLDP, requests TEP address, and boot file via DHCP.

⑤ Fabric can be discovered and initialized from multiple sources concurrently.

② Leaf switch discovers attached APIC via LLDP, requests TEP address, and boot file via DHCP.

⑦ APIC Cluster will form when members discover each other via Appliance Vector (AV).

◇ **APIC**   **APIC Cluster**   ◇ **APIC**   ◇ **APIC**

APIC Bootstrap Configuration

① 1. APIC Cluster Configuration
2. Fabric Name
3. TEP Address Space (Infra-VRF)

④ All nodes in the same APIC cluster should contain the same bootstrap information if they are intended to form a cluster.

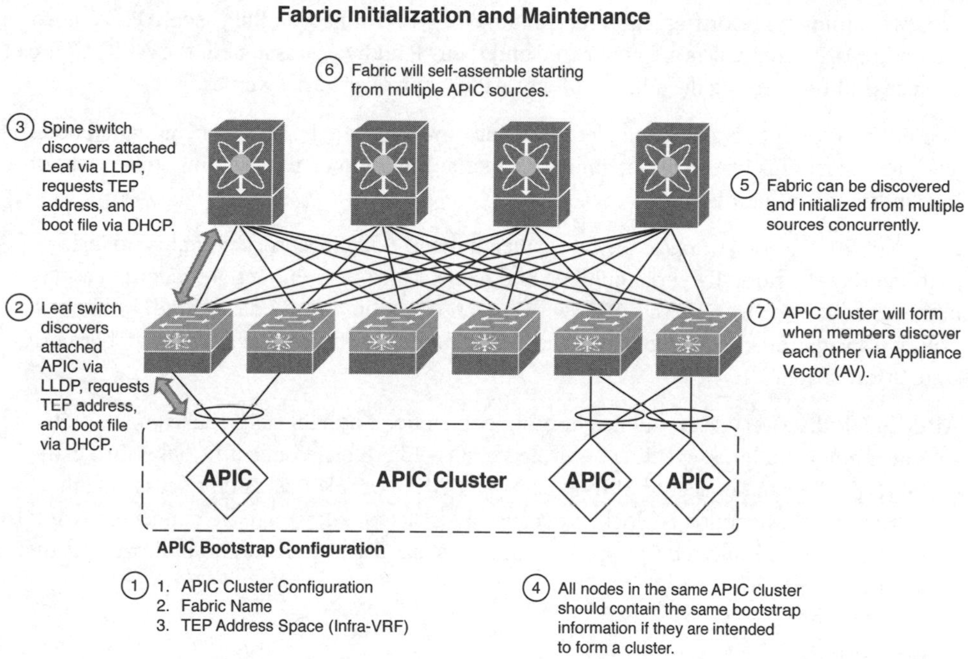

Figure 12-27 *Cisco ACI Fabric Initialization and Maintenance*

The following describes the APIC cluster discovery process:

- Each APIC in the Cisco ACI uses an internal private IP address to communicate with the ACI nodes and other APICs in the cluster. The APIC discovers the IP address of other APIC controllers in the cluster through the LLDP-based discovery process.

12

- APICs maintain an appliance vector (AV), which provides a mapping from an APIC ID to an APIC IP address and a universally unique identifier (UUID) of the APIC. Initially, each APIC starts with an AV filled with its local IP address, and all other APIC slots are marked as unknown.

- When a switch reboots, the policy element (PE) on the leaf gets its AV from the APIC. The switch then advertises this AV to all its neighbors and reports any discrepancies between its local AV and neighbors' AVs to all the APICs in its local AV.

Using this process, the APIC learns about the other APIC controllers in the ACI through switches. After validating these newly discovered APIC controllers in the cluster, the APIC controllers update their local AV and program the switches with the new AV. Switches then start advertising this new AV. This process continues until all the switches have the identical AV and all APIC controllers know the IP address of all the other APIC controllers.

The ACI fabric is brought up in a cascading manner, starting with the leaf nodes that are directly attached to the APIC. LLDP and control-plane IS-IS convergence occurs in parallel to this boot process. The ACI fabric uses LLDP- and DHCP-based fabric discovery to automatically discover the fabric switch nodes, assign the infrastructure VXLAN tunnel endpoint (VTEP) addresses, and install the firmware on the switches. Prior to this automated process, a minimal bootstrap configuration must be performed on the Cisco APIC controller. After the APIC controllers are connected and their IP addresses assigned, the APIC GUI can be accessed by entering the address of any APIC controller into a web browser.

The policy model contains a complete real-time inventory of the fabric, including all nodes and interfaces. This inventory capability enables automation of provisioning, troubleshooting, auditing, and monitoring.

For Cisco ACI fabric switches, the fabric membership node inventory contains policies that identify the node ID, serial number, and name. Third-party nodes are recorded as unmanaged fabric nodes. Cisco ACI switches can be automatically discovered, or their policy information can be imported. The policy model also maintains fabric member node state information.

After LLDP discovery learns all neighboring connections dynamically, these connections are validated against a loose specification rule such as "LEAF can connect to only SPINE-L1-*" or "SPINE-L1-* can connect to SPINE-L2-* or LEAF." If a rule mismatch occurs, a fault results and the connection is blocked because a leaf is not allowed to be connected to another leaf, or a spine connected to a spine. In addition, an alarm is created to indicate that the connection needs attention.

Reference List

Unleashing IT: http://www.unleashingit.com/aci/

Software Defined Networking Cisco Guide: http://www.cisco.com/web/offers/sdn01/software-defined-networking/index.html?KeyCode=000748195

Open Networking Foundation: http://www.openflow.org, https://www.opennetworking.org/

Mark Burgess, Todd Craw, Mike Dvorkin, and Paul Borrill. *A Promise Theory Perspective on Data Networks* http://arxiv.org/pdf/1405.2627.pdf, 2014

OpFlex Control Protocol: https://tools.ietf.org/html/draft-smith-opflex-02

Cisco Development Network: https://developer.cisco.com/web/unifiedcomputing/ucsemulatordownload

Avramov, Lucien, and Portolani Maurizio. *The Policy Driven Data Center with ACI: Architecture, Concepts, and Methodology.* Cisco Press, 2015.

APIC Visore Tool Introduction: http://www.cisco.com/c/en/us/support/docs/cloud-systems-management/application-policy-infrastructure-controller-apic/118839-technote-visore-00.html

Programmability and Automation with Cisco Open NX-OS: http://www.cisco.com/c/dam/en/us/td/docs/switches/datacenter/nexus9000/sw/open_nxos/programmability/guide/Programmability_Open_NX-OS.pdf

Cisco Data Center GitHub: https://github.com/datacenter

Exam Preparation Tasks

Review All Key Topics

Review the most important topics in the chapter, noted with the key topic icon in the outer margin of the page. Table 12-7 lists a reference of these key topics and the page numbers on which each is found.

Table 12-7 Key Topics for Chapter 12

Key Topic Element	Description	Page
List	Description of Four Main API Components	436
Table 12-2	"Comparison of REST, NETCONF, and SNMP"	436
List	REST Interface Guiding Principles	437
Figure 12-1	"SDN Stack"	438
Figure 12-2	"OpenFlow Components"	439
Figure 12-3	"Network Programmability Models"	440
Figure 12-5	"Cisco Data Center Software-Defined Network Solutions"	442
Table 12-3	"Cisco Solutions"	442
Figure 12-6	"Cisco Software-Defined Networking Solutions"	443
List	SDN Common Use Cases	443
List	Advantages of Group-Based Policy	444
Figure 12-7	"Group-Based Policy"	445
List	Imperative and Declarative Management Models	445
List	Clos Network Architecture	448
Figure 12-10	"ACI Physical Topology"	450
List	The Main Features of APIC	456
Figure 12-15	"Centralized Automation and Fabric Management"	457
List	The APIC Appliance	458
Figure 12-16	"Unified Information Model of Cisco ACI"	458
Figure 12-18	"The APIC Distributed Multi-Active Database"	461
Figure 12-19	"Cisco Application Infrastructure Controller"	461
List	The Configuration of APIC	462
Figure 12-20	"Different Ways to Access and Make Configuration on APIC"	462
Figure 12-21	"Different Ways to Access Leaf and Spine ACI Switches"	463
List	Different Tools to Access the APIC	463

Key Topic Element	Description	Page
Figure 12-22	"VXLAN Frame Format and Cisco FabricPath Frame Format Comparison"	464
Figure 12-23	"VXLAN Frame Format"	465
Figure 12-24	"VTEPs in a Cisco ACI Fabric"	465
Figure 12-25	"VXLAN Header"	466
Figure 12-26	"Encapsulation Normalization"	467
Figure 12-27	"Cisco ACI Fabric Initialization and Maintenance"	469

Complete Tables and Lists from Memory

Print a copy of Appendix B, "Memory Tables" or at least the section for this chapter, and complete the tables and lists from memory. Appendix C, "Memory Tables Answer Key" includes completed tables and lists to check your work.

Define Key Terms

Define the following key terms from this chapter, and check your answers in the Glossary:

Software-Defined Networking (SDN), Application Programming Interface (API), LLDP (Link Layer Discovery Protocol), Representational State Transfer (REST), Web Services Description Language (WSDL), Cisco Application Policy Infrastructure Controller Enterprise Module (APIC EM), OpenDaylight (ODL), Border Gateway Protocol and Ethernet VPN (BGP-EVPN), Virtual Topology System (VTS), Infrastructure as a Service (IaaS), Platform as a Service (PaaS), Software as a Service (SaaS), Internet of Things (IoT), Internet of Everything (IoE), Cisco Application Virtual Switch (AVS)

12

This chapter covers the following exam topics:

5.4 Describe the ACI logical model

   5.4.a Tenants

   5.4.b Context

   5.4.c Bridge domains

   5.4.d EPG

   5.4.e Contracts

CHAPTER 13

ACI Logical Model and Policy Framework

The Cisco Application Infrastructure policy model enables the specification of application requirements policies. The goal of this chapter is to introduce the reader to a basic level of understanding about the model, what this policy model contains, and how to work with it. The complete object model contains a hierarchy of data center interactions. The most extensive information resource that is available at this moment is the APIC Management Information Model Reference packaged with the application policy infrastructure controller (APIC).

The policy model manages the entire Cisco application centric infrastructure (ACI) fabric, including the infrastructure, authentication, security, services, applications, and diagnostics. Logical constructs in the policy model define how the fabric meets the needs of any of the functions of the fabric. This chapter is written to clearly outline the ACI policy model logical constructs. This is not an official product or configuration guide, however; refer to the appropriate official documents to evaluate products and design and configure solutions with Cisco ACI. This chapter goes directly into the key concepts of ACI and discusses topics relevant to "The 200-155 DCICT: Introducing Cisco Data Center Technologies" certification.

"Do I Know This Already?" Quiz

The "Do I Know This Already?" quiz enables you to assess whether you should read this entire chapter thoroughly or jump to the "Exam Preparation Tasks" section. If you are in doubt about your answers to these questions or your own assessment of your knowledge of the topics, read the entire chapter. Table 13-1 lists the major headings in this chapter and their corresponding "Do I Know This Already?" quiz questions. You can find the answers in Appendix A, "Answers to the 'Do I Know This Already?' Quizzes."

Table 13-1 "Do I Know This Already?" Section-to-Question Mapping

Foundation Topics Section	Questions
"Abstraction"	1
"ACI Policy Object Model"	2–4
"Different Models"	5
"ACI Logical Constructs"	6–11

> **CAUTION**   The goal of self-assessment is to gauge your mastery of the topics in this chapter. If you do not know the answer to a question or are only partially sure of the answer, you should mark that question as wrong for purposes of the self-assessment. Giving yourself credit for an answer you correctly guess skews your self-assessment results and might provide you with a false sense of security.

1. Which of the following statements are correct for Cisco Application Centric Infrastructure? (Choose two.)

    a. The Application Network Profile expresses relationships between compute segments.

    b. In ACI, devices autonomously update the state of the network depending on the configured policy requirements.

    c. ACI works with the imperative model.

    d. Application architects can build stateful policies in ACI fabric.

2. Which of the following programmatic entities are included in Cisco Application Infrastructure Controller's API model? (Choose three.)

    a. Classes

    b. Types

    c. Methods

    d. MIT

    e. Visore

3. What is the name of an object browser that is used for querying the tree for classes or objects for Cisco APIC?

    a. Firefox

    b. Visore

    c. Chrome

    d. MO

    e. DME

4. Which of the following options are correct for managed objects (MOs) in the ACI object model? (Choose three.)

    a. Each node in the management information tree (MIT) represents a MO.

    b. MO instances are unique, and they cannot form a parent-child relationship.

    c. Users create all MOs.

    d. When any MO is created because of a user-initiated action, an event is generated.

    e. In an API operation to create a specific MO, the resource path consists of /mo/ followed by the DN of the MO.

5. Which of the following stages are implemented within the ACI object model? (Choose three.)

   a. The logical model

   b. The resolved model

   c. The concrete model

   d. The universe model

   e. The shared model

6. Which of the following options are correct for ACI logical constructs? (Choose three.)

   a. A tenant is a folder for application policies.

   b. A context is a representation of a private Layer 3 namespace or a Layer 3 network.

   c. A tenant can contain one or more virtual routing and forwarding contexts.

   d. A tenant can contain only one outside network object.

   e. An EPG contains one or more tenants.

7. Which of the following options are correct for ACI endpoint groups (EPGs)? (Choose three.)

   a. EPGs act as a container for a collection of applications.

   b. EPGs are fully decoupled from the physical and logical topology.

   c. Endpoint membership in an EPG can be dynamic or static.

   d. Within an EPG, separate endpoints can exist in only one subnet.

   e. The use of EPGs is similar in different fabric deployments.

8. Which of the following EPG communications are correct for contracts in ACI? (Choose three.)

   a. Between ACI fabric application EPGs, both intra-tenant and inter-tenant

   b. Between ACI fabric application EPGs and Layer 2 external outside network instance EPGs

   c. Between labeled EPGs and intra-tenant EPGs

   d. Between ACI fabric application EPGs and Layer 3 external outside network instance EPGs

   e. Between ACI fabric out-of-band management and common EPGs.

9. Which of the following options are correct for application profiles in ACI? (Choose two.)

   a. An application profile is a convenient logical container for grouping EPGs.

   b. An application profile contains three EPGs and their policies.

   c. An application profile is an expression of the logical model.

   d. An application profile contains ACLs based on the bridge domains.

13

10. Which of the following options are correct for the ACI policy model? (Choose two.)

   a. The policy model allows for both unidirectional and bidirectional policies.

   b. The application policy model defines application requirements.

   c. The policy is pushed into spine switches in the ACI fabric.

   d. The policy cannot be enforced within a subnet or across subnets.

11. Which of the following options are correct for contracts in the ACI logical model? (Choose three.)

   a. Subjects are contained in filters.

   b. One or more subjects within a contract may use filters.

   c. Labels can be applied to a variety of provider and consumer-managed objects.

   d. Labels are applied to bridge domains.

   e. A unidirectional filter is used in one direction.

Foundation Topics

Abstraction

For many years, network administrators created the connectivity between different segments by using VLANs, IP addresses, routing, and access control lists (ACLs) and translating the requirements of the IT organization to support a specific application. Network administrators have no way to really express such configurations directly in a format that can be mapped to the network, leaving administrators with no choice but to focus primarily on expressing an open connectivity policy to ensure that servers can talk to each other if they are internal to the company and can talk to the outside if they are on the DMZ or extranet. This requires administrators to harden ACLs and put firewalls to restrict the scope of which service clients and other servers can use from a given set of servers.

This approach results in nonportable configurations. They are hard-coded in the specific data center environment where they are implemented. If the same environment must be built in a different data center, somebody must perform that time-consuming job of reconfiguring IP addresses and VLANs and deciphering ACLs.

ACI is revolutionizing this process by introducing the ability to create an application network profile, a configuration template to express relationships between compute segments. ACI then translates those relationships into networking constructs that routers and switches can implement (that is, in VLANs, virtual extensible LANs (VXLANs), virtual routing and forwardings (VRFs), IP addresses, and so on). IP addresses become fully portable within the fabric, while security and forwarding are decoupled from any physical or virtual network attributes.

The abstraction (as shown in Figure 13-1) of the infrastructure allows stateless application policies. Abstraction also means that the policy defining application requirements is no longer tied to traditional network constructs, and thus removes dependencies on the infrastructure and increases the portability of applications. The application policy model defines application requirements, and based on the specified requirements, each device will instantiate a set of required changes. Devices autonomously and consistently update the state of the network based on the configured policy requirements set within the application profile definitions.

13

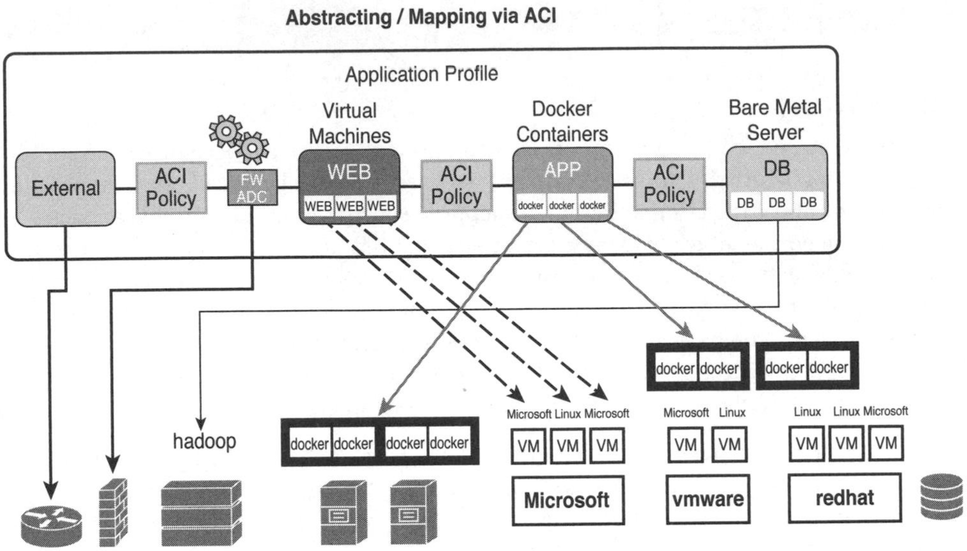

Abstracting / Mapping via ACI

Application Profile

Figure 13-1 *Abstracting/Mapping via ACI*

ACI Policy Object Model

Underlying the promise theory-based model, Cisco ACI builds an object model to focus on the deployment of applications. The abstracted model utilized in ACI is object oriented. Everything in the Cisco ACI infrastructure is represented as a class or a *managed object* (abbreviated "MO"). Each managed object is identified by a name and contains a set of typed values, or properties. For instance, a given tenant is an object of the same type and with a specific name, such as DC.com. A routing instance in the fabric is an object, as is a port on a switch. Objects can be concrete (labeled "C" in the Cisco APIC REST API User Guide) or abstract (labeled "A" in the Cisco APIC REST API User Guide); a tenant, for instance, is an abstract object, whereas a port is a concrete object.

All configurations in Cisco ACI consist of creating such objects, modifying their properties, deleting the objects, or querying the tree. For instance, to create or manipulate objects, you use REST calls with a URL of this example: https://<APIC IP Address>/api/mo/uni/.xml. To perform an operation on a class, use a REST call with a URL of this type: https://<APIC IP Address>/api/class/uni/.xml. Figure 13-2 illustrates the URL structure of a REST API Read call and examples.

You navigate the object data store (that is, the current tree saved in the distributed database) with a tool called *Visore*, which is accessible by pointing your browser to the APIC controller with the following URL: https://<APIC or Switch IP Address>/visore.html.

The Managed Object Browser, or Visore, is a utility built into the APIC that provides a graphical view of the MOs using a browser. The Visore utility uses the APIC REST API query methods to browse MOs active in the ACI fabric, allowing you to see the query that was used to obtain the information. The Visore utility cannot be used to perform configuration operations. Figure 13-3 illustrates the name of a class, such as **tenant**, and gets the list of instances of this class. Or, if you can enter the distinguished name of a particular tenant object, you get the information about that specific tenant.

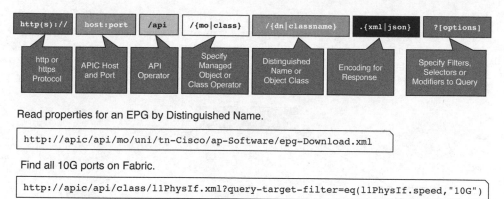

Read properties for an EPG by Distinguished Name.

```
http://apic/api/mo/uni/tn-Cisco/ap-Software/epg-Download.xml
```

Find all 10G ports on Fabric.

```
http://apic/api/class/l1PhysIf.xml?query-target-filter=eq(l1PhysIf.speed,"10G")
```

Figure 13-2 *REST API: Read Operations*

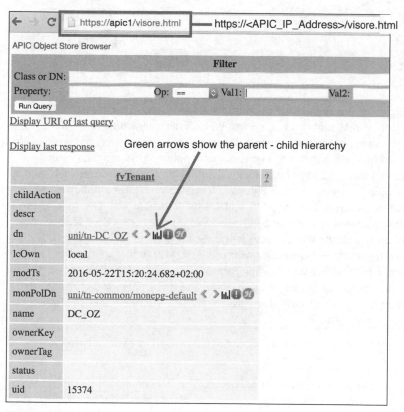

Figure 13-3 *Visore*

All the physical and logical components that comprise the ACI fabric are represented in a hierarchical management information model (MIM), also referred to as the management information tree (MIT). Each node in the tree represents a managed object (MO) or group of objects that contains its administrative state and its operational state.

13

Managed object instances can contain other instances that form a parent-child relationship as part of a tree. Figure 13-4 provides a high-level view of the object tree organization. At the root is "the class universe." Next are the classes that belong to the infrastructure (that is, physical concepts such as ports, port channels, and VLANs) and classes that belong to logical concepts (such as the tenant and networks within the tenant).

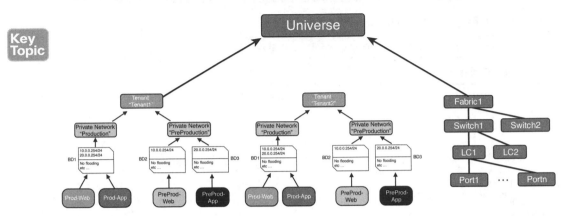

Figure 13-4 *Hierarchy of the Object Model*

Configuration policies are the majority of the policies in the system. They describe the configurations of different ACI fabric components. Policies determine how the system behaves under specific circumstances. Certain MOs are not created by users but are automatically created by the fabric (for example, power supply objects and fan objects). The information model is centrally stored as a logical model by the APIC, while each switch node contains a complete copy as a concrete model. When a user creates a policy in the APIC that represents a configuration, the APIC updates the logical model. The APIC then performs the intermediate step of creating a fully elaborated policy from the user policy and pushes the policy into all the switch nodes where the concrete model is updated. The models are managed by multiple data management engine (DME) processes that run in the fabric. When a user or process initiates an administrative change to a fabric component, the DME first applies that change to the information model and then applies the change to the actual managed endpoint. As we discussed in Chapter 12, "ACI Architecture," this approach is called a model-driven framework.

You can identify a specific object by its distinguished name (DN) or by its relative name (RN).

The DN enables you to identify a specific target object. The DN consists of a series of RNs:

dn = {rn}/{rn}/{rn}/{rn}...

In this example, the DN provides a fully qualified path for fabport-1 from the top of the object tree to the object. The DN specifies the exact managed object on which the API call is operating.

< dn ="sys/ch/lcslot-1/lc/fabport-1" />

The RN identifies an object from its siblings within the context of its parent object. The DN contains a sequence of RNs.

The application programming interface (API) operates in forgiving mode, which means that missing attributes are substituted with default values (if applicable) that are maintained in the internal DME. The DME validates and rejects incorrect attributes. The API is also atomic. If multiple MOs are being configured (for example, virtual NICs) and any of the MOs cannot be configured, the API stops its operation. It returns the configuration to its prior state, stops the API operation that listens for API requests, and returns an error code.

Updates to MOs and properties conform to the existing object model, which ensures backward compatibility. If existing properties are changed during a product upgrade, they are managed during the database load after the upgrade. New properties are assigned default values.

Full event subscription is enabled. When any MO is created, changed, or deleted because of a user- or system-initiated action, an event is generated. With an API query, you can create a subscription to any future changes in the results of that query.

Operation of the API is transactional and terminates on a single data model. The APIC is responsible for all endpoint communication, such as state updates; users cannot communicate directly to endpoints. In this way, developers are relieved from the task of administering isolated, individual component configurations.

The API model includes these programmatic entities:

- **Classes:** Templates that define the properties and states of objects in the MIT.

- **Methods:** Actions that the API performs on one or more objects.

- **Types:** Object properties that map values to the object state (for example, equipmentPresence).

In an API operation to create, read, update, or delete a specific MO, the resource path consists of /mo/ followed by the DN of the MO as described in the *Cisco APIC Management Information Model Reference*. Figure 13-5 illustrates how to access the *APIC Management Information Model Reference* from the APIC GUI.

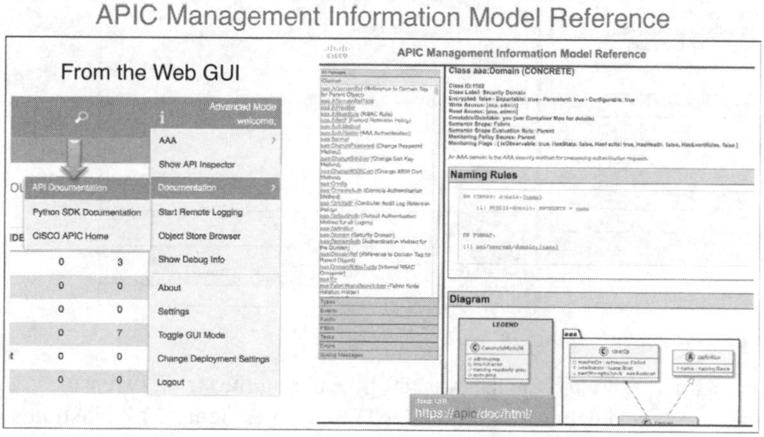

Figure 13-5 *APIC Management Information Model Reference*

All classes are organized as members of packages. Cisco ACI defines, among others, the following packages:

- **Aaa:** User class for authentication, authorization, and accounting
- **fv:** Fabric virtualization
- **callhome:** Provides an email-based notification for critical system policies

Figure 13-6 illustrates the list of classes that are part of the package fv.

The class for tenant is named fv:Tenant, where fv indicates the package that the class belongs to. The distinguished name of a tenant is uni/tn-[name], where uni is the class universe and tn stands for target name. Figure 13-6 illustrates the information that you can find for the class tenant in the *APIC Management Information Model Reference.*

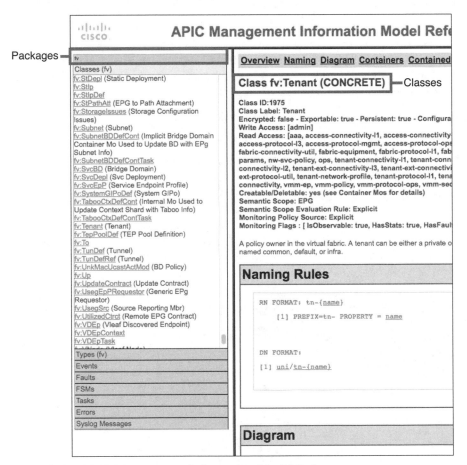

Figure 13-6 *APIC Management Information Model Reference*

You can explore the object data store for the class tenant by entering the string fvTenant (without a colon) in the search field (labeled "Class or DN") of Visore. Figure 13-7 illustrates a search on Visore, where the fvTenant class name equals DC_OZ. The same result can be achieved by searching with the DN name of the object, which is uni/tn-DC_OZ.

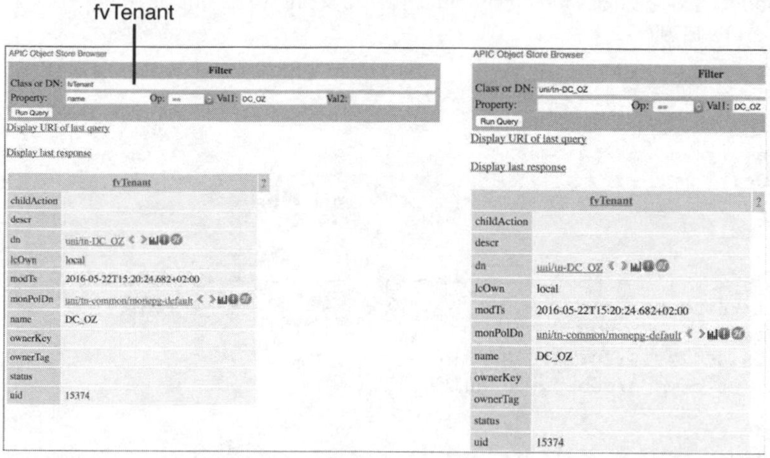

Figure 13-7 *APIC Object Store Browser—Visore*

The managed objects can be also queried by the Managed Object Browser "*moquery*" from the APIC CLI. First the admin user connects to the APIC via SSH using the command **ssh admin@APIC_IP_Address** and connects to the bash shell to run the moquery, as demonstrated in Figure 13-8.

```
$ ssh admin@<APIC_IP_Address>
Application Policy Infrastructure Controller
admin@10.48.22.122's password:
APIC1# bash
admin@APIC1:~> moquery -h              Moquery help to display all arg.
usage: Command line cousin to visore [-h] [-i HOST] [-p PORT] [-d DN]
                                      [-c KLASS] [-f FILTER] [-a ATTRS]
                                      [-o OUTPUT] [-u USER]
                                      [-x [OPTIONS [OPTIONS ...]]]


optional arguments:
  -h, --help            show this help message and exit
  -i HOST, --host HOST  Hostname or ip of apic
  -p PORT, --port PORT  REST server port
  -d DN, --dn DN        dn of the mo
  -c KLASS, --klass KLASS
                        comma separated class names to query
  -f FILTER, --filter FILTER
                        property filter to accept/reject mos
  -a ATTRS, --attrs ATTRS
                        type of attributes to display (config, all)
  -o OUTPUT, --output OUTPUT
                        Display format (block, table, xml, json)
  -u USER, --user USER  User name
  -x [OPTIONS [OPTIONS ...]], --options [OPTIONS [OPTIONS ...]]
                        Extra options to the query
```

Figure 13-8 *APIC Bash Shell Access and Moquery*

13

You can use the moquery for the class tenant by entering the string fvTenant or the DN name, as shown in Figure 13-9.

```
                        Query for a dn -d returns the exact dn used as an arg.
admin@APIC1:~> moquery -d uni/tn-DC_OZ
Total Objects shown: 1
# fv.Tenant                  The class of the MO which is displayed.
name           : DC_OZ
childAction    :
descr          :
dn             : uni/tn-DC_OZ    Dn : The "address" of the MO in the MIT.
lcOwn          : local
modTs          : 2016-05-22T15:20:24.682+02:00
monPolDn       : uni/tn-common/monepg-default
ownerKey       :
ownerTag       :
rn             : tn-DC_OZ
status         :                Other query option for a class -c
uid            : 15374          returns all MO of that class.

admin@APIC1:~> moquery -c fvTenant | grep name
name           : infra
name           : common
name           : DC_West
name           : VitaminC
name           : test1
name           : mgmt
name           : DC_OZ
```

Figure 13-9 *Managed Object Query—Moquery via APIC CLI*

In creating objects and forming their relationships within the ACI fabric, a relationship is expressed when an object is a provider of a service and another object is a consumer of that provided service. If a relationship is formed and one side of the service is not connected, the relationship is considered to be **unformed**. If a consumer exists with no provider or a provider exists with no consumer, this is an unformed relationship. If both a consumer and a provider exist and are connected for a specific service, that relationship is fully **formed**.

There are a couple of places to locate the DN and RN of the objects from the APIC GUI. In the upper-right corner of the APIC GUI, click on the welcome, <username> message to view the drop-down. In the drop-down list, choose Show Debug Info and click on the object on the GUI that you want to get the DN information. Figure 13-10 illustrates all the steps required to get the DN and RN of the objects.

When you perform a task in the APIC GUI, the GUI creates and sends internal API messages to the operating system to execute the task. By using the API Inspector, which is a built-in tool of the APIC, you can view and copy these API messages. A network administrator can replicate these messages to automate key operations, or you can use the messages as examples to develop external applications that will use the API. In the upper-right corner of the APIC GUI window, click on the welcome, <username> message to view the drop-down list. In the drop-down list, choose Show API Inspector. The API Inspector opens in a new browser window and displays all the API messages. Figure 13-11 illustrates the usage of the API Inspector on the APIC GUI.

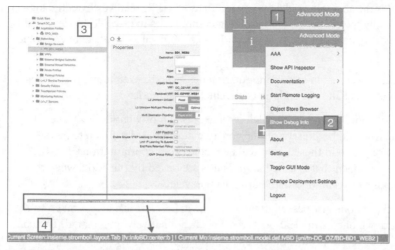

Figure 13-10 *Show Debug Info*

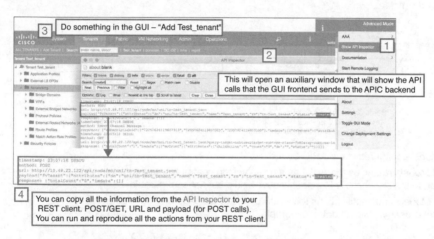

Figure 13-11 *API Inspector*

Different Models

Within the ACI application model, the primary object that encompasses all the objects and their relationships to each other is called an *application profile*. This is also referred to as an *application network profile* interchangeably.

Within the ACI object model, there are essentially three stages of implementation of the model: the logical model, the resolved model, and the concrete model.

The *logical model* is the logical representation of the objects and their relationships. The application profile is an expression of the logical model. This is the declaration of the "end-state" expression that is desired when the elements of the application are connected and the fabric is provisioned by the APIC, stated in high-level terms.

13

The *resolved model* is the abstract model expression that the APIC resolves from the logical model. This is essentially the elemental configuration components that would be delivered to the physical infrastructure when the policy must be executed (such as when an endpoint connects to a leaf).

The *concrete model* is the actual in-state configuration delivered to each fabric member based on the resolved model and the endpoints attached to the fabric.

In general, the logical model should be the high-level expression of what exists in the resolved model, which should be present on the concrete devices as the concrete model expression. If there is any gap in these, there will be inconsistent configurations. In ACI, there is a feedback mechanism that is called *fault*. Faults are raised by the APIC when there are transitions through more than one state during its lifecycle.

There are some configurations just passed down to the switches. For instance, you go to the APIC GUI and shut down one of the leaf ports the switch can natively understand. The configuration does not need to go through all the steps of abstraction to logical to resolved to concrete models. In Figure 13-12, this situation is represented as a direct line from the logical to the concrete model.

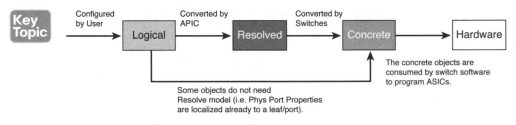

- Logical Model configured in the APIC by the user.
- Resolved Model created by the APIC as a unit/object to communicate and pass information to the switches. This model is user visible but not configurable.
- Concrete Model sends notifications to iNXOS by the switches to program hardware. This model is user visible but not configurable.

Figure 13-12 *Logical Model, Resolved Model, and Concrete Model*

ACI Logical Constructs

At the top level, the APIC policy model is built on a series of one or more tenants, which allow the network infrastructure administration to segregate the data flows. One or more tenants can be used for customers, business units, or groups, depending on organizational needs. For instance, a given enterprise might use one tenant for the entire organization, whereas a cloud service provider might have customers using one or more tenants to represent its organization.

Tenants further break down into private Layer 3 networks, which directly relate to a VRF instance or separate IP space. Each tenant may have one or more private Layer 3 networks depending on the business needs of that tenant. Private Layer 3 networks, which are called context, offer a way to further separate the organizational and forwarding requirements below a given tenant. Because contexts use separate forwarding instances, IP addressing can be duplicated in separate contexts for the purpose of multitenancy.

Below the context, the model provides a series of objects that define the application itself. These objects are endpoints, endpoint groups (EPGs), and the policies that define their relationship. It is important to note that policies in this case are more than just a set of ACLs and include a collection of inbound/outbound filters, traffic quality settings, marking rules/redirection, rules, and Layer 4 through 7 service device graphs. Figure 13-13 illustrates the ACI logical constructs.

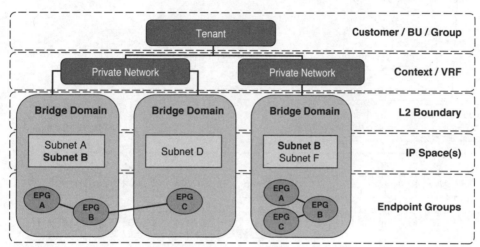

Figure 13-13 *ACI Logical Constructs*

A *tenant* is a logical container or a folder for application policies. It can represent an actual tenant, an organization, or a domain, or it can just be used for the convenience of organizing information. A normal tenant represents a unit of isolation from a policy perspective, but it does not represent a private network. Tenants can provide isolation and play into the role-based access control (RBAC) model that ACI uses. For example, you could have three tenants called Development, Production, and Test. Only certain admins are allowed to make configuration changes in Development, and some others in Production tenants. Some admins may also just have read only access to these tenants. In addition, there is a fabric administrator who has access to everything. You can use multitenancy to separate workloads into a network-centric tenant and an application centric tenant. One tenant can be used for existing workloads in the network-centric model, a second tenant can be used for new applications deployed in application centric mode, thereby giving you a safe separation between legacy workloads and new workloads brought directly into ACI at inception.

A special tenant named *common* has sharable policies that all tenants can use. A *context* is a representation of a private Layer 3 namespace or Layer 3 network. It is a unit of isolation in the Cisco ACI framework. A tenant can rely on several contexts. Contexts can be declared within a tenant (contained by the tenant) or can be in the "common" tenant. Figure 13-14 illustrates ACI Logical constructs with common and private tenants. This approach provides

13

both multiple private Layer 3 networks per tenant and shared Layer 3 networks used by multiple tenants. This way, you do not dictate a specific rigidly constrained tenancy model. The endpoint policy specifies a common Cisco ACI behavior for all endpoints defined within a given virtual ACI context.

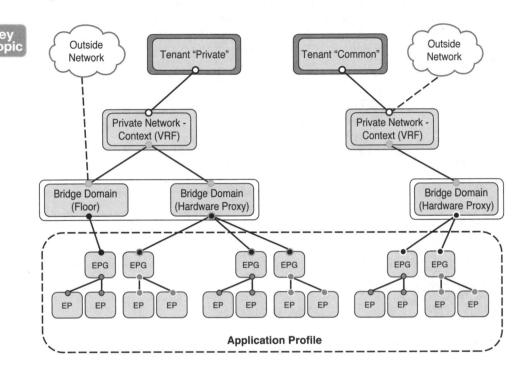

Figure 13-14 *ACI Logical Constructs*

Tenants do not actually separate traffic inherently in ACI, but they do allow for the implementation of security domains, endpoint policy, and RBAC both within and between tenants.

A separate VRF (context) can be created allowing overlapping IP space between tenants. VRF stands for virtual routing and forwarding and simply means you can have overlapping logical routers in the same switch (or same switch fabric, in the case of ACI). ACI actually uses VRF-lite within the fabric. The VRF allows for the separation of traffic between tenants, or more accurately between VRFs. ACI is flexible in that each tenant can have its own VRF, or you can share a given VRF among tenants or any mix of the two.

Figure 13-15 provides an overview of the tenant portion of the MIT. Tenants can be isolated from one another, or they can share resources. The primary elements that the tenant contains are filters, contracts, outside networks, bridge domains, contexts, and application profiles that contain EPGs. Entities in the tenant inherit its policies. A tenant can contain one or more VRF instances or contexts; each context can be associated with multiple bridge domains.

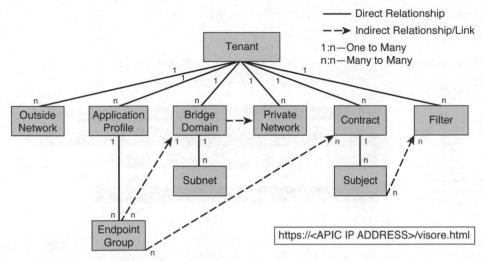

Figure 13-15 *ACI Management Information Tree*

A tenant can contain multiple outside network objects. Outside network policies specify the relevant Layer 2 or Layer 3 properties that control communications between an outside public or private network and the ACI fabric. External devices—such as routers that connect to the WAN and enterprise core—or existing Layer 2 switches connect to the front panel interface of a leaf switch. The leaf switch that provides such connectivity is known as a *border leaf*. The border leaf switch interface that connects to an external device can be configured as either a bridged or a routed interface. In the case of a routed interface, static or dynamic routing can be used. The border leaf switch can also perform all the functions of a normal leaf switch.

The relationship of managed objects expresses the relationship between managed object instances that do not share containment (parent-child) relations. MO relations are established between the source MO and a target MO in one of the following two ways:

■ An *explicit relation* defines a relationship based on the target MO domain name (DN).

■ A *named relation* defines a relationship based on the target MO name.

The dotted lines in Figure 13-15 show several common MO relations. For example, the dotted line between the EPGs and the bridge domain defines the relationship between those two MOs. The EPG (fvAEPg) contains a relationship MO (fvRsBD) that is named with the target bridge domain MO (fvDB). For example, if production is the bridge domain name (tnFvBDName=production), then the relation name would be production (fvRsBdName=production).

In the case of policy resolution based on named relations, if a target MO with a matching name is not found in the current tenant, the ACI fabric tries to resolve in the common tenant. If a named relation cannot be resolved in either the current tenant or the common tenant, the ACI fabric attempts to resolve to a *default policy*. If a default policy exists in the current tenant, it is used. If it does not exist, the ACI fabric looks for a default policy in the common tenant. Bridge domain, context, and contract (security policy) named relations do not resolve to a default.

13

Figure 13-16 illustrates the ACI logical constructs in the APIC GUI.

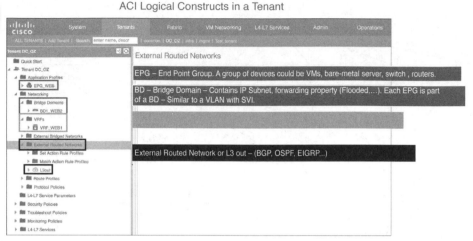

Figure 13-16 *ACI Logical Constructs in a Tenant*

Bridge Domains and Subnets

A bridge domain represents a Layer 2 forwarding construct within the fabric. Figure 13-15 shows the location of bridge domains in the MIT and their relation to other objects in the tenant. A bridge domain can be defined similarly to VLANs. The bridge domain contains a gateway, or switch virtual interface (SVI). The SVI acts as a pervasive gateway for endpoints. In network-centric mode, you have only one SVI, or subnet, contained within a bridge domain.

A bridge domain must be linked to a context and have at least one subnet that is associated with it. The bridge domain defines the unique Layer 2 MAC address space and a Layer 2 flood domain if such flooding is enabled. Although a context defines a unique IP address space, that address space can consist of multiple subnets. Those subnets are defined in one or more bridge domains that reference the corresponding context.

The options for a subnet under a bridge domain or under an EPG are as follows:

■ **Public:** The subnet can be exported to a routed connection.

■ **Private:** The subnet applies only within its tenant.

■ **Shared:** The subnet can be shared with and exported to multiple contexts (VRFs) in the same tenant or across tenants as part of a shared service. An example of a shared service is a routed connection to an EPG present in another context (VRF) in a different tenant. This enables traffic to pass in both directions across contexts (VRFs). An EPG that provides a shared service must have its subnet configured under that EPG (not under a bridge domain), and its scope must be set to advertise externally and be shared between VRFs.

There is one noticeable difference between traditional networks and ACI: ACI uses the white list model. Hence, by default no traffic is allowed between subnets, although traffic is allowed within the bridge domains, by default. This default behavior can be easily changed to match traditional networking concepts. To change this white list model, contracts need to be configured. Contracts will be discussed later in this chapter.

Bridge domain packet behavior can be controlled as outlined in Table 13-2.

Table 13-2   Bridge Domain Packet Behavior

Packet Type	Mode
ARP	Unicast/Flood
NOTE If the `limitIpLearnToSubnets` in `fvBD` is set, endpoint learning is limited to the bridge domain only if the IP is in a configured subnet of the bridge domain or in an EPG subnet that is a shared service provider.	
Unknown Unicast	Proxy/Flood
Unknown IP Multicast	Flood Mode/Optimized Multicast Flooding Mode
L2 Multicast, Broadcast, Link Local	BD-flood: flood in bridge domain Encap-flood: flood in encapsulation Drop: drop the packet
NOTE Because the following protocols are always flooded in a bridge domain, bridge domain mode settings do not apply: OSPF/OSPFv6, BGP, EIGRP, CDP, LACP, LLDP, ISIS, IGMP, PIM, ST-BPDU, ARP/GARP, ND.	

Bridge domains can span multiple switches. A bridge domain can contain multiple subnets, but a subnet is contained within a single bridge domain. If the bridge domain (fvBD class) `limitIPLearnToSubnets` property is set to yes, endpoint learning will occur in the bridge domain only if the IP address is within any of the configured subnets for the bridge domain or within an EPG subnet when the EPG is a shared service provider. Subnets can span multiple EPGs; one or more EPGs can be associated with one bridge domain or subnet.

In-Band and Out-of-Band Management Networks

An APIC controller has two routes to reach the management network. One is by using the in-band management interface, and the other is by using the out-of-band management interface.

The in-band management network allows APIC to communicate with the leaf switches and with the outside using the ACI fabric, and it makes it possible for external management devices to communicate with the APIC or the leaf switches and spine switches using the fabric itself.

The out-of-band management network configuration defines the configuration of the management port on the controllers, the leaf switches, and the spine switches.

The APIC controller always selects the in-band management interface over the out-of-band management interface if the in-band management interface is configured. The out-of-band management interface is used only when the in-band management interface is not configured

13

or if the destination address is on the same subnet as the out-of-band management subnet of the APIC. This behavior cannot be changed or reconfigured. The APIC management interface does not support an IPv6 address and cannot connect to an external IPv6 server through this interface. The APIC out-of-band management connection link must be 1 Gbps. Figure 13-17 illustrates the in-band and out-of-band network connectivity within the ACI fabric.

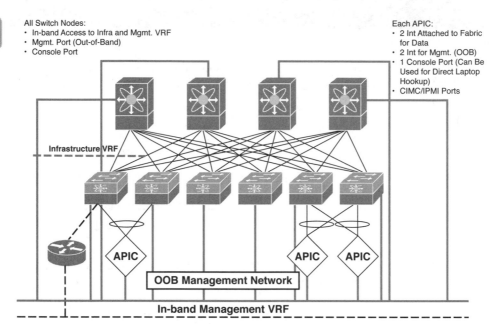

- Infrastructure VRF—Used for in-band APIC to switch node communication.
- In-band Management Network—'tenant' VRF created for in-band access to switch nodes.
- Out-of-Band (OOB) Management Network—APIC and All Switch Nodes have dedicated mgmt. ports.

Figure 13-17 *In-Band and Out-of-Band Management Networks*

In-band management addresses can be provisioned on the APIC controller only through a policy (Postman REST API, NX-OS Style CLI, or GUI). Additionally, the in-band management addresses must be configured statically on each node. Out-of-band management addresses can be provisioned on the APIC controller either at the time of bootstrap or by using a policy (Postman REST API, NX-OS Style CLI, GUI). Additionally, the out-of-band management addresses must be configured statically on each node or by specifying a range of addresses (IPv4/IPv6) to the entire cluster. IP addresses are randomly assigned from a range to the nodes in the cluster.

The Cisco APIC automatically configures an infrastructure VRF instance that is used for in-band communication between the Cisco APIC and the switch node communication; it is nonroutable outside the fabric.

The Cisco APIC serves as DHCP and TFTP server for the fabric. The Cisco APIC assigns the tunnel endpoint (TEP) addresses for each switch. Core links are unnumbered.

The Cisco APIC allocates three types of IP addresses from private address space:

- **Switch TEP IP address:** Switches inside a pod share a common prefix.
- **Cisco APIC IP address:** The management IP address of the Cisco APIC appliance.
- **VXLAN tunnel endpoint (VTEP) IP address:** VTEPs behind a leaf share a common prefix.

Two tenants are created by default in Cisco ACI for management purposes:

- **Infrastructure:** This tenant is used for TEP-to-TEP (or leaf-to-leaf) traffic within the fabric and for bootstrap protocols within the fabric.
- **Management:** This tenant is used for management connectivity between the APICs and switch nodes, as well as for connectivity to other management systems (authentication, authorization, and accounting [AAA] servers, vCenter, and so on).

The in-band management configuration lets you define the IP addresses for APIC controllers, leaves, and spines so that they can share a bridge domain for management purposes. The configuration includes the definition of a VLAN, which is used to enable communication between the controller and the fabric. This VLAN must be configured on the mgmt tenant and enabled on the port that connects to the controller from the infrastructure configuration.

The infrastructure tenant is preconfigured for the fabric infrastructure, including the VRF instance and bridge domain used for the fabric VXLAN overlay. The infrastructure tenant can be used to extend the fabric infrastructure to outside systems that support overlay protocols such as VXLAN. Administrators are strongly advised against modifying the infrastructure tenant. This tenant is not used for general management functions.

The management tenant is used for general in-band and out-of-band management of Cisco ACI. Figure 13-18 illustrates the configuration of in-band management in APIC Basic GUI. The management tenant has a default VRF instance and private network named inb (for "in band"). A single bridge domain is created by default, also named inb.

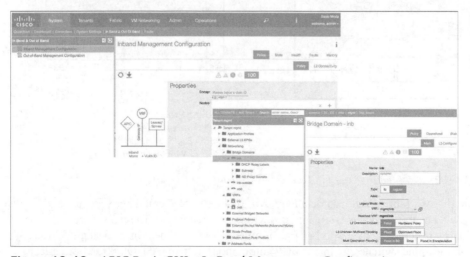

Figure 13-18 *APIC Basic GUI—In-Band Management Configuration*

To employ existing firewalls (or other Layer 3 gateways like routers with Internet connections), you can use an ACI concept called Layer 3 Out. It is important to note that an ACI fabric is effectively a big L3 routed fabric that advertises local routes and learns external routes. For example, you connect a firewall or a router to a leaf switch using a single line or a port channel, and then you use a routing protocol like Open Shortest Path First (OSPF), Enhanced Interior Gateway Routing Protocol (EIGRP), or Border Gateway Protocol (BGP) to exchange routes between the device and the ACI fabric. Inside the fabric, you build the connection using a combination of SVI and VLAN and then create and apply this via an external routed domain. You do not need to make changes to the default gateways or FHRP on your traditional networks. In other words, leave them where they are currently in the classical Ethernet environment, and later migrate from the old network to the ACI fabric. Once you migrate all workloads completely to ACI, you can move the gateways for those VLANs and subnets inside the fabric. It is possible to do this on a per-VLAN basis. Figure 13-19 summarizes Layer 3 Out in ACI fabric.

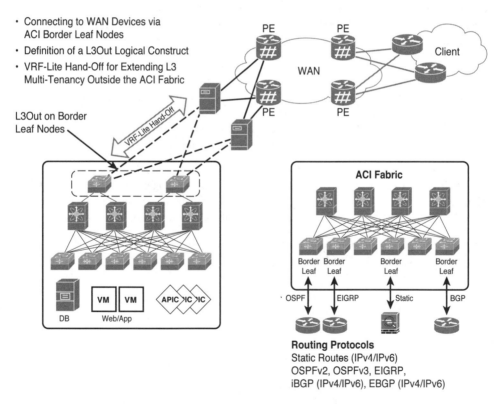

Figure 13-19 *Connecting ACI via Layer 3—Routing*

Within the ACI fabric, Multiprotocol BGP (MP-BGP) is implemented between leaf and spine switches to propagate external routes within the ACI fabric. The BGP route reflector technology is deployed to support a large number of leaf switches within a single fabric. All the leaf and spine switches are in one BGP autonomous system (AS). Once the border leaf learns the external routes, it can then redistribute the external routes of a given VRF to an MP-BGP address family VPN version 4 (or VPN version 6 when IPv6 routing is supported in ACI). With address family VPN version 4, MP-BGP maintains a separate BGP routing table for each VRF. Within MP-BGP, the border leaf advertises routes to a spine switch, which is a BGP route reflector. The routes are then propagated to all the leaves where the VRFs are instantiated. If you bring external routes into the fabric, it will be necessary to enable MP-BGP, which is not enabled by default, and use an AS number. Note that this will only run within the fabric and not between the fabric and any external device or network. For the OSPF leaf to tell the rest of the fabric about any routes it learns, it will have to use route redistribution. Because ACI is multitenant, the protocol of choice is BGP; it carries more information than just routes.

Endpoint Groups

ACI EPGs provide a new model for mapping applications to the network. EPGs provide a logical grouping for objects that require similar policy. Rather than using forwarding constructs such as addressing or VLANs to apply connectivity and policy, EPGs use a grouping of application endpoints. EPGs act as a container for collections of applications, or application components and tiers that can be used to apply forwarding and policy logic. They allow the separation of network policy, security, and forwarding from addressing and instead apply it to logical application boundaries. They are a logical grouping with varying use options depending on the application deployment model in use. They have an address (identity), a location, and attributes (such as version or patch level), and they can be physical or virtual. Knowing the address of an endpoint also enables access to all its other identity details. EPGs are fully decoupled from the physical and logical topology. Endpoint examples include servers, virtual machines, network-attached storage (NAS), and clients on the Internet. Endpoint membership in an EPG can be dynamic or static. Figure 13-20 depicts the relationship between endpoints, EPGs, and applications.

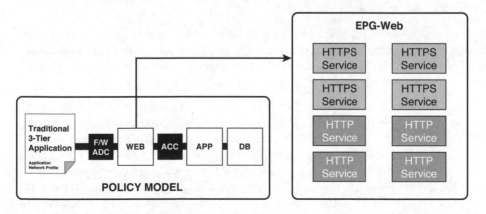

Figure 13-20 *ACI Policy Model Brings the Concept of Endpoint Group (EPG)*

Figure 13-20 shows a grouping of HTTP and HTTPS services as a single group of endpoints known as an EPG. This grouping is independent of addressing, VLAN, and other network constructs as opposed to traditional network environments that must rely on these for groupings.

Within an EPG, separate endpoints can exist in one or more subnets, and subnets can be applied to one or more EPGs based on several other design considerations. Layer 2 forwarding behavior can then be applied independently of the Layer 3 addressing. Figure 13-21 shows the relationship between EPGs and subnets. Figure 13-21 shows two subnets being applied to two different services within two EPGs. HTTPS endpoints reside in 10.11.12.x, whereas HTTP endpoints reside in 10.11.13.x. Regardless of the separate subnets, policy is applied to both HTTPS and HTTP services within this EPG in this example. This illustrates the complete decoupling of addressing from policy enforcement. Within the ACI fabric, subnets are utilized for forwarding only. Policy can be enforced granularly within a subnet or consistently across subnets.

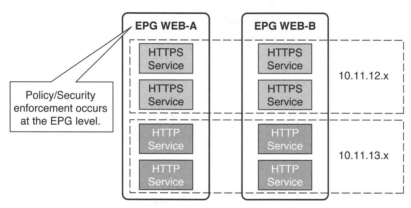

Figure 13-21 *EPGs, Subnets, and Policies*

Endpoint groups not only allow for better mapping of applications to the network, but better mapping of the network to application owners and developers. Rather than application owners and developers being required to maintain mappings to IP addressing and subnets, they can group applications or application components to logical EPGs.

In Legacy mode, there is no routing, L3 context, or contract enabled in the L2 fabric profile. A tenant can be represented by a set of EPGs instead. To improve the load sharing among APIC controller nodes, you must distribute EPGs and bridge domain across an ACI tenant. The ACI L3 fabric solution provides a feature-rich, highly scalable solution for public cloud and large enterprise. With this design, almost all supported features are deployed at the same time and are tested as a solution. The fabric scalability numbers represent the overall number of objects created on the fabric. The per-leaf scale numbers are the objects created and presented on an individual leaf switch. The fabric-level scalability numbers represent APIC cluster scalability and the tested upper limits. Some of the per-leaf scalability numbers are subject to hardware restrictions. The per-leaf scalability numbers are the maximum limits tested and supported by leaf switch hardware. The maximum verified scalability limits for ACI parameters are documented in *Verified Scalability Guide* depending on the specific software release.

EPGs are designed as flexible containers for endpoints that require common policy. Several methods exist for defining endpoints and placing them in EPGs. Once grouped, policy is applied based on the logical grouping rather than addressing and forwarding constructs. The use of EPGs can and will differ across customer environments and even across a single fabric deployment.

EPGs contain endpoints that have common policy requirements such as security, virtual machine mobility (VMM), quality of service (QoS), and Layer 4 to Layer 7 services. Rather than configure and manage endpoints individually, they are placed in an EPG and managed as a group. Figure 13-22 illustrates endpoint classifications. The ACI fabric can contain the following types of EPGs:

- Application endpoint group
- Layer 2 external outside network instance endpoint group
- Layer 3 external outside network instance endpoint group
- Management endpoint groups for out-of-band or in-band access

Endpoint Classification

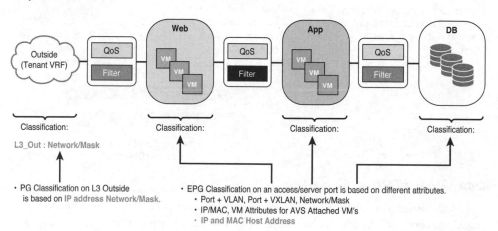

Figure 13-22 *Endpoint Classification*

Policies apply to EPGs, never to individual endpoints. An EPG can be statically configured by an administrator in the APIC or dynamically configured by an automated system such as vCenter or OpenStack.

Virtual machine management connectivity to VMware vCenter is an example of a configuration that uses a dynamic EPG. Once the virtual machine management domain is configured in the fabric, vCenter triggers the dynamic configuration of EPGs that enable virtual machine endpoints to start up, move, and shut down as needed.

13

Although encapsulation-based EPGs are commonly used, IP-based EPGs are suitable in settings needing large numbers of EPGs that cannot be supported by Longest Prefix Match (LPM) classification. IP-based EPGs do not require allocating a network/mask range for each EPG, unlike LPM classification. Also, a unique bridge domain is not required for each IP-based EPG. The configuration steps for an IP-based EPG are like those for configuring a virtual IP based EPG that is used in the Cisco AVS vCenter configuration.

Policy within a Cisco ACI fabric is applied between two EPGs. It can be utilized in either a unidirectional or a bidirectional mode between any given pair of EPGs. The policy then defines the allowed communication between EPGs. Figure 13-23 illustrates the independent communication policy between EPGs.

EPGs and Class IDs

- Each EPG is identified by a specific Group Policy 'Class ID'.

- All traffic sourced from an endpoint is identified by the class ID corresponding to its EPG membership.

- When one endpoint communicates with another endpoint the Fabric checks that the class ID of the *source* is permitted to communicate to the class ID of the *destination* using the specific ports as defined by the filters in the contract.

- Communication policy is 'directional' (policy checks both Web to App and App to Web are allowed).

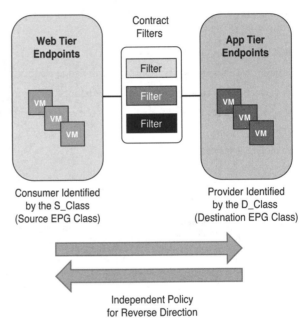

Figure 13-23 *EPGs and Class IDs*

EPGs are designed to abstract the instantiation of network policy and forwarding from basic network constructs (VLANs and subnets). This allows applications to be deployed on the network in a model consistent with their development and intent. Endpoints assigned to an EPG can be defined in several ways: by virtual port, physical port, IP address, and DNS name. In the future, they will be able to be defined through identification methods such as IP address plus Layer 4 port and others.

EPG as a VLAN

The EPG as a VLAN method is useful for both an initial mapping of existing applications onto the ACI fabric and for incorporating existing systems in mixed environments. In this model, the VLAN and all the devices within that VLAN are mapped into an EPG.

This method can be utilized both logically for migrating applications and physically when connecting to existing network infrastructure. In the logical usage, the devices attached to an existing VLAN are defined as members of a single EPG within the ACI fabric. Once the logical configuration is in place, the actual devices—virtual or physical—can be migrated onto the ACI fabric.

EPG as a Subnet

EPG as a subnet is another method for mapping applications onto the ACI fabric in a method mirroring traditional networking. Rather than redesigning the application layout for a given application, existing subnets can be configured as EPGs. All devices in the assigned IP address range will become members of the EPG and receive consistent policy.

This model will fall in line with many current service appliance (firewall, application delivery controller [ADC], and so on) deployment models that utilize the IP subnet to identify and apply policy to traffic. Policy will be applied based on the EPG that is equal to the original subnet. Additionally, this model allows for a quick and straightforward migration to the ACI fabric.

EPG as a VXLAN VNID/NVGRE Virtual Subnet ID (VSID)

Many virtualized environments have moved toward overlay models that utilize VXLAN or NVGRE for tunneling. This tunneling allows virtual machine connectivity independent of the underlying network. In these environments, one or more virtual networks are built using the chosen overlay technology, and traffic is encapsulated as it traverses the physical network. The ACI fabric is designed to provide overlay independence and can bridge frames to and from VXLAN, NVGRE, VLAN, and 802.1x encapsulation. This provides flexibility for heterogeneous environments, which may have services residing on disparate overlays. The virtual networks or VNIDs created by these overlays can be translated directly into EPGs within the ACI fabric. This provides a method for quickly migrating onto the ACI fabric as well as providing policy instantiation for these networks in production use.

EPG as a VMware Port Group

This model of EPG use is similar to the EPG as a VLAN method because the connectivity from the ACI leaf perspective is still VLAN based. The difference is that the configuration and integration of the VLAN constructs on the VMware Distributed Virtual Switch (DVS) within the VMware environment are automated by the Cisco APIC. Both Microsoft HyperV and Linux-based hypervisors rely on standard VLAN configuration for switching and are typically configured using EPG as a VLAN for existing workloads being moved to the ACI fabric.

A DVS mapped to the ACI environment is created, uplinks (physical network interface cards, known as pNICs) are added to the construct, and port groups are created. Each port group receives a user-friendly name and a VLAN or a trunk (multiple VLANs), or it is left untagged. VMs are provided connectivity by assigning their virtual NICs (vNIC) to a specific port group.

13

EPG as an Application Component Group

EPG as an application component group is the primary basis of EPG design. In this method, EPGs are designated as logical groups of endpoints that represent a specific component or tier of an application. For example, an EPG may represent the endpoints serving as the web portal of a multitier application.

This model typically aligns most closely to the design driven by application architects. Additionally, this model frees application architects from needing knowledge of underlying constructs such as VLANs and subnets. Using EPGs to designate application component groups allows for clear policy application between tiers in a fashion organic to the way in which they are designed. In this model, EPGs can be thought of as having a provider/consumer relationship with one another, where the communication between them is defined by policy contracts.

EPG as a Zone

Utilizing EPG as a zone allows resource grouping based on security or compliance rules without the need to segregate these resources by VLAN or subnet. Examples of zones include demilitarized zone (DMZ), internal, shared services, PCI, HIPPAA, and others. This allows for a logical segregation of devices that require specific security and compliance policies to be applied.

EPG as a zone alleviates the traditional network reliance on addressing and VLAN for segregation of resources and application of policy. Using this method allows developers and network teams to more closely coordinate policy and definition without the need for translation between common terminologies. It also decreases the complexity of the design and application of those defined policies.

There is no dedicated manner in which EPGs should be deployed and utilized. The use of EPGs is intended to be extremely flexible to allow the right fit for the right task, rather than a one-size-fits-all methodology.

Policy Enforcement

The relationship between EPGs and policies can be thought of as a matrix with one axis representing the source EPG (sEPG) and the other representing the destination EPG (dEPG.) One or more policies will be placed at the intersection of the appropriate sEPGs and dEPGs. The matrix will be sparsely populated in most cases because many EPGs have no need to communicate with one another.

Policies are divided by filters for QoS, access control, service insertion, and more. Filters are specific rules for the policy between two EPGs. Filters consist of inbound and outbound rules: permit, deny, redirect, log, copy, and mark. Policies allow wildcard functions in the definitions. Policy enforcement typically uses a most-specific-match-first approach. Figure 13-24 illustrates the flow of the policy enforcement on the fabric.

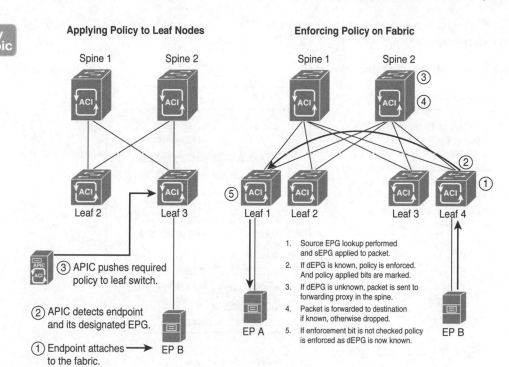

Figure 13-24   *Policy Enforcement Flow Diagrams*

Enforcement of policy within the fabric is always guaranteed; however, policy can be applied in one of two places. Policy can be enforced opportunistically at the ingress leaf; otherwise, it is enforced on the egress leaf. Whether or not policy can be enforced at ingress is determined by whether the destination EPG is known. The source EPG will always be known, and policy rules pertaining to that source as both an sEPG and a dEPG are always pushed to the appropriate leaf switch when an endpoint attaches. After policy is pushed to a leaf, it is stored and enforced in hardware. Because the Cisco APIC is aware of all EPGs and the endpoints assigned to them, the leaf to which the EPG is attached will always have all policies required and will never need to punt traffic to a controller, as might be the case in other systems.

If the destination EPG is not known, policy cannot be enforced at ingress. Instead, the source EPG is tagged, and policy applied bits are not marked. Both of these fields exist in the reserved bits of the VXLAN header. The packet is then forwarded to the forwarding proxy, typically resident in the spine. The spine is aware of all destinations in the fabric; therefore, if the destination is unknown, the packet is dropped. If the destination is known, the packet is forwarded to the destination leaf. The spine never enforces policy; the egress leaf will handle this.

When a packet is received by the egress leaf, the sEPG and the policy applied bits are read. (These were tagged at ingress.) If the policy-applied bits are marked as applied, the packet is forwarded without additional processing. If instead the policy-applied bits do not show that policy has been applied, the sEPG marked in the packet is matched with the dEPG (always known on the egress leaf), and the appropriate policy is then applied. Figure 13-25 illustrates the distributed policy enforcement with VXLAN header.

Fabric Policy—Distributed Policy Enforcement

- ACI Fabric leverages an application centric policy model.
- VXLAN Source Group is used as a tag/label to identify the specific endpoint for each application function (EPG).
- Policy is enforced between an ingress or source application tier (EPG) and an egress or destination application tier (EPG).
- Policy can be enforced at source or destination.

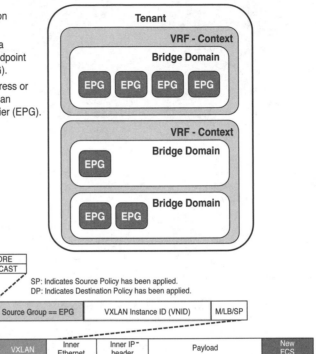

Figure 13-25 *Fabric Policy—Distributed Policy Enforcement*

Another benefit of EPGs is in the way in which policy is enforced for an EPG. The physical ternary content-addressable memory (TCAM) where policy is stored for enforcement is an expensive component of switch hardware and therefore tends to lower policy scale or raise hardware costs. Within the Cisco ACI fabric, policy is applied based on the EPG rather than the endpoint itself. This policy size can be expressed as $n * m * f$, where n is the number of sources, m is the number of destinations, and f is the number of policy filters. Within the Cisco ACI fabric, sources and destinations become one entry for a given EPG, which reduces the number of total entries required.

Multicast Policy Enforcement

The nature of multicast makes the requirements for policy enforcement slightly different. Although the source EPG is easily determined at ingress because it is never a multicast address, the destination is an abstract entity; the multicast group may consist of endpoints from multiple EPGs. In multicast cases, the Cisco ACI fabric uses a multicast group for policy enforcement. The multicast groups are defined by specifying a multicast address range or ranges. Policy is then configured between the sEPG and the multicast group.

The multicast group (EPG group corresponding to the multicast stream) will always be the destination and never used as a source EPG. Traffic sent to a multicast group will be from either the multicast source or a receiver joining the stream through an IGMP join. Because multicast streams are nonhierarchical and the stream itself will already be in the forwarding table (using IGMP join), multicast policy is always enforced at ingress. This prevents the need for multicast policy to be written to egress leaves.

Microsegmentation

Microsegmentation associates endpoints from multiple EPGs into a microsegmented EPG according to virtual machine attributes, IP address, or MAC address. Virtual machine attributes include VNic domain name, VM identifier, VM name, hypervisor identifier, VMM domain, datacenter, operating system, and custom attribute.

Some advantages of microsegmentation include the following:

■ Stateless white list network access security with line rate enforcement.

■ Per-microsegment granularity of security automation through dynamic Layer 4 through Layer 7 service insertion and chaining.

■ Hypervisor agnostic microsegmentation in a broad range of virtual switch environments.

■ ACI policies that easily move problematic VMs into a quarantine security zone.

■ When combined with intra-EPG isolation for bare metal and VM endpoints, provides policy-driven endpoint isolation within application tiers.

For any EPG, the ACI fabric ingress leaf switch classifies packets into an EPG according to the policies associated with the ingress port. Microsegmented EPGs apply policies to individual virtual or physical endpoints that are derived based on the VM attribute, MAC address, or IP address specified in the microsegmented EPG policy.

Intra-EPG Endpoint Isolation

Intra-EPG endpoint isolation policies provide full isolation for virtual or physical endpoints; no communication is allowed between endpoints in an EPG that is operating with isolation enforced. Isolation-enforced EPGs reduce the number of EPG encapsulations required when many clients access a common service but are not allowed to communicate with each other.

An EPG is isolation enforced for all ACI network domains or none. Although the ACI fabric implements isolation directly to connected endpoints, switches connected to the fabric are made aware of isolation rules according to a primary VLAN (PVLAN) tag.

If an EPG is configured with intra-EPG endpoint isolation enforced, these restrictions apply:

■ All Layer 2 endpoint communication across an isolation-enforced EPG is dropped within a bridge domain.

■ All Layer 3 endpoint communication across an isolation-enforced EPG is dropped within the same subnet.

13

Application Profiles

An application profile models the logical representation of the entire application and its requirements on the Cisco ACI fabric. An application profile is a convenient logical container for grouping EPGs. Figure 13-15 shows the location of application profiles in the MIT and their relationship to other objects in the tenant.

Application profiles within the fabric are a collection of the EPGs, their connections, and the policies that define those connections. They can contain one or more EPGs. Modern applications have multiple components. For example, an e-commerce application could require a web server, a database server, data located in a storage-area network, and access to outside resources that enable financial transactions. The application profile contains as many (or as few) EPGs as necessary that are logically related to providing the capabilities of an application. Figure 13-26 illustrates an application profile.

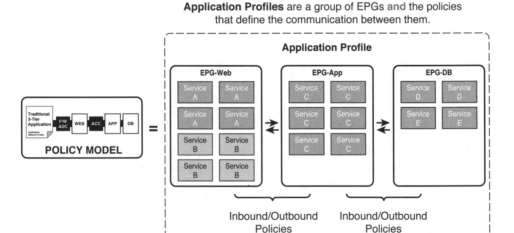

Figure 13-26 *Application Profile*

EPGs can be organized according to one of the following:

- The application they provide
- The function they provide (such as infrastructure)
- Where they are in the structure of the data center (such as DMZ)
- Whatever organizing principle that a fabric or tenant administrator chooses to use

Contracts

In addition to EPGs, contracts are key objects in the policy model. EPGs can only communicate with other EPGs according to contract rules. Figure 13-27 shows the location of contracts in the MIT and their relation to other objects in the tenant.

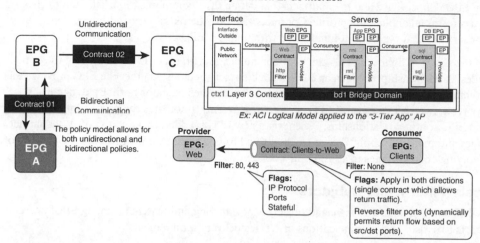

Figure 13-27 *Applying Policy Between EPGs: ACI Contracts*

An administrator uses a contract to select the type(s) of traffic that can pass between EPGs, including the protocols and ports allowed. If there is no contract, inter-EPG communication is disabled by default. There is no contract required for intra-EPG communication; intra-EPG communication is always implicitly allowed.

Contracts govern the following types of endpoint group communications:

■ Between ACI fabric application EPGs, both intra-tenant and inter-tenant

■ Between ACI fabric application EPGs and Layer 2 external outside network instance EPGs

■ Between ACI fabric application EPGs and Layer 3 external outside network instance EPGs

■ Between ACI fabric out-of-band or in-band management EPGs

Contracts govern the communication between EPGs that are labeled providers, consumers, or both. EPG providers expose contracts with which a would-be consumer EPG must comply. The relationship between an EPG and a contract can be either a provider or a consumer. When an EPG provides a contract, communication with that EPG can be initiated from other EPGs as long as the communication complies with the provided contract. When an EPG consumes a contract, the endpoints in the consuming EPG may initiate communication with any endpoint in an EPG that is providing that contract.

An EPG can both provide and consume the same contract. An EPG can also provide and consume multiple contracts simultaneously.

Contracts define inbound and outbound permits, denies, QoS, redirects, and service graphs. They allow for both simple and complex definitions of how a given EPG communicates with other EPGs depending on the requirements of a given environment.

13

In Figure 13-27, you see the relationship between the three tiers of a web application defined by EPG connectivity and the contracts that define their communication. The sum of these parts forms an application profile. Contracts also provide reusability and policy consistency for services that typically communicate with multiple EPGs.

In the Cisco ACI fabric, EPGs can only communicate with other EPGs according to contract rules. A relationship between an EPG and a contract specifies whether the EPG provides the communications defined by the contract rules, consumes them, or both. By dynamically applying contract rules to all EPGs in a context, vzAny automates the process of configuring EPG contract relationships. Whenever a new EPG is added to a context, vzAny contract rules automatically apply. The vzAny one-to-all EPG relationship is the most efficient way of applying contract rules to all EPGs in a context.

Labels, Filters, and Subjects

Label, subject, and filter-managed objects enable mixing and matching among EPGs and contracts to satisfy various applications or service delivery requirements.

Contracts can contain multiple communication rules, and multiple EPGs can both consume and provide multiple contracts. Labels control which rules apply when communicating between a specific pair of EPGs. A policy designer can compactly represent complex communication policies and reuse these policies across multiple instances of an application. Figure 13-28 illustrates the contracts and the communication policies within ACI fabric.

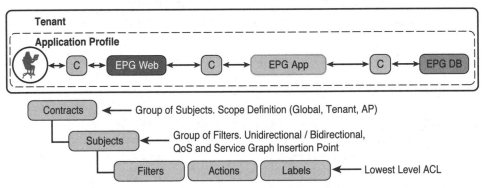

Figure 13-28 *Contracts—Communication Policies*

Labels, subjects, and filters define EPG communications according to the following options:

■ Labels are managed objects with only one property: a name. Labels classify which objects can and cannot communicate with one another. Label matching is done first. If the labels do not match, no other contract or filter information is processed. The label match attribute can be one of these values: at least one (the default), all, none, or exactly one. Labels can be applied to a variety of provider and consumer managed objects, including EPGs, contracts, bridge domains, DHCP relay policies, and DNS policies. Labels do not apply across object types; a label on an application EPG has no relevance to a label on a bridge domain. Labels determine which EPG consumers and EPG providers can use to communicate with one another. Label matching determines which subjects of a contract are used with a given EPG provider or EPG consumer of that contract. There are two types of labels:

- Subject labels that are applied to EPGs. Subject-label matching enables EPGs to choose a subset of the subjects in a contract.

- Provider/consumer labels that are applied to EPGs. Provider/consumer label matching enables consumer EPGs to choose their provider EPGs and vice versa.

■ Filters are Layer 2 to Layer 4 fields, TCP/IP-header fields such as Layer 3 protocol type, Layer 4 ports, and so forth. According to its related contract, an EPG provider dictates the protocols and ports in both the in and out directions. Contract subjects contain associations to the filters (and their directions) that are applied between EPGs that produce and consume the contract. When a contract filter match type is All, best practice is to use the context (VRF) unenforced mode. Under certain circumstances, failure to follow these guidelines results in the contract not allowing traffic among EPGs in this context (VRF).

Subjects are contained in contracts. One or more subjects within a contract use filters to specify the type of traffic that can be communicated and how it occurs. For example, for HTTPS messages, the subject specifies the direction and the filters that identify the IP address type (for example, IPv4), the HTTP protocol, and the ports allowed. Subjects determine if filters are unidirectional or bidirectional. A unidirectional filter is used in one direction. Unidirectional filters define in or out communications but not the same for both. Bidirectional filters are the same for both; they define both in and out communications.

EPGs in one tenant can communicate with EPGs in another tenant through a contract interface contained in a shared tenant. The contract interface is an MO that can be used as a contract consumption interface by the EPGs that are contained in different tenants. By associating to an interface, an EPG consumes the subjects represented by the interface to a contract contained in the shared tenant. Tenants can participate in a single contract, which is defined at some third place. More strict security requirements can be satisfied by defining the tenants, contract, subjects, and filter directions so that tenants remain completely isolated from one another.

Reference List

APIC Visore Tool Introduction: http://www.cisco.com/c/en/us/support/docs/cloud-systems-management/application-policy-infrastructure-controller-apic/118839-technote-visore-00.html

Cisco Data Center GitHub: https://github.com/datacenter

ACI Toolkit: https://datacenter.github.io/acitoolkit/

Avramov, Lucien, and Portolani Maurizio. *The Policy Driven Data Center with ACI: Architecture, Concepts, and Methodology.* Cisco Press, 2015.

ACI Cobra SDK: http://cobra.readthedocs.io/en/latest/

13

Cisco APIC REST API User Guide: http://www.cisco.com/c/en/us/td/docs/switches/data-center/aci/apic/sw/1-x/api/rest/b_APIC_RESTful_API_User_Guide.html

ACI Cisco Support Community: https://supportforums.cisco.com/community/12206936/application centric-infrastructure

Vega, Andres, Bryan Deaver, Jerry Ye, Kannan Ponnuswamy, Loy Evans, Mike Timm, Paul Lesiak, and Paul Raytick. *ACI Troubleshooting* book: http://aci-troubleshooting-book.readthedocs.io/en/latest/

Exam Preparation Tasks

Review All Key Topics

Review the most important topics in the chapter, noted with the key topic icon in the outer margin of the page. Table 13-3 lists a reference of these key topics and the page numbers on which each is found.

Table 13-3 Key Topics for Chapter 13

Key Topic Element	Description	Page
Section	"ACI Policy Object Model"	480
Figure 13-2	"REST API: Read Operations"	481
Figure 13-4	"Hierarchy of the Object Model"	482
List	The API Model Programmatic Entities	483
Figure 13-9	"Managed Object Query—Moquery via APIC CLI"	486
Figure 13-11	"API Inspector"	487
Section	"Different Models"	487
Figure 13-12	"Logical Model, Resolved Model, and Concrete Model"	488
Figure 13-13	"ACI Logical Constructs"	489
Section	"Tenant"	489
Figure 13-14	"ACI Logical Constructs"	490
Figure 13-15	"ACI Management Information Tree"	491
Figure 13-16	"ACI Logical Constructs in a Tenant"	492
Section	"Bridge Domains and Subnets"	492
Section	"In-Band and Out-of-Band Management Networks"	493
Figure 13-17	"In-Band and Out-of-Band Management Networks"	494
Figure 13-19	"Connecting ACI via Layer 3—Routing"	496
Section	"Endpoint Groups"	497
Figure 13-22	"Endpoint Classification"	499
Figure 13-23	"EPGs and Class IDs"	500
Section	"Policy Enforcement"	502
Figure 13-24	"Policy Enforcement Flow Diagrams"	503
List	Policy Enforcement When the Destination EPG Is Unknown	503
Figure 13-25	"Fabric Policy—Distributed Policy Enforcement"	504
Section	"Application Profiles"	506

13

Key Topic Element	Description	Page
Section	"Contracts"	506
Figure 13-27	"Applying Policy Between EPGs: ACI Contracts"	507
Section	"Labels, Filters, and Subjects"	508
Figure 13-28	"Contracts—Communication Policies"	508

Define Key Terms

Define the following key terms from this chapter, and check your answers in the Glossary:

Bridge Domain, Class Name, Consumer, Context, Contract, Distinguished Name (DN), Endpoint Group (EPG), Filter, Subject, Managed Object (MO), Management Information Tree (MIT), Outside Network, Policy, Profile, Provider, Subject, Target DN (tDn), Tenant, VRF, Source Endpoint Group (sEPG), Destination Endpoint Group (dEPG), Ternary Content-Addressable Memory (TCAM), Private Network Virtual Routing and Forwarding (VRF), Application Profile (AP)

This chapter covers the following exam topic:

5.3 Describe the policy-driven, multi-tier application deployment model and its benefits

CHAPTER 14

Operating ACI

Cisco application centric infrastructure (Cisco ACI) simplifies the deployment and management of policies across all virtual switch and bare metal server environments for any type of workload (physical, virtual, or container) based on virtual machine or network attributes or endpoint-group isolation policy.

Cisco ACI was designed to bring together physical and virtual networking to offer an end-to-end solution. For example, Cisco ACI provides transparent support for a mission-critical physical database workload working in conjunction with virtualized web servers and applications. This feature allows operators to support multiple hypervisors, including Citrix Xen, Linux kernel-based virtual machine (KVM), VMware hypervisors, and Microsoft Hyper-V. It also allows them to connect physical servers on the same Cisco ACI network fabric. As open projects such as OpenStack continue to evolve, the capability to span these different environments will become an essential element of any cloud. The Cisco ACI network fabric allows OpenStack Neutron networks to transparently span physical and multihypervisor virtual environments.

This chapter is written to outline the ACI hypervisor integration from multiple vendors, service integration, Cisco application virtual switch (AVS), and OpenStack integration. This is not an official product or configuration guide, however; refer to the appropriate official documents to evaluate products, design, and configure solutions with Cisco ACI. This chapter goes directly into the key concepts of ACI and discusses topics relevant to "The 200-155 DCICT Introducing Cisco Data Center Technologies" certification.

"Do I Know This Already?" Quiz

The "Do I Know This Already?" quiz enables you to assess whether you should read this entire chapter thoroughly or jump to the "Exam Preparation Tasks" section. If you are in doubt about your answers to these questions or your own assessment of your knowledge of the topics, read the entire chapter. Table 14-1 lists the major headings in this chapter and their corresponding "Do I Know This Already?" quiz questions. You can find the answers in Appendix A, "Answers to the 'Do I Know This Already?' Quizzes."

Table 14-1 "Do I Know This Already?" Section-to-Question Mapping

Foundation Topics Section	Questions
"Telemetry"	1, 2, 3, 4
"Open Policy Framework"	5
"Hypervisor Integration"	6, 7
"OpenStack"	8
"Layer 4 to Layer 7 Services Integration"	9
"Microsegmentation"	10

> **CAUTION**   The goal of self-assessment is to gauge your mastery of the topics in this chapter. If you do not know the answer to a question or are only partially sure of the answer, you should mark that question as wrong for purposes of the self-assessment. Giving yourself credit for an answer you correctly guess skews your self-assessment results and might provide you with a false sense of security.

1. Which of the following technologies are used to deliver telemetry for ACI fabric? (Choose two.)

    a. Atomic counters

    b. Health scores and health monitoring

    c. QOS

    d. Late metrics

    e. OpFlex

2. Which of the following options of ACI tenant can atomic counters provide? (Choose two.)

    a. Application-specific counters

    b. Fabric misrouting detection

    c. Endpoint group debugging

    d. PPS port synchronization

    e. Fault counts

3. Which of the following options are available for ACI fabric health information? (Choose three.)

    a. System

    b. POD

    c. Tenant

    d. Filters

4. Which of the following options are different stages of the fault life cycle? (Choose three.)

    a. Soaking

    b. Soaking-clearing

    c. Raised

    d. Cleared

    e. Retaining-clearing

5. What are the meaningful services that ACI applies while moving the traffic from physical and virtualized servers and bringing it in the best possible way to its destination? (Choose three.)

    a. Traffic optimization that improves application performance

    b. Telemetry services

    c. Extensible policy model

    d. Overall health monitoring

    e. Northbound controller

6. How many modes of traffic forwarding does Cisco AVS support?

    a. Four

    b. Three

    c. Two

    d. One

    e. Five

7. Which of the following options are the main characteristics of Microsoft SCVMM integration? (Choose three.)

    a. Policy management through APIC

    b. VM discovery via OpFlex

    c. Manual plug-in installation

    d. Cisco application virtual switch (AVS)

    e. Integrated plug-in installation

8. Which of the following components of OpenStack provides storage volume for compute?

    a. Horizon

    b. Nova

    c. Quantum

    d. Cinder

9. Which of the following parts are in the ACI device package? (Choose four.)

    a. Device specification

    b. Device script

    c. Function profile

    d. Device-level configuration parameters

    e. Group container

10. Which of the following options work for ACI Microsegmentation? (Choose three.)

    a. VMware

    b. Microsoft Azure

    c. OpenStack

    d. IBM

    e. OpFlex

Foundation Topics

ACI and Three-Tier Application Model

Within a layer of virtualization, different traffic can run IP or Ethernet application traffic, video, voice, and storage. Therefore, the virtual data center design offers various quality of service (QoS) capabilities to prioritize the various traffic patterns that take the same uplink toward the first top-of-rack (ToR) switch. The typical type of application running in a virtualized data center is what is often called the *three-tier application model*: consisting of the combination of a specific application, a database, and a web server. Each typically runs on a dedicated virtual machine. In enterprise deployment, databases are often hosted on bare metal servers. In Figure 14-1, notice the relationship between the three tiers of a web application defined by endpoint group (EPG) connectivity and the contracts that define their communication. An "application" in the context of Cisco ACI is the end-to-end components that make up a business application. An application network profile is a collection of EPGs, contracts, and connectivity policy. In other words, it is a collection of groups of workloads that together form what the administrator defines as the application. The sum of these parts becomes an application network profile (ANP, otherwise known as an application profile).

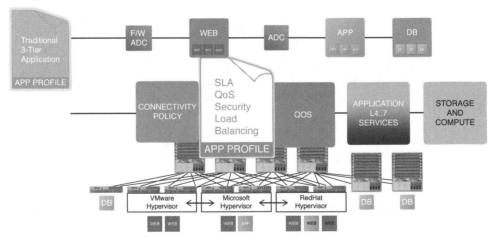

Figure 14-1   *Cisco ACI Three-Tier Application Model*

With traditional networks, application teams put in requirements for their infrastructure teams who then translate them into networking constructs like VLANs, subnets, ports, and routes, oftentimes using spreadsheets. Figure 14-2 depicts a simple case for a three-tier application. As you can see, the workflow for how application requirements are translated can be slow, labor intensive, and vulnerable to manual errors.

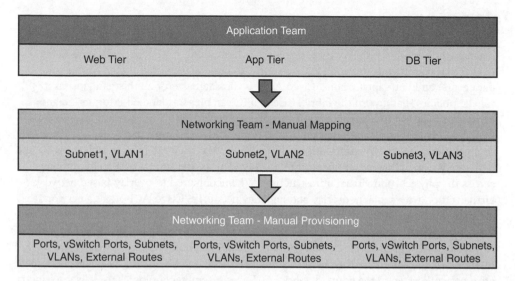

Figure 14-2   *Three-Tier Application Model*

Application deployment is a slow, arduous process often hindered by difficulty translating application and business requirements to infrastructure configuration. Application teams and network teams speak different languages. The network needs to understand the needs of the application, but frequently there is no one to translate.

Network teams are pressed to quickly assess these needs by configuring multiple devices using multiple interfaces when a new application is deployed or modified. Modern applications also have demands the network was not originally designed to provide. Now imagine adding security, load balancing for the web tier, and any other Layer 4 through Layer 7 services into the diagram shown in Figure 14-2. The problem quickly gets out of hand, and this explains why it takes days to weeks to deploy a new application. Now that you appreciate the complexity of configuration, what about day-to-day operational challenges?

The application owner specifies tiers, security constraints between these tiers, how the web server connects to the outside world, and, as needed, firewall, load balancer, and any other Layer 4 through Layer 7 services. The application policy infrastructure controller (APIC) takes these inputs and provisions the entire application automatically.

Under the covers, APIC handles all the complexity of diverse network infrastructure and mapping to the physical or virtual elements. Because APIC already knows the relationship of an application's policy model to the real infrastructure elements, it automatically correlates infrastructure events and failures to each tenant and application.

Just to give you a sense of visibility and troubleshooting, imagine today's situation with a network link failure. For most customers, an event/failure is logged in some management system. The network administrator may, at best, know the server or set of servers affected. The application owner has no idea what happened and perhaps can only see degraded performance. In APIC, as soon as the link is down, the impact will be reflected on the health score of the application.

Telemetry

Cisco ACI is designed to offer a combination of software and hardware that can provide real-time hop-by-hop visibility and telemetry. You can think of the fabric as a telemetry device that collects information for Cisco APIC to provide meaningful data to run your data center and your applications. Cisco APIC is the database for all this data, just as it is for the policies that govern the fabric. Cisco APIC can present detailed information about the performance of individual endpoint groups and tenants in the network. This information includes details about latency, packet drops, and traffic paths and can be sliced at the group or tenant level. Telemetry information can be useful for a wide range of troubleshooting and debugging tasks, allowing an operator to quickly identify the source of a tenant problem across the physical and virtual infrastructure. When compared to overlay-based network virtualization with separate overlay and underlay networks, Cisco ACI offers a network that is easier to manage and that can be debugged more efficiently: an extremely valuable feature because it allows inter-tenant and intra-tenant networking problems to be identified and resolved quickly. ACI offers telemetry services combining comprehensive troubleshooting methodologies that enable the network administrator to quickly identify, isolate, and remediate a network issue on the network fabric. ACI uses several technologies to deliver telemetry for the ACI fabric:

- Atomic counters
- Latency metrics
- Health scores and health monitoring

Atomic Counters

The ACI fabric atomic counters are packet and byte counters that are read atomically across the entire ACI fabric. *Atomic* means that the values in the counters are consistent regardless of where they are in the fabric or the amount of latency or distance that exists between them.

This is accomplished by updating the counters (incrementing the packet count and adding packet length to byte count) atomically with respect to the packet, not with respect to time. In other words, all the counters across the network that a given packet updates are revised before the counters are read. Once all the counters have been updated, the fabric stops revising them until they have been read.

To avoid missing some counts (updates), two sets of counters are kept. While one set is being read, the other set is being updated, and vice versa. These sets are called the *even* set and the *odd* set. The two sets make a counter pair. There is a marker bit set in the packet header that distinguishes the counters that need to be updated for each packet. When the bit is clear, the even counters are updated, and when the bit is set, the odd counters are updated. To make the feature much more useful, a filter is applied to each packet to determine which of N counters are updated. The header fields from the packet are applied to a TCAM (ternary content-addressable memory is a specialized type of high-speed memory that searches its entire contents in a single clock cycle), and the result of the TCAM tells the hardware which counter pair to update. The marker bit in the packet header then informs the hardware which of the two counters in the pair to update. This allows the system to be configured to count multiple kinds of traffic simultaneously.

In conventional settings, it is nearly impossible to monitor the amount of traffic from a bare metal NIC to a specific IP address (an endpoint) or to any IP address. Atomic counters allow an administrator to count the number of packets that are received from a bare metal endpoint without interference to its data path. In addition, atomic counters can monitor per-protocol traffic that is sent to and from an endpoint or an application group.

Leaf-to-leaf (Tunnel Endpoint to Tunnel Endpoint) atomic counters can provide the following:

- Counts of drops, admits, and excess packets

- Short-term data collection such as the last 30 seconds, and long-term data collection such as 5 minutes, 15 minutes, or more

- A breakdown of per-spine traffic (available only when the number of TEPs, leaves, or virtual port channels [VPCs] is less than 64)

- Ongoing monitoring

Figure 14-3 illustrates atomic counters configuration in APIC GUI.

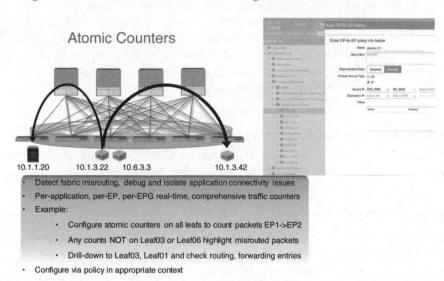

Figure 14-3 *Atomic Counters*

Tenant atomic counters can provide the following:

- Application-specific counters for traffic across the fabric, including drops, admits, and excess packets

Modes include the following:

- Endpoint-to-endpoint MAC address, or endpoint-to-endpoint IP address. Note that a single target endpoint could have multiple IP addresses associated with it.

- EPG to EPG

- EPG to endpoint

- EPG to * (any)
- Endpoint to external IP address

Latency Metrics

The ACI fabric offers a submicrosecond type of latency for forwarding and for troubleshooting per leaf or per spine. The ACI fabric switches are equipped with a pulse per second (PPS) hardware input port. This allows the switch to be connected to an external clock source that has nanosecond accuracy and to use the source clock to set its own time.

The PPS port synchronization is not mandatory for the Precision Time Protocol (PTP) feature. However, it provides better accuracy to the fabric time synchronization because it avoids the multiple hops of the IEEE 1588 protocol to be transmitted. After the switches have the time synchronized, via the support of PTP as defined in IEEE 1588, they serve as a boundary PTP clock source to the remaining switches in the ACI fabric. With PTP, the time synchronizes across switches, and packets are tagged with a PTP timestamp. With PTP, the timestamp is enforced on all fabric switches. This monitors hardware-level latency performance of the ACI fabric, where each switch reads and tags with a PTP timestamp the traffic traversing it. It provides an end-to-end hardware latency real-time knowledge of the traffic going through the ACI fabric. The data is useful for understanding the baseline end-to-end latency performance. It also helps to identify where there could be delays of latency introduced in the fabric due to such things as buffering. With the ACI application programming interface (API) model, it is possible to build real-time tools to monitor the latency at any given place of the ACI fabric.

Health Scores and Health Monitoring

The ACI fabric uses a policy model to combine data into a health score. Health scores can be aggregated for a variety of areas such as for the system, infrastructure, tenants, applications, or services.

ACI fabric health information is available for the following views of the system:

- **System:** Aggregation of system-wide health, including pod health scores, tenant health scores, system fault counts by domain and type, and the APIC cluster health state.
- **Pod:** Aggregation of health scores for a pod (a group of spine and leaf switches), and pod-wide fault counts by domain and type.
- **Tenant:** Aggregation of health scores for a tenant, including performance data for objects such as applications and EPGs that are specific to a tenant, and tenant-wide fault counts by domain and type.
- **Managed Object:** Health score policies for managed objects (MOs), which includes their dependent and related MOs. An administrator can customize these policies.

The system and pod health scores are based on the leaf and spine switches health scores as well as the number of endpoints learned on the leaf switches. The GUI System Dashboard also displays system-wide fault counts by domain type, along with the APIC cluster per-node admin state, operational state, and health state.

Tenant health scores aggregate the tenant-wide logical objects health scores across the infrastructure they happen to use. The APIC GUI tenant dashboard screen also displays tenant-wide-fault counts by domain and type.

Each MO belongs to a health score category. By default, the health score category of an MO is the same as its MO class name. Figure 14-4 illustrates the MO health score.

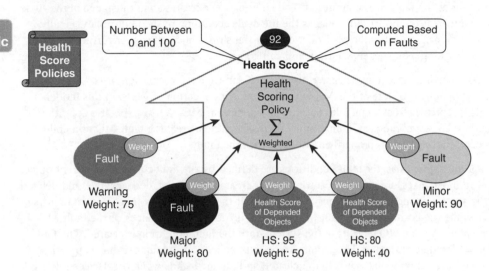

Figure 14-4 *Managed Object (MO) Health Score*

Each health score category is assigned an impact level. The five health score impact levels are Maximum, High, Medium, Low, and None. For example, the default impact level of fabric ports is Maximum, and the default impact level of leaf ports is High. Certain categories of children MOs can be excluded from health score calculations of its parent MO by assigning a health score impact of None. These impact levels between objects are user configurable. However, if the default impact level is None, the administrator cannot override it.

The following factors are the various impact levels:

Maximum: 100% High: 80% Medium: 50% Low: 20% None: 0%

The category health score is calculated using an Lp-Norm formula. The health score penalty equals 100 minus the health score. The health score penalty represents the overall health score penalties of a set of MOs that belong to a given category and are children or direct relatives of the MO for which a health score is being calculated.

The health score category of an MO class can be changed by using a policy. For example, the default health score category of a leaf port is eqpt:LeafP, and the default health score category of fabric ports is eqpt:FabP. However, a policy that includes both leaf ports and fabric ports can be made to be part of the same category called ports.

Faults

Faults that occur in the ACI fabric are monitored by the fault agent. They have explicit representation as managed objects such as policies and ports. Faults have properties such as severity, ID, and description. They are stateful and mutable, and their life cycle is controlled by the system. Finally, faults, like any other ACI health category, are queried using standard APIs.

Faults are originally detected by the switch operating system (NX-OS). The NX-OS process notifies the fault manager on the switch. The fault manager then processes the notification according to the fault rules configured. The fault manager creates a fault instance in the ACI object information model and manages the life cycle according to the fault policy. Finally, the fault manager notifies the controller of state transitions and can trigger further actions such as a syslog message, SNMP trap, and call home.

The APIC maintains a comprehensive, up-to-date, run-time representation of the administrative and operational state of the ACI fabric system in a collection of MOs. In this model, a fault is represented as a mutable, stateful, and persistent MO. When a specific condition occurs, such as a component failure or an alarm, the system creates a fault MO as a child object to the MO that is primarily associated with the fault.

For a fault object class, the fault conditions are defined by the fault rules of the parent object class. In most cases, a fault MO is automatically created, escalated, de-escalated, and deleted by the system as specific conditions are detected. If the same condition is detected multiple times while the corresponding fault MO is active, no additional instances of the fault MO are created. A fault MO remains in the system until the fault condition is cleared. The fault MO is deleted according to the settings in the fault collection and fault retention policies. A fault MO is read-only unless it is in the cleared and retained state, when the user can delete it by acknowledging it. The creation of a fault MO is triggered by internal processes such as finite state machine (FSM) transitions, detected component failures, or conditions specified by various fault policies, some of which are user configurable. For instance, you can set fault thresholds on statistical measurements such as health scores, data traffic, or temperatures. Figure 14-5 illustrates how to check the details of a fault in APIC GUI.

APIC Faults

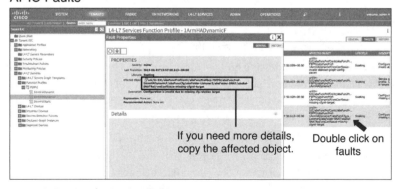

Figure 14-5 *Faults in APIC GUI*

The details of the fault can be investigated in the APIC Visore tool, as shown in Figure 14-6.

Example L4-L7 fault details using Visore Tool
https://apic/visore.htm

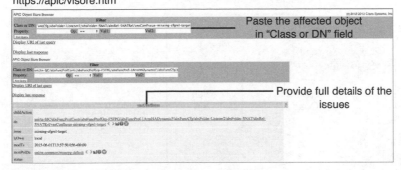

Figure 14-6 *Fault Details Using Visore Tool*

For every fault, a fault record object (fault:Record) is created in the fault log. A fault record is an immutable object that records a state transition for a fault instance object. Record creation is triggered by fault instance MO creation or deletion or by modification of key properties such as severity, life cycle, or acknowledgment of the fault instance object. Although a fault instance object is mutable, the fault record object is not. All properties of the record are set at the time the record object is created.

A record object contains a complete snapshot of the fault instance object and is logically organized as a flat list under a single container. The record object contains properties from the corresponding instance object (fault:Inst), such as severity (original, highest, and previous), acknowledgment, occurrence, and life cycle, as well as inherited properties that provide a snapshot of the fault instance and the nature and time of its change. The record is meant to be queried using time-based filters or property filters for severity, affected DN, or other criteria.

The fault monitoring has a life cycle. APIC fault MOs are stateful. They are faults raised by the APIC when there are transitions through more than one state during its life cycle. In addition, the severity of a fault might change due to its persistence over time, so modification in the state may cause a change in severity. Each change of state causes the creation of a fault record and, if external reporting is configured, can generate a syslog or other external report. Only one instance of a given fault MO can exist on each parent MO. If the same fault occurs again while the fault MO is active, the APIC increments the number of occurrences.

The different stages of the fault life cycle are soaking, soaking-clearing, raised, raised-clearing, and retaining. In more detail, a **soaking** fault is the state for a fault when it is first detected. During this state, depending on the type of fault, it may expire if it is a nonpersistent fault, or it will continue to persist in the system. When a fault enters the **soaking-clearing** state, that fault condition has been resolved at the end of a soaking interval. If a fault has not been cleared by the time the soaking interval has been reached, it will enter the **raised** state and potentially have its severity increased. The new severity is defined by the policy for the particular fault class and will remain in the raised state until the fault condition is cleared. The fault life cycle is shown in Figure 14-7.

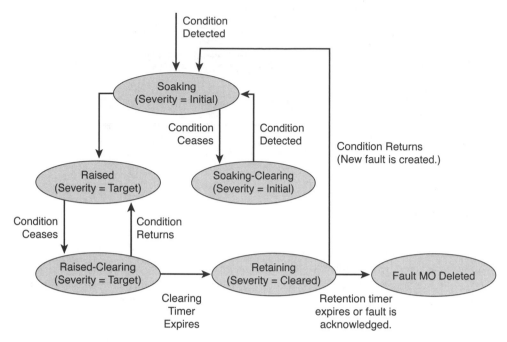

Figure 14-7   *The Fault Life Cycle*

Once a fault condition has been cleared, it will enter the **raised-clearing** state. At this point a clearing interval begins, after which if the fault has not returned it will enter the **retaining** state, which leaves the fault visible so that it can be inspected after an issue has been resolved. At any point during which a fault is created, changes state, or is cleared, a fault event log is generated to keep a record of the state change.

Summary of Cisco ACI Telemetry

Cisco ACI and the policy model bring a centralized approach for diagnostics and provide aggregated metrics for the health of the system by leveraging monitoring technology on each node such as atomic counters, latency monitoring, and fault and diagnostic information. To troubleshoot the ACI fabric, take a fabric-wide approach: examine the global fabric statistics, faults, and diagnostics provided for all elements of the fabric. When thresholds are reached, the health score and faults reflect the changes and globally alert the administrator. At that point, drilling down on particular nodes, looking at the atomic counters or on-demand diagnostics such as show tech-support, provides the relevant information to the administrator, as illustrated in Figure 14-8.

Cisco ACI delivers simplified operations and visibility to the network. Figure 14-9 summarizes all the advanced tools in APIC GUI to ease the life of network administrators.

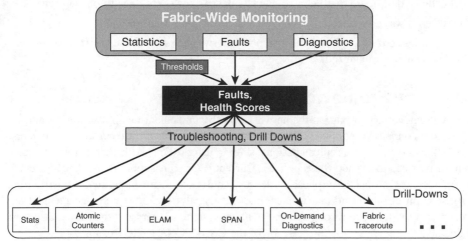

Figure 14-8 *Faults, Health Scores*

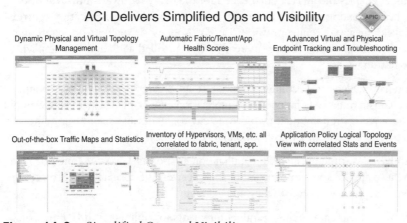

Figure 14-9 *Simplified Ops and Visibility*

These advanced features can be summarized here:

- ACI offers rich troubleshooting tools with topology visualization, specific packet counters, and a wealth of information that relates to the troubleshooting process.

- ACI calculates health scores for every object (including tenants and applications), including a root cause analysis tool that shows the underlying reason for why an application might not be at 100%. These application health scores can help operators focus on those problems impacting the most critical customers/applications.

- ACI offers a single GUI/CLI/API for the whole network, instead of a fragmented management concept (one CLI per DLR/ESG).

- ACI includes an impact analysis that shows which objects are using any specific policy. This helps at evaluating the impact of network changes.

- ACI offers a dashboard that helps to quickly identify the overall health of the network.

- ACI offers a way to snapshot the complete network configuration.

- ACI includes zero-touch deployment of physical switches so that the effort of scaling up the data center is minimized.

Open Policy Framework

Cisco ACI removes complexity at the network layer by implementing application, tenant, security, and connectivity policies automatically in multivendor infrastructure deployments. Cisco ACI also offers open, representational state transfer (REST) APIs that enable an ecosystem of partners to expand these policies. Currently, Cisco has more than 40 ecosystem partners in areas that include application delivery control, security, integrated infrastructure, enterprise applications, cloud management platforms, analytics, and system management. In this chapter we will not go through all those 40 ecosystem partners and their integrations to ACI because these will not be in the scope of the Cisco CCNA DCICT exam.

Cisco ACI simplifies and accelerates the application deployment and production life cycle, while also optimizing the underlying infrastructure to meet your ever-changing application requirements. It enables the automation needed for the many hardware infrastructure changes and application endpoint configurations that are essential in an application centric, DevOps-style development environment. With Cisco ACI policy-driven network configuration, DevOps application environments are more closely controlled and aligned to application release automation needs.

Cisco ACI multitenancy, along with context configurations, creates a powerful partitioning and security mechanism to manage independent application environments. This enables rapid release for applications that require their own private environments and secure endpoint management, as part of the enterprise application DevOps life cycle.

It is important to have real-time telemetry on application endpoints. Cisco ACI provides the ability to probe these application components for their network performance and to accelerate virtualization of services with consistency and accuracy.

Cisco ACI addresses fundamental architectural requirements for policy-based IT infrastructure automation:

- **Centralized policy store and infrastructure controller:** In software-defined networking (SDN) and Cisco ACI, this feature is generally known as the controller (Cisco Application Policy Infrastructure Controller [APIC] for Cisco ACI).

- **Programmable, or automated, network devices:** All infrastructure devices, such as servers and network nodes, must be able to respond to and implement policies according to commands from the controller. This feature may involve agents running on the device, APIs in the devices themselves, or management hooks to the devices that are implemented in the controller.

- **Controller southbound protocol to communicate with the managed or controlled devices and to communicate policy information:** Initially, the OpenFlow protocol was used in SDN architectures, and vendors released OpenFlow-compliant switches. In Cisco ACI, OpFlex is the primary protocol used, although other mechanisms for integrating devices into the Cisco ACI policy model are supported. For virtual overlay networks, OpenFlow has been complemented with the Open vSwitch Database (OVSDB) management protocol to control virtual switches.

- **Northbound controller interfaces for integrating higher-level automation solutions on top of the policy and controller framework, including workflow automation tools and analytics:** Modern SDN controllers include northbound APIs allowing for the integration of OpenStack or other vendor-specific cloud automation tools.

The main purpose of a Cisco ACI data center fabric is to move traffic from physical and virtualized servers, bring it in the best possible way to its destination, and while doing so apply meaningful services (see Figure 14-10) such as these:

- Traffic optimization that improves application performance
- Telemetry services that go beyond classic port counters
- Overall health monitoring for what constitutes an application
- Applying security rules embedded with forwarding

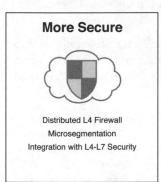

More Secure

Distributed L4 Firewall
Microsegmentation
Integration with L4-L7 Security

Easier to Automate

REST API, API Tools
Github Repository with Many Examples
SDKs (Python, Ruby, Powershell)

Easier to Operate

Single Point of Management
Zero-Touch Deployment
Embedded Network Management
Troubleshooting Wizard
NXOS-Like CLI

Figure 14-10   *More Secure, Easier to Automate, and Easier to Operate*

The main benefits of using a Cisco ACI fabric are illustrated in Figure 14-10. Those benefits can also be summarized as such:

- Single point of provisioning either via GUI or via REST API
- Connectivity for physical and virtual workloads with complete visibility on virtual machine traffic
- Hypervisor compatibility and integration without the need to add software to the hypervisor
- Ease (and speed) of deployment
- Simplicity of automation
- Multitenancy (network slicing)
- Capability to create portable configuration templates
- Hardware-based security
- Elimination of flooding from the fabric

- Ease of mapping application architectures into the networking configuration
- Capability to insert and automate firewall, load balancers, and other L4 through L7 services
- Intuitive and easy configuration process

Basic or Advanced GUI?

The Cisco ACI Release 1.2(1) and later has two GUI options (advanced and basic) that guide the user through the tasks of managing fabrics of various sizes.

- APIC Basic GUI enables network administrators to configure leaf ports and configure tenants without the need to configure switch profiles, interface profiles, policy groups, and so on.
- The Advanced GUI instead has a 1:1 mapping with the object model.

The main differences between the Advanced GUI and the Basic GUI are in the workflows that need to be performed to achieve the same configuration. For instance, with the Basic GUI the user configures one port at a time, as was the case prior to Cisco ACI; hence, the GUI creates one object for each port.

If you want to configure many ports simultaneously and identically, the preferred tool is the Advanced GUI. If you want to create configurations using interface profiles, selectors, policy groups, and so on, or if you plan to automate the fabric, you also should use the Advanced GUI.

Changes made through the Basic GUI can be seen, but cannot be modified, in the Advanced GUI, and changes made in the Advanced GUI cannot be rendered in the Basic GUI. The GUI also prevents you from changing objects that are created in one GUI from the other GUI. Figure 14-11 illustrates how to change or log on with one of the modes in the APIC GUI. Enter the URL **https://<mgmt_ip-address>** and use the out-of-band management IP address that you configured during the initial setup.

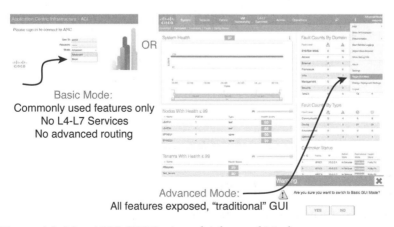

Figure 14-11   *APIC GUI Basic and Advanced Modes*

The Basic GUI is kept synchronized with the NX-OS CLI, so that if you make a change from the NX-OS CLI, these changes are rendered in the Basic GUI, and changes made in the Basic GUI are rendered in the NX-OS CLI. Cisco recommends that you do not mix configuration modes (Advanced or Basic). When you make a configuration in either mode and change the configuration using the other mode, unintended changes can occur.

From Cisco APIC Release 1.0 until Release 1.2, the default CLI was a Bash shell with commands to directly operate on MOs and properties of the Management Information Model. Beginning with Cisco APIC Release 1.2, the default CLI is a NX-OS style CLI. The object model CLI is available by typing the **bash** command at the initial CLI prompt. Figure 14-12 illustrates the NX-OS and Object Model CLI accesses.

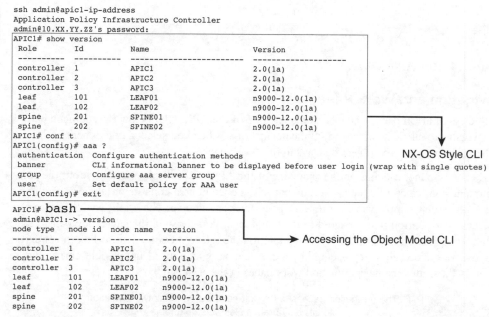

Figure 14-12 *NX-OS Style CLI and Object Model CLI*

Menu Bar and Submenu Bar

The menu bar is displayed across the top of the APIC GUI (see Figure 14-13). It provides access to the main tabs. You can navigate to the submenu bar by clicking on one of the tabs in the menu bar. When you click on a menu bar tab, the submenu bar for that tab is displayed. The submenu bar is different for each menu bar tab and might differ depending upon your specific configurations.

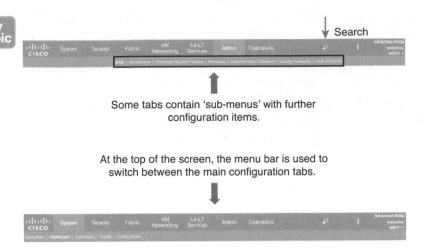

Search

Some tabs contain 'sub-menus' with further configuration items.

At the top of the screen, the menu bar is used to switch between the main configuration tabs.

Figure 14-13   *APIC GUI*

Navigation and Work Pane

The Navigation pane, which is on the left side of the APIC GUI below the submenu bar, navigates to all elements of the submenu category. When you select a component in the Navigation pane, the object displays in the Work pane.

The Work pane, which is on the right side of the APIC GUI, displays details about the component you selected in the navigation pane. The content area consists of tabs. See Figure 14-14 for an example view of the work pane and content area. These tabs enable you to access information that is related to the component you chose in the navigation pane. The tabs displayed in the content area depend upon the selected component. A link to context-sensitive online help is represented by a question mark icon in the upper-right corner. Figure 14-14 illustrates the navigation and work panes in the APIC GUI.

The navigation pane is on the left-hand side and allows navigation to all configuration elements on a tab.

The work pane displays information about the component selected in the navigation pane.

Figure 14-14   *Navigation Pane and Work Pane in APIC GUI*

System Tab

The System tab collects and displays a summary of the overall system health, its history, and a table of system-level faults.

Tenants Tab

The Tenants tab in the menu bar performs tenant management. In the submenu bar, you see an Add Tenant link and a drop-down list that contains all the tenants. Up to five of the most recently used tenants are displayed on the submenu bar.

A tenant contains policies that enable qualified users domain-based access control. Qualified users can access privileges such as tenant administration and networking administration.

A user requires read/write privileges for accessing and configuring policies in a domain. A tenant user can have specific privileges into one or more domains.

In a multitenancy environment, a tenant provides group user access privileges so that resources are isolated from one another (such as for endpoint groups and networking). These privileges also enable different users to manage different tenants. Figure 14-15 illustrates the Tenants tab in the APIC GUI.

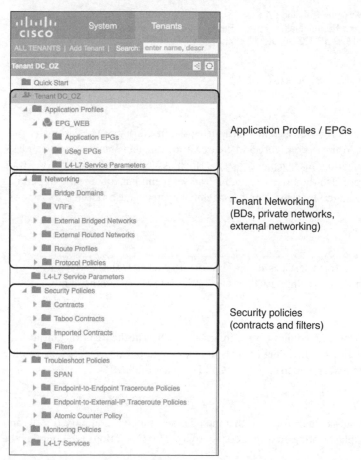

Figure 14-15 *The Tenants Tab in the APIC GUI*

Fabric Tab

The Fabric tab contains the following tabs in the submenu bar:

- **Inventory:** Displays the individual components of the fabric.
- **Fabric Policies:** Displays the monitoring and troubleshooting policies and fabric protocol or fabric maximum transmission unit (MTU) settings.
- **Access Policies:** Displays the access policies that apply to the edge ports of the system. These ports are on the leaf switches that communicate externally. Figure 14-16 illustrates the Fabric tab.

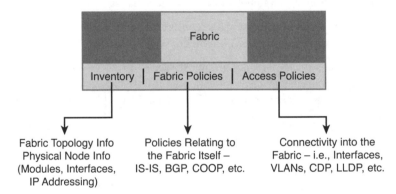

Figure 14-16 *The Fabric Tab in the APIC GUI*

VM Networking Tab

The VM Networking tab is for viewing and configuring the inventory of the various virtual machine (VM) managers. You can configure and create various management domains under which connections to individual management systems (such as VMware vCenters or VMware vShield) can be configured. Use the Inventory tab in the submenu bar to view the hypervisors and VMs that are managed by these VM management systems (also referred to as controllers in API).

L4-L7 Services Tab

The L4-L7 Services tab perform services such as importing packages that define Layer 4 to Layer 7 devices. You can view existing service nodes in the Inventory submenu tab.

Admin Tab

The Admin tab is for performing administrative functions such as authentication, authorization, and accounting functions, scheduling policies, retaining and purging records, upgrading firmware, and controlling features such as syslog, Call Home, and SNMP.

Operations Tab

The Operations tab provides a single location that includes several commonly used tools and outputs required for troubleshooting endpoint connectivity. The Operations tab contains the following subtabs:

■ **Enhanced Troubleshooting Wizard (Visibility & Troubleshooting) tab:** Quickly identifies connectivity issues when troubleshooting connectivity between endpoints within the fabric. The Enhanced Troubleshooting Wizard provides a single location that includes several commonly used tools and outputs required for troubleshooting endpoint connectivity.

■ **Capacity Dashboard tab:** Gets a summary of critical fabric resource thresholds.

■ **ACI Optimizer tab:** Enables you to enter your network requirements to determine how many leafs you will need for your network and to learn how to deploy each application and external endpoint group on each leaf without violating constraints.

■ **EP Tracker tab:** Allows you to enter an endpoint IP or MAC address and quickly see the location of this endpoint, the endpoint group that it belongs to, the VLAN encapsulation used, and if any transitions (flaps) have occurred for this endpoint.

■ **Visualization tab:** Allows you to view traffic statistics for a set of spine and leaf switches.

Figure 14-17 illustrates VM Networking, L4-L7 Services, Operations, and Admin tabs in the APIC GUI.

Figure 14-17   *APIC GUI*

Hypervisor Integration

Cisco ACI virtual machine networking provides hypervisors from multiple vendors programmable and automated access to high-performance scalable virtualized data center infrastructure. The ACI open REST API enables virtual machine (VM) integration with and orchestration of the policy-model-based ACI fabric. ACI VM networking enables consistent enforcement of policies across both virtual and physical workloads managed by hypervisors from multiple vendors. Attachable entity profiles easily enable VM mobility and placement of workloads anywhere in the ACI fabric.

Virtual Machine Manager Domain Main Components

ACI fabric virtual machine manager domains enable an administrator to configure connectivity policies for virtual machine controllers. The essential components of an ACI virtual machine manager domain policy include the following:

- **Virtual Machine Manager Domain Profile:** Groups VM controllers with similar networking policy requirements. For example, VM controllers can share VLAN pools and application EPGs. The APIC communicates with the controller to publish network configurations such as port groups that are then applied to the virtual workloads. The virtual machine manager domain profile includes the following essential components:

  - **Credential:** Associates a valid VM controller user credential with an APIC VMM domain.

  - **Controller:** Specifies how to connect to a VM controller that is part of a policy enforcement domain. For example, the controller specifies the connection to a VMware vCenter that is part a VMM domain.

- **EPG Association:** Endpoint groups regulate connectivity and visibility among the endpoints within the scope of the VMM domain policy. Virtual machine manager domain EPGs behave as follows:

  - The APIC pushes these EPGs as port groups into the VM controller.

  - An EPG can span multiple virtual machine manager attachable entity profile (AEP) domains, and a virtual machine manager domain can contain multiple EPGs.

- **Attachable Entity Profile Association:** Associates a virtual machine manager domain with the physical network infrastructure. An attachable entity profile (AEP) is a network interface template that enables deploying VM controller policies on a large set of leaf switch ports. An AEP specifies which switches and ports are available and how they are configured.

- **VLAN Pool Association:** A VLAN pool specifies the VLAN IDs or ranges used for VLAN encapsulation that the virtual machine manager domain consumes.

An APIC virtual machine manager domain profile is a policy that defines a virtual machine manager domain. The virtual machine manager domain policy is created in APIC and pushed into the leaf switches. Figure 14-18 illustrates hypervisor integration with ACI and virtual machine manager domain VM controller integration.

Virtual machine manager domains provide the following:

- A common layer in the ACI fabric that enables scalable fault-tolerant support for multiple VM controller platforms

- Virtual machine manager support for multiple tenants within the ACI fabric

14

**Hypervisor Integration with ACI
Control Channel - VMM Domains**

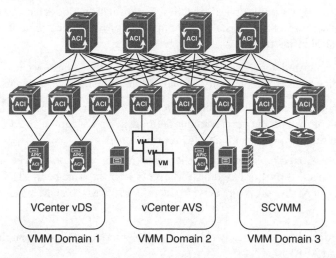

- Relationship is formed between APIC and Virtual Machine Manager (VMM).

- Multiple VMMs likely on a single ACI Fabric.

- Each VMM and associated Virtual hosts are grouped within APIC.

- Called VMM Domain.

- There is 1:1 relationship between a Distributed Switch and VMM Domain.

VCenter vDS	vCenter AVS	SCVMM
VMM Domain 1	VMM Domain 2	VMM Domain 3

Figure 14-18 *Hypervisor Integration—ACI Virtual Machine Manager Domains*

Virtual machine manager domains contain VM controllers such as VMware vCenter or Microsoft Service Center Virtual Machine Manager (SCVMM) Manager and the credential(s) required for the ACI API to interact with the VM controller. A virtual machine manager domain enables VM mobility within the domain but not across domains. A single virtual machine manager domain can contain multiple instances of VM controllers, but they must be the same kind. For example, a virtual machine manager domain can contain many VMware vCenters managing multiple controllers, each running multiple VMs, but it may not also contain SCVMM Managers. A virtual machine manager domain inventories controller elements (such as pNICs, vNICs, VM names, and so forth) and pushes policies into the controller(s), creating port groups and other necessary elements. The ACI virtual machine manager domain listens for controller events such as VM mobility and responds accordingly.

The ACI fabric associates tenant application profile EPGs to virtual machine manager domains, either automatically by an orchestration component such as Microsoft Azure, or by an APIC administrator creating such configurations. An EPG can span multiple virtual machine manager domains, and a virtual machine manager domain can contain multiple EPGs.

Attachable Entity Profile (AEP)

The ACI fabric provides multiple attachment points that connect through leaf ports to various external entities such as bare metal servers, virtual machine hypervisors, Layer 2 switches (for example, the Cisco UCS fabric interconnect), and Layer 3 routers (for example, Cisco Nexus 7000 Series switches). These attachment points can be physical ports, FEX ports, port channels, or a virtual port channel (vPC) on leaf switches.

An AEP represents a group of external entities with similar infrastructure policy requirements. The infrastructure policies consist of physical interface policies that configure various protocol options, such as Cisco Discovery Protocol (CDP), Link Layer Discovery Protocol (LLDP), maximum transmission unit (MTU), and Link Aggregation Control Protocol (LACP).

An AEP is required to deploy VLAN pools on leaf switches. Encapsulation blocks (and associated VLANs) are reusable across leaf switches. An AEP implicitly provides the scope of the VLAN pool to the physical infrastructure.

The following AEP requirements and dependencies must be accounted for in various configuration scenarios, including network connectivity and virtual machine manager domains:

■ The AEP defines the range of allowed VLANs, but it does not provision them. No traffic flows unless an EPG is deployed on the port. Without defining a VLAN pool in an AEP, a VLAN is not enabled on the leaf port even if an EPG is provisioned.

■ A particular VLAN is provisioned or enabled on the leaf port that is based on EPG events either statically binding on a leaf port or based on VM events from external controllers such as VMware vCenter or Microsoft Azure Service Center Virtual Machine Manager (SCVMM).

A virtual machine manager domain automatically derives physical interface policies from the interface policy groups of an AEP.

An override policy at the AEP can specify a different physical interface policy for a virtual machine manager domain. This policy is useful when a VM controller is connected to the leaf switch through an intermediate Layer 2 node, and a different policy is desired at the leaf switch and VM controller physical ports. For example, you can configure LACP between a leaf switch and a Layer 2 node. At the same time, you can disable LACP between the VM controller and the Layer 2 switch by disabling LACP under the AEP override policy.

VMware vSphere Distributed Switch and VMware vShield Integration

The APIC integrates with a third-party virtual machine manager (for example, VMware vCenter) to extend the benefits of ACI to the virtualized infrastructure. The APIC enables its administrator to use the ACI policies inside the virtual machine manager system.

The following modes of Cisco ACI and VMware virtual machine manager integration are supported:

■ **VMware vDS and vShield:** When integrated with Cisco ACI, the VMware vSphere Distributed Switch enables you to configure VM networking in the ACI fabric.

■ **Cisco Application Virtual Switch (AVS)**: It is a distributed virtual switch solution that is fully integrated within the VMware virtual infrastructure, including VMware vCenter for the virtualization administrator. This solution allows the network administrator to configure virtual switch and port groups in order to establish a consistent data center network policy.

Figure 14-19 illustrates details of each integration option.

VMware Integration Options

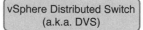

vSphere Distributed Switch (a.k.a. DVS)	vCenter + vShield	Application Virtual Switch (AVS)

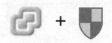

- Encapsulations: VLAN
- Installation: Native
- VM Discovery: LLDP
- Data Path Learning: Distributed Switch
- Control Plane Learning: Out-of-Band Handshake vCenter APIs In-Band Handshake: LLDP or CDP
- Software/Licenses: vCenter with Enterprise+ License

- Encapsulations: VLAN,VXLAN
- Installation: Native
- VM Discovery: LLDP
- Data Path Learning: Distributed Switch
- Control Plane Learning: Out-of-Band Handshake vCenter APIs In-Band Handshake: LLDP or CDP
- Software/Licenses: vCenter with Enterprise+ License, vShield Manager with vShield License

- Encapsulations: VLAN, VXLAN
- Installation: VIB Through VUM or Console
- VM Discovery: OpFlex Data Path Learning: Distributed Switch
- Control Plane Learning: In-Band Handshake: OpFlex-Enabled Host
- Software/Licenses: vCenter with Enterprise+ License

Figure 14-19 *VMware Integration Options*

In the above options, the APIC administrator should configure the vCenter domain policies in the APIC as a prerequisite. The APIC administrator provides the following vCenter connectivity information:

- vCenter IP address, vCenter credentials, virtual machine manager domain policies, and virtual machine manager domain SPAN

- Policies (VLAN pools, switch type such as VMware vDS, Cisco AVS)

- Connectivity to physical leaf interfaces using AEPs

Figure 14-20 illustrates a sequential operational workflow among the components.

Cisco ACI Hypervisor Integration – VMware vSphere Distributed Switch

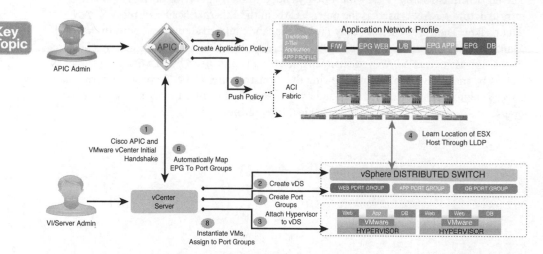

Figure 14-20 *Cisco ACI Integration with VMware vDS*

Following is an overview of the tasks performed:

1. The APIC automatically connects to the vCenter.

2. The APIC creates a VDS under a specified data center on the vCenter. The VDS name is the virtual machine manager domain name.

3. The vCenter administrator or the compute management tool adds the ESX host or hypervisor to the APIC VDS and assigns the ESX host hypervisor ports as uplinks on the APIC VDS. These uplinks must connect to the ACI leaf switches.

4. The APIC learns the location of the hypervisor host to the leaf connectivity using LLDP or CDP information of the hypervisors.

5. The APIC administrator creates and associates application EPG policies.

6. The APIC administrator associates EPG policies to virtual machine manager domains.

7. The APIC automatically creates port groups in the VMware vCenter under the VDS. This process provisions the network policy in the VMware vCenter. The port group name is a concatenation of the tenant name, the application profile name, and the EPG name. The port group is created under the VDS, and it was created earlier by the APIC.

8. The vCenter administrator or the compute management tool instantiates and assigns VMs to the port groups.

9. The APIC learns about the VM placements based on the vCenter events. The APIC automatically pushes the application EPG and its associated policy (for example, contracts and filters) to the ACI fabric.

VMware vCenter and vShield Domain Operational Workflow

The APIC integrates with the vShield Manager to use the hypervisor VXLAN functionality provided by VMware. The APIC controls and automates the entire VXLAN preparation and deployment on the vShield Manager so that users are not required to perform actions on the vShield Manager.

The fabric infrastructure VLAN must be extended to the hypervisor ports. The fabric infrastructure VLAN is used as the outer VLAN in the Ethernet header of the VXLAN data packet. The APIC automatically pushes the fabric infrastructure VLAN to the vShield Manager when preparing the APIC VDS for the VXLAN. This is accomplished by checking Enable Infrastructure VLAN in the attachable entity profile used by this domain profile, as well as by manually enabling and allowing the infrastructure VLAN ID on any intermediate Layer 2 switches between the fabric and hypervisors. Figure 14-21 illustrates a sequential operational workflow of the VMware vShield Integration.

14

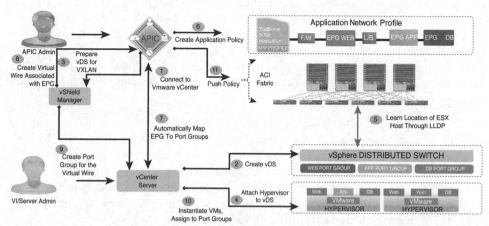

Figure 14-21 *Cisco ACI Integration with VMware vShield*

The APIC administrator configures the vCenter and vShield domain policies in the APIC. The APIC administrator must provide the association between vShield Manager and the vCenter Server on the APIC. The APIC administrator must provide the segment ID and multicast address pool that is required for the VXLAN. The segment ID pool in the vShield Manager must not overlap with pools in other vShield Managers that are configured on the APIC. An overview of the tasks performed follows:

1. The APIC connects to vCenter and creates the vDS.

2. The APIC creates a vDS under a specified data center on the vCenter. The vDS name is the virtual machine manager domain name.

3. The APIC connects to the vShield Manager, pushes the segment ID and multicast address pool, and prepares the vDS for VXLAN.

4. The vCenter administrator or the compute management tool attaches the hypervisors to the vDS. All hypervisors in the cluster must be attached to the vDS. Only after that will vShield start vDS preparation.

5. The APIC learns the location of the hypervisor host to the leaf connectivity using LLDP or CDP information from the hypervisors.

6. The APIC administrator creates application profiles and EPGs.

7. The APIC administrator associates them to virtual machine manager domains.

8. The APIC automatically creates virtual wires in the vShield Manager under the vDS. The APIC reads the segment ID and the multicast address from the VXLAN virtual wire sent from the vShield Manager.

9. The vShield Manager creates virtual wire port groups in the vCenter server under the vDS.

10. The vCenter administrator or compute management tool instantiates and assigns VMs to the virtual wire port groups.

11. The APIC automatically pushes the policy to the ACI fabric.

VMware AVS Integration—Cisco Application Virtual Switch (AVS)

The Cisco AVS is a key part of the Cisco application centric infrastructure (ACI). The Cisco AVS is a hypervisor-resident distributed virtual switch that is specifically designed for the Cisco ACI and managed by the Cisco APIC. It offers different forwarding and encapsulation options and extends across many virtualized hosts and data centers defined by the VMware vCenter Server. The Cisco AVS is integrated with the Cisco ACI architecture as a virtual leaf and is managed by the Cisco APIC. The Cisco AVS implements the OpFlex protocol for control plane communication.

The Cisco AVS can use either VXLAN or VLAN encapsulation to forward traffic to the leaf and back. The encapsulation type is selected during the Cisco AVS installation. If VXLAN encapsulation mode is used, only the infra-VLAN must be available between the Cisco AVS and the VXLAN. VXLAN is the recommended encapsulation mode if there are one or more switches between the Cisco AVS and the leaf. If VLAN encapsulation mode is used, a range of VLANs must be available for use by the Cisco AVS. These VLANs have significance only within the L2 network between the Cisco AVS and the leaf.

The Cisco AVS supports two modes of traffic forwarding: **Local Switching mode**, formerly known as FEX disable mode; and **No Local Switching mode**, formerly known as FEX enable mode. You choose the forwarding mode during Cisco AVS installation. Figure 14-22 illustrates AVS traffic forwarding modes. At the time of writing this book, there were two modes.

Cisco AVS works in two modes:

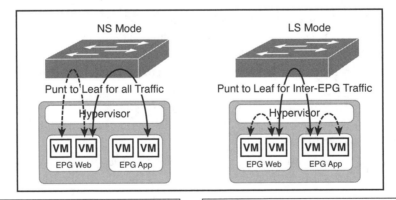

Figure 14-22   *Cisco AVS Switching Modes*

Local Switching Mode

In Local Switching mode, all intra-EPG traffic is locally forwarded by the Cisco AVS, without the involvement of the leaf. All inter-EPG traffic is forwarded through the leaf. In this mode, the Cisco AVS can use either VLAN or VXLAN encapsulation for forwarding traffic to the leaf and back. You choose the encapsulation type during Cisco AVS installation.

If you choose VLAN encapsulation, a range of VLANs must be available for use by the Cisco AVS. These VLANs have local scope in that they have significance only within the Layer 2 network between the Cisco AVS and the leaf. If you choose VXLAN encapsulation, only the infra-VLAN needs to be available between the Cisco AVS and the leaf. This results in a simplified configuration and is the recommended encapsulation type if there are one or more switches between the Cisco AVS and the physical leaf.

No Local Switching Mode

In No Local Switching mode, all traffic is forwarded by the leaf. In this mode, VXLAN is the only allowed encapsulation type.

Figure 14-23 illustrates a topology that includes the Cisco AVS with the Cisco APIC and VMware vCenter.

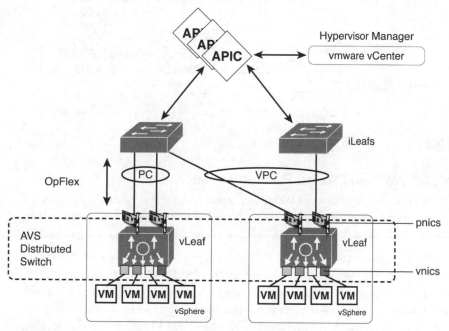

Figure 14-23 *Cisco AVS Architecture View*

Virtual extensible LAN (VXLAN) load balancing allows you to ensure that data moves efficiently between Cisco AVS and the leaf switch (a Nexus 9000) over multiple uplinks when you have a MAC pinning policy and VXLAN encapsulation.

The specific combination of VXLAN encapsulation and MAC pinning does not provide a built-in load-balancing mechanism when there are multiple uplinks between Cisco AVS and the leaf switch. This limitation does not apply if either VLAN encapsulation or LACP are used. When the host (server) is added into a vSphere Distributed switch (vDS) in VMware vCenter, the Cisco APIC creates a VMware kernel NIC (vmknic) that is used for VXLAN encapsulation to send data packets. This vmknic uses only one of the many available uplinks to send packets if MAC pinning is the link aggregation method. So we recommend that you enable VXLAN load balancing if you use VXLAN encapsulation and use MAC pinning as your link aggregation method. Figure 14-24 illustrates a sequential operational workflow for the VMware AVS integration in ACI fabric.

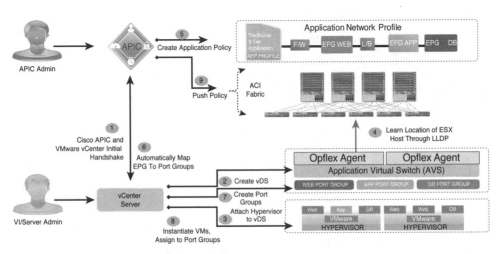

Figure 14-24 *Cisco ACI VMware AVS Integration*

Microsoft SCVMM and Azure Pack Integration

The APIC integrates with Microsoft VM management systems and enhances the network management capabilities of the platform. The Cisco ACI integrates at the following levels of the Microsoft VM Management systems:

- **Cisco ACI with Microsoft SCVMM:** When integrated with Cisco ACI, SCVMM enables communication between ACI and SCVMM for network management.

- **Cisco ACI and Microsoft Windows Azure Pack:** ACI resource provider in Windows Azure Pack drives the Application Policy Infrastructure Controller (APIC) for network management. Networks are created in System Center Virtual Machine Manager (SCVMM) and are available in Windows Azure Pack for respective tenants.

At the time of writing this chapter, the APIC and SCVMM communicate with each other for network management. EPGs are created in APIC as VM networks in SCVMM. Compute is provisioned in SCVMM and can consume these networks. Figure 14-25 illustrates these two modes of operation with Microsoft integration.

Microsoft Interaction with ACI
Two modes of Operation

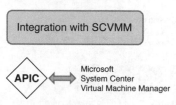

| Integration with SCVMM | Integration with Azure Pack |

APIC ⟷ Microsoft System Center Virtual Machine Manager

APIC ⟷ Windows Azure + Microsoft System Center Virtual Machine Manager

- Policy Management: Through APIC
- Software/License: Windows Server with HyperV, SCVMM
- VM Discovery: OpFlex
- Encapsulations: VLAN
- Plugin Installation: Manual

- Superset of SCVMM
- Policy Management: Through APIC or Through Azure Pack
- Software/License: Windows Server with HyperV, SCVMM, Azure Pack (Free)
- VM Discovery: OpFlex
- Encapsulations: VLAN
- Plugin Installation: Integrated

Figure 14-25 *Microsoft Interaction with ACI*

Microsoft SCVMM provides an object called "Cloud" that acts as a container of logical and physical fabric resources. ACI integration with SCVMM automatically creates the various logical networking pieces and enables the logical networks at your designated cloud. When configuring ACI integration with SCVMM, the fabric cloud is the one that is specified as the root container on the APIC, whereas the tenant cloud is an SCVMM cloud that contains a subset of the host groups specified in the fabric cloud. SCVMM contains all the host groups that will be used to deploy the logical switch. Once the fabric cloud is set up and the logical switch has been deployed to the hosts in the host groups, an SCVMM admin can create tenant clouds and enable the apicLogicalNetwork on that tenant cloud, allowing Windows Azure Pack tenants to create and deploy tenant networks on the fabric.

Cisco ACI integrates in Microsoft Windows Azure Pack to provide a self-service experience for the tenant. Microsoft Windows Azure Pack is built on top of an existing Microsoft SCVMM installation. Cisco ACI has integration points at each of these layers, enabling you to leverage the work performed in a SCVMM environment and use it in a Microsoft Windows Azure Pack installation. Windows Azure Pack for Windows Server is a collection of Microsoft Azure technologies, available to Microsoft customers at no additional cost for installation into the data center. It runs on top of Windows Server 2012 R2 and System Center 2012. Figure 14-26 illustrates a sequential operational workflow for the Cisco ACI Azure Pack integration.

Cisco ACI Azure Pack Integration

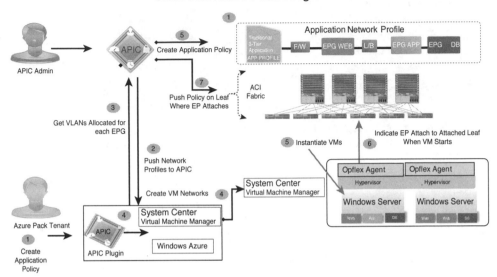

Figure 14-26 *Cisco ACI Azure Pack Integration*

OpenStack

OpenStack is an open source software platform for orchestration and automation in data center environments. It is typically used for private and public clouds. OpenStack is designed to automate, supervise, and manage compute, network, storage, and security in virtualized environments. The goal of the OpenStack project is to deliver solutions for all types of clouds by being simple to implement, feature rich, scalable, and easy to deploy and operate. OpenStack consists of several projects that deliver components of the OpenStack solution.

OpenStack has different components. The software suite is available for download online and can operate on multiple Linux distributions. The current main components of OpenStack are Compute (Nova), Networking (Neutron), Storage (Cinder and Swift), Dashboard GUI (Horizon), Identity (Keystone), and Image Service (Glance).

- Dashboard (**Horizon**) provides a web front end to the other OpenStack services.
- Compute (**Nova**) stores and retrieves virtual disks (images) and associated metadata in Image (**Glance**).
- Network (**Quantum**) provides virtual networking for Compute.
- Block Storage (**Cinder**) provides storage volumes for Compute.
- Image (**Glance**) can store the actual virtual disk files in the Object Store (**Swift**).
- All the services authenticate with Identity (**Keystone**).

Figure 14-27 illustrates the relationships between the OpenStack services.

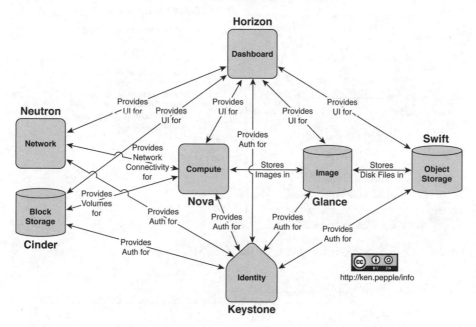

Figure 14-27   *OpenStack Conceptual View*

OpenStack defines a flexible software architecture for creating cloud-computing environments. The reference software-based implementation of OpenStack allows for multiple Layer 2 transports, including VLAN, GRE, and VXLAN. The Neutron project within OpenStack can also provide software-based Layer 3 forwarding. When utilized with ACI, the ACI fabric provides an integrated Layer 2 and Layer 3 VXLAN-based overlay networking capability that can offload network encapsulation processing from the compute nodes onto the ToR or ACI leaf switches. This architecture provides the flexibility of software overlay networking in conjunction with the performance and operational benefits of hardware-based networking.

The APIC driver supports Neutron APIs, including network, router, subnet, and security group APIs. The APIC driver works as part of the Neutron Modular Layer 2 (ML2) plug-in architecture (see Figure 14-28). It also automates configuration of external networks and the creation and attachment of Neutron ports to virtual machines. With the exception of security groups, which are supported through IP address tables, each of these APIs automatically triggers configuration on the controller.

The Cisco ACI fabric offers distributed Layer 2 behavior, allowing complete flexibility in the placement of virtual machines within the OpenStack cloud. It also serves as a distributed default gateway between Neutron networks, eliminating the need for a software-based Layer 3 agent.

The APIC can manage Open vSwitch (OVS) in an OpenStack environment using the OpFlex protocol. The OpFlex agent, an open-source software component running on each hypervisor, communicates with one or more physical leaf switches within the Cisco ACI fabric and manages a local instance of OVS. Figure 14-29 highlights OpenStack with OpFlex features.

ML2 Solution

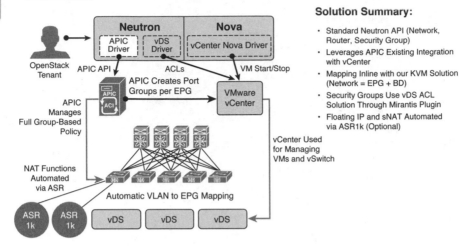

Solution Summary:

- Standard Neutron API (Network, Router, Security Group)
- Leverages APIC Existing Integration with vCenter
- Mapping Inline with our KVM Solution (Network = EPG + BD)
- Security Groups Use vDS ACL Solution Through Mirantis Plugin
- Floating IP and sNAT Automated via ASR1k (Optional)

Figure 14-28 *OpenStack Neutron Modular Layer 2 (ML2) Solution*

ACI OpenStack – With OpFlex Support

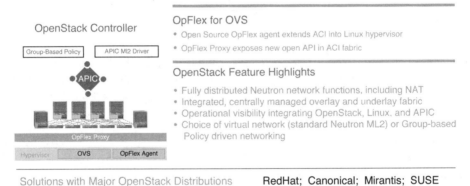

Figure 14-29 *OpenStack with OpFlex Support*

This approach allows tight integration between the APIC and OpenStack using the controller's native virtual machine networking tools and interfaces. This link between OpenStack and the APIC offers a number of advantages:

- It enables the controller to track each OpenStack computing node, including its virtual machines, internal networking configuration, and traffic metrics.

- It provides operational visibility into the OpenStack environment and simplifies troubleshooting across the physical and virtual environments.

- It supports local response to Dynamic Host Configuration Protocol (DHCP) and metadata requests on each OpenStack computing node rather than relying on responses through a centralized network node.

- It enables efficient virtual machine migration by automatically sending a Gratuitous Address Resolution Protocol (GARP) request.

The Cisco ACI OpenStack plug-in can be deployed in either ML2 or GBP mode. In Modular Layer 2 (ML2) mode, standard neutron API is used to create networks. This is the traditional way of deploying VMs and services in OpenStack. In group-based policy (GBP) mode (see Figure 14-30), a new API is provided to describe, create, and deploy applications as policy groups without worrying about network-specific details.

Group-Based Policy Solution

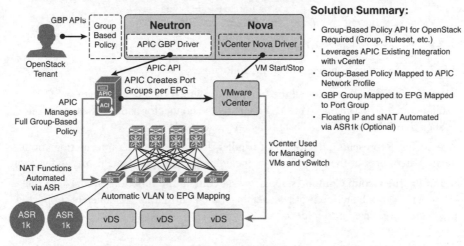

Solution Summary:

- Group-Based Policy API for OpenStack Required (Group, Ruleset, etc.)
- Leverages APIC Existing Integration with vCenter
- Group-Based Policy Mapped to APIC Network Profile
- GBP Group Mapped to EPG Mapped to Port Group
- Floating IP and sNAT Automated via ASR1k (Optional)

Figure 14-30 *OpenStack Group-Based Policy Solution*

Cisco ACI, with the GBP APIC driver, supports the capability to create floating IP addresses and dynamically assigns them to virtual machines. Using OpFlex and OVS, the floating IP address capability is fully distributed within each hypervisor host. The solution also allows virtual machines in private tenant networks to access external networks through source network address translation (SNAT).

Layer 4 to Layer 7 Services Integration

The Cisco ACI policies are used to insert services. APIC service integration provides a life cycle automation framework that enables the system to dynamically respond when a service comes online or goes offline. Shared services that are available to the entire fabric are administered by the fabric administrator. Services that are for a single tenant are administered by the tenant administrator.

The APIC provides automated service insertion while acting as a central point of policy control. APIC policies manage both the network fabric and the services appliances. The APIC can configure the network automatically so that traffic flows through the services. Also, the APIC can automatically configure the service according to the application's requirements. This approach allows organizations to automate service insertion and eliminate the challenge of managing all the complex traffic-steering techniques of traditional service insertion.

The Layer 4 to Layer 7 service device type policies include key managed objects such as services supported by the package and device scripts. Figure 14-31 shows the objects of the Layer 4 to Layer 7 service device type policy model.

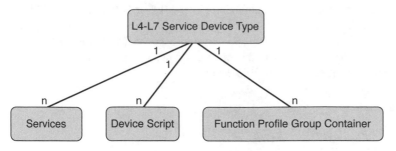

Figure 14-31 *Layer 4 to Layer 7 Policy Model*

Layer 4 to Layer 7 service policies contain the following:

■ **Services:** Contains metadata for all the functions provided by a device, such as SSL offloading and load-balancing. This MO contains the connector names; encapsulation type, such as VLAN and VXLAN; and any interface labels.

■ **Device Script:** Represents a device script handler that contains meta information about the related attributes of the script handler, including its name, package name, and version.

■ **Function Profile Group Container:** Objects that contain the functions available to the service device type. Function profiles contain all the configurable parameters supported by the device organized into folders.

Service Graphs

The Cisco ACI treats services as an integral part of an application. Any services that are required are treated as a service graph that is instantiated on the ACI fabric from the Cisco APIC. Users define the service for the application, whereas service graphs identify the set of network or service functions that the application needs. Each function is represented as a node.

After the graph is configured in the APIC, the APIC automatically configures the services according to the service function requirements that are specified in the service graph. The APIC also automatically configures the network according to the needs of the service function that is specified in the service graph, which does not require a change in the service device. A service graph is represented as two or more tiers of an application with the appropriate service function inserted between. A service appliance (device) performs a service function within the graph. One or more service appliances might be required to render the services required by a graph. One or more service functions can be performed by a single-service device.

Service graphs and service functions have the following characteristics:

■ Traffic sent or received by an EPG can be filtered based on a policy, and a subset of the traffic can be redirected to different edges in the graph.

■ Service graph edges are directional.

■ Taps (hardware-based packet copy service) can be attached to different points in the service graph.

- Logical functions can be rendered on the appropriate (physical or virtual) device, based on the policy.

- The service graph supports splits and joins of edges, and it does not restrict the administrator to linear service chains.

- Traffic can be reclassified again in the network after a service appliance emits it.

- Logical service functions can be scaled up or down or can be deployed in a cluster mode or 1:1 active-standby high-availability mode, depending on the requirements.

A service graph is most often used for the following things:

- Automation

- Integration of Cisco ACI and services for advanced features

You do not need to use a service graph all the time. For example, you might want to use unmanaged mode, or you might only want to create endpoint groups and plug a firewall and load balancer into the endpoint groups. In such cases, you do not need a service graph. Figure 14-32 illustrates a flowchart that can help you determine if you should use a service graph.

Service Graph Decision Flowchart

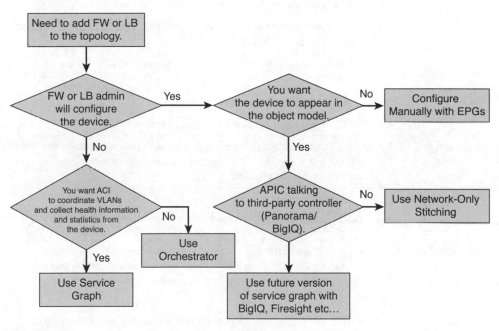

Figure 14-32 *Service Graph Decision Flowchart*

There are three main deployment modes for a service graph:

- **GoTo:** The Layer 4 to Layer 7 device is a Layer 3 device that routes traffic; it is the default gateway for servers or the next hop.

■ **GoThrough:** The Layer 4 to Layer 7 device is a transparent Layer 2 device; the next-hop or the outside bridge domain provides the default gateway.

■ **One-arm:** The bridge domain of the servers is the default gateway.

Device Packages

The APIC requires a device package to configure and monitor service devices. A device package manages a class of service devices and provides the APIC with information about the devices so that the APIC knows what the device is and what the device can do. A device package allows an administrator to add, modify, or remove a network service on the APIC without interruption. Adding a new device type to the APIC is done by uploading a device package. Table 14-2 summarizes the content of a device package.

Table 14-2 A Device Package Is a Zip File That Contains the Following Parts

Device specification	An XML file that defines the following properties:
	Device properties:
	■ **Model:** Model of the device.
	■ **Vendor:** Vendor of the device.
	■ **Version:** Software version of the device.
	Functions provided by a device, such as load balancing, content switching, and SSL termination.
	Interfaces and network connectivity information for each function.
	Device configuration parameters.
	Configuration parameters for each function.
Device script	A Python script that performs the integration between the APIC and a device. The APIC events are mapped to function calls that are defined in the device script.
Function profile	A profile of parameters with default values that the vendor specifies. You can configure a function to use these default values.
Device-level configuration parameters	A configuration file that specifies parameters that a device requires at the device level. The configuration can be shared by one or more of the graphs that are using the device.

Figure 14-33 shows the APIC service automation and insertion architecture through the device package.

Service Automation Through Device Package

- Service automation requires a vendor device package.
  It is a zip file containing:
  - Device Specification (XML File)
  - Device Scripts (Python)
- APIC interfaces with the device using device Python scripts.
- APIC uses the device configuration model provided in the package to pass appropriate configurations to the device scripts.
- Device script handlers interface with the device using its REST or CLI interface.

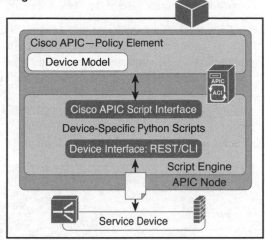

Figure 14-33 *Device Package Architecture*

A device package can be provided by a device vendor or can be created by Cisco. The device package enables an administrator to automate the management of the following services:

- Device attachment and detachment
- Endpoint attachment and detachment
- Service graph rendering
- Health monitoring
- Alarms, notifications, and logging
- Counters

When a device package is uploaded through the GUI or the northbound APIC interface, the APIC creates a namespace for each unique device package.

Microsegmentation

Data center architectures have continually evolved to meet the needs of mobile, social, big data, and cloud applications. Security architectures have been evolving as well to support the security needs of these distributed applications in distributed data centers.

Organizations are under unrelenting attack, and security breaches are happening every day. According to Cisco, 75 percent of all attacks begin stealing data within minutes, but detection takes longer. After an attack has been discovered, several weeks may pass before full containment and remediation are achieved.

To address this problem, Cisco ACI provides embedded security and policy-based automation using the EPG and contract constructs. An EPG by definition is a microsegment, and its security enforcement policy is defined by a contract that consists of a built-in stateless whitelist firewall and Layer 4 through Layer 7 (L4-L7) service insertion policy that supports a robust ecosystem of L4-L7 partners for next-generation firewall (NGFW) and next-generation intrusion prevention system (NG-IPS) solutions, application analytics, and more.

Cisco ACI extends microsegmentation and intra-EPG isolation security for physical and virtual workloads in a data center using simple policy constructs. Cisco ACI now normalizes policy-based microsegmentation to secure any type of workload regardless of the application topology or the location of the workload (see Figure 14-34).

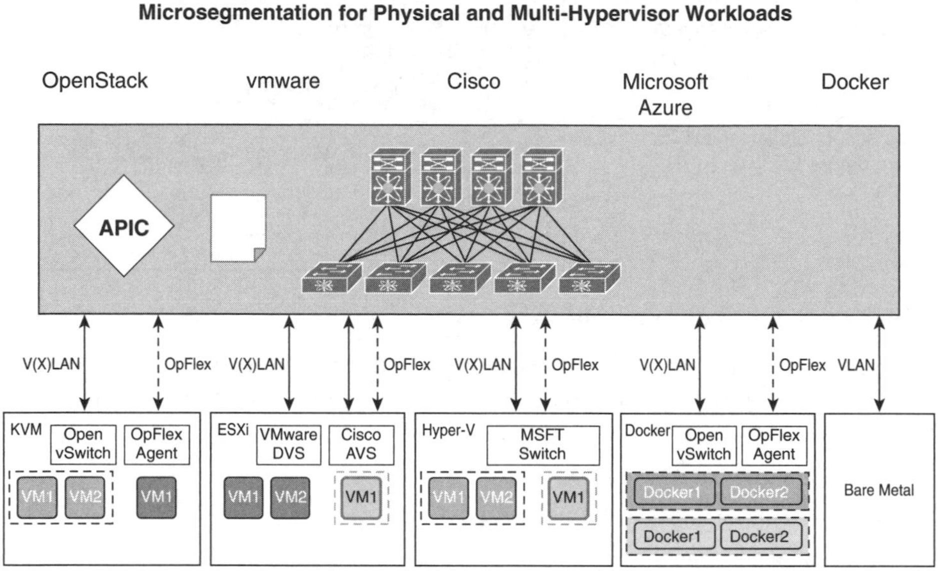

Microsegmentation for Physical and Multi-Hypervisor Workloads

Figure 14-34 *Cisco ACI Microsegmentation Works Across VMware, Microsoft, and OpenStack Virtual Machines, Bare metal Servers, and Containers*

Why Microsegmentation Matters

Although the broad constructs of segmentation are relevant, today's application and security requirements mandate increasingly specific methods that are more secure and operationally simpler. This need has led to the evolution of microsegmentation, which has the following goals:

■ Programmatically define segments on an increasingly specific basis, achieving greater flexibility (for example, limit the lateral movement of a threat or quarantine a compromised endpoint within a broader system).

■ Automatically program segment and policy management across the entire application life cycle (from deployment to decommissioning).

■ Enhance security and scalability by enabling a zero-trust approach for heterogeneous workloads.

Cisco ACI microsegmentation embodies four main functions: isolation, segmentation with integrated security, closed-loop feedback, and automated remediation.

Main Features

Cisco ACI takes an elegant approach to microsegmentation, with policy definition separating segments from the broadcast domain.

It uses a new application-aware construct called the endpoint group, or EPG, that allows application designers to define the endpoints that belong to the EPG regardless of their IP addresses or the subnets to which they belong. In addition, the endpoint can be a physical server, a virtual machine, a Linux container, or even traditional mainframe computers; that is, the type of endpoint is normalized and therefore irrelevant, thereby offering simplicity and flexibility in the treatment of endpoints.

Cisco ACI provides microsegmentation support for VMware vSphere Distributed Switch (VDS), Microsoft Hyper-V virtual switch, and bare metal endpoints, allowing highly specific endpoint security enforcement. Customers can dynamically enforce forwarding and security policies, quarantine compromised or rogue endpoints based on virtual machine attributes (such as the name, guest OS, or virtual machine identifier) and network attributes (such as the IP address), and restore cleaned endpoints to the original EPG.

Data center microsegmentation can offer enhanced security for east-west traffic within the data center. Its true value lies in its integration with application design and holistic network policy. It must interoperate transparently with a variety of hypervisors, bare metal servers, L4-L7 devices, and orchestration platforms.

Reference List

ACI Solution Overview: http://www.cisco.com/c/dam/en/us/solutions/collateral/data-center-virtualization/unified-fabric/aci-ecosystem-so-v6-final.pdf

OpFlex Control Protocol: https://tools.ietf.org/html/draft-smith-opflex-02

Cisco Development Network: https://developer.cisco.com

Avramov, Lucien, and Portolani Maurizio. *The Policy Driven Data Center with ACI: Architecture, Concepts, and Methodology.* **Cisco Press, 2015.**

Programmability and Automation with Cisco Open NX-OS: http://www.cisco.com/c/dam/en/us/td/docs/switches/datacenter/nexus9000/sw/open_nxos/programmability/guide/Programmability_Open_NX-OS.pdf

Virtualization Compatibility List Solution Overview: http://www.cisco.com/c/en/us/solutions/collateral/data-center-virtualization/application centric-infrastructure/solution-overview-c22-734588.html

OpenStack: http://www.openstack.org/

Pepple, Ken. *Deploying OpenStack.* O'Reilly, 2011.

Exam Preparation Tasks

Review All Key Topics

Review the most important topics in the chapter, noted with the key topic icon in the outer margin of the page. Table 14-3 lists a reference of these key topics and the page numbers on which each is found.

Table 14-3   Key Topics for Chapter 14

Key Topic Element	Description	Page
Section	"Telemetry"	520
Figure 14-3	"Atomic Counters"	521
List	The List of Tenant Atomic Counters	521
Section	"Health Scores and Health Monitoring"	522
Figure 14-4	"Managed Object (MO) Health Score"	523
List	The Different Stages of the Fault Life Cycle	525
Figure 14-8	"Faults, Health Scores"	527
List	Cisco ACI Advanced Features	527
List	Cisco ACI Fundamental Architectures	528
Figure 14-10	"Secure, Easier to Automate, and Easier to Operate"	529
Figure 14-11	"APIC GUI Basic and Advanced Modes"	530
Figure 14-12	"NX-OS Style CLI and Object Model CLI"	531
Figure 14-13	"APIC GUI"	532
Figure 14-14	"Navigation Pane and Work Pane in APIC GUI"	532
Figure 14-15	"The Tenants Tab in APIC GUI"	533
Figure 14-16	"The Fabric Tab in APIC GUI"	534
Figure 14-17	"APIC GUI"	535
Section	"Virtual Machine Manager Domain Main Components"	536
Figure 14-18	"Hypervisor Integration with ACI"	537
Section	"Attachable Entity Profile"	537
Section	VMware vSphere Distributed Switch and VMware vShield Integration"	538
Figure 14-19	"VMware Integration Options"	539
Figure 14-20	"Cisco ACI Integration with VMware vDS"	539
Figure 14-21	"Cisco ACI Integration with VMware vShield"	541

Key Topic Element	Description	Page
Section	"VMware AVS Integration—Cisco Application Virtual Switch (AVS)"	542
Figure 14-22	"Cisco AVS Switching Modes"	542
Figure 14-23	"Cisco AVS Architecture View"	543
Figure 14-24	"Cisco ACI VMware AVS Integration"	544
Figure 14-25	"Microsoft Interaction with ACI"	545
Figure 14-26	"Cisco ACI Azure Pack Integration"	546
Section	"OpenStack"	546
Figure 14-28	"OpenStack Neutron Modular Layer 2 (ML2) Solutions"	548
Figure 14-29	"OpenStack with OpFlex Support"	548
Figure 14-30	"OpenStack Group-Based Policy Solution"	549
Section	"Layer 4 to Layer 7 Services Integration"	549
Section	"Service Graphs"	550
Section	"Device Packages"	552
Table 14-2	"A Device Package Parts"	552
Figure 14-33	"Device Package Architecture"	553
Section	"Microsegmentation"	553

Complete Tables and Lists from Memory

Print a copy of Appendix B, "Memory Tables" or at least the section for this chapter, and complete the tables and lists from memory. Appendix C, "Memory Tables Answer Key" includes completed tables and lists to check your work.

Define Key Terms

Define the following key terms from this chapter, and check your answers in the Glossary:

Cisco Application Virtual Switch (AVS), OpenStack, Graphical User Interface (GUI), Hypervisor, Open vSwitch (OVS), Git/GitHub, SCVMM (System Center Virtual Machine Manager), Segmentation, Soaking, Service Insertion, Service Graph, Telemetry, vCenter Virtual Machine Manager Domain, Service Chaining, Attach Entity Profile (AEP), OpFlex, Atomic Counters

Part IV Review

Keep track of your part review progress with the checklist shown in Table PIV-1. Details on each task follow the table.

Table PIV-1 Part IV Review Checklist

Activity	First Date Completed	Second Date Completed
Repeat all "Do I Know This Already?" questions		
Answer "Part Review" questions		
Review Key Topics		
Self-assessment questionnaire		

Repeat All "Do I Know This Already?" Questions: For this task, answer the "Do I Know This Already?" questions again for the chapters in this part of the book, using the PCPT software. Refer to "How to View Only 'Do I Know This Already?' Questions by Part" in the Introduction to this book for help with how to make the PCPT software show you "Do I Know This Already?" questions for this part only.

Answer "Part Review" Questions: For this task, answer the "Part Review" questions for this part of the book, using the PCPT software. Refer to "How to View Only Part Review Questions by Part" in the Introduction to this book for help with how to make the PCPT software show you "Part Review" questions for this part only.

Review Key Topics: Browse back through the chapters and look for the Key Topic icons. If you do not remember some details, take the time to reread those topics.

Self-Assessment Questionnaire: Each chapter of this book introduces several key learning items. This might seem overwhelming to you initially, but as you read through each new chapter, you will become more familiar and comfortable with them, which will help you remember the concepts and technologies of these key topics as you progress with the book.

For this self-assessment exercise in the book, without looking back at the chapters or your notes, you should try to answer these self-assessment questions to the best of your ability. This exercise lists a set of key self-assessment questions, which are relevant to the particular chapter, shown in the following list. There will be no written answers to these questions in this book; if you are not certain, you should go back and refresh on the key topics.

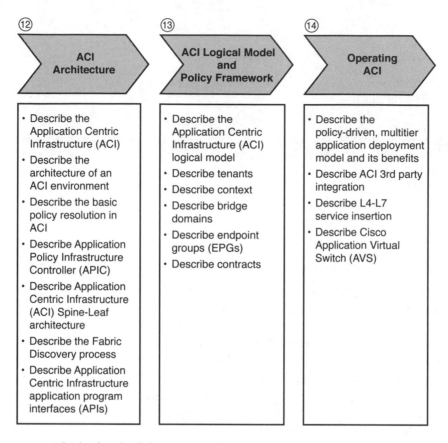

⑫ **ACI Architecture**

- Describe the Application Centric Infrastructure (ACI)
- Describe the architecture of an ACI environment
- Describe the basic policy resolution in ACI
- Describe Application Policy Infrastructure Controller (APIC)
- Describe Application Centric Infrastructure (ACI) Spine-Leaf architecture
- Describe the Fabric Discovery process
- Describe Application Centric Infrastructure application program interfaces (APIs)

⑬ **ACI Logical Model and Policy Framework**

- Describe the Application Centric Infrastructure (ACI) logical model
- Describe tenants
- Describe context
- Describe bridge domains
- Describe endpoint groups (EPGs)
- Describe contracts

⑭ **Operating ACI**

- Describe the policy-driven, multitier application deployment model and its benefits
- Describe ACI 3rd party integration
- Describe L4-L7 service insertion
- Describe Cisco Application Virtual Switch (AVS)

■ Think of each of these open self-assessment questions as being about the chapters you have read. You might or might not find the answer explicitly, but the chapter is structured to give you the knowledge and understanding to be able to discuss and explain these self-assessment questions. For example, number 12 is about *ACI* architecture, number 13 is about *ACI* logical model and policy framework, and so on.

■ Note your answer and try to reference key words in the answer from the relevant chapter. For example, tenant would apply to Chapter 13, "ACI Logical Model and Policy Framework."

Exam topics covered in Part V:

- 4.1 Explain the purpose and value of using APIs

- 4.2 Describe the basic concepts of cloud computing

- 4.3 Describe the basic function of a UCS Director

  - 4.3a Management

  - 4.3b Orchestration

  - 4.3c Multitenancy

  - 4.3d Chargeback

  - 4.3e Service offerings

  - 4.3f Catalogs

- 4.4 Interpret and troubleshoot a UCS Director workflow

Part V

Automation and Orchestration

Chapter 15: Cloud Computing

Chapter 16: UCS Director

Chapter 17: Understanding and Troubleshooting UCSD Workflows

This chapter covers the following exam topics:

4.1 Explain the purpose and value of using APIs

4.2 Describe the basic concepts of cloud computing

Cloud Computing

Cloud computing introduces a new model where compute, network, storage, and virtualization resources are consumed in a utility-like shared fashion leveraging key principles of elasticity, service provisioning, service charge, and so on. In this chapter we are going to look at main concepts behind different types of cloud computing models and see how they enable various use cases for application deployment. We will also see how application programming interfaces (APIs) play a key role in enabling a programmatic approach with unprecedented agility in provisioning and operating private and public cloud computing environments.

"Do I Know This Already?" Quiz

The "Do I Know This Already?" quiz enables you to assess whether you should read this entire chapter thoroughly or jump to the "Exam Preparation Tasks" section. If you are in doubt about your answers to these questions or your own assessment of your knowledge of the topics, read the entire chapter. Table 15-1 lists the major headings in this chapter and their corresponding "Do I Know This Already?" quiz questions. You can find the answers in Appendix A, "Answers to the 'Do I Know This Already?' Quizzes."

Table 15-1 "Do I Know This Already?" Section-to-Question Mapping

Foundation Topics Section	Questions
Describe the Basic Concepts of Cloud Computing	1-7
Explain the Purpose and Value of Using APIs	8-10

CAUTION The goal of self-assessment is to gauge your mastery of the topics in this chapter. If you do not know the answer to a question or are only partially sure of the answer, you should mark that question as wrong for purposes of the self-assessment. Giving yourself credit for an answer you correctly guess skews your self-assessment results and might provide you with a false sense of security.

1. What is cloud computing? (Choose two.)

    a. Model for enabling ubiquitous, convenient, on-demand network access to a shared pool of configurable computing resources

    b. Model for manual provisioning of compute, network, storage, and virtualization infrastructure

    c. Model for automated and rapid provisioning with minimal or no management effort

    d. Model for rapid provisioning of wireless connectivity

2. What are the key characteristics of cloud computing? (Choose three.)

   a. Self-service portal

   b. Resource elasticity

   c. Manual provisioning

   d. Pay-per use

3. What are cloud computing service models? (Choose three.)

   a. Infrastructure as a service

   b. Platform as a service

   c. Software as a service

   d. Cloud computing service models have not been defined.

4. True or false? Cloud computing is equal to virtualization.

   a. True

   b. False

5. Which of the following technologies are examples of network virtualization? (Choose three.)

   a. VLAN

   b. VXLAN

   c. ACL

   d. VRF

6. Which of the following are the cloud computing deployment models? (Choose all that apply.)

   a. Public

   b. Private

   c. Hybrid

   d. Community

7. What is the main purpose of a hybrid cloud approach?

   a. Ability to keep private cloud resources isolated from the public cloud

   b. Ability to use both private and public cloud resources to complete required computational tasks

   c. Ability to discontinue the use of the public cloud and shift all resources to the private cloud

   d. None of the above

8. What is an application programming interface? (Choose two.)

   a. It is a software-to-software interface.

   b. It is a user-to-software interface.

   c. It is a switch port connecting to the server, which is running the application.

   d. It is a remotely accessible software interface.

9. True or false? Application programming interfaces always leverage HTTP or HTTPS protocols.

    a. True

    b. False

10. What are the common data formatting schemes for web APIs? (Choose two.)

    a. Extensible Markup Language (XML)

    b. JavaScript Object Notation (JSON)

    c. Representational State Transfer (REST)

    d. Remote Procedure Call (RPC)

15

Foundation Topics

What Is Cloud Computing?

Many attempts have been made over the years to come up with a clear definition of cloud computing. In September 2011, the Information Technology Laboratory (ITL) at the National Institute of Standards and Technology (NIST) provided a formal definition of the cloud computing as a "model for enabling ubiquitous, convenient, on-demand network access to a shared pool of configurable computing resources (e.g., networks, servers, storage, applications, and services) that can be rapidly provisioned and released with minimal management effort or service provider interaction" (http://nvlpubs.nist.gov/nistpubs/Legacy/SP/nistspecialpublication800-145.pdf). It also defined the cloud model composed of five essential characteristics, three service models, and four deployment models. This definition accurately represents the essence of cloud computing, but it still keeps it open to individual vendor and analyst interpretation.

In the most simplistic way, we can view cloud computing as a type of utility service, similar to water and electricity encountered on a daily basis. The ubiquitous availability of those resources makes us consume them without fully understanding how they are being generated and delivered. When we turn on the light switch at our house, we expect the light to come on. We do not spend time thinking about how the electricity was generated, how it was delivered to our house, and by which energy company. We just expect it to be there. This type of utility model is comparable to the principles behind cloud computing. Imagine being able to "turn on" compute, network, storage, virtualization, and application resources and then consume them from a computer terminal to execute on-demand computational tasks. This is, in fact, what cloud computing is about, and it does so without your thinking about which servers are carrying out those computations, where they are located, what kind of storage resources they have, how the network is set up between them, and which virtualization platform is leveraged on top of them.

Cloud computing deployment models differ by the amount of abstraction they provide between the customers and the cloud resources. Software as a service (SaaS) provides the highest level of abstraction, most often exposing only a web-based interface, which can be consumed by an Internet browser running on a client machine. On the other hand, infrastructure as a service (IaaS) provides the lower level of abstraction, exposing raw elements of compute, network, storage, and virtualization to the customer. The IaaS model is most often used to build the service offering from the ground up. Platform as a service (PaaS) caters to the application development community by offering the ability to develop, run, and manage applications without building the infrastructure required for this task, while exposing the tools required for higher-level programming with dramatically reduced infrastructure complexity.

With various levels of abstractions in place, the issue of where the actual infrastructure elements of compute, network, storage, and virtualization are actually deployed still remains. The answer depends on defining the target customer population and the desired target infrastructure. Cloud computing networks, which service internal users, are called private clouds, and they are deployed in organizational data centers or colocation facilities. Cloud computing networks, which are offered as a service by the service providers, are called public clouds, and they are deployed in service provider facilities. Cloud computing networks that allow augmenting private cloud resources with resources consumed out of the public cloud, otherwise known as cloud bursting, are called hybrid clouds.

In addition to defining deployment models and cloud computing types, we can identify five distinct key characteristics inherent to many cloud computing deployments:

■ *Self-service portal* for an on-demand provisioning of cloud computing resources. Think about it as logging into a secure portal, making selections for the desired resources, and having them be available after they have been spun up by the cloud computing orchestrator.

■ *Ubiquitous access* for the ability to access and consume cloud computing resources leveraging a variety of thin and thick client platforms, such as mobile phones, smart watches, tablets, laptops, virtual desktops, workstations, and so on.

■ *Resource elasticity* for the ability to scale up and scale down cloud computing resources based on administrative actions or dynamic workload demands.

■ *Resource pooling* for the ability to consider compute resources as a pool of geographically independent resources to be assigned to individual customers based on either required performance characteristics or locality. The multitenant nature of cloud computing environments allows you to offer per-tenant resource allocation.

■ *Pay-per use* for the ability to charge customers based on the resource type and consumption. For private clouds, it also allows IT organizations, usually owning the infrastructure that the cloud computing is built on top of, to perform charge-back to individual organizational units consuming cloud resources. It helps IT departments create a return on investment (ROI) behind upfront investments in the cloud computing infrastructure.

Before continuing, let's have a quick look into the history behind cloud computing.

Brief History of Cloud Computing

Cloud computing as a term exploded in its popularity during the 2000s. Its ability to offer a utility-like consumption model to traditional IT disciplines of compute, storage, and networking had given rise to a more agile and resource-friendly infrastructure delivery. Where did cloud computing come from, and was it the invention of the new millennia? Absolutely not!

Cloud computing principles can be traced back as far as the 1950s, to the era largely dominated by the massive (and very expensive) computers performing centralized computational operations. Computing time was rented out to whoever was willing to pay the price. If you rented this computer, you could run your required computational tasks, but no one else could do it at the same time.

The evolution of cloud computing into the 1960s and 1970s introduced ideas of timesharing, where centralized computers could be shared to perform multiple parallel computational tasks to drive higher efficiency into the system. The access into the centralized computer was achieved through the terminals, which used communication protocols to send and receive data back and forth between the centralized computer and the terminals.

This approach laid down the foundation for the Defense Department's DARPA (Defense Advanced Research Project Agency), which later on became the Internet.

The continuous evolution of computing technology in the 1980s and 1990s produced increasingly more sophisticated machines capable of executing complicated computational tasks at dramatically faster speeds and at a fraction of the previous cost. Computers became smaller, smarter, and faster. Computational tasks shifted from a centralized to decentralized approach.

The economical turmoil of the early 2000s, also known as the dot-com bubble, shook the technology industry to its foundation. More cost-efficient methods of delivering compute capacity were sought, giving birth to the modern era of cloud computing. Cloud computing of the 2000s offered the ability to modernize organizational IT infrastructure by enabling utility-like consumption models, powered by the virtualization technologies for shared physical resources. Due to its private nature, this type of cloud computing was labeled as the private cloud. For the service providers, it opened new revenue-generating opportunities of offering IaaS, where organizations could conduct their business without relying on the local data center resources, which offered a great relief to budget- and resource-constrained customers. Because of its public nature, this type of cloud computing was labeled as the public cloud.

Some organizations look at augmenting their existing private cloud capacity by leveraging pay-per-use public cloud resources. For example, this could be the case of a retailer needing to accommodate increased capacity associated with end-of-year or holiday seasonal sales. In term of cloud computing, such a model was labeled as the hybrid cloud, and the ability to leverage public cloud resources to run computational tasks alongside the private cloud resources was labeled as bursting.

The final chapter of cloud computing is far from being written by the industry. In the subsequent sections of this chapter, we are going to take a closer look at different types of cloud computing models and some of their most distinct characteristics.

Cloud Computing and Virtualization

Many mistakenly consider virtualization and cloud computing as the same. This is because virtualization introduces flexibility and efficiency compatible with the cloud computing philosophy. Virtualization is indeed an important element of cloud computing, but it is not the only one. In fact, it is possible to build the cloud computing environment without leveraging virtualization techniques. Some of the largest public clouds demonstrated the ability to build massive scale clouds without use of server virtualization technology.

Virtualization can be defined as a layer of abstraction that can exist throughout the infrastructure stack. It allows representing infrastructure as a collection of sharable resources instantiated in software and having scheduled access to the underlying physical resources. The resources primarily are made up of servers, network, and storage.

Several types of server virtualization are in existence, with the most popular one being the ability to run multiple instances of the server operating system on the same physical server by leveraging the construct of a virtual machine. Virtual machines can be created, started, moved/migrated, stopped, and destroyed. Virtual machines run on top of the virtual hypervisor, which abstracts underlying physical server resources, such as CPU, memory, and disk. Alternative to virtual machines, cloud computing can leverage software constrainers as the means of operating system level virtualization. Containers provide a more resource-friendly footprint, but they lack the ability to run dissimilar operating systems, such as Windows and Linux on the same physical server. The use of virtual machines and containers allows cloud computing deployments to achieve the flexibility and agility they are meant to achieve. For example, additional virtual machines or containers can be created to accommodate increased workload demand based on the computational tasks required by the customer. Virtual machines or containers can also be migrated from one physical host to another in accordance with underlying physical server resource availability.

Storage virtualization aims to represent a pool of physical data storage capacity as a single virtual device presented to the physical or virtual servers. Many cloud computing environments are evolving from dedicated storage arrays and storage area networks to a distributed storage approach based on x86 server platforms, local hard drives, and ubiquitous IP fabric accommodating both network and storage traffic. This distributed storage approach is also known as the hyper-convergence, and it allows cloud computing environments to drive more cost-efficient models as an alternative to a traditionally expensive monolithic data storage approach.

Finally, network virtualization aims to introduce flexibility and efficiency into delivering network connectivity services for the cloud computing environments. Network virtualization and segmentation solutions range from the rudimentary VLANs and virtual routing and forwarding (VRF) to more sophisticated multiprotocol label switching virtual private networks (MPLS VPNs), IPsec VPNs, overlay transport virtualization (OTV), Locator/ID Separation Protocol (LISP), Network Virtualization Using Generic Routing Encapsulation (NVGRE), and virtual extensible LAN (VXLAN) overlay networks. Overlay networks are established on top of the physical networks; they allow linking cloud computing resources into private isolated network topologies. Overlay networks also abstract the physical networks and allow construction of transport-independent topologies. Network virtualization is not limited to just overlay networking. Mechanisms for network device virtualization, such as virtual device contexts (VDCs) available on Cisco Nexus 7000/7700 series data center switches or virtual contexts available on Cisco ASA firewalls, cater to cloud computing environments' shared resource approach.

Cloud Computing Deployment Models

As mentioned earlier, over the years cloud computing evolved to include several deployment models based on the target customers and the infrastructure leveraged for the deployment. In this section we are going to look at various deployment models existing for cloud computing environments.

Private Cloud

Private cloud deployment is defined as a cloud computing environment provisioned for internal organizational use, which may include various internal divisions, business units, internal consumers, and so on.

Private clouds offer an ideal way to solve some of the most significant business and technology challenges faced by organizations today. A private cloud can deliver IT-as-a-service. It helps reduce costs, raise efficiency, and introduce innovative new business models, while simplifying operations and infrastructure. The Cisco philosophy on delivering a private cloud is predicated on the principles of the Unified Data Center, which consists of Unified Fabric, Unified Compute System, and Unified Management. This holistic approach unifies and dynamically optimizes compute, storage, and network resources, allowing them to be securely and rapidly provisioned on-demand.

Unified Fabric allows running multiple types of traffic—specifically network and storage traffic—over the same Ethernet infrastructure. The use of ACI brings extreme automation and application centricity into the private cloud network infrastructure to deliver optimal user experience and IT agility. The Unified Computing System allows you to run private cloud workloads on a highly capable and scalable server platform, while leveraging service profiles for hardware provisioning automation. Unified Management completes the story by providing private cloud holistic automation, orchestration, and self-service portal capabilities.

Infrastructure pieces leveraged for the private cloud can come in the form of individually provisioned elements of compute, network, and storage, but they can also come in the pre-validated and preintegrated form offered as a Cisco VCE Vblock system or as a validated reference design offered as Cisco FlexPod.

Public Cloud

In contrast with the private cloud, the public cloud is usually owned and operated by a service provider as a service to customers. The key characteristic of the public cloud is its ability to accommodate multiple customers, called tenants, over the shared infrastructure, while keeping them segregated from a security and resource perspective. Similar segregation requirements may appear in the private cloud deployment in a form that internal organizational units may be viewed as private cloud tenants, but this requirement may not be as stringent, and the implications of sharing the data between the two tenants may not be as significant or as legally binding.

Think of a public cloud as a hotel you can check into, pay the room rate, and use the hotel facilities as needed. Now the question is if it's financially feasible for you to permanently live in the hotel. Does it make sense for an organization to conduct its entire business in the public cloud? The answer depends on the use case.

For smaller organizations, buying, deploying, and maintaining in-house IT infrastructure many times becomes cost prohibitive. For such organizations, public clouds provide an excellent solution by offering a service model where organizations consume cloud resources on an as-needed basis and only pay for the services or resources consumed. This largely eliminates the need for a local IT infrastructure beyond the basic Internet connectivity services.

For larger organizations where IT budgets are simply a normal part of running their business, public clouds offer the ability to shift certain—and in many cases lower priority—computational tasks into the public cloud to free up resources for higher priority tasks executed in the local (private) cloud. This balanced approach is beneficial for larger organizations to keep IT budgets under control for lower priority or unplanned projects requiring infrastructure or capacity deployment.

Hybrid Cloud

The hybrid cloud offers a hybrid approach between the private and the public cloud. The premise of the hybrid cloud is to extend the existing private cloud environment into the public cloud as needed, on demand, and with consistent network and security policies. There are several use cases behind using a hybrid cloud approach, but the most predominant one is to augment in-house private cloud capacity when such capacity comes to demand. Figure 15-1 depicts the philosophy behind hybrid clouds.

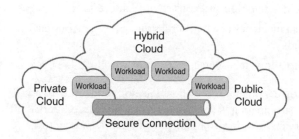

Figure 15-1 *Hybrid Cloud Philosophy*

Let's discuss a simple example of a retailer conducting business leveraging its private cloud infrastructure hosted in the organizational data center or colocation facilities. Private cloud compute, network, storage, and virtualization capacities are defined for projected use with headroom for additional growth. During peak seasonal or holiday sales, this retailer can experience a significant surge in capacity demand to accommodate increased sales activities. This additional capacity can be accommodated by provisioning further infrastructure elements, such as more servers, more disk space, more network bandwidth, and so forth. However, the question becomes what this extra capacity is going to be used for during the normal sales cycles when infrastructure demands subside. It seems wasteful to provision additional capacity, at times bearing significant costs, for it just to be leveraged during short periods of high demand and otherwise being idle most of the time. This is exactly the case where hybrid cloud can come to the rescue. The retailer can request additional capacity from the public cloud service provider, establish secure connectivity to the allocated public cloud resources, and extend organizational network and security policies to the public cloud resources. Increased demand for capacity can be accommodated by shifting some of the workloads and computational tasks from the organizational private cloud to the service provider–owned public cloud, while complying with all organizational policies. The retailer bears the cost for consuming public cloud resources, but when such resources are no longer needed, they can be relinquished, ceasing any additional charges.

Cisco InterCloud Fabric offers highly secure, open, and flexible solution for establishing hybrid cloud connectivity for both businesses and service providers. It allows freedom of placing organization workloads ubiquitously across public and private clouds based on the business needs. In accordance with our earlier discussion, Cisco InterCloud Fabric applies the same network, security, QoS, and access control policies in the public cloud, the same way they are applied in the private cloud environment. The end result is that there is no real demarcation point between public and private cloud environments, and an organization can ubiquitously leverage resources and capacity of this heterogeneous environment regardless of its geographical location or ownership.

Following are the key features of Cisco InterCloud Fabric:

- Automated format conversion between workload types created in different environments

- Ability to migrate workloads between the public and private clouds leveraging secure transport between the two, with consistent organizational security policy enforcement

- Ability to extend Layer 2 connectivity securely between private and public cloud environments to allow live virtual machine migration and consistent IP addressing

- Workload monitoring for the virtual machines residing across the heterogeneous environment of private and public clouds

- Automation and programmability to allow managing all aspects of workload life cycle

Cisco InterCloud Fabric for business offers organizations the choice of connecting to a variety of public cloud service providers participating in the cloud ecosystem. Cisco InterCloud Fabric for service providers allows service providers to easily join and participate in the cloud ecosystem, offering their public cloud services to the business customers.

Community Cloud

The community cloud is a lesser known emerging cloud deployment model. It is a model that provides shared infrastructure resources to specific groups that share common interests or have common concerns. The community cloud can be deployed either on-premises or off-premises, and it can be owned and operated by either a third-party managing service provider, the participating organizations themselves, or a combination of both.

Community clouds help alleviate common challenges across a diverse set of organizations, such as universities, government agencies, and enterprises in regard to financial pressures, technology complexity, security concerns, industry compliance, and potentially lack of sector-specific services from the service provider community.

Cloud Computing Services Models

The cloud computing philosophy allows delivering anything as a service. In this section we are going to look at three main models offered as part of cloud computing. These models are IAAS, PaaS, and SaaS.

Infrastructure as a Service

IT departments often face significant challenges when trying to address the organizational needs for cost reduction, scalability, agility, security of data and applications, rollout of new services, and so on. The common inability of traditional IT to deliver on the organizational needs results in what is called a shadow IT, where organizational departments start investing in their own purpose-delivered infrastructure instead of relying on the IT delivered services. Services rolled out using shadow IT often lack the elements of resiliency, security, and cost arbitrage. Simply put, shadow IT puts organizations at risk, but it is an inevitable outcome of the traditionally rigid and slow IT infrastructure and service delivery. This is exactly where consuming IaaS comes to the rescue.

Traditional organizational IT infrastructure consists of elements such as network devices, servers, storage devices, transport links, and facility systems. These elements are provisioned, managed, and operated by the organizations. With the IaaS cloud computing service model, these IT infrastructure elements are hosted by the service provider and are offered as a service to the customer organizations, which eliminates the need for the organizations to purchase and own these IT elements themselves.

To allow efficient sharing of the underlying physical resources, service providers many times employ principles of virtualization to present virtual servers (virtual machines), virtual networks (overlay networks), and virtual storage (distributed storage) to customers as part of IaaS offering. Customers can start leveraging these cloud resources as if they were provisioned in the organizational data centers by installing operating systems and applications. IaaS environments also can be provisioned to have access to the Internet to provide remote connectivity and extranet services. Figure 15-2 depicts the difference between delivering infrastructure as a private on-prem cloud versus consuming it as a service from the public IaaS service provider.

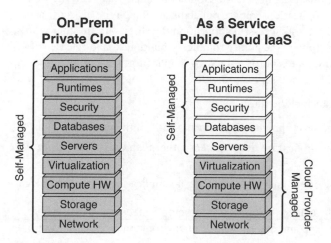

Figure 15-2 *On-Prem Owned Private Cloud Versus Public as a Service IaaS*

IaaS addresses common concerns about moving to the cloud:

- Provide secure, scalable, and extensible infrastructure.

- Roll out services with significant cost savings compared to implementing them in organizational data centers. Shift from upfront capital investments to an ongoing pay-as-you-go or pay-as-you-grow model.

- Ease to accommodate local in-county regulations and compliance by consuming in-county or in-region infrastructure services.

- Raise efficiencies by leveraging as a service load balancing, application acceleration, and other advanced features to help ensure optimal utilization of resources.

- Operational excellence through highly trained personnel managing physical and virtual infrastructure adjusted to organizational specifications and needs, while retaining management visibility and decision-making authority.

The service provider infrastructure, which serves as the foundation for IaaS services offering, is often delivered out of regional owned, leased, or colocated facilities. This allows service providers to achieve a global reach, while keeping their infrastructure as close to their customers as possible for the best possible performance. It also helps to address any regulations in regard to data locality.

Nothing, of course, precludes IaaS from being delivered as part of a private cloud offering. In this case, organizational IT departments still benefit from the agility of delivering IaaS to their internal customers. IaaS does, however, require IT to host and own the cloud computing physical infrastructure elements.

Platform as a Service

PaaS is a little less known cloud computing service model. It is best described as a development environment hosted on the cloud infrastructure to facilitate rapid design, testing, and deployment of the new applications. PaaS targets the cloud consumers that need the flexibility to configure and develop applications yet are reluctant to take on the tasks of managing the elements and tools required for successful application development. In other words, the PaaS service model offers customers the ability to quickly build, test, and release software products using infrastructure that is purpose-built for application development, yet is delivered as a service by the public cloud service provider.

Some of the main benefits of PaaS include these:

- Rapidly provision application development environments with all the necessary toolsets
- Allow developers to focus on application development rather than on infrastructure management
- Shift the management framework from a VM-centric to an application centric approach

PaaS environments can also be leveraged as application development "sandboxes," where developers are free to quickly create and experiment in an environment where the cost of consuming resources is greatly reduced.

Software as a Service

SaaS is common in today's IP industry, and it is the most comprehensive way of abstracting IT infrastructure elements, while exposing only easily consumable interfaces and APIs. Many SaaS applications are in existence today. These applications include collaboration, messaging, e-mail, enterprise resource planning (ERP), human resources (HR), customer relationship management (CRM), and even gaming. SaaS applications can be consumed by a simple means of an Internet web browser, or they can be based on a thin client approach.

With SaaS, independent software vendors (ISVs) have a choice of offering their software product leveraging their own private cloud IT infrastructure, leveraging public cloud computing platforms, or combining the two in the form of a hybrid cloud. In fact, delivering SaaS can be seen as a culmination of the process that had started with building IaaS to provide an agile, scalable, and cost-effective IT infrastructure, moved to PaaS for effective application- and feature-rich application development environment, and finally ended with SaaS to deliver the software on demand to the user population. Figure 15-3 depicts the hierarchical relationship of delivering software on demand, taking advantage of the IaaS and PaaS foundation.

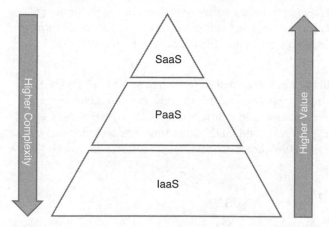

Figure 15-3   *Hierarchical Approach for Software on Demand*

SaaS is, of course, not predicated on the existence of IaaS and PaaS. However, the overwhelming advantages of using it as a service approach for end-to-end delivery are mostly appealing.

Application Programming Interfaces

APIs are essential elements of a successful cloud computing strategy. They are instructions, routines, protocols, and tools leveraged to build applications. APIs define how different software elements interact, and they allow developers to treat these software elements as a collection of building blocks that can be put together to produce the desired result. Think of APIs as software-to-software interfaces, which can also be automated, rather than interfaces leveraged by users. If invoked, these interfaces expose certain functionality and allow access to information or trigger processing. The API itself is just a piece of programming code that governs the rule of how one software element can communicate with another software element; as such, APIs are pervasively leveraged in the software development community for a myriad of use cases.

One rather simple example of API use could be an online shopping website, where once a shopper provides payment details, an API call can be issued to the bank to validate payment method validity and fund availability. Once that is successful, the shopper can be notified and the transaction completed.

APIs allow open information exchange between multiple software elements, but they can also offer a form of application security, where rather than exposing the internals of software elements, developers can only expose programmatic API interfaces that other software elements can interact with. This way, communication methods and types of requests are tightly controlled.

The de facto standard for today's web APIs is in the form of representational state transfer (REST). It is an architectural style and an approach to communications that is often used in the development of web services. REST is a popular building style for cloud-based APIs, and the major public cloud providers existing in the market at the time of writing this book offer it. The popularity of REST comes from its lightweight communications between the software element acting as producer (server) and a software element acting as consumer (client). REST uses HTTP/HTTPS for transport and exposes a set of methods as uniform resource identifiers (URIs). When Web services use REST architecture, they are called RESTful or REST APIs.

Data returned through REST APIs is usually encoded or formatted as XML or JSON. XML stands for Extensible Markup Language, and it is ideal for highly structured information. JSON stands for JavaScript Object Notation, and it differs from XML by being more lean and more easily human-readable. Both XML and JSON data formatting are extensively used in today's programmatic APIs. Figure 15-4 shows two sample API call responses with XML and JSON formatting for comparison.

XML

```
<?xml version="1.0"?>
<book id="123">
    <title>CCNA DC Guide</title>
    <author>Cisco</author>
    <published>
      <by>Cisco Press</by>
      <year>2016</year>
    </published>
</book>
```

JSON

```
{
    "id": 123,
    "title": "CCNA DC Guide",
    "author": "Cisco",
    "published": {
       "by": "Cisco Press",
       "year": 2016
    }
}
```

Figure 15-4 *XML and JSON Formatting Examples*

In recent years, REST APIs have increasingly replaced previously popular Simple Object Access Protocol (SOAP). SOAP had been around for a long time, and as such it enjoys the benefits of long-term use. However, SOAP's heavyweight and at times inflexible approach makes it a less preferred choice for application developers. Of course, not all APIs are web based; one example is the Java API.

APIs have significant implications on the cloud computing environments, their success, and the flexibility of services they offer. The most successful public cloud offering to date comes from Amazon Web Services (AWS). AWS was the first to burst into the scene as a viable IaaS service provider. It kept up to date with changing market trends. The use of APIs was a major enabler behind its success, allowing customers to consume its resources by automating creation, modification, and deletion tasks. Automation is the key to unlocking the cloud's agility.

For private cloud deployments, APIs also play an invaluable role by enabling services such as self-service, billing, and chargeback. Self-service allows customers to opt in for the cloud service and request resources or modify existing settings in a completely automated way, while relying on APIs to deliver instructions to various cloud computing infrastructure elements to instantiate or alter the service, as requested. Billing and chargeback are also part of API-enabled automation, where organizational IT departments responsible for the rollout of private cloud infrastructure can establish a process of charging other organizational units for the resources based on their consumption. APIs can also play a significant role at the infrastructure layer. APIs leveraged in the compute, network, storage, and virtualization layers can be used for provisioning and operational tasks, assisting IT teams in monitoring and expanding underlying infrastructure based on the customer demands.

Reference List

Cloud Computing Definition: http://nvlpubs.nist.gov/nistpubs/Legacy/SP/nistspecialpublication800-145.pdf

Cisco Cloud Infrastructure Solutions: http://www.cisco.com/c/en/us/solutions/data-center-virtualization/cloud-infrastructure/index.html

Cisco Powered Cloud Services: http://www.cisco.com/c/en/us/solutions/cisco-powered/overview.html

Exam Preparation Tasks

Review All Key Topics

Review the most important topics in the chapter, noted with the key topic icon in the outer margin of the page. Table 15-2 lists a reference of these key topics and the page numbers on which each is found.

Table 15-2   Key Topics for Chapter 15

Key Topic Element	Description	Page
Paragraph	Private Cloud	571
Paragraph	Public Cloud	572
Paragraph	Hybrid Cloud	573
List	Key Features of Intercloud Fabric	574
Paragraph	Infrastructure as a Service	574
Paragraph	Software as a Service	576
Paragraph	Application Programming Interfaces	577
Paragraph	Implication of APIs on the Cloud	578

Define Key Terms

Define the following key terms from this chapter, and check your answers in the Glossary:

IaaS, PaaS, SaaS, Private Cloud, Public Cloud, Hybrid Cloud, Community Cloud, Intercloud, API, REST, XML, JSON

This chapter covers the following exam topics:

4.3 Describe the basic functions of a Cisco UCS Director

4.3a Management

4.3c Multitenancy

4.3d Chargeback

4.3e Service offerings

4.3f Catalogs

CHAPTER 16

UCS Director

Data centers contain multiple technology stacks, such as compute, storage, networking, and virtualization, working together to provide IT services for an organization. These technology stacks can be from different vendors and they are often managed manually in silos by using separate management software for each technology. However, using a manual process and a separate tool for each technology is not efficient. Cisco UCS Director (UCSD) is a software solution that provides unified management and automated provisioning of computing, network, storage, and virtualization technologies within the data center. Based on the role, IT team members can use UCSD as a unified management platform to manage their devices and to automate the tasks for faster service delivery.

This chapter gives you an overview of UCSD features and functions that are relevant to the DCICT exam. It also provides configuration and troubleshooting guidelines, and information about using UCSD to simplify data center management.

"Do I Know This Already?" Quiz

The "Do I Know This Already?" quiz allows you to assess whether you should read this entire chapter thoroughly or jump to the "Exam Preparation Tasks" section. If you are in doubt about your answers to these questions or your own assessment of your knowledge of the topics, read the entire chapter. Table 16-1 lists the major headings in this chapter and their corresponding "Do I Know This Already?" quiz questions. You can find the answers in Appendix A, "Answers to the 'Do I Know This Already?' Quizzes."

Table 16-1 "Do I Know This Already?" Section-to-Question Mapping

Foundation Topics Section	Questions
"Features and Functions of UCS Director"	1–4
"Unified Infrastructure Management"	5–9
"UCSD Administration"	10–11
"Chargeback"	12
"ACI Integration"	13–14
"Catalogs"	15

CAUTION The goal of self-assessment is to gauge your mastery of the topics in this chapter. If you do not know the answer to a question or are only partially sure of the answer, you should mark that question as wrong for purposes of the self-assessment. Giving yourself credit for an answer you correctly guess skews your self-assessment results and might provide you with a false sense of security.

1. Which of the following are key benefits of UCS Director? (Choose all that apply.)

    a. Faster service delivery

    b. Business agility and operational efficiency

    c. Improved service quality

    d. Multivendor support

    e. Virtualization of computing resources

2. Which of the following statements describes the adaptive provisioning feature of UCS Director?

    a. Provides orchestration engine to automatically provision network, compute, and storage.

    b. Provides a real-time available capacity, internal policies, and application workload requirements to optimize the availability of your resources.

    c. Provides a policy-based framework to offer infrastructure as a service (IaaS).

    d. Provides the XML and REST API for integration.

3. Which of the following statements are correct about UCS Director? (Choose three.)

    a. UCS Director provides a single interface for the administrator to monitor, provision, and manage the IT infrastructure across physical, virtual, and bare metal environments.

    b. UCS Director is used to monitor, provision and manage only Cisco products such as Cisco routers, Cisco switches, Unified Computing System, and Application Centric Infrastructure.

    c. UCS Director provides complete life cycle management of virtual machines such as VM power management, VM resizing, VM snapshot management, and other VM actions.

    d. UCS Director has an open XML API and a REST API that can be used to assess the capabilities of UCSD with a higher level management platform.

4. Which of the following server virtualization platforms are supported by UCS Director? (Choose three.)

    a. VMware vSphere

    b. VMware Fusion

    c. Microsoft Hyper-V

    d. Red Hat KVM

    e. Microsoft Terminal Server

5. Which of the following statements are correct about UCS Director sites? (Choose two.)

    a. Sites are used to logically group the pods.

    b. Creating sites is mandatory in UCS Director.

    c. Creating sites is optional in UCS Director.

    d. Sites are used to group users and to provide role-based access control.

6. Which of the following statements describes the function of pods in UCS Director?

    a. Pods manage the quota and provide QoS features.

    b. Pods are used to group sites.

    c. Pods are used to group resources.

    d. Pods provide isolation between tenants.

7. Which of the following virtual accounts are supported in UCS Director? (Choose three.)

    a. VMware vSphere

    b. Openstack Account

    c. Rackspace Cloud

    d. Amazon Web Services EC2

    e. Linux Containers

8. Which of the following servers are valid physical account types in UCS Director? (Choose three.)

    a. UCS Manager

    b. Cisco ASA

    c. EMC VNX

    d. NetApp OnCommand

    e. Microsoft Terminal Server

9. Which of the following statements best describes a multidomain manager account in UCS Director?

    a. A multidomain manager account is a physical account that represents a software application that can manage more than one domain.

    b. A multidomain manager account is used for representing the domain name system.

    c. A multidomain manager account is for the admin account.

    d. A multidomain manager account is a virtual account for cloud platforms such as AWZ and Azure.

    e. A multidomain manager account is used for managing Microsoft Terminal Server

10. To enable multitenancy in UCS Director, which feature should be enabled?

    a. MSP Organization

    b. Service provider feature

    c. Groups

    d. Role-based access control

11. UCS Director supports which of the following multitenancy features?

   a. Delegated administration to tenant

   b. Portal branding for tenant

   c. Tenant ability to act as a cloud broker

   d. Resource allocation to the tenant

12. What are the valid cost models supported by the chargeback feature of UCS Director? (Choose two.)

   a. Hybrid Cost Model

   b. Standard Cost Model

   c. Normal Cost Model

   d. Advanced Cost Model

13. Which of the following statements is correct about UCS Director service offerings?

   a. A service offering defines the resources needed to provision an application.

   b. A service offering defines the integration options of UCS Director.

   c. A tenant profile is also called a service offering.

   d. A service offering is needed for integration with Cisco Prime Service Catalog (PSC).

14. In a service offering, you can define usage of resource groups as one of the following. (Choose two.)

   a. Shared among the applications or tenants

   b. Reserved for the administrator

   c. Reserved for users

   d. Dedicated to a single application or tenant

15. Which of the following statements are correct about the UCS Director self-service catalog? (Choose two.)

   a. Administrators deploy new infrastructure instances by logging into the UCS Director catalog and ordering the services.

   b. Administrators publish catalog items for IT services by using predefined policies and governance practices.

   c. Users deploy new infrastructure instances by logging into the UCS Director catalog and ordering the services.

   d. Users publish catalog items so the administrator can receive the order for automation of infrastructure service.

Foundation Topics

What Is UCS Director?

Cisco UCS Director (UCSD) is data center management software that simplifies IT operation by administering both the physical and the virtual infrastructure from a single web-based service portal. It provides a unified view of compute, network, storage, and virtualization resources to the IT administrators. UCSD software also provides visibility to the capacity and utilization of the resources it manages. It offers policy-based orchestration for both physical and virtual resources by abstracting hardware and software into programmable tasks. These tasks can be performed in a sequence, using predefined or custom workflows. UCSD workflows can span hypervisor, compute, network, and storage components in the data center. UCSD communicates with all the elements in the data center and acts as the orchestra conductor for IT operations. The software automates end-to-end IT processes and helps ensure that the infrastructure layer is synchronized, optimized, and available on demand. The automation and orchestration processes of UCSD speed up the delivery of the IT infrastructure and increase the quality of delivery using a consistent policy across different technology domains. UCSD supports northbound APIs that enable other IT tools to use its functions by making application programming interface (API) calls. UCSD also provides a software development kit (SDK) allowing ecosystem partners to develop custom integration for their devices. Figure 16-1 shows that UCSD can perform end-to-end automation and life cycle management of the IT infrastructure in the data center.

NOTE At the time of writing this chapter, UCSD 5.5 is the latest version, and UCSD 6.0 is planned for upcoming release. Most of the features discussed in this chapter are generic and valid for all versions of UCSD. There might be a slight variation in the features depending on the version of UCSD. Please check product documentation for details.

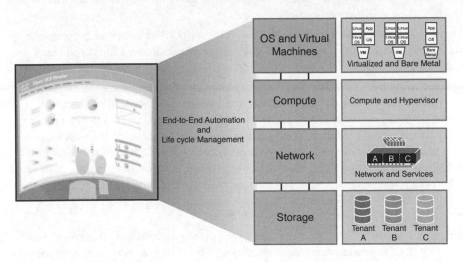

Figure 16-1 *UCS Director*

You can use UCSD to build a private cloud for your organization. You can also extend your internal IT policies to public clouds by managing public clouds from UCSD in the same way you manage your internal resources. This approach provides a consistent, reliable, and predictable IT process across public and private clouds.

Benefits of UCS Director

Some of the benefits of using UCSD are as follows:

- **Faster Service Delivery:** UCSD provides faster services by automating the end-to-end task for IT service delivery.

- **Cost Savings:** Efficient use of resources and visibility into the capacity results in cost savings. UCSD allows IT departments to experience the full benefits of their converged infrastructure investment by continuing to reduce TCO and save staff time with transparent unified management for the industry's leading converged and hyper converged infrastructure solutions.

- **Business Agility and Operational Efficiency:** Cisco UCSD improves business agility and increases efficiency by automating infrastructure management and services delivery. It provides unified infrastructure provisioning and automation across computing, networking, and storage resources to drastically reduce the complexity of IT operation and administration.

- Cisco UCSD improves consistency, efficiency, and speed within your organization. It accomplishes this by replacing time-consuming, manual provisioning and deprovisioning data center resources with automated workflows. Cisco UCSD reduces delivery time from weeks to minutes.

- **Ease of Use:** Cisco UCSD automates and simplifies IT processes. It provides a single point from which the IT infrastructure can be automated and orchestrated, including compute, network, and storage, with physical and virtual resources treated equally. This results in easy provisioning of infrastructure from single IT tools by IT administrators and by clients using a self-service catalog.

- **Improved Service Quality:** A well-tested automation workflow can provide consistent results for IT services. UCSD delivers IT services that are no longer subject to human errors.

- **Improved Security:** Cisco UCSD supports multitenancy to keep the tenant users, policies, reports, and application workloads isolated from each other for better security. Internal applications can be isolated from external applications, and development/testing environments can be isolated from production environments using the multitenancy model of the UCSD platform. Role-based access control (RBAC) is used to manage user privileges and to make sure that users can only perform the operation they are authorized for. Further, resource management and tracking are fully built into UCSD. All IT operations performed via UCSD are fully logged and can be reversed as needed. This provides improved security compliance and change tracking.

- **Multivendor Support:** The data center comprises diverse technologies from many vendors. Cisco UCSD provides a management platform for such heterogeneous infrastructure. It supports multiple hypervisor platforms, multiple compute platforms, multiple converged, and hyper-converged solution stacks.

UCSD provides a task library that supports the creation, manipulation, and editing of virtual machines, hosts, and virtual networks for hypervisors such as VMware ESXi, Microsoft Hyper-V, and Red Hat KVM. It also includes broad guest operating system support to facilitate cloning of Windows and Linux virtual machines, and monitoring of CPU, memory, and resource usage.

UCSD supports NetApp FlexPod and ExpressPod, EMC VSPEX, and Virtual Computing Environment (VCE) vBlock systems, based on the Cisco UCS and Cisco Nexus platforms. It is also possible to integrate a third-party solution into the UCSD with a publicly available SDK.

Features and Functions of UCS Director

Some of the key features and functions of UCSD are outlined in Table 16-2.

Table 16-2   Features and Functions of UCSD

Features and Functions of UCSD	Description
Unified Management	UCSD provides a single interface for the administrators to monitor, provision, and manage the IT infrastructure across physical, virtual, and bare metal environments. With UCSD, there is no need to log into multiple IT tools and switch between the tools to perform day-to-day tasks. There are several benefits of this approach, including ease of use, increased productivity, and centralized policy-based infrastructure provisioning for consistent results.
Self-Service Catalog	Administrators, using predefined policies and governance practices, publish catalog items for each IT service. Users deploy new infrastructure instances by logging into UCSD and ordering the service.
Adaptive Provisioning	Provides a real-time available capability, internal policies, and application workload requirements to optimize the availability of your resources.
Dynamic Capacity Management	UCSD continuously monitors all resources in real time and provides visibility to the infrastructure consumption to improve capacity planning and management of these resources. UCSD also identifies the underutilized and overutilized resources.
Reporting Capabilities	UCSD has many out-of-the-box reporting capabilities, such as unified dashboards, infrastructure assessment reports, resource utilization reports, trend monitoring, and heat maps. These reports help administrators reduce troubleshooting time and identify performance bottlenecks. You can also create your own reports using the report builder module.

Features and Functions of UCSD	Description
Multitenancy	UCSD offers the ability to manage network, compute, and storage resources for multiple tenants. In multitenant configuration, infrastructure resources can be allocated to the tenant, where each tenant can only manage his own resources.
Multiple Hypervisor Support	UCSD supports VMware ESXi, Microsoft Hyper-V, and Red Hat KVM hypervisors.
Computing Management	UCSD monitors, manages, and provisions physical, virtual, and bare metal servers and blades from Cisco and other vendors.
Network Management	UCSD provides policy-based provisioning of physical and virtual switches and dynamic network topologies. It allows administrators to configure VLANs, virtual network interface cards (vNICs), port groups and port profiles, IP and Dynamic Host Control Protocol (DHCP) allocation, and access control lists (ACLs) across network devices.
Storage Management	Provides policy-based provisioning and management of filers, virtual filers (vFilers), logical unit numbers (LUNs), and volumes.
Converged and Hyper Converged Infrastructure Management	UCSD supports converged infrastructure solutions, including NetApp FlexPod and FlexPod Express, EMC VSPEX, EMC VPLEX, and VCE Vblock. It also supports hyper converged storage with Cisco VSAN ready node and VMware VSAN.
Out-of-Box Task Library	UCSD provides a library of common tasks to manage the network, storage, and compute infrastructure that spans Cisco and third-party hardware solutions. These libraries help you build your infrastructure in minutes.
Orchestration Capabilities	UCSD replaces time-consuming manual provisioning and deprovisioning of data center resources with automated workflows. You can use built-in product capabilities or write your own custom workflows to automate and orchestrate infrastructure. These orchestration capabilities improve consistency, efficiency, and speed of IT operation within your organization.
Virtual Application Container Service (VACS)	Cisco VACS is a complete infrastructure solution with preconfigured and integrated virtual services, switching, and workflow automation tools. It streamlines infrastructure policy definitions, integration, and deployment. Cisco VACS accelerates the application deployment process with compliant containers, or logical network and services descriptions, that work immediately after installation.
Application Centric Infrastructure (ACI) Support	Supports ACI provisioning, management, and monitoring. UCS Director provides automation of common ACI tasks, such as defining service graphs, EPGs, contracts, and other ACI policies.

Features and Functions of UCSD	Description
Infrastructure as a Service (IaaS)	Delivers VDC and application containers to the tenants with their own virtual firewall, virtual load-balancer, and virtual machines.
Life Cycle Management	UCSD supports complete life cycle management of virtual machines, such as virtual machine (VM) power management, VM resizing, VM snapshot management, and other VM actions.
Extensible Platform	Easy extensibility of platform using SDK.
Billing & Charge Back	You can define billing and chargeback policies to the resources.
XML and REST API	UCSD has an open XML API and a REST API that can be used to assess the capabilities of UCSD with higher-level management platforms.

UCS Director Solution Overview

This section is an overview of the UCSD solution.

UCS Director Components

UCSD software is available as a virtual appliance that can be deployed on Microsoft Hyper-V and VMware vSphere virtualization platforms. This virtual appliance contains CentOS 6.6, Apache Tomcat application, Java 1.8, MySQL database, and several UCSD internal services. After installing UCSD, verify that all internal services are running. Figure 16-2 shows the components of UCSD.

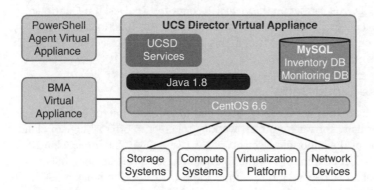

Figure 16-2 *Components of UCS Director*

The UCSD internal services are as follows:

- **broker:** Java Message Service (JMS) Broker
- **controller:** UCSD Policy Engine
- **eventmgr:** Event Manager
- **client:** Console Client

- **idaccessmgr:** Identity and Access Manager
- **inframgr:** Infrastructure Manager
- **tomcat:** Web Application Server
- **websock:** Virtual Network Computing (VNC) Proxy, for console access to virtual machine

UCSD keeps all the information it receives about data center infrastructure in the MySQL database. There are two separate databases on MySQL. The first database is for inventory, and the second database is for monitoring. The inventory database contains physical and virtual accounts and their related inventory data. It also keeps the data used in the normal operation of Cisco UCSD for all supported features. The monitoring database contains the data that Cisco UCS director uses for historical computations, such as aggregations and trend reports. The size of these databases depends on the number of devices and VMs that you would like to manage through Cisco UCSD.

Another important component of UCSD is Bare Metal Agent (BMA). BMA is a separate virtual appliance that is used to install an operating system directly on the bare metal hardware, such as a UCS blade. BMA can install several operating systems, including Windows and Linux, or hypervisor software such as VMware ESXi. Installation and configuration of BMA is discussed in the "UCS Director Deployment" section of this chapter.

UCSD also requires a PowerShell Agent (PSA) virtual appliance. This virtual appliance is a lightweight Microsoft Windows virtual machine to manage applications that expose Windows PowerShell–based northbound API calls. PSA acts as an interfacing layer between Cisco UCSD and applications such as XenDesktop Controller and Microsoft SCVMM that are managed through Windows PowerShell. Once Cisco UCSD PowerShell Agent is installed and running on a Windows Server VM, you need to add it to Cisco UCSD. After adding PowerShell Agent to UCSD, you can set up the virtual account for XenDesktop Controller, or Hyper-V SCVMM, to collect inventory and for other management functions for these applications. Virtual accounts are explained later in this chapter under the section "Unified Infrastructure Management."

Cisco ONE Enterprise Cloud Suite

Cisco ONE Enterprise Cloud Suite is a comprehensive end-to-end solution for building a private cloud. It includes many software products working together to offer a range of cloud capabilities. UCSD is one of the important elements of the Cisco ONE Enterprise Cloud Suite; however, there are other components of the solution. These additional components expand the solution capabilities beyond infrastructure and provide tools to quickly design and implement current and next-generation application stacks that can be located on-premises or in the hybrid cloud. Figure 16-3 shows the components of Cisco ONE Enterprise Cloud Suite.

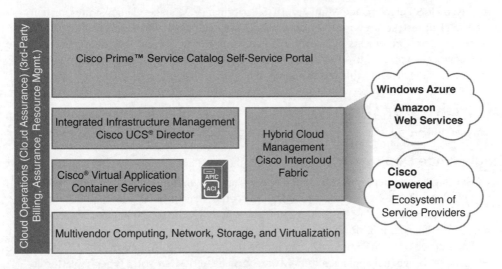

Figure 16-3 *Cisco ONE Enterprise Cloud Suite*

Key components of the Cisco ONE Enterprise Cloud Suites are described here:

- **Cisco Prime Service Catalog (PSC):** The PSC is a self-service portal to order and manage any type of IT service. It delivers data center, workplace, and application services to the users, using an on-demand, automated, and repeatable process. It provides a simple process for ordering, delivery, tracking, and resource management. In Cisco ONE Enterprise Cloud Suite, PSC integrates other components of the solution to provide out-of-box infrastructure as a service (IaaS). It also has an embedded stack designer that can be used to design, configure, and automate the delivery of application stacks. PSC also gives more control over the IT governance using the following:

  - Policy-based controls and approvals

  - User entitlements and role-based access to the services

  - Life cycle management and tracking of services

  - Financial and demand management with pricing, quota, and lease

- **Cisco UCSD:** In Cisco ONE Enterprise Cloud Suite, UCSD provides the function of infrastructure manager. It performs unified provisioning and management of physical and virtual resources across compute, network, storage, security, and virtualization layers. PSC integrates with UCSD using northbound APIs for ordering of infrastructure services. In this solution, UCSD manages Cisco ACI and Cisco Virtual Application Container Service (VACS).

- **Cisco VACS:** This service works in conjunction with Cisco UCSD to accelerate application deployment through preconfigured virtual networking, virtual security and L4-L7 services, and workflow automation for the Cisco Nexus 1000V Switch, Cisco Carrier Services Router (CSR), Cisco Virtual Security Gateway (VSG), and the open-source HAProxy.

- **Cisco Intercloud Fabric:** Cisco Intercloud Fabric software extends your exiting data center to public clouds as needed, on demand and with consistent network and security policies. Cisco Intercloud Fabric is installed within your existing data center to allow connectivity to a large ecosystem of cloud providers to support hybrid cloud deployment.

- **Cisco UCS Performance Manager:** UCS Performance Manager demonstrates visibility into IT infrastructure for performance monitoring and capacity planning. It helps maintain service-level agreements by allowing IT staff to optimize resource allocation. Performance Manager can also be used to identify performance issues, forecast future capacity needs, and provide customizable reports across many device categories.

UCS Director Deployment

This section provides an overview of UCSD single-node and multinode deployment models.

Single-Node Deployment

UCSD single-node deployment is suitable if you are planning to manage 2000 to 5000 virtual machines. In this deployment mode, all the components of the UCSD are installed on a single virtual machine. Installation steps of single-node UCSD for 2000 virtual machines are the same as installation for 5000 virtual machines. The only difference is in CPU, memory, and disk space of virtual appliance, and tuning of database configuration. The UCSD is available as a 64-bit virtual appliance for VMware vSphere and Microsoft Hyper-V platforms. You can download UCSD virtual appliance in the following two formats:

- VMware vSphere open virtualization format (OVF)
- Microsoft Hyper-V virtual hard disk (VHD)

Installation steps for single-node deployment are simple. You can install UCSD software by deploying an OVF template on VMware vSphere. The installation wizard will guide you through the installation steps, where you can specify the root password, shelladmin password, and IP addressing information. Once OVF is deployed, you can access UCSD using your web browser and install licenses. The BMA and PowerShell agents require separate virtual machines; therefore, they are installed separately. Figure 16-4 illustrates the installation steps of UCSD on VMware vSphere.

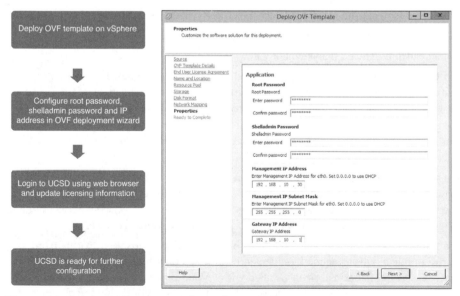

Figure 16-4 *UCS Director Single-Node Deployment Steps*

Multinode Deployment

UCSD multinode configuration is suitable to support a large number of devices and virtual infrastructure. In this deployment mode UCSD components are installed on different virtual machines or nodes. For each node in multinode setup, the CPU, memory hard disk, and database configuration depends on the size of deployment. A multinode UCSD configuration includes the following nodes:

- **Primary Node:** There is only one primary node in a multinode setup. The primary node performs scheduling of system tasks. It contains the configuration of services nodes, node pools, and a list of system tasks that can be offloaded to service nodes for processing. UCSD licenses are installed only on the primary node.

- **Service Nodes:** The service nodes execute the system task assigned to them by the primary node. You can have one or more service nodes in a multinode setup. The number of service nodes required by a multinode setup depends on the number of devices and virtual machines you would like to support. If the primary node is unable to reach service nodes, it will execute the system tasks locally on primary node. If the primary node is not available, a service node can be promoted to the primary node.

- **Database Nodes:** In a multinode setup, you can have only one inventory database and one monitoring database. Once you configure a node as an inventory database or a monitoring database, it cannot be changed to any other type of node.

Figure 16-5 shows the multinode deployment topology of UCSD.

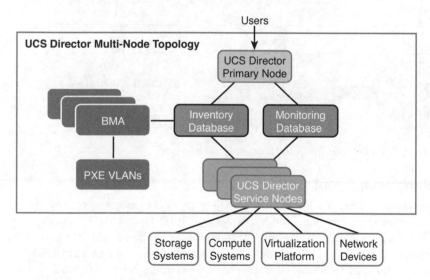

Figure 16-5 *UCS Director Multinode Topology*

You can determine the size of a multinode deployment based on the number of virtual machines you are planning to support. Table 16-3 shows the recommended number of UCSD nodes and number of virtual machines supported by a small, medium, and large implementation of UCSD.

Table 16-3   Multinode Deployment Size

	Small	Medium	Large
Number of VMs supported	5,000–10,000	10,000–20,000	20,000–50,000
Primary Node	1	1	1
Service Nodes	2	3	6
Inventory Database	1	1	1
Monitoring Database	1	1	1

Figure 16-6 illustrates the multinode installation steps for UCSD.

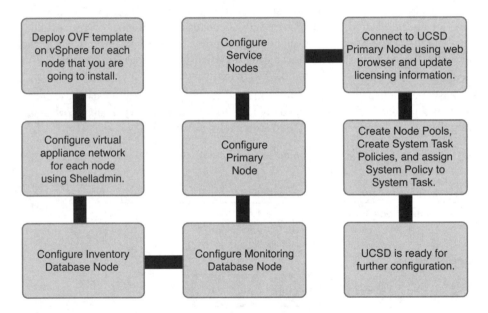

Figure 16-6   *UCS Director Multinode Deployment Steps*

Deploying Baremetal Agent

BMA uses the Preboot Execution Environment (PXE) to install the operating system on a bare metal server or virtual machine. BMA provides DHCP, HTTP, and TFTP services that are required for a functional PXE install. When UCSD is configured with BMA and the environment is operational, you can build PXE installation tasks on BMA and UCSD infrastructure workflows to automate installation of the operating system. You can access BMA through Secure Shell (SSH). A single Cisco UCSD node can support multiple BMA applications.

BMA software is available as a virtual appliance that can be deployed on Microsoft Hyper-V and VMware vSphere virtualization platforms. For Microsoft Hyper-V, BMA is available in VHD (virtual hard disk) format. To install BMA on Hyper-V, create a new VM and attach

BMA VHD file to it. For VMware vSphere, BMA is available as an OVF (open virtualization format) file. To install BMA on vSphere, deploy a new VM using the OVF file.

Once BMA appliance is installed, you can use the following steps to configure bare metal provision of the server:

Step 1.   Decide if you would like to use a single network for management and PXE, or if you want to create separate management and PXE networks. The management network is used for communication between BMA and UCSD or other devices and appliances. The PXE network is used for services provided by BMA, such as DHCP, TFTP, and HTTP. If you decided to use a single network, the topology is simple. There is only one NIC required on BMA. This NIC is used for both management and PXE traffic. If you decided to create separate networks for management and PXE, then you need an IP address on the second NIC of BMA, so it can communicate with the bare metal server on the PXE network. Figure 16-7 shows the two possible topologies of BMA implementation.

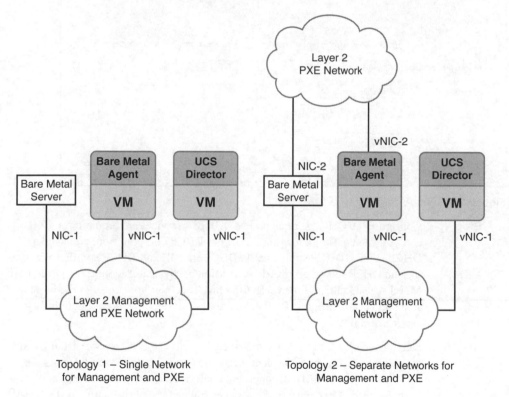

Figure 16-7   *Bare Metal Agent Network Topology*

Step 2.   Configure management of the IP address of BMA. You can figure the management IP address manually or via DHCP. If DHCP is used, make sure that the IP address is reserved so it does not change on reboot of the BMA. UCSD uses a management IP address to communicate with BMA. Therefore, the management IP address of BMA must be reachable from UCSD.

Step 3. Add a BMA account into UCSD. This allows you to control BMA from UCSD for bare metal server provisioning. For adding BMA, you need the IP address of BMA, the login ID and password, the IP address of the PXE network (in case you are using a separate network for PXE), and the database address. BMA uses the UCSD database. If you have multinode deployment, then use the IP address of the inventory database node. To add a BMA account, go to **Administration > Physical Account**, select the **Bare Metal Agents** tab, and click **Add**. Figure 16-8 shows how to add BMA in UCSD.

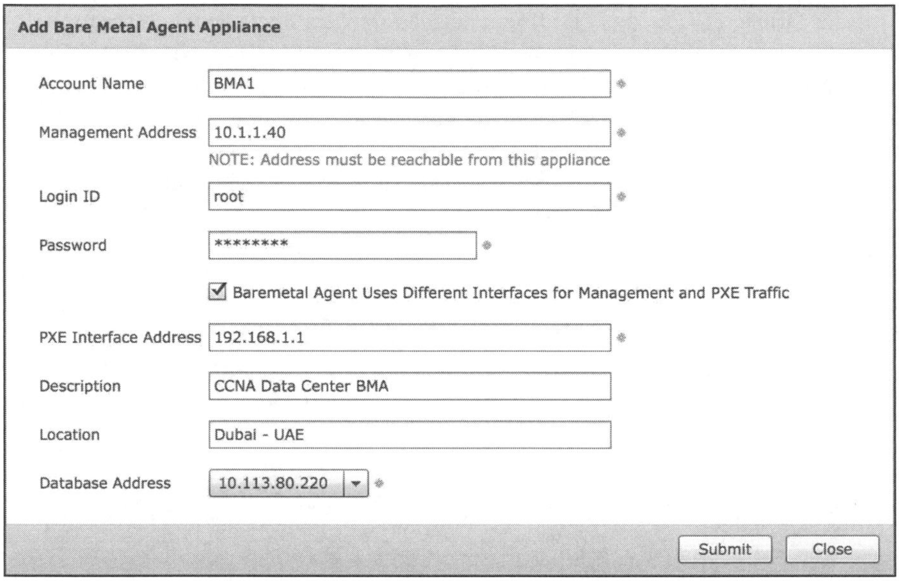

Figure 16-8 *Add BMA to UCS Director*

Step 4. Configure the DHCP service on BMA. DHCP services are required for PXE, and you can configure it from UCSD. For DHCP configuration, you need a DHCP subnet, DHCP subnet mask, DHCP start IP, and DHCP end IP. To configure the DHCP server, go to **Administration > Physical Account**, select the **Bare Metal Agents** tab, and then select the BMA account you added in the previous step and click **Configure DHCP**. Figure 16-9 shows how to configure DHCP service on a BMA.

Step 5. Start the service for the BMA appliance. To start the BMA service from UCSD, go to **Administration > Physical Account**, select the **Bare Metal Agents** tab, and then select the BMA account you configured in the previous step and click **Start Service**. After starting the service, you can check the status of the BMA by clicking on **Service Status**.

Step 6. The operating system images that you want to use in a PXE boot request must be configured correctly and available in BMA. You can copy OS images (ISO files) directly on BMA or to an NFS mount point that you added to BMA. Steps required to prepare the OS image may differ based on the operating system. It is recommended that you check the UCSD BMA document for your operating system. This step is necessary before setting up the PXE boot request in UCSD.

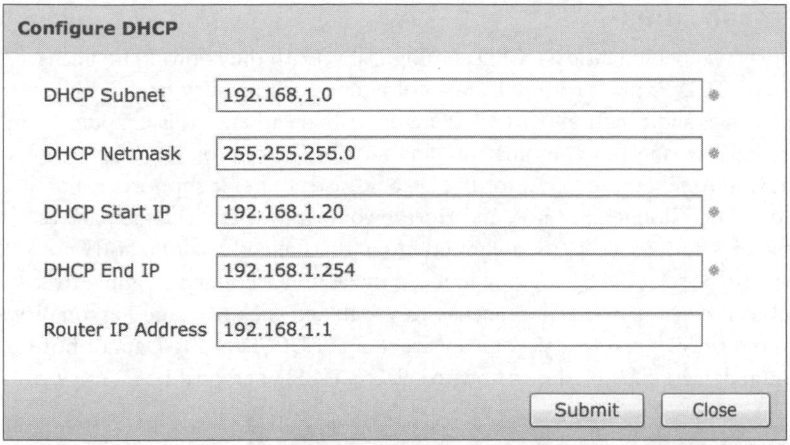

Configure DHCP

DHCP Subnet   192.168.1.0

DHCP Netmask   255.255.255.0

DHCP Start IP   192.168.1.20

DHCP End IP   192.168.1.254

Router IP Address 192.168.1.1

Submit   Close

Figure 16-9 *Configure DHCP Server for PXE*

Step 7.   Create a PXE boot request in UCSD. This request indicates that you want to provision a new bare metal server using BMA. Server provisioning starts when you reboot the server after creating the PXE boot request. You can perform this step manually or by using an orchestration workflow. To create a PXE boot request manually, go to **Physical > Compute**, and in the left pane, navigate to the pod for which you want to set up the PXE boot request. In the right pane select the **PXE Boot Requests** tab, and click **Add PXE Request**. Figure 16-10 shows how to create a PXE boot request in UCSD.

PXE Boot Request Add

Server MAC Address   0025B5BC000F

Host Name   server1

Root Password   *******

Confirm Password   *******

                      ☐ PXE Request for Windows

Management VLAN   80

Server Address   10.1.1.100
                      Specify a static IP address for the server

Network Mask   255.255.255.0

Gateway   10.1.1.1

Name Server   ns1.cisco.com

Timezone   US/Pacific

Additional Parameters

Name	Value

Submit   Close

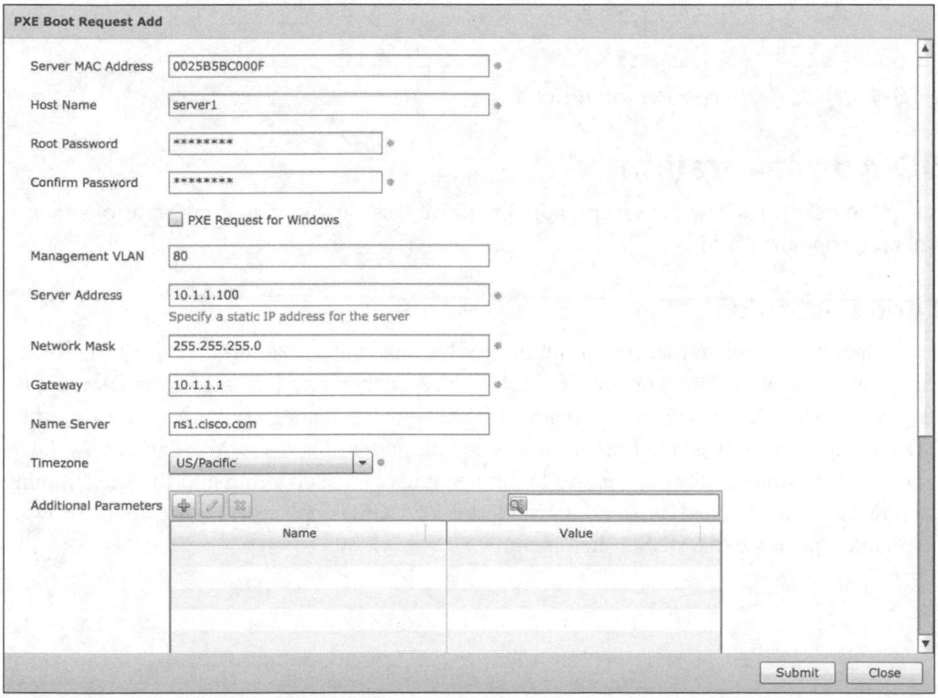

Figure 16-10 *Creating PXE Boot Request*

UCS Director Personalities

Cisco UCSD supports two personalities: UCSD and Big Data. With the appropriate licenses, you can enable Cisco UCSD Express for Big Data features and functionality from within Cisco UCSD. The features and functions of UCSD are described earlier in this chapter. UCSD Express for Big Data is used to automate deployment of Hadoop on the Cisco UCS Common Platform Architecture (CPA) for Big Data infrastructure. It supports major Hadoop distributions from Cloudera, MapR, and Hortonworks, providing a single pane of glass management across both Cisco UCS integrated infrastructure and Hadoop software. UCSD personalities can be selected by logging in using the admin account and going to the **Administration > License** menu. Select the **License Keys** tab and click **Manage Personality** to choose the required UCSD personality. You can select either UCSD or Big Data or both personalities if required. Figure 16-11 shows how to select a UCSD personality.

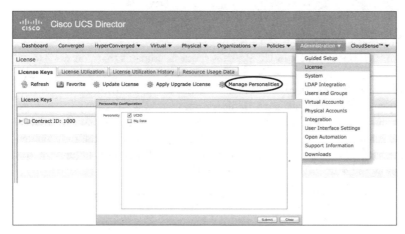

Figure 16-11   *UCS Director Personalities*

UCSD Administration

This section describes how to perform administrative tasks and system configurations that you need to operate UCSD.

Shell Administration

You use the UCSD shell to perform common troubleshooting and administration tasks such as changing a password, stopping and starting services, generating log and report data, applying a patch to UCSD, backing up and restoring the database, managing BMA, rebooting the UCSD appliance, as well as other common system administration tasks. You can access the UCSD shell by using any SSH client and log in using user id: **shelladmin** and the shell admin password that you specified during the installation of UCSD appliance. Figure 16-12 shows the available options in the UCSD shell menu.

```
                Cisco UCS Director Shell Menu
Node:Standalone | Version:5.5.0.0 | UpTime:  04:18:01 up 4 days, 19:16

1)   Change ShellAdmin Password
2)   Display Services Status
3)   Stop Services
4)   Start Services
5)   Stop Database
6)   Start Database
7)   Backup Database
8)   Restore Database
9)   Time Sync
10)  Ping Hostname/IP Address
11)  Show Version
12)  Generate Self-Signed Certificate and Certificate Signing Request
13)  Import CA/Self-Signed Certificate
14)  Configure Network Interface
15)  Display Network Details
16)  Enable Database for Cisco UCS Director Baremetal Agent
17)  Add Cisco UCS Director Baremetal Agent Hostname/IP
18)  Tail Inframgr Logs
19)  Apply Patch
20)  Shutdown Appliance
21)  Reboot Appliance
22)  Manage Root Access
23)  Login as Root
24)  Configure Multi Node Setup (Advanced Deployment)
25)  Clean-up Patch Files
26)  Collect logs from a Node
27)  Collect Diagnostics
28)  Quit

SELECT> ▮
```

Figure 16-12   *UCS Director Shell Menu*

UCS Director REST API

The Cisco UCSD northbound REST API allows an application to interact with Cisco UCSD programmatically. These requests provide access to resources in Cisco UCSD. With an API call, you can execute Cisco UCSD workflows and make changes to the configuration of switches, adapters, policies, and other hardware and software components. The API accepts and returns HTTP messages that contain JavaScript Object Notation (JSON) or Extensible Markup Language (XML) documents. The JSON or XML payload contained in an HTTP message describes a method or managed object (MO) in Cisco UCSD. You can use any programming language to generate the messages and the JSON or XML payload.

Installing and Managing a License

You can order a free 60-day evaluation license online from Cisco. For a production system, you need a base license for every installation of UCSD. In high-availability mode, you need a separate base license for each instance of UCSD. Other licenses can be installed on top of the base license to enable additional features. UCSD supports a counted license model that defines the number of servers, networks, and storage systems, as well as license bundles for PODs such as ExpressPod and FlexPod.

You can update license information, monitor license utilization, and view resource usage data by going to the **Administration > License** menu.

Mail Setup

You can configure UCSD to sends e-mails about system alerts, provisioning status, and approval notifications. All of these outgoing e-mails from UCSD require a SMTP server. To configure an outgoing SMTP server, choose **Administration > System** and go to the **Mail Setup** tab. You can specify the SMTP server by using an IP address or fully qualified domain name (FQDN). Figure 16-13 shows how to configure the SMTP server.

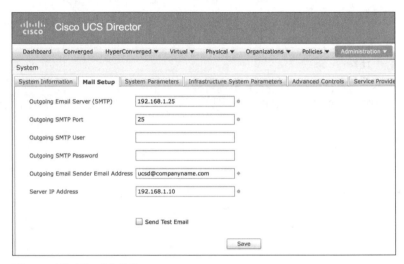

Figure 16-13 *Mail Setup*

Configuring System Parameters

UCSD is installed with default values for the retention period of data and type of currency. These values are defined in system parameters. You can edit these parameters only if you would like to change the defaults. The system parameters define following:

- Number of days that the system retains VM data
- Number of days that the system retains all events
- Number of days that the system retains trend data or historical data of the inventory (such as CPU, storage, and memory usage)
- Number of days that the system retains VM metering records
- Type of currency and precession

You can configure system parameters by going to the **Administration > System** menu and selecting the **System Parameters** tab. Figure 16-14 shows the default values for system parameters.

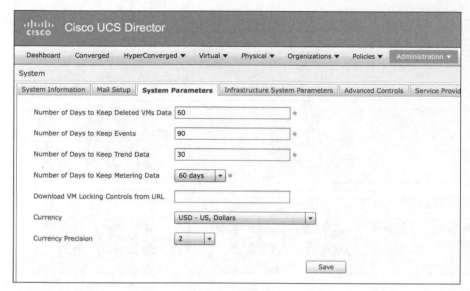

Figure 16-14 *Configuring System Parameters*

Multitenancy

UCSD supports multitenancy by using the service provider feature. If this feature is enabled, you can create managed services provider (MSP) organizations and suborganizations. The first-level MSP organization is the parent organization that can contain multiple second-level organizations. By default, the first-level organization is called the **MSP Organization**, and the second-level organization is called the **Customer Organization**. At the time of enabling the service provider feature, you can change these defaults.

In UCSD, a tenant can be created as an MSP organization. Tenants can further create multiple customer organizations for their departments, business units, or different IT environments. Administration of the MSP organization and customer organization can be delegated using predefined user roles. UCSD user roles are discussed later in this chapter. For example, you can create MSP organizations for tenants such as Company-A and Company-B. Within these MSP organizations, you can create multiple customer organizations. Company-A would like to create suborganizations for its HR, Finance, and Operations department. Company-B would like to divide the IT infrastructure into Development/Testing and Production environments. Figure 16-15 shows the tenancy model of UCSD.

To enable the service provider feature, select **Administration > System** and go to the **Service Provider Feature** tab. Click on **Enable Service Provider Feature** and type the first-level and second-level MSP organization names. You must reboot UCSD after enabling or disabling the service provider feature. Figure 16-16 shows how to enable the service provider feature in UCSD.

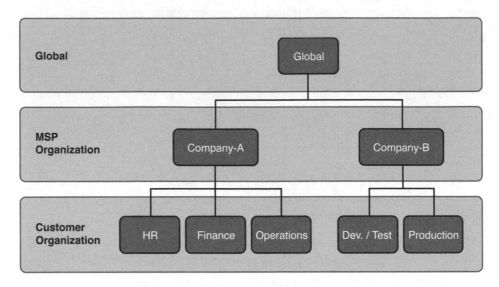

Figure 16-15 *UCS Director Tenancy Model*

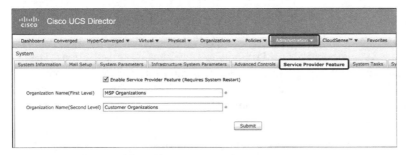

Figure 16-16 *Enabling Service Provider Feature*

Some of the important multitenancy features supported by UCSD are described here:

- **Delegated Administration:** Tenant self-administration using MSP Admin and Customer Admin roles.

- **Portal Branding:** UCSD supports branding of portal for the organizations, with customized logos, application labels, URLs, and custom links. Portal branding can be done at the global level, MSP organization level, and customer organization level.

- **Resource Allocation:** Resources can be allocated and limited for each MSP organization.

- **Cost Model:** A cost model can be defined for each MSP organization. This cost model is used for chargeback.

- **Reporting:** UCSD provides hierarchal control of the CloudSense report. These reports can be generated and viewed at the MSP organization or customer organization level.

User Roles

The role defines the menus and tabs that a user can access and actions that can be performed in Cisco UCSD. When you define a new user role, you must select a role type. There are two role types available in UCSD:

    Admin: For different administrative roles in UCSD

    End-User: For end users consuming IT services from the UCSD catalog

There are a number of system-defined user roles available in UCSD. These predefined roles are created with a set of permissions to access Cisco UCSD. These built-in roles can be modified, and additional custom roles can be created with appropriate permissions. To implement RBAC, you can assign a role to the user. A user can also be assigned to more than one role by using user access profile. For example, a user might log into Cisco UCSD as a Network Administrator and a Storage Administrator, if both roles are mapped to the user, in the access profile.

The system-defined user roles are as follows:

- **All Policy Admin:** Users associated with this role can modify all policies with UCSD.
- **Billing Admin:** This role can perform chargeback and billing-related activities such as resource accounting, budgeting, and reporting.
- **Computing Admin:** This role has read-only access to most parts of UCSD. Users associated with this role can manage physical computing, modify computing policies, approve service requests, perform orchestration, and do the device discovery.
- **Group Admin:** The users associated with this role have the privilege of adding other users. These users can use the self-service portal.
- **IS Admin:** This role has read-only access to most parts of UCSD. Users associated with this role can manage vDC, modify service delivery policies, modify deployment policies, approve service requests, and perform orchestration.
- **MSP Admin:** An administrator is required for each MSP in Cisco UCSD. This administrator is referred to as the MSP Admin. This administrator manages the MSP organization and all the customer organizations within it.
- **Network Admin:** This role has read-only access to most parts of UCSD. Users associated with this role can manage the physical network, modify network policies, approve service requests, perform orchestration, and do the device discovery.
- **Storage Admin:** This role has read-only access to most parts of UCSD. Users associated with this role can manage physical storage, modify storage policies, approve service requests, perform orchestration, and do the device discovery.
- **System Admin:** This role has full access to UCSD. The built-in admin account belongs to this role.
- **Operator:** This role has read-only access to most parts of UCSD. This role is designed to monitor the status of UCSD.
- **Service End User:** This role is assigned to the users ordering the service from UCSD. Users associated with this role can only view and use the Self-Service portal.

Users and Group Management

Users need an ID and password to access UCSD so they can order services and perform day-to-day administration of their IT resources. UCSD comes with two default local user accounts. These user accounts are **admin** and **infraUser**. The admin account has full rights on UCSD. You will use the admin account for initial system configuration and to add more users to the system. In UCSD, the admin account cannot be deleted. The user account **infraUser** is for UCSD internal use only, and it cannot be modified or deleted. To add new users to UCSD, go to **Administration > Users and Groups**, select the **Users** tab, and click **Add**. At the time of creating a user, you can assign a role and add it to a group. User group filed is only visible when you select **service end-user** or **group admin** as the user role. You can also assign account disable date and time for each user. Figure 16-17 shows how to add a new user account in UCSD.

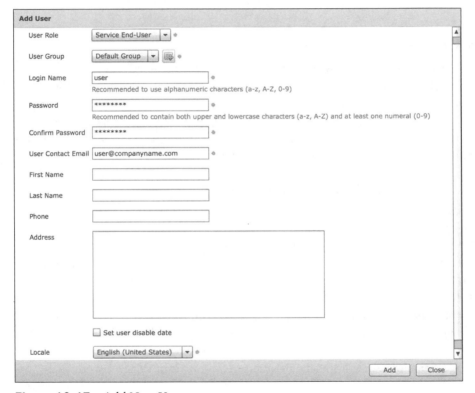

Figure 16-17 *Add New User*

An administrator is required for each MSP in Cisco UCSD. You can create an MSP administrator by creating a user with the role MSP Admin and selecting the appropriate MSP organization for which he will be the administrator. This administrator manages the MSP organization and all the customer organizations within it. You can add the groups in UCSD in the same way you created users. Groups are available only if the MSP feature is disabled. If MSP is enabled, then you will see Customer Organization instead of groups.

Authentication Preference

UCSD supports multiple ways to authenticate users. You can configure UCSD to authenticate users using the local database, Lightweight Directory Access Protocol (LDAP), and VeriSign Identity Protection (VIP) two-factor authentication. For local authentication and VIP, you can configure a preference with no fallback option. For local authentication and LADP, you can configure a preference with fallback option on each other. Table 16-4 shows authentication preference options of UCSD.

Table 16-4   Authentication Preference

Authentication Preference	Description
Local Authentication	Authentication is local only (Cisco UCSD) and not through the LDAP server.
Local first, fallback to LDAP	Authentication is done first at the local server (Cisco UCSD). If the user is unavailable at the local server, the LDAP server is checked.
LDAP first, fallback to Local	Authentication is done first at the LDAP server. If the user is unavailable at the LDAP server, the local server is checked (Cisco UCSD).
VeriSign Identity Protection	VIP Authentication Service (two-factor authentication) is enabled.

Lightweight Directory Access Protocol (LDAP) Integration

UCSD can integrate with LDAP and synchronize the LDAP server's groups and users. LDAP synchronization can be done automatically or manually. Once synchronization is complete, the synchronized users can authenticate with the LDAP server. You can integrate multiple LDAP servers to UCSD. When a new LDAP server account is added, a system task for this account is created, and synchronization of data starts automatically. The users and groups from the LDAP server are then added to the UCSD system. UCSD adds all LDAP users to the service end-user profile. When integrated with multiple LDAP servers, UCSD appends the domain name to the user ID to avoid username conflict between LDAP servers. This rule also applies to user groups. When a single LDAP account is used, the user can log in to the system by specifying only the username. In this case, UCSD uses authentication preference to identify the local or external LDAP user.

To integrate LDAP server, go to **Administration > Users and Groups**, select the **LDAP Integration** tab, and then click **Add**.

Support Information

UCSD provides you information and logs for troubleshooting and debugging. To collect system information and logs you can go to **Administration > Support Information** and select the appropriate option. UCSD provides you the following options to collect system information:

- **System Information (Basic):** This option provides UCSD version, system clock, uptime, service status, system licenses status, system resource usage, status of different accounts, system catalogs, devices status, and clouds status.

■ **System Information (Advanced):** This option provides all the information in basic system information, and product configuration, top process information, processor information, memory information, disk information, log files information, network information, system login information, system tasks status, cloud inventory, monitoring status, and database tables summary.

■ **Show logs:** This option provides the last few lines of the selected log files. You can select the log files related to Infra Manager, web context cloud manager, Tomcat log, authentication log, mail delivery log, and patch log.

■ **Download All Log:** This option creates and downloads all relevant log files.

■ **Debug Logging:** This option starts and stops debug logging. The debug logging is limited to 30 minutes only and stops automatically if you do not stop before the 30-minute time limit. When you stop debug logging, a link appears to download the log file.

Unified Infrastructure Management

UCSD provides a friendly user interface to administer the entire data center infrastructure. You can monitor and manage infrastructure elements by logging into the UCSD. With this feature, users do not need a separate login for each infrastructure element. Different IT teams can manage relevant infrastructure elements based on their role, using a common UCSD user interface. RBAC is used to make sure that they have access to the elements they are responsible for. During initial setup, you add IT resources to the UCSD. These resources are represented by the accounts, and accounts are arranged using sites and pods for ease of management.

Site

Sites are used to logically group the pods. This grouping can be done based on geographical location, administrative domain, department, and customer. If you have multiple data centers across the world, you can create sites based on the name of the city where the data center is located. For example, site names can be Bangalore, Brussels, Dubai, and Toronto. Creating sites is an optional step. You can assign multiple pods to a site. During initial setup, you can skip the sites, and later as needed you can create sites and organize your pods using sites.

You can create a site by going to the **Administration > Physical Accounts** menu and selecting the **Site Management** tab. Figure 16-18 shows how to add a site in UCSD.

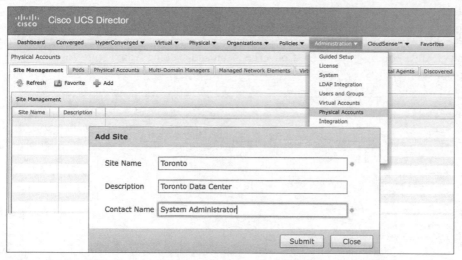

Figure 16-18 *Add New Site*

Pods

A pod is a logical structure in UCSD where resources are placed. These resources are typically physical or virtual infrastructure components, and they are represented by accounts in UCSD. The accounts contain the information that UCSD requires to discover and manage the component, such as IP address, login name and password, port, and protocol. Two major categories of accounts are physical and virtual. Types of accounts supported in UCSD are discussed later in this chapter. A pod can have multiple accounts, such as UCS domain for physical computing, Nexus 7000 switches for network, and EMC and NetApp for storage.

When you create a new pod, you must consider the reason to group the resources in a pod. For example, you can create a pod to represent the following:

- A single converged infrastructure stack such as FlexPod, Vblock, or VSPEX
- A specific customer or tenant
- An environment such as development, testing, or production

Each pod is a module on its own with network, compute, storage, and application components to provide infrastructure services within your data center. Multiple pods can be created in UCSD. If needed, you can assign pods to the sites. A site can have multiple pods; however, a pod can belong to only one site. UCSD comes with a default pod that cannot be deleted. You can hide a pod by editing pod properties.

UCSD supports the following types of pods:

- FlexPod
- ExpressPod Small
- ExpressPod Medium
- Vblock

- VSPEX
- Generic

You can create a pod by going to the **Converge** menu and clicking **Add.** Figure 16-19 shows how to add a pod in UCSD.

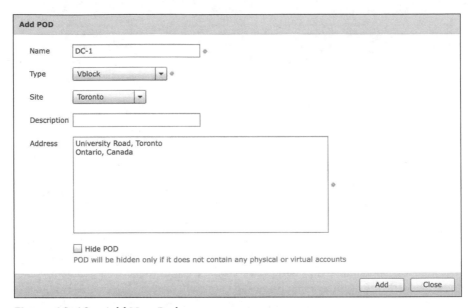

Figure 16-19   *Add New Pod*

Virtual Account

A virtual account represents a cloud environment that UCSD manages. This cloud environment is a supported hypervisor platform or a supported public cloud service. When a cloud account it added to the UCSD, an automatic discovery is performed to find the existing configuration and inventory of virtual machines and images. You can create multiple virtual accounts for the following types:

- VMware vSphere
- Microsoft Hyper-V
- RedHat KVM
- Rackspace Cloud
- Amazon Web Services EC2

To create virtual accounts in UCSD, go to the **Administration > Virtual Accounts** menu and select the **Virtual Accounts** tab. Figure 16-20 shows how to add a VMware vSphere virtual account.

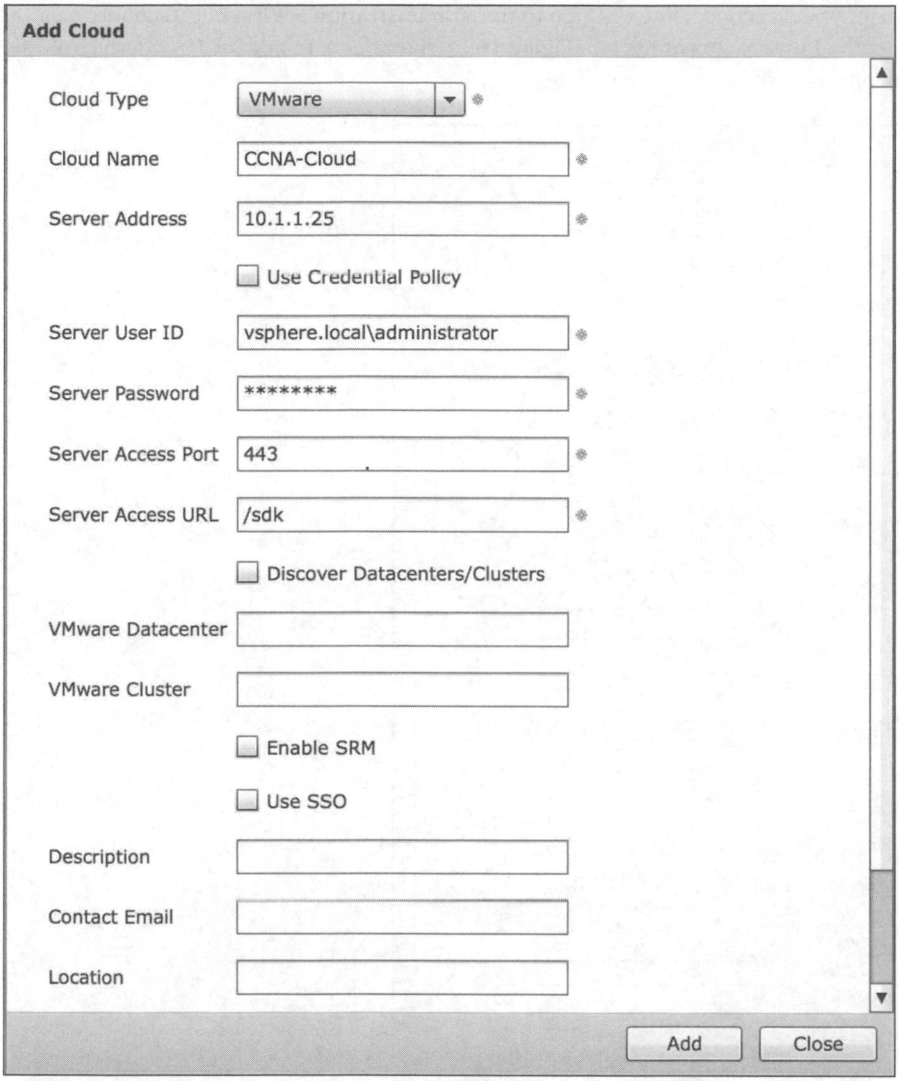

Add Cloud

Cloud Type	VMware ▾	✷
Cloud Name	CCNA-Cloud	✷
Server Address	10.1.1.25	✷
	☐ Use Credential Policy	
Server User ID	vsphere.local\administrator	✷
Server Password	********	✷
Server Access Port	443	✷
Server Access URL	/sdk	✷
	☐ Discover Datacenters/Clusters	
VMware Datacenter		
VMware Cluster		
	☐ Enable SRM	
	☐ Use SSO	
Description		
Contact Email		
Location		

Add   Close

Figure 16-20   *Add VMware vSphere Account*

Physical Account

Physical accounts represent a supported compute or storage device or domain. The element manager of the component such as the following identifies physical accounts in UCSD:

- UCSM account for UCS Domain
- HP OA account or HP iLO account for HP Servers
- NetApp OnCommand account or NetApp OnTAP account for NetApp storage arrays
- EMC VNX account, EMC VNXe account, or EMC VMAX account for EMC storage arrays

To create physical accounts in UCSD, go to the **Administration > Physical Accounts** menu, and select the **Physical Accounts** tab. Figure 16-21 shows how to add a UCS Manager physical account.

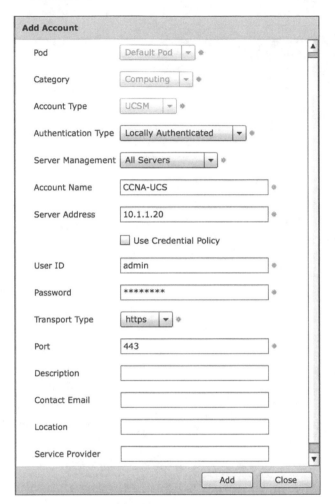

Figure 16-21 *Add UCS Manager Account*

Multidomain Managers

A multidomain manager is a physical account that represents a software application that can manage more than one domain. Multidomain manager accounts are identified by the software name, such as the following:

■ UCS Central

■ Prime Data Center Network Manager (DCNM)

■ Prime Network Service Controller (PNSC)

■ Application Policy Infrastructure Controller (APIC)

- EMC Recovery Point
- EMC VPLEX

To create multidomain manager accounts in UCSD, go to the **Administration > Physical Accounts** menu and select the **Multi-Domain Managers** tab. Figure 16-22 shows how to add an application policy infrastructure controller (APIC) multidomain manager account.

Add Account

Account Type	APIC
Account Name	CCNA-APIC
Description	
Pod	Select Pod
Server IP	10.1.1.21
	☐ Use Credential Policy
Username	admin
Password	********
Protocol	https
Port	443
Contact	
Location	

Submit   Close

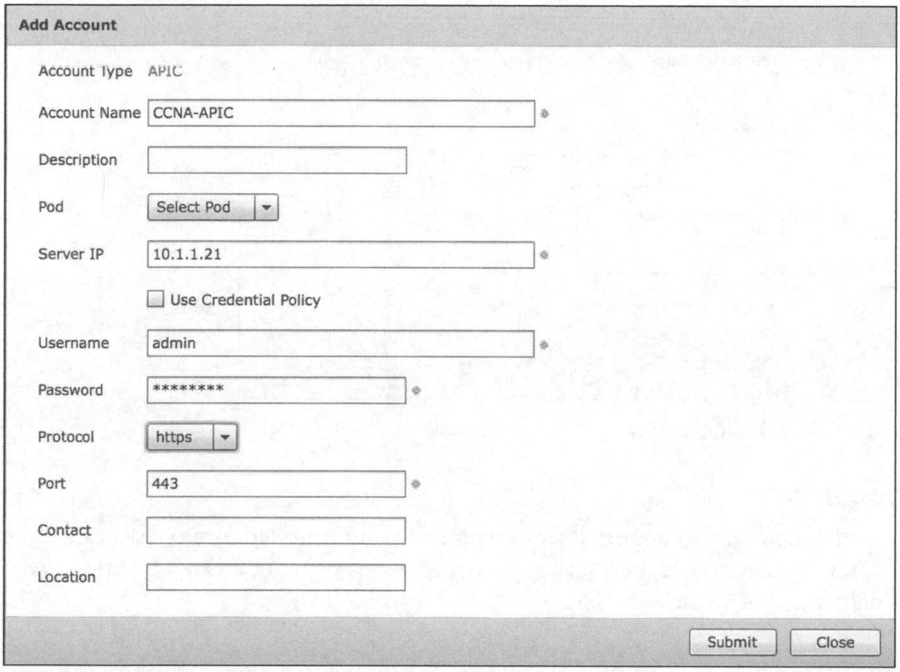

Figure 16-22 *Add APIC Account*

Managed Network Elements

A managed network element is a physical account that represents a supported network device, switch, firewall, or load balancer. Managed network elements are identified by the operating system or name of the network device, such as the following:

- Cisco Nexus OS
- Cisco IOS
- Cisco ASA
- F5 Load Balancer
- Brocade Fabric OS
- Brocade Network OS

To create managed network element accounts in UCSD, go to the **Administration > Physical Accounts** menu and select the **Managed Network Elements** tab. Figure 16-23 shows how to add a Cisco Nexus OS device account.

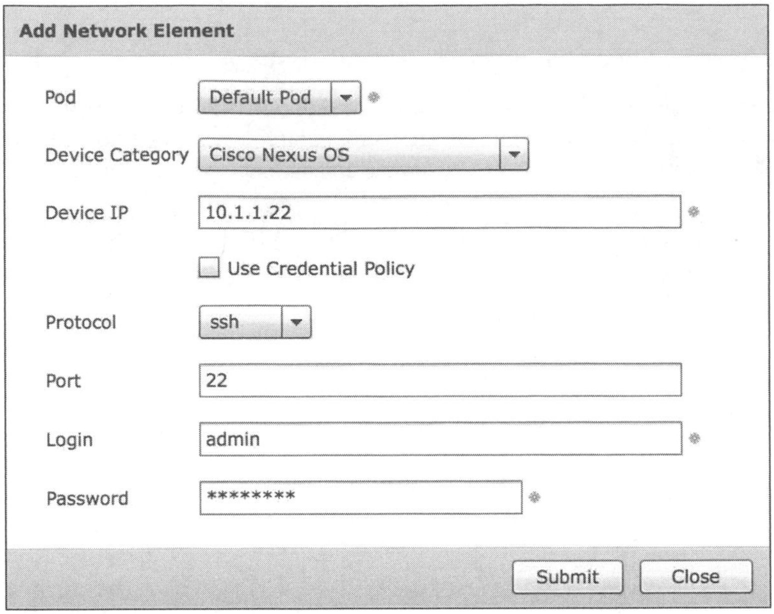

Add Network Element

Pod	Default Pod ▼ ✱
Device Category	Cisco Nexus OS ▼
Device IP	10.1.1.22 ✱
	☐ Use Credential Policy
Protocol	ssh ▼
Port	22
Login	admin ✱
Password	******** ✱

Submit   Close

Figure 16-23 *Add NX-OS Device*

Rack Accounts

A rack account represents a supported rack server that is not managed by a physical account or a multidomain manager account, such as a Cisco C-Series server or a Cisco E-Series server. There is only one type of rack account.

Device Discovery

Device discovery can be performed manually or by using device discovery guided setup. The purpose of device discovery is to learn about the device and assign its accounts to the pods. There are two ways you can perform this task. The first method is to manually add an account and assign it to a pod. In this method, you add device accounts one at a time by repeating the manual process for each device. The second method is to use the device discovery guided setup wizard. Some setups are the same whether you add an account manually or use the guided setup wizard. By using the setup wizard, you can discover many devices quickly and add them to a pod. However, if you choose to use the wizard, you must use the credential policy. Credential policies are discussed later in this chapter. To access the device discovery guided setup wizard, go to the **Administration > Guided Setup** menu and select **Device Discovery, Discover Pod Components**. Figure 16-24 shows the guided setup wizard for device discovery.

During the device discovery, UCSD communicates with the device and retrieves the inventory. The protocol used to communicate with the device depends on the type of device. For example, Cisco UCS director uses XML to communicate with Cisco UCS manager and CLI to communicate with Nexus devices.

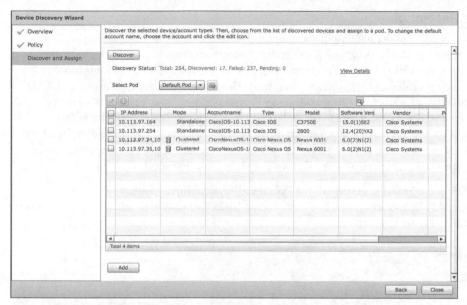

Figure 16-24 *Device Discovery Wizard*

Cisco UCSD creates a system task that polls the device at regular intervals and retrieves the inventory. The polling time for the system task is different for each device type. However, you can customize the interval to meet your data center needs. For some devices, Cisco UCS director creates additional system tasks to retrieve other information such as faults and statistics.

Policies and Policy-Based Provisioning

UCSD simplifies IT operations by defining a reusable policy framework. These policies help in IT governance, compliance, and deployment of infrastructure with greater speed and accuracy. The administrator can define policies and use them to limit user capabilities. A policy-based model is also used to automate the IT process necessary to accomplish infrastructure provisioning and decommissioning in a consistent manner.

In UCSD, a policy is a group of rules that determines where and how new virtual or physical services are provisioned based on the availability of system resource. The policies about the physical infrastructure are available under the menu **Policies > Physical Infrastructure Policies**. The physical infrastructure policies include UCS manager, rack server, UCS central, NetApp, and credential policy. The policies about the virtual infrastructure are available under the menu **Policies > Virtual/Hypervisor Policies**. The virtual infrastructure policies include VDC, service delivery computing, storage, and network. Cisco UCSD requires that you define computing, storage, network, and system policies to provision a virtual machine. It is important to make sure that necessary accounts are present in the system before you start defining the policies.

Credential Policies

When you add a physical or virtual account to UCSD, you provide information such as user ID, password, protocol, and port number. This information is used for logging into the device to collect inventory and perform configuration of devices. In an organization with a large number of devices, it is difficult to provide this information for each account. UCSD credential policies store this information in a central place and use it to log in to the devices. Credential policies contain the login, port, and protocol information. With a credential policy, it is easy to change the password of the devices. When the password is changed on devices, you only need to change the password in the credential policies for those devices. There is no need to update the account for every device in UCSD.

To define a credential policy, go to the **Policies > Physical Infrastructure Policies > Credential Policies** menu, and click **Add**. Figure 16-25 shows how to add a credential policy for a Cisco Nexus OS account.

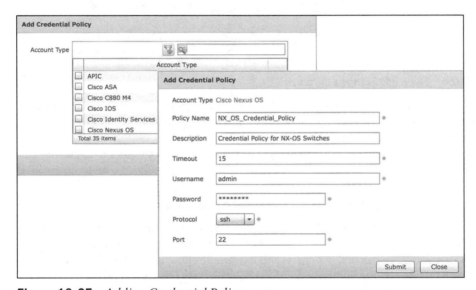

Figure 16-25   *Adding Credential Policy*

Each credential policy represents a specific type of account because information stored in the credential policy may vary based on the type of account. You can use the same credential policy for one or more of the same types of devices that share the same login user ID, password, port, and protocol. For example, you can use the same credential policy for all Cisco Nexus OS devices in your organization. However, you cannot use the same credential policy for different types of accounts, even if they use the same login ID, password, protocol, and port. For example, you cannot use the same credential policy for a Cisco Nexus OS device and a Cisco UCS Manager domain.

Computing Policies

Computing policies define conditions to determine the compute resources that can be used during the provisioning. As an admin, you can mix and match various conditions in the computing policy based on group or workload requirements for virtual machine setup. It is important to thoroughly evaluate all the conditions in computing policy because some combination of the conditions can result in no resources being available for virtual machine provisioning. UCSD supports computing policies for multiple server virtualization platforms such as VMware vSphere, RedHat Enterprise Virtualization (RHEV) Kernel-based Virtual Machine (KVM), and Microsoft HyperV. You can also define computing policies for the Citrix XenDesktop platform.

To define computing policies, go to the **Policies > Virtual/Hypervisor Policies > Computing** menu, and select the appropriate tab for your virtualization platform. As an example, for VMware you will select **VMware Computing Policy** and click **Add**.

For VMware vSphere, computing policies define computing resources such as host/cluster, resource pool, ESX type, filter conditions, resizing options, and installation folder.

Network Policies

The network policy defines settings and resources such as DHCP pools, Static IP pools, IP subnet pools, VLAN pools, and VXLAN pools. UCSD supports network policies for multiple server virtualization platforms such as VMware vSphere, RHEV KVM, and Microsoft HyperV. Network policies define network requirements for virtual machine provisioning, such as cloud name, network port group name, vNIC, and IP configuration. You can also define an option to add multiple vNICs to the virtual machine.

To define network policies, go to the **Policies > Virtual/Hypervisor Policies > Network** menu, and select the appropriate tab to define your policies. As an example, for VMware you would select **VMware Network Policy** and click **Add**.

Storage Policies

Storage policy defines resources and conditions such as the datastore scope, type of storage to use, minimum conditions on the storage, resizing of disk, and deployment options. Datastore scope specifies which disks are included and excluded. Type of storage can be local, SAN, or NFS. You can allow users to configure additional disk policies for multiple disks. The storage policy also provides data store choices for use during a service request creation. The datastores listed in the choice depend upon the scope conditions specified in the storage policy. If you are using the datastore selection feature, the VM template used for provisioning must have all disk types assigned as system disk. UCSD supports storage policies for multiple server virtualization platforms such as VMware vSphere, RHEV KVM, and Microsoft HyperV.

To define storage policies, go to the **Policies > Virtual/Hypervisor Policies > Storage** menu, and select the appropriate tab to define your policies. As an example, for VMware you would select **VMware Storage Policy** and click **Add**.

System Policies

System policies are part of service delivery policies. System policies define the system information such as VM name template, host name template, DNS information, time zone, and VM image type. The VM name template is used to automatically generate a unique virtual machine name, and the host name template is used to generate unique names for hosts. For the Windows operating system, you can also define the licensing information.

Virtual Data Center (VDC)

A virtual data center (VDC) is a logical group of virtual resources, operational details, rules, and policies. VDCs are created to manage a specific group or organization requirements. They provide an administrative boundary to the tenant for the resources such as virtual machines, images, templates, and policies. A tenant represented by a customer organization or group can have multiple VDCs. However, a VDC can only belong to one customer organization or group. You can manage capacity by enforcing quotas and assigning resource limits at the VDC level.

There is a default VDC in Cisco UCSD. A VM that is created outside of the UCSD is discovered automatically and assigned to the default VDC. If a VM is provisioned using a UCSD service request, it can be assigned to a VDC at the time of provisioning by choosing the appropriate VDC from the list. While creating a service request, users can only see the list of VDCs that are available to their organization or group. If you like to enforce an approval process for provisioning of virtual machines in a VDC, you can do it by defining approvers. You can define two levels of approvals in a VDC. The approvers assigned to the VDC must approve all service requests for VM provisioning.

Figure 16-26 shows components of VDC in UCSD.

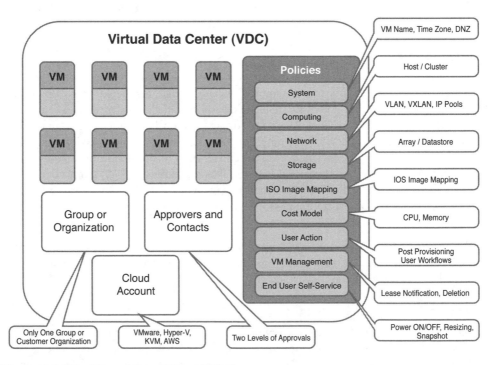

Figure 16-26 *Virtual Data Center (VDC)*

To create a VDC, go to the **Policies > Virtual/Hypervisor Policies > Virtual Data Center** menu, select the **VDC** tab, and click **Add**.

When you are creating a VDC, you must select system, computing, network, and storage policies. These policies are discussed earlier in this chapter. Other policies are optional, and they are described here:

- **IOS Image Mapping Policy** defines the IOS image mapping available to the users.

- **Cost Model** defines the model used for chargeback.

- **User Action Policy** is used for execution of orchestration workflow after provisioning of the VMs. The workflow you pick in the user action policy appears as an action button for VMs within the VDC.

- **VM Management Policy** defines lease notification durations and deletion settings after the lease is expired.

- **End User Self-Service Policy** defines virtual machine self-service options for users, such as power on, power off, resizing, and snapshot.

You can also create a VDC service profile. A service profile is used as a template for creating a VDC from a task in the orchestration workflow. You can create multiple VDC service profiles to meet your business requirements. For example, you can create VDC service profiles based on class of service such as Gold, Silver, and Bronze VDCs.

Catalogs

Catalogs provide a list of IT services that an end user can order from UCSD. A user can log in to the UCSD and self-provision VMs using a predefined catalog. A catalog is a logical construct that defines parameters such as the user group, VM image, cloud name, OS information, application information, user credentials, customization, and VM access to present it as a single "Menu Item" for Self-Service user. You can publish VMs, predefined workflows, and application containers in catalogs.

To manage a catalog, UCSD provides a structure similar to the file folders. While creating a catalog, you can place items in a folder. You can group similar items in one folder. A folder is visible to the users only if it has at least one catalog. Users can create service requests from a catalog page.

The following catalog types are available by default in UCSD. These catalog types are represented by folders. You cannot edit or delete these folders:

- **Standard:** It provides VM self-provisioning based on prebuilt image templates. You have to specify user groups or customer organizations for which this catalog is available. In a standard catalog, the cloud name and image template identifies virtual resources. You can also specify post-provisioning workflows.

- **Advanced:** It represents a complex orchestration workflow. You have to specify user groups or customer organizations for which this catalog is available. You can build your own custom orchestration workflow and publish it as an advanced catalog.

- **Service Container:** It provides application containers, such as fenced containers and VACS containers.

- **VDI:** It provides a virtual desktop infrastructure (VDI) for XenDesktop.

Application Container

Application containers offer a template-based approach to provisioning application stacks for end users. An application stack is a group of servers working together to provide a business function. To allow users to order an application stack, you must create one or more application containers with the appropriate policies, workflows, and templates. An application container has all the necessary information to provision the components of an application. An application container can define the following:

- Physical server or virtual machines
- Storage information
- CPU and memory information
- Operating system versions
- Network information such as VLAN, firewall, load-balancer, and gateway
- Required approvals
- Cost associated with the application container

NOTE UCSD application containers are not the same as dockers containers. These are two different concepts, and there is no relationship between them.

UCSD supports multiple types of containers. You can select the type of application container based on your requirements and deployment configuration. Application container types supported by UCSD are as follows:

- **Fenced Virtual:** This container type is commonly used with VM.
- **VSG:** This container type provides application segmentation using Cisco Virtual Security Gateway. It offers improved security over Fenced Virtual.
- **APIC:** This container type uses the Cisco ACI infrastructure for application segmentation.
- **Fabric:** This container type is used in dynamic fabric automation (DFA) network deployments.
- **VACS:** This container type is used in Cisco Virtual Application Cloud Segmentation Service deployments. It requires additional VACS licenses.

Self-Service Provisioning

You can provision VMs or applications through self-service provisioning. To provision a VM or an application, you must first create a service request. This action initiates a VM creation workflow that includes the following:

- Budget validation
- Dynamic resource allocation
- Approval

- Provisioning
- Life cycle setup

After you create a service request, you can check the status and workflow, cancel the request, and resubmit the request. A typical service request to provision a virtual machine involves the following steps:

1. **Initiation:** Initiate the service request.
2. **Resource Allocation:** Allocate required resources such as CPU, memory, network, and storage to the VM.
3. **Approval:** Send an e-mail to the approver; workflow will wait for approval. Proceed to the next step after approval.
4. **Provisioning:** Create and provision the VM.
5. **Life Cycle Schedule:** Configure life cycle scheduling with the setup, schedule, and termination times.
6. **Notify:** Send an e-mail to the user to notify him that the VM is ready.

ACI Integration

UCSD integrates with APIC to support automation and orchestration of the data center where Cisco ACI is used. UCSD leverages the APIC REST-based API of ACI to automate the various operational tasks within the ACI fabric. An example of these tasks is creation and modification of tenants, private networks, bridge domains, application profiles, EPGs, and service graphs. UCSD also complements the automation of ACI with the endpoint automation. Therefore, it provides end-to-end workflows encompassing operational tasks across all infrastructure layers, such as ACI fabric, virtual servers, physical server, storage, and network-based services.

UCSD uses an out-of-the-box ACI application container framework for defining, provisioning, and managing tenants and applications in an ACI environment. Following are the two components of the ACI application container framework.

- Tenant life cycle
- Application life cycle

Resource Groups

In UCSD, tenants are represented by user groups and customer organization. Resource groups are part of tenant life cycle management, which enables you to secure onboard resources for tenants. You assign device accounts to the resource group to create a pool of physical and virtual resources with specific capacities and capabilities. You can use these capabilities and capacities in resource allocation. Resources are assigned to tenants based on specific requirements. You can share resources in resource groups across tenants, or you can dedicate them to a specific tenant. The framework provided by a resource group is only used for the Cisco ACI infrastructure. Resources are divided into categories such as virtual compute, virtual network, virtual storage, physical compute, physical network, and physical storage. Figure 16-27 shows the resource groups in UCSD.

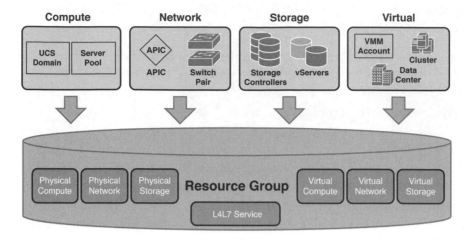

Figure 16-27   *Resource Groups*

Resource groups also contain environment-specific inputs. These inputs provide connectivity details about devices in a resource group. In addition, resource groups contain information such as IP and VLAN pools.

Resource Tags

Resource tags are optional. They enable more granular control of resources within the resource group. They provide a mechanism to tag resources with certain attributes or values. UCSD can use these tags in resource selection and allocation. For example, you can create tiers of resources within a resource group by tagging the resources as gold, silver, and bronze.

Service Offerings

Service offerings define tenant or application requirements. They outline the resources needed to provision an application. A service offering must include service classes to represent the required capability and capacity for the following resource layers:

- Virtual Compute
- Virtual Storage
- Virtual Network
- Physical Compute
- Physical Storage
- Physical Network
- Layer 4 to Layer 7 Service

In a service offering, you can specify the usage of resource groups as one of the following:

- **Shared** among the applications or tenants
- **Dedicated** to a single application or tenant

Tenant Profile

Tenant profiles represent the pairing of service offerings to a resource groups. Each tenant profile defines infrastructure and application requirements for that tenant. You can associate a tenant profile with multiple service offerings and select the appropriate resource groups for each service offering. You can share a tenant profile among multiple tenants.

Chargeback

The chargeback module in UCSD tracks and measures IT expenses so you can charge them back accordingly. It provides visibility into the cost of the virtual infrastructure. It supports definition and assignment of the cost model where you can consider fixed overhead cost as well as variable cost of resources. You can assign the cost model to the group or a customer organization. Metering data is collected from virtual machines at frequent intervals. You can export this information to PDF, XLS, and CSV format to integrate with reporting and billing tools. Key features of UCSD chargeback are as follows:

- Based on organization requirements, you can provide fixed costs, one-time costs, allocation costs, usage costs, and a combination as required.

- You can use a template-based approach by creating standardized cost models. These cost models are assigned to the VMs.

- VM metering information can be monitored and analyzed in real time with the built-in dashboard and extensive set of graphical widgets.

- You can view the top five reports for VMs with highest CPU, memory, storage, and network costs.

- You can see summary and comparison reports of costs and resource usage for the virtual infrastructure.

- View reports via a web browser or export them into PDF, CSV, and XLS formats.

Budget Policies

The UCSD Chargeback module is responsible for overall accounting and tracking of resources in the system. In addition to the chargeback, you can also enforce budget policies for user groups and customer organizations. The budget policy allows you to control resource usage based on pre-defined thresholds. You can enable or disable budget watch features at the group level. You can also allow users to go over budget, and specify policy to shutdown VMs if there are no funds available to the group.

Cost Model

UCSD supports the following cost models:

Standard cost model: This defines cost in a linear format. In the standard cost model, cost is defined at the unit level and chargeback is based on how many units are provisioned for a particular VM.

Advanced cost model: This defines cost in a nonlinear format. In the advanced cost model, cost is defined in the form of a package, such as CPU and memory.

Reporting and Monitoring

UCSD provides extensive reporting and monitoring across the entire data center infrastructure. It can monitor the virtual as well as the physical infrastructure and system resources by providing a wide range of reports and views. These reports are useful to understand end-to-end system performance and health. In addition to the reports that are available out of the box, you can create custom report templates and build your own reports. Some important monitoring and reporting capabilities are discussed next.

Dashboard

The dashboard is the first screen that you see when you log in to the UCSD. If you do not see the Dashboard tab in UCSD, it means it is disabled. You can make the Dashboard tab visible by clicking on your login ID at the top-level menu and enabling it under the Dashboard tab. The UCSD dashboard is flexible and customizable. You can add any report widget on the dashboard. You can change the size of dashboard widgets by moving the scrollbar on the top right of your screen. You can also set the refresh rate of widget data. You can customize it from 5 minutes to a maximum of 60 minutes. You can disable or enable widget refresh by using the automatic refresh button on the dashboard.

Summary

The Summary window is available for each physical and virtual account in the system. It allows you to view system capacity and performance status at a glance. You can add summary widgets of an account to dashboard by clicking on the down arrow in the upper-right corner of the widget and selecting the option Add to Dashboard. The Summary window shows a range of tabular and graphical reports. To access the Summary tab of the account, select the account under the Physical or Virtual menu and click on the pod name in the left pane.

Reports

Cisco UCSD can monitor the virtual infrastructure and system resources by displaying a wide array of reports. These reports help you understand system details and provide insight into the system usage, capacity, and performance.

UCSD provides the following types of reports:

- **Tabular Reports:** These reports provide system information in tabular format such as system overview, host nodes, new VMs, and deleted VMs.

- **Bar and Pie Graph:** These reports provide comparisons of different information within the system, such as active VMs versus inactive VMs, total CPU capacity versus provisioned CPU, and total memory verses allocated memory.

- **Trend graphs:** These reports provide trending information about system resources and operations, such as CPU trends, memory trends, VM addition trends, and VM deletion trends.

- **Top-five reports:** There reports provide information about the top-five trends of resource utilization. Top-five reports include information such as highest number of VMs, user groups with high CPU usage, VDCs with the highest number of VMs, and host nodes with high CPU usage. These reports are available at the group, VDC, host node, and VM level.

- **Map reports:** These reports provide system resource utilization and other information in the heat maps or color-coded map format. This view is extremely useful for operations staff to identify the problem areas and view overall system utilization.

CloudSense Reports

UCSD CloudSense is built on a reporting and analytics engine that provides visibility into many areas of data center infrastructure. The administrator can set up CloudSense reporting to understand critical performance metrics across multiple technology stacks in your data center. You can use CloudSense to monitor infrastructure resources utilization and capacity in real time. CloudSense also helps you in capacity planning, trending, and forecasting of your virtual and cloud infrastructure. You can generate the following reports with CloudSense:

- Billing Report for a Customer
- EMC Storage Inventory Report
- NetApp Storage Inventory Report
- NetApp Storage Savings Per Group
- NetApp Storage Savings Report
- Network Impact Assessment Report
- Organizational Usage of Virtual Computing Infrastructure
- PNSC Account Summary Report
- Physical Infrastructure Inventory Report for a Group
- Storage Deduplication Status Report
- Storage Inventory Report For A Group
- Thin Provisioned Space Report
- UCS Data Center Inventory Report
- VM Activity Report by Group
- VMware Host Performance Summary

Report Builder

The Report Builder module allows you to create custom reports. You can create report templates with specific parameters and run reports using these templates. The template provides reporting flexibility, enabling you to specify the context, the type of report to run, and the duration of the data samples for the report. You can create multiple report templates and generate several reports using these templates.

With the help of report templates, you can generate a report in PDF or HTML format and send it to users via e-mail. You can review and archive a report outside Cisco UCSD. In addition to creating a template, you can edit, clone, and delete your custom report templates.

Reference List

UCS Director Installation Guides: http://www.cisco.com/c/en/us/support/servers-unified-computing/ucs-director/products-installation-guides-list.html

Getting Started with Cisco UCSD: http://www.cisco.com/c/dam/en/us/products/collateral/servers-unified-computing/ucs-director/le-41601-ucsd-gsd.pdf

Application Infrastructure on Demand with Cisco UCSD and Cisco Application Centric Infrastructure: http://www.cisco.com/c/dam/en/us/products/collateral/servers-unified-computing/ucs-director/application centric-infrastructure.pdf

Exam Preparation Tasks

Review All Key Topics

Review the most important topics in the chapter, noted with the key topics icon in the outer margin of the page. Table 16-5 lists a reference of these key topics and the page numbers on which each is found.

Table 16-5   Key Topics for Chapter 16

Key Topic Element	Description	Page
Section	"Benefits of UCS Director"	588
Table 16-2	"Features and Functions of UCSD"	589
Section	"UCS Director REST API"	601
Paragraph	Multitenancy	603
Paragraph	Multitenancy Features	604
List	User Roles	605
Section	"Site"	608
Section	"Pods"	609
Section	"Virtual Account	610
Section	"Physical Account"	611
Section	"Multidomain Managers"	612
Section	"Managed Network Elements"	613
Section	"Device Discovery"	614
Bullet Points	Catalogs	619
Section	"Service Offerings"	622
List	Chargeback Features	623

Complete Tables and Lists from Memory

Print a copy of Appendix B, "Memory Tables," or at least the section for this chapter, and complete the tables and lists from memory. Appendix C, "Memory Tables Answer Key," includes completed tables and lists to check your work.

Define Key Terms

Define the following key terms from this chapter, and check your answers in the Glossary:

Role-Based Access Control (RBAC), Bare Metal Agent (BMA), PowerShell Agent (PSA), Cisco ONE, Prime Service Catalog (PSC), Intercloud, Open Virtualization Format (OVF), Preboot Execution Environment (PXE), REST API, JSON, XML, Multitenancy, Managed Service Provider (MSP), Lightweight Directory Access Protocol (LDAP), VeriSign Identify Protection (VIP), UCS Manager (UCSM), UCS Central, Data Center Network Manager (DCNM), Prime Network Service Controller (PNSC), Virtual Data Center (VDC), Catalogs, Fenced Virtual Container, Virtual Security Gateway (VSG), Fabric Container, Virtual Application Container Service (VACS), Chargeback

This chapter covers the following exam topics:

4.3.b Orchestration

4.4 Interpret and troubleshoot a Cisco UCS Director workflow

CHAPTER 17

Understanding and Troubleshooting UCSD Workflows

Provisioning of the IT infrastructure, platforms, and application requires configuration of multiple technology components within a data center. In a conventional data center, different IT teams collect user requirements, exchange necessary information between the teams, and perform the configuration changes manually. The manual process is time consuming and costly. It also results in inconsistent and inefficient configuration that is error prone and hard to troubleshoot. A modern data center uses a cloud management platform such as UCS Director to automate the provisioning and management of various IT components. UCS Director orchestrator combines different IT tasks into a sequence called workflow. You can execute a workflow to complete a complex provisioning task within minutes.

This chapter gives you an overview of UCS Director orchestration. It provides necessary information about workflow designer to create, validate, execute, and troubleshoot UCS Director workflows.

"Do I Know This Already?" Quiz

The "Do I Know This Already?" quiz allows you to assess whether you should read this entire chapter thoroughly or jump to the "Exam Preparation Tasks" section. If you are in doubt about your answers to these questions or your own assessment of your knowledge of the topics, read the entire chapter. Table 17-1 lists the major headings in this chapter and their corresponding "Do I Know This Already?" quiz questions. You can find the answers in Appendix A, "Answers to the 'Do I Know This Already?' Quizzes."

Table 17-1 "Do I Know This Already?" Section-to-Question Mapping

Foundation Topics Section	Questions
"Orchestration"	1–4
"Understanding UCS Director Workflow"	5–8
"Using Workflow Designer"	9–10

CAUTION The goal of self-assessment is to gauge your mastery of the topics in this chapter. If you do not know the answer to a question or are only partially sure of the answer, you should mark that question as wrong for purposes of the self-assessment. Giving yourself credit for an answer you correctly guess skews your self-assessment results and might provide you with a false sense of security.

1. Which of the following statements is correct about cloud orchestration?

   a. Cloud orchestration can only deliver virtual resources "as a service."

   b. Cloud orchestration can use multiple lower level automation tasks to deliver a resource or set of resources "as a service."

   c. Cloud orchestration can only provide infrastructure as a service (IaaS).

   d. Cloud orchestration is only possible in a public cloud.

2. Cloud orchestration is delivered by which of the following software?

   a. Network Management System (NMS)

   b. Cloud Portal/Catalog

   c. Cloud management platform (CMP)

   d. Virtual Machine Manager

3. Which of the following statements correctly identifies different layers of the cloud management platform?

   a. The cloud management platform includes the following layers: Portal, API, Service Management, Orchestration, and Resource Management.

   b. The cloud management platform includes a data link layer, a network layer, and a transport layer.

   c. The cloud management platform has only an orchestration and a resource management layer.

   d. The cloud management platform includes a virtualization layer and a network management layer.

4. The Orchestration layer of the CMP is used for automating and standardizing which of the following IT processes? (Choose three.)

   a. Service delivery management

   b. Workload automation

   c. Network function virtualization

   d. Infrastructure management

   e. Virtualization of compute resources

5. What is a task in UCS Director?

   a. A task is a Python script that the cloud administrator writes.

   b. A task defines policy-based infrastructure provision.

   c. A task is a manual operation the cloud administrator performs.

   d. A task is the smallest unit of work. It represents specific action or operation performed by UCS Director.

   e. A task refers to virtualization of compute resources.

6. A UCS Director task can have how many inputs and outputs?

   a. A task can have only one input and one output.

   b. A task can have any number of inputs and any number of outputs.

   c. A task can have any number of inputs but only one output.

   d. You cannot define input or output to a task.

7. What is a UCS Director workflow?

   a. A UCS Director workflow is a JavaScript created by the cloud admin to fulfill a user request.

   b. A UCS Director workflow is a Python script the admin creates.

   c. A UCS Director workflow is a sequence of tasks linked to fulfill a user request.

   d. UCS Director workflows are the policies defined in the system.

8. Which of the following are valid states of a service request? (Choose three.)

   a. Scheduled

   b. Stopped

   c. Running

   d. Completed

9. What is a compound task?

   a. A task that represents a workflow is called a compound task.

   b. A complex task is called a compound task.

   c. A task written in JavaScript is called a compound task.

   d. A task that can provision multiple networks is called a compound task.

10. When you create a new workflow, which of the following tasks are populated automatically in the workflow designer? (Choose three.)

   a. Start Task

   b. Stop Task

   c. Completed (Success)

   d. Completed (Failure)

   e. Finish

17

Foundation Topics

Orchestration

The cloud-based data center uses various automation tasks to perform operations such as spinning up a virtual machine (VM), deploying a bare metal server, installing an operating system image, creating a new storage logical unit number (LUN), deploying an application, implementing a network function, and configuring a device or application. These automation tasks implement a specific function in a data center that is required to deploy cloud resources. This automation is achieved using tools such as custom scripts and configuration management software.

Cloud orchestration can use multiple lower level automation tasks to deliver a resource or set of resources "as a service." It receives the user request for a cloud resource and provides end-to-end automation workflow or a process that coordinates the automation tasks to fulfill the user request. Cloud orchestration defines the arrangement of the automation task in a workflow by considering technical requirements and interdependencies of these automation tasks. It makes sure that a task is completed successfully before proceeding to the next task in the workflow. Cloud orchestration can also integrate with the IT processes such as approvals, change management, configuration management, assurance, and billing.

The cloud management platform (CMP) is software that delivers cloud orchestration in the data center. The CMP includes several layers of functionality. These layers are as follows:

- **Portal/Catalog:** Provides access to the CMP for ordering, managing, monitoring, and troubleshooting the cloud services.

- **Application Programming Interface (API):** Provides programmatic access to the CMP for actions that can be performed using a portal/catalog. A portal/catalog may also use the same API that is available to the users.

- **Service Management Layer:** Presents service offerings to the cloud consumers. It allows users or automation processes to define and administer the service in real time. The services may be predefined in a service catalog for end user consumption, or they can be modified or built using dynamic service design and infrastructure modeling tools.

- **Orchestration Layer:** Provides automation of the service delivery process and handles the control, governance, and coordination of those tasks. It interacts with underlying resources via the resource management layer. Orchestration workflows are normally fixed and not exposed to the end users. However, some cloud management platforms offer integrated orchestration authoring, and some provide that orchestration in a visual form. This layer also helps in standardizing the IT processes.

- **Resource Management Layer:** Provides an open and abstracted interface to all the cloud resources, such as storage services, bare metal servers, networking, virtualization, L4-L7 services, and applications within the data center.

The orchestration layer of the CMP is used for automating and standardizing IT processes such as these:

- **Service Delivery Management:** Request and approval
- **Virtual Infrastructure Administration:** VM provisioning

- **Virtual Infrastructure Operations:** VM life cycle actions

- **Workload Automation:** Scale up, scale down, and VM consolidation

- **Disaster Recovery Automation:** Backup and recovery

- **Infrastructure Management:** Bare metal provisioning and compute, storage, and network provisioning

UCS Director Orchestrator

The UCS Director orchestrator enables the cloud administrator to standardize IT services by automating delivery of IT resources, administration, and provisioning tasks. In a large cloud environment where hundreds of provisioning requests are received every day, manually performing actions such as provisioning a network, creating VMs, customizing an operating system, and configuring storage is costly and time consuming. An IT administrator can use a Cisco UCS Director workflow designer GUI to automate many of these infrastructure provisioning, administrative, and operational tasks. The self-service capabilities of UCS Director reduce the delivery time and increase the compliance. There is a built-in task library in UCS Director where many common automation tasks are available for the IT administrator. These automation tasks can be used to build a complex orchestration workflow, where output from one automation task can be used as input of the next automation task. In this manner, the UCS Director orchestrator can automate a complex administrative process that includes many technology domains, such as provisioning the virtual machine (VM), setting up bare metal servers, creating and mounting storage, configuring compute, and managing network resources.

NOTE At the time of writing this chapter, UCS Director version 5.5 is the latest, and UCS Director 6.0 is on the roadmap. Most of the features discussed in this chapter are generic and valid for all versions of UCS Director. There might be slight variation in the features depending on the version of UCS Director. Please check product documentation for details.

UCS Director Orchestrator provides the following orchestration capabilities:

- Visually design infrastructure automation workflows with an easy-to-use GUI designer

- Automate manual and labor-intensive operational and administrative tasks

- Monitor for alerts on the system using predefined or custom workflows

- Simplify IT management by automating the IT process

- Orchestrate complex IT workflows

- Execute and schedule workflows

Understanding UCS Director Workflows

UCS Director performs orchestration using the workflows. Therefore, the first step in setting up orchestration is to create a workflow. This section explains some important concepts required to create UCS Director workflow.

Task

A task is a specific action or operation performed by UCS Director orchestrator. It is the smallest unit of work that can be performed by UCS Director. A task can take inputs and generate outputs. In some cases, a task does not need input or output. UCS Director has numerous predefined tasks that an administrator needs for the orchestration, as shown in Figure 17-1. These predefined tasks are for compute, storage, and network in both virtual and physical infrastructures. If you are unable to find a suitable per-defined task, you can create a custom task or import custom tasks that other administrators create. Some examples of predefined tasks are as follows:

- **SSH Command Task:** Execute a command in a secure shell (SSH) session.

- **Collect Inventory Task:** Gather information about available devices.

- **Create New User:** Add a user to the system.

- **New VM Provision:** Create a new VM (hypervisor specific).

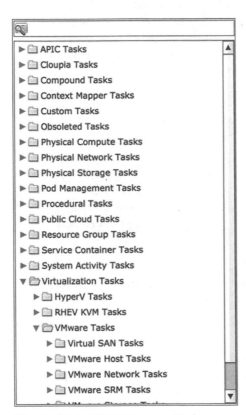

Figure 17-1 *UCS Director Tasks*

Input and Output

Task input and output are stored in variables. A task can have any number of input and output variables. They are defined in the format **Task_Name.Input_Name** or **Task_Name. Output_Name**. Task input can be provided using one of the following methods:

- An administrator can preset the value of the input variable.

- A user can be prompted for the value in the GUI.

- An input variable can be set via custom approval.

- An input variable can be set from output of another task.

Input of a task can be mandatory or optional. If a task has several mandatory input variables, all of these inputs must be provided to run the task. Whether an input is mandatory or optional, it is defined at the time of creating the task. UCS Director supports many input types that represent a broad selection of categorical, numeric, and text parameters. Some examples of input data types are as follows:

- Generic text input

- Date time

- Password

- IPv4 address

- OS type

- UCS VLAN group

Figure 17-2 shows a task called Add Domain to EPG. This task has multiple input and output variables associated with it. Some of these inputs are mandatory and must be provided to execute the task. Once a task is completed successfully, it generates multiple output variables that can be used as input of subsequent tasks.

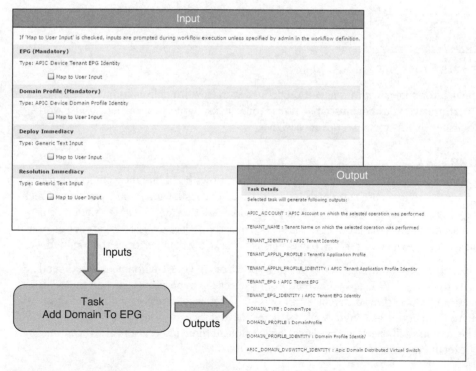

Figure 17-2 *Task Input and Output*

Workflow

Workflow defines the sequence of tasks that are required to fulfill user requests. The UCS Director workflow is built using a series of automation tasks linked to perform a complex IT operation. The workflow determines the order in which the tasks are executed. It also links the output of one task into the input of another task. The simplest workflow can contain only one task, but workflows can be complex with any number of tasks linked to perform operations across multiple IT domains. UCS Director orchestrator uses workflows to automate processes of any level of complexity on your physical and virtual infrastructure. Figure 17-3 shows how tasks are arranged in a workflow:

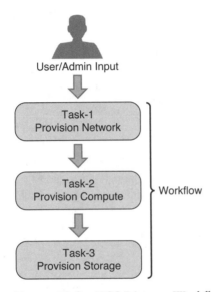

Figure 17-3 *UCS Director Workflow*

UCS Director comes with a range of predefined workflows to deliver common IT services and perform everyday administrative tasks. You can also write your own customer workflows using UCS Director workflow designer.

Activities

UCS Director activities provide abstraction of workflows by hiding their implementation details. An activity is used as a placeholder for a generic task, which is independent of technology. You can point an activity to multiple workflows that are specific to the implementation according to your product or platform. An activity uses decision logic such as user input to decide which workflow to execute. The workflow then performs the required work.

For example, you are using three types of hypervisors in your environment. Users send a request to create a VM, and you would like to select the hypervisor based on the available capacity. You have three different workflows—one for each hypervisor type—to create a VM. You can define an activity called Create VM and then associate these workflows with it. The activity will check the available capacity on all three hypervisors at the runtime and then execute the correct workflow to provision the VM.

In addition, an activity can be used as a workflow task. This provides additional flexibility to perform tasks according to the context within workflows.

Service Request

UCS Director service requests are closely related to the workflows. When you run a workflow, it creates a service request in the system. A service request is a process that runs under the control of UCS Director. You can monitor the status of a service request to determine if a workflow completed successfully. Execution of a workflow can be scheduled for a later time. The details of a completed service request are stored in the system, and the user can review its status. A service request can have one of the following states depending on its execution status:

- **Scheduled:** Waiting for execution at a later time
- **Running:** In the process of executing the request
- **Blocked:** For example, request is waiting for approval
- **Completed:** Request has been completed successfully
- **Failed:** One of the component tasks has failed to execute properly

Task Libraries

Task libraries are collections of predefined tasks in UCS Director. You can build your own workflows using the tasks that are available in the libraries. You can also make a copy of an existing workflow and modify it according to your requirements. UCS Director provides online help for the tasks in the library. Figure 17-4 shows UCS Director online help of the task libraries.

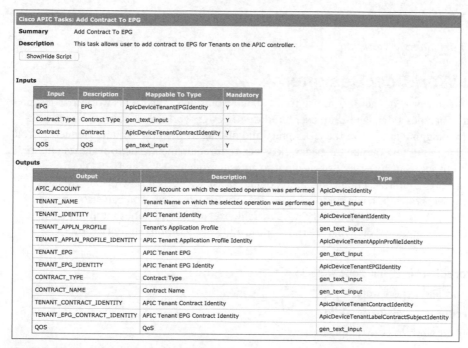

Figure 17-4 *Task Library Online Help*

Sample Workflow

This sample UCS Director workflow adds a new hypervisor host in the system. To provision a new hypervisor host, the workflow first performs multiple network configuration tasks so the network is ready for this installation. After configuring a network, the workflow does necessary configuration on the compute platform. When the compute platform is ready, it installs a hypervisor using a bare metal provisioning task. The storage and SAN are configured next. After that, the workflow registers the hypervisor with virtual machine manager and notifies the user that the provisioning task is complete. Figure 17-5 shows the sample workflow.

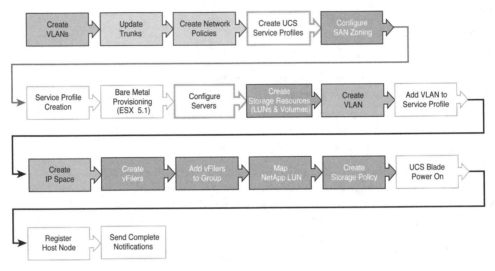

Figure 17-5   *Sample Workflow*

Using Workflow Designer

UCS Director provides an easy-to-use tool to build workflows. The tool is workflow designer, and it includes a drag-and-drop user interface to design workflows. You can build workflows by dragging tasks from the task library and placing them in the required sequence. You can define inputs and outputs of each task as per your requirement. The tool allows you to use the output from an earlier task as input to any subsequent task. The UCS Director workflow supports conditional branching and looping by using a special flow-of-control task. Once the workflow design is complete, you can save the workflow. You can also convert your workflow to a template, modify it, validate it, execute it, and publish it into a catalog for user consumption. Following are the workflow life cycle actions supported by UCS Director:

- Add, edit, delete, and clone workflows
- Import and export workflows
- Execute and schedule workflows
- Convert workflows to templates

Creating Workflows

To create a new workflow, go to **Policies > Orchestration**, select the **Workflow** tab, and click on **Add**. Figure 17-6 shows how to add a new workflow to UCS Director.

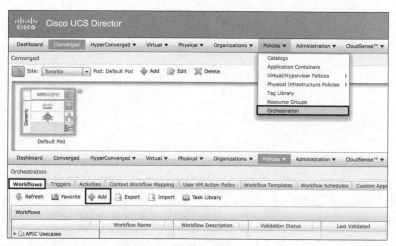

Figure 17-6 *Creating New Workflow*

When you click **Add** to create a new workflow in UCS Director, you see an Add Workflow Wizard. This wizard provides necessary information about the workflow, such as workflow name, version, input variables, and output variables. There are three steps in the Add Workflow Wizard. In the first step, you can provide workflow properties as mentioned here:

- **Workflow Name:** Use a name that will help you easily identify the workflow in the list of other workflows.

- **Version:** You can keep track of the changes in the workflow by assigning versions. The initial version of a workflow is always zero. Before making changes to an existing workflow, you can create a new version from the workflow designer.

- **Workflow Context:** This specifies if the workflow should be used within a context. You have two options for workflow context: Any Context and VM Context. If VM Context is selected, the workflow is only allowed to execute when you choose a VM.

- **Save as Compound Task:** Select this option if you want to save your workflow as a task in the task library. This will allow you to use your workflow as a task in another workflow. A task that represents a workflow is called a compound task.

- **Place in New Folder:** You can organize your workflows in folders. You can select an existing folder or create a new folder. If you want to create a new folder, select this option.

- **Notify Status of Execution to Initiating User:** You can select this option if you would like to notify the user about the workflow execution.

Figure 17-7 shows workflow properties in the Add Workflow Wizard.

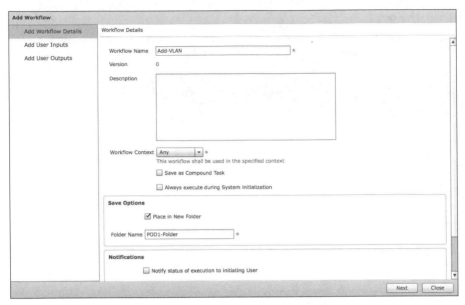

Figure 17-7 *Add Workflow Wizard—Workflow Properties*

In the second step of the Add Workflow Wizard, you can define the inputs of the workflow. Workflow input is the information that you would like to receive from a user at the time of workflow execution. Click the Add Input Field button (the plus sign) to add inputs to the workflow. You can add multiple inputs to the workflow based on your requirements. You will provide the following information about each input you add to the workflow.

- **Input Label:** This is the label for the input that the user needs to provide.

- **Input Type:** This is the category of the input that the user needs to provide.

- **Optional:** This allows you to execute the workflow; without this, input is missing.

- **Admin Input:** If you select this option, an administrator needs to provide this input. Admin inputs are not available for users. This allows you to restrict users from providing certain inputs.

Figure 17-8 shows the User Input dialog in the Add Workflow Wizard.

In the third step, Add Workflow Wizard, you can define the outputs of the workflow. You define the outputs in the same way that you added inputs to the workflow. You can add necessary information to workflow outputs that you would like to share with the user when workflow execution is completed. If you forget to define an input or output to the workflow, you can add it later by editing the workflow.

Once you define workflow properties, inputs, and outputs, you can add tasks to your workflow. Some tasks are populated automatically in the workflow designer. The following list and Figure 17-9 show these tasks:

- **Start task icon:** This is a blue icon, and it represents the beginning of a workflow.

- **Completed (Success):** This is a green icon, and it represents the successful completion of a workflow.

- **Completed (Failure):** This is a red icon, and it represents the failed state.

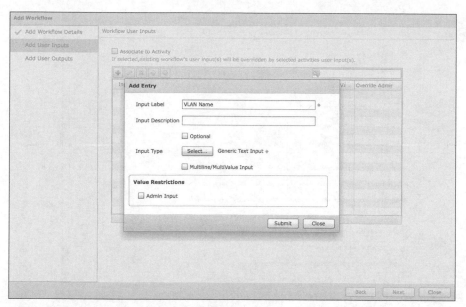

Figure 17-8 *Add Workflow Wizard—Inputs*

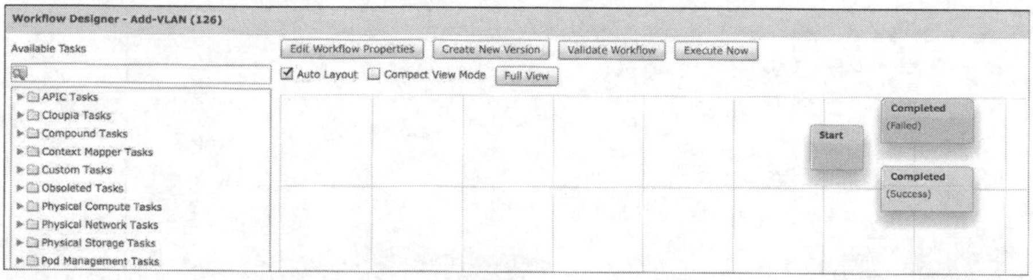

Figure 17-9 *Workflow Designer Window*

Workflow inputs are used to start the workflow. Each task provides outputs after an action is completed. These outputs can be consumed by other tasks later in the workflow. You can add a task to the workflow by dragging it from the task library and placing it in the work pane of the workflow designer. Each task appears as an icon in the workflow designer. When you place a new task in the workflow designer, you see an Add Task Wizard. You can use this wizard to review the task information, perform user input mappings, provide task inputs, and do the user output mappings. Figure 17-10 shows the Add Task Wizard.

After adding multiple tasks that are required to fulfill a user request, you will link these tasks (icons) in a required sequence to assemble a complete workflow. Each task is embedded with two buttons. These buttons are On Success (green button) and On Failure (red button). You can see these buttons when you bring your mouse over the task icon. You can select which task is executed next by clicking the down arrow on the On Success button of the task icon. Figure 17-11 shows how to link the tasks in a workflow.

Add Task (Create APIC Tenant)

Task Information	Workflow Task Basic Information - Enter task name and comments.
User Input Mapping	
Task Inputs	
User Output Mapping	

Task Name   CreateAPICTenant_1474   *

Task Category   Cisco APIC Tasks   ▼   *

Task Type   Create APIC Tenant   ▼   *

Comment

☐ Retry Execution
Enables retry if the task supports retry

☐ Disable Roll Back
Disables rollback if the task supports rollback

Task Details

Selected task will generate following outputs:

DATACENTER : Name of the Datacenter on which the selected operation was performed

DEVICE_IP : IP address of the APIC device on which the selected operation was performed

APIC_ACCOUNT : APIC Account on which the selected operation was performed

TENANT_NAME : Tenant Name on which the selected operation was performed

TENANT_IDENTITY : APIC Tenant Identity

DEVICE_TENANT_MONITORING_POLICY : Apic Monitoring Policy

DEVICE_TENANT_MONITORING_POLICY_IDENTITY : Apic Monitoring Policy Identity

Next   Close

Figure 17-10   *Add Task Wizard*

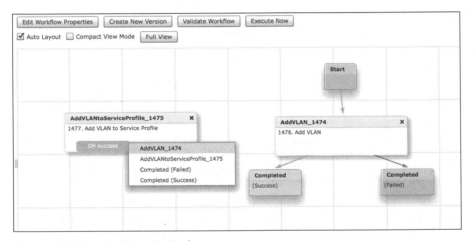

Figure 17-11   *Linking the Tasks*

You will begin with the blue icon task with the name Start and click the On Success button of all your tasks to stitch them with the next task in the workflow. Similarly, On Failure of all the tasks in the workflow needs to be linked to the red icon task with the name Completed (Failed). You will link the On Success button of your final task to the green icon task with the name Completed (Success). Figure 17-12 shows a complete workflow with all the tasks linked with each other.

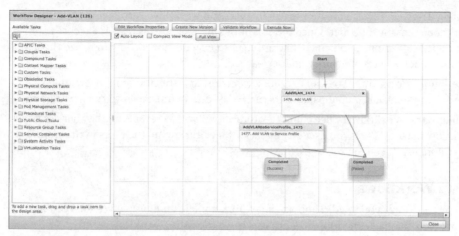

Figure 17-12 *Complete Workflow in Workflow Designer*

Validating Workflow

When the workflow design is complete, you can validate it by clicking on the Validate Workflow button in the workflow designer. UCS Director performs the workflow validation and ensures that there are no inconsistencies in the workflow. The validation process of the workflow checks for the following inconsistencies:

- Each task has a Complete action and a Fail action. Each task also validates that these actions are linked to another task or to the end of the workflow.

- There are no mapping mismatches.

- There are no missing values for mandatory input variables of a tasks

- There are no instances of the task handler not being found.

- There are no missing admin/task inputs after import or upgrade.

Executing Workflows

When you execute a workflow, it begins with the Start task and executes all the tasks in the sequence that you defined during the design phase until it reaches the Completed task. There are many different ways you can execute a workflow in UCS Director orchestrator. The different methods of executing the workflow are outlined here:

- **Using Service Requests:** You can view and generate workflow executions using a service request.

- **Using the Execute Now Action:** You can execute a workflow using the Execute Now action. You can highlight the required workflow and select Execute Now in the top menu, from the drop-down list on the right of the interface, or by right-clicking on the workflow. You can select the version of the workflow that you would like to execute and provide necessary user input.

- **Using a VM Action Policy:** You can execute workflows on VMs by using custom actions in the VM user action policy. Custom action policies can contain one or more actions pointing to different workflows. You can select a user action policy for VMs within a virtual data center (vDC).

- **Using a Trigger:** You can create triggers to execute a workflow. A trigger defines specific conditions that must be met. Once the conditions are met, a workflow is executed automatically. For example, you can define a trigger to execute a workflow to resize the VM memory when a certain memory limit is reached.

- **Scheduling Workflows:** You can execute a workflow at a specific time by creating a schedule. Several scheduling parameters can be used to define when to run a workflow.

- **Rolling Back Workflows:** The rollback feature allows you to reverse all the changes a workflow makes. When you execute rollback of a workflow, all the tasks in the workflow are undone by executing the workflow in reverse order.

Managing Workflows

UCS Director allows you to edit, import and export, and create multiple versions of the workflow. You can make the following changes to your existing workflow:

- **Rename the workflow:** You can edit a workflow and give it a new name. When you change the name of the workflow, it is changed for all versions.

- **Reorder inputs:** You can change the order in which the workflow process user inputs during the execution of workflow. To reorder workflow inputs, select the workflow and go to Edit Workflow properties, and then advance to the User Input screen. Select the user input and press the up arrow or down arrow icon to change the order of input.

- **Change an input type:** You can change input from optional to mandatory. However, you cannot change a mandatory input to optional. To change the input type, select the workflow and go to Edit Workflow properties; then advance to the User Input screen. Select the user input, and change it from optional to mandatory.

- **Edit tasks:** You can modify the workflow by adding and deleting or modifying the task in workflow designer.

- **Delete workflow:** You can delete a selected version of the workflow or completely delete all versions of it. To delete a workflow, select the workflow and select Delete from the menu.

- **Create a new version:** UCS Director supports version history of the workflows. With the version history, you can go back to an earlier version of the workflow, create a new version of the workflow before making changes, or delete a version if it is not required.

- **Exporting and importing workflows:** You can export and import the workflow artifacts.

Workflow Templates

The UCS Director workflow template is like a blueprint to create workflows. You can create a workflow and export it as a template. You can import this workflow template to another UCS Director. You cannot execute a workflow template. However, you can instantiate a new workflow using the workflow template. For example, you can develop a new custom workflow in your test environment using workflow designer. When you are finished with the testing, you can export it as a workflow template. This workflow template can be imported into your production environment for quick implementation of the custom workflow.

Certain workflow templates come predefined with the system. You can review these templates under the Workflow Templates tab of orchestration. A workflow template contains the following information:

- **Task names:** Only the names of tasks are exported in the template. The tasks must exist in the system where the template is imported.

- **Workflow structure:** This is the sequence of tasks and connections between these tasks.

- **Input names:** These are details about input variables.

If your workflow template is using custom tasks, you must import these tasks separately in the system where your workflow template is imported. The admin inputs must be defined again after importing the workflow template to a new system.

Workflow Troubleshooting

This section provides step-by-step guidelines for troubleshooting UCS Director workflows.

The first step in troubleshooting is to make sure that the workflow is valid. You can validate the workflow by going to **Policies, Orchestration**, selecting your workflow from the Workflows tab, and clicking **Workflow Designer, Validate Workflow**, as shown in Figure 17-13. You can then execute the workflow to see what the issue is.

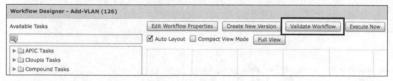

Figure 17-13   *Validating Workflow*

The next troubleshooting step is to check service request logs. The service request logs are generated during the execution of the workflow. You can check the service request logs to see if there were any errors the workflow generated. You can also check whether the correct values of Input/Output variables are used during the workflow execution. You can view service request logs and Input/Output variables by going to **Organizations, Service Requests** and then selecting the service request and clicking **View Details, Log** or selecting **View Details, Input/Output.** Figure 17-14 shows UCS Director service request logs.

In the service request logs, you can check the status of each task during the execution. The logs tell you if a task in the workflow was executed successfully or if there were any errors during the execution. Figure 17-15 shows a log of a successful and failed service request.

Figure 17-14 *Service Request Logs*

```
Successful:
Mar 11, 2016 13:49:48 EDT Executing custom action Send Test Email (#0: Send Email)
Mar 11, 2016 13:49:48 EDT Executing action Send Test Email (#0: Send Email) (VM <none>)
Mar 11, 2016 13:49:48 EDT Sending email to shelladmin@localhost, with Subject Test Email
Mar 11, 2016 13:49:50 EDT Context Start task after -1
Mar 11, 2016 13:49:50 EDT setting start after in workflow handler -1
Mar 11, 2016 13:49:50 EDT Task #3 (Send Test Email (#0: Send Email)) completed successfully in 1
seconds

Failed:
Mar 11, 2016 14:55:14 EDT Executing custom action Send Test Email (#0: Send Email)
Mar 11, 2016 14:55:14 EDT Executing action Send Test Email (#0: Send Email) (VM <none>)
Mar 11, 2016 14:55:15 EDT Sending email to test@cisco.com, with Subject Test Email
Mar 11, 2016 14:01:32 EDT Request cancelled by user admin
Mar 11, 2016 14:01:34 EDT Action Handler for Send Test Email (#0: Send Email) failed with error
Could not connect to SMTP host: out.cisco.com, port: 25 (VM <none>)
Mar 11, 2016 14:01:34 EDT Task #3 (Send Test Email (#0: Send Email)) failed after 379 seconds
```

Figure 17-15 *Successful and Failed Service Requests*

If you are unable to find the problem within service request logs, you can check inframgr logs. You can execute the workflow and check inframgr logs for error messages. To access inframgr logs, you must access UCS Director using SSH and log in as shelladmin. Select the option to tail the Inframgr logs, and then select log file sequence 0. You can wait for the system log events to pass before you execute the workflow. Then execute the workflow and examine the logs for any errors during the process.

An important troubleshooting step is to verify inputs and linking of tasks in the workflow. You can edit the workflow in workflow designer. Make sure that inputs of all the tasks are mapped correctly. Also make sure that the success or failure of each task is linked to the appropriate task in the sequence that is desired in workflow.

To make sure the system has correct information about the state of infrastructure, you can manually re-collect the inventory for the physical and virtual accounts in UCS Director. Manually re-collecting information will ensure that all recent changes made on the physical and virtual accounts are collected by the system. To re-collect inventory, go to **Administration, System** and select **the System Tasks** tab. Search for Inventory and select the corresponding task for each account and select **Run Now**.

Within certain tasks, there is a **Revalidate** button (see Figure 17-16) to read the information from the UCS Director database if there are no options available for certain inputs that are required.

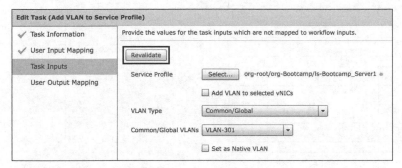

Figure 17-16   *Revalidate*

Workflow Resources

UCS Director allows you to write your own workflows. However, writing a workflow from scratch can be time consuming. Cisco provides a community for UCSD developers where they can discuss ideas, exchange information, and share custom workflows. You can find prebuilt UCS Director workflows on github and communities.cisco.com. Many ready-made workflows are available to download from these sites. When you download a workflow, it is possible that it will not fit all your requirements, and you will have to modify the workflow to fit your needs. You can also share your custom workflows with other UCSD developers in this community. Figure 17-17 shows some workflows that are available on communities. cisco.com.

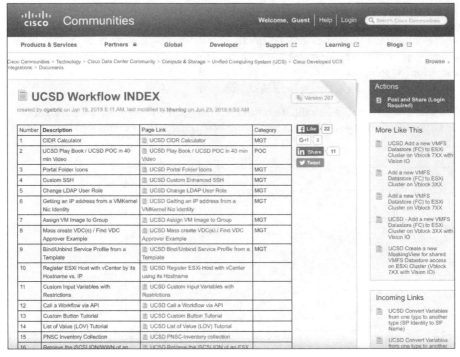

Figure 17-17 *Workflow Resources*

Open Automation

UCS Director provides an open automation framework so you can develop your own integration and features within UCS Director. You can download open automation software development kit (SDK) and sample code to write your own UCS Director modules. A module is the topmost logical entry point into Cisco UCS Director. A module can include tasks, reports, and triggers. Using the UCS Director modules, you can perform the following functions:

- Develop your own Cisco UCS Director reports and report actions
- Inventory your devices
- Track changes made to the system through your module
- Develop tasks that can be used for workflows
- Develop and schedule repeatable tasks
- Set up new resource limits

Reference List

UCS Director Orchestration Guide: http://www.cisco.com/c/en/us/td/docs/unified_computing/ucs/ucs-director/orchestration-guide/5-5/b_UCS_Director_Orchestration_Guide_5_5.html

UCS Director Workflow Index: https://communities.cisco.com/docs/DOC-56419

DevNet—UCS Director Page: https://developer.cisco.com/site/ucs-director/overview/

Exam Preparation Tasks

Review All Key Topics

Review the most important topics in the chapter, noted with the key topics icon in the outer margin of the page. Table 17-2 lists a reference of these key topics and the page numbers on which each is found.

Table 17-2   Key Topics for Chapter 17

Key Topic Element	Description	Page
List	CMP Functionality	634
List	IT Process Automation by CMP	634
Paragraph	Task	636
List	Methods of Providing Task Input	637
Paragraph	Workflow	638
Paragraph	Activities	638
Paragraph	Service Request	639
List	Inconsistencies Checked by Workflow Validation	645
List	Methods of Executing Workflows	645
List	Changes That Can Be Made to an Existing Workflow	646
List	Information in Workflow Template	647

Define Key Terms

Define the following key terms from this chapter, and check your answers in the Glossary:

Orchestration, Cloud Management Platform (CMP), Application Programming Interface (API), Workflow, Service Request, Workflow Designer, UCSD Compound Task, UCSD Activity

Part V Review

Keep track of your part review progress with the checklist shown in Table PV-1. Details on each task follow the table.

Table PV-1 Part V Review Checklist

Activity	First Date Completed	Second Date Completed
Repeat all "Do I Know This Already?" Questions		
Answer "Part Review" Questions		
Review Key Topics		
Self-Assessment Questionnaire		

Repeat All "Do I Know This Already?" Questions: For this task, answer the "Do I Know This Already?" questions again for the chapters in this part of the book, using the PCPT software. Refer to "How to View Only 'Do I Know This Already?' Questions by Part," in the Introduction for help with how to make the PCPT software show you "Do I Know This Already?" questions for this part only.

Answer "Part Review" Questions: For this task, answer the "Part Review" questions for this part of the book, using the PCPT software. Refer to "How to View Only Part Review Questions by Part," in the Introduction to this book for help with how to make the PCPT software show you "Part Review" questions for this part only.

Review Key Topics: Browse back through the chapters and look for the Key Topic icons. If you do not remember some details, take the time to reread those topics.

Self-Assessment Questionnaire: Each chapter of this book introduces a number of key learning items. This might seem overwhelming to you initially, but as you read through each new chapter, you will become more familiar and comfortable with them, which will help you remember the concepts and technologies of these key topics as you progress with the book.

For this self-assessment exercise in the book, without looking back at the chapters or your notes, you should try to answer these self-assessment questions to the best of your ability. This exercise lists a set of key self-assessment questions, which are relevant to the particular chapter, shown in the following list. There will be no written answers to these questions in this book; if you are not certain, please go back and refresh on the key topics.

⑮

Cloud Computing

- Describe the five key characteristics of cloud computing
- Describe different deployment models of the cloud
- Explain the difference between private cloud and public cloud
- Describe key features of Intercloud fabric
- Describe API and common data formatting schemes used in API

⑯

UCS Director

- List the benefits and key functions of Cisco UCS Director
- List the key components of Cisco ONE Enterprise Cloud Suite and UCS Director
- Describe the multi-tenancy features supported by UCS Director
- Explain different user roles in UCS Director
- Describe unified infrastructure management
- Describe application containers supported in UCS Director

⑰

Understanding and Troubleshooting UCSD Workflows

- Explain the difference between automation and orchestration
- Describe workflow, task, compound task, activity, and service request
- Explain different methods of executing a workflow in UCS Director
- Explain the changes that can be made to an existing workflow
- Describe the use of workflow template

■ Think of each of these open self-assessment questions as being about the chapters you have read. You might or might not find the answer explicitly, but the chapter is structured to give you the knowledge and understanding to be able to discuss and explain these self-assessment questions. For example, number 15 is about cloud computing, number 16 is about UCSD, number 17 is about UCSD workflows, and so on.

■ Note your answer and try to reference key words in the answer from the relevant chapter. For example, VACS would apply to Chapter 16, "UCS Director."

Part VI

Final Preparation

Chapter 18: Final Preparation

Congratulations! You made it through the book, and now it is time to finish getting ready for the exam. This chapter covers the following topics:

Advice About the Exam Event: This section provides an overview of the exam structure and the types of questions you will encounter. It also provides some strategies for managing your time during the exam.

Pearson IT Certification Practice Test Engine and Questions: This section describes how to install and use the Pearson online exam engine in order to access and take 200-155 DCICT practice exams to better prepare you for the exam day.

Exam Review: This section suggests some new activities and repeats some old ones.

Final Thoughts: This section gives you encouragement about your exam results.

Final Preparation

This chapter begins by talking about the exam itself. At this moment, you know the content and the topics. Now you need to think about what happens during the exam and what you need to do in these last few weeks before taking the exam. At this point, everything you do should be focused on getting yourself ready to pass so that you can finish up. Although you are close to the finish line, you need to make one last effort. Everything is possible; you just need to believe it. The secret sauce of getting ahead is getting started, so what are you waiting for?

Advice About the Exam Event

Now that you have finished most of this book, you could register for your Cisco 200-155 DCICT exam, show up, and take the exam. However, if you spend a little time thinking about the exam event itself, learning more about the user interface of the real Cisco exams, and the environment at the Vue testing centers, you will be better prepared—particularly if this is your first Cisco exam. This first of three major sections in this chapter gives some advice about the Cisco exams and the exam event itself.

Learn the Question Types Using the Cisco Certification Exam Tutorial

In the weeks leading up to your exam, you should think more about the different types of exam questions and have a plan for how to approach those questions. One of the best ways to learn about the exam questions is to use the Cisco Exam Tutorial.

To find the Cisco Certification Exam Tutorial, go to http://www.cisco.com/ and search for "exam tutorial." The tutorial sits inside a web page with a Flash presentation of the exam user interface. The tutorial even lets you take control as if you were taking the exam. The example questions in this section are from the Cisco Certification Exam Tutorial, and they have nothing to do with the actual CCNA Data Center 200-155 exam content. You can expect to find the following types of questions on the exam:

- **Multiple choice, single answer:** The question has several possible answers, but only one correct one. Try to click Next on the multi-choice, single-answer question without clicking an answer, and see that the testing software tells you that you have too few answers. Figure 18-1 shows an example.

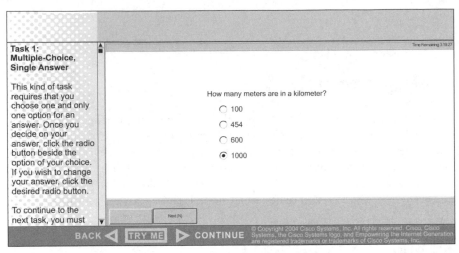

Figure 18-1 *Example Multiple-Choice, Single-Answer Exam Question*

■ **Multiple choice, multiple answer:** The question has several possible answers, with a given number of correct ones. Try to select too few answers and click Next to again see how the user interface responds. Figure 18-2 shows an example.

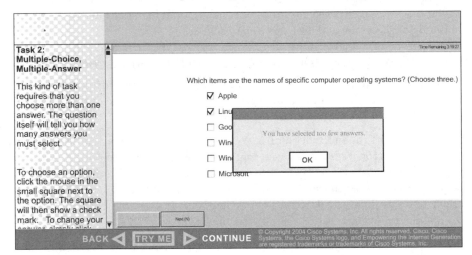

Figure 18-2 *Example Multiple-Choice, Multiple-Answer Exam Question*

■ **Drag and drop:** In the drag-and-drop questions, drag the answers to the obvious answer locations, but then drag them back to the original location. (You might do this on the real exam, if you change your mind when answering the question.) Figure 18-3 shows an example.

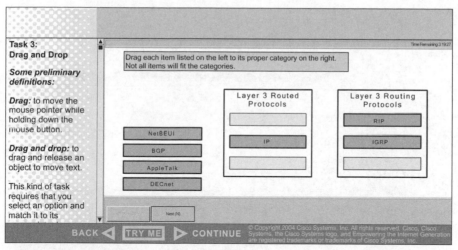

Figure 18-3   *Example Drag-and-Drop Exam Question*

- **Fill in the blank:** In this type of questions there is one or more blank answers that you must fill in. Figure 18-4 shows an example.

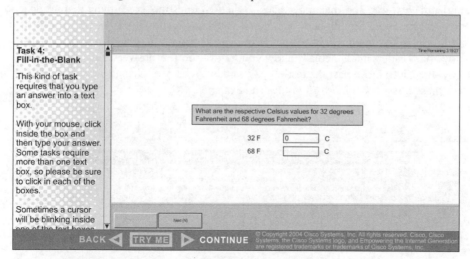

Figure 18-4   *Example Fill-in-the-Blank Exam Question*

- **Simulation:** The question includes a description and a network diagram. You can click a network device and interact with it through a simulated command-line interface (CLI). On the simulation question, first make sure that you can get to the CLI on one of the routers. To do so, you have to click the PC icon for a PC connected to the router console; the console cable appears as a dashed line, and network cables are solid lines. (Note that the exam tutorial uses the IOS CLI, not NX-OS, but it is similar enough for you to get the idea.) Figure 18-5 shows an example.

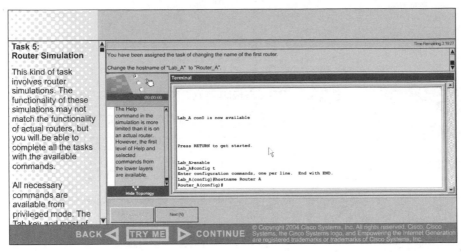

Figure 18-5 *Example Router Simulation Question*

■ **Testlet:** The question includes a detailed scenario and a set of questions that you select and answer. On the testlet question, answer one multiple choice question, move to the second and answer it, and then move back to the first question, confirming that inside a testlet, you can move around between questions. On the testlet question, click the Next button to see the pop-up window that Cisco uses as a prompt to ask whether you want to move on. Testlets might actually allow you to give too few answers and still move on. After you click to move past the testlet, you cannot go back to change your answer for any of these questions. Figure 18-6 shows an example.

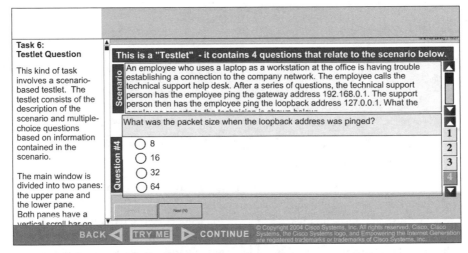

Figure 18-6 *Example Testlet Question*

■ **Simlet:** The question includes a scenario and a set of questions that you must answer based on interaction with a simulated network device. Make sure that you look at the scroll area. On the Sim question, make sure that you can toggle between the topology window and the terminal emulator window by clicking Show Topology and Hide Topology. Figure 18-7 shows an example.

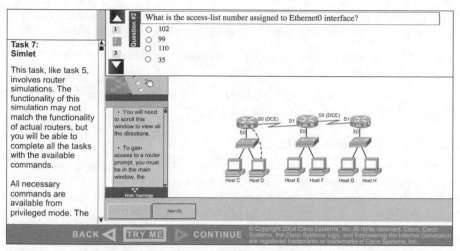

Figure 18-7   *Example Simlet Question*

Think About Your Time Budget Versus the Number of Questions

On exam day, you need to keep an eye on your speed. Going too slowly hurts you because you might not have time to answer all the questions. Going too fast can hurt as well if your fast speed is because you are rushing and not taking the time to fully understand the questions. You need to be able to somehow know whether you are moving quickly enough to answer all the questions, while not rushing.

The exam user interface shows some useful time information—namely, a countdown timer and a question counter. The question counter shows a question number for the question you are answering, and it shows the total number of questions on your exam.

Unfortunately, treating each question as equal does not give you an accurate time estimate. For example, if your exam allows 90 minutes, and your exam has 45 questions, you would have two minutes per question. After answering 20 questions, if you had taken 40 minutes, you would be right on time. However, several factors make that kind of estimate difficult.

First, Cisco does not tell us beforehand the exact number of questions for each exam. For example, Cisco.com (at press time) listed DCICT as a 90-minute exam with 65–75 questions. So, you know only a range of questions. But you do not know how many questions are on your exam until it begins, when you go through the screens that lead up to the point where you click Start Exam.

Next, some questions (call them time burners) clearly take a lot more time to answer:

Normal-time questions: Multi-choice and drag and drop, approximately 1 minute each

Time burners: Sims, simlets, and testlets, approximately 4 to 5 minutes each

Finally, the exam software counts each testlet and simlet question as one question in the question counter. For example, if a testlet question has four embedded multiple-choice questions, in the exam software's question counter, that counts as one question.

You need a plan for how you will check your time—a plan that does not distract you from the exam. It might be worth taking a bit of a guess to keep things simple, like this:

60 questions, 90 minutes equals exactly 1:15 per question. Then guess a little based on how many time-burner questions you have seen so far.

No matter how you plan to check your time, think about it before exam day. You can even use the method listed under the next heading.

A Suggested Time-Check Method

The following math can be used to do your time check in a way that weights the time based on those time-burner questions. You do not have to use this method. But this math uses only addition of whole numbers to keep it simple. It gives you a pretty close time estimate.

The concept is simple. Do a simple calculation that estimates the time you should have used so far. Basically, this process gives you one minute for normal questions and six minutes per time burner; here is the math:

Number of Questions Answered So Far + 6 Per Time Burner

Then you check the timer to figure out how much time you have spent:

- You have used exactly that much time or a little more: Your timing is perfect.
- You have used less time: You are ahead of schedule.
- You have used noticeably more time: You are behind schedule.

For example, if you have already finished 17 questions, 2 of which were time burners, your time estimate is 17 + 6 + 6 = 29 minutes. If your actual time is also 29 minutes, or maybe 30 or 31 minutes, you are right on schedule. If you have spent less than 29 minutes, you are ahead of schedule.

So, the math is pretty easy: Questions answered, plus 6 per time burner, is the guesstimate of how long you should have taken so far if you are right on time.

> **NOTE** This math is an estimate; we make no guarantees that the math will be an accurate predictor on every exam.

Miscellaneous Pre-Exam Suggestions

Here are a few more suggestions for things to think about before exam day:

- Get some earplugs. Testing centers often have some, but if you do not want to chance it, come prepared. The testing center is typically a room inside the space of a company that does something else as well, often a training center. So, there are people talking in nearby rooms and other office noises. Earplugs can help. (Headphones, as electronic devices, would not be allowed.)
- Some people like to spend the first minute of the exam writing down some notes for reference. For example, maybe you want to write down the table of magic numbers for finding IPv4 subnet IDs. If you plan to do that, practice making those notes. Before each

practice exam, transcribe those lists, just like you expect to do at the real exam. Do not forget to ask for a pen and paper from your proctor. The proctor will not allow you to enter in the exam room with your own note papers.

- Plan your travel to the testing center so that you will not be rushing to make it just in time.

- If you tend to be nervous before exams, practice your favorite relaxation techniques for a few minutes before each practice exam.

Exam-Day Advice

We hope the exam goes well for you. Certainly, the better prepared you are, the better chances you have on the exam. But these small tips can help you do your best on exam day:

- Rest the night before the exam rather than staying up late to study. Clarity of thought is more important than one extra fact, especially because the exam requires so much analysis and thinking rather than just remembering facts.

- If you did not bring earplugs, ask the testing center for some, even if you cannot imagine you would use them. You never know whether it might help.

- You can bring personal effects into the building and the testing company's space, but not into the actual room in which you take the exam. Take as little extra stuff with you as possible. If you have a safe place to leave briefcases, purses, electronics, and so on, leave them there. However, the testing center should have a place to store your things. Simply put, the less you bring, the less you have to worry about storing.

- The exam center will give you a laminated sheet and pen as a place to take notes. (Test center personnel typically do not let you bring paper and pen into the room, even if supplied by the testing center.)

- Leave for the testing center with extra time so you do not have to rush.

- Plan to find a restroom before going into the testing center. If you cannot find one, of course you can use one in the testing center, and test personnel will direct you and give you time before your exam starts.

- Do not drink a liter (34 ounce) of drink on the trip to the testing center. After the exam starts, the exam timer will not stop while you go to the restroom.

- On exam day, use any relaxation techniques that you have practiced to help get your mind focused while you wait for the exam.

Pearson IT Certification Practice Test Engine and Questions

Register this book to get access to the Pearson IT Certification test engine and other study materials plus additional bonus content. Check this site regularly for new and updated postings written by the author that provide further insight into the more troublesome topics on the exam. Be sure to check the box that you would like to hear from us to receive updates and exclusive discounts on future editions of this product or related products.

Companion Website

To access this companion website, follow these steps:

1. Go to www.pearsonITcertification.com/register and log in or create a new account.

2. Enter the ISBN: 9781587205910.

3. Answer the challenge question as proof of purchase.

4. Click on the "Access Bonus Content" link in the Registered Products section of your account page to be taken to the page where your downloadable content is available.

Please note that many of our companion content files can be large, especially image and video files. If you are unable to locate the files for this title by following the steps at the left, please visit www.pearsonITcertification.com/contact and select the "Site Problems/ Comments" option. Our customer service representatives will assist you.

The companion website includes the Pearson IT Certification Practice Test engine—software that displays and grades a set of exam-realistic multiple-choice questions. Using the Pearson IT Certification Practice Test engine, you can either study by going through the questions in Study Mode or take a simulated exam that mimics real exam conditions. You can also serve up questions in a Flash Card Mode, which will display just the question and no answers, challenging you to state the answer in your own words before checking the actual answers to verify your work.

The installation process requires two major steps: installing the software and then activating the exam. The website has a recent copy of the Pearson IT Certification Practice Test engine. The practice exam (the database of exam questions) is not on this site.

NOTE   The cardboard case in the back of this book includes a piece of paper. The paper lists the activation code for the practice exam associated with this book. Do not lose the activation code. On the opposite side of the paper from the activation code is a unique, one-time-use coupon code for the purchase of the Premium Edition eBook and Practice Test.

Install the Software

The Pearson IT Certification Practice Test is a Windows-only desktop application. You can run it on a Mac using a Windows virtual machine, but it was built specifically for the PC platform. The minimum system requirements are as follows:

- Windows 10, Windows 8.1, or Windows 7
- Microsoft .NET Framework 4.0 Client
- Pentium-class 1 GHz processor (or equivalent)
- 512 MB RAM
- 650 MB disk space plus 50 MB for each downloaded practice exam
- Access to the Internet to register and download exam databases

The software installation process is routine as compared with other software installation processes. If you have already installed the Pearson IT Certification Practice Test software from another Pearson product, there is no need for you to reinstall the software. Simply launch the software on your desktop and proceed to activate the practice exam from this book by using the activation code included in the access code card sleeve in the back of the book. The following steps outline the installation process:

1. Download the exam practice test engine from the companion site.

2. Respond to windows prompts as with any typical software installation process.

The installation process will give you the option to activate your exam with the activation code supplied on the paper in the cardboard sleeve. This process requires that you establish a Pearson website login. You need this login to activate the exam, so please do register when prompted. If you already have a Pearson website login, there is no need to register again. Just use your existing login.

Activate and Download the Practice Exam

Once the exam engine is installed, you should activate the exam associated with this book (if you did not do so during the installation process) as follows:

1. Start the Pearson IT Certification Practice Test software from the Windows Start menu or from your desktop shortcut icon.

2. To activate and download the exam associated with this book, from the My Products or Tools tab, click the **Activate Exam** button.

3. At the next screen, enter the activation key from the paper inside the cardboard sleeve in the back of the book. Once you have entered it, click the **Activate** button.

4. The activation process will download the practice exam. Click **Next**, and then click **Finish**.

When the activation process completes, the My Products tab should list your new exam. If you do not see the exam, make sure that you have selected the **My Products** tab on the menu. At this point, the software and practice exam are ready to use. Simply select the exam and click the **Open Exam** button.

To update a particular exam you have already activated and downloaded, display the Tools tab and click the **Update Products** button. Updating your exams will ensure that you have the latest changes and updates to the exam data.

If you want to check for updates to the Pearson Cert Practice Test exam engine software, display the **Tools** tab and click the **Update Application** button. You can then ensure that you are running the latest version of the software engine.

Activate Other Exams

The exam software installation process, and the registration process, only has to happen once. Then, for each new exam, only a few steps are required. For instance, if you buy another Pearson IT Certification Cert Guide, extract the activation code from the cardboard sleeve in the back of that book; you do not even need the exam engine at this point. From there, all you have to do is start the exam engine (if not still up and running) and perform Steps 2 through 4 from the previous list.

Premium Edition

In addition to the free practice exam provided with this book, you can purchase additional exams with expanded functionality directly from Pearson IT Certification. The Premium Edition of this title contains an additional two full practice exams as well as an eBook (in both PDF and ePub format). In addition, the Premium Edition title has remediation for each question to the specific part of the eBook that relates to that question.

Because you have purchased the print version of this title, you can purchase the Premium Edition at a deep discount. There is a coupon code in the cardboard sleeve in the back of the book that contains a one-time-use code, as well as instructions for where you can purchase the Premium Edition.

To view the Premium Edition product page, go to http://www.ciscopress.com/title/9780134469683.

Using the Exam Engine

The Pearson IT Certification Practice Test (PCPT) engine lets you access a database of questions created specifically for this book. The PCPT engine can be used either in study mode or practice exam mode, as follows:

■ **Study mode** is most useful when you want to use the questions for learning and practicing. In study mode, you can select options such as randomizing the order of the questions and answers, automatically viewing answers to the questions as you go, testing on specific topics, and many others.

■ **Practice exam mode** presents questions in a timed environment, providing you with a more exam-realistic experience. It also restricts your ability to see your score as you progress through the exam and view answers to questions as you are taking the exam. These timed exams not only allow you to study for the actual 200-155 DCICT exam, but also help you simulate the time pressure that occurs on the actual exam.

When doing your final preparation, you can use study mode, practice exam mode, or both. However, after you have seen each question a couple of times, you will likely start to remember the questions, and the usefulness of the exam database may decrease. So, consider the following options when using the exam engine:

■ Use the question database for review. Use study mode to study the questions by chapter, just as with the other final review steps listed in this chapter. Consider upgrading to the Premium Edition of this book if you want to take additional simulated exams.

■ Save the question database, not using it for review during your review of each book part. Save it until the end so that you will not have seen the questions before. Then use practice exam mode to simulate the exam.

To select the exam engine mode, click on the **My Products** tab. Select the exam you wish to use from the list of available exams, and then click the **Use** button. The test engine should display a window from which you can choose **Study Mode** or **Practice Exam Mode**. When in study mode, you can further choose the book chapters, limiting the questions to those explained in the specified chapters of the book.

Exam Review

This exam review completes the Study Plan materials as suggested by this book. At this point, you have read the other chapters of the book, and you have done the chapter review Exam Preparation Tasks and Part Review Tasks. Now you need to do the final study and review activities before taking the exam, as detailed in this section.

The Exam Review section suggests some new activities, as well as repeats some old ones. However, whether new or old, all the activities focus on filling in your knowledge gaps, finishing off your skills, and completing the study process. Although repeating some tasks you did at the chapter review and the part review can help, you need to be ready to take an exam, so the exam review asks you to spend a lot of time answering exam questions.

The exam review walks you through suggestions for several types of tasks and gives you some tracking tables for each activity. The main categories are as follows:

- Practicing for speed
- Taking practice exams
- Finding what you do not know well yet (knowledge gaps)
- Configuring and verifying functions from the CLI
- Repeating the chapter and part review tasks

Take Practice Exams

One day soon, you will take a Cisco exam at a Vue testing center. So it is time to practice the real event as much as possible.

A practice exam using the Pearson IT Certification Practice Test (PCPT) exam software lets you experience many of the same issues as when taking a real Cisco exam. The software gives you a number of questions, with a countdown timer shown in the window. After you answer a question, you cannot go back to it (yes, that's true on Cisco exams). If you run out of time, the questions you did not answer count as incorrect.

The process of taking the timed practice exams helps you prepare in three key ways:

- To practice the exam event itself, including time pressure, the need to read carefully, and a need to concentrate for long periods
- To build your analysis and critical thinking skills when examining the network scenario built into many questions
- To discover the gaps in your networking knowledge so that you can study those topics before the real exam

As much as possible, treat the practice exam events as if you were taking the real Cisco exam at a Vue testing center. The following list gives some advice on how to make your practice exam more meaningful, rather than as just one more thing to do before exam day rolls around:

- Set aside two hours for taking the 90-minute timed practice exam.

- Make a list of what you expect to do for the 10 minutes before the real exam event. Then visualize yourself doing those things. Before taking each practice exam, practice those final 10 minutes before your exam timer starts. (The earlier section "Exam-Day Advice" lists some suggestions about what to do in those last 10 minutes.)

- You cannot bring anything with you into the Vue exam room, so remove all notes and help materials from your work area before taking a practice exam. You can use blank paper, a pen, and your brain only. Do not use calculators, notes, web browsers, or any other app on your computer.

- Real life can get in the way, but if at all possible, ask anyone around you to leave you alone for the time you will practice. If you must do your practice exam in a distracting environment, wear headphones or earplugs to reduce distractions.

- Do not guess, hoping to improve your score. Answer only when you have confidence in the answer. Then if you get the question wrong, you can go back and think more about the question in a later study session.

Practice Taking the DCICT Exam

To take a DCICT practice exam, you need to select one or both of the DCICT exams from PCPT. If you followed the study plan in this book, you will not have seen any of the questions in these two exam databases before now. After you select one of these two exams, you choose the Practice Exam option in the upper right and start the exam.

You should plan to take between one and three DCICT practice exams with these exam databases. Even people who are already well prepared should do at least one practice exam, just to experience the time pressure and the need for prolonged concentration. For those who want more practice exams, these two exam databases have enough questions for more than two exams. As a result, if you take a fourth practice exam with these exam databases, you will have seen almost all the questions before, making the practice exam a little too easy. If you are interested in purchasing more practice exams, check out the *CCNA Data Center DCICT 200-155 Official Cert Guide Premium Edition eBook and Practice Test* product at www.ciscopress.com/title/9780134469683 and be sure to use the 70% off coupon included in the cardboard sleeve in the back of this book.

Table 18-1 gives you a checklist to record your different practice exam events. Note that recording both the date and the score is helpful for some other work you will do, so note both. Also, in the Time Notes section, if you finish on time, note how much extra time you had; if you run out of time, note how many questions you did not have time to answer.

Table 18-1   DCICT Practice Exam Checklist

Exam	Date	Score	Time Notes
DCICT			
DCICT			
DCICT			
DCICT			

Advice on How to Answer Exam Questions

Open a web browser. Yes, take a break and open a web browser on any device. Do a quick search on a fun topic. Then, before you click a link, get ready to think where your eyes go for the first 5–10 seconds after you click the link. Now click a link and look at the page. Where did your eyes go?

Interestingly, web browsers, and the content on those web pages, have trained us all to scan. Web page designers design content with the expectation that people will scan with different patterns. Regardless of the pattern, when reading a web page, almost no one reads sequentially, and no one reads entire sentences. They scan for the interesting graphics and the big words, and then they scan the space around those noticeable items.

Other parts of our electronic culture have also changed how the average person reads. For example, many of you grew up using texting and social media, sifting through hundreds or thousands of messages—but each message barely fills an entire sentence. (In fact, that previous sentence would not fit in a tweet, being longer than 140 characters.)

Those everyday habits have changed how we all read and think in front of a screen. Unfortunately, those same habits often hurt our scores when taking computer-based exams.

If you scan exam questions like you read web pages, texts, and tweets, you will probably make some mistakes because you missed a key fact in the question, answer, or exhibits. It helps to start at the beginning and read all the words—a process that is amazingly unnatural for many people today.

When taking the practice exams and answering individual questions, here are two suggestions. First, before the practice exam, think about your own personal strategy for how you will read a question. Make your approach to multiple-choice questions in particular be a conscious decision on your part. Second, if you want some suggestions on how to read an exam question, use the following strategy:

Step 1.   Read the question itself, thoroughly, from start to finish.

Step 2.   Scan any exhibit (usually command output) or figure.

Step 3.   Scan the answers to look for the types of information. (Numeric? Terms? Single words? Phrases?)

Step 4.   Reread the question thoroughly, from start to finish, to make sure that you understand it.

Step 5. Read each answer thoroughly while referring to the figure/exhibit as needed. After reading each answer, do the following before reading the next answer:

A. If correct, select as correct.

B. If definitely incorrect, mentally rule it out.

C. If unsure, mentally note it as a possible correct answer.

> **NOTE** Cisco exams will tell you the number of correct answers. The exam software also helps you finish the question with the right number of answers noted. For example, the software prevents you from selecting too many answers. Also, if you try to move on to the next question but have too few answers noted, the exam software asks if you truly want to move on.

Use the practice exams as a place to practice your approach to reading. Every time you click to the next question, try to read the question following your approach. If you are feeling time pressure, that is the perfect time to keep practicing your approach to reduce and eliminate questions you miss because of scanning the question instead of reading thoroughly.

Take Other Practice Exams

Many people add other practice exams and questions other than the questions that come with this book. Frankly, using other practice exams in addition to the questions that come with this book can be a good idea, for many reasons. The other exam questions can use different terms in different ways, emphasize different topics, and show different scenarios that make you rethink some topics.

No matter where you get additional exam questions, if you use the exam questions for a timed practice exam, it helps to take a few notes about the results. Table 18-2 gives you a place to take those notes. Also, take a guess at the percentage of questions you have seen before taking the exam, and note whether you think the questions are less, more, or the same challenge level as the questions that come with this book. And as usual, note whether you ran out of time or had extra time left over at the end.

Table 18-2 Checklist for Practice Exams from Other Sources

Exam Source	Other Exam Notes	% Questions Repeated (Estimate)	Challenging?	Date	Score	Time Notes

> **NOTE** The publisher does sell products that include additional test questions. The *CCNA Data Center DCICT 200-155 Official Cert Guide Premium Edition eBook and Practice Test* product is basically the publisher's eBook version of this book. It includes a soft copy of the book in formats you can read on your computer or on the most common book readers and tablets. The product includes all the content you would normally get with the print book, including all the question databases mentioned in this chapter. Additionally, this product includes two more DCICT exam databases for extra practice tests.

Find Knowledge Gaps Through Question Review

You just took a number of practice exams. You probably learned a lot, gained some exam-taking skills, and improved your networking knowledge and skills. But if you go back and look at all the questions you missed, you might be able to find a few small gaps in your knowledge.

When doing your final exam preparation, one of the hardest things is to discover gaps in your knowledge and skills. In other words, what topics and skills do you need to know that you do not know? Or what topics do you think you know, but you misunderstand about some important fact? Finding gaps in your knowledge at this late stage requires more than just your gut feeling about your strengths and weaknesses.

This next task uses a feature of PCPT to help you find those gaps. The PCPT software tracks each practice exam you take, remembering your answer for every question and whether you got it wrong. You can view the results and move back and forth between seeing the question and seeing the results page. To find gaps in your knowledge, follow these steps:

Step 1.   Pick and review one of your practice exams.

Step 2.   Review each incorrect question until you are happy that you understand the question.

Step 3.   When finished with your review for a question, mark the question.

Step 4.   Review all incorrect questions from your exam until all are marked.

Step 5.   Move on to the next practice exam.

Figure 18-8 shows a sample "Question Review" page, in which all the questions were answered incorrectly. The results list a "Correct" column with no check mark, meaning that the answer was incorrect.

To review questions and mark them as complete, you can move between this Question Review page and the individual questions. Just double-click a question to move back to that question. From the question, you can click Grade Exam to move back to the grading results and to the Question Review page shown in Figure 18-8. The question window also shows the place to mark the question, in the upper left, as shown in Figure 18-9.

18

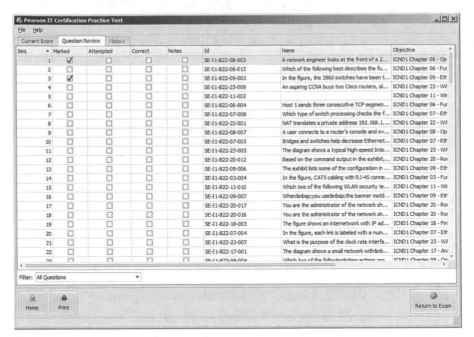

Figure 18-8 *PCPT Grading Results Page*

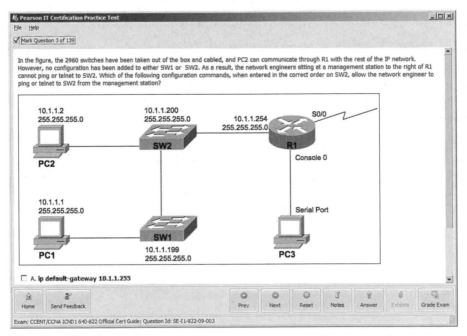

Figure 18-9 *Reviewing a Question, with Mark Feature in Upper Left*

If you want to come back later to look through the questions you missed from an earlier exam, start at the PCPT home screen. From there, instead of clicking the Start button to start a new exam, click the View Grade History button to see your earlier exam attempts and work through any missed questions.

Track your progress through your gap review in Table 18-3. PCPT lists your previous practice exams by date and score, so it helps to note those values in the table for comparison to the PCPT menu.

Table 18-3   Tracking Checklist for Gap Review of Practice Exams

DCICT Exam	Original Practice Exam Date	Original Exam Score	Date Gap Review Was Completed

Practice Hands-On CLI Skills

To do well on sim and simlet questions, you must be comfortable with many Cisco NX-OS commands, as well as how to use them from the CLI. As described in the introduction to this book, sim questions require you to decide what configuration command(s) need to be configured to fix a problem or to complete a working configuration. Simlet questions require you to answer multiple-choice questions by first using the CLI to issue **show** commands to look at the status of routers and switches in a small network.

Other Study Tasks

If you get to this point and still feel the need to prepare more, this last topic gives you three suggestions.

First, the chapter review Exam Preparation Tasks and Part Review sections give you some useful study tasks.

Second, take more exam questions from other sources. You can always get more questions in the Cisco Press Premium Edition eBook and Practice Test products, which include an eBook copy of this book plus additional questions in additional PCPT exam banks. However, you can search the Internet for questions from many sources, and review those questions as well.

NOTE   Some vendors claim to sell practice exams that contain the exact exam questions from the exam. These exams, called "brain dumps," are against the Cisco testing policies. Cisco strongly discourages using any such tools for study.

Finally, join in the discussions on the Cisco Learning Network. Try to answer questions asked by other learners; the process of answering makes you think much harder about the topic. Cisco provides a wide variety of CCNA Data Center preparation tools. Resources found there include sample questions, forums on each Cisco exam, video-based learning games, and information about each exam.

To reach the Cisco Learning Network, go to https://learningnetwork.cisco.com, or use a search engine to search for "Cisco Learning Network." To access some of the features and resources, you need to use the login you created. If you do not have such a login, you can register for free. To register, simply go to Cisco.com, click **Register** at the top of the page, and supply some information.

Final Thoughts

You have studied quite a bit, worked hard, and sacrificed time and money to be ready for the exam. We hope your exam goes well, that you pass, and that you pass because you really know your stuff and will do well in your IT and networking career. At the end of the CCNA Data Center exam, you will receive your score and news of your passing or failing. If you fail, take a few minutes to write down as many exam questions as you can remember. Note which questions left you uneasy. Next, schedule to take the same exam again. Allow a few days so that you can study the topics that gave you trouble. The exam score should also break down the entire exam into major topics, each with its respective score. Do not be discouraged about starting over with your studies; the majority of it is already behind you. Just spend time brushing up on the "low spots" where you lack knowledge or confidence. Go for it and do your best!

We would encourage you to celebrate when you pass, and ask advice when you do not. Congratulations on achieving a major milestone in your career.

Answers to the "Do I Know This Already?" Quizzes

Chapter 1

1. A, B, and D. **Explanation:** There are several benefits of using port channels. Bundling multiple Ethernet links into a logical port channel provides increased capacity. Traffic is load-balanced across the port channel member ports. If one of the member ports goes down, the port channel is still operational; therefore, it provides high availability.

2. A, B, and D. **Explanation:** To create a port channel, the following port attributes must match: speed, duplex, and flow control.

3. A, C, and D. **Explanation:** Static port channel is created using mode On. Port Channel with LACP can use mode Active or Passive.

4. B. **Explanation:** Passive mode puts the port into a passive negotiating state in which the port responds to LACP packets that it receives, but it does not initiate LACP negotiation.

5. D. **Explanation:** LACP Active Mode puts the port into an active negotiating state in which the port initiates negotiations with a peer switch by sending LACP packets.

6. A, B, and C. **Explanation:** The Cisco Nexus family supports load balancing based on source and destination MAC address, source and destination IP address, and source and destination TCP/UDP port number.

7. B and C. **Explanation:** vPC is supported by all Nexus family switches, which includes Nexus 9000, Nexus 7000, Nexus 6000, and Nexus 5000.

8. A, B, and C. **Explanation:** vPC combines ports from two switches into one port channel. It utilizes all available bandwidth by load-balancing traffic across vPC member ports. Because ports from two switches are bundled together in vPC, STP blocking is eliminated, and faster convergence is achieved. vPC is supported only by Nexus family switches.

9. B. **Explanation:** Cisco Fabric Services over Ethernet (CFSoE) uses vPC peer link to synchronize control and data plane information.

10. A and C. **Explanation:** Cisco Fabric Services over Ethernet (CFSoE) is used as a primary control plane protocol to perform consistency and compatibility checks, to exchange the Layer 2 forwarding table, and to monitor the status of vPC member ports.

11. A. **Explanation:** Only one vPC domain ID can be configured on a single switch or VDC. It is not possible for a switch or VDC to participate in more than one vPC domain.

12. C. **Explanation:** In a FabricPath network, Dynamic Resource Allocation Protocol (DRAP) automatically assigns a unique switch ID to each FabricPath switch.

13. A, B, and C. **Explanation:** In FabricPath, the root for multidestination tree is elected based on root priority, system ID, and switch ID. A higher value of these parameters is preferred.

14. C. **Explanation:** When an Ethernet frame enters the FabricPath, the switch encapsulates the frame with a 16-byte FabricPath header. This header includes a 48-bit outer MAC destination address (ODA), a 48-bit outer MAC source address (OSA), and a 32-bit FabricPath tag. The ODA and SDA contain a 12-bit unique identifier called Switch ID. In a FabricPath network, the packet is forwarded using a destination switch ID within the ODA.

15. A. **Explanation:** Cisco FabricPath uses a single control plane that functions for unicast, broadcast, and multicast packets by leveraging the Layer 2 Intermediate System-to-Intermediate System (ISIS) protocol.

Chapter 2

1. C. **Explanation:** Data plane of switch is responsible for forwarding traffic, which is why it is also called forwarding plane.

2. C. **Explanation:** Management plane is responsible for configuration and monitoring of switch. Network administrator and network monitoring tools use management plane to configure and monitor the device.

3. A. **Explanation:** Control plane maintains the information necessary for data plane to operate. This includes routing and switching tables within a switch.

4. C and D. **Explanation:** Spanning Tree Protocol (STP) and Link Aggregation Control Protocol (LACP) are examples of control plane protocol. Simple Network Management Protocol (SNMP) and NETCONF are examples of management plane.

5. A and B. **Explanation:** Spanning Tree Protocol (STP) and Link Aggregation Control Protocol (LACP) are examples of control plane protocol. Simple Network Management Protocol (SNMP) and NETCONF are examples of management plane.

6. B. **Explanation:** The CMP only exists on Nexus 7000 SUP1.

7. A, B, and C. **Explanation:** The NX-API supports JSON-RPC, XML, and JSON as message formats.

8. A and B. **Explanation:** The Nexus 5000 Series switch provides the following default user roles:

   - **network-admin (superuser):** Complete read and write access to the entire Nexus 5000 Series switch.

   - **network-operator:** Complete read access to the Nexus 5000 Series switch.

9. B. **Explanation:** It has only read access to a specific VDC.

10. D. **Explanation:** 256 rules can be assigned to a single role.

Appendix A: Answers to the "Do I Know This Already?" Quizzes   681

A

Chapter 3

1. B. **Explanation:** Multilayer design makes use of a "stove-pipe" architecture, which best fits traditional north south predominantly client/server type of traffic.

2. B and C. **Explanation:** Deploying separate application-specific dedicated environments can be one possible solution for solving the problem of different application needs that cannot be reconciled over a single environment. At the same time, modern data center fabrics, such as Cisco ACI, are also capable of discovering application requirements eliminating the need to deploy separate application specific dedicated environments.

3. A, B, C, and D. **Explanation:** Unified Fabric is built on Ethernet technology, leveraging enhancements introduced by the IEEE data center bridging standards. It consolidates multiple traffic types over a unified transport medium while supporting physical, virtual, and cloud environments.

4. B and D. **Explanation:** Unified Fabric consolidates many types of traffic over ubiquitous Ethernet fabric; network and SAN are the most commonly deployed.

5. C. **Explanation:** vPC leverages port channels to create all-forwarding switch uplink topology. There are no blocked ports with vPC.

6. C. **Explanation:** Cisco Virtual Security Gateway (VSG) allows securing VM-to-VM traffic within the same tenant space. Adaptive Security Virtual Appliance (ASAv) secures inter-tenant communication.

7. D. **Explanation:** vPath is used on the Cisco Nexus 1000v virtual switches to steer the traffic toward virtual service nodes.

8. A, B, and D. **Explanation:** Cisco Data Center Network Manager products can manage many data center components, including LAN and SAN. DCNM can be used to provision vPC.

9. A. **Explanation:** OTV does not forward unknown unicast frames. OTV edge devices drop unicast frames with destination MAC addresses not found in the MAC address table.

10. B. **Explanation:** In LISP, ITR stands for Ingress Tunnel Router.

Chapter 4

1. B and D. **Explanation:** The main challenge is to get VM level network visibility and the fact that, without Cisco Nexus 1000V Series switches, it was impossible to enforce policies at the VM level, at the vNIC. Policies could only be enforced at the physical hosts uplink interfaces.

2. B. **Explanation:** It was impossible to manage a VM's vNIC, as it was not visible to the outside network. The standard static switch in VMware did not expose it to be managed like a physical switch.

3. A and B. **Explanation:** The VMware static vSwitches posed numerous challenges, including the fact that all port-groups needed to be maintained manually on each and every vSwitch and with an ever increasing number of ESX/ESXi hosts, the virtual access layer started to grow and server/virtualization admins with little networking background needed to manage that access layer. Also, if a VM was compromised, it couldn't be quarantined and could only be traced up to a VLAN/physical port without VN-Tag capabilities.

4. C. **Explanation:** These are the fundamental building blocks of virtual networking in a server-virtualized environment. They make the primary constructs that work in tandem to deliver network connectivity to virtual machines.

5. A. **Explanation:** The VMware Virtual Distributed Switch (vDS) was introduced with VMware vSphere 4. As opposed to managing static vSwitches on every ESX or ESXi host, the vDS brings the capability to configure and manage a collection of vSwitches in an ESX or ESXi host/multiple hosts within a VMware Cluster.

6. B and C. **Explanation:** The VMware vDS and vSwitch can be used in tandem, depending on your design requirements and circumstances. However, the centralized management of this distributed switch does reduce the burden on virtual access layer administrative tasks and most importantly it allows policies assigned to VMs to travel with it, as a VM is vMotioned from one host to another.

7. B. **Explanation:** The Cisco Nexus 1000V Series switch is based on Cisco's next generation advanced networking operating system known as NX-OS.

8. B. **Explanation:** The Cisco Nexus 1000V Series switch consists of a VSM and a VEM, which are analogues to a Cisco physical modular switch. The VSM is the supervisory module, while the VEM is the line card.

9. A. **Explanation:** Cisco Nexus 1000V introduced Layer 3 mode for control, packet and management traffic since version 1.2. At that time, Layer 3 connection mode was optional; at the time of writing this book the default when installing the VSM is to establish Layer 3 connectivity instead of Layer 2.

10. A. **Explanation:** Port-profiles are the Cisco Nexus 1000V series switch equivalent of port-groups in VMware. When a port-profile is created, you will see a corresponding port group being created in VMware vCenter server.

11. B. **Explanation:** After login as admin user from the config terminal, execute the **show svs connections** command. Identify the operational and config status to confirm connection with VMware vCenter has been established.

12. A. **Explanation:** If you have SSH enabled on your ESX or ESXi host, you can log into your host by opening an SSH connection, log in with valid credentials and at the CLI of the host, you can execute the **vem status** command.

13. A. **Explanation:** Use the **show port-profile name** *<name>* command to verify the details of that port-profile configuration and parameters. With this command, you can check which switchport mode this port-profile uses, which VLANs are associated with this port-profile, and which virtual interfaces are assigned to this port-profile.

Appendix A: Answers to the "Do I Know This Already?" Quizzes   683

A

Chapter 5

1. A and C. **Explanation:** The ASR 1000 and Nexus 7000 series support OTV.

2. A. **Explanation:** You can statically add the MAC address of the silent host to the edge device MAC address table.

3. C. **Explanation:** You need to enable IGMPv3 on the OTV join interface.

4. A. **Explanation:** You can have only one join interface per overlay in the current NX-OS.

5. A. **Explanation:** You need to bring up the overlay interface after it is added; it is in a shutdown state by default.

6. B. **Explanation:** VXLAN uses MAC-in-UDP/IP encapsulation.

7. C. **Explanation:** The VNID is 24-bit and is able to create 16M segments.

8. A. **Explanation:** EVPN routes are advertised through the L2VPN EVPN address family.

9. A. **Explanation:** NVGRE has a 24-bit virtual subnet identifier (VSID).

10. C. **Explanation:** NVGRE has a 24-bit virtual subnet identifier (VSID).

Chapter 6

1. D. **Explanation:** SUP 1 supports up to four VDCs, and SUP 2E supports up to eight VDCs.

2. A, B, and C. **Explanation:** We can have default VDC, non-default VDC, Admin VDC, and Storage VDC.

3. B. **Explanation:** We cannot assign physical interfaces to the admin VDC.

4. B. **Explanation:** the **switchto vdc** command is used to access a nondefault VDC from the default VDC or the admin VDC.

5. B. **Explanation:** The Nexus 2000 Series switch cannot run as a standalone switch and requires a parent switch; this can be Nexus 7000, Nexus 6000, and Nexus 5000.

6. C. **Explanation:** The VNTag is being standardized under IEEE 802.1BR.

7. B. **Explanation:** VIF stands for virtual interface.

8. B. **Explanation:** Rapid PVST+, which is the IEEE 802.1w, is the default spanning tree mode for the NX-OS.

9. A. **Explanation:** Example 6-17 shows how to verify STP root bridge for all VLANs for a specific switch

    Explanation: Example 6-16 shows how to verify STP root bridge for all VLANs for a specific switch.

10. A and B. **Explanation:** The Cisco Adapter FEX requires an adapter that supports VNTag technology like the Cisco UCS Virtual Interface Card VIC-1225/1385 for the Cisco UCS C-Series rackmount server, the Cisco UCS VIC-1240/1380 for the Cisco UCS B-Series server.

Chapter 7

1. C. **Explanation:** Cisco UCS consists of multiple computing hardware, components, and management software that formulates the unified compute system offering from Cisco.

2. B and D. **Explanation:** High performance or grid computing and cloud computing, because they are logical architectures in computing and not physical form factors or classes of server.

3. A. **Explanation:** By disaggregating the server components, UCS M-Series helps provide a component life cycle management strategy as opposed to a server-by-server strategy. UCS M-Series provides a platform that offers flexible and rapid deployment of compute, storage, and networking resources. All of the customization is configured through standard Cisco UCS Manager service profiles to programmatically define these server instances from central policy. This configuration is independent of the physical hardware, which streamlines life cycle management, serviceability, and deployment of the infrastructure.

4. True. **Explanation:** The x86 microprocessor architecture belongs to the CISC family of microprocessors used by Intel and AMD. CISC architecture processors, such as Intel's Nehalem, Sandy-Bridge, and so on, are becoming faster and cheaper in the market. With operating systems like Linux evolving to provide reliability, availability, and scalability features, this combination of CISC + Linux operating systems are gaining acceptance in the marketplace. Cisco UCS server products do not produce RISC architecture-based blade or rackmount servers.

5. C. **Explanation:** Cisco UCS B- and C-series naming is strictly refers to their form factors. The M# numbering refers to the current processor family it supports, which can be found by referring to their respective spec sheets.

6. B. **Explanation:** The E5-2600 CPU consists of four memory channels per socket. Each channel can accommodate 3 DIMMS. By populating 2DPC, it's a total of 16 DIMMS per blade. Each channel can achieve speeds of 1866 MHz.

7. D. **Explanation:** The Cisco UCS C460 M2 C-series server is a high-performance system that is typically used to host CPU and I/O intensive workloads, such as database, ERP applications, and high-performance computing systems. This is a four-socket system with the capability to host 12 disk drives and 2 TB of DRAM.

8. A, B, D, and E. **Explanation:** Regardless of the IO module, the number of links can only be a power of 2. The second-generation UCS 2208 I/O module supports a maximum of eight links, whereas the first-generation Cisco UCS 2104XP I/O module supports a maximum of four links, similar to the third generation 2304 IOM; the main difference is that the 2304 IOMs support 40GE interfaces.

9. A. **Explanation:** The integrated management of a Cisco UCS platform is embedded in various locations. There are chassis management controllers (CMC) located in every chassis along with a Chassis Management Switch (CMS). The CMS carries the management traffic to a CIMC, located on every blade server.

10. B. **Explanation:** An I/O module should be connected to only a single fabric interconnect, even in the case of clustered fabric interconnects. If you had two modules, the I/O module should be connected to a Fabric Interconnect (A) and the second IOM module must be connected to Fabric Interconnect (B).

Chapter 8

1. C. **Explanation:** The Cisco UCS Manager is embedded into the Cisco UCS Fabric Interconnects and provides a single pane of glass to manage and monitor the entire Cisco UCS domain.

2. B. **Explanation:** It is not possible to perform the initial setup of a Cisco UCS Fabric Interconnect via its virtual IP address, simply because it is not configured yet. They have not been assigned to the Cisco UCS Fabric Interconnect.

3. A and B. **Explanation:** The L1 and L2 ports are used as Cisco UCS Fabric Interconnects, they are used for heartbeat and master database synchronization between the primary and subordinate Fabric Interconnects.

4. B. **Explanation:** On a Cisco UCS Fabric Interconnect, there is only one console port, which is a RJ-45 port. You will require a standard Cisco DB-9 to RJ-45 console cable. If your workstation does not have a COM port, you will require a DB-9 to USB converter and appropriate software drivers installed.

5. B and C. **Explanation:** Both commands can be used to verify roles and cluster status. The primary difference between answers b and c is that the latter shows details of chassis members selected to participate in HA. The Cisco UCS Fabric Interconnects utilizes the Cisco UCS 5108 blade server chassis SEEPROM to identify latest configuration database version and prevent split-brain syndromes etc.

6. C. **Explanation:** There are three major panes in the UCS Manager GUI, and they are different from the UCS Manager GUI Tabs. The panes are a Navigation Trail, Navigation Pane, and a Content Pane. Each pane gives you a single line folder structure, current selection, and configurable items, respectively.

7. A. **Explanation:** Though it is possible to configure the entire system via CLI, it is recommended to utilize the Cisco UCS Manager GUI, as it is very intuitive and easy to use. The CLI is primarily used to set specific parameters, troubleshoot, and if need be utilized in scripts.

8. B. **Explanation:** These "Tabs" in the Cisco UCS Manager represent the following: hardware/firmware, service profiles, network connectivity, storage connectivity, integration with vCenter and UCS administrative tasks, respectively.

9. B. **Explanation:** The Cisco UCS Manager is always in discovery mode. Through a series of presence sensors and voltage indications, the Cisco UCS Manager detects that new hardware is added to its domain and displays it in the equipment tab.

10. B. **Explanation:** The FSM runs in the DME (Data Management Engine) and manages Cisco UCS endpoints, with regard to physical components (chassis, I/O modules, servers), logical components (policies), and workflows (all discoveries, backup, service profiles etc).

Chapter 9

1. A. **Explanation:** A Service Profile is a collection of unique attributes that defines a server. That definition is known as a service profile and it can be bound to a Cisco UCS blade/rackmount server and also can be associated/dis-associated from server-to-server, while maintaining the same identities.

2. B. **Explanation:** Hardware identities and all required attributes to instantiate a server will be needed prior to installation of an operating system on a Cisco UCS blade/rackmount server. A service profile must be associated prior to installing an operating system.

3. B and C. **Explanation:** The Cisco UCS Service Profile is not a hypervisor. It is a software object that contains the identities and parameters that are required to instantiate a physical server. By associating a Cisco UCS Service Profile to a blade or rackmount server, you have only software defined the server identities and settings. Only then is it ready to be installed with an operating system.

4. B. **Explanation:** Logical resource pools are user defined identities e.g. MAC, WWN pools etc. and are consumed by Cisco UCS service profiles and/or templates. Physical resource pools are server hardware grouped together based on a qualification criteria defined by the user e.g. CPU type, DRAM qty.

5. D. **Explanation:** This is a hardware device ID, assigned to the manufacturer of that device and it is used in Fiber Channel Protocol to register with a storage-area network. It is analogues to the MAC address in Ethernet networks. There are two types of WWNs (World Wide Number) used in the FC protocol i.e. physical (Node, port) and logical (LUN). Based on the logical/physical element being identified, this address can be either a 64-bit or 128-bit address, assigned by the IEEE 803.2 extended.

6. A, C, and D. **Explanation:** Primarily utilized for consistency and automated, rapid provisioning of service profiles. It allows a Cisco UCS administrator to pre-create all the necessary identities with future scale in mind and allows the user to utilize them when provisioning service profiles. It also allows you to create initial and updating templates, whereas in the latter, changes made to the template are reflected onto every child service profile automatically.

7. B. **Explanation:** You cannot move a service profile. However, you can copy, clone a service profile; when you do, Cisco UCS Manager will create a new object utilizing the same properties but with unique identities.

8. B. **Explanation:** The adapter policy allows you to set host-side attributes of an adapter. There are pre-set attribute values available, based on OS, software vendor recommendations. This policy is useful to tune an adapter based on the target application requirements and their performance tuning recommendations by the appropriate vendor.

9. C. **Explanation:** These UCS power management policies are used to define a maximum threshold of power utilization. They can be specific to a blade, rackmount server, chassis wide or applied to a user-defined group of server hardware. Further, with power control policies you can define the priority to be allocated power. Utilized to maximize power usage efficiencies within a Cisco UCS domain.

10. A. **Explanation:** A blade server can belong to multiple blade server pools at the same time. Cisco UCS manager will select a non-associated blade from the pool; the service profile associated with that blade owns the blade, not the server pool.

Chapter 10

1.   A. **Explanation:** If a server/device needs to be managed via its data access path (server data traffic), this is known as in-band management access. However, if a server/device consists of a separate NIC (network interface) that can be accessed separately via a switch or directly, it is known as out-of-band access. Most networking devices, blade enclosures, and individual rack servers offer the option to access their management and administration capabilities out-of-band, because it's a best practice to separate management and data traffic in a data center.

2.   A. **Explanation:** Cisco UCS Manager offers the option to access a blade's KVM functions via in-band management access. However, if you need to access the Cisco UCS Manager, the only option is to use its out-of-band management access interface.

3.   C. **Explanation:** The host firmware packages allow Cisco UCS to abstract the firmware levels of blade servers and their components. You can create a host firmware package consisting of multiple firmware levels for those components and attach it to a Cisco UCS service profile or template. When a Cisco UCS service profile is disassociated and associated with another server, it ensures that the same firmware levels are also enforced.

4.   B. **Explanation:** There are three main bundles of firmware for Cisco UCS (Infrastructure, B-Series, and C-Series bundles). Since the release of Cisco UCS Manager version 2.1, Cisco UCS supports running different versions of infrastructure and server-level firmware. This allows you to run one version for all infrastructure components (UCSM, FIs, IOMs) and another for server-level components (BIOS, CIMC, Adaptor).

5.   A. **Explanation:** Different types of backups are available on the Cisco UCS Manager. These backup types exist to protect the various states of the Cisco UCS Manager configuration and allow full bare metal restoration needs. The available backup types are logical, system, all configurations, and a full state backup.

6.   B. **Explanation:** Only the full state backup file, which is a binary file that includes a snapshot of the entire system, can be used to restore a new Cisco UCS Fabric Interconnect during a disaster recovery situation. This file can restore or rebuild the configuration of the original fabric interconnect, or re-create it.

7.   A. **Explanation:** In the Cisco UCS Manager you can suppress SNMP traps and faults and call home notifications due to planned maintenance activities, if necessary. You can also utilize fault suppression policies to suppress transient faults.

8.   A. **Explanation:** They are a set of policies that can be used to determine the collection interval of statistics from adapter, chassis, host (future use), port, and server, and the threshold policy is utilized to set upper or lower limits, in the event that this threshold is true. Accordingly notifications can be sent to the operations and support teams.

9.   C. **Explanation:** The goUCS enables the ability to perform the action in the UCSM GUI manually, use goUCS to filter the Java log file from the UCSM GUI for the exact XML method that the UCSM GUI used, and then provide a mechanism to replace the unique data in the XML document with variables enabling the UCS admin to reuse the XML code over and over programmatically.

10. **D. Explanation:** Cisco UCS XML API consists of a set of well-documented APIs that can be used to interact with Cisco UCS Manager. These XML APIs consist of four types of methods: Authentication, Query, Configuration Change, and Event Subscription. Under each of these methods, XML APIs can be used to perform various operations mimicking all Cisco UCS Manager GUI-based operations.

11. **B. Explanation:** Cisco UCS Manager supports SNMP v1, v2, and v3. Cisco UCS Manager generates SNMP notifications as traps or informs. The SNMP MIBs can only be accessed read-only. SNMP can be configured from the Cisco UCS admin tab, under communication services.

Chapter 11

1. **A and C. Explanation:** Hypervisor is a shim layer of software installed on top of a bare metal server. It allows access to physical server resources in a shared manner, and it operates at Ring level 0 or -1 depending on the implementation. Hypervisor is also sometimes referred to as Virtual Machine Monitor. Virtual Machine Manager is often used to describe the management tool used for the virtualization environment, such as VMware vCenter or Microsoft System Center.

2. **A. Explanation:** Type 2 hypervisor is a type of hypervisor that does not run directly on top of physical server hardware; instead, it runs as an application on top of the server operating system.

3. **C. Explanation:** The link between virtualized server and the physical switch it is connected to most often leverages IEEE 802.1Q trunking technology to carry VLANs used in the virtual switching environment.

4. **C. Explanation:** Only guest operating systems approved by the server virtualization vendor are allowed to be installed inside the virtual machine powered by that vendor's server virtualization products.

5. **A. Explanation:** With paravirtualization, the guest operating system is allowed additional communication channels with the underlying hypervisor to make better use of the physical server hardware. The guest operating system must be modified to be compatible with paravirtualization.

6. **B. Explanation:** With the operating system virtualization technique, all virtual machines rely on the same shared host operating system kernel, which does not allow running different flavors of the guest operating system. In other words, you cannot run Linux and Microsoft Windows on the same server leveraging the operating system virtualization model.

7. **D. Explanation:** Virtual machine mobility events can be triggered automatically or manually. The automatic trigger can be failure of the physical host where the virtual machine resides, shortage of physical resources where the virtual machine resides, and so on. Administrators can also manually trigger virtual machine mobility events.

8. **A.** The virtual machine retains its TCP/IP settings across the mobility events, so it anticipates to be placed in the same IP subnet as it moves from source to destination host. To accommodate such requirements, Layer 2 connectivity (VLAN), which is mapped to the subnet where the virtual machine's IP address resides, must be stretched between source and destination hosts.

9. B. **Explanation:** Traditional data center POD architecture creates discontiguous Layer 2 domains, which limit virtual machine mobility domain and have an adverse effect on overall server virtualization efficiency.

10. B. **Explanation:** Traffic between two virtual machines residing on the same physical server and belonging to the same Layer 2 domain does not pass through the physical network; therefore, the physical network cannot provide security for this type of traffic.

Chapter 12

1. A and B. **Explanation:** APIs have four primary components: methods, actions, objects, and formats.

2. A and B. **Explanation:** The payload must be human readable. The payload must be text based for ease of revision control. Transactions must follow ACID rules: they must be atomic, consistent, independent, and durable.

3. A, B, and D. **Explanation:** SDN is decoupling of the control plane and the data plane. In SDN architecture, network intelligence is centralized in a controller. The programmable control APIs are exposed in the SDN environment.

4. A, B, and D. **Explanation:** The core components of OpenFlow are Controller, OpenFlow Agent, Northbound APIs, and OpenFlow Protocol.

5. A, B, and C. **Explanation:** Some common use cases for SDN beyond general cloud, data center, and IT automation include DevOps, Big Data and Everything-as-a-Service, Mobility apps, and the Internet of Things (IoT).

6. A, B, and C. **Explanation:** A group-based policy offers a number of advantages: an easier, application-focused way of expressing policy, improved automation, consistency, and an extensible policy model.

7. A, B, and C. **Explanation:** Following are the main benefits of Cisco ACI:

   - Simplified automation with an application-based policy model
   - Common platform for managing physical, virtual, and cloud-based environments
   - Centralized visibility with real-time application health monitoring
   - Operation simplicity, with common policy, management, and operation models across application, network, and security resources (and computing and storage resources in the future)
   - Open software flexibility for development and operations (DevOps) teams and ecosystem partner integration
   - Scalable performance and secure multitenancy

8. A, B, and D. **Explanation:** Cisco ACI consists of Cisco APIC, Cisco Nexus 9000 Series switches and Cisco ACI Ecosystem, and Cisco AVS.

9. B. **Explanation:** It is based on the declarative management model.

10. A, B, and D. **Explanation:** There are different tools to access the APIC, such as GUI, CLI on Cisco APIC, POSTMAN, Python scripts, PHP, advanced orchestration tools like OpenStack, CIAC, and Cisco UCS Director.

11. A, C, and E. **Explanation:** VXLAN provides greater scalability in the number of Layer 2 segments that are supported. VXLAN uses MAC-in-UDP. Cisco ACI uses VXLAN in ACI Fabric.

12. A, B, and C. **Explanation:** The administrator can statically program the identity-to-location mapping. Dynamic Host Configuration Protocol (DHCP) packets can be used to learn identity-to-location mapping. Learning can occur through Address Resolution Protocol (ARP), Gratuitous ARP (GARP), and Reverse ARP (RARP) traffic. The CPU on the leaf switch, upon receiving a copy of the ARP, GARP, or RARP packet, updates its local mapping cache with a static entry for this host and informs the centralized mapping database of the update for the host address through the Council of Oracles Protocol (COOP).

13. A, B, and C. **Explanation:** Four spine switches are available at the time of writing this book. These switches are Cisco Nexus 9516, Nexus 9508, Nexus 9504, and Nexus 9336PQ.

14. A and B. **Explanation:** LLDP and DHCP are the two protocols that are used in ACI Fabric discovery.

Chapter 13

1. A and B. **Explanation:** ACI is revolutionizing this process by introducing the ability to create an application network profile, a configuration template to express relationships between compute segments. In ACI, devices autonomously update the state of the network depending on the configured policy requirements. ACI works with the declarative model.

2. A, B, and C. **Explanation:** Classes, types, and methods are included in the Cisco APIC API model.

3. B. **Explanation:** Visore is the object browser that is used for querying the tree for classes or objects for the Cisco APIC.

4. A, D, and E. **Explanation:** Each node in the management information tree (MIT) represents a MO. When any MO is created because of a user-initiated action, an event is generated. In an API operation to create a specific MO, the resource path consists of /mo/ followed by the DN of the MO.

5. A, B, and C. **Explanation:** The logical model, the resolved model, and the concrete model are the three stages that are implemented in the ACI object model.

6. A, B, and C. **Explanation:** A tenant is a folder for application policies. A context is a representation of a private Layer 3 namespace or a Layer 3 network. A tenant can contain one or more virtual routing and forwarding contexts.

7. A, B, and C. **Explanation:** EPGs act as a container for a collection of applications. EPGs are fully decoupled from the physical and logical topology. Endpoint membership in an EPG can be dynamic or static.

Appendix A: Answers to the "Do I Know This Already?" Quizzes   691

A

8. A, B, and D. **Explanation:** The ACI fabric application EPGs that are located in intra-tenant and inter-tenant can communicate to each other. The ACI fabric application EPGs and Layer 2 external outside network instance EPGs can communicate to each other. The ACI fabric application EPGs and Layer 3 external outside network instance EPGs can also communicate.

9. A and C. **Explanation:** An application profile is a convenient logical container for grouping EPGs. An application profile is an expression of the logical model.

10. A and B. **Explanation:** The ACI policy model allows for both unidirectional and bidirectional policies. The application policy model defines application requirements.

11. B, C, and E. **Explanation:** In the ACI logical model, one or more subjects within a contract may use filters. Labels can be applied to a variety of provider and consumer-managed objects. A unidirectional filter is used in one direction.

Chapter 14

1. A and B . **Explanation:** ACI uses several technologies to deliver telemetry for ACI fabric:

   - Atomic counters
   - Latency metrics
   - Health scores and health monitoring

2. A and B. **Explanation:** Tenant atomic counters can provide application-specific counters for traffic across the fabric, including drops, admits, and excess packets.

3. A, B, and C. **Explanation:** ACI fabric health information is available for the following systems: System, Pod, Tenant, and Managed Object.

4. A, B, and C. **Explanation:** The different stages of the fault life cycle are soaking, soaking-clearing, raised, raised-clearing, and retaining.

5. A, B, and D. **Explanation:** These meaningful services follow:

   - Traffic optimization that improves application performance
   - Telemetry services that go beyond classic port counters
   - Overall health monitoring for what constitutes an application
   - Applying security rules embedded with forwarding

6. C. **Explanation:** The Cisco AVS supports two modes of traffic forwarding: Local Switching mode, formerly known as FEX disable mode, and No Local Switching mode, formerly known as FEX enable mode.

7. A, B, and C. **Explanation:** The main characteristics of SCVMM follow:

   - Policy management through APIC
   - Software/license: Windows Server with HyperV, SCVMM
   - VM discovery: OpFlex
   - Encapsulation: VLAN
   - Plug-in installation: Manual

8. D. **Explanation:** Block Storage (Cinder) provides storage volumes for compute.

9. A, B, C, and D. **Explanation:** A device package is a zip file that contains the following parts:

    ■ Device specification

    ■ Device script

    ■ Function profile

    ■ Device-level configuration parameters

10. A, B, and C. **Explanation:** Cisco ACI Microsegmentation works across VMware, Microsoft, and OpenStack virtual machines, bare metal servers, and containers.

Chapter 15

1. A and C. **Explanation:** According to NIST, the formal definition of cloud computing is a "model for enabling ubiquitous, convenient, on-demand network access to a shared pool of configurable computing resources (such as networks, servers, storage, applications, and services) that can be rapidly provisioned and released with minimal management effort or service provider interaction." Three main service models are infrastructure as a service (IaaS), platform as a service (PaaS), and software as a service (SaaS).

2. A, B, and D. **Explanation:** There **are** several key characteristics of the cloud computing environment: self-service portal, ubiquitous access, resource elasticity, resource pooling, and pay-per-use.

3. A, B, and C. **Explanation:** Three primary service models are available in a cloud computing environment. These are infrastructure as a service (IaaS), platform as a service (PaaS), and software as a service (SaaS). Generally speaking, cloud computing philosophy allows delivering anything as a service.

4. B. **Explanation:** False. Virtualization is one of the elements **that** can be leveraged to build cloud computing environments. It is not a mandatory element.

5. A, B, and D. **Explanation:** There are many examples of network virtualization, such as VLANs, VRFs, MPLS VPNs, IPsec VPNs, OTV, LISP, NV-GRE, and VXLAN.

6. A, B, C, and D. **Explanation:** Public, private, hybrid, and community are the deployment models of a cloud computing environment.

7. B. **Explanation:** Hybrid cloud philosophy advocates the ability to leverage both private and public cloud resources to complete computational (and other) tasks. With a hybrid cloud, private cloud workloads can "burst" to the public cloud based on resource availability or administrative action.

8. A and D. **Explanation:** An application programming interface (API) is a set of instructions, routines, protocols, and tools leveraged to build applications. APIs define how different software elements can interact with each other through a series of calls.

9. B. **Explanation:** False. Web APIs do indeed leverage HTTP or HTTPS; however, there are other types of interfaces **that** do not, **including** JAVA APIs.

10. A and B. **Explanation:** XML and JSON define data formatting.

Chapter 16

1. A, B, C, and D. **Explanation:** The key benefits of UCS Director are faster service delivery, cost savings, business agility and operational efficiency, ease of use, improved service quality, improved security, and multivendor support.

2. B. **Explanation:** The adaptive provisioning feature of UCS Director provides a real-time available capacity, internal policies, and application workload requirements to optimize the availability of your resources.

3. A, C, and D. **Explanation:** UCS Director unified management feature provides a single interface for the administrator to monitor, provision, and manage IT resources. The life cycle management feature of UCS Director provides control over VM actions. UCS Director also supports northbound XML and REST API.

4. A, C, and D. **Explanation:** UCS Director supports multiple hypervisors, such as VMware vSphere, Microsoft Hyper-V, and Red Hat KVM hypervisors.

5. A and C. **Explanation:** Sites are used to logically group the pods. You can create sites based on geographical location, administrative domain, department, and customer. Creation of a site is optional in UCS Director.

6. C. **Explanation:** A pod is a logical structure in UCS Director where resources are placed. You can create a pod to represent a single converged infrastructure such as FlexPod and vBlock, a specific customer or tenant, and an environment such as development, testing, and production.

7. A, C, and D. **Explanation:** UCS Director supports the following virtual accounts: VMware vSphere, Microsoft Hyper-V, RedHat KVM, Rackspace Cloud, and Amazon Web Services EC2.

8. A, C, and D. **Explanation:** UCS Director supports the following physical accounts: UCS Manager, HP OA, HP iLO, NetApp On Command, NetApp OnTAP, EMC VNX, EMC VNXe, and EMC VMAX.

9. A. **Explanation:** A multidomain manager account is a physical account that represents a software application that can manage more than one domain. Examples of multidomain managers are UCS Central, Prime Data Center Network Manager (DCNM), Application Policy Infrastructure Controller (APIC), EMC Recovery Point, and EMC VPLEX.

10. B. **Explanation:** UCS Director supports multitenancy by using the service provider feature. If this feature is enabled, you can create managed service provider (MSP) organizations and suborganizations.

11. A, B, and D. **Explanation:** UCS Director multitenancy features include delegated administration, portal branding, resource allocation, cost model reporting.

12. B and D. **Explanation:** UCS Director chargeback supports two cost models. The Standard Cost model defines cost in a linear format. The Advanced Cost Model defines cost in a nonlinear format.

13. A. **Explanation:** A UCS Director service offering defines the resources needed to provision an application.

14. A and D. **Explanation:** In a service offering, you can specify the usage of resource groups as shared among the application or tenants or dedicated to a single application or tenant.

15. B and C. **Explanation:** There are many benefits of using UCS Director in data center. Some of these benefits are a faster service delivery, cost savings, business agility, operational efficiency, ease of use, improved service quality, improved security, and multivendor support.

Chapter 17

1. B. **Explanation:** Cloud orchestration can use multiple lower level automation tasks to deliver a resource or set of resources "as a service." Cloud orchestration works across physical and virtual resources. It can deliver services such as IaaS, PaaS, and SaaS in any deployment model of cloud.

2. C. **Explanation:** The cloud management platform (CMP) is software that delivers cloud orchestration in the data center.

3. A. **Explanation:** The cloud management platform includes the following layers: Portal, API, Service Management, Orchestration, and Resource Management.

4. A, B, and D. **Explanation:** The Orchestration layer of the CMP is used for automating and standardizing service delivery management, virtual infrastructure administration, virtual infrastructure operations, workload automation, disaster recovery automation, and infrastructure management.

5. D. **Explanation:** A task is a specific action or operation performed by the UCS Director orchestrator. It is the smallest unit of work that UCS Director can perform.

6. B. **Explanation:** Task input and output are stored in variables. A task can have any number of input and output variables.

7. C. **Explanation:** Workflow defines the sequence of tasks that are required to fulfill a user request. The UCS Director workflow is built using a series of automation tasks linked to perform a complex IT operation. The workflow determines the order in which the tasks are executed.

8. A, C, and D. **Explanation:** A service request can have one of the following states depending on its execution status: Scheduled, Running, Blocked, Completed, or Failed.

9. A. **Explanation:** A task that represents a workflow is called a compound task. You can save a workflow as a task and use it in another workflow.

10. A, C, and D. **Explanation:** When you create a new workflow, the following tasks are populated automatically in workflow designer: Start Task, Completed (Success), and Completed (Failure).

Memory Tables

Chapter 1

Table 1-2   Port Channel Modes

Port Channel Mode	Description
	This mode represents a static port channel configuration. In this mode, member ports join the port channel without exchanging information with the peer switch. This mode also means that LACP is not running.
	LACP is enabled, and LACP packets are sent on the port. This mode puts the port into an active negotiating state in which the port initiates negotiations with the peer switch by sending LACP packets.
	LACP is enabled, but LACP packets are not initiated. This mode puts the port into a passive negotiating state in which the port responds to LACP packets that it receives but does not initiate LACP negotiation.

Chapter 4

Table 4-2   Network Visibility and Configuration Comparison

Features	Physical Network	Virtual Network
Network visibility		
Port configuration		
Network configuration		
Security policies		

Table 4-3   Administrator Tasks Before and After Cisco Nexus 1000V Series Switch

Tasks	VMware Administrator Before	VMware Administrator After	Network Administrator Before	Network Administrator After
vSwitch config				
Port group config				
Add ESX host				
NIC teaming config				

Tasks	VMware Administrator Before	VMware Administrator After	Network Administrator Before	Network Administrator After
Virtual machine creation				
Security				
VM visibility				
Management				

Chapter 7

Table 7-4   Cisco UCS Fabric Interconnects

	First Generation		Second Generation		*Third Generation	
Item	Cisco UCS 6120XP	Cisco UCS 6140XP	Cisco UCS 6248UP	Cisco UCS 6296UP	Cisco UCS 6332	Cisco UCS 6332-16UP
Description	20-Port Fabric Interconnect	40-Port Fabric Interconnect	48-Port Fabric Interconnect	96-Port Fabric Interconnect	32-Port Fabric Interconnect	40-Port Fabric Interconnect with Unified Ports
Form Factor	1 RU	2 RU	1 RU	2 RU	1RU	1RU
Number of Fixed 40 GB Interfaces					32	24
Number of Fixed 10 GB Interfaces						
Number of 1 GB/10 GB Interfaces (Depending on SFP Module Installed)	Ports 1–8	Ports 1–16	—	—	—	Ports 1–16
Unified Ports (1 GB/10 GB, 8 Gb/s FC, FCoE)	No	No				
Throughput	520 Gbps	1.04 Tbps	960 Gbps	1920 Gbps	2.56 Tbps	2.43 Tbps

	First Generation		Second Generation		*Third Generation	
Compatibility with all IOMs						
Expansion Slots						
Fan Modules	2	5	2	5	4	4
Power Supplies	2 (AC only)	2 (AC only)	2 (AC/DC available)	2 (AC/DC available)	2	2

Table 7-5   Cisco UCS Fabric Interconnect—Expansion Modules

Description	Cisco UCS 6120XP	Cisco UCS 6140XP	Cisco UCS 6248UP	Cisco UCS 6296UP
16-Port Unified Expansion Module				
8-Port 1, 2, 4 Gbps Fibre Channel (FC)				
6-Port 1, 2, 4, or 8 Gbps Fibre Channel (FC)				
6-Port 10 GE				
4-Port 10 GE/4-Port Fibre Channel				

Table 7-6   Cisco UCS I/O Module Details

Description	Cisco UCS 2104 IOM	Cisco UCS 2204 IOM	Cisco UCS 2208 IOM	Cisco UCS 2304 IOM
Fabric Interconnect facing ports (Fabric Ports)	4	4	8	4
Fabric Interconnect facing bandwidth	40	40	80	160
Port channeling fabric ports	No	Yes	Yes	Yes
Host/blade facing ports/per IOM	8	32	32	8
Host/blade facing bandwidth/per IOM				
Compatibility with different generation fabric interconnects				
Max bandwidth per blade (per I/O module)				

Table 7-7   Cisco UCS B-Series Blade Server Products

Description	B22 M3	B200 M3	B230 M2	B260 M4	B420 M3	B420 M4	B460 M4	B200 M4
Width	Half	Half	Half	Half	Half	Half	Half	Half
Processor Sockets	Up to 2	Up to 2	Up to 2	Up to 2	2 or 4	2 or 4	2 or 4	Up to 2
Processors Supported	E5-2400	E5-2600 (Sandy Bridge), E5-2600 v2 (Ivy Bridge)	E7-2800, E7-8800	E5-2800 v2 / E7-4800 v2 / E7-8800 v2	E5-4600 v2	E5-4600 v3	E7-4800 v2 / E7-8800 v2	E2600 v3
Memory Capacity								
Extended Memory Technology								
Memory DIMM Sizes	4, 8, 16, 32 GB DIMMS	4, 8, 16, 32 GB DIMMS	4, 8, 16 GB DIMMS	8, 16, 32 GB DIMMS	4, 8, 16, 32 GB DIMMS	8, 16, 32, 64 GB DIMMS	8, 16, 32 GB DIMMS	8, 16, 32 GB DIMMS (DDR4)
Internal Disk Drives	Max 2 (SATA, SAS)	Max 2 (SATA, SAS)	Max 2 (SATA)	Max 2 (SAS, SATA)	Max 4 (SAS, SATA)	Max 4 (SAS, SATA)	Max 4 (SAS, SATA)	Max 2 (SAS, SATA,)
Maximum Internal Storage (Raw)	2 TB	2 TB	800 GB	2.4 TB	4 TB	6.4 TB	4.8 TB	3.2 TB
Integrated RAID Controller	0,1	0,1	0,1	0,1	0,1,10, 5	0,1,10, 5, 6,50,60	0,1	0,1
I/O Throughput								

Table 7-8   Cisco UCS Blade Server Populating DRAM

Description	Best Practice
B22 M3	
B200 M3, M4	
B230 M2	
B260 M4	

Description	Best Practice
B420 M3, M4	
B460 M4	

Table 7-10   Cisco UCS Virtual Interface Cards

Description	Cisco UCS Virtual Interface Card 1240	Cisco UCS Virtual Interface Card 1280	Cisco UCS Virtual Interface Card 1340	Cisco UCS Virtual Interface Card 1380	Cisco UCS M81KR Virtual Interface Card (Palo)
Port Interface Speeds	10 GbE	10 GbE	10–40 GbE	10–40 GbE	10 GbE
Total Virtual Interfaces					
Interface Type	Dynamic	Dynamic	Dynamic	Dynamic	Dynamic
Ethernet Interfaces	0–256	0–256	0–256+	0–256+	0–128
FC Interfaces	0–256	0–256	0–256+	0–256+	0–128
Virtual Machine Fabric Extender	VM-FEX or Cisco Adapter FEX	VM-FEX or Cisco Adapter FEX	VM-FEX		VM-FEX or Cisco Adapter FEX
Compatibility					
Interface Fabric Failover Support	Hardware, no driver needed	Hardware, no driver needed	Hardware, no driver needed	Hardware, no driver needed	Hardware, no driver needed
RoCE, NVGRE, VXLAN Offload, Netflow Support	No	No	Yes	Yes	No

Table 7-13 Cisco UCS C-Series Rackmount Server Populating DRAM

Description	C22 M3	C24 M3	C220 M3	C240 M3	C260 M2	C420 M3	C460 M2	C460 M4	C220 M4	C240 M4
Best Practice										

Table 7-14 Common RAID Configurations

RAID Level	RAID 0 (Stripe)	RAID 1 (Mirror)	RAID 5, Distributed Parity	RAID 6, Dual Distributed Parity	RAID 1+0	RAID 0+1	RAID 5+0	RAID 6+0
Minimum Disks						4		
Redundancy	No	Yes		Yes		Yes		Yes
Parity						No		
Performance (Read/ Write)	Excellent	Good		Good writes Excellent for read-intensive operations		Excellent		Excellent
Popular Use	Noncritical data	Critical data		Critical data		Critical data Slightly less fault tolerant		Critical data

Table 7-22 Cisco UCS 2100XP and 2200UP Series IOM Discrete-Mode Connectivity Ratios

Device	Blade Pinning	Based on Cisco UCS 2104XP	*Based on Cisco UCS 2204XP	*Based on Cisco UCS 2208XP with VIC 1280	*Based on Cisco UCS 2208XP with VIC 1240	Cisco UCS 2304
I/O Module Mode	Discrete	Discrete	Discrete	Discrete	Discrete	Discrete
I/O Module Links	Blade slot to FEX link pinning	Over-subscription	Over-subscription	Over-subscription	Over-subscription	Over-subscription

Device	Blade Pinning	Based on Cisco UCS 2104XP	*Based on Cisco UCS 2204XP	*Based on Cisco UCS 2208XP with VIC 1280	*Based on Cisco UCS 2208XP with VIC 1240	Cisco UCS 2304
	Blade slot (1–8)		16:1		16:1	
	Blade slot (1, 3, 5, 7), (2, 4, 6, 8)		8:1		8:1	
	Blade slot (1, 5), (2, 6), (3, 7), (4, 8)		1:1		4:1	
	Blade slots (1–8)		—		2:1	

Chapter 9

Table 9-2   Cisco UCS Identity Pools and Their Advantages

The Challenge	With Identity Pools	Without Identity Pools
Managing virtual identities	Consumed and associated, if resources are available, or waits	Must manually assign, reassign, and manage identities
Templates		
Cloning		

Chapter 12

Table 12-2   Comparison of REST, NETCONF, and SNMP

	REST	NETCONF	SNMP
Transport			
Payload formatting			BER
Schema			
Identification of resources	URLs	Paths	OIDs

Table 12-3 Cisco Solutions

Category	Use Case	Cisco Solution
Data Center		Cisco ACI
Data Center	Overlay Automation	
Data Center, Campus, and WAN		OpenDaylight Version Supported by Cisco
Campus, Branch, and WAN	WAN and LAN Automation	

Chapter 14

Table 14-2 A Device Package Is a Zip File That Contains the Following Parts

Device specification	An XML file that defines the following properties:
	Device properties:
	■ **Model:** Model of the device.
	■ **Vendor:** Vendor of the device.
	■ **Version:** Software version of the device.
	Functions provided by a device, such as load balancing, content switching, and SSL termination.
	Interfaces and network connectivity information for each function.
	Device configuration parameters.
	Configuration parameters for each function.
Device script	
Function profile	
Device-level configuration parameters	

Chapter 16

Table 16-2   Features and Functions of UCSD

Features and Functions of UCSD	Description
	UCSD provides a single interface for the administrators to monitor, provision, and manage the IT infrastructure across physical, virtual, and bare-metal environments. With UCSD, there is no need to log into multiple IT tools and switch between the tools to perform day-to-day tasks. There are several benefits of this approach, including ease of use, increased productivity, and centralized policy-based infrastructure provisioning for consistent results.
	Administrators, using predefined policies and governance practices, publish catalog items for each IT service. Users deploy new infrastructure instances by logging into UCSD and ordering the service.
	Provides a real-time available capability, internal policies, and application workload requirements to optimize the availability of your resources.
	UCSD continuously monitors all resources in real time and provides visibility to the infrastructure consumption to improve capacity planning and management of these resources. UCSD also identifies the underutilized and overutilized resources.
	UCSD has many out-of-the-box reporting capabilities, such as unified dashboards, infrastructure assessment reports, resource utilization reports, trend monitoring, and heat maps. These reports help administrators reduce troubleshooting time and identify performance bottlenecks. You can also create your own reports using the report builder module.
	UCSD offers the ability to manage network, compute, and storage resources for multiple tenants. In multitenant configuration, infrastructure resources can be allocated to the tenant, where each tenant can only manage his own resources.
	UCSD supports VMware ESXi, Microsoft Hyper-V, and Red Hat KVM hypervisors.
	UCSD monitors, manages, and provisions physical, virtual, and bare-metal servers and blades from Cisco and other vendors.
	UCSD provides policy-based provisioning of physical and virtual switches and dynamic network topologies. It allows administrators to configure VLANs, virtual network interface cards (vNICs), port groups and port profiles, IP and Dynamic Host Control Protocol (DHCP) allocation, and access control lists (ACLs) across network devices.
	Provides policy-based provisioning and management of filers, virtual filers (vFilers), logical unit numbers (LUNs), and volumes.
	UCSD supports converged infrastructure solutions, including NetApp FlexPod and FlexPod Express, EMC VSPEX, EMC VPLEX, and VCE Vblock. It also supports hyper converged storage with Cisco VSAN ready node and VMware VSAN.

B

Features and Functions of UCSD	Description
	UCSD provides a library of common tasks to manage the network, storage, and compute infrastructure that spans Cisco and third-party hardware solutions. These libraries help you build your infrastructure in minutes.
	UCSD replaces time-consuming manual provisioning and deprovisioning of data center resources with automated workflows. You can use built-in product capabilities or write your own custom workflows to automate and orchestrate infrastructure. These orchestration capabilities improve consistency, efficiency, and speed of IT operation within your organization.
	Cisco VACS is a complete infrastructure solution with preconfigured and integrated virtual services, switching, and workflow automation tools. It streamlines infrastructure policy definitions, integration, and deployment. Cisco VACS accelerates the application deployment process with compliant containers, or logical network and services descriptions, that work immediately after installation.
	Supports ACI provisioning, management, and monitoring. Service graph creating, EPG creation, contracts, and other policies.
	Delivers VDC and application containers to the tenants with their own virtual firewall, virtual load-balancer, and virtual machines.
	UCSD supports complete lifecycle management of virtual machines, such as virtual machine (VM) power management, VM resizing, VM snapshot management, and other VM actions.
	Easy extensibility of platform using SDK.
	You can define billing and chargeback policies to the resources.
	UCSD has an open XML API and a REST API that can be used to assess the capabilities of UCSD with higher-level management platforms.

Memory Tables Answer Key

Chapter 1

Table 1-2 Port Channel Modes

Port Channel Mode	Description
On	This mode represents a static port channel configuration. In this mode, member ports join the port channel without exchanging information with the peer switch. This mode also means that LACP is not running.
Active	LACP is enabled, and LACP packets are sent on the port. This mode puts the port into an active negotiating state in which the port initiates negotiations with the peer switch by sending LACP packets.
Passive	LACP is enabled, but LACP packets are not initiated. This mode puts the port into a passive negotiating state in which the port responds to LACP packets that it receives but does not initiate LACP negotiation.

Chapter 4

Table 4-2 Network Visibility and Configuration Comparison

Features	Physical Network	Virtual Network
Network visibility	Individual server	Physical server
Port configuration	Individual server	Physical server
Network configuration	Network administrator	VM and network administrator
Security policies	Individual server	Physical server

Table 4-3 Administrator Tasks Before and After Cisco Nexus 1000V Series Switch

Tasks	VMware Administrator Before	VMware Administrator After	Network Administrator Before	Network Administrator After
vSwitch config	Per ESX host	Automated	—	Same as physical network
Port group config	Per ESX host	Automated	—	Policy-based

Tasks	VMware Administrator Before	VMware Administrator After	Network Administrator Before	Network Administrator After
Add ESX host	vCenter-based	vCenter-based	—	—
NIC teaming config	Per vSwitch	Automated	—	Port channel optimized
Virtual machine creation	vCenter-based	vCenter-based	—	—
Security	—	Policy-based	—	ACL, PVLAN, port security, TrustSec
VM visibility	vCenter	VM-specific	—	VM-specific
Management	vCenter	vCenter-based	—	Cisco CLI, XML API, SNMP, DCNM

Chapter 7

Table 7-4 Cisco UCS Fabric Interconnects

	First Generation		Second Generation		*Third Generation	
Item	Cisco UCS 6120XP	Cisco UCS 6140XP	Cisco UCS 6248UP	Cisco UCS 6296UP	Cisco UCS 6332	Cisco UCS 6332-16UP
Description	20-Port Fabric Interconnect	40-Port Fabric Interconnect	48-Port Fabric Interconnect	96-Port Fabric Interconnect	32-Port Fabric Interconnect	40-Port Fabric Interconnect with Unified Ports
Form Factor	1 RU	2 RU	1 RU	2 RU	1RU	1RU
Number of Fixed 40 GB Interfaces					32	24
Number of Fixed 10 GB Interfaces	20	40	32	48	96 + 2 (Using breakout cables + QSA module)	72 + 16 (Using breakout cables)

	First Generation		Second Generation		*Third Generation	
Number of 1 GB/10 GB Interfaces (Depending on SFP Module Installed)	Ports 1–8	Ports 1–16	—	—	—	Ports 1–16
Unified Ports (1 GB/10 GB, 8 Gb/s FC, FCoE)	No	No	All	All	—	1–16
Throughput	520 Gbps	1.04 Tbps	960 Gbps	1920 Gbps	2.56 Tbps	2.43 Tbps
Compatibility with all IOMs	First Generation only	First Generation only	All	All	Second and Third Generation	Second and Third Generation
Expansion Slots	1	2	1 (16 port)	3 (16 port)	—	—
Fan Modules	2	5	2	5	4	4
Power Supplies	2 (AC only)	2 (AC only)	2 (AC/DC available)	2 (AC/DC available)	2	2

Table 7-5   Cisco UCS Fabric Interconnect—Expansion Modules

Description	Cisco UCS 6120XP	Cisco UCS 6140XP	Cisco UCS 6248UP	Cisco UCS 6296UP
16-Port Unified Expansion Module	No	No	Yes	Yes
8-Port 1, 2, 4 Gbps Fibre Channel (FC)	Yes	Yes	—	—
6-Port 1, 2, 4, or 8 Gbps Fibre Channel (FC)	Yes	Yes	—	—
6-Port 10 GE	Yes	Yes	—	—
4-Port 10 GE/4-Port Fibre Channel	Yes	Yes	—	—

Table 7-6 Cisco UCS I/O Module Details

Description	Cisco UCS 2104 IOM	Cisco UCS 2204 IOM	Cisco UCS 2208 IOM	Cisco UCS 2304 IOM
Fabric Interconnect facing ports (Fabric Ports)	4	4	8	4
Fabric Interconnect facing bandwidth	40	40	80	160
Port channeling fabric ports	No	Yes	Yes	Yes
Host/blade facing ports/per IOM	8	32	32	8
Host/blade facing bandwidth/per IOM	80G	160G	320G	320G
Compatibility with different generation fabric interconnects	No	Yes	Yes	No
Max bandwidth per blade (per I/O module)	5G	40G	80G	40G

Table 7-7 Cisco UCS B-Series Blade Server Products

Description	B22 M3	B200 M3	B230 M2	B260 M4	B420 M3	B420 M4	B460 M4	B200 M4
Width	Half	Half	Half	Half	Half	Half	Half	Half
Processor Sockets	Up to 2	Up to 2	Up to 2	Up to 2	2 or 4	2 or 4	2 or 4	Up to 2
Processors Supported	E5-2400	E5-2600 (Sandy Bridge), E5-2600 v2 (Ivy Bridge)	E7-2800, E7-8800	E5-2800 v2 / E7-4800 v2 / E7-8800 v2	E5-4600 v2	E5-4600 v3	E7-4800 v2 / E7-8800 v2	E2600 v3

Description	B22 M3	B200 M3	B230 M2	B260 M4	B420 M3	B420 M4	B460 M4	B200 M4
Memory Capacity	Up to 384 GB (12 slots)	Up to 768 GB (24 slots)	Up to 512 GB (32 slots)	Up to 3 TB (48 slots)	Up to 1.5 TB (48 slots)	Up to 3 TB (48 slots)	Up to 6 TB (96 slots)	Up to 768 GB (24 slots)
Extended Memory Technology	No	No	Yes	Yes	No	No	Yes	No
Memory DIMM Sizes	4, 8, 16, 32 GB DIMMS	4, 8, 16, 32 GB DIMMS	4, 8, 16 GB DIMMS	8, 16, 32 GB DIMMS	4, 8, 16, 32 GB DIMMS	8, 16, 32, 64 GB DIMMS	8, 16, 32 GB DIMMS	8, 16, 32 GB DIMMS (DDR4)
Internal Disk Drives	Max 2 (SATA, SAS)	Max 2 (SATA, SAS)	Max 2 (SATA)	Max 2 (SAS, SATA)	Max 4 (SAS, SATA)	Max 4 (SAS, SATA)	Max 4 (SAS, SATA)	Max 2 (SAS, SATA)
Maximum Internal Storage (Raw)	2 TB	2 TB	800 GB	2.4 TB	4 TB	6.4 TB	4.8 TB	3.2 TB
Integrated RAID Controller	0,1	0,1	0,1	0,1	0,1,10, 5	0,1,10, 5, 6,50,60	0,1	0,1
I/O Throughput	Up to 80 Gbps	Up to 80 Gbps	Up to 80 Gbps	Up to 160 Gbps	Up to 160 Gbps	Up to 160 Gbps	Up to 160 Gbps	Up to 80 Gbps

Table 7-8   Cisco UCS Blade Server Populating DRAM

Description	Best Practice
B22 M3	1DPC or 2DPC
B200 M3, M4	2DPC
B230 M2	2DPC
B260 M4	2DPC
B420 M3, M4	2DPC
B460 M4	2DPC

Table 7-10 Cisco UCS Virtual Interface Cards

Description	Cisco UCS Virtual Interface Card 1240	Cisco UCS Virtual Interface Card 1280	Cisco UCS Virtual Interface Card 1340	Cisco UCS Virtual Interface Card 1380	Cisco UCS M81KR Virtual Interface Card (Palo)
Port Interface Speeds	10 GbE	10 GbE	10–40 GbE	10–40 GbE	10 GbE
Total Virtual Interfaces	256	256	256 and above	256 and above	128
Interface Type	Dynamic	Dynamic	Dynamic	Dynamic	Dynamic
Ethernet Interfaces	0–256	0–256	0–256+	0–256+	0–128
FC Interfaces	0–256	0–256	0–256+	0–256+	0–128
Virtual Machine Fabric Extender	VM-FEX or Cisco Adapter FEX	VM-FEX or Cisco Adapter FEX	VM-FEX		VM-FEX or Cisco Adapter FEX
Compatibility	Requires second generation UCS hardware	Requires second generation UCS hardware	Second and third generation UCS hardware Exclusive for B200 M3, M4	Second and third generation UCS hardware Exclusive for B200 M3, M4	Supports first and second generation UCS hardware
Interface Fabric Failover Support	Hardware, no driver needed	Hardware, no driver needed	Hardware, no driver needed	Hardware, no driver needed	Hardware, no driver needed
RoCE, NVGRE, VXLAN Offload, Netflow Support	No	No	Yes	Yes	No

Table 7-13 Cisco UCS C-Series Rackmount Server Populating DRAM

Description	C22 M3	C24 M3	C220 M3	C240 M3	C260 M2	C420 M3	C460 M2	C460 M4	C220 M4	C240 M4
Best Practice	1 DPC	1 DPC	1 DPC/2 DPC	1 DPC/2 DPC	2 DPC	3 DPC	2 DPC	2 DPC	2DPC	2DPC

Table 7-14   Common RAID Configurations

RAID Level	RAID 0 (Stripe)	RAID 1 (Mirror)	RAID 5, Distributed Parity	RAID 6, Dual Distributed Parity	RAID 1+0	RAID 0+1	RAID 5+0	RAID 6+0
Minimum Disks	2.	2.	3.	3.	4.	4.	6.	8.
Redundancy	No.	Yes.	Yes.	Yes.	Yes.	Yes.	Yes.	Yes.
Parity	No.	No.	Yes.	Yes.	No.	No.	Yes.	Yes.
Performance (Read/Write)	Excellent.	Good.	Good writes. Excellent for read-intensive operations.	Good writes. Excellent for read-intensive operations.	Excellent.	Excellent.	Excellent.	Excellent.
Popular Use	Noncritical data.	Critical data.	Critical data.	Critical data.	Critical data. Better fault tolerance. Best option, but needs more disks.	Critical data. Slightly less fault tolerant.	Critical data. Most cost effective.	Critical data.

Table 7-22   Cisco UCS 2100XP and 2200UP Series IOM Discrete-Mode Connectivity Ratios

Device	Blade Pinning	Based on Cisco UCS 2104XP	*Based on Cisco UCS 2204XP	*Based on Cisco UCS 2208XP with VIC 1280	*Based on Cisco UCS 2208XP with VIC 1240	Cisco UCS 2304
I/O Module Mode	Discrete	Discrete	Discrete	Discrete	Discrete	Discrete
I/O Module Links	Blade slots to FEX link pinning	Over-subscription	Over-subscription	Over-subscription	Over-subscription	Over-subscription
1	Blade slots (1–8)	8:1	16:1	32:1	16:1	8:1
2	Blade slots (1, 3, 5, 7), (2, 4, 6, 8)	4:1	8:1	16:1	8:1	4:1
4	Blade slots (1, 5), (2, 6), (3, 7), (4, 8)	2:1	1:1	8:1	4:1	2:1
8	Blade slots (1–8)	—	—	1:1	2:1	-

Chapter 9

Table 9-2   Cisco UCS Identity Pools and Their Advantages

The Challenge	With Identity Pools	Without Identity Pools
Managing virtual identities	Consumed and associated, if resources are available, or waits	Must manually assign, reassign, and manage identities
Templates	Allows greater speed and flexibility in server creation and in conjunction with updating templates; many service profiles can be updated	Must manually assign, reassign, and manage identities
Cloning	Allows greater speed and flexibility in server creation	Must manually assign, reassign, and manage identities

Chapter 12

Table 12-2   Comparison of REST, NETCONF, and SNMP

	REST	NETCONF	SNMP
Transport	HTTP/HTTPS	SSH	UDP
Payload formatting	XML, JSON	XML	BER
Schema		YANG	MIBs
Identification of resources	URLs	Paths	OIDs

Table 12-3   Cisco Solutions

Category	Use Case	Cisco Solution
Data Center	Integrated Overlay and Underlay Policy-Based Automation	Cisco ACI
Data Center	Overlay Automation	Virtual Topology System
Data Center, Campus, and WAN	OpenFlow Traffic Engineering Other Open-Source Modules	OpenDaylight Version Supported by Cisco
Campus, Branch, and WAN	WAN and LAN Automation	APIC EM

Chapter 14

Table 14-2 A Device Package Is a Zip File That Contains the Following Parts

Device specification	An XML file that defines the following properties: Device properties: ■ **Model:** Model of the device. ■ **Vendor:** Vendor of the device. ■ **Version:** Software version of the device. Functions provided by a device, such as load balancing, content switching, and SSL termination. Interfaces and network connectivity information for each function. Device configuration parameters. Configuration parameters for each function.
Device script	A Python script that performs the integration between the APIC and a device. The APIC events are mapped to function calls that are defined in the device script.
Function profile	A profile of parameters with default values that the vendor specifies. You can configure a function to use these default values.
Device-level configuration parameters	A configuration file that specifies parameters that a device requires at the device level. The configuration can be shared by one or more of the graphs that are using the device.

Chapter 16

Table 16-2 Features and Functions of UCSD

Features and Functions of UCSD	Description
Unified Management	UCSD provides a single interface for the administrators to monitor, provision, and manage the IT infrastructure across physical, virtual, and bare-metal environments. With UCSD, there is no need to log into multiple IT tools and switch between the tools to perform day-to-day tasks. There are several benefits of this approach, including ease of use, increased productivity, and centralized policy-based infrastructure provisioning for consistent results.
Self-Service Catalog	Administrators, using predefined policies and governance practices, publish catalog items for each IT service. Users deploy new infrastructure instances by logging into UCSD and ordering the service.

Features and Functions of UCSD	Description
Adaptive Provisioning	Provides a real-time available capability, internal policies, and application workload requirements to optimize the availability of your resources.
Dynamic Capacity Management	UCSD continuously monitors all resources in real time and provides visibility to the infrastructure consumption to improve capacity planning and management of these resources. UCSD also identifies the underutilized and overutilized resources.
Reporting Capabilities	UCSD has many out-of-the-box reporting capabilities, such as unified dashboards, infrastructure assessment reports, resource utilization reports, trend monitoring, and heat maps. These reports help administrators reduce troubleshooting time and identify performance bottlenecks. You can also create your own reports using the report builder module.
Multitenancy	UCSD offers the ability to manage network, compute, and storage resources for multiple tenants. In multitenant configuration, infrastructure resources can be allocated to the tenant, where each tenant can only manage his own resources.
Multiple Hypervisor Support	UCSD supports VMware ESXi, Microsoft Hyper-V, and Red Hat KVM hypervisors.
Computing Management	UCSD monitors, manages, and provisions physical, virtual, and bare-metal servers and blades from Cisco and other vendors.
Network Management	UCSD provides policy-based provisioning of physical and virtual switches and dynamic network topologies. It allows administrators to configure VLANs, virtual network interface cards (vNICs), port groups and port profiles, IP and Dynamic Host Control Protocol (DHCP) allocation, and access control lists (ACLs) across network devices.
Storage Management	Provides policy-based provisioning and management of filers, virtual filers (vFilers), logical unit numbers (LUNs), and volumes.
Converged and Hyper Converged Infrastructure Management	UCSD supports converged infrastructure solutions, including NetApp FlexPod and FlexPod Express, EMC VSPEX, EMC VPLEX, and VCE Vblock. It also supports hyper converged storage with Cisco VSAN ready node and VMware VSAN.
Out-of-Box Task Library	UCSD provides a library of common tasks to manage the network, storage, and compute infrastructure that spans Cisco and third-party hardware solutions. These libraries help you build your infrastructure in minutes.

Features and Functions of UCSD	Description
Orchestration Capabilities	UCSD replaces time-consuming manual provisioning and deprovisioning of data center resources with automated workflows. You can use built-in product capabilities or write your own custom workflows to automate and orchestrate infrastructure. These orchestration capabilities improve consistency, efficiency, and speed of IT operation within your organization.
Virtual Application Container Service (VACS)	Cisco VACS is a complete infrastructure solution with preconfigured and integrated virtual services, switching, and workflow automation tools. It streamlines infrastructure policy definitions, integration, and deployment. Cisco VACS accelerates the application deployment process with compliant containers, or logical network and services descriptions, that work immediately after installation.
Application Centric Infrastructure (ACI) Support	Supports ACI provisioning, management, and monitoring. Service graph creating, EPG creation, contracts, and other policies.
Infrastructure as a Service (IaaS)	Delivers VDC and application containers to the tenants with their own virtual firewall, virtual load-balancer, and virtual machines.
Lifecycle Management	UCSD supports complete lifecycle management of virtual machines, such as virtual machine (VM) power management, VM resizing, VM snapshot management, and other VM actions.
Extensible Platform	Easy extensibility of platform using SDK.
Billing & Charge Back	You can define billing and chargeback policies to the resources.
XML and REST API	UCSD has an open XML API and a REST API that can be used to assess the capabilities of UCSD with higher-level management platforms.

C

10BASE-2   An older 10-Mbps baseband Ethernet standard that uses a relatively thick coaxial cable that runs to each device, without the need for a networking device. Also known as thicknet.

10BASE-T   The 10-Mbps baseband Ethernet specification using two pairs of twisted-pair cabling (Categories 3, 4, or 5): One pair transmits data and the other receives data. 10BASE-T, which is part of the IEEE 802.3 specification, has a distance limit of approximately 100 m (328 feet) per segment.

100BASE-T   A name for the IEEE Fast Ethernet standard that uses two-pair copper cabling, a speed of 100 Mbps, and a maximum cable length of 100 meters.

1000BASE-T   A name for the IEEE Gigabit Ethernet standard that uses four-pair copper cabling, a speed of 1000 Mbps (1 Gbps), and a maximum cable length of 100 meters.

802.1Q   The IEEE standardized protocol for VLAN trunking.

802.1AB   The IEEE standard for Link Layer Discovery Protocol, which is formally referred to as Station and Media Access Control Connectivity Discovery Protocol. It is a vendor-neutral link layer protocol in the Internet Protocol Suite used by network devices for advertising their identity, capabilities, and neighbors on an IEEE 802 local-area network, principally Ethernet.

802.1Qau   The IEEE standard for data center bridging (DCB) enhancements to Ethernet local-area networks for congestion notification. It provides end-to-end congestion management for protocols that are capable of transmission rate limiting to avoid frame loss. It is expected to benefit protocols such as TCP that have native congestion management, as it reacts to congestion in a timelier manner.

802.1Qaz   The IEEE standard for data center bridging (DCB) enhancements to Ethernet local-area networks for enhanced transmission selection (ETS). It provides a common management framework for assignment of bandwidth to frame priorities.

802.1Qbb   The IEEE standard for data center bridging (DCB) enhancements to Ethernet local-area networks for priority flow control (PFC). It provides a link level flow control mechanism that can be controlled independently for each frame priority. The goal of this mechanism is to ensure zero traffic loss under congestion in DCB networks.

802.11a   The IEEE standard for wireless LANs using the U-NII spectrum, OFDM encoding, at speeds of up to 54 Mbps.

802.11b   The IEEE standard for wireless LANs using the ISM spectrum, DSSS encoding, and speeds of up to 11 Mbps.

802.11g   The IEEE standard for wireless LANs using the ISM spectrum, OFDM or DSSS encoding, and speeds of up to 54 Mbps.

802.11n   The IEEE standard for wireless LANs using the ISM spectrum, OFDM encoding, and multiple antennas for single-stream speeds up to 150 Mbps.

802.11w   The IEEE standard that defines the changes necessary to the operation of a MAC Bridge to provide a rapid reconfiguration capability for STP.

802.2   The IEEE standard for the portion of the data link layer feature in common across LANs, known more commonly as Logical Link Control (LLC).

802.3   The IEEE standard for Ethernet.

802.3ad   The IEEE standard for Ethernet. The Link Aggregation Control Protocol (LACP) (802.3ad) for the Gigabit Interfaces feature bundles individual Gigabit Ethernet links into a single logical link that provides the aggregate bandwidth of up to four physical links.

802.4   The IEEE standard for Token Bus.

802.5   The IEEE standard for Token Ring.

A

AAA   Authentication, authorization, and accounting. Authentication confirms the identity of the user or device. Authorization determines what the user or device is allowed to do. Accounting records information about access attempts, including inappropriate requests.

ACI   Application centric infrastructure. Cisco data center architecture with centralized automation and policy-driven application profiles. ACI delivers software flexibility with the scalability of hardware performance. Key characteristics of ACI include simplified automation by an application-driven policy model, centralized visibility with real-time application health monitoring, open software flexibility for DevOps teams and ecosystem partner integration, scalable performance, and multitenancy in hardware.

AD   Active Directory. A distributed directory service.

Adapter-FEX   Converged network adapter virtualization technology that enables you to create logical instances of network interface cards and host bus adapters instantiated on a single physical adapter. Adapter-FEX is part of Cisco Fabric Extender technologies.

adapter port channel   A channel that groups all the physical links from a Cisco UCS virtual interface card (VIC) to an IOM into one logical link.

AED   Authoritative edge device. OTV elects a designated forwarding edge device per site for each VLAN to provide loop-free multihoming. It is part of the OTV control plane and does not need additional configuration. The forwarder is known as the AED.

AEP   Attach entity profile represents a group of external entities with similar infrastructure policy requirements. The ACI fabric provides multiple attachment points that connect through leaf ports to various external entities such as bare metal servers and hypervisors. These attachment points can be physical ports, port channels, or a vPC on the leaf switches.

ANSI   American National Standards Institute. A private nonprofit organization that oversees the development of voluntary consensus standards for products, services, processes, systems, and personnel in the United States.

AP   Application profile is a convenient logical container for grouping endpoint groups (EPGs). It models application requirements.

API   Application programming interface. Specifies a software component in terms of its operations, its inputs and outputs, and its underlying types. Cisco UCS exposes APIs to the external world for programmatic control.

APIC EM   Cisco Application Policy Infrastructure Controller Enterprise Module. Its applications are part of the Cisco ONE portfolio. The controller provides a low-risk, incremental approach to adopting software-defined networking (SDN) technologies in branch and campus environments. Using a policy-based approach, the controller automates provisioning of the end-to-end infrastructure to rapidly deploy applications and services.

arbiter   An electronic device that allocates access to shared resources. A bus arbiter is a device used in a multimaster bus system to decide which bus master will be allowed to control the bus for each bus cycle. The most common kind of bus arbiter is the memory arbiter in a system bus system. A memory arbiter is a device used in a shared memory system to decide, for each memory cycle, which CPU will be allowed to access that shared memory.

ARP   Address Resolution Protocol. An Internet protocol used to map an IP address to a MAC address. Defined in RFC 826.

ARP table   A list of IP addresses of neighbors on the same VLAN, along with their MAC addresses, as kept in memory by hosts and routers.

ASAv Cisco Adaptive Security Virtual Appliance.   Cisco virtual security solution for traditional multitier and fabric environments. In multitenant environments, ASAv provides tenant edge security services.

ASIC   Application-specific integrated circuit. An integrated circuit (IC) customized for a particular use, rather than intended for general-purpose use.

Atomic counters   Packet and byte counters that are read atomically across the entire ACI fabric. Atomic means that the values in the counters are consistent regardless of where they are in the fabric or the amount of latency or distance that exists between them.

AVS   Cisco application virtual switch is a hypervisor-resident virtual network switch that is specifically designed for the application centric infrastructure (ACI) architecture. Based on the Cisco Nexus 1000V virtual switch, AVS provides feature support for the ACI application policy model, full switching capabilities, and more advanced telemetry features.

B

BFD   Bidirectional forwarding detection. A network protocol used to detect faults between two forwarding engines connected by a link. It provides low-overhead detection of faults even on physical media that do not support failure detection of any kind, such as Ethernet, virtual circuits, tunnels, and MPLS Label Switched Paths.

BGP-EVPN   Border Gateway Protocol and Ethernet VPN. Ethernet VPN (EVPN) encompasses next-generation Ethernet L2VPN solutions that use Border Gateway Protocol (BGP) as a control plane for MAC address signaling/learning over the core as well as for access topology and VPN endpoint discovery.

BIC   Binary increase congestion. One of the congestion control algorithms that can be used for TCP. BIC is optimized for high-speed networks with high latency: so-called long fat networks. BIC has a unique congestion window (cwnd) algorithm. This algorithm tries to find the maximum TCP window size that can be maintained for a long period of time by using a binary search algorithm.

Big Data   An all-encompassing term for any collection of data sets so large and complex that it becomes difficult to process using traditional data processing applications.

BIOS   Basic Input Output System. In a computer system, it performs the Power on Self-Test procedure, searches, and loads to the Master Boot Record in the system booting process.

BMA   Bare metal agent is a virtual appliance used with UCS Director to install an operating system directly on the bare metal hardware such as a UCS blade. BMA can install several operating systems, including Windows, Linux, and hypervisor software such as VMware ESXi.

booting   The initialization of a computerized system. Booting is a process or set of operations that loads and hence starts the operating system, starting from the point when a user switches on the power button.

BPDU   Bridge protocol data unit. A frame that contains information about the Spanning Tree Protocol (STP). Switches send BPDUs using a unique MAC address from its origin port and a multicast address as destination MAC (01:80:C2:00:00:00). For STP algorithms to function, the switches need to share information about themselves and their connections, which are BPDUs. BPDUs are sent out as multicast frames to which only other Layer 2 switches or bridges are listening.

Bridge domain   A set of logical ports that share the same flooding or broadcast characteristics. Like a virtual LAN (VLAN), bridge domains span multiple devices.

C

Catalogs   Provide a list of IT services that an end user can order. In UCS Director, users can log in and self-provision virtual machines (VMs) using a predefined catalog. UCS Director catalog is a logical construct that defines parameters such as the user group, VM image, cloud name, OS information, application information, user credentials, customization and VM access to present it as a single "Menu Item" for Self Service use. Virtual machines, predefined workflows, and application containers can be published in catalogs.

CDP   Cisco Discovery Protocol. A media- and protocol-independent device-discovery protocol that runs on most Cisco-manufactured equipment, including routers, access servers, and switches. Using CDP, a device can advertise its existence to other devices and receive information about other devices on the same LAN or on the remote side of a WAN.

CDP neighbor   A device on the other end of some communications cable that is advertising CDP updates.

CFS   Cisco Fabric Services. Offers a common infrastructure for automatic configuration synchronization in the network. It provides the transport function and a set of common services to the features. CFS can discover CFS-capable switches in the network and discover feature capabilities in all CFS-capable switches.

CFS   Compact file set. An open archive file format and software distribution container file format. Basic CFS files are compatible with ISO files. It is intended to be similar enough to ISO-9660 that many systems and applications will be able to read CFS, and other applications will require only minor modifications.

CFSoE   Cisco Fabric Services over Ethernet. A reliable state transport mechanism that can be used to synchronize the actions of the vPC peer devices. CFSoE carries messages and packets for many features linked with vPC, such as STP and IGMP. Information is carried in CFS/CFSoE protocol data units (PDUs).

CH   Cisco Call Home. A feature in Cisco UCS Manager that allows notification of faults in Cisco UCS hardware.

Chargeback   An ability of an IT organization to track and measure IT resource utilization per business unit or department and charge them back for the usage of resources.

CIM   Common information model. An open standard that defines how managed elements in an IT environment are represented as a common set of objects and relationships between them. This is intended to allow consistent management of these managed elements, independent of their manufacturer or provider.

CIMC   Cisco Integrated Management Controller. Present in both Cisco UCS blade chassis and blade/rack servers, allowing integrated management control of the Cisco UCS infrastructure without needing separate hardware modules.

CISC   Complex instruction set computing. A CPU design in which single instructions can execute several low-level operations (such as a load from memory, an arithmetic operation, and a memory store) or are capable of multistep operations or addressing modes within single instructions. The term was retroactively coined in contrast to reduced instruction set computer (RISC).

Cisco InterCloud   A highly secure, open, and flexible solution for establishing hybrid cloud connectivity for both businesses and service providers alike. It offers organizations the choice of connecting to a variety of public cloud service providers participating in the cloud ecosystem.

Cisco MDS   A family of Cisco storage-area network switches supporting Fibre Channel, Fibre Channel over Ethernet, and Fibre Channel over IP-based storage environments.

Cisco Nexus   A family of Cisco network physical and virtual switches primarily targeted at the data center environments.

Cisco NX-OS   Device operating system running on the Cisco Nexus data center family of switches.

Cisco ONE   A software licensing model that offers a valuable and flexible way to buy software for your data center, WAN, and access domains. Cisco ONE Enterprise Cloud Suite uses this licensing model to offer a comprehensive end-to-end software bundle for building a private cloud. It includes many software products working together to offer a wide range of cloud capabilities.

ClassName   Specifies the name of the targeted class. This name is a concatenation of the package name of the object queried and the name of the class queried in the context of the corresponding package. For example, the class aaa:User results in a className of aaaUser in the URI.

CLI   Command-line interface. An interface that enables the user to interact with the operating system by entering commands and optional arguments.

CLOS   A multistage switching network.

CMP   Connectivity management processor. A separate processor on the Cisco Nexus 7000 Series Supervisor 1 module that is in addition to the main control processor (CP). The CMP provides a second network interface to the switch for use even when the CP is not reachable. CMP can be accessed to configure it and to perform system operations, such as taking over the CP console or restarting the CP.

CMP   Cloud management platform. A software stack such as UCS Director that delivers cloud services in the data center. CMP includes several layers of functionality such as portal, catalog, application program interface (API), service management layer, orchestration layer, and resource management layer.

CNA   Converged network adapter. A computer input/output device that combines the functionality of a host bus adapter (HBA) with a network interface controller (NIC). In other words, it "converges" access to a storage-area network and a general-purpose computer network.

Community cloud   A cloud computing environment that provides shared infrastructure resources to specific groups that share common interests or have common concerns. Community cloud can be deployed either on-premises or off-premises, and it can be owned and operated by either a third-party managing service provider, the participating organizations themselves, or a combination of both.

Consumer   An endpoint group (EPG) that consumes a service.

Context   Also known as VRF. Defines a Layer 3 address domain that allows multiple instances of a routing table to exist and work simultaneously. This increases functionality by allowing network paths to be segmented without using multiple devices.

Contract   A set of rules that specify what and how communications in a network are allowed. In ACI, contracts specify how communications between EPGs take place.

Crossbar   Also known as cross-point switch or matrix switch. A switch connecting multiple inputs to multiple outputs in a matrix manner. Originally the term was used for a matrix switch controlled by a grid of crossing metal bars. Later it was broadened to matrix switches in general. It is one of the principal switch architectures, together with a rotary switch, a memory switch, and a crossover switch. A crossbar switch is an assembly of individual switches between multiple inputs and multiple outputs. The switches are arranged in a matrix. If the crossbar switch has M inputs and N outputs, a crossbar has a matrix with $M \times N$ cross points or places where the "bars" cross. At each cross point is a switch; when closed, it connects one of M

inputs to one of *N* outputs. A given crossbar is a single layer, nonblocking switch. "Non-blocking" means that other concurrent connections do not prevent connecting an arbitrary input to any arbitrary output. Collections of crossbars can be used to implement multiple layer and/or blocking switches.

CWDM   Course wavelength-division multiplexing. A technology that multiplexes a number of optical carrier signals onto a single optical fiber by using different wavelengths (that is, colors) of laser light. This technique enables bidirectional communications over one strand of fiber and multiplication of capacity.

D

DCB   Data center bridging. A set of IEEE standards enhancing Ethernet networks to be able to accommodate convergence of network and storage traffic.

DCBX   Data center bridging exchange. A discovery and capability exchange protocol to discover peers and exchange configuration information between DCB-compliant bridges. DCBX leverages functionality provided by IEEE 802.1AB (LLDP).

DCI   Data center interconnect. Solutions that, in general, extend LAN and SAN connectivity between geographical dispersed data centers that allow us to have data replication, server clustering, and workload mobility.

DCNM   Cisco Prime Data Center Network Manager. Designed to help efficiently implement, visualize, and manage Cisco Unified Fabric. It includes a comprehensive feature set, along with a customizable dashboard that provides enhanced visibility and automated fabric provisioning of dynamic data centers.

dEPG   Destination endpoint group. A destination endpoint group in the relationship between EPGs.

DFA   An evolution of the Cisco Unified Fabric. It simplifies the deployment of the data center fabric and automates consumption of network services. It provides a scale-out architecture without congestion points in the network while providing optimized forwarding for all types of applications.

DHCP   Dynamic Host Configuration Protocol. Client/server protocol that automatically provides a host with its IP address and other related configuration information, such as the subnet mask, default gateway IP address, and DNS server IP address.

DHCP client   Any device that uses DHCP protocols to ask to lease an IP address from a DHCP server, or to learn any IP settings from that server.

DHCP relay   The name of the router IOS feature that forwards DHCP messages from a client to servers by changing the destination IP address from 255.255.255.255 to the IP address of the DHCP server.

DHCP server   Software that waits for DHCP clients to request to lease IP addresses, with the server assigning a lease of an IP address as well as listing other important IP settings for the client.

DME   Data management engine. Residing within the Cisco UCS Manager, DME is the repository of all the objects managed, FSM, and business logic defined in the Cisco UCS Manager.

DMZ   Demilitarized zone. In computer security, a DMZ (sometimes referred to as a perimeter network) is a physical or logical subnetwork that contains and exposes an organization's external-facing services to a larger and untrusted network, usually the Internet.

DN   Distinguished name. Specifies the DN of the targeted managed object (MO).

DNS   Domain Name System. An application layer protocol used throughout the Internet for translating hostnames into their associated IP addresses.

DRAM   Dynamic Random Access Memory. Stores each bit of data in a separate capacitor. The main memory in a server utilizes DRAM.

DRAP   Dynamic Resource Allocation Protocol. An extension to FabricPath IS-IS that ensures networkwide unique and consistent switch IDs and FTAG values.

E

EOBC   Ethernet out-of-band channel. Various forms of communication between line cards, fabric modules, and supervisors are required within a normal system operation. This communication occurs over an internal switching infrastructure called the EOBC.

EoMPLS   Ethernet over MPLS. Any Transport over MPLS (AToM) transports Layer 2 packets over an MPLS backbone. AToM uses a directed Label Distribution Protocol (LDP) session between edge routers for setting up and maintaining connections. EoMPLS is one of the AToM transport types. EoMPLS works by encapsulating Ethernet PDUs in MPLS packets and forwarding them across the MPLS network. Each PDU is transported as a single packet.

EoR   End-of-row. In the EOR network design, each server in individual racks is connected to a common EOR aggregation switch directly, without connecting to individual switches in each rack. Bigger cables are used to connect each server to chassis-based EOR/aggregation switches. There might be multiple such EOR switches in the same data center, one for each row or certain number of racks.

EPG   Endpoint group. A logical entity that contains a collection of physical or virtual network endpoints. In ACI, endpoints are devices connected to the network directly or indirectly. They have an address (identity), a location, and attributes (such as version and patch level), and they can be physical or virtual. Endpoint examples include servers, virtual machines, storage, or clients on the Internet.

EPLD   Erasable programmable logic device. An integrated circuit composed of an array of programmable logic devices (PLD) that do not come preconnected; the user programs the connections electrically.

Ethernet   A series of LAN standards defined by the IEEE, originally invented by Xerox Corporation and developed jointly by Xerox, Intel, and Digital Equipment Corporation.

Ethernet address   A 48-bit (6-byte) binary number, usually written as a 12-digit hexadecimal number, used to identify Ethernet nodes in an Ethernet network. Ethernet frame headers list a destination and source address field used by the Ethernet devices to deliver Ethernet frames to the correct destination.

Ethernet frame   A term referring to an Ethernet data link header and trailer, plus the data encapsulated between the header and the trailer.

Ethernet link   A generic term for any physical link between two Ethernet nodes, no matter what type of cabling is used.

Ethernet port   A generic term for the opening on the side of any Ethernet node, typically in an Ethernet NIC or LAN switch, into which an Ethernet cable can be connected.

EtherType   Jargon that shortens the term Ethernet Type, which refers to the Type field in the Ethernet header. The Type field identifies the type of packet encapsulated inside an Ethernet frame.

ETS   Enhanced transmission selection. *See* 802.1Qaz.

F

Fabric container   An infrastructure solution offered by Cisco UCS Director for the networks that use dynamic fabric automation (DFA).

FabricPath   Cisco FabricPath is a crucial element in Cisco Unified Fabric architecture. It brings the stability and performance of Layer 3 routing to Layer 2 switched networks to build a highly resilient and scalable Layer 2 fabric. Cisco FabricPath is a foundation for building massively scalable and flexible data centers.

Fabric port channel   Fibre Channel uplinks defined in a Cisco UCS Fabric Interconnect, bundled together and configured as a port channel, allowing increased bandwidth and redundancy.

FCIP   Fibre Channel over IP. An Internet Protocol (IP) created by the Internet Engineering Task Force (IETF) for storage technology. An FCIP entity functions to encapsulate Fibre Channel frames and forward them over an IP network. FCIP entities are peers that communicate using TCP/IP. FCIP technology overcomes the distance limitations of native Fibre Channel, enabling geographically distributed storage-area networks to be connected using existing IP infrastructure, while keeping fabric services intact. The Fibre Channel fabric and its devices remain unaware of the presence of the IP network.

FCoE   Fibre Channel over Ethernet. A computer network technology that encapsulates Fibre Channel frames over Ethernet networks. This allows Fibre Channel to use 10 Gigabit Ethernet networks (or higher speeds) while preserving the Fibre Channel protocol characteristics. The specification is part of the International Committee for Information Technology Standards T11 FC-BB-5 standard published in 2009. FCoE maps Fibre Channel directly over Ethernet while being independent of the Ethernet forwarding scheme.

FCS   Frame check sequence. A field in many data link trailers used as part of the error-detection process.

Fenced Virtual Container   An infrastructure solution offered by Cisco UCS Director. It is the most common type of application container for use with VMs.

FEX   Fabric Extender. Cisco Fabric Extender technology delivers an extensible and a scalable fabric that provides a flexible and comprehensive solution as part of Cisco Unified Fabric. It is based on the emerging standard IEEE 802.1BR (Bridge Port Extension). Allows the switching fabric access layer to extend and expand all the way to the server hypervisor as your business grows. Helps enable operational simplicity at scale, with a single point of management and policy enforcement on the access parent switch.

FHRP   First Hop Redundancy Protocol. A networking protocol that offers default gateway redundancy by allowing two or more routers to provide backup for the IP address of the default gateway.

Fibre Channel (FC)   A high-speed network technology (commonly running at 2-, 4-, 8- and 16-gigabit per second rates) primarily used to connect computer data storage. Fibre Channel is standardized in the T11 Technical Committee of the International Committee for Information Technology Standards (INCITS), an American National Standards Institute (ANSI)-accredited standards committee.

Fibre Channel over Ethernet N-Port Virtualization (FCoE-NPV)   Secure method to connect FCoE-capable hosts to an FCoE-capable FCoE forwarder (FCF) device. Switches operating in FCoE-NPV mode proxy all Fibre Channel processing and functions to the upstream switch operating in FCoE-NPIV mode.

Fibre Channel over Ethernet N-Port ID virtualization (FCoE-NPIV)   Fibre Channel mechanism to assign multiple Fibre Channel IDs on the same physical interface. FCoE-NPIV can work with FCoE-NPV to enable a scaled-out SAN access layer.

FIFO   First in, first out. A method for organizing and manipulating a data buffer, where the oldest (first) entry, or "head" of the queue, is processed first.

Filter   A TCP/IP-header field such as L3 protocol type, L4 ports, and so on that are used to allow inbound or outbound communications between EPGs in ACI fabric. ACI uses a whitelist model—all communication is blocked by default; communication must be given explicit permission.

FPGA   Field-programmable gate array. This is an integrated circuit designed to be configured by a customer or a designer after manufacturing—hence, "field-programmable."

Fport-channel-trunk   Trunking F ports allow interconnected ports to transmit and receive tagged frames in more than one VSAN, over the same physical link.

frame   A term referring to a data link header and trailer, plus the data encapsulated between the header and trailer.

FSM   Cisco UCS Finite State Machines that monitor the state transition of Cisco UCS objects.

full duplex   Generically, any communication in which two communicating devices can concurrently send and receive data. In Ethernet LANs, the allowance for both devices to send and receive at the same time, allowed when both devices disable their CSMA/CD logic.

full mesh   A network topology in which more than two devices can physically communicate and, by choice, all pairs of devices are allowed to communicate directly.

full virtualization   Server virtualization technique used to provide an environment completely simulating underlying server hardware. With full virtualization, guest operating systems running inside virtual machines are fully isolated from one another. No guest operating system modification is required to support full virtualization.

G

Git/GitHub   A web-based Git repository hosting service. It offers all the distributed revision control and source code management (SCM) functionality of Git and adds its own features. Unlike Git, which is strictly a command-line tool, GitHub provides a Web-based graphical interface and desktop as well as mobile integration.

GOLD   Generic online diagnostics. Defines a common framework for diagnostics operations across Cisco platforms running Cisco IOS Software. The GOLD framework specifies the platform-independent fault-detection architecture for centralized and distributed systems.

guest operating system   Operating system software running inside the virtual machine in addition to the main operating system or the hypervisor.

GUI   Graphical user interface. In computing, a type of interface that allows users to interact with electronic devices through graphical icons and visual indicators such as secondary notation, as opposed to text-based interfaces, typed command labels, or text navigation. GUIs were introduced in reaction to the perceived steep learning curve of command-line interfaces (CLIs), which require commands to be typed on the keyboard.

H

HBA   Host bus adapter. Host controller, host adapter, or host bus adapter (HBA) connects a host system (the computer) to other network and storage devices.

HDD   Hard disk drive. A disk drive that can read/write bits of information and is nonvolatile.

head-of-line blocking (HOL Blocking)   A performance-limiting phenomenon in computer networking that occurs when a line of packets is held up by the first packet, for example in input buffered network switches, out-of-order delivery, and multiple requests in HTTP pipelining.

HIF   Host interface. Front panel port on FEX, connecting to a server.

host-based virtualization   It requires additional software running on the host, as a privileged task or process. In some cases volume management is built in to the operating system, and in other instances it is offered as a separate product. Volumes (LUNs) presented to the host system are handled by a traditional physical device driver. However, a software layer (the volume manager) resides above the disk device driver, intercepts the I/O requests, and provides the metadata lookup and I/O mapping.

HSRP   Hot Standby Router Protocol. A Cisco proprietary redundancy protocol for establishing a fault-tolerant default gateway, described in detail in RFC 2281.

HTML   Hypertext Markup Language. A simple document-formatting language that uses tags to indicate how a given part of a document should be interpreted by a viewing application, such as a web browser.

HTTP   Hypertext Transfer Protocol. The protocol used by web browsers and web servers to transfer files, such as text and graphics files.

Hybrid cloud   A cloud computing environment that offers a hybrid approach between the private and public cloud. The premise of the hybrid cloud is to extend the existing private cloud environment into the public cloud as needed, on demand, and with consistent network and security policies.

hypervisor   A software allowing multiple operating systems, known as guest operating systems, to share a single physical server. Guest operating systems run inside virtual machines and have fair scheduled access to underlying server physical resources.

I

IaaS   Infrastructure as a service. A form of cloud computing that provides virtualized computing resources over the Internet. IaaS is one of three main categories of cloud computing services, alongside software as a service (SaaS) and platform as a service (PaaS).

IANA   Internet Assigned Numbers Authority. An organization that owns the rights to assign many operating numbers and facts about how the global Internet works, including public IPv4 and IPv6 addresses.

ICMP   Internet Control Message Protocol. A TCP/IP network layer protocol that reports errors and provides other information relevant to IP packet processing.

IDS   Intrusion detection system. A security function that examines more complex traffic patterns against a list of both known attack signatures and general characteristics of how attacks can be carried out, rating each perceived threat and reporting the threats.

IEEE   Institute of Electrical and Electronics Engineers. A professional organization that develops communications and network standards, among other activities.

IEEE 802.2   An IEEE LAN protocol that specifies an implementation of the LLC sublayer of the data link layer.

IEEE 802.3   A set of IEEE LAN protocols that specifies the many variations of what is known today as an Ethernet LAN.

IETF   Internet Engineering Task Force. The IETF serves as the primary organization that works directly to create new TCP/IP standards.

IGMP   Internet Group Management Protocol. A communications protocol used by hosts and adjacent routers on IP networks to establish multicast group memberships. IGMP is an integral part of IP multicast.

IGP   Interior Gateway Protocol. *See* Interior Routing Protocol.

In-band   A storage virtualization method that places the virtualization engine directly in the data path so that both block data and the control information that governs its virtual appearance transit the same link.

INCITS   International Committee for Information Technology Standards. An ANSI-accredited forum of IT developers. It was formerly known as the X3 and NCITS.

initiator   All SCSI devices are intelligent, but SCSI operates as a master/slave model. One SCSI device (the initiator) initiates communication with another SCSI device (the target) by issuing a command, to which a response is expected. Thus, the SCSI protocol is half-duplex by design and is considered a command/response protocol.

Intel VT   Intel Virtualization Technology or hardware-assisted Intel Virtualization Technology (Intel VT) assists the hypervisors and their virtual machines to utilize hardware assists for better performance and features.

Inter-VLAN routing   The ability of a device to route between two or more VLANs.

Interior Routing Protocol   A routing protocol designed for use within a single organization.

I/O Accelerator (IOA)   The Cisco MDS 9000 family I/O Accelerator (IOA) feature provides Small Computer System Interface (SCSI) acceleration in a SAN where the sites are interconnected over long distances using Fibre Channel or Fibre Channel over IP (FCIP) Inter-Switch Links (ISLs).

IoE   Internet of everything. Cisco defines the IoE as bringing together people, processes, data, and things to make networked connections more relevant and valuable than ever before—turning information into actions that create new capabilities, richer experiences, and unprecedented economic opportunity for businesses, individuals, and countries.

IOPS   Input/Output Operations per Second, pronounced "eye-ops." A common performance measurement used to benchmark computer storage devices like hard disk drives (HDD), solid state drives (SSD), and storage-area networks (SAN).

IOS   Cisco Internetwork Operating System Software that provides the majority of a router or switch's features, with the hardware providing the remaining features.

IOS image   A file that contains the IOS.

IoT   Internet of things. The network of physical devices, vehicles, buildings, and other items—embedded with electronics, software, sensors, and network connectivity—that enables these objects to collect and exchange data.

IP   Internet Protocol. The network layer protocol in the TCP/IP stack, providing routing and logical addressing standards and services.

IP address (IP version 4)   In IP version 4 (IPv4), a 32-bit address assigned to hosts using TCP/IP. Each address consists of a network number, an optional subnetwork number, and a host number. The network and subnetwork numbers together are used for routing, and the host number is used to address an individual host within the network or subnetwork.

IP address (IP version 6)   In IP version 6 (IPv6), a 128-bit address assigned to hosts using TCP/IP. Addresses use different formats, commonly using a routing prefix, subnet, and interface ID, corresponding to the IPv4 network, subnet, and host parts of an address.

IP network   Communication network that uses Internet Protocol (IP) to send and receive messages between multiple hosts.

IP packet   An IP-header, followed by the data encapsulated after the IP-header, but specifically not including any headers and trailers for layers below the network layer.

IP subnet   Subdivisions of a Class A, B, or C network, as configured by a network administrator. Subnets allow a single Class A, B, or C network to be used instead of multiple networks, and still allow for a large number of groups of IP addresses, as is required for efficient IP routing.

IP version 4   Literally, the version of the Internet Protocol defined in an old RFC 791, standardized in 1980, and used as the basis of TCP/IP networks and the Internet for more than 30 years.

IP version 6   A newer version of the Internet Protocol defined in RFC 2460, as well as many other RFCs, whose creation was motivated by the need to avoid the IPv4 address exhaustion problem.

IPMI   Intelligent platform management interface. A set of specifications for a computer subsystem that provides management and monitoring capabilities independently of the host system's CPU, firmware (BIOS), and operating system.

IPS   Intrusion prevention system. A security function that examines more complex traffic patterns against a list of both known attack signatures and general characteristics of how attacks can be carried out, rating each perceived threat, and reacting to prevent the more significant threats.

IPv4 address exhaustion   The process by which the public IPv4 addresses, available to create the Internet, were consumed through the 1980s until today, with the expectation that eventually the world would run out of available IPv4 addresses.

IPv6 neighbor table   The IPv6 equivalent of the ARP table. A table that lists IPv6 addresses of other hosts on the same link, along with their matching MAC addresses, as typically learned using Neighbor Discovery Protocol (NDP).

iSCSI   Internet Small Computer Interface. An Internet Protocol (IP)-based storage networking standard for linking data storage facilities. By carrying SCSI commands over IP networks, iSCSI is used to facilitate data transfers over intranets and manage storage over long distances. iSCSI can be used to transmit data over local-area networks (LANs), wide-area networks (WANs), or the Internet and can enable location-independent data storage and retrieval. The protocol allows clients (called *initiators*) to send SCSI commands (*CDBs*) to SCSI storage devices (*targets*) on remote servers. It is a storage-area network (SAN) protocol, allowing organizations to consolidate storage into data center storage arrays while providing hosts (such as database and web servers) with the illusion of locally attached disks. iSCSI can be run over long distances using existing network infrastructure. iSCSI was pioneered by IBM and Cisco in 1998 and submitted as a draft standard in March 2000.

ISL   Inter-Switch Link. A Cisco-proprietary protocol that maintains VLAN information as traffic flows between switches and routers.

ISO   International Organization for Standardization. An international organization that is responsible for a wide range of standards, including many standards relevant to networking. The ISO developed the OSI reference model, a popular networking reference model.

ISSU   In-service software upgrade. The industry's first comprehensive, transparent software upgrade capability for the IP/Multiprotocol Label Switching edge router.

J

JSON   JavaScript Object Notation. A lightweight data-interchange format that is based on a subset of JavaScript programming language. It can be considered an alternative to XML.

K

keepalive   A proprietary feature of Cisco routers in which the router sends messages on a periodic basis as a means of letting the neighboring router know that the first router is still alive and well.

KVM   Keyboard, video, and mouse functions.

L

LACP   Link Aggregation Control Protocol. *See* 802.3ad.

LAN   Local-area network. A computer network that interconnects computers within a limited area, such as a home, school, computer laboratory, or office building, using network media. The defining characteristics of LANs, in contrast to wide-area networks (WANs), include their smaller geographic area and noninclusion of leased telecommunication lines.

LDAP   Lightweight Directory Access Protocol. An open, vendor-neutral, industry standard application protocol for accessing and maintaining distributed directory information services over an Internet Protocol (IP) network.

LIF   Logical interface. Presentation of a front panel port in a parent switch.

LISP   Locator ID Separation Protocol. Routing architecture that provides new semantics for IP addressing by decoupling device identify, such as IP address, from its location in the network topology.

LLC   Logical link control. The higher of the two data link layer sublayers defined by the IEEE. Synonymous with IEEE 802.2.

LLDP   Link Layer Discovery Protocol. *See* 802.1AB.

LUN   Logical unit number. In computer storage, a number used to identify a logical unit, which is a device addressed by the SCSI protocol or protocols that encapsulate SCSI, such as Fibre Channel or iSCSI. A LUN may be used with any device that supports read/write operations, such as a tape drive, but it most often refers to a logical disk as created on a SAN.

M

MAC   Media Access Control. The lower of the two sublayers of the data link layer defined by the IEEE. Synonymous with IEEE 802.3 for Ethernet LANs.

MAC address   A standardized data link layer address that is required for every device that connects to a LAN. Ethernet MAC addresses are 6 bytes long and are controlled by the IEEE. Also known as a *hardware address*, a *MAC layer address*, and a *physical address*.

MDS   Cisco MDS 9000 Series Multilayer SAN Switches allow building highly available, scalable storage networks with advanced security and unified management.

metadata   Data about data. The term is ambiguous because it is used for two fundamentally different concepts (types). Structural metadata is about the design and specification of data structures and is more properly called "data about the containers of data;" descriptive metadata, on the other hand, is about individual instances of application data, the data content. The main purpose of metadata is to facilitate in the discovery of relevant information, more often classified as resource discovery. Metadata also helps organize electronic resources, provides digital identification, and helps support archiving and preservation of the resource.

metric   A unit of measure used by routing protocol algorithms to determine the best route for traffic to use to reach a particular destination.

MIB   Management information base. A database used for managing the entities in a communications network. Most often associated with the Simple Network Management Protocol (SNMP), the term is also used more generically in contexts such as in OSI/ISO Network management model.

MIT   Management information tree. Cisco ACI managed object instances can contain other instances, forming a parent-child relationship as part of a tree, known as the managed information tree.

MO   Managed object. Everything in the Cisco ACI infrastructure is represented as a class or a managed object. Each managed object is identified by a name and contains a set of typed values, or properties. It specifies whether the target of the operation is a managed object (MO) or an object class.

MPLS   Multiprotocol label switching. A mechanism in high-performance telecommunications networks that directs data from one network node to the next based on short path labels rather than long network addresses, avoiding complex lookups in a routing table. The labels identify virtual links (*paths*) between distant nodes rather than endpoints.

MS   Microsoft.

MSP   Managed service provider. An information technology (IT) services provider that manages and provides a defined set of services to its clients. UCS Director supports multitenancy by using a service provider feature that allows you to create multiple MSP organizations and suborganizations. In UCS Director, an MSP organization represents a tenant, and a suborganization may represent departments, business units, or different IT environments.

MTU   Maximum transmission unit. In computer networking, the MTU of a communications protocol of a layer is the size (in bytes) of the largest protocol data unit that the layer can pass onward.

multihop FCoE   Set of technologies and designs to extend convergence of network and storage traffic beyond the data center access layer.

multilayer switch   A LAN switch that can also perform Layer 3 routing functions. The name comes from the fact that this device makes forwarding decisions based on logic from multiple OSI layers (Layers 2 and 3).

multimode   A type of fiber-optic cabling with a larger core than single-mode cabling, allowing light to enter at multiple angles. The main difference between multimode and single-mode optical fiber is that the former has a much larger core diameter, typically 50–100 micrometers—much larger than the wavelength of the light carried in it. The equipment used for communications over multimode optical fiber is less expensive than that for single-mode optical fiber because of lower light source requirements.

multipathing   A technique that lets you use more than one physical path that transfers data between the host and an external storage device.

multitenancy   A mode of operation whereby IT resources are securely shared among multiple users. It utilizes virtualization technologies to create logical segments of a physical resource to create isolation between the users.

MUX   A device that combines several input information signals into one output signal, which carries several communication channels by means of some multiplex technique.

N

NBAR   Network-Based Application Recognition. A mechanism that classifies and regulates bandwidth for network applications to ensure that available resources are utilized as efficiently as possible. Cisco Systems developed NBAR as part of its Content Networking platform for implementing intelligent network services.

network   A collection of computers, printers, routers, switches, and other devices that can communicate with each other over some transmission medium.

network address   *See* network number.

network-based virtualization   In computing, network virtualization is the process of combining hardware and software network resources and network functionality into a single, software-based administrative entity, a virtual network. Network virtualization involves platform virtualization, often combined with resource virtualization.

network broadcast address   In IPv4, a special address in each classful network that can be used to broadcast a packet to all hosts in that same classful network. Numerically, the address has the same value as the network number in the network part of the address and all 255s in the host octets—for example, 10.255.255.255 is the network broadcast address for classful network 10.0.0.0.

network number   A number that uses dotted-decimal notation like IP addresses, but the number itself represents all hosts in a single Class A, B, or C IP network.

network part   The portion of an IPv4 address that is either 1, 2, or 3 octets/bytes long, based on whether the address is in a Class A, B, or C network.

NIC   Network interface card. A computer card, sometimes an expansion card, and sometimes integrated into the motherboard of the computer that provides the electronics and other functions to connect to a computer network. Today, most NICs are specifically Ethernet NICs, and most have an RJ-45 port, the most common type of Ethernet port.

NIF   Network interface port on FEX, connecting to the parent switch.

N_Port   Node port. Used to connect a device port to the SAN fabric.

NMI   Nonmaskable interrupt. A hardware interrupt that standard interrupt masking techniques in the system cannot ignore. It is typically used to signal attention for nonrecoverable hardware errors.

NPIV   N_port ID virtualization. A technique that enables the sharing of a single Fibre Channel N-Port between multiple N-Ports. It is used in storage networking techniques that utilize Fibre Channel-based ports to send and receive data between virtual machines (VMs) and virtual storage-area networks (SANs). NPIV is a component of the Fibre Channel Link Services (FC-LS) specification.

NPV   N-Port virtualization. A feature that has growing importance in the data center. In a traditional SAN fabric, each switch is assigned a domain ID. The domain ID is an 8-bit field in the FCID. There are officially 255 domain IDs. In reality, some of these IDs are reserved and cannot be assigned to switches, leaving us with 239 switches. In large environments, that hard limit can become a serious issue as you try to scale the fabric. The solution to this problem is NPV. NPV allows SAN switches to essentially become N-Port proxies.

NTP   Network Time Protocol. A protocol used to synchronize time-of-day clocks so that multiple devices use the same time of day, which allows log messages to be more easily matched based on their timestamps.

NVGRE   Network Virtualization Using Generic Routing Encapsulation. A network virtualization technology similar to VXLAN; it allows creating Layer 2 overlay networks on top of Layer 3 underlying networks by encapsulating original frames in GRE tunnels.

NVRAM   Nonvolatile RAM. A type of random-access memory (RAM) that retains its contents when a unit is powered off.

O

ODL   OpenDaylight. A collaborative open source project hosted by The Linux Foundation. The goal of the project is to accelerate the adoption of software-defined networking (SDN) and create a solid foundation for network functions virtualization (NFV). The software is written in Java.

OpenStack   A free and open-source software platform for cloud computing. Mostly deployed as an infrastructure as a service (IaaS).

operating system virtualization   Server virtualization technique where the kernel of an underlying operating system allows for multiple isolated user space instances, instead of just one. Such instances are often called containers.

operational plane   Networking devices typically have different entry points to access, control, and allow normal data operations. These are known as different operational planes (Control, Management, and Data).

Opflex   An extensible policy protocol designed to exchange abstract policy between a network controller and a set of smart devices capable of rendering policy. OpFlex relies on a separate information model understood by agents in both the controller and the devices.

Orchestration   Coordination of multiple lower level automation tasks to deliver an IT resource or set of IT resources "as a service."

OS   Operating system. Software that manages computer hardware and software resources and provides common services for computer programs. The operating system is an essential component of the system software in a computer system. Application programs usually require an operating system to function.

OSI   Open System Interconnection reference model. A network architectural model developed by the ISO. The model consists of seven layers, each of which specifies particular network functions, such as addressing, flow control, error control, encapsulation, and reliable message transfer.

OTV   Overlay transport virtualization. Innovative Layer 2 LAN extension technology over any core transport infrastructure.

out-of-band   A storage virtualization method that provides separate paths for data and control, presenting an image of virtual storage to the host by one link and allowing the host to directly retrieve data blocks from physical storage on another.

outside network   In ACI, inside networks are associated with a particular bridge domain of a tenant network. In other words, all workloads that have been discovered in a given tenant belong to an inside network. Outside networks are learned via a border leaf. An exception is made for Layer 2 extension. An L2 extension maps to a bridge domain but is "external." All devices that are not connected via Layer 2 or Layer 3 extension are "internal."

OVF   Open virtualization format. An open standard for packaging and delivering virtual appliances. Software vendors use this format to ship their software as a virtual machine. This format is commonly used on the VMware vSphere platform.

OVS   Open vSwitch. A production-quality open-source implementation of a distributed virtual multilayer switch. The main purpose of Open vSwitch is to provide a switching stack for hardware virtualization environments, while supporting multiple protocols and standards used in computer networks.

P

PaaS   Platform as a service. A category of cloud computing services that provides a platform allowing customers to develop, run, and manage applications without the complexity of building and maintaining the infrastructure typically associated with developing and launching an app.

paravirtualization   Server virtualization technique that presents a software interface to virtual machines that is similar to, but not identical to, that of the underlying server hardware. Guest operating systems require modification to support paravirtualization.

PBR Cisco policy-based routing.   Provides a flexible mechanism for network administrators to customize the operation of the routing table and the flow of traffic within their networks.

PFC   Priority Flow Control. *See* 802.1Qbb.

PIM   Protocol Independent Multicast. Has multiple multicast routing protocols, each optimized for a different type of environment. There are two main PIM protocols: PIM Sparse Mode and PIM Dense Mode. A third PIM protocol, Bidirectional PIM, is less widely used.

PNSC   Prime Network Service Controller. Software is a management platform for virtual network appliances. PNSC can be used to execute configuration changes quickly and consistently on virtual services elements like firewalls, load-balancers, routers, and switches.

POAP   Power On Auto Provisioning. Automates the process of upgrading software images and installing configuration files on Cisco MDS and Nexus switches that are being deployed in the network.

Policy   Named entity that contains generic specifications for controlling some aspect of system behavior. For example, a Layer 3 Outside Network Policy would contain the BGP protocol to enable BGP routing functions when connecting the fabric to an outside Layer 3 network.

port channel   An aggregation of multiple physical interfaces that creates a logical interface.

POST   Power-on self-test. In a computer system, the foremost routine that checks and tests the basic hardware. If it fails, it displays an error.

private addresses   IP addresses in several Class A, B, and C networks that are set aside for use inside private organizations. These addresses, as defined in RFC 1918, are not routable through the Internet.

Private cloud   A cloud computing environment provisioned for internal organizational use, which may include various internal divisions, business units, internal consumers, and so on.

processing delay   The amount of time a router or firewall takes to inspect and forward the packet.

profile Named entity that contains the necessary configuration details for implementing one or more instances of a policy. For example, a switch node profile for a routing policy would contain the entire switch-specific configuration details needed to implement the BGP routing protocol.

propagation delay A technical term that can have a different meaning depending on the context. It can relate to networking, electronics, or physics. In general, it is the length of time taken for the quantity of interest to reach its destination.

provider An EPG that provides a service in ACI fabric.

PSA PowerShell Agent. A virtual appliance used with UCS Director to manage applications that expose Windows PowerShell–based northbound API calls. PSA acts as an interfacing layer between Cisco UCS Director and applications such as XenDesktop Controller and Microsoft SCVMM that are managed through Windows PowerShell.

PSC Prime Service Catalog. A self-service portal to order and manage any type of IT service. It delivers data center, workplace, and application services to the users, using an on-demand, automated, and repeatable process. It provides a simple process for ordering, delivery, tracking, and resource management. It also has an embedded stack designer that can be used to design, configure, and automate the delivery of application stacks.

PTP Port Trunking Protocol. Used to carry tagged frames.

public cloud A cloud computing environment usually owned and operated by a service provider and offered as a service to customers.

public IP address An IP address that is part of a registered network number, as assigned by an Internet Assigned Numbers Authority (IANA) member agency, so that only the organization to which the address is registered is allowed to use the address. Routers in the Internet should have routes allowing them to forward packets to all the publicly registered IP addresses.

PVLAN Private VLAN. A construct to segment traffic within a VLAN, within a broadcast domain. A private VLAN partitions one broadcast domain into multiple smaller broadcast subdomains.

pWWN *See* WWPN.

PXE Preboot Execution Environment. An industry standard protocol used for booting a machine via the network. In the data center, this protocol is often used to automate installation of an operating system on new servers.

Q

QCN Quantized congestion notifications. IEEE 802.1Qau standard defines a Layer 2 traffic management system that pushes congestion to the edge of the network by instructing rate limiters to shape the traffic causing the congestion.

QoS Quality of service. The overall performance of a telephony or computer network, particularly the performance seen by the users of the network.

R

RADIUS   Remote Authentication Dial-In User Service. A networking protocol that provides centralized authentication, authorization, and accounting (AAA) management for users who connect and use a network service.

RAID   Redundant array of independent disks. Configured on disks allowing them to be presented as one logical unit with redundancy, availability, performance, and optimal usage of hard disk capacity.

RAM   Random-access memory. A type of volatile memory that a microprocessor can read and write.

RBAC   Role-based access control. An approach to restricting system access to authorized users for the purpose of computer systems security. It can implement mandatory access control (MAC) or discretionary access control (DAC).

REST   Representational state transfer. An architectural style consisting of a coordinated set of architectural constraints applied to components, connectors, and data elements, within a distributed hypermedia system. REST ignores the details of component implementation and protocol syntax to focus on the roles of components, the constraints upon their interaction with other components, and their interpretation of significant data elements.

RISC   Reduced instruction set computing. A CPU design strategy based on the insight that a simplified instruction set (in contrast to a complex set) provides higher performance when combined with a microprocessor architecture capable of executing those instructions using fewer microprocessor cycles per instruction.

RMON   Remote monitoring. RMON is a standard monitoring specification that enables various network monitors and console systems to exchange network-monitoring data. The IETF developed RMON MIB to support monitoring and protocol analysis of LANs.

ROM   Read-only memory. A type of nonvolatile memory that can be read but not written to by the microprocessor.

RSTP   Rapid Spanning Tree Protocol. The IEEE introduced RSTP as 802.1w. RSTP provides significantly faster spanning tree convergence after a topology change, introducing new convergence behaviors and bridge port roles to do this. RSTP was designed to be backward compatible with standard STP.

S

SaaS   Software as a service. A software licensing and delivery model in which software is licensed on a subscription basis and is centrally hosted. It is sometimes referred to as "on-demand software." SaaS is typically accessed by users using a thin client via a web browser.

SACK   Selective acknowledgement. An improvement over the conventional cumulative acknowledgement TCP algorithm that facilitates fewer data retransmissions in lossy networks. The selective acknowledgement extension uses two TCP options. The first is an enabling option, SACK-permitted, which can be sent in a SYN segment to indicate that the SACK option can be used after the connection is established.

SAN   Storage-area network. A dedicated network that provides access to consolidated, block-level data storage. SANs are primarily used to enhance storage devices, such as disk arrays, tape libraries, and optical jukeboxes, accessible to servers so that the devices appear like locally attached devices to the operating system. A SAN typically has its own network of storage devices that are generally not accessible through the local-area network (LAN) by other devices.

SAN-boot   The process of booting a computer operating system from a centralized online storage device, via a storage-area network, in contrast to having it boot from its local hard disk.

SCH   Cisco Smart Call Home. A feature in Cisco UCS Manager that allows proactive notifications of faults in Cisco UCS hardware both internally and to Cisco TAC, where cases are created automatically. Cisco TAC maintains a full inventory of your system, too.

SCSI   Small Computer System Interface. A set of standards for physically connecting and transferring data between computers and peripheral devices. The SCSI standards define commands, protocols, and electrical and optical interfaces.

SCVMM   System Center Virtual Machine Manager. Forms part of Microsoft's System Center line of virtual machine management and reporting tools, alongside previously established tools such as System Center Operations Manager and System Center Configuration Manager. SCVMM is designed for management of large numbers of virtual servers based on Microsoft Virtual Server and Hyper-V.

SDK   Software development kit. Typically, a set of software development tools that allows the creation of applications for a certain software package, software framework, hardware platform, or computer system.

SDN   Software-defined networking. A collective name for network modernization technologies that intend to introduce characteristics such as automation and programmability into data center, campus, backbone, and wide-area networks.

SDS   Software-defined storage. A term for computer data storage technologies that separate storage hardware from the software that manages the storage infrastructure. The software enabling a software-defined storage environment provides policy management for feature options such as deduplication, replication, thin provisioning, snapshots, and backup. By definition, SDS software is separate from hardware it is managing. That hardware may or may not have abstraction, pooling, or automation software embedded.

SEEPROM   Serial (PC) Electrically Erasable Programmable Read Only Memory. Uses a serial connection on the circuit board that can read/write bits. It is nonvolatile.

segmentation   One of the principal requirements of large-scale data centers is the capability to segment several tenants, each of which is a hosted enterprise or a department. Segmentation is achieved by leveraging the VNID field of the VXLAN header and the ACI extensions for the EPG. Traditionally, segmentation was performed with VLANs that incidentally were also broadcast and flooding domains.

SEL   System event log. Resides on the CIMC in NVRAM. It records most server-related events, such as over and under voltage, temperature events, fan, and so on.

sEPG   Source Endpoint Group. The relationship between EPGs.

serialization delay   The delay in moving packets from the network interface card's (NIC's) transmit buffer to the wire.

service chaining   The Cisco ACI fabric offers a native service-chaining capability that allows a user to transparently insert or remove services between two endpoints.

service graph   Cisco application centric infrastructure (ACI) technology provides the capability to insert Layer 4 through Layer 7 functions using an approach called a service graph.

service insertion   The capability to add Layer 4 through Layer 7 devices in the path between endpoints. The Cisco ACI service graph technology is considered a superset of service insertion.

service request   A request from a user for a standard IT service or changes to an existing service. UCS Director service requests are closely related to the workflows. When a workflow is run, it creates a service request in the system. The status of a service request can be monitored to find if the workflow has completed successfully.

SFP   Small form-factor pluggable. A compact, hot-pluggable transceiver used for both telecommunication and data communications applications. The form factor and electrical interface are specified by a multisource agreement (MSA). It interfaces a network device motherboard (for a switch, router, media converter, or similar device) to a fiber optic or copper networking cable.

SFP+   Enhanced small form-factor pluggable. An enhanced version of the SFP that supports data rates up to 10 Gbps. The SFP+ specification was first published on May 9, 2006, and version 4.1 was published on July 6, 2009.

SMB   Server Message Block. Operates as an application-layer network protocol mainly used for providing shared access to files, printer serial ports, and miscellaneous communications between nodes on a network.

SNIA   Storage Networking Industry Association. An association of producers and consumers of storage networking products; a registered 501 nonprofit trade association incorporated in December 1997. Its members are dedicated to "ensuring that storage networks become complete and trusted solutions across the IT community."

SNMP   Simple Network Management Protocol. An Internet-standard protocol for managing devices on IP networks. Devices that typically support SNMP include routers, switches, servers, workstations, printers, modem racks, and more.

SOA   Service-oriented architecture. A software design and software architecture design pattern based on distinct pieces of software providing application functionality as services to other applications.

Soaking   A fault managed object (MO) is created when a fault condition is detected. The initial state is Soaking, and the initial severity is specified by the fault policy for the fault class.

SoL   Serial over LAN. A mechanism that enables the input and output of the serial port of a managed system to be redirected over IP.

Spine-Leaf   In modern data centers, an alternative to the core/aggregation/access layer network topology. In leaf-spine architecture, a series of *leaf* switches form the access layer. These switches are fully meshed to a series of *spine* switches.

SSD   Solid-state drive. A data storage device using integrated circuit assemblies as memory to store data persistently. SSD technology uses electronic interfaces compatible with traditional block input/output (I/O) hard disk drives, thus permitting simple replacement in common applications.

SSH   Secure Shell. A TCP/IP application layer protocol that supports terminal emulation between a client and a server, using dynamic key exchange and encryption to keep the communications private.

store-and-forward switching   One of three internal processing options on some Cisco LAN switches in which the Ethernet frame must be completely received before the switch can begin forwarding the first bit of the frame.

STP   Spanning Tree Protocol. A protocol that uses the spanning tree algorithm, allowing a switch to dynamically work around loops in a network topology. Switches exchange bridge protocol data unit (BPDU) messages with other switches to detect loops and then remove the loops by blocking selected switch interfaces.

STP   Shielded twisted-pair. A type of cabling that has a layer of shielded insulation to reduce electromagnetic interference (EMI).

subject   In ACI, subjects in a contract specify what information can be communicated and how.

SUP   Supervisor engine. Refers to specific modules that can be placed in a modular chassis, such as Nexus 7000, Nexus 9000, and MDS 9000 switches. It has the management plane and the control plane for the switch.

sWWN   Switch WWN. The interface of a switch identified by the sWWN.

synchronous mirroring   Writes to both the local and the remote sites at the same time, keeping your disaster recovery site up to date. Although having both sites up to date is advantageous, the time that it takes to write to the remote physical volumes can affect application response time.

T

T11   Responsible for standards development in the areas of intelligent peripheral interface (IPI), high-performance parallel interface (HIPPI), and Fibre Channel (FC).

TAC   Cisco technical assistance center. Offers post-sales technical assistance on all Cisco products.

TACACS   Terminal Access Controller Access Control System, usually pronounced "tack-axe." Refers to a family of related protocols handling remote authentication and related services for networked access control through a centralized server.

target   A typical name for SCSI storage devices.

TCAM   Ternary content-addressable memory. A specialized type of high-speed memory that searches its entire contents in a single clock cycle.

TCP   Transmission Control Protocol. A connection-oriented transport layer TCP/IP protocol that provides reliable data transmission.

TCP/IP   Transmission Control Protocol/Internet Protocol. A common name for the suite of protocols developed by the U.S. Department of Defense in the 1970s to support the construction of worldwide internetworks. TCP and IP are the two best-known protocols in the suite.

tDn   Target DN. To create or manipulate objects in ACI Fabric, REST calls identify the resources by their distinguished name (DN). A DN identifies a managed object directly.

telemetry   The ACI fabric new telemetry tools provide a comprehensive troubleshooting methodology that enables the network administrator to quickly identify, isolate, and remediate a network issue on the network fabric.

Telnet   The standard terminal-emulation application layer protocol in the TCP/IP protocol stacks. Telnet is used for remote terminal connection, enabling users to log in to remote systems and use resources as if they were connected to a local system. Telnet is defined in RFC 854.

tenant   A secure and exclusive virtual computing environment. In ACI, a tenant is a unit of isolation from a policy perspective, but it does not represent a private network. Tenants can represent a customer in a service provider setting, an organization or domain in an enterprise setting, or just a convenient grouping of policies. ACI tenants can contain multiple private networks (VRFs).

TLV   Type, length, value. Link Layer Discovery Protocol (LLDP) data units consist of an untagged Ethernet header and a sequence of short, variable-length information elements known as TLV. TLVs have Type, Length, and Value fields. Type identifies the kind of information being sent. Length indicates the length (in octets) of the information string. Value is the actual information being sent.

ToR   Top-of-rack. A small port count switch that sits on the top or near the top of a Telco rack in data centers or colocation facilities. ToR solutions complement rack-at-a-time deployment by simplifying and shortening cable runs and facilitating the replication of rack configurations.

trace   Short for traceroute. A program available on many systems that traces the path that a packet takes to a destination. It is used mostly to troubleshoot routing problems between hosts.

trunk   In campus LANs, an Ethernet segment over which the devices add a VLAN header that identifies the VLAN in which the frame exists.

trunk interface   A switch interface configured so that it operates using VLAN trunking (either 802.1Q or ISL).

trunking   Also called VLAN trunking. A method (using either the Cisco ISL protocol or the IEEE 802.1Q protocol) to support multiple VLANs, allowing traffic from those VLANs to cross a single link.

TTL   Time to live, or hop limit. A mechanism that limits the lifespan or lifetime of data in a computer or network. TTL may be implemented as a counter or timestamp attached to or embedded in the data. After the prescribed event count or timespan has elapsed, data is discarded. In computer networking, TTL prevents a data packet from circulating indefinitely. In computing applications, TTL is used to improve performance of caching or to improve privacy.

U

UCF   Unified crossbar fabric. A single UCF is a 58-by-58 single-stage crossbar switch; it is therefore sufficient to support all 56 internal fabric interfaces from the 14 UPCs.

UCS   Unified Computing System. An (x86) architecture data center server platform, introduced in 2009, that is composed of computing hardware, virtualization support, switching fabric, and management software.

UCS Central   A Cisco product to centrally manage policies of multiple UCS domains.

UCSD activity   Used as a placeholder for a generic task that is independent of technology. UCSD activity can be pointed to multiple workflows that are specific to the implementation according to your product or platform. UCSD activity uses the decision logic based on user input to select which technology-specific workflow to execute. The required work is then performed by the workflow.

UCSD Compound Task   Represents a complex operation that runs as a workflow. When a compound task is executed, the workflow is called to perform the complex operation. The workflow can be created and saved as a task and used in another workflow as a compound task.

UCSM   Cisco UCSM or UCS Manager. The single pane of management of the Cisco UCS infrastructure.

UDLD   Unidirectional Link Detection. A data link layer protocol from Cisco Systems to monitor the physical configuration of the cables and detect unidirectional links. UDLD complements the Spanning Tree Protocol, which eliminates switching loops.

UDP   User Datagram Protocol. Connectionless transport layer protocol in the TCP/IP protocol stack. UDP is a simple protocol that exchanges datagrams without acknowledgments or guaranteed delivery.

Unified Fabric   Architectural approach of running storage, data networking, and network services over a single physical network infrastructure.

Unified port   Switch interface capable of functioning as either Ethernet, Fibre Channel, or Fibre Channel over FCoE through software configuration.

UPC   Unified port controller. The UPC handles all packet processing operations within the Cisco Nexus 5000 Series server switch.

uplink   In VMware, a trunked interface that allows multiple VLANs to communicate on the same interface.

uplink port channel   Ethernet uplinks defined in a Cisco UCS Fabric Interconnect, bundled together and configured as a port channel, allowing increased bandwidth and redundancy.

UUID   Universally unique identifier. Defined in the RFC 4122. UUIDs are applied for identification purposes.

V

VACS   Virtual Application Container Service. An infrastructure solution with preconfigured and integrated virtual services, switching, and workflow automation tools. It streamlines infrastructure policy definitions, integration, and deployment. Cisco VACS accelerates the application deployment process with compliant containers, or logical network and services descriptions, that work immediately after installation.

vCenter Virtual Machine Manager (VMM) domain   The VMM domain for VMware is VMware vSphere vCenter. Each VMM domain has a local significant association with a VLAN or VXLAN and contains its own mobility domain, which means that mobility is restricted to that VMM domain.

VDC   Virtual device context. Partitions a single physical device into multiple logical devices that provide fault isolation, management isolation, address allocation isolation, service differentiation domains, and adaptive resource management. A VDC instance can be managed within a physical device independently. Each VDC appears as a unique device to the connected users. A VDC runs as a separate logical entity within the physical device, maintains its own unique set of running software processes, has its own configuration, and can be managed by a separate administrator.

VE_Port   Virtual E_Port. FCoE port type allowing formation of FCoE Inter-Switch Links, which enable FCoE multihop topologies.

VF_Port   Virtual F_Port. FCoE port type connecting to a peripheral device (host or disk) operating as a VN_port. A VF_Port can be attached to only one VN_Port.

VFS   Virtual file system. An abstraction layer on top of a more concrete file system. It allows client applications using heterogeneous file-sharing network protocols to access a unified pool of storage resources.

vHBA   Virtual host bus adapter. The virtual representation of a typical host bus adapter used to connect to a Fibre Channel storage device or network.

VIC   Cisco Virtual Interface Cards, Converged Adapter for Physical and Virtual Networks. This adapter provides acceleration for the various new operational modes introduced by server virtualization.

VIF   Virtual interface. Logical construct that consists of a front panel port, VLAN, and several other parameters.

VIP   VeriSign Identity Protection. A product that offers an extra layer of security by using two-factor authentication. The VIP credential provides a dynamic security code that can be used in addition to the username and password for safe and secure access to the system.

Virtual Ethernet Module   A component providing data forwarding functions in the Cisco Nexus 1000V virtual switch.

Virtual Supervisor Module   A component providing control and management functions in the Cisco Nexus 1000V virtual switch.

VLAN   Virtual LAN. A group of devices, connected to one or more switches, with the devices grouped into a single broadcast domain through switch configuration. VLANs allow switch administrators to separate the devices connected to the switches into separate VLANs without requiring separate physical switches, gaining design advantages of separating the traffic without the expense of buying additional hardware.

VLAN configuration database   The name of the collective configuration of VLAN IDs and names on a Cisco switch.

VLAN interface   A configuration concept inside Cisco switches, used as an interface between IOS running on the switch and a VLAN supported inside the switch, so that the switch can assign an IP address and send IP packets into that VLAN.

vLUN   Virtual logical unit number. A LUN that is virtual for the real-time server and is exposed by the real-time target mode driver. An application host treats a vLUN as a normal LUN.

VM   Virtual machine. In computing, an emulation of a particular computer system.

vMAC   Virtual MAC address. A floating entity shared by the primary and the secondary nodes in an HA setup.

VM-FEX   Technology extending Cisco Fabric Extender architecture to virtualized servers by assigning virtual machine vNIC to a vNIC instantiated by the Cisco Adapter-FEX.

VMKernel   The interface between virtual machines (VMs) and the physical host hardware that supports them.

VMM   Virtual machine monitor. A piece of computer software, firmware, or hardware that creates and runs virtual machines.

VMNIC   In VMware, a physical NIC that is assigned to a hypervisor as an uplink or trunked interface.

vNIC   Virtual network interface card. The virtual representation of a typical network interface card, used to connect to an Ethernet network.

VNP_Port   Virtual NP_Port. FCoE port type on FCoE-NPV device emulating FCoE-capable host with multiple ENodes, where each ENode has its own unique MAC address. In FCoE multihop topology, VNP_Ports on FCoE-NPV devices are connected to VF_Ports on FCoE-NPIV devices.

VN-Tag   The format of the information tag inserted into each frame exchanged between the Cisco fabric extenders and the Nexus parent switch, which enables the advanced functions provided by such architecture. The IEEE defines a similar tag, referred to as E-Tag, under the IEEE 802.1BR working group (Bridge Port Extension). E-Tag provides the same functions as VN-Tag but uses a slightly different format.

VOQ   Virtual output queues. The technique used in input-queued switches where, rather than keeping all traffic in a single queue, separate queues are maintained for each possible output location. It addresses a common problem known as head-of-line blocking.

vPath   Redirection mechanism to intelligently steer network traffic from the virtual switch to the services appliance for policy enforcement.

vPC   Virtual port channel. Allows links that are physically connected to two different Cisco Nexus 5000, 7000, 9000, and UCS Series devices to appear as a single port channel to a third device. The third device can either be a Cisco Nexus 2000 Series Fabric Extender, a switch, a server, or any other networking device. vPC can provide Layer 2 multipathing, which allows creating redundancy by increasing bandwidth, enabling multiple parallel paths between nodes, and load-balancing traffic where alternative paths exist.

vPC host mode   On the Nexus 1000V, a capability of the Virtual Ethernet Module (VEM) in a host to group two or more physical uplinks into an Etherchannel bundle, with those uplinks being connected to two different upstream physical switches.

VPLS   Virtual Private LAN Services. Similar to EoMPLS, VPLS uses an MPLS network as the underlying transport network. However, instead of point-to-point Ethernet pseudo wires, VPLS delivers a virtual multiaccess Ethernet network.

VRF   Private network virtual routing and forwarding. Defines a Layer 3 address domain that allows multiple instances of a routing table to exist and work simultaneously. This increases functionality by allowing network paths to be segmented without using multiple devices. ACI tenants can contain multiple private networks (VRFs).

VRRP   Virtual Router Redundancy Protocol. Specifies an election protocol that dynamically assigns responsibility for a virtual router to one of the VRRP routers on a LAN. The VRRP router controlling the IP address(es) associated with a virtual router is called the master, and it forwards packets sent to these IP addresses. The election process provides dynamic failover in the forwarding responsibility should the master become unavailable. This allows any of the virtual router IP addresses on the LAN to be used as the default first hop router by end-hosts.

VSAN   Virtual storage-area network. In computer networking, a VSAN is a collection of ports from a set of connected Fibre Channel switches that form a virtual fabric. Ports within a single switch can be partitioned into multiple VSANs, despite sharing hardware resources. Conversely, multiple switches can join a number of ports to form a single VSAN. VSANs were designed by Cisco modeled after the virtual local-area network (VLAN) concept in Ethernet networking, applied to a storage-area network. In October 2004, the Technical Committee T11 of the International Committee for Information Technology Standards approved VSAN technology to become a standard of the American National Standards Institute (ANSI).

VSG   Cisco Virtual Security Gateway. Cisco virtual security solution integrated with Cisco Nexus 1000V virtual switch to provide virtual machine context-aware intratenant security services.

VSID   Virtual subnet identifier. A 24-bit field in NVGRE encapsulation that identifies a virtual network. It can provide more than 16 million virtual network identifiers.

VTS   Virtual Topology System. An open, scalable, SDN framework for data center virtual network provisioning and management. It is designed to address the requirements of today's multitenant data centers for cloud and network function virtualization (NFV) services without sacrificing the security, reliability, and performance of traditional data center architectures.

VUM   VMware Update Manager. A centralized, automated update and patch management tool.

VXLAN   Virtual extensible LAN. Uses MAC in User Datagram Protocol (MAC-in-UDP) encapsulation technique, which allows extending Layer 2 and Layer 3 connectivity services over IP routed network. VXLAN header carries a 24-bit identifier, known as VXLAN VNID, which enables you to build more than 16 million logical segments.

VXLAN VNID   The 24-bit value used in the VXLAN packet header to identify virtual segments.

W

WAN   Wide-area network. A part of a larger network that implements mostly OSI Layer 1, 2, and Layer 3 technology, connects sites that typically sit far apart (geographically dispersed areas), and uses a business model in which a consumer (individual or business) must lease the WAN from a service provider (often a Telco).

Workflow   Defines the sequence of tasks that are required to fulfill a user request. The UCS Director workflow is built using a series of automation tasks linked together to perform a complex IT operation. It also determines the order in which the tasks are executed, and if required it can link output of one task into the input of another.

Workflow Designer   A tool provided by UCS Director to build workflows. It provides a drag-and-drop user interface to design workflows. Workflows can be built by dragging tasks from the task library, placing them in required sequence, and defining their input and outputs. Once workflow design is complete, you can save it, test it, and publish it to a catalog for user consumption.

WWNN   Worldwide node name. A name assigned to a node (an endpoint, a device) in a Fibre Channel fabric. It is valid for the same WWNN to be seen on many different ports (different addresses) on the network, identifying the ports as multiple network interfaces of a single network node.

WWPN   Worldwide port name. A name assigned to a port in a Fibre Channel fabric. Used on storage-area networks, it performs a function equivalent to the MAC address in the Ethernet protocol because it is supposed to be a unique identifier in the network.

X

XFP   10 Gigabit Small Form Factor Pluggable. A standard for transceivers for high-speed computer network and telecommunication links that use optical fiber. An industry group defined it in 2002, along with its interface to other electrical components, which is called XFI.

XML   Extensible Markup Language. A markup language that defines a set of rules for encoding documents in a format that is both human-readable and machine-readable. It is defined in the XML 1.0 specification produced by the W3C, and several other related specifications, all free open standards.

Index

PXE (Preboot Execution Environment), UCSD and BMA deployments, 596-599

Python SDK, UCS management, 386-387

Q

QoS (Quality of Service), server virtualization, 417, 420

QSA Modules, UCS Fabric Interconnects, 247

questions

advice on answering, 671-672

drag-and-drop questions, example of, 660

multiple choice questions, example of, 659-660

reviewing, 673-675

simlet questions, example of, 662

simulation questions, example of, 661

testlet questions, example of, 662

time budgets versus number of questions, 663-664

R

rack accounts, UCSD, 614

rackmount servers (UCS C-Series), 258-260

connectivity, 278-279

DRAM population, 261-262

HBA, 268-269

NIC, 267

NPIV, 269

OEM CNA adapters, 265-267

RAID adapters, 262-265

storage accelerator adapters, 270

VIC, 265-267

Rapid-PVST+, VDC STP, 207

RBAC (Role-Based Access Control)

characteristics of, 72

guidelines, 72

Nexus switches, 70-73

privilege levels, 72-73

UCS administration, 369

redundancy modes, UCS 5108 blade server chassis, 248

reference notes, exam strategies, 664

registering for exams, 7

relaxation techniques, exam strategies, 665

remote accessibility, UCS management, 382

remote shared storage, 410

replication, Layer 2 extensions, 163

reporting/monitoring in UCSD

bar graphs, 624

CloudSense reports, 625

dashboard, 624

map reports, 625

pie charts, 624

Report Builder, 625

Summary window, 624

tabular reports, 624

top-five reports, 624

trend graphs, 624

resolved model (ACI), 488

resource groups, ACI/UCSD integration, 621

resource tags, ACI/UCSD integration, 622

T

U

X-Y

Z